Gendering Bodies

THE GENDER LENS SERIES

SERIES EDITORS

Judith A. Howard
University of Washington

Barbara Risman
University of Illinois, Chicago

Joey Sprague
University of Kansas

The Gender Lens series has been conceptualized as a way of encouraging the development of a sociological understanding of gender. A "gender lens" means working to make gender visible in social phenomena; asking if, how, and why social processes, standards, and opportunities differ systematically for women and men. It also means recognizing that gender inequality is inextricably braided with other systems of inequality. The Gender Lens series is committed to social change directed toward eradicating these inequalities. Originally published by Sage Publications and Pine Forge Press, all Gender Lens books are now available from The Rowman & Littlefield Publishing Group.

BOOKS IN THE SERIES

Gendering Bodies

Sara L. Crawley
Lara J. Foley
Constance L. Shehan

ROWMAN & LITTLEFIELD PUBLISHERS, INC.
Lanham • Boulder • New York • Toronto • Plymouth, UK

ROWMAN & LITTLEFIELD PUBLISHERS, INC.

Published in the United States of America
by Rowman & Littlefield Publishers, Inc.
A wholly owned subsidiary of The Rowman & Littlefield Publishing Group, Inc.
4501 Forbes Boulevard, Suite 200, Lanham, Maryland 20706
www.rowmanlittlefield.com

Estover Road, Plymouth PL6 7PY, United Kingdom

The photograph on page i courtesy of Vanessa Lopez. Photographs on pages 86, 87, 88, 89, 123, 124, 217, 230 courtesy of Getty Images. All other photographs were provided by the subjects and are reproduced by permission.

British Library Cataloguing in Publication Information Available

Library of Congress Cataloging-in-Publication Data

Crawley, Sara L., 1966–
   Gendering bodies / Sara L. Crawley, Lara J. Foley, and Constance L. Shehan.
      p. cm. — (The gender lens series)
   Includes bibliographical references and index.
   ISBN-13: 978-0-7425-5956-1 (cloth : alk. paper)
   ISBN-10: 0-7425-5956-4 (cloth : alk. paper)
   ISBN-13: 978-0-7425-5957-8 (pbk. : alk. paper)
   ISBN-10: 0-7425-5957-2 (pbk. : alk. paper)
   1. Sex role—United States. 2. Sex—Social aspects—United States. 3. Sexual orientation—United States. 4. Gender identity—United States. I. Foley, Lara J., 1972– II. Shehan, Constance L. III. Title.
   HQ1075.5.U6C73 2008
   306.701—dc22   2007006366

Printed in the United States of America

∞™ The paper used in this publication meets the minimum requirements of American National Standard for Information Sciences—Permanence of Paper for Printed Library Materials, ANSI/NISO Z39.48-1992.

For all of us who have felt the pain of conformity in big and small ways.

Contents

Series Editors' Foreword

It is now more than twenty years since feminist sociologists identified gender as an important analytic dimension in sociology. In the intervening decades, theory and research on gender have grown exponentially. With this series, we intend to further this scholarship, as well as ensure that theory and research on gender become fully integrated into the discipline as a whole.

In their classic edited collection *Analyzing Gender: A Handbook of Social Science Research* (1987), Beth Hess and Myra Marx Ferree identify three stages in the study of women and men since 1970. Initially, the emphasis was on sex differences and the extent to which such differences might be based on the biological properties of individuals. In the second stage, the focus shifted to the individual sex roles and socialization, exposing gender as the product of specific social arrangements, although still conceptualizing it as an individual trait. The hallmark of the third stage is the recognition of the centrality of gender as an organizing principle in all social systems, including work, politics, everyday interaction, families, economic development, law, education, and a host of other social domains. As our understanding of gender has become more social, so has our awareness that gender is experienced and organized in race- and class-specific ways.

In the summer of 1992, the American Sociological Association (ASA) funded a small conference organized by Barbara Risman and Joey Sprague to discuss the evolution of gender in these distinctly sociological frameworks. The conference brought together a sampling of gender scholars working in a range of substantive areas with a diversity of methods to focus on gender as a principle of social organization. The discussions of the state of feminist scholarship made it clear that gender is pervasive in society and operates at multiple levels. Gender shapes identities and perception, interactional practices, and the very forms of social institutions, and it does so in race- and class-specific ways. If we did not see gender in social phenomena, we were not seeing them clearly.

The participants in the ASA-sponsored seminar recognized that although these developing ideas about gender were widely accepted by feminist sociologists and many others who study social inequalities, they were relatively unfamiliar to many who work within other sociological paradigms. This book series was conceived at that conference as a means of introducing these ideas to sociological colleagues and students and of helping to develop gender scholarship further.

As series editors, we believe it is time for gender scholars to speak to our other colleagues and to the general education of students. There are many sociologists and scholars in other social sciences who want to incorporate scholarship on gender and its intersections with race, class, and sexuality in their teaching and research but lack the tools to do so. For those who have not worked in this area, the prospect of the bibliographic research necessary to develop supplementary units or transform their own teaching and scholarship is daunting. Moreover, the publications necessary to penetrate a curriculum resistant to change and encumbered by inertia have simply not been available. We conceptualize this book series as a way of meeting the needs of these scholars and thereby also encouraging the development of the sociological understanding of gender by offering a "gender lens."

What do we mean by a *gender lens*? We mean working to make gender visible in social phenomena, asking if, how, and why social processes, standards, and opportunities differ systematically in women and men. We also mean recognizing that gender inequality is inextricably intertwined with other systems of inequality. Looking at the world through a gendered lens thus implies two seemingly contradictory tasks. First, it means unpacking the assumptions about gender that pervade sociological research and social life in general. At the same time, looking through a gender lens means revealing how central assumptions about gender continue to be the organization of the social world, regardless of their empirical reality. We show how our often unquestioned ideas about gender affect the words we use, the questions we ask, the answers we envision. The Gender Lens series is committed to social change directed toward eradicating these inequalities. Our goals are consistent with initiatives at colleges and universities across the United States that are encouraging the development of more-diverse scholarship and teaching.

The books in the Gender Lens series are aimed at different audiences and have been written for a variety of uses, from assigned readings in introductory undergraduate courses to graduate seminars and as professional resources for our colleagues. The series includes several different styles of books that address these goals in distinct ways. We are excited about the series and anticipate that it will have an enduring impact on the direction of both pedagogy and scholarship in sociology and other related social sciences. We invite you, the reader, to join us in thinking through these difficult but exciting issues by offering feedback or by developing your own project and proposing it for us in the series.

ABOUT THIS VOLUME

In the twentieth century, feminist scholarship was born (and it could be argued it began before this!) and "sex differences" were re-conceptualized as being centered as much in inequality as in body types. At first, even feminists focused on the social construct of gender and left bodies to the "hard" "natural" sciences. But before long, it became clear that there could be no clear dichotomy between biological sex as natural and gender as social, since how we conceive of the body *is* social, and we do gender in our physical bodies. In this work, *Gendering Bodies*, Sara Crawley, Lara Foley, and Constance Shehan argue convincingly that gender constructs bodies, that biological potentialities are shaped by cultural contexts. They build on the feminist tradition of blurring the analytical distinctions between the biological and the social. While much of the previous writing on the topic was very technical, and hard for students to understand, this book is both analytically creative and accessible.

This revisioning of the body, and the centrality of social context for understanding gender, bodies, and ourselves, is theoretically innovative. What makes this work unique is that the original ideas are presented in clear and precise enough language that every first-year college student can follow the intellectual journey. *Gendering Bodies* will be useful in every class in which students and faculty are engaging the questions of how we become women and men, how we come to learn, internalize, accept, reject, and re-frame our identities and bodies. It will be equally germane to every course about social interaction, what we expect from each other, and how we conform to or resist those expectations. While the authors are feminist sociologists, and the analysis sociologically sophisticated, this volume is well suited also to courses in psychology, human development, communication, and women's and gender studies.

One unusual aspect of this volume is that the authors write not only from their own standpoints—all authors do—but these authors do so self-reflectively and bring the reader into the narrative. We learn how gender conformity and resistance in the authors' lives helped shape their intellectual understandings.

A major strength of this book is that the authors lay out for us a Gendered Feedback Loop model that helps us to conceptualize how we make gender and bodies, how we create a world of difference by categorizing sexed and gendered cultural messages. The authors go on to illustrate clearly how we do gender as performance in sports, at work, and in sexuality. This sharp analysis then helps us understand how we become our own jailers, doing both surveillance of ourselves and others. But they do not leave us stranded with a view of gender as an oppressive power of irresistible constraints. They show clearly how gender resistance can change lives—our own and others—and suggest that we all can help create a more just society if we move beyond gender dichotomies. This is the kind of book that just may change your life.

Judith A. Howard
Barbara Risman
Joey Sprague

Preface

Gendering and Embodiment

If gender is socially constructed, why do women and men seem to enact gender so consistently? Isn't it true that females tend to walk "like women" and males tend to walk "like men"? Doesn't that imply that gender really is an innate part of the body? In this book, we argue no. Just because women tend to use their bodies in a consistent manner and so do men, this is not proof of a biological imperative. It is entirely probable that the way you move (embody your self) is something you learned and are continuing to learn through cultural practices over the course of your life. In this book we want to push the idea that you *learn* how to be women and men to a very radical level—we ultimately suggest your interactions in the world shape your body. Although bodies vary in a variety of ways (height, weight, genital size and shape, hair color and texture, musculature, etc.), the conformity we come to know around femininity and masculinity tends to train us toward conformity to bodily ideals, not just demonstrate biological necessities. Are you intrigued? Keep reading.

Human bodies are not simply biological organisms. Humans are also social organisms whose bodies bear the imprint of social interaction. In the history of science, research on the body has overemphasized biological, chemical, and medical studies, under the assumption that the size and shape of physical bodies are purely the result of synapses firing or hormones pumping or chemicals reacting. While each of these studies adds to knowledge of the human body, they largely neglect the effects of culture and society on the body. Sociologists have long asserted that meanings about the body are developed in social interaction. But only recently have theorists begun to consider how those meanings actually shape the size and use of physical bodies.

In Western culture, messages about and practices of gender have developed as a rigid, dichotomous (two-part) system. Feminist researchers have long questioned the effectiveness of forcing all people into one of two sex/gender categories.[1] Until recently, sociology as a discipline left studies of the body to the biologists and medical scientists under the strict disciplinary split that determined that bodies were "natural" and societies were social (Frank 1991; Hall 1996).

In this book, we turn that ideology on its head, arguing that bodies *are* the purview of social theory. Past social theorists have taken seriously the notion that uses and meanings of bodies could be studied by social science (Foucault 1973, 1977, 1978; Goffman 1959, 1963, 1967). More recently, social theorists have refused to recognize a split between nature and nurture (Fausto-Sterling 1986, 2000; Lorber 1994). Shilling (1993) famously recognizes the body as a project that is emerging from physiological and social process, not a static thing. We agree with Shilling and argue that social ideas determine behaviors that affect the sizes, shapes, and uses of bodies. Specifically, we argue that, although we are each born with different bodily potentialities, *our bodies are constantly being gendered—that is, encouraged to participate in (heterosexual) gender conformity.*

Embodied knowledge is gained through bodily practices. Mind and body are not experienced as separate. All thoughts and feelings are experienced through the physical body, and bodily practices and behaviors that result *from ideas and cultural messages* shape the physical body in various ways. These behaviors include nutrition practices, dieting, working out, cosmetic surgery, and training (or lack of training) in sports or fitness, to name a few. And our experiences of the body reflect our experiences of our lived worlds (e.g., feelings of bodily competence in work or leisure settings, understandings of sexuality and reproduction), which are constantly gendered (Connell 2002:17; Jackson and Scott 2001).

In this book we concentrate on the gendered cultural messages that have developed about bodies and the physical effects of those messages on bodies. In doing so, we question the rigid binary of normative gender interactions and the science that has done as much to uphold that binary as it has to create knowledge about bodies. Therefore, we have attempted to be specific in our use of language. To be true to our own theory, we have been careful to talk about females and males where we refer to bodies and to talk about masculinity, femininity, men, and women where we refer to gendered presentations and experiences. Also, we try to avoid unnecessary gendering in our own language and use the generic pronoun "they" rather than the dualistic pronouns "he or she" when we mean some person, not a particular person. While this may be grammatically incorrect, we use these constructions purposefully to be attentive to and to minimize gendering in our language.

The book is intended to be an introduction to studying the gendering of bodies.[2] For that reason, we have attempted to write in accessible language rather than academic jargon. We have also worked hard to include examples of everyday interaction in common settings—at work, in leisure and sports settings, and in sexual and reproductive experiences—that we hope give personal context to clarify theoretical concepts. We have included stories of real experiences from ourselves and our students in boxed insets. We hope that students and scholars might use this book to introduce themselves to the sociology of the gendered body. In most chapters we have included endnotes that provide significant detail about theoretical differences among authors cited. We hope that presenting this detail in endnotes rather than in the text provides researchers with the details they need while not overburdening undergraduate readers. If you find the endnotes too detailed, feel free to read past them. We hope that our style of writing and storytelling will make the ideas widely accessible and useful to the broadest audience.

NOTES

1. Some have approached this problem from a social psychological or interactional perspective (e.g., Hollander and Howard 2000; Howard and Hollander 1997; P. Martin 2003; West and Zimmerman 1987) and others from a structural perspective (e.g., Lorber 1994, 2005; Martin 2004; Risman 1998, 2004). But only recently have gender theorists begun to push their theories from the world of language and meaning into the physical world of bodies, asking "How is dichotomous biological sex accomplished through gendered social interaction?" (Fausto-Sterling 1986, 2000; Kessler and McKenna 1978; Lorber 1994).

2. Studying the construction of physical bodies as gendered is a relatively new focus of sociological study. For two exemplary studies see Lorber and Martin (1998) and Martin (1998).

Acknowledgments

Writing this book has been a journey. Since the beginning of the project, our bodies have aged and, between the three of us, we have celebrated one wedding and seven job title changes; lost family members, close colleagues, and pets; and moved households a cumulative total of six times. In thought, writing, and grunt work, this book has been a truly collaborative process. The book might never have been written if Connie hadn't suggested it, if Lara hadn't made a few subtle threats to speed up the process and been fanatical about details, and if Sara hadn't stubbornly insisted that we write *this* book and not one of the many inferior drafts that came before it.

We appreciate the support we have received from the Gender Lens editors, Judy Howard, Joey Sprague, and especially Barbara Risman, who not only invented this wonderful series, but have been so patient with us. We want to thank Mindy Stombler and Peter Nardi for their careful and thoughtful reviews of the manuscript. We would also like to thank the publishing team at Rowman & Littlefield, especially Alan McClare and Alex Masulis for working with us on the photographs, and Jehanne Schweitzer and Ginny Perrin for blending an understanding and appreciation of the arguments in the book with meticulous technical editing.

Writing a book with three authors who live in three different cities makes keeping track of references quite a headache. We owe a special debt of appreciation to Rebecca Willman for helping to track down mystery citations in the final hour. We'd also like to thank Jessie Finch, Patrick Foley, and Don Geesling for teaching us how to properly cite music lyrics.

Our colleagues and support staffs in the sociology departments at The University of Tulsa and the University of Florida and the Women's Studies and sociology departments at the University of South Florida have supported us through this long endeavor. We would like to thank The University of Tulsa Office of Sponsored Research, College of Arts and Sciences, and Department of Sociology for assistance with publication costs. Sara would also like to thank her former colleagues in Women's Studies at Florida International University and in sociology at the University of New Orleans. Our students have inspired and encouraged us and many of our colleagues have either directly or indirectly helped this book take shape. In particular we would like to thank Jean Blocker, Kendal Broad, Spencer Cahill, Susan Chase, Joe Feagin, Jay Gubrium, Jim Holstein, Ron Jepperson, Doni Loseke, Susan Mann, Pat Martin, Marilyn Myerson, and Kim Spencer for their mentoring, collegiality, and friendship.

The idea for this book came about when Sara and Lara were in graduate school at the University of Florida where Connie was their professor and mentor. Endless conversations and experiences with the graduate school cohort of Helena Alden, Mark Cohan, Susan Eichenberger, Chris Faircloth, Leslie Houts Picca, Shannon Houvouras, Laurel Tripp, and Melanie Wakeman were the original inspiration for the book.

We have to thank our partners, Barbara Bonanno, Andrew Wakeman, and Paul Mueller, for their patience and encouragement. They have each asked many times, "Aren't you finished with that book yet?" Finally, we thank our parents (for giving us bodies) and our families and friends for giving us the social laboratory that helped us develop our thinking. In particular, Sara would like to thank Nin, all the University of Peanut Island crowd, especially Ray (I'm sorry I never said it before now), Dianne, Aneeza, and Tiffany (for pink and blue jobs).

We would like to thank the people who contributed photographs and personal essays to this book, many developing theorists themselves. They remind us that the arguments we make are not merely academic or abstractly theoretical, but are about real bodies and real lives.

1

Creating a World of Dichotomy

Categorizing Sex and Gendering Cultural Messages

> With the courage to confront, understand, and redefine our incorrigible propositions, we can begin to discover new scientific knowledge and to construct new realities in everyday life. (Kessler and McKenna 1978:167)

In U.S. culture, we commonly assume that our physiological bodies (in particular notions of femaleness or maleness and presumptions about physical size, strength, and reproductive capacities) determine our social roles. Here we argue that this is a premature conclusion. There is no necessary relationship between one's capacity to produce ova or sperm (or lack of capacity to produce either) and acting "ladylike" or "manly." We too commonly assume that social expectations come from bodily necessity. In our everyday lives we are so practiced at conforming the uses of our bodies to gendered expectations that we assume our comfort with those practices comes from nature. In this book, we wish to reverse the causal direction and turn that commonsense argument on its head. We argue that *cultural messages*[1] that form our expectations and "rules" about gender determine the gendered experiences of our bodies—our *embodied knowledge*, and that these messages and our resulting gendered practices help to shape our physical bodies as well. Thus, social messages and physical ("natural") bodies are inextricably inseparable. There is no physical body separate from social practices (which originate from gendered messages). There is no social experience separable from physical bodies. The imprint of physical propensities and social experiences exists in each person. In essence, the social world and the physical world co-construct gendered bodies.

1

As an example of how we (incorrectly) assume physical necessity determines social practices, let's consider bathroom use. Specifically: Why do women and men use different rooms to—shall we say—evacuate waste? Clearly evacuation of waste is a physiological necessity on the micro level. If one cannot evacuate waste, the body shuts down and one dies. Additionally, at a macro level, waste disposal is a physical necessity given that if, as a society, we do not determine how to dispose of waste, there will be sanitation concerns and grave potential for disease. This is clearly a process of the physical world. Still, is it necessary to segregate women from men while doing it? In U.S. culture, we take this as a foregone conclusion and rarely question this practice. The very idea of walking into the "wrong" restroom is such a social taboo that most Americans feel extremely uncomfortable even thinking about it. You may even experience a visceral reaction to such an event (heart beats faster, adrenaline rush from breaking the taboo). Why?[2]

Is it physiologically necessary to separate women's rooms from men's rooms? Well, no. Perhaps you imagine that having a penis or a vulva necessitates different bathroom equipment—urinal vs. toilet. Although it seems to be culturally preferred for male-bodied people to urinate while standing, it is not physically necessary. Similarly, it is not absolutely necessary for female-bodied people to sit while urinating. Have you ever seen separate "men's" and "women's" rooms or a urinal installed in a private home? Commonly, private homes have one or more bathrooms that accommodate any sort of person. So, physiological necessity cannot be the reason for separate rooms or different bathroom equipment.

Is it a matter of privacy and efficiency in public facilities? Perhaps. It is clear that public restrooms are often designed to maximize efficiency by accommodating more than one person at a time, while preserving privacy. Of course, privacy is a social notion. There is no physical reason for privacy. Animals do not require privacy. Additionally, privacy in the sense of separate bathrooms only extends to not interacting with someone who has different genitalia in those rooms. It is perfectly socially permissible for women to change clothes in front of women and men in front of men (e.g., in locker rooms). Privacy is also a limited notion when you recognize that men urinate openly in front of each other in most public restrooms in the United States.[3] So, "privacy" means keeping female-bodied people from witnessing male-bodied people and vice versa.

So, maybe we separate restrooms because we assume people who potentially are sexually attracted to each other should not have an opportunity to see each other's bodies? Perhaps this expectation is how the construction of public restrooms evolved. However, given that people with same-sex attraction have been documented to exist throughout time (Adam 1987; Halperin 1989; Katz 1995; Trumbach 1994), this premise is akin to the proverbial ostrich with its head in the sand. We do not construct separate facilities for gay and straight people. Further, separating facilities for females and males does not happen even in all industrialized countries. While traveling in Belgium some years back, one author happened upon a bar with a joint facility wherein a male-bodied person was utilizing a partitioned urinal while she utilized a partitioned toilet. None of the locals seemed to give this situation a second thought.

A former female student suggested that she would not want to use the same restroom as male people for safety reasons; she was afraid of being raped. Unless we are willing to suggest that all male-bodied people have a biological propensity to rape (which we are not!), we must recognize that this concern, however valid, is a result of the social landscape in the United States, where sexual assault crimes are far too common and relatively underpunished, and men's violence and sexuality are symbolically linked in so many ways.

Although the "necessity" of separate restroom use is a social construction, the depth and pervasiveness of our gendered expectations with regard to bathroom use permeate the experience of our entire lives. Every time we use the (gendered) restroom, we re-create and reify the expected "real" differences between women and men (Goffman 1977; Halberstam 1998; Lucal 1999); *we make gender a real part of the embodiment of our intimate, everyday lives*. The constant, foregone conclusion of that difference impacts our entire experience of self.[4] Take note of an important and very practical point: If you are in a public place and need to use a restroom, it does not matter that gender is constructed. In every practical sense, you have two choices— the women's room or the men's room—and you must comply with the requisite gender rules, however constructed. Imagine if you were a person who had difficulty deciding which room to use. We often assume that every person is unambiguously female or male, but this is not so. We will return to this point shortly.

Gendered expectations produce the very real effect of dichotomizing in body knowledge—how we come to know, understand, and use our bodies and how we understand our relationship to each other and the world. Restroom use is only one example of the myriad things throughout our culture that demonstrate the socially constructed character of gender.

What we argue in this book is that each of us has become gendered and is continually being gendered in our everyday experiences in the world. Every thought, every action, every interaction with others in this world is gendered.[5] That is how deeply our cultural messages about the importance of biological sex affect our lives. We become those messages. Others hold us accountable to those messages constantly. In this book we explain how social processes can become part of our bodies and embodiments. We explain how gender becomes real.

GENDER DOES NOT EXIST, BUT IT IS REAL

Gender is a bit of a conundrum. On the one hand, *social constructionism* suggests that the differences between women and men that we identify as significant (i.e., femininity and masculinity) are products of the social world, not nature. So, like laws, U.S. currency, and the Western calendar, gender is a system of organizing that Western cultures have devised to organize and make sense of our lives. (All cultures use gender as an organizing system, but may not all use the system in exactly the same ways.) Importantly, because gender is "done" by us rather than innate within us, we can decide whether and how to allow the organization of gender to affect us in the future, if we choose to be attentive to its effects. Social constructionism stands in sharp contrast to the essentialist notion of biological determinism. *Essentialism* is the notion that there is an enduring truth to be found if only we look hard enough. For example, to believe that a real difference between women and men resides in the body is an essentialist belief. This belief is the basis of evolutionary theory or *biological determinism*—the notion that women and men have been bred to be different animals, adapting to evolutionary functional necessities. Social constructionism is the response to evolutionary theory that argues that what we understand as "appropriately" feminine and masculine are social evaluations, not physical necessities, and are based on social organization, not physiological adaptation. Clearly, in this book we lean much more strongly in the direction of social constructionism.

On the other hand, gender inequality exists (as do inequalities based on race, class, sexuality, age, and ability, among others). That is, there are a number of very measurable, and hence seemingly real, social disadvantages experienced by people who are not members of the dominant group (e.g., income and wealth inequality, unequal access to jobs, unequal representation in politics, etc.). Hence, even though socially constructed phenomena are not "real" in terms of being an innate part of our bodies, they are real in their effects on our lives and life chances (and in many ways their effects may leave a mark on our bodies as well).

So, while it seems clear that gender is socially constructed, it seems equally clear that the effects of gender are quite real. As a result, we argue that *gender does not exist* (in nature) *but it is real* (in terms of real consequences, including various structural inequalities, physical violence, etc.). In this way, we can remain attentive to both the theoretical perspectives that understand gender as constructed, as well as the material effects that the system of gender has on the lives of real people. In other words, we see both the theoretical relevance of gender theory and the practical application of gendered experiences in the lives of actual people.

A social constructionist perspective on social problems argues that people live in two worlds simultaneously (and inseparably): the physical world and the symbolic world (Loseke 1999). We only know the physical world through the interpretations that we make of it, and conversely, there is no world of meaning outside of our physical place in the world—in the body.

We see gender and *embodied knowledge* (knowledge of self and others via experiences of one's body) in the same way. Gender exists in both the world of language, images, and interactions (which always have significance attached) and the physical practices and experiences of the body (Paechter 2003, 2006). Every use of the body has meaning. Every meaning and interpretation is experienced through the body. Hence, each body is an ever-developing process that begins with a physiological basis but on which constant social intervention makes its mark (Shilling 1993; Turner 1996). Therefore, we will never ask the question: Is it nature *or* nurture? We always understand gendered experiences as a combination of both physiological experience and social interpretation.

Nonetheless, we suggest that the physical effects of social practices are far more flexible than has been popularly imagined. The sizes and shapes of bodies are a result of social practices (e.g., nutrition, dieting, fitness, surgical alteration, contraceptive practices, female and male circumcision), just as social practices are designed to meet physical needs (e.g., food preparation and distribution, creating and obtaining shelter, sanitary practices) (Cashmore 2005; Connell 2002; Lorber 1994). Therefore, in this book we are attentive to cultural messages and social practices. Like Lorber (1994), we see gender as something that most of us first *believe* to be true of bodies and that we then *find* selectively in the world of social practice. Lorber writes, "Gendered people do not emerge from physiology or hormones but from the exigencies of social order, from the need for reliable division of the work of food production and the social (not physical) reproduction of new members" (19).

In other words, although our physiological bodies emerge from nature, gender—as a part of social organization—defines what is "appropriate" in the uses of our bodies. Lorber continues, "I am not saying that physical differences between male and female bodies don't exist, but that these differences are socially meaningless until social practices transform them into social facts" (18).

To suggest that gender is a social construction is to argue that there are "rules" (which originate in cultural messages) of appropriate behavior for women and men, and that those rules do not inhere in nature (that is, they do not originate from within our bodies), but they are mandated by social participation. In other words, "we" made them up—what we consider appropriate comes from the social world. Much like laws, the "rules" of gender have developed *over time through social participation*. While these rules of behavior are based on expectations about bodies (femaleness or maleness), they rarely have to do with bodily capacities. For example, it is traditional for men to open doors for women. However, there is no physiological reason for this expectation. Women and men both have hands with opposable thumbs such that door opening is generally not problematic (unless a particular person has a physical difference, such as being wheelchair bound). Genitalia are not commonly used in the opening of doors. Hence, there is no necessary reason to expect that maleness or femaleness renders one a better door opener. Nonetheless, the tradition of door opening is based on a social expectation about female and male bodies. This example demonstrates how the "rules" of appropriate gender behavior are more about gender performance than physiological necessity. They are more about what we expect of female or male people than about what female or male bodies require or can accomplish physically. (We discuss gender as performance in greater depth in chapter 2.)

To suggest that gender—the rules of "appropriate" participation—is socially constructed is not to suggest that gender expectations are not serious. Gender is serious business. If you have broken the rules, you will know about it. Your peers, mentors, families, friends, authority figures, and sometimes even strangers will indicate it to you with more or less formalized types of sanctions: perhaps by giving you a nasty look, making an unpleasant remark, or beating you up or arresting you. Oftentimes if you have broken the rules, you will feel it intuitively or viscerally; even without comment or response from another person (because these rules are so practiced you already know what response to expect).

Additionally, recognizing gender as a social construction does not suggest that physiology and the social world are fully separable. Indeed, the overarching argument throughout this book is that, while gender is socially constructed, it is so "real," serious, and pervasive as to change the way in which we experience our bodies and the ways we use our bodies—over time resulting in changes to physical capacities (e.g., strength, size, proportion).

But to further shore up our argument, we can demonstrate that gender is socially constructed because *gender expectations change over time and across cultures.* While some gendered system has always historically existed in the United States, what is considered appropriately masculine or feminine has changed considerably over just the past 50 years. For example, Feinberg (1996) reports that in the 1950s in Albany, New York, a person could have been arrested for dressing inappropriately for one's gender (sometimes called cross-dressing). The law required each person to be wearing at least three pieces of gender-appropriate clothing. Feinberg reports that this law was primarily applied to arrest people who attended lesbian and gay bars, above all drag queens and butch women, who she reports were regularly beaten and raped by the police. Given that cross-dressing performances, such as drag queen and drag king performances, are common in most major cities today (Berkowitz, Belgrave and Halberstein, forthcoming 2007; Halberstam 1998; Newton 1972; Rupp and Taylor 2003), and that celebrities such as David Bowie, RuPaul, Boy George, k.d. lang, Dennis Rodman, Ellen DeGeneres, and Marilyn Manson, among others, have become famous while gender bending (nonconforming in terms of styles of dress and fashion) since the 1950s example above, we can say that expectations about gender performances have changed and are changing. Similarly, the once common notion of the stay-at-home mom as the core of the (white) nuclear family (as seen in the television shows *Leave It to Beaver* and *Father Knows Best*) has shifted considerably out of economic necessity in the twenty-first century to the extent that it is much more likely today than in the past to expect mothers to work (Coontz 1992; Ruane and Cerulo 2000). In actuality throughout U.S. history the notion of a stay-at-home mom was only reserved for economically privileged, mostly white families. Women of color, especially immigrant women, have always been expected to work, even in extremely arduous jobs—such as domestic labor and migrant farming. In the nineteenth century, during the U.S. transition to capitalist industrialism, an ideology referred to as the *cult of true womanhood* (Welter 1978) emerged. It reflected the movement of economic work out of the home and into separate workplaces. The division between public and private worlds prescribed a division of labor by gender, with men following production out of the home and women remaining in the home to tend to reproductive issues. The home became the proper sphere for women's interests and influence. This gendered division of labor was accompanied by new beliefs about women's "natural superiority" as caregivers and moral custodians of the home. This ideology of women's true place, although aspired to by families of all social classes, was not easily attainable. Many families depended on the paid labor of women and could not afford to have them sitting "idle" at home. Thus, the cult of true womanhood functioned as a class ideology. It was a way for white, middle-class families to distinguish themselves from people of color and working-class white people. However, even for white middle-class wives, the cult of true womanhood restricted life options to home and family. So, notions of appropriate femininity (including expectations of physical strength of female bodies) have always been a matter of context and have shifted across time and social strata.

Further, notions of appropriate behavior for female and male people differ considerably across cultures and religious traditions. With the renewed sensationalism in the U.S. media during the Second Gulf War about Muslim women in Iraq and Afghanistan wearing *burquas,* and the various interpretations of this practice, it is clear that clothing imperatives differ greatly between the United States and other countries. Beyond mere clothing imperatives, other cultures allow for gender switching or gender ambiguity in ways to which U.S. culture provides no recognizable parallels. For example, Brown (1997) writes about the existence of "Two Spirit People" among some Native American cultures who he argues occupy six different gender positions, some of which are not analogous to any gender position in Western cultures. Additionally, Young (2000) writes about "women who become men" in rural Albania—female-bodied people who become "sworn virgins" and legitimately live their lives and dress as men in Albanian culture. Again, this form of gender switching has no legitimated and recognized parallel in the United States. So, while we regularly take current-day notions of masculinity and femininity as normative—a given—in our everyday lives, it need not be so.

CONSTRUCTING DICHOTOMOUS BODIES

Woman is a pair of ovaries with a human being attached, whereas man is a human being furnished with a pair of testes.

—Dr. Rudolf Virchow

The ancient Greek physician Hippocrates introduced the idea of a "wandering uterus," to explain hysteria and many other ailments in women. He argued that the uterus would detach itself and wander around the body. The only "cure" for this, according to Hippocrates, was to anchor the uterus through impregnation or to keep the uterus moist, and thus keep it from seeking out the moisture of other organs, through sexual intercourse. Aristotle (writing between 384 and 322 BCE) argued that women provided only the raw material for conception, while men contributed form and soul to a fetus (cited in Tuana 1989). In the second century CE, Galen believed that men and women had the same genitals, but that women's were inverted (Laqueur 1990). In other words, embryos that did not receive enough heat in utero to become male babies became female babies, whose genitals were upside down (or downside up perhaps is a better description). Drawings of the female reproductive system in medical texts in the seventeenth and eighteenth centuries depict the uterus as an inverted phallus. In these early writings and drawings, we see the notion of men as active creators and women as passive vessels. Ancient theories of reproduction sound laughable to our modern ears, but they give us an idea of the historical constructions of difference between women and men that have lingered well into modern times.

Metaphors and Medical Texts

Not surprisingly, today essentialist notions of "true" difference between women and men arise from the presumed effects of genital differences—such that people with penises and people with vaginas are presumed to be wholly different kinds of people with predictable sexualities (always assumed to have attractions to the other sex), reproductive interests (always assumed to want to reproduce), and capabilities (always assumed to be able to reproduce). In other words, presumptions about reproductive capacity (whether accurate or not) fuel the notion that men are primarily active people and women are primarily passive people. As we stated earlier, there is no universal definition of masculinity or femininity. The "rules" change over time and across cultures (which is how we know them to be socially constructed). But one common notion in many Western cultures regardless of the specifics of dress and action of the place or time period is the expectation of males as aggressive and females as passive and receptive.

Emily Martin (1987, 1991) shows how the construction of the sperm as "active" (swims, is strong, is healthy, digs, wags, fertilizes) and the ovum (or "egg") as "passive" (waits, is released, attracts) in medical textbooks contributes to the gendering of cultural messages about heterosexual reproductive bodies. Expanding on this idea, Lisa Jean Moore (2003) examines the representation and personification of sperm in children's books. She shows an example of the *romantic sperm*, a cartoon sperm dressed in a top hat and bowtie, sitting on a heart, with a caption reading "How could an egg resist a sperm like this?" As it turns out, the language commonly used to describe the activities of eggs and sperm is not necessarily descriptive of what actually happens during the reproductive process. Scientific research suggests that the sperm and the egg actually work interactively. They seem to recognize each other, and stick to each other. One might even argue that the egg actively "catches" the sperm (Martin 1991). Other language or images could be chosen to describe the process.

Additionally, medical texts have described women's reproductive bodies using many telling metaphors. Most frequently, perhaps, female bodies have been thought of and treated as vessels or containers, as we will see in chapter 3. Another common metaphor in the modern age has been that of a machine that "produces" in the case of pregnancy and birth and "fails to produce" in the case of menstruation and menopause (Martin 1987). While the metaphor of a machine may bring to mind images of power and active production, we must also realize that machines often require humans to control the machine. For this reason, many feminist scholars have criticized the machine model of women's bodies, claiming that it takes away from women's power in reproductive functioning. In other words, while the woman may be the machine, the (presumably male) doctor would be the operator or mechanic.

Men's sexual and reproductive bodies are also likened to machines, not as passive instruments, but rather as powerful, high-performance machines. In "Pills and Power Tools," Susan Bordo (1998) describes how our language shapes cultural expectations of and for men:

> Think of our slang terms, so many of which encase the penis, like a cyborg, in various sorts of metal or steel armor. Big rig. Blow torch. Bolt. Cockpit. Crank. Crowbar. Destroyer. Dipstick. Drill. Engine. Hammer. Hand tool. Hardware. Hose. Power tool. Rod. Torpedo. Rocket. Spear. Such slang—common among teenage boys—is violent in what it suggests the machine penis can do to another,

"softer" body. But the terms are also metaphorical protection against the failure of potency. (88)

Hence, men's bodies are understood as active and women's bodies as passive. This dichotomy is an interesting reduction of all bodily difference
and capability into two greatly oversimplified groups, ignoring most of
women's actions and capabilities and men's inabilities or choices to be less
active (as well as a whole category of intersexed people, whom we discuss
shortly).

Not only are whole bodies gendered, body parts come with their own
gendered and sexualized messages. Whereas hands are not often seen as sex
organs (even though we may use them in behaviors we would refer to as
sexual), certain body parts (especially penises, testicles, and vulvas) are seen
as inherently sexual and, hence, as "private parts." In public in the United
States, a naked hand is commonplace, but naked genitals are often cause for
calling the police. Interestingly, breasts are only sexualized on women, even
though breast structures on men (nipples and the pectoral area) are similar
to those of women, albeit usually with less fatty tissue and without milk-
producing capabilities. So essentially, women are precluded from having
naked breasts in public and their breasts are sexualized primarily because
they have more fat tissue. Paradoxically, some larger male-bodied people
have fatty breasts (because weight gain throughout the body usually results
in fatty development of breasts as well), yet they are not commonly considered undressed if they are shirtless in public, even if their breasts are
larger than a female person who is "flat-chested."

Much of this gendering of body parts happens in the use of slang terms
in everyday life. Like the words Bordo outlines above, slang for the penis often implies violence. Slang commonly used to describe female body parts
tends to emphasize breasts—"hooters," "knockers," "boobs"—rather than
genitals, and breasts are not envisioned as powerful, but as objects to be
manipulated (Young 2005: 77). Slang for female genitalia often implies the
absence of something (vaginas described as a "hole," or envisioned as a
dangerous, bottomless pit) or does not speak of anything at all (e.g., the eu-
phemism "down there"). Indeed, Eve Ensler's (1998) wildly famous play,
The Vagina Monologues, is entirely premised on the concept that women are
encouraged to ignore their genitals and develop an absence of knowledge
about their bodies and sexualities.

The cultural message of dichotomy between females and males clearly
ignores a host of human bodily *similarities*, including the ways that human maleness and femaleness *arise from each other*. Take, for example, the
egg and sperm metaphors above. The notion of sperm as active and egg as
passive ignores the reality that sperm are needed to create female babies
and an ovum (an "egg") is needed to create a male baby. In other words,

making the father active where the mother is passive ignores the "male" component of female children and the "female" component of male children. Further, humans have far more similarities, even genital similarities, than differences. It is less often recognized outside of scientific circles that the genital sex of a child is not determined at conception. All embryos remain genitally undifferentiated until about six weeks into embryonic development (LeVay and Valente 2002; Strong et al. 2005). For this reason, females and males (all humans) have homologous reproductive structures. A clitoris will arise from *the same* fetal material as a penis. Labia and scrotum are similarly homologous structures that arise from the same previously undifferentiated tissue. Similarly, ovaries or testes arise from the same material in the pre-sexed embryo. Indeed, adult human bodies are sexually similar. Although it is clear that male bodies tend to have external organs while female bodies tend to have internal organs, both react physically in much the same way. As Masters and Johnson (1966) mapped several decades ago, the human sexual response cycle is similar between female- and male-bodied people, beginning with excitement, then plateau, then orgasm, then resolution. And, while it is common to note that male body tissues engorge with blood (in the corpus cavernosa and corpus spongeosum within the penis) and experience muscle reaction during orgasm, it is less publicly recognized that female bodies also engorge with blood (in the corpus cavernosa and corpus spongeosum within the labia and surrounding the vagina) and experience muscle reaction during orgasm (Strong et al. 2005). In other words, female and male genitals actually work in somewhat similar ways during orgasm with the exception that male erection and orgasm is more visible because male genitals are external.

Additionally, most components of human bodies are similar. Most human bodies have 10 fingers and 10 toes, two arms and legs, similar facial components (although many humans have all manner of differences as well). The size and shape of bodies and body components vary widely, and human bodies are amazingly plastic; we survive and thrive in many forms. There are female and male bodies that are less than five feet tall and female and male bodies that are more than seven feet tall. There are females who bench-press more than 200 pounds and males who weigh less than 100 pounds. There are recognizably female or male people who cannot reproduce and people who are not recognizably "female" or "male." Hence, the gendered notion that women and men are polar opposites ignores the vast majority of similarities among all human bodies and the myriad ways male and female populations overlap or simply do not meet our gendered expectations. Gendered messages and practices are at work here to keep us from recognizing the vast diversity among humans. How does this happen?

Why Only Two? Understanding Dualisms and Typifications

Before understanding how gender works, we need to first examine two important attributes about Western thought—dualistic thinking and typification. Both dualistic thinking and typification create the categorization system that allows us to believe in the naturalness of femaleness and maleness.[6]

In Western cultures, we tend to practice *dualistic thinking* (Bordo 1986; Jay 1981; Sprague 1997). In other words, we tend to think in terms of two options (i.e., either/or). That is, we utilize the most simple category system—one or the other. Common sense tells us there are "two sides to every argument" or "two sides of a coin." Of course, we could think of coins as continuous circles or arguments as having an unlimited number of complex sides (5? 27?). But we commonly refer to most issues in terms of simple dualisms or binaries. Some examples are as follows: right/wrong, white/black, man/woman, straight/gay, citizen/alien, rational/emotional, abstract/concrete, public/private, up/down, high/low, divine/mortal, capitalist/worker, masculine/feminine. Not only do we conceptualize in terms of dualisms, but we imagine them as polar opposites—mutually exclusive categories with no gray area in between.

While this practice may seem innocent enough, there are at least two particular problems with dualistic thinking. First, thinking in terms of two and only two possible options masks the complexity of the world. Imagine trying to describe all the variety of flowers in terms of one type or the other. Can you describe trees in terms of two options? Let's assume all trees can be described as deciduous (those that shed their leaves once a year) or evergreens. If someone giving you directions were to tell you to turn left at the deciduous tree, would you have any idea to which tree they were referring? Categorizing in terms of twos greatly reduces the variability with which we can describe the world—and falsely so. It too narrowly focuses our attention to very limited criteria. Not only can we not describe wide variety, but we are continually focused on the simple categories created.

The second problem with dualisms is that we rarely create equal and opposite options within our dualisms. We tend to think hierarchically. That is, we rank the options. Rational is imagined as better than emotional. Even space is understood hierarchically—up is better than down; high is better than low. Of course, in many ways this is nonsensical. Exactly how up is "up" enough? If high is better than low, how do we know how high is high? Is four feet off the ground "high" or "low"? Is it "high" if the other option is two feet off the ground? Or is it that high is good but higher is always better? Clearly the ideas of high and low are relative and never provide enough information to fully understand a complex situation. Nonetheless, we use this dualism to be somehow informative.

Gender expectations fall into Western practices of thinking dualistically (Bem 1993; Kessler and McKenna 1978; Lorber 1996). We think in terms of masculine = male and feminine = female. We often think this is linked to expectations of "natural" reproduction. Interestingly, we do not categorize based on actual reproductive capacity—those who can reproduce (the fertiles) and those who cannot (the nonfertiles) (Kessler and McKenna 1978). Perhaps we avoid this dualism because it is not readily apparent upon sight exactly who falls into each group. After all, the nonfertiles would be comprised of the very young (not yet fertile) and the old (beyond fertile age), as well as some younger adults who simply will never be fertile. Similarly, the gender binary is based on presumptions about the clothed, visible body— presumptions about genitalia and reproductive capacity (Kessler 1998; West and Zimmerman 1987). We will follow this up in depth shortly.

In addition to dualistic thinking, we tend to think categorically using what Schutz (1970) calls *typification*, or the idea that human thought is the process of categorizing—the process of linking objects abstractly into categories such that we can think in terms of what is typical. So while desks can come in a variety of styles comprised of a variety of materials, when one thinks of "desk," one has a mental picture of the thing that is typical of desk. Indeed, language is categorical. You do not have to be thinking of a particular desk (your desk, for example) to imagine "desk" as a type of thing that is used in typical ways. The word d-e-s-k is a marker for that typical thing into which a wide variety of actual objects fall.[7] Typifications are abstract notions that group physical objects into manageable categories (Zerubavel 1996). If you could not typify, you would have to figure out each object that you encounter as if it were new to you each time you encounter it. For Schutz, typifications are useful and necessary. Without the ability to typify, language itself would not exist. So typifications are very efficient and useful in the development of language.

Of course, people are objects about which typifications can be applied. When applied to people, typifications may be thought of by the more familiar term *stereotypes*. Stereotyping is the use of commonsense (often discriminatory) assumptions about groups of people to make predictions about characteristics of an individual. Indeed, as physical objects, people are readily stereotyped based on visual cues of the physical body.

There are some qualities of typifications that make it problematic to apply them to people. First, typifications are acquired in the everyday world of interaction. That is, they develop through our interactions into what we call common sense—the collections of our experiences within a culture. In other words, our typifications are not based on scientific measurement and testing, but rather on acting and interacting within our culture, specifically that part of our culture that is most familiar to us. So what you believe is true or typical is based only on the biases of your own cultural experiences.

Also, the existing category system blinds us to other possibilities. Once we have developed notions of the typical, we focus our attention on the typical, not the aberration, often even when the aberration is common. That is, rather than upset our category system, we simply call that thing that doesn't fit "atypical" ("Oh, that's not typical!") and dismiss it.

Let's consider an example of typification. Imagine the following situation. A woman is in the kitchen at 7 o'clock on a Tuesday morning browning meat for the family. What is she doing? Easy enough, she's "cooking." Now imagine another situation. It's Saturday afternoon. A man is outside browning meat over a propane stove (perhaps even drinking a beer while flipping burgers) for the family. What's he doing? He's "grilling" or "barbecuing" (depending on the part of the country from which you originate). In each situation, we imagine both are just being "mom" and "dad" respectively. We imagine that if a woman is preparing food on a weekday morning, she is demonstrating her nurturing "nature" by acting as mom, whereas if a man is preparing food on a weekend afternoon, he is recreating or acting as "dads" do. Of course, *both scenarios are exactly the same activity*—preparing a meal. But we have cultural stories about how we typically understand each situation and whom we expect to find in each situation. It is useful to note that what moms do, we expect to be done inside; whereas what dads do, we expect to be done outside. Hence, context is extremely important in our understanding of each situation. Consider this: how would your idea of the first situation have shifted if we asked you to imagine that the female person preparing meat on a Tuesday morning at 7 o'clock was drinking a beer while flipping meat? My guess is that your expectations about "good, nurturing mother" would have disappeared completely, even though the same activity is perfectly acceptable by "dads" on weekend afternoons. Hence, gender is an engagement of our notions of the typical, which is always about context, even when the same activity is being conducted.

Now imagine it is Tuesday morning at 7 o'clock and a man is browning meat for some kids for breakfast. What is he doing? He's "helping" or perhaps he is a "very nurturing father" or "a catch" as a husband. That is, our cultural script says that moms cook breakfast. So if a male person is cooking, we imagine he must be exceptional as a person or perhaps there is some aberrant situation ("Mom had to go to work early today for a meeting"). That is, we begin to make up a narrative in our minds to understand the situation that does not fit our expectations. In other words, because the situation does not fit our idea of the typical, we throw it out—declare it an outlier, rather than allow it to change our categories of "mom" and "dad." So the typifications that already exist blind us to the possible ways in which we might see or imagine each interaction.

Another favorite example of this effect comes from a true story of a real group of friends (female and male) who have known each other for many years. One friend, Dianne, is a marathon runner. She has always been an accomplished athlete, having been a four-year All American in field hockey and a three-year All American in softball during her four-year college career. Indeed, she was one person short of making the alternate position on the U.S.

Olympic field hockey team during that time. Having now aged out of competitive sports in her early forties, she trains for and runs marathons for fun. One year, she ran the Boston Marathon (for which one must be invited) in 26.2 consecutive 7-minute-48-second miles. It is safe to say she is an amazing athlete. Most of the rest of this crowd of friends are more known for their beer-drinking abilities than athletics. It probably would not be contested by the male friends that Dianne can outrun them all consecutively (if the rest of them run as a group, one after another, against her alone) and she would whip the group pretty handily for speed and distance even when she is not training. Nonetheless, everyone involved, including Dianne, would likely agree to the idea that "men are naturally physically superior to women." That's right, in the face of pure empirical evidence that some women are physically superior in some physical characteristics to many men, we tend to hold on to our typifications, rather than open up our categories. That is, we see Dianne as an outlier and we "throw her out." All of a sudden, she becomes "athlete" and not "woman," so our category for "woman" does not have to be amended. This is how gender typification works.

You might suggest that if the guys had trained, they could beat Dianne, but they did not train and they do not train. Actually Dianne trains regardless of whether or not she is preparing for a race. It is simply true in every testable sense that she is a better runner. If you doubt it or imagine that she can't be representative of "women," then you have proven our point—typifications blind us from seeing things that fall outside our categories, even those things that are easily verifiable. It is much easier to ignore Dianne than to change our categories.

Heteronormativity and the Gender Box Structure

Our binary notions of "typical" bodies suggest our rules for interaction have a basis in the "natural" body. True to our Western intellectual origins, these so-called "natural" bodies are also understood in hierarchical ways. We see male bodies (and hence men) as strong, tall, powerful, and aggressive; and female bodies (and hence women) as small, petite, elegant, and in need of protection. In our culture, the male body is understood as physically better than the female body—that is, we see males as "naturally physically superior" to females. This means that we as a culture do not understand the ability to give birth to human life as strength or an indicator of any sort of physical superiority; it is attributed to the "weak" female body.

Notice that all this discussion relies on typification—generalized ideas about everyone falling into the groups "women" and "men." Whereas we know that not all men are stronger than all women and that not all men are taller than all women, we typify "women" as small and "men" as tall and ignore any evidence to the contrary. If we notice the differences, we have to amend our categories, and that is often too challenging.

Heteronormativity is the belief that institutionalized heterosexuality should be the standard for legitimate intimate relationships (Ingraham 1996:169). Within the heteronormative paradigm, sex, gender, and sexual orientation are ideologically fused and are assumed to be based on innate characteristics of the body, rather than social prescriptions (Butler 1990; Jackson and Scott 2001; Kessler 1998; Kessler and McKenna 1978; Lorber 1996; West and Zimmerman 1987). That is, they are presumed to be "natural" and reliant on whether one has a penis or a vagina (which has historically been understood as lack of a penis [de Beauvoir 1952; Kessler 1998]). So in practice, when we see a person (or even imagine the sight of someone, for example, when interacting virtually via the Internet), we first attribute biological sex (femaleness or maleness) to that person, then implicitly apply expectations for gendered behavior (modes of dress, uses of the body) and heterosexual practices (coupling with an "opposite" partner). That is, we typify each person or "place them in a box"—the female box or the male box (figure 1.1).

Two points are particularly pertinent in this figure. First, notice that sex, gender, and sexual orientation are fused and assumed to be attached to biological bodies. So, if we believe we know the sex of the person, we also believe we know the gender and sexual orientation of the person. Second, notice that there is a space between the boxes where presumably no one can exist. That is, this is an instance of Western dualistic thought that provides for two and only two options that are understood as mutually exclusive

Figure 1.1. Gender Box Structure. Binary gender messages in the social world tell us to typify each person as either "female" or "male" and apply assumptions about bodies, gender, and sexual orientation.

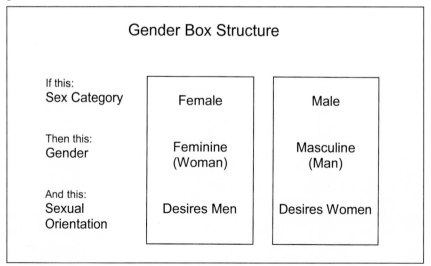

(not overlapping). In other words, we understand all people to fit in either one box or the other. Anyone not fitting in these boxes is understood as "unnatural," "not normal," aberrant, an outlier. And so, we "throw them out"—place them outside the realm of our acknowledgment or understanding. Like all dualisms, this box structure is far too narrowly focused to accurately and colorfully describe the human diversity that we know to exist. We know people who do not fit our typifications; we just choose not to figure them into our categories. And, like all dualisms, we implicitly create a hierarchy in which to have a penis (be masculine, be the "active" sexual participant) is understood as better than to have no penis (be feminine, be the "passive" sexual recipient).

In this book, we argue that the gender box structure is both unnecessary and inaccurate in understanding and describing human experience. Far greater diversity of humanity exists than is imagined and described by heteronormative paradigms. We provide an alternative theory of how gender works shortly, but first—a note on variation within gender messages.

A Note on Race, Class, and Sexual Orientation

We have stated so far that notions of masculinity and femininity are dualistic. This should not imply that femininity and masculinity do not vary by racial or cultural experience, social class experience, or by participating in groups based on sexual orientation. Just as gender messages differ across cultures and over time, notions of masculinity and femininity vary somewhat by cultural subgroup affiliation.

Like gendered messages, racialized messages affect bodies and interaction (Schiebinger 1993; Somerville 2000). Beliefs in the "natural" racialized body ("white," "Latin," "black," "Asian") have been used to justify all manner of racist and discriminatory interactions in U.S. history. Expectations about race continue to affect interactions among people today (Combs-Jones 2004; Houts 2004; Tripp 2003). As recently as 2004, a significant study by Sampson and Raudenbush found that white and Latin respondents' perceptions that neighborhoods are in "disorder" (that is, they are perceived as bad or dangerous neighborhoods) increased as the percentage of black people living in that neighborhood increased (in other words, not based on the increase in physical disarray—broken windows, trash in the street, etc.).[8] So, racist notions about bodies still exist in practice today even if overtly racist attitudes are less popular to express in public than they used to be.

Like gender, the belief in "natural" races compels cultural performances of ethnicity (Nagel 2000). Ideas about gender may not be exactly the same for African Americans on the West Coast or Puerto Rican Americans living in the heartland or white Americans from New England (and the differences may vary quite a bit across social classes). Despite these differences across ethnic groups, social class, and geographic location, gendered messages still prevail within each group. For example, while waiflike thinness has been the ideal image of beauty for white women (Rooks 1996), African American and Latin cultures have idealized a curvier woman's body. Sir Mix-A-Lot's very popular song, "Baby Got Back," attests to the urban legend that African American subcultures in the United States eroticize larger backsides for women than do white subcultures. Look specifically at the following lyrics that offer a cultural protest for a different beauty standard than what is exemplified by the dominant paradigm of the white Hollywood supermodel.

> I like big butts and I can not lie
> You other brothers can't deny
> That when a girl walks in with an itty bitty waist
> And a round thing in your face
> You get sprung, . . .
> I'm tired of magazines
> Sayin' flat butts are the thing
> Take the average black man and ask him that
> She gotta pack much back
> So, fellas! (Yeah!) Fellas! (Yeah!)
> Has your girlfriend got the butt? (Hell yeah!)
> Tell 'em to shake it! (Shake it!) Shake it! (Shake it!)
> Shake that healthy butt!
> Baby got back! (Sir Mix-A-Lot 1992)

The point here is not to suggest there are real differences of beauty between different kinds of bodies, but rather that standards of fashion and beauty are related to culture and subculture and need not be consistent across groups even if they are gendered.

Similarly, standards of black masculinity arising from urban hip-hop culture differ from white masculinity. Interestingly, country-and-western standards of masculinity (which of course are also bound by social class) might prescribe tight blue jeans and large cowboy hats for men; whereas "thug" masculinity from hip-hop culture might prescribe loose pants (that nearly fall off one's butt) and oversized gold necklaces, yet both are intended to display the independent man who may use physical violence to get what he wants. Even more compelling, in the last decade or so, young white men in working-class, urban, and suburban cultures (often fans of hip-hop) have followed a trend of copying "black" masculinity and hip-hop styles. Clearly, these styles are about cultural associations, not real differences between people of certain body types.

Nonetheless, for each subgroup, there tends to be a very distinct set of messages that establish the "rules" for femininity and masculinity as separate. They exist as a dualism within subcultures even if they vary between subcultures. In other words, the belief that maleness = masculinity and femaleness = femininity tends to exist within various subgroups. Heteronormative cultural messages exist even if the specific rules vary. Interestingly, notions of race and class tend to be dualisms as well (black vs. white, poor vs. rich), even though it is clear that skin color and financial solvency exist in various ranges, not as either/or categories. While racialized bodies and ethnic performativity could be the topic of its own book, we include some examples of them and the ways they intersect with gender throughout this book. Where specific racial or class-based issues emerge, we will provide some specific examples.

STEPPING OUT OF THE GENDER BOX STRUCTURE

The Mirror of Nature

The mirror hanging on the wall dictates through the reflection of our image, reminds us of the codes inscribed on our flesh. Our bodies become sites of deeply felt contention. Refusing conformity, confinement, we struggle for the right of acceptance, for the ability to celebrate our own experience of embodiment. Yet, it is a conflict without end, reemerging with each day, with each new interaction, with each glance thrown at that mirror whose reflection disguises its insidious intent behind the veneer of the natural body.

When younger, I found myself in growing unease with the image of male bodies around me: the muscular bulk, the prominently round

stomachs, the coarseness of arms darkened by the sun. I refused the appearance offered me, broad and heavy mass that I am supposed to be. Without knowing why, I found any explicit sign of masculinity insufferable. Though I was very physically active throughout my youth, I refused to lift weights with my father or friends, not wanting those torn muscles to expand into the ripped mold of the macho form. However, I might also add that I did not substitute running over weightlifting or elect to shave my arms and legs simply out of emotive reaction to masculine appearances. These were choices in which I also took great pleasure. However, my decisions have been motivated in part by discomfort with what I perceived as the materiality of masculinity—the white supremacy, homophobia, and sexist domination that converged in my particular socialization as a masculine person. All those masculinities that I found difficult to redefine as anything except imposing and destructive. I have never come to terms with my body. My body's terms are in constant flux, demanding to be redefined, reread, embraced, and then emptied of all meaning.

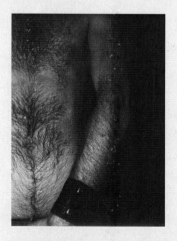

Body hair is one aspect that has always leant itself to a feeling of distress. By age 13 my chest and stomach had cultivated a considerable spread of hair, relentless in its conquest of my skin. As I write this, the hair that I frequently shave from my arms and torso spreads the surface of my skin like wild foliage, as I am too lazy and busy this week to divest of that layer. Throughout my life such physical appearances have proven to be occasions of severe discomfort within me to the point of utter revulsion. At certain times I determined to clear away those markings by shaving my body in its entirety. I also had the luxury of possessing thick hair that I usually grew long, allowing me to obtain, to an extent, a certain androgyny that I most treasured. If "Miss" was a designation I occasionally received, I accepted it with gratitude and pleasure against the apologies of the speaker.

And yet, there are times, though much more rare, when I manage certain appreciation for that bristled growth spanning the length of my arms and legs. I remember distinctly one such moment, occurring during travels in Guatemala. I was volunteering at a children's day care on the outskirts of the city, where kids from surrounding rural homes would

spend the morning and afternoon. They came because their parents were busy tending to the harvest or away pleading for work in the city; they came with a tenderness and force of will that could melt all resistance.

Because day care volunteers are often female, I was uncertain how my presence as a male would be met. The first day one of the children opened the front door and before I could offer a salutary spread of teeth or an introduction in my lumbering Spanish tongue, one of the young girls, without a word, took me by the hand to guide me through a hall brimming with smiles widened by their curiosity. In a short span of time, our friendship began to unfold and blossom into laughter and trust.

Two months living in Latin America, outside my familiar social spaces that keep me conscious of physical grooming, I allow my hair to grow out in abandon. One afternoon, before preparing the afternoon meal, I am sitting at the table drawing with the children. One of the boys, Walter, pulls up my denim sleeve and giggles: "Tienes mucho vello. . .you're so hairy." I expect the sight to repel him, but to my surprise he runs his fingers up my arms like a gust of wind parting a path through a grassy field. Another boy and girl approach and begin to do the same. I am arrested by the affection of their caresses as they explore the texture of my arm hair, which is normally cause for my own revulsion. And yet, suddenly the way they embrace my body enables me not only to accept its features, but to celebrate them.

—Ryan Mauldin, undergraduate student

Are all girls feminine and all boys masculine? Based on Ryan's story, it would be hard to answer yes to that question. In your everyday experience of the world, you are likely to say no. Each of us knows people who do not readily fit the prescriptions of femininity or masculinity, whether by conscious or seemingly unconscious choice. We know men who enjoy cooking and women who are Marines, and so forth. In fact, not all people who may be considered normatively masculine or feminine engage in masculine or feminine activities all the time. For example, if a woman is good at ice hockey, does that make her masculine? If a man is changing a diaper, does that make him feminine? Perhaps you might say, "It's not fair to question someone's identity just because they are good at sports or because they care for their children!" But isn't that how we assign those identities in the first place? If a man is good at sports, we see him as masculine. If a woman is good at sports, we see her as "pretty good for a girl." Or perhaps we even question whether she is a *real* girl by suggesting she is lesbian. (See chapter 3 for a discussion of "lesbian baiting" of women athletes.) If a woman is changing a diaper, we assume she is enacting her nurturing "nature." If a man is changing a diaper, we avoid seeing him as feminine, rather we say he's a good dad even though nurturing activities are supposed to be related to femininity. Hence, we fall back into the box structure typifications. Yet we know many female-bodied people who are good athletes and male-bodied people who care for children. What we argue, then, is that via the gender box structure, *we understand activities as gendered and then we encourage or discourage people with certain presumed genitalia to or from participating.* We think of sports as typically masculine and cooking as typically feminine[9] and then typify people who do them. Anyone can play ice hockey. Anyone can cook. Yet we make significance out of who does what, when, and how. More importantly, there is a performance style to playing sports and cooking that suggests a "realness" to our understandings of gender assignments. We will follow this idea in depth in the next chapter on performing gender.

We use typifications to think about sexuality also. Is it true that all people are heterosexual? No, quite a large number of people identify as homosexual, some of whom have received a good bit of celebrity in the last 10 years via television and popular culture. It is very likely that you know someone who does not identify as heterosexual. Is it true that all people are either heterosexual or homosexual (another Western binary)? No, there are people who identify as bisexual. Does bisexual mean always preferring women and men at all times? Does it imply serial monogamy (my current partner is x but future partners could be x or y)? Does it mean sexually voracious—or wanting sex all the time with any willing partner? Bisexuality is often understood as a problematic category because it does not easily align with binary notions of homo or hetero and confuses the "naturalness" of binary biological sex urges, and so hence becomes politically confusing to those who prefer neat categories (Rust 1995). Do you believe that someone can have attractions to females and males throughout their entire lives? Many people report just that.

Additionally, do people always identify in one of these categories for their entire lives? What is the defining characteristic of someone's "real" sexual orientation? Sexual practices? Whom they desire? How they choose to self-identify? This, in fact, is the classic question in studies of sexual orientation opened by Kinsey's (1948, 1953) famous studies in which he asserted that a great deal of the U.S. population could be labeled bisexual based on reports of his participants of same-sex sexual practices, desires, or identities.[10] If sexual orientation is an essentially true characteristic about people, how do we determine the "true" orientation of each of us?

Let's assume sexuality is based on with whom you have had sexual contact. If a female-bodied person currently identifies as lesbian but had sex with men until age 30, is she lesbian or bisexual? If a person has never had sex with anyone (i.e., the person is a "virgin"), can they have a sexual orientation?

Perhaps sexuality is based on how people identify themselves. If a man identifies as heterosexual but occasionally has sex with men, is he straight or gay? This scenario is apparently much more common than common-sense knowledge would have predicted or Kinsey's study (1948) would not have caused such lengthy discussion both in and out of the academy. If you said he's gay, then you've admitted that your definition of someone's sexuality is as salient as that person's definition. In other words, identity is co-constructed between a person and the social context in which others label that person. If someone identifies as heterosexual and engages in a three-some with both a male and female partner, is that person bisexual by definition? If you answered no to this and "gay" to the previous question, you have just contradicted your own theory of sexuality.

Perhaps you imagine the answer lies in whom the person desires. So, if the male person who occasionally has sex with another man does not express desire for him ("It's just sex—a way to get off."), is that not "gay" sex? What if the two men are having sex for the voyeuristic enjoyment of a female person: are all three heterosexual? If a female person has always been married heterosexually but secretly dreams of sex with women, is she "really" lesbian—even if she only has sex with her heterosexually married partner?

Sexuality is not nearly as clear-cut as we imagine it. Life experiences and sexual histories of individuals are not continuously consistent over time. Sexual practices, identities, and desires often do not align consistently: some people report desire without sexual contact, or contact without desire, or identities that do not match practices (Schwartz and Rutter 1998). Interestingly, in U.S. culture, the notion of sexual orientation is not based strictly on an individual's characteristics, but on the sex of their partner. Further, this notion of sexuality has not been the definition of appropriate sexuality throughout time or across cultures—that is, it is a socially constructed notion of sexuality (Katz 1995; Rubin 2003; Weeks 2003). Katz (1995) writes that our notion of "heterosexuality" is a modern invention originating in the second half of the nineteenth century. It appeared in the dictionary after the word "homosexual" appeared in the dictionary. Prior to this time frame, various notions of sexuality existed. Of course same-sex sexual practices have been recorded throughout history, but the ways in which people have understood them have changed considerably. Halperin (1989) writes of Ancient Greek cultures in which sexual prerogative was defined by citizenship (land ownership) such that to be a citizen meant that one could have sexual relations with any noncitizen (female or male). Hence, the notion of "orientation" was nonsensical to Ancient Greeks. Further, in current cultures in other areas of the world, if a man is having anal sex with another man, it does not automatically imply that both men are understood as gay. Almaguer (1993) writes that in some subcultures in northern Mexico, the active partner is *activo* or masculine, and hence not stigmatized; whereas the partner who allows himself to be penetrated is *pasivo* and stigmatized as feminine (essentially made a woman). In the United States, some men secretly engage in sex with other men while considering themselves to be heterosexual (Humphreys 1970; King 2005). The slang term for this practice is "on the down low." A significant concern about this practice is that many of these men have female partners or wives to whom they do not reveal their (often unprotected) sexual interactions with men, hence risking HIV infection for their unsuspecting female partners (King 2005).[11]

So notions of sexual practices, sexual identities, gendered activities, and gendered participation in the world are much fuzzier than the dichotomous box structure would predict. Although people regularly use these typifications of gender and sexuality, the dichotomous box structure simply does not describe the vast variability of experiences and practices in the world. But what about so-called biological sex? Can that be dichotomous?

What about Nature?

Isn't it true that all people are born unambiguously female or male? No, a significant portion of the human population (estimated at 1.7% of live births) are born *intersexed*—that is, born with various ambiguities of genital appearance or chromosomal or hormonal differences (Blackless et al. 2000; Fausto-Sterling 2000:51).[12] In other words, some people do not fit into the dichotomous standard of femaleness or maleness, based on some genital, chromosomal, or hormonal difference (Fausto-Sterling 2000; Kessler 1998). The works of Anne Fausto-Sterling and Suzanne Kessler demonstrate to us how the "problem" of intersexuality is a problem of normative categories, not a problem of bodies or intersexed people themselves.

Kessler documents the process of twentieth-century medical practice in the United States that has come to define genital difference as "abnormal" or even "deviant" and in need of surgical change in *intersexed* children. During the so-called progress of twentieth-century medical science, doctors began making surgical changes to "fix" the genitals of intersexed infants that could not be clearly assigned a sex category. In other words, a sex category (female or male) was chosen for the child and normative appearing genitals surgically constructed based on the greatest likeness the doctors felt could be achieved (based on medical abilities of the particular time). The medical premise for such changes was that intersexed bodies were "abnormal" or "a mistake" of nature that medical science proposed to "fix." Having surgically and hormonally "fixed" these so-called aberrant bodies, doctors were purported to have made these children "normal" so they might fit into the "biological" order of femaleness and maleness. In essence, doctors were purporting to make these ambiguous bodies into "normal" women and men (Kessler 1998).

That logic, however, is exactly the inverse of the logic of biological determinism or the notion that there is an essential biological "truth" to femaleness and maleness. We want to be clear on this point: Bodies emerge into the world naturally—that is, birth is a natural process (however, sometimes assisted by human intervention). Only after babies are born do we sometimes socially categorize certain differences as "wrong," different, or in need of "fixing." That is, our social process of understanding these babies as deviant because the appearance of genitalia does not fit within the (humanly constructed) standard of long-enough penises or short-enough clitorises dictates how we respond to these children. Clearly, if these children were born with some life-threatening concern (like inability to defecate or urinate), then surgical intervention seems ethically clear. However, Kessler reports that the vast majority of these children do not have life-threatening physical differences. They are largely differences of appearance. Hence, most frequently, the medical emergency was not that the child could die or face illness, but rather that the parents and doctors could not pronounce the child normatively "a girl" or "a boy" within the heteronormative paradigm.

Further, Kessler discusses the lack of clear, biologically based standards for determining what exactly is normative for penis or clitoris length in favor of "medically acceptable" standards. The practices described below were standard prior to the mid 1990s. Although the critique of these practices has led to many changes in the process, some doctors continue to use the general guideline of clitoral size as less than .9 centimeters, and "medically acceptable" infant penis length between 2.5 and 4.5 centimeters. Notably, the space between .9 and 2.5 centimeters has traditionally been understood as "unacceptable" for would-be males and females. (Notice how readily this spatial difference replicates the gender box structure in figure 1.1). A clitoris longer than .9 cm was considered too long and a penis shorter than 2.5 cm unworkable; hence each were determined to require surgery—for clitorises, to reduce them to a "normal" size, and, for penises, often to excise penis and scrotum entirely and change the child (surgically and hormonally) into a girl. Interestingly, scrotum and labia size were considered less relevant to doctors. Penis and clitoral appearance seemed of utmost concern. Kessler argues (and we agree) that this concern for penis size was predicated on the belief that if the penis were too small the adult person would never be able to penetrate a vagina and, hence, would not be a man (see also Fausto-Sterling 1995). Conversely, if a clitoris were considered a "cosmetic offense" (a term actually quoted from medical literature) because of its large size, the child could not be considered a woman (Kessler 1998:36). Clearly, then, de Beauvoir (1952) and an entire generation of feminists were right that the definition of being a man is to have a penis, whereas to be a woman is to be lacking a penis. And, if a person were born not meeting this clear dichotomy, medical doctors would make it so via surgical intervention.

Unfortunately, these doctors' protocols left little concern for the sexual pleasure of the surgically altered children when they reached adulthood or any consideration of the possibility of sexual pleasure outside the penile-vaginal penetrative model. Hence, any loss of sensation from surgical intervention was considered irrelevant to the medical necessity of knowing gender from birth. Additionally, no latitude was given to allowing the child self-definition. It was not until the early 1990s that adult intersexed persons began to advocate for a change to the treatment of intersexed babies, favoring self-elective surgeries later in life (if at all). The Intersex Society of North America,[13] an advocacy and information-providing organization originated by Cheryl Chase, emerged in the early 1990s to advocate self-determination to the American Medical Association. Only in very recent years has the medical establishment seemed willing to listen.

In addition to Kessler's work, there is a large body of literature from transgendered or transsexual people who testify to not fitting into the heteronormative box structure and, hence, the social problematic of the category system itself (Bornstein 1994; Crawley and Broad 2004; Feinberg 1996; Nestle, Howell, and Wilchins 2002). *Transsexual* (a term generally reserved for those who have undertaken some form of surgical alteration of the body) and *transgendered* (a broader term that denotes anyone who defines themselves as not fitting the requisite body/gender dualism prescribed by heteronormativity) people challenge the preeminence of the body's determination of the person or psyche. If we take seriously the earnest reports of adult transsexuals and transgendered people that their bodies need to be made to conform to fit their own gender expectations (i.e., making some genital surgical changes such that the body matches the person they wish to display), we must recognize that genitals are not the origin of psyche or self.[14] Indeed, the very idea that a person can "change sex" surgically or hormonally (or both) suggests that bodies (and, thus, sex itself) are malleable. If we can surgically change sexes, how fixed or original, then, can biology be? And, how useful is bodily appearance in predicting sex?

As an example, see the pictures in the inset of Andi/6pak, a female-bodied person. Andi performs male impersonation, for fun and for profit, as 6pak.

He has a number of personas during performance, but the one he likes most is the "thug" appearance. Other than gluing a "beard" on his face and taping his breasts to the side for the purpose of these performances, Andi/6pak has taken no steps to physically alter his female body.

The Art of Illusion Is My Passion

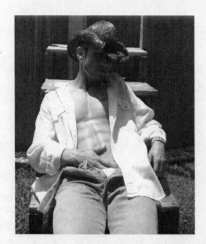

My stage name is 6pak. Some would call me a "drag king"—a gender illusionist—but I prefer male impersonator, and the art of illusion is my passion. Entertaining crowds, especially seeing the audience enjoying a good time, is the reason for my work. Having done shows from Florida to Chicago, I regularly perform in clubs using a unique spectrum of musical genres, taking on all sorts of masculine personas like Kid Rock, Tim McGraw, Eminem, and others. I also have a film credit to my credentials; I played the male lead in a romantic comedy short film called *Miggy N Lil* which filmed in Austin, Texas, and debuted in Manhattan in 2006.

My performance specialty is showing off my 6pak abs and developed biceps; I am the first male impersonator to perform with an open shirt. You should know I am a biological female and completely unaltered from the biology of my birth. I have not taken steroids; I do not use costumes or makeup to enhance my muscles; I have not had surgery or done anything to my body other than live my life. People often assume I have taken steroids or have had surgical alteration, which bothers me because it diminishes my creativity. It's almost as if some people think I am "cheating" or not being truthful because my body does not look like the female body they expect. The person you see is the biology I was born with

and displays the life I have lived. When I think about myself, I do identify with straight men, and my day job, as a house painter, is one that men often have. Maybe I will have "the surgery" some time in the future to transition from female to male, but for now I am doing what I like to do. I want to be clear: this is just me.

I enter the stage with high energy and a lot of charisma. My goal is a good performance and a good time. And, if I have my way, I will be coming to a stage near you.

—Andi Citino (6pak), male impersonator
Photos courtesy of Kate Eichorst and appear with permission.

In his book *Body Alchemy*, Loren Cameron (1996) has provided a spectacular photo essay of female to male transsexuals that documents physiological changes over time.[15] Cameron recognizes that some female to male transsexuals choose various means of transitioning, which may include any number, but not necessarily all, of the following procedures: breast removal (ranging from full double mastectomy to simple fatty tissue removal), hysterectomy, metoidioplasty (lengthening of the clitoris via partial release of clitoral ligaments as well as hormone treatment), phalloplasty (construction of a phallus from skin grafted from other areas of the body), and/or the use of hormonal treatment. Regardless of the means, if any, used to transition genital appearance, the change in overall appearance (change in sex category) is striking.

Fausto-Sterling (1986, 2000) supports our argument that so-called biological sex is more a continuum than a dichotomy, by recognizing that there remains no accurate, consistent, and reliable measure of so-called biological sex. That's right, *there is no specific, distinct measure that will consistently determine maleness or femaleness for all persons.* We have already shown that genital appearance is not a useful test. Sex chromosomes come in more interesting combinations than just XX = female and XY = male, with varying results, some of which are not physically transparent. Hormones are the least well understood component of all. While decades of research have *assumed* that testosterone influences male aggression and estrogen makes people want to cuddle babies, much of this research has not questioned the relationship of hormones to maleness and femaleness. Testosterone and estrogen have been typed as "sex hormones" for little reason, according to Fausto-Sterling (2000), since all bodies possess both kinds of hormones and both function in many ways to affect the body far beyond one's sex organs. She writes:

Why, then, have hormones always been strongly associated with the idea of sex, when, in fact, "sex hormones" apparently affect organs throughout the entire body and are not specific to either gender? The brain, lungs, bones, blood vessels, intestine, and liver (to give a partial list) all use estrogen to maintain proper growth and development. . . . Researchers accomplished this feat by defining as sex hormones what are, in effect, multi-site chemical growth regulators, thus rendering their far-reaching, non-sexual roles in both male and female development nearly invisible. (147)

Most importantly, Fausto-Sterling offers the critique that scientists' social presumptions about bodies originate in the gender box structure that has far too narrowly focused scientific study and, hence, our interpretation of its results. To paraphrase Lorber's (1993) important article, "Believing Is Seeing," first we believed in gender, then we found it in bodies (578).

Before you become too comfortable with your place in the box structure, let us remind you that we are not talking only about intersexed or transgendered people here. We are talking about you too! Regardless of your comfort with your own sexuality, gender expression, or presumed biological sex, you have also been fit into the box structure in ways that may not describe your life or individuality. Most of us probably feel comfortable that the box structure describes our bodies and our lives, but how do you know how normative your body may be? Have you had your chromosomes tested? Have you had your hormone levels tested? Do you even know what is considered in the "normative range" for a person such as you perceive yourself to be? Our guess is you probably have not even considered having physiological testing unless you think (or your doctor has indicated) that something is "wrong." If you presume your genitals are normative appearing, you may assume your body (and hence your life experience?) is "normal." But do you even know what normative appearing might be? How many sets of genitals have you seen in your life? Are you basing your own experiences on assumptions?

Our goal is not to scare you into running to your doctor, but rather to point out that much about our experiences as women and men is based on the mere presumption of genital appearance, not on medical "fact." Our beliefs are based on fitting into the social process of what we believe to be "normal." It is time to look much more closely at how the social performance of gender affects the physical body and how gender messages encourage us to believe in the presumed "natural" chasm between femaleness and maleness.

THE GENDER FEEDBACK LOOP

We propose a new diagram that we call the gender feedback loop (figure 1.2) that we believe describes the lived experience of individuals much better than the heteronormative box structure. Rather than suggest that the human population fits into one of two "natural" boxes, we assert that each person

Figure 1.2. Gender Feedback Loop: Performance / Surveillance / Resistance. More accurate than the Gender Box Structure, the Gender Feedback Loop describes how gender messages affect our thoughts about selves and our practices of the body in everyday life.

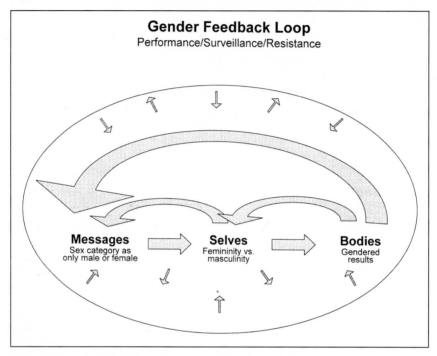

experiences a feedback loop of ideas about bodies and what are deemed appropriate gender expressions that entice each of us to behave as expected. Mapping out her argument for the social embodiment of gender, Connell (2002) agrees with our argument for a gender feedback loop when she writes:

> Bodies are both objects of social practice and agents in social practice. The same bodies, at the same time, are both. . . . There is a loop, circuit, linking bodily processes and social structures. In fact, there is a tremendous number of such circuits. They occur in historical time, and change over time. They add up to the historical process in which society is embodied, and bodies are drawn into history. (47)

This loop ultimately confirms itself by encouraging each of us to produce the gender expression expected of us, which we incorrectly read as "only natural." Throughout this book we explain the details of our argument, but let us take a moment to summarize the argument here.

If this figure looks daunting, it is not surprising. The figure is complex because the operation of gender in our worlds is complex. So here we walk you through the details, adding some crib notes to the figure (see figure 1.3). The figure begins with gendered messages or ideas from our culture that we "inherit" in a sense from previous generations, so, to some extent, the messages are not something we each invent. The messages are notions about how the world exists and are based in the current historical moment in which we have been using science to understand the world around us for about a couple of hundred years. The messages come to us from our families, churches, schools, peers, and media outlets and tell us that there are only two options for biological sex—male or female—and that sex is determinant of the kind of person we are to be in the world. The messages then are a set of ideas that suggest to us how to think about our "selves"—about what is "appropriately" masculine or feminine. They produce expectations for each of our individual selves, which cause us to engage in body practices or gender performances (we discuss this further in the next chapter), both of which shore up our ideas about self and our beliefs in the naturalness of gendered practices.

Of course, you are a thinking person. You do not always do exactly as you are told. The arrows looping back to "messages" and "selves" show us that

Figure 1.3. Gender Feedback Loop: Performance / Surveillance / Resistance. Through gender performance and public surveillance, people put gender messages into action using the body, often confirming and sometimes disrupting those messages in a constant feedback loop.

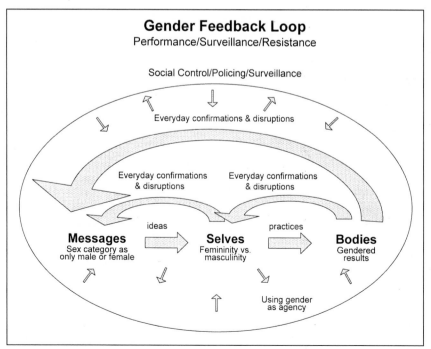

our interactions help to confirm and sometimes change (although usually very modestly) our ideas about self or the cultural messages themselves. Hence, the entire process is a feedback loop of the interplay of personal thought and social interaction for each person. The oval surrounding the figure suggests that all of these experiences exist in an environment of social conformity in interaction (see chapter 3) in which we are encouraged by others and the social setting to act in conformist ways. Although we are given these conformist instructions and we may often follow them, we also resist as individuals and as groups. So the experience is not so much a linear one of conforming to fit appropriately into boxes, but rather a swirling, interactive one of gendered messages, self-measurement and assessment, and finding ways for each of us to conform to certain ideals and also to exercise some latitude to become individuals. All this happens in social interaction with others and is constantly changing but continually referring to messages that pre-existed each of us. Hence, the process is complex, ongoing, interactive, and occurring in real time in every social situation.

As we go through each chapter of this book, we explain each of the components of this figure in detail. You will notice we break the feedback loop into sections in each chapter and we give examples of how each section plays out in various settings, including work, sexual and reproductive relationships, and sports and leisure activities. Below we discuss the format of the rest of the book.

A ROADMAP TO THE BOOK

The theoretical underpinnings for this book are based in a variety of sociological theories that might best be described as social constructionism. As a theoretical cornerstone, we have outlined in chapter 1 an introductory description of gendered cultural messages.

In chapter 2, we explain how messages about gendered bodies become gender practices or performances. We draw from the work of Butler (1990, 1993) and from the ethnomethodological perspective of West and Zimmerman (1987), who note that gender is not only a set of meanings, but a physical accomplishment—gender is something we do, not something we have. Gender is a physical performance that each individual pursues. We also introduce the work of G. H. Mead (1964) and the impact of gendered messages on selves.

In chapter 3, we invoke the work of Foucault in recognizing that bodies are disciplined via public surveillance. We also return to the work of West and Zimmerman, who note that gender is a performance to which others will hold us accountable. Gender is not just something we each do, but it is also something that others do to us—sanctioning behavior that falls outside the realm of what is socially acceptable. Hence, gender is both physically performed and socially mandated. Additionally, as a social mandate, gender is only understood as dichotomous. Little variation is imaginable. We extend that idea with the social constructionist perspective that "what one believes to be real is real in its consequences" (Thomas and Thomas 1928:572). That is, the meanings that emerge about people and bodies through social interaction become real through the practices of the believers. In a society that believes there are only two distinct sexes to which we assign two distinct genders (for which each individual is held accountable), two very different physical bodies will result (Lorber 1994; Lorber and Martin 1998). Here, we argue that gendered meanings about bodies actually shape bodies as much as body sizes and shapes affect the development of gendered meanings. This is certainly a different causal direction than scientists have traditionally asserted.

In chapter 4, we demonstrate the effects of gender messages on the social selves of women and men and how gendered inequalities sustain our beliefs in binary biological sex categories. Using data on a variety of kinds of gender inequality, we argue that gendered messages lead to unequal social access, which confirms our belief that binaries are naturally real. Far from being physiological mandates, female and male bodies operate as symbols that create differential access in the social world. Yet these differential accesses make us believe in our binaries (hence the gender feedback loop). First we believe, then we act in gendered ways, creating gendered bodies, which convinces us our unequal social system is natural (gendered messages again).

While the gender divide is pretty steep, it is not insurmountable. There are many examples of people resisting the gender dichotomy both with and against gender imperatives. In chapter 5 we discuss how gender is practiced in resistance to gender restrictions.

In each chapter, we cover a broad range of topics about the gendered body, including bodies at work, sports and gendered movement, and sexual and reproductive bodies. These substantive areas comprise the major sociological subfields in which theories of the body have become popular. In addition, there are several themes that run throughout theories of the body that we will address in each chapter as appropriate to that subfield. These themes include violence, race, class, age, and ableness.

In the final chapter we suggest some possibilities for *degendering* our interactional worlds (Lorber 2005), in order to increase opportunities for all people to expand their gender expressions. We envision a world with less gender surveillance and more flexibility.

We do not purport to have completed an exhaustive review of the literature on gender in interaction or gendered bodies, but only attempt to open the discussion of social interaction in our lives. Our desire as authors is to encourage students to critically examine how lives (including bodies) become gendered and to question what we perceive to be the overuse of biological explanations for differences between people. We hope the book challenges your imagination and incites you to consider how the social world impacts our most intimate and physical experiences.

NOTES

1. Here we reference the work of Michel Foucault (1977, 1980). We use the term *messages* or *cultural messages* in much the same way that he uses *discourses*, or in the way Dorothy Smith (1987) uses the term *relations of ruling* to imply a discursive form of power as social control.

2. Indeed, during the late 1970s and early 1980s, Phyllis Schlafly argued against the Equal Rights Amendment on the premise that equal rights between women and men entailed co-ed bathrooms in public places. In fact, the ERA did not refer to bathrooms at all, but apparently this was an effective scare tactic.

3. Another interesting gender effect is that women commonly talk to each other throughout the entire event of using a public restroom, while apparently that is not permissible for men. But we digress.

4. Public restroom use is a very socially organized activity with specific local knowledges organizing our bodies (Cahill et al. 1985). Indeed, Weinberg and Williams' (2005) study of restroom etiquette suggests that we tend to learn gendered expectations about bodily control and the appropriateness of defecation and flatulence in public restrooms; that is, heterosexual-identified men tend to feel more free to evacuate their bodies than women or even non-heterosexual-identified men.

5. In this book we are attempting to make an original contribution to gender performance theory by citing Mead's theory of the self as we do in chapter 2 and Foucault's notion of surveillance with West and Zimmerman's ethnomethodological discussion of gender accountability as we do in chapter 3. We argue that gender discourses/messages must be part of our everyday thought processes and interactions because thought is only reactive to social interaction. As such our thoughts and interactions are gendered through and through in every instance. They are not elective performances. In chapter 3, using West and Zimmerman's notion of accountability, we argue that our actions also cannot escape gendering because they are always compelled by others to meet gender discourses/messages.

6. Here, although we are describing closely the important work of Kessler and McKenna (1978), we cite Schutz's notion of *typification*, rather than Garfinkel's notion of *attribution* as Kessler and McKenna do. We do so consciously. Although we concede that Garfinkel's (1967) legendary discussion of Agnes was likely the original "queer theory" in that he was the first to take seriously the idea that binary sex (or "sexual status" as he put it) is a socially constructed reality, we feel Schutz's concept of typification is more accessible to a broader audience than Garfinkel's attribution and more useful for theorizing how gender works than ethnomethodology's goal of only describing lived realities.

7. The study of semiotics moves farther in this direction, but that is beyond our scope here.

8. "Latin" is a racial/ethnic category so large as to be unintelligible, except to mainstream U.S. discourses. Presumably "Latin" means anyone of European Spanish, Caribbean, or Central or South American descent, including both Spanish-

speaking and Portuguese-speaking cultures, even if they are second- or third-generation American citizens. Clearly, this is a grouping made unintelligible by any measure other than comparison to the mainstream U.S. culture. Nonetheless, in the United States there is a common notion of grouping these diverse backgrounds and heritages together as if they do make sense and many people put this identity into use. We use the term "Latin" here to denote people in the United States who self-identify as such on cultural bases. We view this term as preferable to "Hispanic," which we view as having implications for race and genetics that we do not imply in any sense.

9. Interestingly, cooking is understood as masculine and appropriate for males if the person who is cooking is paid well for the skill. So according to the typification, "being a chef" is typically understood as appropriate for men, whom we expect to be highly paid, whereas "cooking" is a feminine thing women do for free on an everyday basis for their families.

10. While Kinsey is often heralded as the father of sexology, the scientific study of human sexuality, other lesser-known writers and scholars were studying these same issues (although perhaps not on such a grand scale) at the same time as Kinsey (see Hohman and Schaffner 1947), and even a decade before Kinsey (see Bromley and Britten 1938).

11. We find it unfortunate that the national discussion of being "on the down low" seems to target primarily black men as those who engage in clandestine sex with other men. As documented famously by Laud Humphreys' *Tea Room Trade* in 1970, this practice is neither new nor specific to black men.

12. The term *hermaphrodite* was formerly used to describe intersexed people, but is now considered a derogatory term.

13. See the Intersex Society of North America's website: http://www.isna.org.

14. Even among transsexuals there is disagreement about the degree to which gender is innate. Some transsexuals argue that gender is a very original, if not genetic, component of their personhood, and that therefore gender is more fixed than sex and can be understood in binary ways (Feinberg 1996; Green 2004; Kotula 2002; Prosser 1995). There are other transsexuals who argue that gender and sex are historically situated and should not be viewed as inflexible or binary (Bornstein 1994; Rubin 2003; Stone 1991; Wilchins 1997, 2004). Often these are diametrically opposed arguments. Nonetheless, most agree that the ability to reconstruct sexual bodies to live as another sex suggests that your genital body at birth does not predict your gender or sexual orientation as the gender box structure would anticipate.

15. See www.lorencameron.com.

2

Doing "Woman"/Doing "Man"

Gender Performances That Produce "Reality"

"It's Pat"

Consider this scenario. You are walking through the mall and some-one you do not know passes by and you cannot determine whether that person is female or male. What do you do? You probably look again. And again. You keep looking until you think you have figured it out. But why? Why do you care? You may never see this person again in your entire life. Why do you feel compelled to know? You have to know because until you know you cannot assign gender or sexuality. You cannot typify according to the gender box structure. That is, *you do not know how to think of that person* through our standard category system (Bem 1993; Kessler and McKenna 1978; West and Zimmerman 1987). But the inability to assign gender is not a problem for that per-son necessarily; it is a problem for *you*. *You* are the one made uncom-fortable by not knowing. Would you ever feel comfortable interacting with a person for whom you could not determine so-called biological sex (that is, for whom you could not assign a sex category)?

This ambiguity, of course, was the joke of the long-running *Saturday Night Live* skit "It's Pat." The character Pat's sex/gender was not obvious to others and so the other characters in the skit were constantly trying to devise clever questions or put Pat in a situation where Pat's sex/gen-der would be revealed. Over and over again, Pat managed to answer questions such as "Do you have a significant other?" without ever using gendered pronouns. It's funny, not because Pat's sex/gender was a prob-lem for Pat, but because it was a problem for the viewer and the other

37

characters in the skit, who might have tumbled into a socially problematic situation because of the inability to assign a pronoun to Pat.*

I experience this kind of discomfort on the part of others on a regular basis. I am regularly called "sir" and mistaken for male, especially when entering women's rooms. It's a little disconcerting when you hear someone behind you in the airport yelling, "Hey, buddy! Hey, buddy! . . . He doesn't know where he is going."

On another occasion, I was ordering food at a McDonald's restaurant. Having ordered a meal of cheeseburger, fries, and a drink, I reached into my pocket and prepared to hand money to the cashier. When she looked up to tell me the total, the young cashier ran into a problem with direct address. "Thank you, s. . .? m. . .?" She ceased to be able to finish the transaction. She couldn't even make change. She literally could not think, speak, or make another move. In other words, her inability to assign sex category (hence, gender) to me brought the entire transaction to a halt. This example is particularly telling, since ordering food at McDonald's is so automated and such a common experience in American life that most Americans can probably operate as either buyer or seller and know what to expect of the entire transaction (Ritzer 1996). For example: "I'd like a number 3 with a Diet Coke." "That will be $4.59." Food is exchanged. "Thank you." "Thank you." And yet, this poor young woman was so transfixed by her lack of ability to assign sex that she could not even make change. I didn't help her out. I never do. Really, why did she need to know?

—Sara L. Crawley (author)

*Julia Sweeney is the actress/comedian who played Pat. See her website for pictures of Pat: http://www.juliasweeney.com.

HOW DOES GENDER WORK?

If gender is constructed, where does gender come from? Often our students look for a specific origin to gender ("Way back in caveman days . . ."). Not only are these origin stories usually ahistorical (out of historical context), but they often greatly overlay our current gender ideals on previous times. Nonetheless, we seem to want a start to it all. We seem to want to find an original function to gender. While there are historical explanations for some components of gender (for example, dividing labor within households during certain economic production systems), suggesting that we've "just always done it that way" ignores our abilities to adapt and overlooks the massive change that has happened in human civilization since "caveman days."

Rather than try to pinpoint an exact beginning of gendered expectations (an impossible and often reductionist endeavor), we use the work of Kessler and McKenna (1978) to focus on *how gender is maintained*. Rather than seek an origin, we ask *how we all participate in maintaining* gendered performances and social structures in the everyday processes of our lives.

In their groundbreaking work, Kessler and McKenna (1978) turned the common knowledge about sex and gender on its head. Rather than suggest that bodies are the origins of social roles that began from some original function (which we can presumably pinpoint if we can just dig up, pun intended, enough archaeological knowledge about our past), they suggest that *gender is something that we assert, create, and re-create now in our everyday lives.* It is not something that originated "back in the day" or "throughout history," but rather a system of *reality construction* (the notion that our understanding and interpretation of the world is constructed through everyday experiences via our culture and languages) that we engage in every moment of every day right now. They write, "The social construction of gender and the gender attribution process are a part of reality construction. No member is exempt, and this construction is the grounding for all scientific work on gender" (162). The cultural messages that form our expectations and supply "rules" about gender merely assume that bodies are dimorphic (either clearly female or clearly male) and that behavior flows from a "natural" origin. But it is that assumption that blinds us to the workings of our everyday production of that reality. The question is not: Where does gender come from? Rather, the question is: How does gender work in our everyday lives to maintain itself?

Gender, then, is a binary set of social meanings that typify female and male bodies as "truly" different. Because we believe in a gender difference on an everyday basis, we put these ideas into practice through and on our bodies (Butler 1990, 1993, 1996; Cahill 1986, 1989; Garfinkel 1967; Kessler and McKenna 1978; West and Zimmerman 1987). Astutely, Butler writes (1996), "Gender is a kind of imitation for which there is no original" (185). She suggests that the *performance of gender* (ways to hold, wear, and use the body to fit social expectations of what is appropriate for females and males) is what comes to be mistaken as an inner, psychic self; it is the illusion of innate sex characteristics (1993, 1996). For Butler, it is the constant, repetitive performativity of social expectations that convinces us that those interests are innate, or originate from within the body, in nature. So, for example, in our culture female-bodied people wear dresses because dresses are a marker of femininity—that which is appropriate for female-bodied people. However, when we see a female wearing a dress, we take that as a display of her "innately" feminine characteristics, disregarding the social fact that we train girls to want to wear dresses because our culture defines dresses as appropriate.

For Butler, it is the reiteration of norms that allows us to claim certain identities—"man," "woman," "masculine," or "feminine." Butler's overarching argument is that bodies are *understood* to be sexed differently. But the body does not precede that understanding, nor does the understanding precede the body. The matter of sex and the symbolic understanding of it emerge together through a continuous process of citing the difference we refer to as sex.[1] It is this continuous process of citation of difference that produces our understanding of difference. Our understandings of difference shape our behavior, which shapes our bodies, which shape our understandings of difference—not in a cyclical pattern, but in reiterative, uneven, cited, practiced, perceived, lived interactions.

Up to this point in Butler's theory, we agree with her understanding of the relationship of bodies to social meanings. However, much of Butler's theory concentrates on linguistic understandings of bodies, which she attempts to make "materialize" by her notion of citationality. As a result, we deem her theory to give short shrift to the empirical, lived experience of actors who experience bodies in *the interactional world* (Dunn 1997; Emery 2002; Jackson and Scott 2001). Shortly we suggest a return to the ethnomethodological/phenomenological arguments of Kessler and McKenna (1978) and West and Zimmerman (1987) that we engage throughout the book. As such, we locate the body as both a target for theorizing and a site of lived experience. Jackson and Scott (2001) summarize this point nicely as follows: "What is lacking in the imaginary bodies of much social theory is the socially located body" (23). Our aim here, then, is to base our theory on the bodies and experiences of people in their everyday lives.

So gender involves both meanings and uses of the body. Or, as Lorber (1993) writes, "believing is seeing"—if we believe something to be true, in our everyday processes of typification we look to find examples of it in the world. Thus, if we believe that gender comes from the body, then we go out and find examples of bodily performances that support our typical categories. Social ideas are overlaid on biology. Like Butler, Lorber argues that it is the belief in the "realness" of gender that produces the effect we see enacted on the bodies of real people. It is not innate, but it need not be if we all perform the expectation until it appears to be real (Garfinkel 1967; Kessler and McKenna 1978; West and Zimmerman 1987).

Both Butler and Lorber rely on the notion of gender as performance. Here we present the work of West and Zimmerman (1987) that *gender is a performance* of the body based on some presumptions about the relationship of so-called biological sex, gender, and sexuality. Then, we present their notion of how gender is "done" via performances of the body.

Understanding Sex, Sex Category, Gender, and Sexuality

In the everyday process of using the gender box structure to make sense out of the events of our lives, we fuse at least three concepts about persons—sex, gender, and sexuality. It is important to recognize how each of these should be understood as separate from the other and also how each is better understood as a continuum of experiences and practices.

Briefly, let's understand how these three characteristics have been defined. The definition of *biological sex* refers to the scientific categorizing of anatomy and physiology as two distinct categories—femaleness and maleness. That is, the idea of biological sex is based on the notion that there are two and only two types of people in the world that are understood as clearly and easily defined based on internal and external genitalia. It is the essentialist belief that the "truth" of difference lies in bodies. Although the notion of biological sex as a "true" binary of nature is socially constructed, given that intersexed people unquestionably exist in nature, notions of appropriate gender and expectations about sexuality are usually understood to be attached to sex.

Gender, then, is the sense of being appropriately masculine or feminine. The key word here is "appropriately." Gender is the notion of what is socially appropriate behavior and presentation for a person with a female or male body. That is, it is the social script for behavior, which is always based on presumptions about (female or male) bodies. Gender is the display of masculinity or femininity. It is the performance of "man" or "woman," as they are culturally defined.

Sexuality (sometimes referred to as sexual orientation) is the way in which a person pursues and practices a sense of the sexual self. In dominant U.S. culture in the nineteenth and twentieth centuries, sexuality has been *assumed* to be heterosexual, or seeking a genital "opposite." That is, heterosexuality has been a compulsory expectation (Ingraham 1996; Katz 1995; Rich 1986; G. Rubin 1984; Seidman 1996).

What we have described above, however, is the heteronormative expectation of the "realness" of biological sex that is assumed to determine gender and sexuality. However, what is not commonly recognized is that, in everyday interaction, each of these characteristics is based on assumption rather than some evidence of realness or "truth." That is, sex, gender, and sexuality are not neatly dichotomous. The gender box structure is based on a belief that we "really" know the sex of each individual we encounter. The big mistake happens in not recognizing the difference between sex and sex category (West and Zimmerman 1987). When each of us sees a body, we tend to immediately assign what we believe to be true about that person's body, their sex. Kessler and McKenna (1978) call this process gender attribution. But in each case, we rarely *know* the person's genital makeup. There are few people we tend to see on a daily basis with naked genitals (unless you have a sexual or intimate relationship with that person, or unless you are a medical service provider). You may know people their entire lives and never see their genitals. Hence, each of us makes assumptions about so-called biological sex based on clothing styles or secondary sex characteristics. What we know about others, then, is not sex, but sex category.

Sex category is the way each of us categorizes people based on their presumed "sex;" we cannot see it, so we presume it. West and Zimmerman write, "People can be seen as members of relevant categories, then we categorize them that way" (133). In other words, we tend to assume all masculine-appearing people are "men," with the same biological, chromosomal, and genital characteristics, hence we typify them as men. Likewise, each of us tends to assume all feminine-appearing people are typically "women." *We base our everyday assumptions about biology on social characteristics*—clothing and hair styles, styles of walking and talking, having facial hair or breasts. In the everyday world of interaction, what each of us knows about others is sex category—how they appear to us—not biological sex. Although often our assumptions about biological sex may be accurate, they *wrongly allow us to presume that there is little variation* among people with penises and among people with vaginas when, in fact, there is great variation among genital shape, size, and reproductive capacity. And, sometimes, we are "wrong" about the genital sex of the person we assign a sex category; some people who cross-dress or are intersexed or transgendered easily fit into our system of sex category based only on their performance of gender. But, in our day-to-day lives, *we would not know this* because sex category is the only "truth" we hold to be informative. In other words, using sex category as a proxy for some bodily "truth" falsely dichotomizes all people into two neat types.

Further, our techniques for gauging another person's sex category are fuzzy at best. We have all seen particularly large male-bodied people (that is, who carry a large amount of body fat) with breasts larger than some female-bodied people. Although we culturally believe that only female-bodied people have "breasts," normatively male-bodied people do have breast structures (i.e., nipples and fatty tissue) that simply lack the ability to lactate. Male-bodied people's "breasts" will increase in size with weight gain just as normatively female-bodied people's do. Similarly, female-bodied people do have facial hair, some of whom feel it is too dark and too thick to allow to grow (otherwise, the beauty industry would not be making so much money on selling plucking devices, bleaching creams, and waxing products).[2] And, perhaps most of us have seen or at least know that drag performances (by drag queens and drag kings) can be very convincing, such that based on appearance, sex category would probably not match so-called biological sex (recall 6pak from chapter 1). In each of these instances, we are accustomed to focusing on the female-male dualism that compels us to attempt sex categorization. It is understood as absolutely necessary—a social imperative—to assign sex category.

To argue that sex category is a narrowly constructed, false binary does not imply that it is not of great importance in a social setting. Indeed, biological sex remains a legal category on the basis of which laws are produced. So, for example, you cannot have whichever sex category you choose on your driver's license, because sex category is still a legal status in the United States. As an example of this, the recent hot-button discussion of same-sex marriage points out that one cannot legally marry anyone of any sex category they choose. So while sex category is socially constructed, it has very real implications for members of U.S. society.

First Impressions

I have been taught my whole life that first impressions are important. You never get another shot at presenting the "real" you. However people first perceive you is how they will continue to view you. This is why, I was told, it is so important to put your best foot forward—just make sure that foot is well-pedicured and outfitted in the newest designer shoe.

I have always known I was from a privileged background. With this recognition came the perceived responsibility to present myself that way. I was advised that with my economic position there was no reason why people's first impression of me shouldn't be pleasing and positive. I took this advice to heart. At a very early age I learned that a well-groomed, very feminine (white) image elicited the most positive responses from people. People started commenting to my parents about what a "lovely young lady" I was. This pleased them, and, in turn, pleased me. I grew comfortable with being labeled a "lovely young lady" and got really good at perfecting the role.

This role transformed into the "rich girl" role by high school. I did not fully understand the rich girl label. Nobody knew what my parents' bank statement said. My parents never handed me free money; I worked for an allowance just like my peers did. Why did people think I was rich? It was in my last years of high school that I got my answer. I finally understood that the rich girl label was directly correlated with my feminine image. In my world, good grooming equaled money. I had perfected the feminine look in order to present a positive first impression—not to look rich—but apparently these were the same thing.

It was during my first year of college that I recognized how difficult it was to keep up this feminine image. After long nights of intense studying, my regular grooming rituals seemed daunting. It seemed much easier to put my hair up in a baseball cap than to spend half an hour straightening it and applying the perfect amount of product to make my hair shine. I also started realizing how much time, effort, and money it took to keep up this image. Getting my hair dyed and nails done took hours, and some sessions were painfully boring. I realized that waxing did not tickle; it was really painful, almost as painful as the heels I wore. I had come to see these grooming techniques as my ticket to the image of a put-together, well-groomed, rich girl—but they were also costly, painful, and time-consuming.

While you might think I would have rebelled and started going around in sweatpants and with bad roots, I did not. I still sit for hours in boring salons and I still walk into my painful waxing sessions wearing my painful heels. As a sociology major, I am well aware of the critiques of gender-appearance norms. I know that some people might take a negative view of my gender presentation, but I have realized that I enjoy being the "prissy" girl and this realization has been liberating. I finally know how to describe myself. I continue with these beauty rituals to produce a feminine image because I like to be put together. It feels good *to me* to dress in designer clothes. Doing "prissy girl" has brought me confidence and self-assurance. I can nail a first impression using my clothes, my hair, *and* my brain. I have yet to find an individual who intimidates me. I can portray the image that I belong in any situation and am just as important as anyone.

While it is possible to find me in old sweats with my hair up in a hat and my nails not done, don't hold your breath. After all, I wouldn't want to give you a bad first impression! I have conquered the rich, feminine girl image and I am using it to boost my own self-confidence and my chances of doing well in this world.

—Sarah Hummel, undergraduate student

GENDER AS PERFORMANCE: "DOING" GENDER

If gender is socially constructed, how then is it possible that in everyday life men are generally masculine appearing and women are generally feminine appearing? If gender is not innate, how is it possible that most people conform to the standards? Simple: we are called upon to perform according to gender expectations—gender is a social performance of the body.

Did you ever notice that most of the manly men in the movies are extremely similar, even across time? Similarly, the womanly women seem to have common characteristics over time. Take a moment to try this exercise. First, make a list of all the celebrities that you can think of that you consider icons of femininity (that is, their status as a celebrity—their persona—exemplifies iconic femininity) and then make a similar list of icons of masculinity. Second, pick one of each that is the most exemplary icon of femininity and of masculinity. Now, make a list for each of the characteristics that give each of them their iconic statuses. What are their attributes that contribute to their celebrity as feminine or masculine icons? Now, compare your lists. We expect you will find at least two noticeable effects.

First, the characteristics of femininity for female icons tend to be opposites of the characteristics of masculinity for male icons, or at least emphasized differently. For example, famous people are usually famous in some way because of their appearance (beauty, fashion, sexual attractiveness). However, what is considered "sexy" for men (large muscles, aggressive, confident) is different than what is considered "sexy" for women (petite and thin, soft spoken, demure). Alternatively, some characteristics are likely to be exemplary for one and not the other, even if both are likely to exemplify the characteristic. For example, most famous people have lots of money (either because riches brought them fame or fame brought them riches). Nonetheless, it is much more common for us to think of money and wealth as characteristic of iconic masculinity, but less likely to think of these things as characteristic of iconic femininity. That is, male icons are usually listed as icons because they have money and power, whereas female icons are usually listed as being with "powerful" men (even when those female celebrities actually have wealth themselves).

Second, the characteristics associated with femininity are likely to be less positive than the characteristics associated with masculinity. For example, men who "get lots of women" might be portrayed in a positive light, whereas many women who are icons receive that status because they "sleep with powerful men," which is portrayed in a negative light. This is the same issue, but is emphasized differently for women than men. Perhaps this is partly because the characteristics for femininity often refer to dependence on men, whereas the characteristics of masculinity often refer to self-reliance. So men and masculinity are often spoken of in positive terms ("gets things done"), whereas women may receive their iconic status from exemplifying femininity, but these traits are seen as less positive than masculine traits ("supports her man").

In the context of iconic celebrities, it's important to remember that *these people do not exist*. The actors exist as human beings, but the way we think of these celebrities is the media image or persona that has been carefully marketed to a wide audience. None of us are likely to actually know the icons we see in the media. Famous people are personas, not people. Some celebrities try hard to avoid exposing their intimate lives (although an entire industry tries to expose such "real life" details). Most carefully groom their public appearance and respond to a carefully planned image. Many do not even use their given names. We know these personas, not the people whose faces are on the personas.

In fact, as media personas or icons, these people demonstrate that *these characteristics are nothing but performance*. We doubt that Vin Diesel ramps cars over his own house on his days off. Will Smith probably does not spend his regular day blowing up the neighbor's car or running down the street after bad guys. We do not expect that Tyra Banks or Heidi Klum have runways in their living rooms. These are nothing but actors putting on performances to suit the public imagination. Indeed, the performances are carefully groomed to push the extremes of fashion—to present the *most* beautiful, handsome, or sexy image as defined by cultural expectations. Nonetheless, people take these ideas into their everyday understanding of the world. While we know these characters are not real, we use them as instructive to us in our everyday lives. So, while we know the performance is pure fantasy, we use the personas to inform our own ideas about self, fashion, appropriateness, and beauty. In other words, gender is a performance of the body (West and Zimmerman 1987).

In their groundbreaking article, West and Zimmerman (1987) created the concept of "doing gender." They argued that *femininity and masculinity are not what you are, they are what you do*. They see gender as performance of self. They write that gender is a "routine, methodical, and recurring accomplishment. We contend that the 'doing' of gender is undertaken by women and men whose competence as members of society is hostage to its production" (126). By accomplishment, they mean it is a performance of the body, a way in which to physically construct the portrayal of self that we wish others to see. That is, gender is not just a set of roles (i.e., men go to work and women do the dishes). It is of far deeper importance than simply getting certain things done. It is the "appropriate" kind of performance of all things understood as appropriate for female-bodied (feminine performance) and male-bodied (masculine performance) people.

For example, we think of the field of building construction as something manly. But building construction is not "manly" just because people with penises work in that field. Building construction is understood as manly because of the way people in that field behave toward each other and themselves (Crawley 2002b). There is a performance to driving a nail that goes beyond actually beating a nail into a board. Imagine this: how would it look if a construction worker were to wear a dress to work and have red painted fingernails? Were you assuming the "construction worker" is male? Okay. Keep that assumption. Does the dress or the painted nails actually affect one's ability to use a hammer? Well, no. One can actually drive a nail into a board while wearing a dress and nail polish, but one is not likely to be taken seriously as a "construction worker" if one does not look the part. In other words, being a construction worker is more than being able to hammer a nail: the clothing worn (worn-out jeans or evening gown?), ornamentation (nail polish or tool belt?), and even uses of the body (swagger versus swish) are all the performance of "construction worker."

Another example is a favorite commercial of ours about the cereal Special K. In it, men are dressed in traditionally manly fashion (jeans, khakis, T-shirts) and sitting at a bar—a very manly setting. The commercial runs through several men in a series speaking to the camera about self-esteem issues. They say, "This year I will not obsess about my weight." "I will not let my dress size determine my self-worth." "I will not freak out if I gain three pounds." "I have my mother's thighs. I have to accept that." "Do these pants make my butt look big?" Of course, the joke is that these are things we expect women to say; they are part of feminine performance. The humor is in the gender inappropriateness of it; although men can say these things, they are not part of appropriate, masculine performance. Indeed, the commercial is funny because it is recognizable as disruptive of our expectations.

In our culture, there is not one form of either masculinity or femininity but there are iconic notions that create a sense of dichotomy (and, of course, with dichotomy comes hierarchy in social binaries) and expectations for those kinds of masculinity and femininity that are most rewarded—most exemplary. Connell (1987) outlines the iconic notions of gender in Western culture as *hegemonic masculinity* and *emphasized femininity*. For Connell, hegemonic masculinity is the kind of masculinity that asserts itself as dominant over other forms of masculinity and over all forms of femininity—a social dominance that is embedded in social messages (i.e., religious doctrine and practice, mass media content, workplace organization, wage structures, family forms) and may include the use of brute force. It is the kind of dominance that is embedded in the fantasy action heroes—Humphrey Bogart, John Wayne, Sylvester Stallone, Steven Segal, Arnold Schwarzenegger, Vin Diesel, Will Smith, Denzel Washington, and so on and so on. These heroes symbolize force, power, control over others, individualism, wealth, and ability to enforce their individual wills. These icons smash up cars/boats/motorcycles, beat the bad guy, single-handedly destroy enemy governments, get the girl, and walk alone into the sunset to save another day—each one is "an army of one." Perhaps more recently, the "thug" or "pimp" persona as exemplified by rap and hip-hop icons and in films about drug kingpins offers a similar kind of icon.[3] Although this image invokes an oppositional or confrontational (toward police and government authority) persona rather than a "saves-the-world" kind of persona, "thug" masculinity still emphasizes physical dominance over others, force, power, individualism, wealth, and the enforcement of their will.

Conversely, emphasized femininity is that kind of femininity that is "oriented to accommodating the interests and desires of men" (Connell 1987: 183). Emphasized femininity is accomplished by making one's physical body sexually attractive to men and derives its social ascendancy (although never dominance) in relation to dominant men. It is exemplified in the figure of the feminine Hollywood icon, the runway model, or perhaps the wife of a powerful man—Marilyn Monroe or Halle Berry, Cindy Crawford or Tyra Banks, Jackie Onassis or Melania Trump. This femininity is characterized by sexual attractiveness to men, thinness, beauty, grace, virtue (characteristics that attract rather than accomplish), and, as women age, by motherhood (bearing men's children) and nurturance. The exemplary woman models her body for men's view, holds her sexuality as the leverage to attract men's wealth, "marries well," requires saving when in distress, and generally competes with other women for the opportunity to hang on the arm of the richest, strongest, best-looking (in that order?) man to function as eye candy for his reputation and secure her a nice house. Notice that each of the above actors, spanning various decades and generations, play essentially the same character—if male, the hero; if female, the beauty queen. Also, notice that neither exists in real life, but we still use them as instructive to our own understanding of self.

These two forms always exist in relation to each other as a gender order, not as simple forms of their own (Connell 2002). Additionally, it is not necessary for each person in the real, everyday world to participate in the exemplary forms of either. Indeed, as icons, both are very hard to achieve and therefore reserved for only a smaller proportion of the culture. But the cultural messages of hegemonic masculinity and emphasized femininity operate as a kind of character (perhaps as caricatures?) or message that defines the extremes of gender and often are produced in the media as the forms we are all intended to pursue. While they are not real, they still operate as exemplars for each of us in our everyday lives—showing us how to walk, talk, dress, cut our hair, or make up our faces (or not), as well as what to drive, how to interact with each other, and what our interests and pursuits should be. They teach us how to perform our gender.

The appropriate performance of gender is something we learn via our participation in social interaction. Gender expectations (notions of what is appropriately feminine or masculine) are pervasive throughout our culture and they organize all our interactions, from going to the bathroom to driving a nail to acting on national television. Gender performances are part of everyday interaction and they are present in every part of our lives. At all times we are expected to act appropriate to the cultural expectations held for female and male bodies. Women are expected to sit up straight and "act ladylike," be clean and tidy, show caring and nurturance toward others, and have a general concern for beauty. Men are expected to be strong and physically competent, to need no direction from others, and to generally show no weakness. These performances are available all around us. As our culture has been increasingly saturated with media, from video games, DVDs, and music videos to the proliferation of channels on cable and satellite TV, to the development and expansion of the Internet, we now have more and more venues to see examples of gender in interaction and can participate in reality construction by virtue of watching fantasy as reality (Baudrillard 1983; Denzin 1991).

Here is an example of emphasized femininity, perhaps the ultimate example—a woman wearing a wedding dress (see photo 2.1). The dress, the hairstyle, the accessories (necklace, flowers) all signify the ultimate in feminine dress and comportment and yet are only surface messages about how you should understand the person wearing them. That is, they are gender performance, not innate bodily composition. They give off messages about how you should view the person pictured. "So what?" you may be saying. Perhaps you are thinking, "Just because a person is dressed a particular way does not cause me to think about them differently." Think again.

Photo 2.1. This photo of author Sara Crawley, taken in 1988, illustrates the pinnacle of emphasized femininity—a bride in wedding dress.

Photo 2.2. This photo of author Sara Crawley, taken in 1997, presents a different narrative about gender, one closer to her current presentation of self. If you saw Sara today, would you think of her differently than if you had seen her in 1988?

The person in photo 2.2 is the same person as in photo 2.1. Both pictures are of the author, Sara Crawley. Neither was staged for this book. Both were taken during significant life events in the everyday course of her life, the first in 1988, the second in 1997. If you only saw Sara today (similar to the second picture), would you think of her differently than if you saw her in 1988? An interesting point about typification and gender performance is that when we interact with others, we never see their histories. This allows us to believe people have clear, static pasts that align easily with the present. In other words, gender performance has a huge impact on how we understand the person because it allows us to see each body as typical of that type of person. It does not allow us to see their histories, thoughts, opinions, feelings. Like all typification, it not only suggests alignment with a particular category, it establishes blinders for what is assumed to be inconsistent with that category. It masks our histories and diversities of self. This is particularly significant for transgendered or transsexual persons, who perhaps most clearly understand the depth of the dichotomy of gender performance and the impact of those performances in everyday lives, because of personal experience presenting each gender.

GENDERED SELVES, GENDERED BODIES:
INTERACTION IN EVERYDAY LIFE

If gender does not exist, how do we make it real? We make it real through our everyday interactions. Through the lifelong process of interaction in a world that holds us accountable to binary gender expectations, each of us develops a gendered self—a notion of who we "really" are based on limited binary categories. While this self may be responsive to some original bodily urges or potentialities, those urges or potentialities are clearly refined and focused by participation in the social world. For example, consider a pianist. How is it possible to know what gives someone the passion to play piano? Perhaps it is possible to inherit some traits suggesting a propensity toward musicality such as manual dexterity or acute ability to differentiate tones (although the status of genetics as a science is far from predicting any of these). Nonetheless, to become a pianist, one must have access to a piano, be encouraged to play, and practice arduously for perhaps years. One may be filled with a passion for piano, but to no avail if one does not develop those potentialities. In other words, even if biological potentialities exist, they are still nurtured—developed, focused, and/or curtailed—in the world of human interaction through thought and practice. Interactionist sociology helps us to understand the depth of that impact on individual life experience; that is, it describes the development of self. In particular the works of Mead ([1934]1964) and Goffman (1959) help us understand how self is developed in thought and action, respectively.[4]

To begin, we must understand the relationship of the self to the body. The self is not the physical body. Rather it is a social structure (Mead [1934]1964). That is, the self is the human inside the body. Self is to body as mind is to brain. Just as the brain (gray matter, hypothalamus, etc.) comprises the physical housing of thought, mind is much more illusive and unbounded, including humanity, self-determination, logic, personality, emotion, and so forth. So the body houses the physical person, but self is the social expression of the person. While a body may die, the self endures in the social setting as the person we ritualize in memory. Self, then, is the idea of a person as an individual actor separate from the group, who expresses interests, has a name, makes decisions, and, most importantly, interacts with others in social settings as an autonomous person (Holstein and Gubrium 2000). In other words, the body is the physical vehicle; the self is "Sara" or "Lara" or "Connie," the social entity we learn from, debate with, and remember when the body is not present. So the self is not reducible to the body; it emerges through social interaction (usually via the body, although not necessarily in the age of virtual communications).

The self emerges out of our interactions in the world, which are fed by social messages that both precede us and are applied to us in everyday life, and that form our expectations and "rules" about gender (see figure 2.1). In

Figure 2.1. Gender Feedback Loop: Performance. Gender messages tell us the "rules" about how we are expected to understand our selves and present our bodies as gendered people.

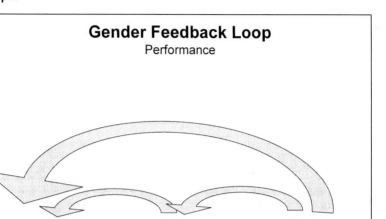

short, each of us forms a self by taking in social messages in interaction, thinking about their application to ourselves, and making decisions about how that will affect our practices (Cahill 1998). Through the performance of self, our bodily practices help to confirm or alter those messages when we interact with others in their self-formation. Think of the arrows as the ways we each make sense of the world. We do not start with a blank slate; we start with what others tell us. Over time we may begin to make our own decisions, but always within the realm of what already makes sense (social messages). From this we form selves and put them into motion on and within our bodies. We examine this idea in more depth by explaining the theories of Mead and Goffman.

For George Herbert Mead ([1934]1964), the social self is much more significant than the body. Mead suggests that self is first and foremost derived from the social setting, not from some original sense of being or personality or individuality.[5] In other words, we are social beings first and individuals later. This notion is especially compelling when we recognize that humans are incapable of survival without assistance in the early years of life. Further, Mead argues that thought is always processed through language and that each specific language pre-exists the individual that later acquires that language and must be taught to each individual based on group participation. Hence, all individuality is focused through group membership.

Specifically, Mead argues that all thought is reaction to an event or person. He argues that thought is essentially an internal conversation between parts of self that he calls "the Me" (the critical, judging part of self) and "the I" (the spontaneous, creative part of self). "The Me" is the generalized attitudes of others gained from interaction in the social world. "The Me" is capable of "taking the role of the other" or judging objects in the world (including self and others) as "the Me" expects others would judge those objects. So part of self ("the Me") has developed the ability to predict how others will respond based on the cumulative experiences with others. "The I" is the individual decision maker that decides how to think about the expected responses of others. The conversation goes something like this: (1) "the Me" (which Mead asserts always processes first) assesses how others will respond to some expression exhibited by self; (2) "the I" decides how to think about that assessment, whether to accept the judgment or reject it for some other idea; (3) then perhaps "the Me" and then "the I" in turn respond until the idea is resolved. Mead's important contribution is that thought is not primarily individual, but always engages the social and reacts to it, even if "the I" eventually rejects "the Me's" assessment.

Here's an example:

Scenario 1: You woke up late this morning and had five minutes to get your clothes on and brush your teeth. You stop to look in the mirror just as you are leaving the house to go to class.

Me: "Oh no, no. Bad hair day. You look rough."

I: "There is no way I can go to class looking like this. It's way too embarrassing. I'll have to take a shower and be late to class."

Scenario 2: Same scenario. Different day.

Me: "Oh no, no. Not good at all. That just isn't good."

I: "I can't be late today or I'll blow my attendance grade. Put on a hat and go."

Notice that regardless of whether the assessment by "the Me" is in agreement with "the I," "the I" can still determine how to proceed. But "the I" never offers the first thought; "the I" only offers reactions to "the Me's" assessment.

Mead does not describe "the Me" and "the I" as actual structures of the brain nor does he see them as having some consistent pattern of order or length of conversation (except that "the Me" makes the initial assessment in each instance), nor does he offer a specific narrative for the content of the interaction between "the Me" and "the I."[6] He is not attempting to understand the self or the social situation in which it finds itself as prescriptive (i.e., determining every thought for the individual). There is individuality in "the I" and in the unbounded form of the internal conversation.

Indeed, he uses the notion of "the Me" and "the I" as analytical tools to get across his point, which is first and foremost that all individuals are social entities—processing all thoughts through shared language and social customs that direct ideas, feelings, logic, and assessments of beauty and appropriateness. While in the United States we like to believe we are freely individual, Mead argues that thinking of the self as a social structure makes fully free individuality impossible. Even choosing to directly oppose the norm is a reaction to the norm. So individuality is always filtered through the social experience.

How does this relate to gender and bodies? Following Mead's argument about the self as a social structure, there is no thought that is not filtered by the gender box structure (i.e., notions of appropriate femininity and masculinity). If all bodies are assessed as female or male and then "appropriate" gender and sexuality assigned, we each judge *ourselves* based on those social notions (i.e., using Mead's "Me") and are judged by others using those social notions (i.e., using West and Zimmerman's accountability, which we discuss at length in the next chapter). Indeed, when others hold us accountable for our gender performances, they are giving us more fodder for future evaluations by "the Me" (because "the Me" is the accumulated set of expectations based on past interactions with others). Mead's notion of self suggests we must evaluate ourselves through the gender box structure (heteronormativity). Since that box structure is based on assessments about bodies that we believe are a binary (i.e., sex category is assessed as either male or female whether or not it "accurately" describes a body), we evaluate the options as either female/feminine/desires men or male/masculine/desires women and assess ourselves and others accordingly. Each of us evaluates how we fit in that pre-established structure. In order to comply with that social expectation, we often conform to the binary. Of course, "the I" need not always conform. Nonconformity and resistance do exist. We address nonconformity and resistance in further detail in chapter 5 of this book.

While Mead concentrates on the development of self in thought, Erving Goffman (1959) focuses on the bodily presentation of self. His contribution is the notion that the body is not the self but the self is performed by the body. That is, we present who we believe we are with our bodies. We present the self we want others to believe us to be. We do not just exist as "mother," "priest," "teacher," "friend," and so forth, we *perform* "mother," "priest," "teacher," "friend," and so forth. We perform whoever we are called upon to be in any given situation, based particularly on the context of the situation. So, for example, while you may know a person who is both a mother and who smokes pot, our guess is that that person will not attempt to do both at the same time. These two performances call for different behaviors in different situations. While this person is being "mother" (interacting with children and with other parents), she will likely speak in certain tones of voice (stern disciplinarian/soft-spoken, nurturing parent), espouse certain ideals ("You should behave like a good little girl/boy"), teach discipline, and so forth. She is likely to avoid any reference to being a "pot smoker." She may even speak out against the use of illicit drugs altogether. However, that same person, when acting as "friend" with a peer and not "mom" in front of children, may pinch a joint between thumb and index finger, puffing smoke and railing against government control. This is not because this person is a "bad mom" or a hypocrite. It is because we are called to perform different selves in different social interactions and, Goffman writes, we generally are happy to oblige. The performance of "mom" and the performance of "pot smoker" are two very different performances and need not be understood by the individual as mutually exclusive in different social situations. Another example is that as "teachers," each of us (the authors) are expected to dress in a particular way and stand at the front of the room speaking authoritatively about ideas while quizzing students about the information on which we are expected to be experts. However, if we tried this at home when we are expected to be "partners" and not "teachers," we might find ourselves in a serious fight with our respective significant others.

So, selves are performed and presented in all social situations. It need not be the exact same self in each situation because each situation may call for a different presentation. Nonetheless, in each situation, each of us presents the self we wish to have taken seriously and this presentation of self is worn on the body and performed via the body. We wear certain clothes to certain occasions, dressing differently for a wedding than for a day at the beach. We hold our bodies differently depending on the social status we expect to present (e.g., CEO or homeless person). We speak more or less authoritatively, given the situation (e.g., performing professor or daughter).

Again, what does this have to do with gender? "Woman" and "man" are two distinctly different performances of self in our culture. Recall, for example, our discussion of icons of femininity and masculinity. Many of the characteristics named for each "icon" were about self-presentation of bodies (Who is expected to wear lipstick and when? Who is expected to be "strong" and how?). As we noted earlier, gender is a performance. It is a performance of self. Returning to the gender feedback loop, we see that gendered messages suggest to us how we should create our selves (as feminine or masculine) and how we should use our bodies to accomplish these performances of femininity or masculinity. The performances themselves operate through the feedback loop as everyday confirmations that the original messages were "right" (see figure 2.2). That is, our performances of self tend to confirm the rightness of the cultural messages, which of course further encourages those performances.

If we take Mead and Goffman's ideas together, it becomes clear that thought and action are focused through the social process. Neither Mead nor Goffman argues that the social process determines all action. Clearly, each indi-

Figure 2.2. Gender Feedback Loop: Performance. Each of our performances of self operates through the feedback loop as everyday confirmations that the original messages were "right."

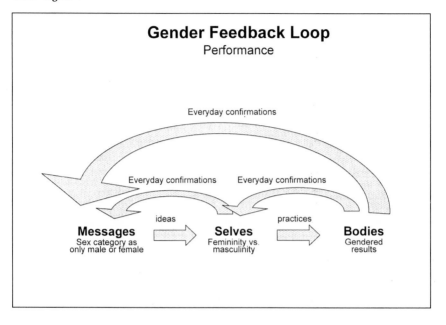

vidual has decision-making capacity and can consciously choose to work against the social expectations. Even so, social expectations are taken into account. No one is ever a fully free-thinking individual exempt from social processes.

GENDERING BODIES IN ACTION

In this and the next three chapters, we follow our theoretical discussion with a section of examples called "Gendering Bodies in Action." In each chapter we interrogate how gender works in three specific realms: sports and leisure, work, and sexuality and reproduction. While we do not purport to give an exhaustive review of all aspects of social life (or even these three areas), we feel these three realms cover a large expanse of the everyday lived experience. Within each section, we cover some common cultural messages, practices, and experiences of gender. For each of these realms of everyday life—sports, work, and sexuality—we give specific examples of how gender performance happens in the everyday world. We hope this section helps to illuminate the theories described above by offering examples from everyday life to which readers can relate.

Sports

Gendered Messages, Gendered Movement, Gendered Sport, Gendered Bodies

One way in which the performance of gender becomes very real is via the institution of sport. As a significant leisure activity and sometimes a professional opportunity, athletics and sports both reflect and re-create our culture (Coakley 2001; Eitzen 1999). Games and sports are created around our value systems but they also reinforce those values. Whereas individuals may participate in physical activities purely for fun (as in the joyful play of a child playing imaginary games), they may also engage in sports as a highly organized form of physical competition that "calls upon the body's capacities and skills merely for the sake of determining what they can achieve" (Young 1979:46). Sport is not only a place for the demonstration of physical skill; it is a cultural site for constructing meanings about bodies (Bryson 1987; Cole 1994; Messner 1988; Messner and Sabo 1990; Willis 1982) and for performing those meanings in gendered ways.

In sport, bodily differences are both emphasized and obscured. On the one hand, bodily differences are always pointed out via the definitions of "women's" and "men's" sports. It is extremely rare that sex category is not *foregrounded* in organizing any sport or an individual game. In other words, it is often assumed that all men are "naturally physically superior" to all women in terms of physical capacities and, hence, each sport and each game is organized under this assumption (Bryson 1987; Cole 1994; Messner 1988; Willis 1982). On the other hand, sport is one arena in which many individual women build bodies and bodily capacities that far exceed the abilities of many (if not most) men. But the abilities of many women to outperform many men are regularly overshadowed by citing only the elite men in that sport or by underreporting women's achievements (Bryson 1987; Burton Nelson 1994).

As an example, during the 1996 Olympics Jackie Joyner-Kersee was depicted in a TV commercial stating, "I can long jump farther than all but seven men in the world." Given this, it is clear that she is much more physically abled at long jump than literally billions of men (including many male Olympians), but as a culture we tend to focus on those seven as though they represent the "truth" of *all* male bodies. That is, we typify all males as aligning with the one or two elite men, and we typify all females as no more capable of beating any man than the elite women are of beating the one or two elite men. As a result, although there is a huge overlap of bodily capabilities of female-bodied and male-bodied people (i.e., women taller, larger, stronger, and more capable at some physical tasks than many men), in the cultural context and cultural messages of sport we almost exclusively focus on male accomplishment, giving the appearance that *all* men are more physically capable than *all* women. In U.S. culture, we tend to think dichotomously, expecting that the male body is always, in every case, stronger than the female body (Birrell and Cole 1994; Hargreaves 1994; Messner 1990; Theberge 1991). We argue here that this notion that male bodies are "naturally physically superior" to female bodies, coupled with the required performances of masculinity and femininity, combine to achieve a social differentiation between women and men that actually builds dichotomous bodies.

Sport, then, is a site in which the performance and surveillance of masculinity and femininity are rampant. And, we argue, a site where gender becomes "real"—that is, where male-bodied people are encouraged far more than female-bodied people to perform and learn bodily competence and, as a result, where men are more likely than women to feel and become larger, more self-confident, and expectant that they can use their bodies to accomplish goals. In essence, because of the cultural message of gender difference, so-called "average" (i.e., not just athletes, but everyday people who engage in many types of activities beyond athletics) men tend to believe in their bodily potential, perform it consistently, and actually build their own physical capabilities more readily than "average" women.

How do *social* processes actually create physically more-abled male bodies and physically "dis-abled" female bodies (in relationship to both male and female bodily potentials)?[7] On the one hand, this question seems simple. If you work a muscle, it gets bigger. If you do not work it, it atrophies. On the other hand, the question is much more complex: How does U.S. culture systematically teach females to understand themselves as "naturally" physically less capable and males as physically more capable in ways that seem irrefutable? In this section we theorize how bodies are constantly physically gendered and how individuals come to know themselves as more or less physically abled.

Sport = Masculinity

Accomplishment in sports is the quintessential performance of masculinity in our culture. For any individual man, performing well in sports *is* performing masculinity well. Our gender messages tell us sport is what men do well, and when they do it well they become "real men." So we should not be surprised that women playing sports disturbs our gender messages and is much less encouraged in our culture.

A significant difference between women's and men's experience of physical embodiment in the world is learned through training (or lack of training) in sport (Connell 1983; Whitson 1994; Young 1980). The works of Raewyn Connell[8] and Iris Marion Young point out the phenomenal difference in the systematic gender training of male-bodied and female-bodied people to become men and women.[9] Read together, these works argue that women and men are differentially trained in social settings to experience and practice the body differently, which results in very different understandings of self, body, and physical ability, as well as resulting in differential body size and capacity (Whitson 1994). Sport is a significant mechanism for training these differential experiences and embodiments; as such, it is one setting where we learn to perform gender.

Over the last century, sport has been a central site for teaching masculinity to boys and men (Bryson 1990; Connell 1983; Crossett 1990; Kimmel 1990; Messner and Sabo 1990; White and Vagi 1990; Whitson 1990, 1994). Indeed, masculine participation in sport teaches the use of the body to attain power (Connell 1983; Whitson 1990, 1994). That is, sport is created and maintained for the purpose of teaching masculinity (which is the use of the body for power) to boys and men. Connell (1983) argues that the purpose of each sport is to teach the combination of force and skill in order to embody power. According to Connell, it is a simple equation: Power = force (i.e., taking up/controlling space) + skill. This is the purpose of each sport's construction. Hence, the well-trained athlete learns these bodily capacities. Connell (1983) argues that boys and men are taught to constantly and consciously measure their physical abilities. Connell writes, "To be an adult male is distinctly to occupy space, to have a physical presence in the world. Walking down the street, I square my shoulders and covertly measure myself against other men. . . .What it means to be masculine is, quite literally, to embody force, to embody competence" (19, 27). Because the male sporting experience teaches the use of force and skill in the pursuit of power, it allows males to practice masculinity.

Modern sporting practices and the celebration of masculinity in sport are the result of historical cultural shifts (Crossett 1990). During the significant social changes that occurred from the nineteenth to the twentieth centuries—the shift from an agrarian economy to an industrial-service economy, the democratizing of bourgeois social classes to a large (so-called) middle class, the rise of the women's and civil rights movements—the so-called "natural" differences that defined women's and men's "roles" became less clear (Crossett 1990). The pursuit of "manliness" became important, and such manliness could be demonstrated symbolically via economic success or via success in sport. Because of industrialism, the image of the previously self-employed, autonomous male working in manual labor had shriveled (as it were) causing a "crisis of masculinity" (Kimmel 1990). For those previously successful men who moved from the fields and frontiers to the assembly line and the office desk, another means of proving masculinity—bodily empowerment—was necessary. From the 1880s to the 1920s, pro-male organizations sprang up to fill the void, including the YMCA, the Boy Scouts, and organized sports, especially baseball (Kimmel 1990).

Of course, the men who moved into desk jobs in the late 1880s were primarily white men, not men of color. Hence, the notion of this sort of crisis of masculinity applies particularly to white men moving into less physical work. This should not suggest that men of color have not experienced a related form of bodily presentation of masculinity. Because of legalized discrimination of that time, many men of color were not able to demonstrate masculinity via economic success. For many African American men (and probably for all people of color on a symbolic level), status as men could be gained in particular through athletic success. To demonstrate prowess at a sport, especially beating white men, was to gain respect as men in the face of racial discrimination. For example, Joe Lewis's prize fights and Jesse Owens representing the United States by running against Nazi athletes in the Olympics are examples of African Americans' athletic achievements, symbolizing resistance to racism as well as gaining a sense of masculinity for African American men in the popular imagination (Evans 1997).[10]

The practice and organization of modern sport, then, aligns masculinity with physical prowess. To be fully, appropriately masculine, a male person must exhibit physical control of his space and be able to act on objects and bodies in it. He must exude power and confidence (Connell 1983). Fortunately for men, sport teaches this—the use of the body as a tool for accomplishing one's intentions. In short, sport equals masculinity. Importantly, though, sport is not a fully elective experience for boys. It is considered part of the requisite training to become a man.

"Throwing Like a Girl" and Other Messages of Femininity

Are you familiar with the concept of "throwing like a girl"? Have you seen people (female and male) do it—"throw like a girl"? Most of us have. It implies physical inability—failure at throwing, throwing poorly, but it also implies girl-ness. In other words, we do not say, "You throw like a wimp" (sex unassigned); we say, "you throw like a girl," as though the female body is implicated, as though there is something deficient about the female body. But let's take a minute to think about it. What does "throwing like a girl" look like? What does the body actually do when "throwing like a girl"? How does it look? Weak? Unfocused? Restricted? No follow-through?

Iris Marion Young makes an argument for women's embodied understanding of femininity as specifically the opposite of masculinity.[11] In "Throwing Like a Girl," Young (1980) discusses the tendency of girls to concentrate motion in one body part, rather than fully extending the entire body. Young (1980) states, "The girl learns actively to hamper her movements. She is told that she must be careful not to get hurt, not to get dirty, not to tear her clothes, . . . " (153). In short, by learning femininity, girls learn the opposite of empowerment; they are taught and practice to be "ladylike." Young argues that girls learn notions of femininity that make them timid about their own bodily abilities. Were girls trained through sports like boys to learn bodily empowerment, they would not "throw like a girl," but might use their bodies in more engaging and powerful ways (and those who *have* been trained may exhibit more forceful bodily abilities). It is women's lack of sports participation, lesser expectations for sporting abilities, or participation in "gender-appropriate" sports that bars them from learning about the body as both forceful and competent (Connell 1983; Kane and Snyder 1989; Lenskyj 1986; Messner 1988; Whitson 1994; Willis 1982). This differential style of motion actually shapes women's bodies to be smaller and toned rather than larger and powerful.

Young argues that women's physical embodiment of femininity is the practice of bodily restriction; in other words, throwing like a girl is "failure to make full use of the body's spatial and lateral potentialities" (142) and "the whole body is not put into fluid and directed motion, but rather . . . motion is concentrated in one body part" (143). But this is not about women's natural bodily capacities; it is a learned restriction that has more to do with one's training as a "girl" and the practiced ways that women learn self-restriction. She writes, "Feminine bodily existence is an *inhibited intentionality*, which simultaneously reaches toward a projected end with an 'I can' and withholds its full bodily commitment to that end in a self-imposed 'I cannot'" (emphasis in original, 146). So "throwing like a girl" is throwing without training or without force. It engages bodily restriction more than full bodily ability—which is the definition and physical training of femininity. To be ladylike is to be pretty, graceful, reserved—to be looked at, not to be useful and forceful.

Perhaps you have seen or know girls or women who throw extremely well—hard, fast, accurately, and boys or men who "throw like a girl"—untrained, weak, unintentional. There are women who can break your finger right through the softball glove (if you catch the throw out of the pocket). So the ability to throw is not specifically located in the body—especially not in the possession of a penis or vagina. It is in the training to be a "girl/lady" or in the training to be a "man"—in the training to restrict or to fully utilize bodily capacities. In other words, it begins in the cultural messages about how we expect bodies *should be used*.

Quite the opposite of the cultural messages of masculinity in sport, during the late nineteenth and early twentieth centuries women were discouraged from playing most sport or encouraged to play greatly modified games. The general consensus of doctors, educators, and the clergy of that time was that sport was immoral for women and that it might damage reproductive capacities or encourage inappropriate sexuality (Birrell 1988; Lenskyj 1986).[12] Most kinds of activities were discouraged if they appeared too "mannish," and public sporting events that might create a spectacle of women's bodies were feared to be too sexualizing. Many of the ideas of this period were about preserving women's sexual reputations (that is, controlling women's sexuality). Skimpy uniforms had not yet emerged and, indeed, the full-length head-to-toe clothing expected of women at the time made much physical activity difficult (Lenskyj 1986). Some minimally physical activities were understood to aid in women's "health" and "beauty," but they were not organized around physical exertion or testing bodily capacities.

Of course, the ideal of conserving "ladies'" activity was preserved largely for white middle- and upper-class women of privilege. Women of color and working-class women were never protected from the exertion of hard labor or allowed to be concerned with proprieties. Recall from chapter 1 how the "cult of true womanhood" set up differential expectations of femininity practices for various racial and class-based subgroups? Gissendanner (1994) writes that, because of racial segregation, relatively lower-class status, and an "ideal of active femininity," African American communities encouraged women of the 1920s to 1960s to participate in athletics. Gissendanner suggests that African American women, especially in rural and working-class areas, were not held accountable to upper-class, white femininity standards, especially since notions of feminine "weakness" were already falsified by African American women's relegation to hard labor. Instead, all kinds of achievements by African Americans, including achievements in sports, were seen as advancing the cause of civil rights, so women, like men, were encouraged to play sports. Indeed, Gissendanner documents that African American women's basketball games would frequently be organized along with men's basketball games at which admission was charged for both as one event (hence, making both "professional" events).

Still, because of segregation and discrimination against women of color, white middle- and upper-class women's pursuits were more widely disseminated as the proper way for women to behave. These previously dominant notions of passive femininity have translated into current understandings of femininity, although to some extent with less necessity for passivity. Of course, the passage of Title IX (the federal law that requires all public educational resources to be made equally available to all students regardless of sex/gender) in 1972 has greatly changed opportunities for women in sport. (We discuss this in detail in chapter 4.) However, while women and girls do now participate in sports more readily and more fiercely than in the past, cultural messages and practices of femininity still imply a sense of bodily reserve; whereas men are expected to be controlling and dominant.

Our point here is that this phenomenon is not about male or female bodies or about individual abilities as much as it is about systematic training in gender expectations through sport—that is, requisite training of power for boys and men and lack of training or differential training of body movement for women and girls. In addition, how we are expected to behave in church, at work, in relationships, with children, and so forth also plays into how we know and utilize our bodies. Think about how this dichotomy taught in sport might work its way into other settings. How is movement gendered? For example, is there a way that men walk and a way that women walk? Of course, not all men and not all women walk exactly the same way, but is there a way of walking that is considered masculine and a way of walking that is considered feminine that some people exemplify or perhaps play up in certain settings? Try "walking like a woman" and "walking like a man." Play it up. Be stereotypical. After you try it, think about the actual bodily movements. What is different about them? In what ways are body movements being used to make it look different? We expect you will say that women stand with a straight spine (as if balancing a book on their heads), walk gracefully with flowing movements, place one foot in front of the other (especially if that accentuates hip movement—swish!), take smaller strides (which is especially necessary if wearing high heels or a tight skirt), hold their arms close or wrapped around the waist (to look smaller or cover any appearance of a belly), and avert their eyes so as not to look someone in the eye directly. Conversely, we expect you will say that men walk as if with a purpose—taking long, uncontrolled strides; walking with their upper body first as if their pecs are inflated; controlling the sidewalk; taking care not to shake their hips; with hands in their front pockets or clenched in fists but never covering their stomachs. Clearly these are caricatures of feminine and masculine ways of walking and not all people engage these forms of movement, or at least not all the time. But if you recognize any part of these descriptions as related to how women or men are supposed to walk, you must recognize that movement is gendered. Because not all women or all men exhibit this behavior, it is safe to say this movement has little to do with genital differences and more to do with how we are compelled by others to perform femininity and masculinity.

Similarly, is there a way that women and men are expected to sit? You'd probably say that women sit upright with a straight back, legs and arms held closely. In contrast, you'd say that men sit with a bit of a slouch, taking up the armrests, relaxed with arms and legs open and comfortable. What about crossing legs? Is there a way that women are supposed to cross their legs? With knee over knee, or perhaps with one ankle in front of the other and knees pressed together? What about for men? With ankle over knee and legs open and relaxed? Try it. Sit in each of these positions. Does any feel more "wrong" for you than the other? Does that feeling have to do with gender?

The point here is that movement is gendered; it is part of the performance of gender—doing gender. We perform gender expectations with our bodies— for men, using the body as a power tool; for women, constraining body size and capacity in order to appear small. Of course, not all of us comply or even need to comply. We will talk more about how elective these forms of movement are in the next chapter when we discuss surveillance and in chapter 5 when we talk about agency. But these forms of movement fit the cultural messages about masculinity and femininity (the gender box structure) and they are specifically learned and practiced via sport.

Performing Gender through Sport

Many individual sports compel athletes to perform gender through sport. Certain sports have a sense of gender appropriateness. Kane and Snyder

(1989) call this *sport typing*—the notion that certain sports are understood as appropriate for girls while others are appropriate for boys. For example, gymnastics, figure skating, and cheerleading are understood as gender appropriate for women and girls (i.e., feminine); whereas football, basketball, baseball, hockey, and bodybuilding are understood as gender appropriate for men and boys (i.e., masculine). Hence, engaging in these sports enhances one's gender performance.[13] Football is consistent with performing masculinity, so boys and men who play it are seen as masculine; while gymnastics is consistent with performing femininity, so girls and women who engage in gymnastics are seen as feminine. In each of these examples, the sport itself is organized and designed to teach and train stereotypical masculine or feminine performances.

The Feminine Apologetic and Fear of Gender Inappropriateness

You might argue that some men engage in gymnastics, skating, and cheerleading and that some women play football and basketball, right? Not all women play "feminine sports" and not all men play "masculine sports." This is true, but most athletes who play these sports, and, indeed, most games in which gender appropriateness is in question, change the performance to fit back into the paradigm. After all, if sport is designed to teach masculinity to men, what happens to women when they play?

For women who compete in very masculine sports, many will compensate for their athletic prowess on the field by enhancing their feminine performances off the field. This effect is called the feminine "apologetic" (Clasen 2001; Messner 1988).[14] Seriously athletic women are still expected to emerge from the locker room in full makeup with hair styled and sassy. In order not to be questioned about appropriate womanliness, female athletes may be especially attentive to primping and accentuating femininity while not playing. At times, this effect will play out during the practice of the sport itself. For example, many collegiate softball players wear ponytails with ribbons or other frilly hair accessories during the game. Female body builders frequently wear extra makeup and sexualizing swimsuits or skimpy dresses with long earrings and highly styled hair in order to specifically point out their femaleness (which often appears very culturally ambiguous on such pumped-up, muscle-bound bodies). Hence, women in masculine sports go out of their way to perform femininity in order to appear gender appropriate. Likewise, collegiate programs often highlight femininity in their promotional materials for women's teams. Buysee and Embser-Herbert (2004) report that college media guides used to promote and market college sports teams are much more likely to portray the members of men's sports teams as athletes—in uniform, on the court, or in action—whereas the members of women's sports teams will often be posed in feminine ways—in dresses rather than uniforms, or in sexy poses, not in athletic action. This kind of promotion shores up gender performances and stereotypes in ways that tend to display men as actively sporty and aggressive while demonstrating the feminine apologetic for women.

As for men in "feminine" sports, the men's activity in that sport is often changed completely to showcase masculine performances. For example, men in figure skating will do more daring stunts than the women (a triple or quadruple jump will be required, whereas women must attempt a double) or, in pairs skating, a male skater will lift his female partner or skate behind her as if to suggest she needs his strength or that she fits neatly under his wing. (Notice this also fits the heteronormative imperative of matching males and females, not males and males or females and females, in pairs.) Similarly, male cheerleaders usually do not engage in the same activities as female cheerleaders—instead of dancing, they will stand and clap or do push-ups or, instead of jumping themselves, they will lift a female cheerleader.[15] In certain sports, the entire game and pursuit changes to meet masculine performances. For example, in gymnastics, many of the events that men perform in are different from the women's events. Unlike the graceful tumbling routines performed to music that women engage in, men's gymnastics tumbling routines are not performed to music and do not include dance moves. Most of the other men's events, such as the high bar, parallel bars, pommel horse, and rings emphasize upper-body strength and control—much more masculine pursuits. Interestingly, the vaulting event is performed by both men and women on the same piece of equipment.[16]

So, gender is performed through sport, and gender identities are enhanced by sports performances, which, of course, act as everyday confirmations of gender messages. But these performances carry into other social settings as well.

Work

Strength versus Servitude: Messages about Gendered Performances at Work

Gender messages about "truly" different bodies also encourage gender performances at work. In spite of the fact that a great deal of legislation addressing gender-based inequities in the labor force has been passed, there remains a persistent belief about the "nature" of women and men and the proper place for each in the world of work. Many jobs are still regarded as most appropriate for workers of one sex or the other because the jobs call upon skills we see as masculine or feminine (Williams 1989). An important consequence of this gender labeling of jobs is the segregation of women and men in the workplace. Many workers have jobs in which the majority of their co-workers are people of the same sex as themselves. A significant reason for this segregation may be the way in which certain types of jobs enhance or detract from our understandings of our gender performances. Hard labor jobs are seen as masculine, so doing hard labor enhances the masculine performances of the people who do it. Office jobs are seen as feminine and thus enhance the feminine performances of the people who do them. In many instances, jobs may be selected because they contribute to our gender performances.

Table 2.1, for instance, presents a list of blue-collar jobs that are male-dominated; that is, at least 90 percent of the workers in the jobs are men. Included in this list are a number of skilled crafts jobs, such as carpentry, plumbing, and masonry. Because many of these jobs are presumed to require a great deal of strength or involve physical danger, they are generally considered inappropriate for women. Of course, for men, these kinds of jobs also aid in their performances of masculinity, whether the individual plays up that performance or not. What could be more "manly" than working as a pipe fitter or welder?

Whether any of these jobs, in fact, do require extreme physical strength may vary according to the situation. For example, being a crane operator or truck driver may be associated with masculinity but requires no more special strength than driving a car might. Whereas lifting masonry may be quite physically taxing, connecting electrical wire is not in itself terribly heavy work. So while some of these jobs may engage physical labor, many do not require special strength. Nonetheless, all are seen as masculine jobs, and the people who do them may be seen as inherently "doing" masculinity. Interestingly, the majority of these jobs are associated with being outside, especially outside the home, whereas many "women's" jobs are associated with working inside.

Table 2.1. Blue-Collar Jobs: Occupations in Which the Workforce Is at Least 90% Male

Occupations	% Female
Truck drivers	4.6
Firefighters	3.5
Crane operators	3.3
Construction laborers	3.0
Loggers	2.5
Electricians	2.1
Carpenters	1.6
Auto mechanics	1.4
Roofers	1.3
Plumbers, pipe fitters	1.0
Electric power line installers/repairers	0.9
Brick/stone masons	0.9
Structural iron and steel workers	<0.1

Source: U.S. Department of Labor, Women's Bureau, 2003a. "20 Nontraditional Occupations for Women." www.dol.gov/wb/factsheets/nontra2003.htm.

Conversely, "women's" jobs play into gender messages about femininity. Table 2.2 presents a list of "pink-collar" or female-dominated jobs.[17] Many of these involve caring for people who need help (such as the young, the old, the sick or infirm, or the poor) or in some other way represent an extension of women's traditional work in the home and family (e.g., cleaning). Others involve processing paperwork in industry or greeting clients or customers. In popular perception, these jobs do not require a great deal of strength or expose workers to physical risks. In fact, they are viewed as requiring skills women possess simply by virtue of being female. They are presumed to require no special training or strength. They are "clean" jobs that typically take place indoors. Engaging in these kinds of jobs enhances one's performance of femininity.

But these images of ease and simplicity may be more mythical than real. Lifting and carrying babies and children or moving/lifting sick patients in hospital beds may require a great deal of strength, as does carrying buckets of water for mopping floors and loads of wet laundry from industrial washing machines to a dryer or clothesline. Nor can it be accurately said that pink-collar jobs are cleaner than the blue-collar jobs mentioned above. Changing diapers and soiled sheets, cleaning toilets, and chipping plaque from someone's teeth challenge this assumption. So while these jobs are seen as feminine and "clean" and working in them enhances one's performance of femininity, the degree to which they require little strength or allow the worker to actually remain clean is often questionable. Nonetheless, workers are expected to perform their gender on the jobs and, regardless of actual job requirements, jobs are often understood to shore up gendered expectations of each of us. In the sections that follow, we discuss doing gender in segregated work environments as well as ways that men and women working in gender-nontraditional jobs use their bodies to emphasize masculinity and femininity.

Table 2.2. Pink-Collar Jobs: Occupations in Which Approximately 90% (or more) of Workers Are Female (2003)

Occupations	% Female
Preschool and kindergarten teachers	97.9
Secretaries and administrative assistants	96.4
Child care workers	94.9
Receptionists and information clerks	94.1
Registered nurses	92.9
Teacher assistants	92.8
Bookkeeping, accounting, and auditing clerks	92.1
Hairdressers, hairstylists, and cosmetologists	90.6
Health aides	90.5
Maids and housekeepers/cleaners	89.4

Source: U.S. Department of Labor, Women's Bureau, 2003b. "20 Leading Occupations of Employed Women." www.dol.gov/wb/factsheets/20lead2003.htm.

It is important to keep in mind that jobs are not *inherently* masculine or feminine (intended to be done by males or females). Historical studies of occupations show that their gender labels and composition change over time (Brandth and Haugen 2005; Kwolek-Folland 1994; Mills 1998; Pringle 1993). Clerical work—which is now female-dominated[18]—was at one time a "men's" job. Before offices were mechanized, neat penmanship and accurate arithmetic were essential to clerical work, which was regarded as a highly skilled occupation that offered great potential for upward mobility.[19] Men who started as clerks in small offices could work their way up to manage or even own the business. As offices grew and paperwork proliferated, adding machines and typewriters were introduced. Clerical work became female-dominated. It was argued that women had better manual dexterity and could more efficiently operate the machines. The work became understood to be feminine, and not surprisingly, the status of the work declined, along with its wages and opportunities for advancement. Some observers have said that the introduction of office machines reduced the skill level. Others argue that when the gender label of the job changed, the status and salary declined (Pringle 1993).

Another occupation that is currently occupied predominantly by women is that of flight attendant. Historically, however, men performed this job but were called air stewards. During the 1920s, airlines began to recruit bellhops from luxury hotels to serve as "cabin boys" and to use the image of the male air steward to promote the safety of air travel. This occupation was modeled after the service positions that existed in first-class travel by rail and sea (Mills 1998). The image of the air steward was described in a 1936 *Imperial Airlines News Bulletin* and relied in part on a description of the bodies of the men occupying this position. The men were described as "completely dedicated to the passengers and their 'comfort'; experienced and consistent; part psychologist and part actor; methodical and meticulous; 'small, agile, quick-moving', 'deft' and 'proud'" (cited in Mills 1998:178). It was not until the 1940s that many airlines began to hire female flight attendants.[20]

Selling Your Smile: Flight Attendants

Today we understand the job of the flight attendant to be "women's work," or highly feminized work. It is seen as involving skills that women possess simply by virtue of being women. No special training is understood to be required—no special skills involved. Simply responding to situations with "common sense" that a woman is assumed to possess is thought to be sufficient. One female flight attendant is quoted as saying, "This job is more natural for a woman than for a man . . . because females in general are more caring than men . . . women are just more helpful, they are kinder and more instinctive" (Tyler and Taylor 1998:167). The job is constructed as a nurturing position that requires nurturing workers—presumably women. Although, as Hochschild (1983) points out, it is interesting that things presumed to be "natural" have to be meticulously outlined in employee manuals. What are the qualifications for becoming a flight attendant with a U.S. airline, beyond a high school diploma (or its equivalent), U.S. citizenship, and fluency in English? Two essential considerations are customer service experience and appearance.

Relevant customer service, according to the website www.cabincrewjobs .com, includes retail sales, waiting tables in restaurants, and answering phones in a corporate environment. The website advises prospective flight attendants that they will be

> working in front of the public on a regular basis. From greeting, serving, and assisting passengers to making announcements, you will always be representing the company in a customer service role. Because it is very important to project a positive image, airlines are very careful about selecting candidates who have experience working with the public. ("Minimum Qualifications to Become a Flight Attendant" 2006)

In *The Managed Heart*, sociologist Arlie Hochschild (1983) introduces the notion of *emotion work*. Emotions are put into use to complete the job. In essence, they are performed for the job. The flight attendant's job is to deliver a service and create further demand for it, to enhance the status of the customer and be "nicer than natural." Hence, femininity—nurturing, caring, being "nicer than natural"—*is* the job for flight attendants. It is part of job performance.

For flight attendants, the concern for appearance, another component of feminine performance, is closely tied to this customer service dimension. The cabincrewjobs.com website states that

> the airlines are very particular about hiring individuals who have a neat and attractive appearance. . . . Typically, airlines do not permit visible tattoos, body piercings (save for your ears), long hair on men, "rebellious" hairstyles, bizarre or offensive-looking makeup or jewelry, poorly manicured hands, etc. . . . During training you will be given specific grooming regulations which must be strictly adhered to. ("Minimum Qualifications to Become a Flight Attendant" 2006)

So while men can be flight attendants, the expectation for nurturing work and appearance is consistent with the performance of femininity, which is more readily consistent with gender messages for women.

Although flight attendant work is discussed as a polite, feminine kind of job, Wendy Stafford, a former flight attendant, describes one unexpected aspect of the work:

> No one told me about cleaning the airplane. Sometimes we go to cities where aircraft cleaners are not available, and guess who has to clean and straighten up the plane? Vomit-filled barf bags, seatbacks stuffed with dirty tissues, diapers,

and God-only-knows what else, and surprises left in the lavatories! ("Things I Never Anticipated" 2006)

Apparently there are less "clean" components to the job. Although this may be "dirty" work, it is also consistent with housework that women are expected to do.

In addition, flight attendant work is not necessarily as easy or safe as the promotional materials suggest. According to a study conducted by the Association of Flight Attendants (AFA)[21] and the AFL-CIO, 10 percent of more than 31,000 flight attendants reported an injury that required medical attention beyond first aid or caused them to lose time from work. Injuries result from poorly designed food and beverage carts, slipping on galley floors, handling or being struck by heavy carry-on baggage, falling on icy walkways, and sustaining cuts and burns from galley equipment and oven racks. The injury rate of air transportation workers, which includes flight attendants (14.5%) was higher than that in construction (8.8%), agriculture (7.9%), or mining (4.9%), yet the workforce is not offered occupational and safety health protection by either the Occupational Safety and Health Administration or the airlines (*Professional Safety* 2000).

From Men in Trees to Men in Suits: Social Class and Occupational Masculinity

While our imagination leads us to associate stereotypical women's jobs with being indoors, being "clean," and not requiring much strength, we typically imagine stereotypical men's jobs as being outdoors, being dirty, and requiring a great deal of strength. Think of a logger or a lumberjack; what kind of image comes to mind? Probably a man in a flannel shirt and cap, with weathered skin and a generally rugged appearance, using a chain saw or ax to do physically demanding and dangerous work (Brandth and Haugen 2000, 2005). Doing highly masculinized work creates desirable masculine bodies and culturally less-desirable female bodies, as Kris Paap (2006) discovered in her ethnographic study of construction workers. Rather than suggesting that construction work should be men's work because men are physically stronger than women (an argument one might expect to hear), the men Paap worked with seemed to suggest that women could probably do the work, but that they should not as it would create a less-attractive female body. Paap (2006) shows an exchange recorded in a focus group sponsored by the National Institute of Occupational Safety and Health in which men were questioning the training women received before entering into construction work:

"Are you preparing them mentally? Do they also understand what they're going to look like after . . . when they're 50 years old?" "We can look wrinkled and craggly and humped up, and at 37, when they're wrinkled up and crippled up . . ." Another carpenter interjects, "They're old." And the first carpenter agrees, ". . . they're old." The moderator of the focus groups asks, "Yeah? Does

it bother them or does it bother you?" "I think it bothers them. Well, it bothers me, too. I just don't, I'm still from the old school, I don't think a woman
has to look old just because of work." (111)

Jobs like the ones described above are typically thought of as blue-collar,
working class jobs. How do men in white-collar jobs *perform* masculinity?
Brandth and Haugen (2000, 2005) use an analysis of Norwegian forestry
magazines to show the changing nature of occupational masculinity. As the
forestry industry has changed over the years, images of masculinity must
also change. The authors show that the dominant image of the rugged individual battling nature's forces in the 1970s gave way to images of a more
professional forest worker in the 1980s. This image of masculinity involved
younger bodies displayed as extensions of more efficient machines than
used in the past. The 1990s brought images of the organization man, with
bodies displayed in powerful positions in indoor settings like boardrooms,
surrounded by computers and cell phones. The performance of white-collar
masculinity seems to employ the body less directly than blue-collar masculinity. Clothes and technological props fill in for bulging muscles, visible
scars, and weathered skin, making distinctions between performances of
masculinity and femininity more subtle in white-collar settings.

Performance Strategies

We have discussed the segregation of workers by gender that occurs in the
labor market today. In many workplaces, though, women and men do interact closely even when they do different types of work. There is a gender
differentiation (and hierarchy) in the workplace just as there is in the wider
society. *Social distancing techniques* are social practices or strategies that create and exaggerate the social distance between groups by differentiating
them in appearance or behavior (Reskin and Roos 1987:7). In gender-
mixed workplaces, male workers tend to have jobs with more masculine
components—higher status, more power, and more privileges than female
workers. Moreover, when the women and men interact in the economic sphere,
men (employers, co-workers, and even customers) perform masculinity by
using a wide range of techniques to distance themselves from women in order to legitimize and reinforce their masculinity (LaPointe 1992).

Distancing techniques used by men may be subtle or blatant, but often
bodies are implicated in the performance of masculinity. Either bodies are
used to perform masculinity or nonmasculine bodies are targeted to highlight
difference. Williams (1995) describes how men in gender-nontraditional
jobs sometimes emphasize the physical aspects of the job to highlight masculinity. For example, in her study, a school teacher at a school for autistic
children "explained that men were needed for 'restraining' the children,
some of whom were 'very, very violent'" (127). Another example includes

restaurant work, where, for instance, men tend to perform the "masculine" jobs of cook and bartender (producing things), while women are food servers (working with people).

In mixed-gender workplaces, a common "distancing technique" men use in the workplace involves demeaning women through the use of sexual comments to create and reinforce gender performance through demonstrating overt masculine sexuality and sexual control. Often restaurant owners or managers will select uniforms that degrade women by sexualizing or infantilizing them. Sexual harassment is also used by male employers, co-workers, and customers to keep waitresses in a subordinate position (LaPointe 1992). We write in more detail about sexual harassment in chapter 4.

Women working in gender-nontraditional occupations also manage their gender performance, sometimes emphasizing femininity as a distancing technique and other times employing a masculine performance, to be thought of "as one of the guys." Melissa Herbert (1998) surveyed more than 250 women who had served or were currently serving in the U.S. military. The majority of the women surveyed felt that there were penalties for being perceived as either "too feminine" or "too masculine." Being perceived as too feminine often meant being thought of as weak and incompetent and (hetero)sexually available. Being perceived as too masculine often meant being thought of as too aggressive or violent and led to one's heterosexuality being brought into question. Since the U.S. military has a "don't ask, don't tell" policy concerning sexual orientation, all women, regardless of sexual orientation, are at risk of sanctions if they are "outed" as lesbians. Nearly half of the women in Herbert's (1998) study employed techniques to emphasize either femininity or masculinity in their day-to-day interactions on the job. Many of these techniques involved altering their appearance and/or body. Women who emphasized femininity did so by wearing makeup and jewelry both on-duty and off-duty, wearing long hair, wearing skirts and high-heeled shoes whenever possible, and trying to maintain a thin body build. Women who emphasized masculinity chose pants uniforms over skirt uniforms and camouflage uniforms over dress uniforms, lifted weights, and did not ask for help when doing physical tasks like lifting heavy objects.

Hence, both women and men are expected to perform femininity and masculinity (respectively) on the job. These performances are often the basis of job selection but also shore up the expectation that women and men are feminine and masculine people off the job as well.

Sexuality and Reproduction

Producing Heterosexuality: Embodying Sexuality

So, there is a performance of gender for sport and for work. But isn't reproduction biological? Is sex natural? In many ways, sex has biological, "natural" components. But sex is also as gendered and filled with social messages as any realm of everyday life. In other words, there are rules for interaction when one is flirting or courting or even engaging in sex acts. One could say sex is scripted.

Here's an example: If you are kissing someone, are your eyes supposed to be open or closed? We bet you said closed. It's as though for kissing to look "good" and be done well—that is, if you want to be a good kisser, your eyes must be closed. How did you know that? Where did you learn it? You probably learned it from watching movies, television, or music videos, or maybe your friends instructed you. You learned it in a social setting (probably following those media icons). There are other rules too. Who is supposed to open doors for whom? Who is supposed to ask whom on a date? Who is supposed to make the sexual advances? We bet you know the answers to all these questions. Although we do not always perform as scripted, each of us tends to know the rules, and to know that we are breaking them. Sex is scripted and these scripts are gendered (Gagnon 1977; Gagnon and Simon [1973] 2005; Jackson and Scott 2001; Schwartz and Rutter 1998). Gagnon originated the idea that we follow *sexual scripts.* The scripts tell us how we are to behave—when and how we are expected to perform in sexual interactions.

For example, what is the first step when you think you like a person? Do you introduce yourself and say, "Gee, you're good-looking. Would you like to have sex?" Probably not. Do you indicate your interest by walking up to a person and shaking their genitals? Probably not. There is a step-by-step process for indicating interest and starting a sexual relationship with someone. A protracted example of this is the baseball metaphor "getting to first base." Have you heard that term? What does "first base" mean? Who is getting there with whom? Who is expected to be resistant? Is she getting to first base with him? (Or, is she getting to third base with her—another woman? Can he be getting to third base with him?) Is it possible for her to hit a "home run"? What is "second base"? "Third"? What's a "home run"? It is interesting that this is a sports metaphor. We do not think that is by chance. How do we come to such a shared set of ideas about how sex is supposed to progress? The sexual scripts indicate who is supposed to do what to whom and in what order. And, they are very gendered; he is supposed to pursue, she is supposed to resist (at least a little). The scripts are also very heteronormative; they do not suggest two males or two females interacting.

A component of femininity provides the sexual script for females. It might be understood as the Britney Spears ethic: *Be sexy but not sexual!* Have you noticed that throughout Britney Spears's career the media have been obsessed with her sexuality—not just her sexualized appearance but her actual sexual practices? Prior to getting married and having children, there was a media blitz over whether Britney was a virgin. Had she had premarital sex? Did you ever wonder, Why Britney? Why do we care? We suggest Britney Spears's persona represents the paradox of youthful femininity—be sexy in every overt, teasing way, but do not have sex. It is permissible for her to dance barely clothed, looking like a teen and acting like a sex kitten, as long as we can be certain she "really is pure." Of course we cannot "really" know her true sexual history but that is irrelevant compared to her celebrity persona. She must look the part of the icon. Women are expected to look young, pretty, and be sexually attractive, but also to be virtuous—to be virgins on their wedding nights. Some have called this the virgin/whore dichotomy or the Madonna/whore syndrome. A woman should look alluring—always able to attract a man, always trying to attract a man—but not be having sex. In fact, she is expected to be the sexual gatekeeper (Carpenter 2006); giving the signal to proceed with sex or not. This, then, becomes the performance of femininity in sexual contexts—be alluring, not active; be sexy, not sexual.

For men, the performance of masculinity is quite the opposite. Men are expected to be hypersexual—wanting sex constantly and always pursuing it actively with any available woman (Bordo 1998; Kimmel 1994). They are expected to view sex as a thing to accomplish, and their *penis as a power tool* (Bordo 1998). For men, sex is a job to be done with the right tools. The man must perform! (It is not even a pun in this context, is it?) The performance of masculinity, then, is to exude immense sexual energy and to always be on the prowl. In fact, in his essay "How Men Have (a) Sex," Stoltenberg (1990) argues that the act of penile-vaginal intercourse is the ultimate masculinity-confirming act for men. Men develop the sense that they are "men" through the act of coming to orgasm while inside a vagina.

Interestingly, men do not confirm their "manliness" by coming to orgasm in other orifices. We have often heard the claim that there is a natural "fit" between penises and vaginas that makes intercourse "natural." But penises fit in other orifices as well. And, commonly, vaginas (and clitorises!) can be and are stimulated by many other body parts as well as nonbiological things (vibrators, etc.). Penises and vaginas do not require each other for stimulation or sexual enjoyment. A finger may fit in a nose, but we do not consider that a "natural" fit. The meanings and performances we create around sexual acts are part of the social embodiment and performance of gender.

Here we are not arguing that sexual contact is only a discursive understanding of the world or that certain sexual acts would not happen without the teachings of Western culture. We are arguing that every act of sex in our culture comes loaded with performances and meanings, and that those meanings and performances confirm our beliefs in sexual scripts through body knowledge that makes us believe our gendered performances are natural and only biological. It is a bit of a circular effect. We learn the messages that precede us and perform them accordingly as we make them part of our selves. Our experiences of these performances very often have a bodily feeling of confirming what we thought we already knew about biology. Hence, we gain body knowledge based on socially mediated messages. But it is clear that "first base" is a social construction as is the idea that women are less sexual than men or are more in control of their sexuality. There is no "natural" reason for men to "make the first move." We learn and practice the rules of behavior so well that they come to feel a part of our bodies— that is, they feel "natural," but they are no less performative than the idea that men should be chefs and women should cook for the kids. Sexuality is also performed on and through the body.

Pregnancy and Birth Performances for Women and Men

Reproduction is one of the very few things that we *know* involves biological differences between males and females. Even so, not all females can become pregnant and not all males are fertile. Nonetheless, there are gendered social performances surrounding birth processes and even parenting when the child has been adopted. "Mother" and "father" are specific performances that very likely change how one thinks of self and how one interacts in the world.

Pregnancy used to be something that people tried to hide with large maternity clothes. It was public proof of sexuality and there was a sense that "respectable people" did not talk about such things. Today, many people celebrate the pregnant body, taking pictures or making plaster molds of their bellies.[22] Celebrities have led the way in glamorizing pregnancy. In the early 1990s, Demi Moore's nude, pregnant body was displayed on the cover of *Vanity Fair* magazine. Flip through any entertainment magazine these days and you are likely to see pregnant bellies, or "bumps," as the media like to call them, prominently displayed at the beach, at a restaurant, and even at awards shows. Davis-Floyd (1992) describes pregnancy as a ritual and a rite of passage, involving both personal and public transformations. Personal transformation may include personal growth, fear, wonder, and awe along with simultaneous feelings of alienation from and closeness to self and families. As for public transformation, pregnant women must negotiate the avoidance or special interest of strangers. Paradoxically, while it is commonly held in U.S. culture that the space around a person's body is private and generally should not be intruded upon by strangers, it is also common for people to assume it is acceptable to touch a pregnant woman's stomach. Pregnancy, then, is a very visible marker of femaleness, and may change the way others respond to a woman as well as the way she feels about herself and performs and confirms her femininity.

Bailey (2001) documents pregnant women's experiences of their gendered bodies through sensuality, shape, and space. Many of the women in Bailey's study regretted that they did not feel more sexual during their pregnancies, since pregnancy is a visible affirmation of sexuality (despite the existence of new reproductive technologies that do not require sex for pregnancy to occur). Some women connected the changing shape of their bodies with femininity and with motherhood. Others feared getting "fat" and were pleased when their pregnancies began to "show," so that it was obvious that they were pregnant rather than "fat." In this study, women also talked about the change in the amount of public space they were permitted to occupy. As we discussed earlier in the chapter, women are usually socialized to take up as little space as possible, but these norms are loosened during pregnancy. Bailey (2001) argues that the extra space permitted to pregnant women is less about freedom of movement, as it might be for men, and more about "feminine fragility." One of the respondents in this study commented, "when they see that you're pregnant, people sort of stand back and let you go first. I think it's kind of like you're made of china or something, and they can't get too close to you in case they knock you" (121).

Upton and Han (2003) write about women's experiences of wanting to "get the body back" after childbirth. One of their respondents described no longer having a pregnant body, but "[the body] is not really *yours* again either, not at all what your body used to be and that is really distressing when you think about it . . .you're always trying to get it back, but you never really can have it back" (674). Dworkin and Wachs (2004) examined messages from *Shape Fit Pregnancy* magazine covering the years 1997 to 2003. They found this idea of "getting the body back" to be a prominent theme. Pregnant women were encouraged to work out during pregnancy in order to make labor and delivery quicker and less painful and to make it easier to "bounce back" after the birth. Pay attention to interviews with celebrity moms and you will see this phenomenon at work. We challenge you to find an interview in which a new celebrity mom is not asked the question, "So, how'd you lose the weight?"

Internalized gender norms even influence women's performance of femininity during labor and delivery (Houvouras 2004; K. Martin 2003). In her article "Giving Birth Like a Girl," Karin Martin (2003) argues that childbirth education in the United States instructs us to do things that are gender deviant during labor and birth. Respondents in her study describe "acting bad" and "not being nice" during labor. They tried very hard to be polite and were concerned about bothering others—hospital staff, people in neighboring rooms. Not only did they feel bad about being "nasty," "inflexible," and "out of control," but they often apologized to partners and hospital staff afterward, reconciling their gender nonconformity.

Performances of reproductive capacity apply to men as well. What images come to mind when you think of expectant dads? In popular movies and television shows, men are often portrayed as incompetent and sometimes even bumbling idiots when it comes to childbirth and fatherhood. Think of Steve Martin in *Father of the Bride II* running around like a clown or Hugh Grant fainting in *Nine Months*. While we have pop culture images of dads handing out cigars after the birth of a child and a whole host of new self-help books aimed at expectant fathers, sociologists have written very little about men's experiences during pregnancy and birth. Because they do not have the same direct, embodied experience of pregnancy as women, men report feeling detached or remote from the pregnancy experience (Draper 2002a, 2002b, 2003). Expectant fathers often report enjoying tangible events such as the pregnancy test, the ultrasound, feeling the baby move, or the birth itself. In these moments, men feel more connected to their impending fatherhood. Draper calls these body-mediated moments, or "a kind of proxy embodiment conferred through the medium of technology or his partner's body, signal[ing] the beginning of the reality of the pregnancy" (2003: 254).

Although men may not have a specific bodily experience of pregnancy and birth, the changing shape of a female partner's body may be both pleasurable and problematic for men. Draper (2003) reports men using humor to deflect anxiety about their partners' bodily changes. This is reflected in the nature of the self-help books aimed at expectant fathers. Sprinkled among the "serious" books are books with titles such as *My Boys Can Swim! The Official Guy's Guide to Pregnancy* (Davis 1999) (apparently even sperm can perform masculinity!), and a spoof of the popular women's self-help book, *What to Expect When Your Wife Is Expanding* (Hill 1993).[23] It may be during birth that the baby "becomes a person" to the father for the first time. However, dads report fearing harm or damage to the baby or to their partners' bodies and may also worry about their own reactions to the graphic scenes of blood and other fluids in the delivery room (Draper 2002a, 2002b; Shapiro 1987).

One interesting gendered body performance comes in the form of what anthropologists have termed *couvade syndrome*. Couvade syndrome has also been called sympathetic pregnancy and occurs when men experience somatic symptoms similar to the symptoms of their pregnant partner. For example, in the United States men may experience morning sickness, constipation, and so forth. They might also adhere to cultural expectations for pregnancy, including abstaining from certain foods, drugs, and activities. Anthropologists have documented a variety of these types of practices across cultures (for a detailed account of couvades, see Reed 2005).

A "Good Man" on Paper and a "Good Mom" in the Exam Room

What gendered messages imply is important about male bodies is evident in the advertising of sperm donors. A typical entry in a sperm-donor catalogue looks something like the following:

Donor Code	352
Race	Caucasian
Ethnicity	Irish/Italian
Blood type	A+

Hair	Red
Eyes	Brown
Skin	Fair
Height	5'-8"
Weight	165 lbs.
Education	Master's
Occupation	Sales
Interests	Yoga, tennis, guitar

These catalogues are available online.[24] For serious consumers, a detailed medical history is available for a fee. While it is often low-income women who are recruited to serve as surrogate mothers (see chapter 4), it is often well-educated young men and women (with the potential to earn a high income) who are sought out for sperm and egg donation. There is a sense of virtual masculinity[25] in the descriptions of sperm donors. There is no physical body, so to speak, but potential for a body. Language then is what creates differences and hierarchies among men. High-SAT-scoring, blue-eyed, blond-haired, white "men-on-paper" are the most sought out among sperm donors, which perpetuates dominant forms of masculinity (Schmidt and Moore 1998). The agencies that sell sperm are selling what Schmidt and Moore call "technosemen," a superior-quality sperm imbued with the personality characteristics of the donor.

Women's and men's relationships to reproductive technology often have less to do with performance and more to do with surveillance, inequality, and agency, as we will discuss in the following chapters. However, women may be expected to perform "good mother" by responding properly to ultrasound images and other types of reproductive technology. For example, the character Rachel Green on the television show *Friends* performed as expected when she and the baby's father, Ross, were looking at the ultrasound image of their child. While the doctor was in the room, Rachel pretended to see her baby on the screen. As soon as the doctor left, she started crying because she could not see it. When Ross asked why she said she could see it, she replied that she did not want the doctor to think she was a bad mother.

CONCLUSION

To conclude, gender is produced primarily through our interactions with and performances for each other on the basis of our belief in innate bodily differences. Gendered messages tend to tell us that women should be pretty and nice while men are expected to be daring and strong. While cultural messages suggest to us that these are innate propensities, it is clear there is nothing innate about fashions that require females to use makeup and males to wear baggy pants. The way we wear our bodies is a result of culture and social interaction much more than some innate drive. Most of us perform some recognizable imitation of these notions. An important question is: Why? Just because the messages exist, why do we tend to follow them?

In the next chapter, we discuss the surveillance and accountability that each of us endures and replicates in order to keep conforming to gender performance. Performance is not fully elective in our social world. We will explore how gender performance is not simply an individual choice and why individuality is not as prevalent as you may think.

NOTES

1. Butler (1993) calls this "performativity as citationality."

2. For a portrayal of a woman who lives her everyday life with a full beard, see *Juggling Gender* (1992), a documentary by Tami Gold, produced by Women Make Movies.

3. The authors wish to thank Rebecca Willman for this helpful insight.

4. The literature on the self is much larger and more up-to-date than just the works of Mead and Goffman, and resides in a larger literature of symbolic interactionism. However, for the purposes of introducing the notion of self to readers we choose to briefly introduce the original theorists of this literature. For a more updated and nuanced discussion of self, see Cahill et al. (1998), Holstein and Gubrium (2000), and Branaman (2001).

5. Here Mead is in debate with Freud, who posits an individuality that precedes the social setting. Mead's "Me" and "I," which we discuss next, are in direct confrontation with Freud's notions of "id," "ego," and "superego." Significantly, Mead places emphasis on the social setting, whereas Freud emphasizes something more psychically individual. Not surprisingly, sociologists have claimed Mead as one of their founding theorists, whereas psychologists claim Freud as theirs.

6. Mead's theory can be contrasted to Freud's (1949). Whereas Freud had a specific narrative of the Oedipus complex, Mead does not predict a specific set of thoughts or reactions that comprise the content of the conversation between "the Me" and "the I." As a result, we believe Mead's theory is more flexible in describing a wide variety of identities that can be acquired. We argue here that humans could acquire a variety of identities if the discourses to which we react were not as dichotomous as heteronormativity.

7. Elsewhere Crawley has argued that female bodies are understood by men as physically dis-abled (Crawley 2002b), that is, men tend to think of female bodies as a kind of physical disability. Some researchers in the field of disabilities studies have taken exception to the use of this term in gender studies as overshadowing and diminishing the importance of other forms of physical disability. Diminishing these studies is not our goal here, nor do we intend to suggest female bodies are less physically capable. Rather, we are simply pointing out that gender messages themselves suggest the female body is a "weakness" akin to having reduced physical abilities. Hence, both women and people that are differently abled are viewed as less physically competent than "men" (who are all presumed to be more physically competent as a group).

8. Raewyn Connell is the chosen name of the professor who formerly published under the name R. W. (or Bob) Connell. Connell's influential and productive career in the area of gender studies, especially masculinities and men's studies, is apparent throughout this book as we cite her work widely. In her older work, cited under the names R. W. (or Bob) Connell, she refers to her male experience as a man as reflected in reference to her 1983 piece on "Men's Bodies." It is our understanding that Connell now refers to herself as a woman and prefers feminine pronouns. Out of great respect for her work and her personal choices, we use feminine pronouns here to refer to Connell and all of her work. However, in order to cite her work accurately so that the reader may find it, we have not changed the publication name on previously published works.

9. We cannot overstate the importance of two articles, "Men's Bodies" by Connell (1983) and "Throwing Like a Girl" by Young (1980), in the theorizing of gendered embodiment. Both have affected our thinking immeasurably. Much thanks to Whitson (1994) for putting these authors together so well in his article.

10. As a more current effect of racialized masculinity, Richard Majors (1990) talks about "cool pose," a type of bodily stance and expression taken on by African American men as a kind of resistance to discriminatory treatment intended to impute their masculinities. We discuss this further in chapter 5.

11. See also Whitson (1994).

12. More current science shows that physical activity has no negative effects on reproductive capacities in women. While certain very strenuous sports like marathon running may cause amenorrhea (cessation of the menstrual period), it is a temporary condition due to extreme loss of body fat. When extreme training is stopped or reduced, body fat returns, as well as regular menstrual cycles. Indeed, current science shows that physical activity can be much more beneficial to overall health and reproductive capacities than "ladylike," sedentary lifestyles.

13. Interestingly, in the United States, soccer and tennis are understood as more gender-neutral than other sports where both women and men commonly play. However, men playing these sports receive fewer "masculinity points" for successes in them, unlike in Europe, South America, and Australia, where "football" (and perhaps rugby) is understood as perhaps the most masculine sport.

14. The actual origin of the term "feminine apologetic" is unclear. Clasen (2001) cites Felshin in Gerber et al. (1974); Messner (1988) cites Rohrbaugh (1979). We are unclear about who actually invented the term, but cite Clasen's and Messner's works here.

15. Eric Anderson (2005b) challenges the idea that men in feminized sports always enact a rigid and orthodox masculinity to set themselves apart from women. In his study of two different cheerleading associations, Anderson shows that institutional mandates, along with reduction of homophobia in the general culture, allow for two different normative masculinities to be expressed in these two different organizations. The organization he calls the "Orthodox Cheerleading Association" constructs masculinity as opposite and superior to femininity and stigmatizes homosexuality. In the "Inclusive Cheerleading Association," femininity and homosexuality are both valued. The rules of competition for each association reflect these different gender ideologies. For example, the Orthodox Cheerleading Association sanctions teams when men dance, essentially requiring men to move in rigid, "nonfeminized" ways. On the other hand, the Inclusive Cheerleading Association not

only allows but expects men to dance and expects teams to lift and throw men into the air, a real gender no-no in the Orthodox Cheerleading Association.

16. In the past, men and women used the same piece of equipment for vaulting, but for women it was placed in a horizontal position and for men it was placed in a vertical position. In 2001, a new piece of equipment was introduced called a vaulting table and men and women use it in the same way (of course, men still do "harder" vaults). So the sport continues to evolve. Another interesting point is that while women wear the same outfit for all events, men sometimes wear pants and sometimes wear shorts, depending on the event.

17. Note that because this data is provided by the U.S. Department of Labor's "Women's Bureau," numbers for both tables indicate the percent of females occupying each profession. Hence, the numbers in Table 2.1 are very low (because they measure women in male-dominated professions) whereas the numbers in Table 2.2 are very high (because they measure women in female-dominated professions).

18. More than 96 percent of all secretaries and administrative assistants, 94 percent of receptionists and information clerks, and 92 percent of bookkeepers, accounting, and auditing clerks were women in 2003 (U.S. Department of Labor 2003b).

19. In Charles Dickens's novel *A Christmas Carol*, Tiny Tim's father was a clerical worker in Ebenezer Scrooge's office.

20. For an interesting history of this occupation, see *Footsteps in the Sky: A Pictorial History of Airline Inflight Service*, by Helen McLaughlin (1994).

21. The Association of Flight Attendants is the world's largest labor union organized by flight attendants for flight attendants. It represents over 50,000 flight attendants working for 26 airlines. The goal of the union is to negotiate better pay, benefits, working conditions, and work rules in airlines and to improve flight attendants' safety on the job. Visit the website at http://www.afanet.org.

22. Several organizations sell "do-it-yourself belly mold kits." See http://www.doulashop.com/products/gifts/belly-casting-kit.html.

23. A play on the popular pregnancy/birth advice book *What to Expect When You're Expecting* (Murkoff 2002).

24. See for example http://www.cryobank.com; http://www.thespermbankofca.org; and http://www.cryogeniclab.com.

25. Schmidt and Moore (1998) use the term *disembodied masculinity* but we prefer *virtual masculinity* for our purposes here.

3

Becoming Our Own Jailers

Surveillance and Accountability

> There is no such thing as a natural human body. Never has been; the body has changed physiologically over the years: improvements in nutrition, better sanitation, healthier living conditions, and better understandings of its structure and functions have made an impact on the body. (Cashmore 2005:177)

"His Name Is Aurora," read the September 25, 2000, headline of the *Time* magazine article on then-six-year-old Aurora Lipscomb of suburban Ohio (Cloud 2000). The article detailed how local residents and child protective services were deeply concerned about this child's health and well-being and how national political organizations were getting involved. Why? Because Aurora, born male (and given the name Zachary at birth), wants to wear dresses and call himself a girl. What could be scarier? Even more shocking, his parents were planning to let him do so—in public. Like perhaps thousands of children across the United States, as early as age two, Aurora expressed to his parents a penchant for pretty, sparkly dresses and other things unmasculine. By the time this story was published across the country when Aurora was six, his parents had reportedly given in to his persistent interests, honoring his wishes, and allowed him to express his gender differences in public—at school. Allegedly, this is when the outcry began. A magistrate removed Aurora/Zachary from his parents' custody and placed him in foster care—where Aurora was only referred to as Zachary and was not allowed to wear dresses—until some decision could be reached. At the time of the writing of the 2000 *Time* magazine article, Aurora/Zachary's loving but troubled parents were seeking to regain custody of him.

81

This story is not terribly unique. We regularly see stories about people who do not fit gender expectations in newspapers or news magazines (in this instance as national news), and on TV shows as varied as Jerry Springer-style inflammatory talk shows or the Discovery Channel's ostensibly science-oriented informative programs. Reports on gender-variance cases appear every few years and with varying degrees of empathy for the subject of discussion. Sometimes we are told to feel sorry for the person who is regarded as having a physical ailment; other times we are told to understand the person (and their supportive parents?) as "different," almost criminally deviant. Typically, we are treated to a host of "expert" opinions from groups with a variety of political interests and from medical doctors who attempt to find the physiological source of the "problem." Almost always, pundits attempt to seek explanation in the behavior of the parents (Has the child been beaten or coerced into behaving this way?) or in some event that triggered the behavior (When did she/he first start to talk about her/his gender difference?). What is particularly interesting to us in Aurora's case, as *Time* magazine reports it, is that while there were some concerns expressed about the Lipscombs' alleged history of violent behavior and psychological distress (bipolar disorder), the local child services agency did not respond to either of these specific concerns. The event presumably deserving of intervention by public agencies (and deserving of national press) was Zachary's wish to call himself Aurora and to wear dresses to school.[1] What significant problems can be caused by a simple frock!

So much media and literature has focused on transgendered or gender-bending people as individuals—different from the conforming majority. Invariably, we then focus on medical difference, asking doctors to find the physical and psychological source of difference and asking therapists to find the individual behavioral or psychic source (which always already implies a personal problem—what's wrong with this person!?). Rather than reflect on the social categorizing system that compels each of us to conform to rigid behaviors, we label the differing individual as pathological, diagnosing them with so-called "gender identity disorder." (See, for example, the *Diagnostic and Statistical Manual IV*'s classification of "gender identity disorder" as a diagnosable pathology.) In this chapter (and throughout the book), we focus on the conforming majority—the so-called "normal" people. We shift the camera's lens away from the individual and focus squarely on the social messages that form our expectations and "rules" about gender and the interactional context that compels each of us to create conformity. Instead of asking "What makes Aurora different?" we ask "What makes all the rest of us believe we are the same?" How do the majority of people become convinced to look and act in such consistently masculine and feminine ways? We focus on how we all are compelled to present gendered bodies and gendered selves—on the system of messages and interactions that suggests we conform to one of two behavioral categories, woman or man. That is, we demonstrate how the social world genders the mind and body.

In this chapter we add to our feedback loop (figure 3.1) the notion of surveillance and social control and concentrate on the ways the social world disciplines our behaviors and ideas of self. We have added an oval encompassing the gender feedback loop to figure 2.1 from chapter 2. The oval represents the social context in which each person lives—a context of interaction with people and ideas in which both exert social control over the selves we wish to express. In this chapter, we discuss two specific levels of social control—first, institutional control via social contexts and, second, interactional control through face-to-face interaction—and the ways in which we become accountable to others for our presentation of self.

Both the oval surrounding the feedback loop and the tiny arrows pointing in toward the Messages → Selves → Bodies loop (see figure 3.2) suggest a confining and conforming process that happens at the societal level. Gender messages pervasive throughout a social group are what Foucault (1977) and Bartky (1990) mean by the notion of *surveillance*. Gendered messages that instruct our actions (like the image of a little angel and little devil sitting on each of our shoulders whispering conflicting instructions into our ears) constitute surveillance—a kind of institutional force surrounding us

Figure 3.1. Gender Feedback Loop: Surveillance. Gender messages become a form of social control when we engage in surveillance of ourselves and others, encouraging conformity to those messages.

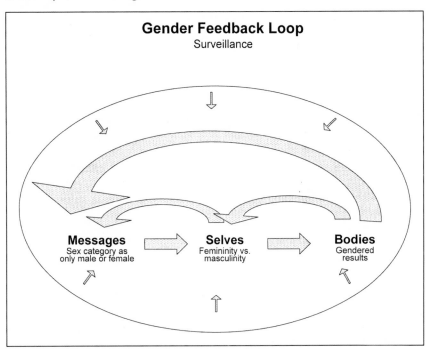

Gender Feedback Loop
Surveillance

Messages
Sex category as
only male or female

Selves
Femininity vs.
masculinity

Bodies
Gendered
results

Figure 3.2. Gender Feedback Loop: Surveillance. In everyday life, others hold us accountable to the ways we perform gender with our bodies, which both encourages conformity and confirms the messages as "true."

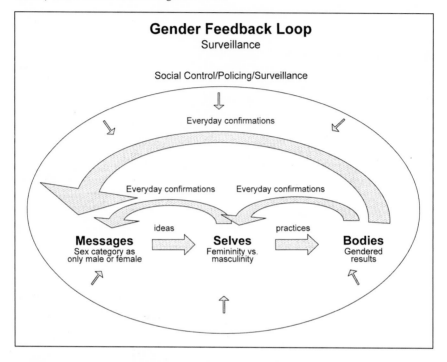

constantly, giving us instructions on how to behave appropriately, how to conform. The messages themselves tend to be pervasive throughout (and perhaps comprise) our culture. But how do these ideas or messages get into our minds? Clearly we observe the instructions and make them our own, but how?

The feedback arrows from bodies to selves, from selves to messages, and from bodies to messages are the *everyday confirmations* that comprise *accountability*. When each of us does as expected—that is, conforms to gendered messages, other people reward us and we confirm for ourselves the "rightness" or "naturalness" of our performances. Accountability, then, is the way others treat us based on how we interact in the world. The combination of gendered performances and accountability in the everyday world of interaction comprise the everyday confirmations of gendered messages that keep the feedback loop in motion.

Such is the notion of both surveillance and accountability—an ever-present force toward conformity—comprised of both pervasive, institutional, gendered messages and interactions with specific people who hold us accountable for our actions. In the next section we describe in detail how these forces play out in everyday interactions.

DISCIPLINING GENDERED BODIES:
SURVEILLANCE AND INSTITUTIONAL MESSAGES

People are typically comfortable with the idea of "the Me" and "the I" and also with the notion that we perform roles (as we discussed in the previous chapter). It makes us feel as though we do make conscious, individualized choices. We all like to feel we are in control of our actions and feelings. In the United States, we tend to be strong proponents of individualism, so we like to feel "the I" is larger than "the Me" and each role is something we freely choose. But look around you. How many people whom you've seen today were wearing absolutely no indicator of femininity or masculinity? Have you seen any female-bodied people with no makeup, no purse, no painted nails, not sitting up straight, not wearing clothing purchased in the "women's" section of the store, not wearing "women's" shoes, nor carrying a "feminine"-style or colored bag? What about any male-bodied people not wearing masculine-appropriate clothing (e.g., lower-waisted, loose-fitting pants, shirts as opposed to "blouses," "men's" shoes)? What exactly are "unisex clothes"? Even blue jeans are cut as "women's jeans" and "men's jeans," and clothing stores are divided into the "women's" section and the "men's" section. Children's clothes are usually gender marked as well.

If you look closely, you are likely to see *gender conformity* in almost all social settings. Fashions may change and vary for women and men over time but what remains fairly consistent is that "women's" fashions and "men's fashions" of any given time maintain a separate demarcation and few people stray completely from that set of expectations. So we ask: If gender is socially constructed and each person has some measure of personal choice, how can we explain so much conformity?

How Do We Convince People to Conform?

Do you think to be thin is to be good-looking (i.e., pretty? handsome? fit?)? You may be saying to yourself, "Well, yes, thin *is* good-looking. Fit *is* fit. It just is." One of the arbiters of beauty in our culture, *People* magazine, each year lists the 50 most beautiful people, and they are invariably thin. But how thin is "thin"? What is the right size of "thin" that is sufficient to be good looking? What makes "thin" good looking?

For women, being thin is not a universal sign of beauty. Not all cultures throughout time have obsessed about thinness as ours does. The beauty of thinness is not an "essential" truth. Other cultures found roundness to be beautiful. Botticelli paintings depict large, round bodies as beautiful—a sign of wealth and leisure. Painting in the late 1400s, Botticelli depicted full hips and round bellies of female bodies. Some current-day Latin cultures value a "healthy" amount of body fat on women as a sign of love, care, and nurturing by one's family (Haubegger 1994; Negron-Mutaner 1997). Even mainstream

U.S. culture has been changing the meaning of feminine body size—
decreasing the size of appropriately fashionable "thinness" over the course
of the last several decades, such that the ultimate symbol of female sexuality
of the twentieth century, Marilyn Monroe (see photo 3.1), appears a little too
full-sized compared to the supermodel standards of today, idealized by Kate
Moss (see photo 3.2). So the current beauty ideal of supermodel waif thinness for women or zero body fat has not always been constant across time
and across cultures. Nonetheless, the current standard has a sense of feeling
very real. If you are female, you may feel bad about yourself if you "feel fat"
(whether you feel it as a constant state or at momentary points in time).
Have you ever said to yourself things such as "I feel fat" or "I really feel un-
happy with my body" and really felt it was true? If beauty is only a product
of the social world, how is it possible that you *really feel* "fat" at any given
size? (100 lbs? 135 lbs? 200 lbs?) Does it make you feel better that large bodies were understood as truly beautiful in Botticelli's time? Perhaps not.

While the standard of beauty for men is not the same as it is for women,
a similar effect is in place. Rather than being "thin" enough, perhaps the
standard for men is to be "buff" or "built." If you are male, have you ever
felt the need to be "buff"? Do you worry about your arms being big
enough? Do you have "pipes?" Are you worried about your abs being
"ripped" enough? That is, have you ever felt your body is not masculine
enough? For men, massive shoulders and six-pack abs have not always been
the cultural standard. In photo 3.3 we see John Wayne, perhaps the preem-
inent figure of masculinity in the United States during the twentieth cen-

*Photo 3.1. In this photo
from 1947, Marilyn
Monroe shows a more
voluptuous notion of
iconic femininity than we
are likely to see in the
media today.*

tury. This promotional shot taken from one of his 1934 films shows his body to be actually quite small by today's masculine standards. Compare this look to Vin Diesel (photo 3.4), a new icon of masculinity with a much more "ripped" appearance. Clearly the newer look is raising the stakes for masculine appearance significantly.

There is no essential truth to fashion or beauty. Even so, we bet you (females and males and especially anyone who feels they fall outside that binary) often poke and prod at your own body, measuring whether you "look good" based on the current beauty standard. The messages of beauty of a given place and time compel you to change your body. In other words, if you believe you are "fat" or "not built" you will likely take measures to change your body to conform to the standard. According to Michel Foucault (1977 and 1980), *discourse* (language, talk, gendered cultural messages) shapes the body.

The most radical notions about conformity of the body come from the ideas of Michel Foucault. Foucault's ideas explain the conundrum that you may feel deeply that your body is not "thin" or "built" enough, even though all fashion (including

Photo 3.2. In this photo from 2006, Kate Moss shows an almost emaciated notion of iconic femininity popular in the media in recent years.

ideas about appropriate body size) is a social concept, not an enduring truth. For, as McHoul and Grace (1993) write about Foucault's notion of power, "The effects of power are quite material, and potentially empowering; and their site is more often than not the body"(22). Here we explain first Foucault's notion of the relationships between discourse, knowledge, history, and power. Then we outline his argument for how our bodies are *disciplined* through institutional *surveillance* to comply with prior established knowledges.

For Foucault, people are never simply free-thinking individuals (McHoul and Grace 1993). Rather, the conceptual categories and practices of a given society at a given point in history define what is *understood as* humanly possible, hence what individuals become. Knowledge and the way we wield cultural messages within a society comprise the power to determine what category is available for a person to become. Foucault (1978, 1980) is the ultimate anti-essentialist. For him, all categories are only the product of what humans believe to be true at that time and in that particular context. That is, there is no "essential" truth (but wide-ranging belief in certain "truths" or cultural messages) that causes individuals within a group to practice those "truths." For example, in *The History of Sexuality*, Vol. 1, Foucault (1978) dates the origin of "homosexuality" as 1870, the year when Westphal first writes about it as a *category* of sexual feeling. Foucault writes, "Homosexuality appeared as one of the forms of sexuality when it was transposed from the practice of sodomy onto a kind of interior androgyny, a hermaphrodism of the soul. The sodomite had been a temporary aberration; the homosexual was now a species" (43).

In other words, Foucault recognizes that same-sex sexual practices have existed for

Photo 3.3. John Wayne, perhaps the twentieth-century pinnacle of iconic masculinity, looks sort of small by today's masculine standards. Photo from the 1934 film The Star Packer.

as long as recorded history. But the notion of "homosexuals" as a subset of the population was only defined—made into a category—in the late nineteenth century. Nonetheless, it is the belief in the truth of the existence of "homosexuals" (and by corollary "heterosexuals") that allows us to understand all people as having a "sexual orientation" (also a historical concept, according to Foucault's configuration).

Foucault arrived at this notion by studying the history of knowledge. At various points throughout history, societies have held notions of what is believed to be invariably true. But it is not the actual truth that impacts how the society organizes. Rather, it is the group's belief in that truth that affects how members interact. Just because the idea of the "homosexual" is a socially constructed, historical phenomenon does not mean that it is of little importance. Indeed, anyone labeled homosexual in the United States can attest to the power of that label in everyday life.

If we accept that categories are social constructs developed by each social group through its own history of knowledge, how do social categories come to feel so deeply a part of who we are? For example, have you ever been somewhere and felt inappropriately dressed—to the point that you felt bad

Photo 3.4. Vin Diesel, pictured here promoting his 2004 film The Chronicles of Riddick, demonstrates the much more pumped-up masculine icon of recent decades.

about yourself? We have often heard women say they wear makeup because they like it; it makes them feel better to wear it. ("I don't like to leave the house without makeup on. I really just don't feel good about myself without it.") Or, perhaps for men, imagine the idea of wearing a pair of pants that is fluorescent pink, or a pair that is way too short in the legs ("high waters"). Could you just be an individual and dress against the fashion? Or would you "just not feel good" wearing that?

Foucault says the reason this is so deeply ingrained is because bodies are disciplined by the knowledge of the society. He basically argues that knowledge disciplines individuals into being what the group "knows" is "true" or "right" or "normal."[2] Power lies in the defining of that which is believed to be "true" or "normal" as well as that which is believed to be "abnormal"—in need of fixing. Individuals learn to discipline their bodies to produce these memberships in the group's "true" or "normal" categories because they are subjected to *panoptical surveillance*—a watchfulness that assesses each individual's relationship to that which is understood as "normal."

According to Foucault, we live in a society of surveillance in which we all "watch" others and are aware at all times that we are being watched. Social interaction involves the expectation of surveillance. We get so used to being watched (judged for our behavior) that we begin to preemptively judge our own behavior and monitor ourselves. In Europe in prior centuries (and in some countries currently), power was exercised as the absolute authority of the regime. If an individual broke the law, the monarch could exercise absolute power by, for example, ordering a beheading—a display that the powerful can exercise their will over the body of their minions who were perceived as property of the monarch. Power works differently in (so-called) modernized, Western societies where we primarily do not practice retribution on the body as a display of power.[3] Instead, we practice a more diffuse style of power in which the "abnormal" individual (or one who has broken a norm) is often disciplined to participate as fits the will of the group. Rather than punish the body, we induce the person to conform to the prescribed behavior. We do so by constant surveillance in all settings such that one always feels as though one is being watched.

Foucault uses the metaphor of the architectural design of the panopticon (the name of the architecture of a particular kind of prison). In the late 1700s, Jeremy Bentham designed the panopticon, a semicircular building with cells for individual prisoners and a tall guard tower in the middle. Because the guard tower is taller than the semicircular building and placed in the middle of the prison yard where a guard can see through all cells at any time, a relatively small guard staff can watch each individual prisoner in each cell constantly. Hence, the prisoners are constantly monitored. Importantly with this prison design, although any guard can see all activities of any prisoner, the prisoners cannot see the guards (because of the angle of looking up at the guard tower). As a result, the prisoners *feel* as though they are being watched at all times, but do not *know for certain* if they are being watched at all times. Because they perceive they are being watched, they behave as though they *are* being watched. After training prisoners to believe in their surveillance, it becomes less necessary for anyone to actually be in the guard tower. *The prisoners become their own jailers;* they monitor their own behavior under the presumption that they are being watched.

The development of this technology of surveillance in the prisons inspired Foucault to recognize the importance of surveillance technologies in our everyday lives. Remember that myth kids tell each other about how swimming pool chemicals have dye in them and if you pee in the pool it will change color and everyone will know you peed? This is an example of surveillance. Everyone will know! So, you begin to feel bad about peeing in pools and avoid doing so. Further, in postmodern society—with our webcams and cell phone cameras, with advertising pop-ups appearing out of seemingly nowhere on our web browsers, with cable and satellites that bring the world into our living rooms and bedrooms, with cell phones ringing and e-mail constantly announcing, "You've got mail," we feel constantly connected to the world of media images and we feel constantly watched (W. Staples 2000). The surveillance feels constant, as does the pressure to present a self that conforms to the images we see. We are all prisoners; we all monitor our own behavior as though we are being watched. *We are our own jailers.* An example of this might be something like picking your nose. Even when you are sure you are alone, very often it just feels inappropriate to pick your nose. Why? Because in a surveillance society, we still feel we are being watched even when we are alone (i.e., in a bathroom with the door closed). There is still a lurking feeling that what we are doing is wrong, even when there is no one there to offend. Indeed, we have seen a letter to Miss Manners (the famed specialist in etiquette) asking whether it is okay to pick one's nose while alone. It is quite telling that, even alone, someone felt the need to ask permission.

What Foucault is arguing is the power of surveillance to encourage conformity. The ever-watching eyes are encouraging us to comply with social expectations. Foucault does not discuss specifically how this surveillance of bodies may be based on *gendered* messages, but of course in our culture, much of this surveillance is gender surveillance (Paechter 2006). The point is that gender messages and gender surveillance are powerful. The surveillance of heteronormativity enforces being good "men" and "women," not just good citizens. Importantly for Foucault, the power to encourage conformity is not like military power. It is not as though someone is standing over you with a gun forcing you to conform. If you do not participate in femininity or masculinity, you do not usually end up in jail (in most Western cultures anyway). The power of surveillance is much more subtle. It is an ever-present expectation that results in ever-present comments from others (we discuss this in more detail later on as accountability). Hence the power of gender and heteronormative surveillance lies not so much in the threat of violence (although clearly sometimes it does) as in the wielding of messages. It is the power to deploy ideas and encourage conformity through those ideas.

Surveillance for Women

Sandra Bartky (1990) specifically relates Foucault's ideas about surveillance and disciplined bodies to practices of femininity. She writes that cultural beauty and fashion "knowledge" about women's bodies are expected to be practiced/disciplined into existence by each individual woman. That is, in the culture of our society, women are constantly watched by women and men (and eventually by themselves) to encourage them (or practically require them) to practice femininity. The surveillance is so ever-present and so institutional that it appears to come from nowhere and everywhere at the same time. It is also so constant and so required that individual women come to feel it is within them, rather than compelled by the social setting. That is, we get so good at practicing it and patrolling our own behavior that it starts to feel innate, even though beauty standards are always a product of social groups.

Bartky writes that there are several ways that physical bodies can be affected by panoptical surveillance—behavior or uses of the body (e.g., restricting movement, practicing poise, "acting ladylike," smiling all the time, swinging one's hips while walking), practices of food intake and exercise (e.g., dieting, doing aerobic exercise to "tone" rather than increase muscle size), and surface ornamentation (e.g., use of makeup to hide or "enhance" features, surgical intervention to control wrinkles, breast implants, tummy tucks, nose jobs, face lifts, etc.). For Bartky, the surveillance of womanhood begins at birth and includes a woman's every behavior.

Women are called to "fix" or change parts of their bodies that do not meet the beauty standards of unnatural thinness, facial perfection, large breasts, and so on. Disciplines of the body, according to Bartky, are more relevant to women than men because men are expected to act, whereas womanhood is understood as the presentation of beauty. While Foucault says all bodies are disciplined, Bartky adds that women's bodies are particularly disciplined as part of patriarchy—the control of women's bodies and lives by men. She writes, "It is also the reflection in women's consciousness of the fact that she is under surveillance in ways that he is not, that whatever else she may become, she is importantly a body designed to please and to excite" (Bartky 1990:80). So, whereas men can make up for bodily imperfections in other ways (e.g., athletic accomplishment or financial success), a woman's value is almost completely understood *to be* the beauty of her body (regardless of her financial success or athletic achievement), and hence the surveillance and discipline of the body is paramount for women.

Worse, this standard of bodily perfection is one that is nearly impossible for most women to attain. Not only is it based on youth and whiteness, but as Hesse-Biber (1996) notes:

> The average fashion model is white, 5 feet 10 inches tall, and weighs 110 pounds. She is approximately 30 pounds less than the average American teenage girl, and almost six inches taller. Her looks are relatively rare, yet her image is so pervasive that it is difficult for girls to see themselves as anything but "wrong" in comparison. (96)

So, while the media imparts an impossible standard of womanhood, girls and women feel compelled to try to meet that standard or risk not being "normal." This results in what Hesse-Biber (1996) calls the "cult of thinness." The goal is to change the size of the entire body—to become a smaller person.

Theorists have argued that women's obsession with thinness is a result of these kinds of body-regulation messages found throughout the media (Bordo 1993; Carlisle Duncan 1994; Hesse-Biber 1996; Kilbourne 1999). Bordo (1993) argues that TV commercials and print advertisements regularly use the notion of "control" as a goal for the presumed female audience, especially the message that control of the body and diet will result in control of the world around them. Women are encouraged to think of being hungry as a good and useful condition for normal women to pursue. As Carlisle Duncan (1994) argues, "fitness" magazines are primarily about dieting and looking good, more so than achieving actual physical health. She notes that these magazines give off the message that "feeling good means looking good"—hence being thin is understood as the precursor to being happy. That these messages happen in the media and are used by women in everyday life to measure themselves is the very definition of surveillance—the constant comparison between the expectation and the actual body.

Marketers have recognized that tactics that have worked well for primarily white, privileged women may be just as effective with men and women of color (Hesse-Biber 1996). Magazines such as *GQ, International Male,* and *Men's Health,* and television shows such as *Queer Eye for the Straight Guy* are beginning to send some similar messages about body image and good looks to men. While African American cultures and Latin cultures have traditionally encouraged and eroticized more natural body size and curviness for women, black and Latin women, particularly those who envision themselves as upwardly mobile, are becoming more affected by the mainstream messages that have traditionally affected white women. As advertisers learn how to capitalize on these effects, surely they will cast their nets more widely.

An example of this is Jennifer Lopez's rise to fame in the late 1990s (Negron-Mutaner 1997). One of Lopez's early career breakthroughs to stardom was playing the role of murdered Mexican icon Selena in the film by the same name. Lopez publicly called attention to her curvaceous figure, especially her butt, arguing that, although she is of Puerto Rican descent, she was well suited to play the role of Selena because both women were full figured. This garnered her popularity from many Latin audiences at the time for portraying Latin women as positive, beautiful, and sexy—as real, full-sized women, not the stick-figure white models of mainstream popular culture. In the mainstream media, a shower of talk ensued over "Jennifer's Butt" (Negron-Mutaner 1997), encouraging Lopez to slim down or lose popularity. In the end (pun intended), she did pursue the more Anglo, slimmed-down body structure of mainstream, Hollywood popularity, abandoning the cause she originally sought to popularize—the more full-figured body embraced by many Latin subcultures. Sadly, at the time of Selena's death, she too was slimming down to meet the standard of the Anglo, mainstream body type, even though her fan base had idolized her specifically because she had championed a more Latin style (Haubegger 1994; Negron-Mutaner 1997).

Thompson (1994:1) points out that although discussions of eating disorders tend to focus on "young, middle- to upper-class, heterosexual white women desperately trying to mold their figures to standards created by advertisers and clothing designers," when women who do not fit into the categories listed above are included in the discussion, the picture of eating disorders changes significantly. Oftentimes eating disorders function as survival strategies "in response to injustices including racism, sexism, homophobia, classism and the stress of acculturation, and emotional, physical, and sexual abuse" (Thompson 1994:2) among various women's subcultures. Interestingly, anorexia is becoming more common in males; however, it tends to take the direction of obsessive body shaping rather than obsessive weight loss (Andersen and Didomenico 1992). This suggests that surveillance of the body is specifically gendered, which leads us to a discussion of the gendered character of surveillance for men.

Wrestling

On one of the last few lazy days before high school graduation, Justin, Randy, and I were hanging out at Randy's house, waiting for a few more players to show up for our biweekly Dungeons & Dragons game. Nerds unite! I'd been out for a year and everyone knew, everyone was cool with it. Indeed for some folks, Steve in particular, I ironically became some sort of a gay mascot, to my continual embarrassment. We were in Randy's room, and for some reason, Justin and Randy were wrestling on the bed. This was playful and not harming anyone, so I was just sitting there. Justin called for me to join in and I froze.

He can't ask me to do that! He knows that I'm gay. I *can't* touch straight guys; I didn't do it before I came out and certainly not after. Touching straight guys means that you risk them thinking that you're coming on to them, or sexually enjoying it. The casual camaraderie can only be there in discussion, in shared activities like watching a movie or in a role-playing game. Touching implies a certain amount of acceptance that I wasn't willing to bet on or risk rejection from. I felt the division between myself as a gay man and these two straight men as a wide, insurmountable gulf. That moment haunts me as a place where I failed to demonstrate a "normal" rough-and-tumble masculinity that the others took for granted. I could play-wrestle with girls like that, or in a flirting way with gay guys, but the intersection of my sexuality and gender placed me outside of that situational, interactional manhood-affirming episode.

The more I learn about the category of man, being a gay man seems like both a contradiction in terms as well as an exemplification of manhood. The contradiction lies in gay men not possessing the societal space that heterosexual men have in our culture. Heterosexuality for men is seen as part and parcel of maleness. The missing element of heterosexuality separates me from being a "real" man. It is the expression of so-called feminine qualities, the type and quality of interactions with women, and the type and quality of interactions with men that separate gay men from our straight brothers. This difference is often seen as effeminate and less powerful; as such it challenges the precepts upon which manhood is constructed. Therein lies the exemplification of the reality of manhood. It is that very instability and inability to fully live up to the masculine code of behavior that drives men's defensiveness and strict controlling of the behavioral borders surrounding manhood. I see most of male "masculine behavior," particularly in the realms of the macho behavioral set and ideals, as a desperate attempt to cover up the inevitable failure of living up to an impossible, inhuman conception of man. If, for no other reason than that they have sex with other men or want to, or even fall in love with other men, gay men fail to be "true men," just as all men do. Gay men are the embodiment of the instability and impossibility of manhood as currently constructed.

I can claim the status of male. I enjoy much of its privilege within the sexist framework for viewing the world. However, in a socially real way, I will never occupy the space of a "genuine" man. Neither will anyone else, since such a goal is unattainable, but I have willfully thrown away the pursuit as a worthwhile one. The ways in which I express "feminine" qualities, interact with women, and interact with men set me apart from that categorical perception of "real" man.

—Michael Rogers, graduate student

Surveillance for Men

Men's bodies are under surveillance as well—however, clearly in different ways. Rather than an ideal of physical beauty, the surveillance of masculinity centers on developing the competent body, especially in the contexts of athletic and sexual performance. Masculinity is often measured in terms of physical competence (i.e., strength) and sexual competence (i.e., potency and ability to give pleasure). As is demonstrated by the obsession with sports by many men, the surveillance of masculinity entails constant measurement of individual men for their physical competence and ability to physically enforce their will (i.e., the ability to "beat someone's ass"). Similarly, the obsession with penis size as a measure of sexual prowess and potency demonstrates the ideal of masculinity as one of ever-present sexual appetite and bodily size as a measure of presumed competence (Bordo 1999).

Interestingly, the greatest surveillance of masculinity does not come from women, as one might expect, but from other men. Kimmel (1994) writes about *masculinity as homophobia*—men's fear that other men will emasculate them.[4] Kimmel does not mean homophobia in the traditional sense of fear or hatred of homosexuals (although bias against homosexual men does follow from the ideal that masculinity is about heterosexual sexual competence). Rather, masculinity as homophobia is the practice and surveillance of a specific masculine ideal by men for men. He writes, "We are afraid of other men. . . . Homophobia is the fear that other men will unmask us, emasculate us, reveal to us and the world that we do not measure up, that we are not real men" (131). Given that women are not expected to possess masculinity, men are understood as most competent to assess an individual man's masculinity. So while women can comment on an individual man's accomplishment of masculinity (which is especially effective in front of other men), the truest assessment—the final word, perhaps—comes from

°Validity from woman doesn't count

other men.[5] Kimmel (1994) writes, "Masculinity is a homosocial enactment" (129). (Again, not a "homosexual" enactment, but one that takes place in a group of men.) Masculinity is of men for men (Bird 1996).

The specific ideal of masculinity that is being enforced is what Kimmel (1994) calls "marketplace masculinity"—a form that would compete well in the public marketplace—"man in power, a man with power, and a man of power" (125). Masculinity is "strong, successful, capable, reliable, in control" (125). Given that this is a competition among men, there is an iconic form of masculinity that comes in the standard of "white, middle-class, early middle aged, heterosexual men with a recent record in sports"(125). While not all men meet this standard, the idea exists as a powerful notion against which all men are measured. Where an individual man might be lacking (e.g., not white), he might make up for that by succeeding in another area (e.g., particular accomplishment in sports). Notice also that the icon entails financial accomplishment (middle class), sexual accomplishment (heterosexual), and physical accomplishment (recent record in sports).[6]

Increasingly, surveillance of men's bodies is moving beyond simple athletic accomplishment to a form of beauty as well. There is a growing industry of men's cosmetics and body-modification products like workout supplements that approximate the surveillance of beauty that women have long experienced. Nonetheless, these products tend to support the large, buff (upper) body (albeit with a thin waist) consistent with masculine accomplishment, unlike women's body surveillance, which is thinness over the entire body. Perhaps this is the result of a growing media obsession with the "perfect" male body as it has traditionally existed for the "perfect" female body.

In any case, this body surveillance exists at an institutional level because it is so pervasive and ever-present in our culture. Representations of "perfect" masculinity and femininity, from body size to appropriate things for a body to do or wear, are in the media, on the Internet, supported by gendered institutions such as the family, the church, work, and leisure and sport. The surveillance of each person's performance of the categories of the gender box structure is ever-present for women and for men. It is institutional in that the messages of femininity and masculinity appear to come from everywhere and nowhere at the same time so that it is hard to locate them in a specific place and time. But there are also specific instances of surveillance in interaction that exist as individual accountability, which we discuss in the next section.

The Gender Police

After years of having long hair, in my senior year of college I had my hair cut to chin length. I just did it to try something new, a little change.

But I noticed that in those last few months of classes, it seemed as though I was taken more seriously in the classroom. That may have been in the back of my mind in graduate school, when I wore my hair very short. Once I even shaved my head or, more precisely, I let some friends shave my head. Because I have pretty much always identified as heterosexual and maintained a relatively feminine gender identity and appearance, friends who knew me before graduate school (and some who met me after graduate school) thought I was making some kind of political statement, rebelling against gender norms. If I were pressed to give a reason, I'd have to say that I just didn't want to bother with all the primping that longer hair involved. It was too time-consuming and too expensive for a graduate student schedule and budget.

Over the years, I would ask various hairstylists to cut my hair short and many would respond, "Let's keep it *soft* in the back." The stylists would then proceed to leave wisps of hair along the neckline. I hated the wisps of hair and would cut them off myself or have a roommate cut them as soon as I got home. One day I entered a fairly trendy salon and showed the stylist a picture of a hairstyle that was about two inches long all over and kind of spiky. The stylist looked at me and exclaimed, "I am not giving you that haircut, it's too butch." I finally understood that *soft* was code for feminine and that all those hairstylists through the years were holding me accountable to gendered appearance norms. I began calling hairstylists the "gender police." I finally found a stylist who gave me the haircut I wanted after I explained to him that my femininity did not reside in my hair.

This is me today. Although I have chosen to return to a more traditionally feminine hairstyle, I still believe that gender identity and expression are much more complex than the way we wear our hair.

—Lara Foley (author)

GENDER IS WHAT OTHERS DO TO YOU:
ACCOUNTABILITY AND FACE-TO-FACE INTERACTION

Foucault's notion of surveillance gives it an ethereal quality—the feeling that it simply exists in space, like the unseen guard in a guard tower. But surveillance takes place in face-to-face interactions as well, in settings where we can see each other and notice how we hold each other accountable to gendered messages. For this we return to West and Zimmerman (1987). It can be difficult to ascertain the difference between surveillance and accountability (and perhaps the difference is only analytically important in theory). But an example of the difference between surveillance and accountability is this: when *Glamour* magazine or TV shows like *What Not to Wear* or hosts of Hollywood events on "the red carpet" say, "That outfit is so last year," it works as surveillance, because it comes from "nowhere" in the sense that the media does not feel like it is real in our everyday lives (unless of course you are the celebrity who is being critiqued). When your sorority sister or your mom or your hair stylist says to you, "That's so last year," it works as accountability to you personally of your own gender performance. Both are surveillance, but accountability is a more specific, personal, interactional type of surveillance.

We stated in the previous chapter that gender is a performance enacted by all people, but there is another half to West and Zimmerman's argument about "doing" gender that is equally important in understanding performance. Gender is not just what you do with your body; it is compelled from you by others (Lucal 1999). *Gender is not just what you do but what others do to you.* That is, we are all held accountable to the socially dictated performance of gender. West and Zimmerman's (1987) notion of *accountability* is that while you can choose not to participate in normative gender performance, people will likely respond to your performance of self in negative ways; they will hold you accountable. Similar to the social rewards you may experience when you do gender "well" (e.g., your parents telling you, "That is such a pretty dress!" or "That's my boy!"), you are likely to experience negative responses for not displaying gender appropriately (e.g., "You're not leaving the house dressed like *that*" or "What are you? A faggot?"). All these cases are instances of accountability—being held personally accountable by others for your performance of gendered messages. While some responses may be mild, relatively neutral comments ("That's not my favorite color"), some may be very extreme, including ostracism from the group or physical violence toward someone breaking a "rule" of gender.

Accountability happens primarily in everyday conversation in face-to-face interaction (Erickson 2004; Garfinkel 1967; Holstein and Gubrium 2000). When we speak to each other, we not only express ourselves but also give others instructions on how to understand their worlds. We comment on each others' looks and behavior by way of encouraging or discouraging those behaviors. So when someone says to you, "Cool shirt!" what they imply is "you are good-looking in that shirt; others will find you attractive in it," or "you have good taste," or maybe even, "I find you attractive when you wear that." Hence, you are encouraged to repeat that behavior because it draws others to you (unless of course you do not return the sentiment! Yikes!). Interestingly, since most clothing is gendered (purchased in the "men's section" and intended for men's use or purchased in the "women's section" and intended for women's use), "Cool shirt!" usually also means that shirt makes you good-looking for a man or good-looking for a woman. It is not usually just a "cool shirt" but usually "cool" for the presentation of masculinity or femininity. Perhaps you are more likely to hear someone say, "that's a pretty blouse" to a woman or "that shirt makes you look handsome" to a man. Hence, accountability is very often gendered. While clothing is a common target for accountability talk, behavior can also be a target for accountability. Recall from chapter 2 the very common example, "You throw like a girl!" which for a female means, "we didn't really expect you to throw well," and for a male means, "you should throw better than you do. You better learn to act like a man." We do not tend to say "you throw like a child" or "you throw badly." We say, "you throw like a girl," always connecting it to gender. Similarly, we also talk about jobs and work as gendered. Certain types of work are referred to as "men's work" or "women's work." Indeed, among people who live aboard boats, it is common to refer to "pink jobs" and "blue jobs" to describe the kinds of work necessary to sail, maintain, and live aboard a boat.[7] Although not all sailors are male-female couples and anyone who lives aboard alone must accomplish all tasks, it is expected that any heterosexual couple that is "cruising" (traveling while living aboard a boat) together divides the labor on the basis of "pink jobs" and "blue jobs." If a woman were to be doing engine repair (a "blue job") while a man were restocking the stores of food (a "pink job"), it would be understood as worthy of comment ("She's got you doing her jobs, huh?").

Parents and family can be perhaps the greatest source of gender accountability. From the moment someone pronounces, "It's a girl," or, "It's a boy" (which often happens before birth these days), the accountability to "girl" and "boy" begins for each of us. And given parents' prescribed role as teachers and disciplinarians for children, it is not surprising that gendered behavior is part of that disciplining process. Parents and grandparents expect their role is to train children to fit in appropriately and so may constantly exact individual surveillance over a child and feel it their duty to hold kids accountable to their behavior. Interestingly, Kane (2006) notes that parents hold boys somewhat more accountable for gender nonconformity than they do girls—that is, girls may be encouraged to pursue some masculine interests, whereas boys are more likely to be discouraged from feminine interests. She writes that the parents of preschool children in her study (who came from various racial and class-based backgrounds) tended to encourage self-sufficiency (so girls would be encouraged to pursue careers and boys encouraged to learn to cook), but parents were much more worried about boys pursuing indicators of femininity like clothing styles and even gendered toys than was the case for girls pursuing typically masculine behaviors (which she interprets as consistent with Kimmel's notion of masculinity as homophobia discussed earlier in this chapter). Heterosexual fathers seemed particularly concerned with the masculinity of their sons as an extension of their own masculinity. Nonetheless, all the parents in the study spoke clearly about their active and intentional role in shaping their children to meet their own moral standards. In other words, they interpret accountability as their specific job as parents.

The notion of accountability is important because it suggests that *gender is unavoidable*. Whether participating in or fully protesting the strictures of cultural gender expectations, others will applaud or scorn our behaviors, often in subtle ways that affect how we think about ourselves, whether we feel safe in the world, and how we think about the gendered messages themselves. In other words, gender accountability in everyday life affects our construction of self, which affects our uses of the body, which affects the physical body, which feeds back to the message that bodies are "naturally" different.

Carlisle Duncan (1994) explains how the combination of public surveillance that favors very specific body types and the individual accountability to those notions can make a very public ideal feel like a private problem. How is it possible that very public fashion and body images come to feel like a personal choice (and often a personal failing)? Using a content analysis of the language used in *Shape* magazine (a purported fitness magazine that puts significant emphasis on beauty as well), Hall (1996) uses the notion of the "gaze" to discuss both very specific accountability offered by others about women's bodies and the self-surveillance that comes from panoptical self-patrolling. She writes:

> How is it that the gaze, which is culturally and socially mandated, disguises itself as private? . . . The invisibility and ambiguity of the source of that gaze encourage women to believe that the body standards they apply to their own bodies are personal and private standards. Thus women may blame themselves—instead of the social institutions and public practices—for their anguished relationships with their bodies. (50)

She goes on to argue, "And private individuals are encouraged to conform to public standards, although those public standards are characterized as private; for example, in the context of *Shape*, 'Look your best' actually means 'Look like Cindy Crawford'" (58).

As we argued throughout this section, we believe this process is also utilized with respect to men, albeit in very different ways. The point to be made is that public standards inaccurately come to be understood as personal choices. The surveillance comes to feel as if it is from everywhere and nowhere at all. But the surveillance is always gendered and it plays out in every aspect of our lives. Ultimately, each of us participates in this surveillance by holding ourselves and others accountable to the gendered messages to which we are exposed and this interaction itself provides the everyday confirmations that our predestined gendered messages are "natural" and "real."

GENDERING BODIES IN ACTION

As in the previous chapter, we use this section to present specific instances of theories we have offered so far in this chapter. How do these theories work for bodies in action in the social world? In the remainder of this section, we describe how surveillance works in sex and reproduction, at work, and in sports. As we will see, bodies are disciplined and gendered by the courts, the prison system, the medical system, workplace policies, athletic rules, and the media, as well as at all social levels, including among individuals and within groups, organizations, and social institutions. In these settings we are held accountable to maintaining gendered bodies through social interaction with others as well as through our own internalized surveillance.

Sexuality and Reproduction

Gender messages are nowhere more pervasive than in talk and images about sex. Messages about sex invariably reinforce the expectation that sex is "natural," meaning it is understood in terms of innate urges and expected to be reserved primarily for reproductive purposes (Myerson et al. 2007; Tiefer 2004). While in our everyday lives sex is usually no longer seen as solely for reproductive purposes, historical, cultural, and religious notions that advocate against sex for pleasure have led us to some very constraining ideas about sexual wants and practices. In particular, we tend to assume there is one "natural" kind of sex act, that female bodies have urges for only male bodies and vice versa, and that our entire sexual lives are ruled by an uncontrollable intent to procreate. Yet, these gendered messages do not necessarily match up with our own interests in and experiences of sexuality. How many people do you know want to have children at some point in their lives? How many of those people hope that their next sexual interaction results in pregnancy? We expect that many people would like to have children at some point, but in most people's everyday lives there are few occasions for engaging in sex for the express purpose of creating a pregnancy. Nonetheless, in Western cultures, we tend to expect to enjoy a sex life for our entire adult lives. So while we imagine that sex is "natural" and reproductive, in our everyday lives we actively work to avoid pregnancy and engage in sex for many other reasons (physical enjoyment/release, intimacy, relationship building, etc.). Clearly, our cultural messages do not match our everyday actions.

We also imagine "the sex act" as a very specific event involving the so-called "missionary position" in which the man is "on top," he initiates all action, and sex begins when a penis enters a vagina and ends when a male has an orgasm. Most other types of sexual, intimate contact are not seen as "sex," or rather, we only call the act just described "sex" (Frye 1983; Myerson et al. 2007; Tiefer 2004). Indeed, Frye argues that, as a culture, we do not fully understand how women "have sex" in any way other than being the recipient of men's orgasms. As such, we don't know how women have sex. We only know how men have sex with women. Indeed, a new phenomenon called the "pinking of Viagra" is a push by pharmaceutical companies to find a female alternative to the sex-enhancing drug for men that is intended to "solve" women's supposedly natural lack of interest in sex (Hartley 2006). (We address the Viagra phenomenon for men in more detail below.) This new initiative by drug companies simply assumes that if a woman is not as interested in sex as a man, she must be broken, and hence, in need of drugs. This is a particularly telling instance where gendered messages control what we "know" about sex, organize how we can imagine our bodies, and focus what we do with them.

Gendered messages about sexual performances constrain how we interact. There is a surveillance about what can be called sex, and individual women and men are held accountable to those messages. For example, Holland, Ramazanoglu, and Thomson ([1996]2002) write that the first act of sexual intercourse for men is considered the passage into adult manhood (having the connotation of a positive event), whereas the passage into womanhood is not the first act of sexual intercourse, but rather the first menstrual period (which has an ambiguous connotation: a little bit positive and a little bit negative). Hence, it is not surprising that when referring to having sex we speak of men "getting some," whereas women "give it up." Indeed, what a woman is supposedly "giving up" is her virginity which is presumed to be her most valuable possession. She is expected to guard it very carefully. So there is a general surveillance for all men to be sexually aggressive and for all women to be sexually passive or guarded.

Individual men and women are held accountable to these ideals in everyday interactions. So, one is not a "real man" if he wants to engage in sex differently than the heteronormative ideal (e.g., to let a partner lead the encounter). Interestingly, in our gendered messages, men are expected to be always sexually aggressive, but not toward other men (Messner 2000). Boys and men who are sexually aggressive toward other boys or men are perceived as not fully masculine (in fact, feminine!) and are often held accountable to this by being called a "fag" or perhaps even suffering physical violence (Smith and Smith 1998). Ironically, while we consider women to be less sexually aggressive than men, it is somewhat more permissible for individual women to engage in same-sex sexual behavior (perhaps if primarily for the eyes of straight men?). So, women are supposed to be "less sexual" but can have a wider array of partners (presumably as long as they end up with a man). Oddly, an individual woman may not be considered "feminine" if she approaches a male partner first about having sex. Then she becomes a "slut" or "whore" and is "too easy." So she can kiss another woman in order to attract a man, but if she simply approaches the man, then she is held accountable as too easy. What an interesting construction! Clearly, "slut" and "fag" as mechanisms of control can have a huge impact on how we behave (Tanenbaum 2000; White 2002).

The messages we receive about what comprises "good sex," then, affect our behaviors toward each other and our understandings of self. The gendered messages we receive about sex are almost entirely heteronormative (Ingraham 1996; Sedgwick 1990); they tell us that only woman-man couples can form socially approved relationships. Although our concept of sex is relatively recent and based in our own historically situated culture (Foucault 1978; Halperin 1989; Katz 1995), we assume that sexual interactions have always been "naturally" ruled by the notion that same-sex behavior is inappropriate. Other cultures at other points in history have not organized sexuality and sexual relationships as U.S. culture does. Halperin (1989) writes that in ancient Greece, sexual relationships were organized around notions of citizenship. Citizens (male landowners) could enforce their will sexually with anyone who was not a citizen (women of any age; "free" men past puberty who were not yet citizens; and noncitizen adult men, usually foreigners or slaves). There was no notion of rape or homosexuality or the "nuclear family"; there was only citizenship as a status that provided legal access to the bodies of noncitizens. As foreign as this may sound by current standards, our notions of homosexuality and women's rights would sound just as foreign in that culture.[8] Nonetheless our gendered messages enforce the surveillance of sexual behavior in our everyday lives. Because heteronormativity tends to rule the day, there are specifically gendered rules to which we are all held accountable and by which our bodies are measured.

Pregnancy, Lesbian Motherhood, and Heterosexual Accountability

I came out as a lesbian in 1996, when I was 14 years old, in Fort Lauderdale, Florida. There was a teen support group at our local GLBT community center; I had the resources to start a gay-straight alliance at my high school; seeing Pride flags downtown was normal; seeing gay people on MTV was normal. Still, I never felt more alone, or scared for my life, or like the life I expected could no longer be counted on. People harassed me at school and administrators did nothing—even when I told them the names and class periods of the boys who threw rocks at my car, my locker, or my head; when my head was bashed into my locker; or when these boys threatened to rape me. I didn't tell my parents what happened at school because I thought they might kick me out or lock me up for being a lesbian. Something else happened too—I stopped thinking that I could be a mother.

Lesbians, in my mind, were just not mothers. As a society we tend to imagine that love, sex, and reproduction come in a neat package. It wasn't just that I thought lesbians weren't mothers, I thought that lesbians weren't reproductive beings. This is the way I felt at 14.

Then, a couple of years ago, something happened to remind me of this feeling. I had been healthy all my life and then, out of nowhere, every time I got my period it felt like somebody was taking an ax to my lower back. General practitioners and emergency room physicians insisted that it was either a problem with my gallbladder or kidney stones; the pain being initiated every month during my period didn't make them wonder if it was gynecological. I got ultrasound after ultrasound until my mother suggested I see a gynecologist.

I didn't take the time to ask friends for doctor recommendations; I went where my health insurance sent me. The room was luxurious, but pretty unfriendly looking. I was wearing a paper-towel-like gown; the nurse had asked that I take off all of my clothes and wear only the gown. The doctor asked that I lie down. To perform the breast exam, he opened the whole gown so that my body was entirely naked. The attending nurse looked down and away, seemingly embarrassed. The doctor looked down to my right hip bone, on it my tattoo in swirled black lettering read "DYKE." He smirked and said, "You're a clever one. What would make you get that? Do you have any other tattoos?" I answered, "One on my lower back." "I shudder to think what that one says," he said while entering me for the pelvic exam.

After the exam we had a short consultation in his office. "We'll need more tests to be sure, but I think you have fibroid tumors in your uterus." "What does that mean—I mean what do we do in that case?" "What we would do in that case is perform a complete hysterectomy." He looked at me blankly, but squarely, in the eye and said, "Would that be a problem?" I was 22 years old.

I told myself that I could still mother. I had other options—my partner could give birth or we could adopt children. Still, some small part of me, planted by our culture's homophobia and reinforced by my physician's assumption that I was not as entitled to keeping my uterus as other women my age, believed that this was my body's way of telling me that I should not be a mother.

Increasingly, especially for women in "childbearing years," radical hysterectomies are not the solution for fibroid tumors. It is perhaps the easiest solution for physicians, especially when they assume that you do not need your uterus for any practical use. I didn't even have fibroid tumors (the second-opinion gynecologist told me). I had a large growth on my right ovary that needed to be removed. It was. And my fertility options haven't changed.

Even though nothing changed in my ability to get pregnant, I realized how far-reaching my internalization of anti-lesbian motherhood rhetoric is and I wonder: knowing how dismissive my gynecologist was of my potential desire to get pregnant, what will it feel like to be pregnant? I have some sense of what will be expected of me if I get pregnant. I will have to respond to every friendly nod when I walk down the street. I will have to smile when strangers touch my body. I will have to take a seat when it's offered to me, even when I don't feel like I need it. I will have to say thank you when people hold doors, lift packages, or say congratulations. I will be expected to display a more extreme version of the already-expected femininity I enact. What I cannot yet imagine is how many times someone will ask me if my husband is excited or what he does for a living. I cannot begin to imagine how many times someone will assume that I'm something I'm not. And I do not yet have a sense of how this will make me feel. I can be nearly sure that with every approving nod, people will be assuming that I am a married, heterosexual woman. I cannot be sure that I will remember that every time I smile back. People usually fail to see me as a lesbian now, because of my femininity and because they assume everyone is heterosexual until proven otherwise. When I'm not seen as a lesbian, it feels like I'm not seen. Pregnancy would make the world see me as a proven heterosexual, as pregnancy is surely the essence of doing femininity. I cannot yet imagine how this will make me feel.

—Maura Ryan, graduate student

Women's Bodies as Always Potentially Pregnant

In the gendered messages of our culture, if men are understood as always needing sex, women are conceptualized as *always potentially pregnant*. This notion has been demonstrated by a Centers for Disease Control and Prevention (CDC) (2006) report entitled "Recommendations to Improve Preconception Health and Health Care." The report focuses attention on reducing risk factors for negative pregnancy-related outcomes for *all* women of childbearing age, regardless of their desire to have children: "The target population for preconception health promotion is women, from menarche to menopause, who are capable of having children, even if they do not intend to conceive" (9).

Men are mentioned in the report, but sparingly, while women are advised to quit drinking and smoking and engaging in any other behaviors that may negatively affect pregnancy and birth outcomes *prior* to conception. Considering that nearly half of pregnancies in the United States each year are unintended or unplanned, at what point *prior* to conception are women supposed to heed this advice? Certainly we might expect the CDC to discourage all people from smoking and drinking since both activities appear to have negative health effects, but notice the campaign is not for women to improve their own health (and apparently not for men at all). Rather, it targets all women as potential mothers.

While the female body is not understood as innately sexual, it is held under the gaze that it might at any time make a baby. Women (who may or may not be of childbearing age, or who may or may not have an interest in childbearing) are barred from certain kinds of jobs where their potential reproductive systems might be damaged. We explore this further in the section on work. Also, remember from chapter 2, throughout the twentieth century women were discouraged from extreme physical exercise under the impression that it might tax their reproductive systems. Commonly, when women seek emergency health care for any number of ailments where drugs might be administered, they receive a pregnancy test as a matter of protocol, regardless of a woman's own reporting of the likelihood of pregnancy or sexual behavior.[9] In almost all settings, women are envisioned to be walking baby vessels, regardless of the individual woman's interest in having children or the relatively short period of time within a woman's life that she might actually be pregnant (9, 18, 27 months out of an entire lifetime?).

Indeed, the notion that we introduced in chapter 2, that women are expected to be *sexy, but not sexual*, follows from the expectation that any woman will become pregnant from each instance of having sex (with a man), even though there are many useful and effective birth control methods available today to prevent conception and many sexual practices that do not put one at risk for pregnancy. As a result, women as *always potentially pregnant* become established as the *gatekeepers* of sexuality. Women make the choice to "say yes" or "say no" to sex. (Men are assumed to always be saying "yes"). As such, we do not hold men accountable to their reproductive capacities in ways that we always in every instance hold women accountable (even when women are not having sex, but are only thinking about having it).

Cultural messages of sex are not only gendered, they are racialized as well. Gendered messages about women and sexual purity have historically applied primarily to white women's bodies. Women of color, especially women of African descent and women of Asian descent, are often viewed as sexually "exotic" and perhaps especially promiscuous. While women's bodies in general are used in commercial advertising under the premise that "sex sells," images of Asian or black women, perhaps posed in leopard print or in a "jungle" scene, are often used to signal wild, exotic sexuality (Collins 2004).

A classic real-life example of the exoticizing of African women is the case of Saartje Bartmann, a South African woman who was enslaved in the early 1800s and put on display naked in Europe because her butt and genitals were considered large and demonstrative of the overt sexuality of African people. She was tellingly put on display as the "Hottentot Venus," a marker of European notions that body shape and size in themselves were understood as indicators of exotic sexuality (Collins 1990; hooks 1992).

Maternal/Fetal Conflict: Women as Baby Vessels

In terms of surveillance and accountability for pregnant bodies, possibly the most critical dilemma for women has been termed the maternal/fetal conflict, in which mother and fetus are seen and treated as separate and sometimes competing entities. Despite the fact that pregnant women and the fetuses they carry are intimately connected, the concept that a fetus is a separate thing from a woman has led to the rhetoric of "fetal rights." When the community begins looking out for the rights of the fetus, often the pregnant woman carrying the fetus is overlooked or is viewed as merely a vessel or container for the "unborn child." As beings that are understood as "always potentially pregnant," individual women are under close surveillance and held especially accountable to their pregnancies in order to be perceived as "good mothers." Women are held accountable by health care providers, restaurant staff, judges, and even total strangers if they are visibly pregnant and smoking or drinking or even eating "unhealthy" foods.

Childbirth has undergone a process of medicalization in the United States. Prior to the twentieth century, pregnancy and childbirth were considered natural events in a woman's life. Today, medicine has defined pregnancy and childbirth as pathological events to be supervised and managed by physicians using various interventions such as pain-relieving medications and technologies such as ultrasound and electronic fetal monitoring. Electronic fetal monitors record fetal heart tones and display them on a screen that health care providers can observe even outside of the physical presence of the birthing woman. Although ostensibly only the fetal heart tones are being monitored, the birthing woman's behavior is also monitored. For example, health care providers will "know" if a woman has moved from the preferred supine position and will come back into the room to correct her (Cartwright 1998).

We are probably all familiar with the ultrasound picture. It has become part of popular culture, appearing in commercials and sent to us via e-mail by friends and family. Ultrasound technology puts the social reality of the baby into "fast forward." Where we once had a period of "quickening," which meant that the mother had felt movement, we now have "technological quickening" (Dunden 1992) in which doctor, mother, and whoever else can "see" the fetus. In a culture that privileges visualization (seeing) over feeling, making the fetus visible somehow makes it more real—perhaps more like a separate entity.

In the United States, sonographers, the technicians who perform ultra-sounds, follow cultural scripts to give personhood to the fetus (Mitchell 2001). They are likely to give commentary about the personality of the "grey blob" on the screen: "Oh look, she's shy" or "Oh, she's being very co-operative today." Often this commentary is also gender specific, perpetuating norms of masculinity and femininity: "What a big, strong boy" or "Isn't she dainty?" These technicians also play a role in the surveillance of pregnant women, holding mothers accountable to appropriate gender performances by deciding if they respond appropriately to the images on the screen and to the narration of the technician. Is she appropriately emotional? Is she actively participating? Does she seem to be interested in the "right" things? On the whole, is she a "good mother"?

As a result of the notion of maternal-fetal conflict, individual women are held accountable to the health of fetuses first and foremost during medical decisions. In early 2004, Melissa Rowland was arrested in Utah and charged with murder when one of her twins was stillborn. Hospital staff claimed that Rowland refused to undergo a cesarean section after repeated warnings by physicians that her twins might not survive without one ("Caesarean Refusal Leads to Murder Charge" 2004). Although performed routinely in the United States, a C-section is major abdominal surgery, replete with all the risks associated with major surgery. The media painted Rowland as mentally unstable and shallow, claiming that her only objection to the surgical procedure was that she did not want a scar.[10] Other women have received court orders to undergo C-sections, including Angela Carder, who was diagnosed with cancer and informed that undergoing a C-section might result in her death. The hospital sought a court order and the court ruled that the fetus had a right to life. Neither Angela nor the baby survived the C-section (Thornton and Paltrow 1991).

In an extreme instance of surveillance and accountability, using drugs while pregnant has led to criminal charges for some women, usually low-income or minority women who receive health care via public hospitals (Balsamo 1999; Roberts 1997). In 2001, the U.S. Supreme Court ruled that South Carolina's practice of drug testing pregnant women without their fully informed consent violated the Fourth Amendment, which protects citizens from unreasonable search and seizure (*Ferguson v. City of Charleston*).[11] However, many states have expanded their child welfare policies to include pregnant women's drug use as sufficient grounds for child abuse charges. Some states have even creatively attempted to charge pregnant women with *distributing illegal substances to a minor*. Regina McKnight was charged with murder in South Carolina when her child was stillborn. Immediately following the birth, both McKnight and the child received a positive drug test (*McKnight v. South Carolina*).[12] In 2003, the U.S. Supreme Court refused to hear the *McKnight* case and thus allowed the murder charge to stand.

The reproductive rights of women prisoners are also limited in many ways. While prison is inherently about restrictions on freedoms, it is still important and humane to provide prisoners with the basic necessities of life such as food, shelter, clothing, and health care. Reproductive surveillances of women in prison have taken the form of both mandating abortions and sterilization *and* restricting access to abortion and contraception. Sometimes women convicted of child abuse or drug abuse are given the "choice" of using Norplant (a long-term contraceptive) or serving jail time (Roberts 1997; Roth 2004a).[13] On the flip side of the coin, women in prison who want an abortion are sometimes denied access (Roth 2004b). For example, in 2004, the Fifth Circuit Court of Appeals held that a Louisiana prisoner's rights were not violated when prison officials prevented her from having an abortion.[14] However, in 2005 when a Missouri prisoner was denied access to an abortion, a federal district court judge ordered transport of the prisoner to an abortion clinic. The U.S. Supreme Court refused to intervene, allowing the district court's ruling to stand (Lane 2005).

In each of these instances, individual women are surveilled by powerful forces such as technology, laws, the media and held accountable by people such as technicians, doctors, and prison guards. They are held accountable not just to their actual reproductive capacities, but also to the cultural messages of women as somehow always about to become pregnant but separate from and perhaps a danger to their own fetuses when they are pregnant. Clearly, in many of the examples above, the accountability is so extreme that individual women lose the control to make decisions about their bodies and their health care in favor of the state making decisions for them (which is an unlikely scenario for other kinds of medical decisions by conscious adults, given our constitutional premises of individualism and right to privacy).

Surveillance of Men as Sexual and Reproductive Beings

In chapter 2 we discussed men's sexual performance of masculinity—meeting expectations of sexual aggressiveness and competence—as based on the message of *penis as power tool* and sex as something to be accomplished and accomplished well (Bordo 1999). According to gendered messages, if the penis is a power tool, it had better be a big power tool. Analogous to women's beauty standard of thinness is men's preoccupation with penis size and function (Bordo 1999; Croissant 2006; Strong et al. 2005).

The "power tool" is often perceived as biologically out of men's control. In popular culture and scientific discourse, men are regularly described as "needing" sex as though it were a biological necessity (Bordo 1999). Calling it the "hot man thesis," Bordo writes that over the last few decades while women have been working to claim a sexuality, "popular science—both 'hard' and 'social'—has been busy reestablishing that men are testosterone-driven, promiscuous brutes whom nature won't permit to keep their peckers in their pants" (230).

Given that men are understood as sex-crazed animals with large power tools, we should not be surprised at the pharmacological phenomenon of Viagra. If we perceive that the penis is the measure of the man, if the tool is broken, it follows that men (and women?) are fixated on fixing it (Baglia 2003; Bordo 1998; Grace et al. 2006; Loe 2004; Marshall 2006; Potts and Tiefer 2006; Tiefer 2006; Tuller 2004; Vares and Braun 2006). The Viagra phenomenon follows from the premise that men accomplish the act of sex for themselves and their (presumably) female partners. Following the "penis as power tool" narrative, the man's job is to be large, potent, and to give the woman an orgasm. So, apparently, if men can't "have sex," then no one can, and there is a crisis for everyone. Thus, if a man fails to have an erection, he is understood as a broken man—that is, no longer a man. His masculinity is centrally at stake. Understood in these terms, it is not surprising that a drug that helps to maintain erection is popular in our culture (even for some men who are not suffering from erectile inabilities, but who hope to use the drug simply for enhancement)[15] and often paid for by health insurance.

Because we tend to assume men always want to have sex, accountability for having (heterosexual) sex tends to be less negative for men. Indeed, if there is accountability for having sex with women, it is generally very positive and masculinity-affirming—hence, the public "pressure" is to have more sex, not less. However, there is accountability for men with regard to sexual aggressiveness that involves rape. One example of how surveillance works through the law and the courts to hold individual men accountable to the stereotype of sexual aggressors (while painting women as always being potentially pregnant) is the 1981 case *Michael M. v. Superior Court of Sonoma County*.[16] In this case, the court upheld a statutory rape law that held a man criminally liable for having intercourse with a woman under the age of 18, but did not impose liability for a woman engaging in similar behavior (Levit 1998). The court's reasoning was as follows:

> Young men and young women are not similarly situated with respect to the problems and risks of sexual intercourse. Only women may become pregnant, and they suffer disproportionately the profound physical, emotional and psychological consequences of sexual activity. (Cited in Levit 1998:70)

Hence, men are blamed as rapists for any instance of contact with (even willing) girls under the age of 18.

Racialized messages of the body extend to men as well. While "Latin" men[17] are often characterized as being aggressive lovers, messages about them do not tend to extend to expectations of the Latin male body itself. But for men of African descent, stereotypes suggest they are innately uncontrollable sexually, especially as marked by the presumption of a large penis. Manning Marable (2000) writes that post-slavery-era fears of black men as sexual predators, especially in the hunt for white women, continue to the present day with myths of the competitively large black male penis. Conversely, Asian men suffer the explicitly emasculating myth of the small or underdeveloped penis (Espiritu 1997). The racism inherent in these myths is particularly apparent. While to have a large penis in U.S. culture is understood as granting masculinity, the myth of black men's large penises has been presented as not favorable, but dangerous, while the myth of Asian men's small penises is understood as unfavorable. This leaves only white men as apparently properly proportioned. While none of these stereotypes has any basis in the actual relationship between race and penis size (Strong et al. 2005), they impact broader public discourse about what kinds of sex relate to what kinds of bodies, and individuals are held accountable to those messages in myriad ways.

Gender messages rarely compel us to think about men as contributors to reproduction. While we see men as "potent" and sexually aggressive, generally the notion of the male contribution to reproductive processes stops at the moment of conception. Consider for example the phrase "to father a child"—as in, "Michael fathered a child." What is implied in that idea? Essentially we believe it means to have contributed sperm for conception. Conversely, what does it mean to "mother a child"—as in "Alice mothered her child"? This term tends to mean a great deal more—a long-term, perhaps a lifetime, commitment. While involved "fathering" may entail a great deal more than just contributing sperm, in our rhetorical lexicon, "to father a child" means a great deal less than "to mother a child," suggesting our notion of fatherhood is much more limited and subject to much different surveillance.

Earlier, we discussed ways that women are implicated in harming fetuses through various activities such as using drugs or refusing medical treatment. Although drug and alcohol use on the part of men can also affect the health of children they might "father," we rarely, if ever, hear about attempts to hold men accountable to male reproductive or procreative bodies by monitoring their behavior or punishing them for harming a fetus (Daniels 1997). Little thought is typically given to the effects of the environment or "hazardous work conditions" on men's reproductive systems. Only since 2004, through the Unborn Victims of Violence Act do we hear of men being punished for harming a fetus.[18] Of course, the harm in this case comes from intentional physical violence rather than from behavior that would damage sperm or otherwise hinder reproductive functioning such as drinking alcohol, using drugs, smoking, having a poor diet, and being exposed to certain chemicals.[19]

Empty Vessels and Shooting Blanks: Cultural Messages of Infertility

Gendered surveillance and accountability also happen when couples (interestingly, women and men interactively) are unable to become pregnant.

Infertility is defined medically as the inability to conceive after 12 months of unprotected intercourse. Socially, though, infertility has a variety of meanings for the men and women who experience it. Women are likely to experience infertility as a failure to fulfill the feminine role of motherhood and to define the experience as very traumatic. Men also may find the experience to be disconcerting, but are less likely to see it as tragic (Greil et al. 1988). In a qualitative study of 236 men and women experiencing infertility, Gay Becker (1994) noted that women experienced infertility as "an assault on embodied knowledge and core sense of self" (394). In this study, women described their bodies as unpredictable and used the metaphor of an "empty vessel." Men also described themselves as "empty," but rather than a vessel metaphor, men compared themselves to an empty gun— "shooting blanks." These descriptions are consistent with messages of gendered bodies (men as active and women as passive). Both men and women also described a sense of inadequacy. For men this revolved around sexual inadequacy and for women around nurturing inadequacy. Men's and women's *experiences* of infertility are likely influenced by social responses to infertility. In other words, we are held accountable to the publicly held messages for our bodies. For women, there is more stigma attached to being childless than for men (Reissman 2000). Women are more likely to receive negative comments and judgments from family, friends, and neighbors.[20]

In these examples, we see men's and women's bodies being disciplined, watched, and held accountable to particular gendered norms. Men are constructed as active, independent, risk-takers *not* in need of protection. They are "loaded guns" or are "shooting blanks." Women, on the other hand, are constructed as passive vessels that house a fetus or empty vessels in need of care and protection. Some of these same themes, as well as some new ones, are also evident in the workplace and in the realm of sports.

Work

As with other social settings, the workplace has been traditionally gendered. Following the historical expectation that public spheres are the realm of men and private spheres the realm of women, jobs have traditionally been gendered in the United States. In fact, as late as the post–World War II era, jobs were advertised as "help wanted—male" and "help wanted—female." The gendered messages of our culture tell us the default worker is a man, except where women are assumed to have special skills in helping, nurturing, and customer relations professions. Widespread assumptions about biologically determined differences in women's and men's physical, mental, and emotional capabilities continue to influence employment patterns.

Gender surveillance for men in the workplace, then, tends not to be much of an impediment. While men may still be held accountable to presenting a masculine appearance at work (e.g., a construction worker is still expected to perform masculinity, although this performance is aided simply by being a construction worker), accountability to masculinity rarely impedes men from succeeding in a chosen profession. Even for men in female-dominated professions (e.g., nursing, education, food preparation), the accountability they experience tends to encourage them to achieve high rankings within those professions (Williams 1989). More often than not, we still expect chefs, principals, and hospital administrators to be men, not women.

Gender surveillance for women in the workplace is quite different indeed. Perhaps the most commonly discussed issue of the U.S. women's rights movement of the 1960s and 1970s, an issue that continues today, was gaining workplace access for women. Even with the greater access earned for individual women today, women are still encouraged to *be women* at work. Dellinger and Williams (1997) found that "appropriate makeup use is strongly associated with assumptions about health, heterosexuality, and credibility in the workplace" (151) for women. So enacting femininity increases a woman's ability to be taken seriously in the workplace. And, being taken seriously is a significant issue for women at work, given that power imbalances in the workplace can result in increased sexual harassment (Krasas Rogers and Henson 1997), which is often a form of gender surveillance at work intended to keep women from surpassing men in rank or to prevent women from accessing men-only workplaces (Benokraitis and Feagin 1995).

Still, even if we are willing to recognize simple attitudinal changes that could make the workplace more equal, many people believe there are some jobs women just cannot do because they do not have the requisite size and strength. (All) men are thought to be stronger than (all) women. Thus, asking women to do "men's" jobs is understood to endanger them. Women's bodies are seen in terms of physical and emotional (or moral) weakness, compared to men, due to their "lack" of testosterone and women's assumed instability tied to hormonal fluctuations associated with menstruation.[21] We examine the reflection of these widespread beliefs about women's lesser physical strength in hiring practices, particularly for jobs that are perceived as dangerous (e.g., firefighting, police work, and space flight/navigation).

Gender Surveillance, Technology, and Fitness Testing

It is clear that extreme physical labor may favor the abilities of many men over many women. Yet individual women may be well suited for physical labor, and in the history of manual labor in the United States, minority women (migrant farmworkers and enslaved women) have rarely been excused from backbreaking work on the basis of being female. And, more recently, as men engage more and more in sedentary service work, these men may be no more suited to physical labor than many women. Further, in the twenty-first century, the use of technology in nearly all jobs is making sheer human force much less necessary than in earlier times. One might think the addition of technology would level the playing field for women's entrance into jobs previously assumed to be all male, but this has not shown itself to be the case. Gender surveillance at work still tends to favor accessibility for male workers and provide impediments for female workers, even where machines are built to do the jobs.

Machinery and technology traditionally have been earmarked as masculine. Indeed, men have used machines (cars, motorcycles) as a homosocial way to bond with each other, such that man and machine have come to signal the ultimate masculine coalescence (Mellstrom 2004). There is no reason to expect that technology could not be used to close any gap in physical abilities among workers, but the gendered messages affixed to machinery continue to engage gender surveillance more so than to counteract it (Grint and Woolgar 1995; Messing et al. 2000).

In a pivotal article outlining the surveillance of gender difference through technology, Cockburn (1981) adapts Marxist notions of socio-political power to understand how men use their "muscle" to distinguish themselves as a class to which women can be subordinated. She writes, "The appropriation of muscle, capacity, tools and machinery by men is an important source of women's subordination, indeed it is part of the process by which females are constituted as women" (44). She suggests men design tools and workplaces to the benefit of their own physiologies to exclude women and maintain workplace dominance. Cockburn argues that the original printing presses *were designed* to require just a bit more strength to use than the average woman could muster; hence, men were "needed" to operate the machines. Important for Cockburn is the recognition that the presses could easily have been designed to require less physical strength, benefiting both female and male workers. Why increase the amount of work necessary, Cockburn asks, unless the goal is simply to prevent women from participating? A more current example is the design of grinding winches on sailboats (Crawley 1998). As described in more detail later in this chapter, Crawley argues that the winches designed to restrain massive sails on racing sailboats tend to favor people with greater upper body strength. Although created to control 100,000 foot-pounds of torque—clearly more force than any human can possibly control without tools—the winches are specifically designed to call attention to the abilities of a person who can bench-press 300 pounds over someone who can bench-press 200 pounds. Pointedly, Crawley asks, "Why not just install larger gears in the winches?" (38). Hence, the design of both printing presses and grinding winches are examples of gender surveillance intended to exclude women from participation in all-male settings.

In the past, employers overtly made hiring decisions based on their own pre-existing beliefs about what types of people could do the work. As a result, many jobs—particularly those in the blue-collar realm—were composed of a nearly 100 percent white male workforce. People from excluded groups (women and minority men) took legal action to get a chance to demonstrate that they could do the jobs as well as white men. The resulting decision institutionalized the use of pre-employment testing in certain occupations to determine which applicants had the necessary strengths and skills.

There are several different types of pre-employment testing. In all types, men's and women's strength levels are compared on specific tasks. Three different approaches are used: *psycho-physiological* (in which people lift weights of increasing levels until they can lift no more), *physiological* (measuring body functions such as oxygen consumption and heart rate during exercise), and *biomechanical* (measuring the amount of muscular effort used in specific tasks). Findings from the best-known psycho-physiological databases show that, on average, men can lift/lower about twice as much weight as women. On tasks involving pushing and pulling rather than lowering and lifting, however, gender differences are considerably smaller, with overlap between women's and men's scores. Gender differences are also smaller for tasks that involve faster lifting rates, smaller boxes, and lifting that involves lower-body strength. When workers are asked to lift things quickly, women's scores are approximately two-thirds as high as men's.

Also, studies of psycho-physiological abilities show that men are more likely to overestimate their lifting ability and may take on tasks that pose risks for them. Women appear to be more careful about overdoing it (Messing, Sirianni, and Rayman 1998). In physiological testing for employment, the focus is on the cardiovascular system's ability to deliver oxygen and food to muscles as they work. Measures of the amount of oxygen consumed and the amount of carbon dioxide produced during physical activity are obtained. Usually results are reported in terms of the absolute amount of oxygen consumed. This type of report fails to take weight and proportion of body fat into consideration, which distorts gender differences in the efficiency of oxygen use. When weight and body fat are controlled, men use approximately 20 to 30 percent more oxygen than women, on average. Some individuals, of course, diverge from these general tendencies. (We will see an example of this in our discussion of the rigorous testing that early American astronauts endured.) When women are allowed to adapt the ways in which their work tasks are performed in order to better fit their own size and strength, they may not need to consume the same amount of oxygen in order to finish a task (Messing, Sirianni, and Rayman 1998).

Biomechanical tests measure the amount of muscular effort that occurs at each joint that is involved in the performance of a task. Usually these tests show that women average about 60 percent of men's strength. However, there is always an overlap between men's and women's scores. And, again, when women are allowed to adapt work methods to better fit their own strengths, differences become less obvious. The amount of force exerted on joints depends on the direction in which the force is exerted. So, the gap between women's and men's scores depends on the angles at which an object is pushed or pulled. For instance, women's grip strength as mea-sured by these tests depends in large part on the distance between the han-dles in the pair of pliers they are squeezing. The difference between women and men is greatest for arms and smallest for legs. Testing was developed with men and then applied to women, so it is not surprising that the tests are better at measuring men's abilities than women's. Tests that are better predictors of women's performance and more closely related to real-life lift-ing tasks are needed (Messing, Sirianni, and Rayman 1998).

The institution of pre-employment testing did allow a few women to en-ter male-dominated occupations but it did not eliminate gender-based dis-crimination in employment. The tests used to screen potential employees were typically based on men's performance of tasks. They rested on the as-sumption that there was only one way to get the work done—the way men had always done it. This approach failed to recognize that women may be able to design different ways to get a job done by taking their own size and strength into account. A prime example of women's adaptation of job tasks to fit their strengths occurs in firefighting. Because women tend to have more lower-body strength than upper-body strength, women firefighters have found that they are better able to safely drag victims from burning buildings rather than carrying them. In fact, some have argued that the dan-gers of smoke inhalation are lower near floor level rather than at shoulder height, so that being dragged from a building rather than carried may re-duce a victim's inhalation of toxic fumes (Messing, Siriani, and Rayman 1998). Additionally, at workstations designed for the average man, many women and some men will be at a disadvantage. If given the chance, all workers usually adapt their workstations, equipment, tools, and procedures to their own capacities. Typically, though, when men are seen as the "nor-mal" worker in the job, women are pressured to try to do the job the way men do.[22] As such, surveillance is in place to see, not whether a job can be accomplished by a worker, but whether women measure up to the way men might do it.

Pregnant Workers Need Not Apply

Related to our previous discussion of women as "always potentially preg-nant," gender surveillance of women at work can take the form of under-standing women as "working wombs." In this section, we will discuss the problems that arise when women workers become—or have the capacity to become—pregnant. The Johnson Controls case, described below, illustrates a long-standing belief in the greater vulnerability of women in the work-place that is linked to expectations of biological reproductive functions.

In the late 1970s, Johnson Controls, a company that produces batteries, issued an official warning to all of its female employees, telling them that if they chose to expose themselves and their unborn children to the lead involved in the production process they would have to accept personal responsibility for any negative outcomes that occurred. Subsequently, eight employees involved in the battery production process became pregnant. The levels of lead in their blood exceeded the critical level set by the Occupational Safety and Health Administration. To avoid potential lawsuits from women workers who might give birth to deformed babies, the company began to exclude all pregnant employees and all women of child-bearing age—regardless of their intentions about pregnancy—from any production jobs that would expose them to lead. Apparently, Johnson Controls was not concerned about male workers' exposure to hazardous chemicals. Indeed related to our discussion about maternal-fetal separation above, this is a classic example of how employers exercise surveillance over the safety of would-be children but not the safety of current female (or male) workers.

In 1984, three women employees filed a class action suit against Johnson Controls because the company kept them out of production jobs because of their sex, a violation of the Civil Rights Act. The court that initially heard the case supported Johnson Controls' right to exclude women from these jobs. But in 1991, the U.S. Supreme Court (in *United Automobile Workers v. Johnson Controls, Inc.*)[23] overturned the ruling of the lower court, saying that by excluding only fertile women employees rather than all fertile workers, male or female, Johnson Controls did indeed violate the Pregnancy Disability Amendment of the Civil Rights Act. This amendment states that as long as pregnant workers continue to perform their jobs effectively they cannot be treated differently than other workers. Johnson Control's policy of excluding fertile women workers from production jobs had nothing to do with their ability to perform the job; and thus, it violated the law, even though its stated purpose in acting was to protect unborn babies from the dangers of exposure to high levels of lead. Exposure to high levels of lead affects male workers as well as female, however, and can potentially harm fetuses through damage to sperm. Brady (2004) argues that "sex specific fetal protection policies (such as that instituted by Johnson Controls), view women as merely 'baby machines,' which is exactly the type of stereotypical thinking that . . . antidiscrimination laws (have) sought to eradicate" (274).

These hiring practices illustrate the presumed instability of women workers due to their social and biological roles in reproduction. On the other hand, men who wish to avoid working in hazardous conditions and request a transfer are typically not given that opportunity. It is assumed that men belong in the workplace and thus their reproductive risks are ignored. Men are constructed as risk-takers who are *not* in need of protection (Levit 1998). For the remainder of this section, we give two extended examples of gender surveillance and accountability.

Women Astronauts: Not the "Right Stuff"

In 1959, the United States was about to enter the "space race" with the Soviet Union. The National Aeronautics and Space Administration (NASA) had been signed into law the previous year by President Dwight D. Eisenhower. Originally, Eisenhower believed that astronauts should come from various occupational backgrounds. But he soon changed his mind and decided to restrict the astronaut corps to people who were military jet test pilots. Doing so would get the program up and going more quickly and enable the United States to jump into the space race sooner, he argued. The director of NASA strongly supported the decision.

Seven military test pilots—all white men—were selected from a pool of 31 to become the first American astronauts, known as the "Mercury 7." In order to qualify for the program, the men had to be military pilots and have a college degree in engineering. They had to prove they had "the right stuff" to undertake the physical and emotional demands of space travel by passing a week's worth of grueling medical, psychological, and flight simulation tests that determined their strength, endurance, and resilience.[24] Martha Ackmann, author of *The Mercury 13: The Untold Story of Thirteen American Women and the Dream of Space Flight* (2003), describes the first astronauts as

> All-American as a John Philip Sousa march, smiling, crew-cut, stand-up-and-salute soldiers from small towns across the country . . . shining embodiments of their middle-class, white, Protestant backgrounds. . . . They were young, energetic, skilled, and attractive and fit the prevailing hero mold in every way, including their appetites for anything fast. (10–11)

At about the same time the men were being tested for the astronaut program, word leaked out to the American space and aeronautics community that the Soviet Union was thinking about sending women into space. Randy Lovelace, who had tested the male astronauts for the Mercury program at his facility in Albuquerque, New Mexico, was curious about women's ability to pass the demanding tests. At an aeronautics conference in Miami, Lovelace was introduced to Jerrie Cobb, a female, award-winning pilot and holder of several world records in aviation. Lovelace invited her to visit his laboratory in Albuquerque to secretly—and unofficially—undergo the astronaut testing program. She passed with flying colors (pun intended). Her test results proved her more qualified for space flight than 98 percent of all the men who were tested.

Determined to gather additional test results from women, Lovelace enlisted Cobb's help to identify other experienced women pilots who might be willing to undergo the testing program. In 1960, there were approximately 10,000 American women involved in aviation, mostly at the student flyer level. Over 780 had commercial pilots' licenses. Cobb and Lovelace subsequently invited 25 women pilots to Lovelace's lab in New Mexico to undergo the same testing process he had used to select the men for the Mercury 7. Nineteen of the women accepted his invitation. The women's performances on the medical and psychological tests equaled and in some cases exceeded that of the men. They used less oxygen, had more endurance, complained less, handled isolation better, and withstood heat, pain, noise, and loneliness better. Also, like the benefit of using less oxygen (using fewer resources), being a smaller body size might be a benefit in the confined spaces of a spacecraft. Thirteen of the women scored high enough to continue with the eligibility process, thus earning the name "the Mercury 13." Yet, as the final phase of the testing was to begin, in an act of sheer accountability to their female bodies, NASA informed the 13 women that it had no interest in admitting women into the astronaut program. The official rationale was that only persons who had experience as military test pilots were eligible for the program. Because women were not permitted to serve as test pilots in the military (gender surveillance) they were automatically excluded from the astronaut program.

Colonel John Staff, then chief of the Wright-Patterson Aeromedical Laboratory, offered an elaborate—but unsupported—justification for excluding women from the astronaut program. According to Martha Ackmann (2003:45), Staff said women were only 85 percent as physiologically efficient as men of the same weight, size, and age, and he was not sure if they could maintain the effort and motivation needed in extremely stressful situations. Using logic that was purely gender surveillance, he doubted if women would be able to be objective and offer sound judgment when they were tired or nervous. Staff claimed that women needed to be protected against exposure to dangerous work. He said "to expose women needlessly to the known as well as the incalculable dangers of pioneer spaceflight would be like employing women as riveters, truck drivers, steel workers, or coal miners" (quoted in Ackmann 2003:45).

Representatives from the Mercury 13 group (including Janey Hart, a pilot and social activist who later became one of the founders of the National Organization for Women) approached then vice president Lyndon Johnson for assistance in appealing to NASA.[25] Johnson refused to help. President Kennedy also declined to help. The group then petitioned the U.S. Congress to convene a special hearing to consider the qualifications of astronauts. During the hearing, astronaut John Glenn testified, "Men go off and fight the wars and fly the planes and women stay at home. It's a fact of our social order" (Ackmann 2003). Glenn, who flew the first "manned" space orbit of the earth, did not note that NASA waived the educational requirement for him to make that flight.[26] In 1963, Valentina Tereshkova, a Soviet textile worker and amateur parachutist, became the first woman in space. She was not a pilot and had no engineering degree or jet piloting experience. The United States opened the astronaut program to women in 1978 but did not have a woman in space until Sally Ride went in 1983. The first U.S. woman space shuttle commander was Eileen Collins in 1999. When it was announced that John Glenn would return to space in 1998 aboard Space Shuttle Discovery's mission STS-95, Jerrie Cobb (the first woman tested for the U.S. space program) began to lobby NASA for a chance to fly, too. She had the support of the National Organization for Women, Hillary Clinton, and many others. Her request was denied.

Firefighters, Police Officers, Gender Surveillance, and Individual Accountability

Firefighting may be the quintessential masculine job (hence, reserved for males) in which gender surveillance and accountability are very common. Carol Chetkovich (1997) highlights this in her book *Real Heat* when she writes:

> Firefighters are expected to be large, strong, athletic, unemotional, cool, good with tools, physically hard-working, brave, aggressive, competitive in the manner of team sports, self-confident, and socially skilled in a loud, group-oriented environment. Women will have a hard time becoming firefighters to the extent that to be a firefighter means to be a man. (37)

Indeed, as table 2.1 from chapter 2 showed, only 3.5 percent of the nation's firefighters are women. Today, more than 5,800 American women work as full-time professional firefighters and another 40,000 work as volunteers (Women in the Fire Services, Inc. 2006), yet fire departments are notorious settings for gender discrimination and sexual harassment (Teicher 1999). One reason for this may be an interest in sex segregation by male firefighters to maintain the perceived masculinity of the job. Maintaining all-male work settings and the performance of individual acts of harassment to discourage women from choosing firefighting as a profession are forms of surveillance and accountability. As such, male firefighters are expected to perform masculinity as part of the job, while female firefighters are held accountable to femininity as the reason why women supposedly cannot accomplish the work.

One of the barriers that keeps women out of firefighting is the physical abilities testing that is required for entrance into the occupation. Many departments have rigid height, weight, and strength tests, even though these have not been clearly shown to be related to the demands of the job. Strength testing for firefighters certainly does increase the surveillance of masculinity and creates a barrier for female-bodied people. In recognition of this pattern of discouraging women, the chief of the Minneapolis Fire Department organized a task force to examine organizational barriers that kept women out of the fire department and instituted a 12-week training program to prepare women for the obstacle course test that is used to determine admission into the ranks. The passing score on the test is now based on the average achieved by all who take the exam each year so that no one can complain that women recruits are lowering the standards of the department (Stern 2001).

In addition to the existence of entrance constraints for women firefighters, male colleagues have offered resistance to accepting women in their ranks. In 2001, firefighters in the San Francisco Fire Department distributed a newsletter in which they referred to their female co-workers as "sisters without backbone, little girls playing pretend firemen, and job thieves" (Stern 2001). In a study of the impact of gender and race in firefighting, Carol Chetkovich (1997) followed the experiences of 26 recruits in the Oakland, California, Fire Department, conducting in-depth interviews, holding discussions with experienced members, making frequent visits to the various fire stations, and responding to emergencies with the crews. She focused on several key issues, including what it means to be a firefighter, how recruits prove themselves and are accepted by "veterans" as firefighters, and how recruits are socialized into the role of firefighter. Chetkovich concluded that gender was a greater impediment to recruitment and acceptance in the department than race, and members of the department agreed. One of the male recruits interviewed by Chetkovich (1997) stated that, "the women know they're not accepted here, by the men—whether they're black, Hispanic, Asian, or white. . . . It would be very, very difficult for a woman to be accepted" (157). Many men who were veteran firefighters in the Oakland Department believed that women were not capable of performing the job, and they regretted the loss of the all-male social environment and the "softening" of the traditional firefighting culture (20). Chetkovich argues that the vehement and persistent opposition to women in firefighting and other male-dominated jobs (such as the military and the police) suggests that gender integration threatens the definition of masculinity. Chetkovich writes:

> The entry of women into fields not only numerically dominated by men but traditionally thought of as masculine proving grounds poses a threat to this distinction, for the fewer the domains from which women can by definition be excluded, the less evidence we have for the validity of a gender distinction. Because the distinction (between men and women) is fundamentally justified by the physical differences between the sexes, work that requires strength is a particularly critical area of contention. (188–89).

So the need to maintain a separation of masculinity from femininity is drawn using a presumption of physical difference between all male and all female bodies that simply does not exist in every instance. Where women may be strong enough to handle the job, the issue becomes a threat to men's performance of masculinity and ensuing surveillance of gender boundaries.

Susan Martin (1980) found a similar kind of effect with police officers:

The objection to patrolwomen on the basis of their physical characteristics is "the bottom line" and therefore, can be expected to be staunchly upheld. In jobs requiring some physical exertion, such as policing,[27] the pressure to exclude women is based not only on men's desire to preserve their superior social and economic status but, more importantly, to preserve the meaning of "manhood." If the physical differences which are visible, measurable, and the traditional basis of the division of labor are irrelevant, how can other, less tangible differences be significant? (207)

In a later study, Martin (1994) looked at the experiences of black women police officers. She noted that, based on historical ideals of white women as frail and in need of protection, they were often "protected from street patrol assignments by being given station house duty and rapid transfers to administrative units" (390). While this treatment serves to limit opportunities for white women, black women's opportunities were limited in different ways. Based on stereotypical, historical notions of black women as strong and comfortable engaging in heavy physical labor, black women police officers could not "count on being protected [by male officers] as females" but because they were still not seen as equals, male partners might demand that they "remain 'back covers'" and then turn around and view them as "lazy" (391) for not participating equally.

In each of these examples, workers are held accountable to their female bodies, not their actual physiological capabilities. It is a common running joke that (assumedly male) police officers spend too much time eating doughnuts, which implies they become overweight. Yet the joke does not imply that this bodily characteristic should be a reason to fire that employee for lack of ability to do the job. The notion of male officers getting fat is understood as a long-running source of humor, not a cause for concern over job performance, unlike simply being female (regardless of athleticism), which is apparently in itself a serious cause for concern.

Sports

"The Stronger Women Get, the More Men Love Football" and the Maintenance of the Sex Divide

Gender is not just an individual performance. As the title of Mariah Burton Nelson's book *The Stronger Women Get, the More Men Love Football* (1994) suggests, gender is an interactive process among people in which sport is a significant site for continually reifying difference between women and men. Sport is not just a setting that encourages individual women and men to perform their femininities and masculinities. It is also a site of gender surveillance. Throughout sport, gender is not just done *by* a person, it is also done *to* a person. That is, there is a surveillance of that which we assume should be male = masculine vs. that which should be female = feminine. Sport is one arena in which sex category is a *central* organizing mechanism and in which individuals are held accountable to sex category and expected to maintain male = masculine and female = feminine body ideals.

Throughout sport, femaleness or maleness are first asserted, and then games are divided into "women's" sport and "men's" sport, even for instances where certain bodily differences (for example, upper-body strength that may favor many males and lower-body strength or endurance that may favor more females) do not have an apparent effect. Indeed, bodily differences do provide advantages in various kinds of games. Whereas basketball, rowing, and boxing favor people with greater height or arm length, horse racing favors very small people as jockeys so that the horses carry less weight and can run faster. In these examples, one might expect sex differences to tend to have an effect. Men as a group tend to be taller than women as a group, suggesting that many men may have a height advantage. Of course, this expectation discounts the reality that many women are much taller than many men. For example, Margo Dydek of the WNBA is seven feet two inches tall (see photo 3.5). If matched with an "average" man of approximately six feet in height, one would expect Dydek to have an advantage. Indeed, in horse racing, one might expect female jockeys to have an advantage, since women, as a group, tend to be shorter and weigh less than men as a group. Yet most professional jockeys are men (see photo 3.6), and of course any woman over 120 lbs. (representing a large proportion

Photo 3.5. Margo Dydek is shown here in a 2004 promotional shot for the Women's National Basketball Association's San Antonio Silver Stars. At seven feet two inches, Dydek is the tallest player in the WNBA.

Photo 3.6. Jockey Edgar Prado is seen following the Preakness Stakes in 2006 in which the horse he rode, Barbaro, injured his leg. Prado's very small stature is in stark contrast to the people aiding him and the crowd standing behind.

of the female population) would have no advantage at all. There are many sports in which expectations of sex difference should have no specific bearing, for example, skeet shooting, pool, or race car driving.[28] Olympic equestrian events are contested between women and men with no regard to the sex of the rider. So, while bodily differences might logically be used to organize sport by height and weight (as in weight classes for boxing), it is not necessary or even logical to segregate all sports into female and male versions.

Regardless, gendered messages that structure sport assume a distinct body type for all males and all females and use this notion to orchestrate specific differences between "women's" and "men's" sports, teams, and games in almost all instances. Usually before any game is organized, the question of the sex of the athletes is the first piece of information that is ascertained. All athletes feel the gendered surveillance of and accountability to sex through sport participation. Boys are expected to be capable. Girls are usually allowed to play, especially in "girls'" leagues or games, but are not taken as seriously as boys. Accountability to sex category is the overriding factor in most sport participation. Even in settings where males and females play together, sex is reported on in the media or is the primary focus of discussion. When the girls play the boys, the meaning of the event is never just a simple game—it is implicitly an enactment of the primordial "battle of the sexes." As exemplified by the 1973 tennis match where professional Billie Jean King famously beat retired professional Bobbie Riggs after much taunting on his part that a woman could never beat a man, each matchup of a woman and a man in direct competition is understood as the test of all women against all men.

In short, surveillance of sex is ever-present in sport and each athlete is held accountable to sex category and appropriate gender performances throughout the sporting experience. In particular, we argue that gender is structured into sports. Surveillance, then, has a significant effect on the kinds of games we play and the way individual athletes are received as "good" or "bad" women or men through playing their chosen sport. Ultimately, the surveillance of sport (including discouragement from participating) facilitates *building feminine and masculine bodies*. Hence, sporting participation or the lack of it affects and shapes our actual physical bodies. Those of us who refuse to follow the "rules" will be held accountable and discouraged at every turn.

Structuring Sport, Gendering Games

As we argued in the previous chapter, the performance of masculinity or femininity in certain sports allows athletes to shore up their gender performances through sport typing. But not only is this an individual performance, games are structured to reinforce and compel gender surveillance. *Games are gendered*. Additionally, when an athlete picks a sport of choice, part of the decision entails considering how they will be held accountable as feminine or masculine persons. Hence, most cheerleaders are female and most football players male.

Even for sports that have female and male equivalents, the rules of the game are usually changed for "women's" sport so that it is different from "men's." For example, why do boys and men play baseball while girls and women play softball? They are essentially the same game, although we consider baseball to be a serious sport, whereas softball is understood primarily as recreation (even though there are now world-class, elite-level opportunities for women to pursue professional softball in the United States and other parts of the world). Why have we, as a society, created separate games? Even if we want to maintain a separation based on gender, we could just separate baseball into women's and men's teams. Why create separate sports—baseball and softball?

We argue that this is a specific example of gender surveillance. Softball is derived from baseball and purposefully made "smaller" in that softball games have fewer innings (seven rather than nine), have a smaller diamond (60-foot baseline rather than 90-foot) and smaller outfield, and pitchers *must* pitch underhand, which necessitates a slower pitch. Also, the ball is larger, as if easier to hit, but it is not "soft" as the game implies. Everything about the way the game is organized suggests it is less significant than baseball. Interestingly, the Olympic website seems to echo this concern and attempts to market softball as a serious sport. The following was taken directly from the official Olympic website:

There is little soft about Olympic softball. One pitch at Atlanta was clocked at 118 kilometres per hour (73.3 mph). Considering the pitcher stands 13.1 metres (43 feet) from the batter, and the hardest-throwing baseball pitchers throw 160 kilometres per hour (99.4 mph) from 18.4 metres (60 feet), softball batters have essentially the same time to react as their baseball counterparts. In addition, a softball is as hard as a baseball. The only difference being the size; a softball is 30.4cm (12 inches) in circumference and a baseball is 22.8cm (9 inches). (Official Website of the Olympic Movement 2006a)

So while the structure of the sport suggests softball is easier or requires less skill or power than baseball, the rule changes from baseball may be deceptive. From the point of view of a batter, approximately the same hair-trigger reaction time is required of both because the distance from the pitcher's mound to the plate is much closer in softball. Further, the larger size of the softball actually inhibits one's ability to hit farther. That is, for any given batter (female or male), one will be able to hit a baseball farther than a softball simply because of the physics of ball size. So although it appears that men who play baseball always hit farther and throw faster than women who play softball, the games themselves make these comparisons spurious. They are not comparable. The question is: Why do women and men play different types of games? Even if women and men play in different leagues, why don't both play by the same rules? We argue that the structure of the game is exemplary of gender surveillance.

Co-ed recreational softball provides another interesting example of the gendering of games (Wachs 2005). While in recreational softball it is common for women and men to play together on the same team, there are often specifically gendered rules written into the sport. For example, co-ed leagues often have such rules as there must be a minimum number of women on a team, the batters must alternate by sex, if the pitcher intentionally walks a male batter, the following female batter also gains a walk, and there must be a line in the outfield behind which all fielders must stand when a female is batting. Each of these rules requires that a player constantly consider the sex of all players on both teams and each implies that female players are expected to be less capable than male players. Hence, even though males and females play together, the rules structure full recognition, surveillance, and accountability of gender into the game, regardless of the quality of any individual player.

An effect similar to the structuring of baseball also happens in basketball. The professional men's game is structured differently than the professional women's game. Men play four 12-minute quarters; women play four 10-minute quarters. Although the court size is not adjusted, the women shoot from a three-point line that is closer than the men's three-point line. And, strangely, while the height of the hoop is not adjusted, the size of the ball is—a regulation WNBA ball is $1\frac{1}{2}$ inches smaller in diameter than the regulation NBA ball. Why? Perhaps we assume the ball is smaller because women, on average, have smaller hands than men. If we are trying to create parity of average body size among female and male populations, why not drop the height of the basket? We guess you imagine that as cheating. Interesting. Some rules are available for revision, while others are held sacred.

Our cultural belief that sex differences exist prompts us to structure the sex divide in sport (Lorber 1993). Most telling is the difference between "women's" and "men's" sport in the Olympic Games, which is perhaps the pinnacle of all worldwide sports competitions.[29] If sport tests the human body's potential "merely for the sake of determining what they can achieve" (Young 1979:46), then the Olympic Games represent the highest level of international performance, but also the highest level of organization, symbolism, and surveillance of sport. As such, it is important to understand how the organization of the Olympics engages the surveillance of "women's" as opposed to "men's" bodies.

From its inception, the modern Olympic Games was intended as a contest of men against men, not of women, wherein sex was the first qualifying (or disqualifying) criteria (Cashmore 2005; Snyder and Spreitzer 1983). There were no women competitors in the first modern Olympics in 1896, although some women competed in the 1900 games. Throughout its history, including the present day, the Olympics has distinguished between women's and men's sports and men have had far more opportunities than women for competition. However, women did compete, and some became so proficient that, by midcentury, there developed some skepticism about the sex of some athletes, prompting the Olympic Committee to institute sex testing in 1966 (Cashmore 2005). Sex ambiguity had apparently become a problem for Olympic officials, as it had in other sports (see Birrell and Cole 1994b). How could we distinguish "men's" sports from "women's" sports if we were not clear who was male and female? Presumably the committee was concerned that truly focused, yet underperforming male athletes might attempt a sex change so as to have an "advantage" when competing as a woman (a scenario that seems a serious unlikelihood to us, the authors). Consequently, intersexed and transsexual people were barred from competition, reinforcing the presumption of a "natural" female-male divide. Sex testing continued until just before the 2000 Sydney games when it became recognized that chromosomal testing does not clearly differentiate sex in every case. In 2004, the International Olympic Committee ruled that transsexuals can now compete but only after having been legally sex-reassigned and after hormone treatments had been ceased for at least two years ("IOC Makes Gender Ruling" 2004). Hence, the segregation of sex in Olympic sports remains in most cases.

Interestingly, the distinction between women's and men's sports and the rules for who can compete remain contested and present some logic puzzles. Not all sports require sex segregation. In badminton, tennis, and sailing, some events are available to mixed-sex doubles teams. In equestrian events, women and men compete on equal terms against each other with no regard to sex differences at all. So, there is a precedent for avoiding sex segregation where femaleness or maleness in itself does not seem to create a need for segregation.

There are some events where women and men compete in parallel events with similar rules but they simply do not compete against each other. Snowboarding, diving, marathon, and triathlon are examples of parallel kinds of competition where the rules are essentially the same regardless of the sex of the competitor even where competition is segregated by sex. Creating parallel events that are structured the same, even where sex is segregated, at a minimum creates an atmosphere of less surveillance of the body. That is, there is no foregone presumption that men will be stronger, faster, or have greater endurance, and the accomplishments of the competitors are comparable in each event.

However, what is much more common than parallel events is to structure each sport so that women and men do not compete in comparable events or so that men have more distance opportunities than women (see table 3.1). Hence, it is laid out in the rule structure of the events that male bodies are expected to be stronger than female bodies in a wide range of events. This is a particularly odd practice in many events (e.g., hurdles where women run 100 m and men run 110 m), given that both women and men compete (separately) in triathlon and marathon—both extreme-endurance sports. These minimal changes to the rules and structure of games that could be parallel engage gender surveillance because results between women and men cannot be compared, even where women and men do not play against each other. Hence, the gender divide remains intact.

Further, some sports remain divided into women's and men's games for reasons that seem unrelated to the potential advantages of would-be body shape and size. For example, in archery, women and men shoot the same distance and participate in the same kinds of events in a game where accuracy, not bodily size or strength, is the key to success. Why, then, should women's and men's events necessarily be divided? Similarly with shooting events, women and men shoot the same distances and with similar weapons (pistol, shotgun, rifle). Interestingly, women's events require shooting fewer shots or they shoot at fewer targets; and only men shoot in running target events, rapid-fire pistol events, and in "50-m rifle *prone* (60 shots)." Both women and men shoot "50-m rifle three positions," but men shoot 3×40 shots, whereas women shoot 3×20 shots.

Winter sports have similarly nonsensical gender distinctions. In luge, a sport in which the goal is to fall down an ice run on a sled (where the fastest takeoff and the most aerodynamic run are the goal), women and men use the same track, but women do not sled down the full length of the track. Could it be that literally falling down the longer track is too tiring for female bodies? We think not. Interestingly, doubles luge teams may

Table 3.1. Olympic Events Constructing Women as Less Competent Than Men

Sport	Maximum Women's Event	Maximum Men's Event
Winter sports:		
Biathlon:		
sprint	7.5 km	10 km
pursuit	10 km	12.5 km
individual	15 km	20 km
relay	4 x 6 km	4 x 7.5 km
Short track speed skating (individual and relay)	3,000 m	5,000 m
Speed skating	5,000 m	10,000 m
Cross-country skiing:		
classical	10 km	15 km
	30 km	50 km
pursuit	5 km	10 km
mass start	15 km	30 km
relay	4 x 5 km	4 x 10 km
Summer sports:		
Swimming—freestyle	800 m	1,500 m
Athletics (track and field)	100 m hurdles Heptathlon (7 events)	110 m hurdles Decathlon (10 events)
Track (true for single, double, and four-person competitions)	500 m	1,000 m
Road cycling	120 km	239 km
Track cycling	500 m	1 km
Mountain biking	30–40 km (5–6 laps)	40–50 km (6–7 laps)
Judo (All competitors are in weight classes.)	Four-minute matches	Five-minute matches

Source: Compiled by authors from the Official Website of the Olympic Games, http://www.olympic.org, as of November 2006.

be mixed—female and male, implying there can be no significant advantage of sex in the sport. In curling, a sport in which the goal is to slide a stone into the middle of a circle marked on the ice while sweeping away at the ice to make a smoother gliding surface, men and women compete separately for no apparent reason. Presumably the sexes are differently abled when it comes to sweeping? These gender distinctions do indeed seem nonsensical.[30]

With all these examples, particularly those in which bodily differences do not seem to grant specific advantages, one question remains: Why separate women and men? Why use sex segregation as the most basic moment of surveillance in sport? An example from the Official Website of the Olympic Movement is quite prophetic:

> At the 1992 Barcelona Olympics, Zhang Shan, a 24-year-old from Nanchong in Sichuan Province, represented China in the skeet shooting event, which included both men and women. Zhang caused a sensation by finishing first and becoming the first woman to win a mixed sex shooting event. The International Shooting Union barred women from shooting against men after the Barcelona Games. Women were not allowed to compete in skeet shooting at the 1996 Olympics, so Zhang was unable to defend her title. A separate women's skeet event was added to the program for the Sydney Games of 2000. Zhang entered and placed eighth. (Official Website of the Olympic Movement 2006b)

Clearly in this instance, Zhang was held accountable to her sex, even when she competed and won against male competitors.

Well-organized, historic institutions such as the Olympics are not the only sports organizations that exclude women from certain events. Perhaps the most glaring example in the United States is the sport of football. Why are there few female equivalents to boys' and men's football leagues? (One might argue that women's rugby is an equivalent of men's football. We discuss rugby extensively in chapter 5.) Perhaps you have a hard time imagining women playing against men at football (although some women have); still, there is no specific reason women should not play against each other. Why not have girls' football leagues and NCAA-sanctioned women's college football? (We also return to this question in chapter 5.) We think the absence is telling.

Gender surveillance is so pervasive throughout sport that football and skeet shooting are not the only examples of female exclusion. Newer, youth-oriented sports are also engaged in gender surveillance. As Kilvert (2002) reports, the 2002 X Games (a competition of nontraditional "extreme" sports such as skateboarding, snowboarding, rollerblading, dirt bike trick jumping, and so forth that was created in the late 1990s as a media spectacle, as opposed to traditionally organized sports, and that tends to appeal to youth cultures) provide another example of gender surveillance. When Jen O'Brien's boyfriend, pro skateboarder Bob Burnquist, asked her to compete with him in the X Games "Men's vert doubles" competition (which entails performing a doubles half-pipe routine) because his regular partner had broken an ankle, neither O'Brien nor Burnquist seemed concerned about entering a mixed-sex doubles team. However, the O'Brien and Burnquist team was disqualified from competition. An event organizer is quoted as saying, "There was a backlash when Bob chose Jen as his partner"

(21). Apparently, many male participants were concerned that the mixed-sex team might beat them. Subsequently, there were no competitions made available to women in skateboarding, BMX, or freestyle motocross in the 2002 X Games. Similar examples of gender accountability and surveillance have been recorded in sports as diverse as sailing (Crawley 1998), auto racing (McKay and Huber 1992), softball (Wachs 2003), street subcultures of skateboarding (Beal 1996), and windsurfing (Wheaton 2000), and in locations as diverse as the United States, Australia, and Great Britain.

Even when women perform well at a sport with or against men, they tend to be held accountable to and denigrated for their femaleness. In recreational or less institutional settings, women tend to be judged more harshly or differentiated from men, regardless of a woman's skill. Wheaton (2000) describes how, in windsurfing subcultures in Great Britain where no actual competition takes place, younger men, in particular, often denigrate women for taking up wave space or getting in the way of male windsurfers. Subtle comments about "men's conditions," implying rough surf conditions, or "men's sails," implying high-performance equipment, differentiate on the basis of sex, not skill, and suggest women are not expected to surf well. Similarly, Beal (1996) encountered gender accountability in street skateboarding subcultures in the United States. A young woman respondent in Beal's study reported, "When you go skating and meet new people you pretty much have to prove yourself and they say, 'oh, a girl skater she probably can't do anything,' so you go to pull off a bunch of tricks and then they say, 'oh, oh, she's pretty cool'" (216–17).

When women do perform well in the face of expectations that females cannot perform, onlookers, particularly men although perhaps not always, often engage in what Wachs (2005) calls ideological repair work—they assess a performance in sexed terms in order to maintain the gender divide and continue to fit women and men into the gender box structure categories. Citing her fieldwork in a co-ed softball league, Wachs writes that women's quality performances are often assessed as "getting lucky" or being "good for a girl." Whereas men are often given the benefit of the doubt regarding competence, women's competence is seemingly always in doubt, even when they perform well. For example, elite male players can make an error and be assessed as being "cheated by bad hops"; when a female player who had performed extremely well all game dropped a ball because the sun blocked her view, all her previous and subsequent excellent plays during that game were reassessed as luck.

It should be noted that men are not the only ones who can use ideological repair work to maintain gendered categories and it is not always the case that men come to expect less of women's bodily performances. Women, too, may assess other women's performances as lesser than men's. Women can learn gender accountability and talk in gendered ways about both female and male athletes.

Why work so hard to separate "women's" and "men's" sports? If men as a group truly are "naturally physically superior" to women, why is such surveillance and each instance of individual accountability necessary? Dunning and several other authors have written about *sport as a male preserve* (Bryson 1987; Dunning 1986; Young 1979). They argue that sport is created for the express purpose of teaching masculinity to men and boys and to continue to reify the sex divide. There can be no other explanation when winning female athletes are later barred from the events. For that matter, this notion explains why some sports are structured differently for the "women's" game and why some endurance events are unavailable to women. The goal of this gender surveillance is to maintain the heteronormative box structure that continues to point out and maintain difference.

Vicarious Masculinity and the Meaning of Competition

The messages about masculinity essentially require individual men to have some background and success in sport. Accordingly, sport provides for boys and men the path to symbolic accomplishment that is compelled by gendered messages *as well as the physical markers of masculinity in the shape of a toned and developed male body.* In this sense, sport seems to provide, not just cultural markers of "success," but something apparently far more concrete in the display of the body. As such, sport is exceedingly important to many boys and men as a way of identifying with masculinity and it reinforces men's identities as masculine (Beneke 1997; Connell 1983, 1987, 1995; Hartmann 2003; Kimmel 1990, 1994; Messner 1988, 1989, 1992; Messner and Sabo 1990; Whitson 1990).

While basketball, baseball, and ice hockey in the United States are important sports for demonstrating masculinity (Messner 2002), football, in particular, conveys perhaps the pinnacle of manhood. Sabo and Panepinto (1990) write that the ritual of football contributes to the reproduction of masculinity by structuring hierarchal relationships between coaches and players. Ultimately, they argue that the football ritual teaches young men what they call "primitive male initiation rites"—to learn conformity and control by older men, deference to older men, and how to inflict and take pain. As such, football operates as a symbolic and actual proving ground for masculinity, and the rewards for conformity are many.

Athletic accomplishment, especially in the major sports—football, basketball, and baseball, can mean nearly godlike status for some men in terms of praise from fathers and teammates, applause of "the crowd," and public accolades (Messner 1992). The celebration of masculine sport in the United States is epic. In terms of accountability, then, sports participation for men is almost always received as positive. Sports participation for individual men—especially in the most masculine sports: football, basketball, baseball, and sometimes hockey—grants masculinity points. The audience of men's sports fans (both men and women) tends to offer positive support for these endeavors and individual men are generally judged more masculine for sporting success (which also acts as an everyday confirmation that men are more naturally fit for sports). Yet, some sports do not grant masculinity to men. If men participate in "unmasculine" sports like figure skating, cheerleading, gymnastics or, other sports marked as feminine (that is, understood as for girls), they may be held accountable to being gay or not sufficiently masculine. Notice how sexuality and masculinity are intertwined in these gendered messages—quite consistent with the gender box structure. This is quite similar to lesbian baiting for women (which we discuss in detail below). Also, some sports, while building fabulously athletic bodies, seem to garner no great celebration from the masses. Track or cross-country, for example, may be cause for some praise for men but do not rate the public celebration of football, basketball, or baseball (unless a man's sprint times allow him to be recruited by a football team). As such, the major "masculine" sports are the central focus of many men's athletic endeavors and certainly are the ones most celebrated by our culture. As we argue throughout this section, this is not coincidental. It is in fact the very basis of gender surveillance.

Athletic accomplishment for men also symbolically implies sexual accomplishment. Successful male athletes are almost across the board assumed to be accomplished heterosexual "studs" and often granted playboy status. Ironically, Connell (1990) points out that truly elite male athletes may have little time to live up to their playboy images while they are actually in training. Also, for each individual man, the godlike status is a conditional status, easily lost with the next game or the end of his athletic career (Messner 1992).

Interestingly, though, the end of athletic success for a man (or never having attained it) is not the end of sport's impact on the notion of masculinity. Many men who were never athletic or who are too old to rely on their athletic successes gain what we call *vicarious masculinity*—status as men via the athletic successes of other men.[31] It is possible for not-so-buff athletes, ex-athletes and non-athletic men to obtain vicarious masculinity from association with those relatively few elite male athletes who develop the extremely large musculature of linebackers or heavyweight boxers, simply because of accountability to the male body. Although only a relatively smaller proportion of the male population actually has this physiology, all men gain vicarious masculinity by association with it.

A classic example comes from Crawley's (1998) account of professional sailing. In 1995 the first women competed as primary crew members in the America's Cup, a 150-year-old competition.[32] The women competed as a "women's" team called America[3] (pronounced "America cubed"), which was entirely privately sponsored by previous cup winner Bill Koch in order to infuse some diversity into this relatively closed elite sport. Why hadn't women competed in the America's Cup prior to 1995? The common response was that women were not strong enough to work the grinding winches as fast as the men, hence, women could not sail. Grinding winches are large tools (which look like old-fashioned coffee grinders and stand about three feet tall) used to control the thousands of pounds of torque placed on the mast and deck when trimming the sails. Generally several large, muscled men work the winches. Noticeably few of the other sailors are muscular, least of all Dennis Conner, the famous beer-bellied captain of the opposing men's team. Indeed, sailing does not actually require muscular men to work winches. In a sport of ever-increasing technology, better winches could be constructed that require less muscle. So why not create winches that require less strength? Why not have women working positions other than the grinder positions? Crawley argues:

> The grinder position serves to bestow masculinity vicariously on other male sailors. Although individual sailors may not necessarily be strong, their masculinity is affirmed via ritual association with the (socially constructed) prowess of the grinders, with whom it is presumed women as a group cannot compete. (39)

That is, all sailors and the sport in general gain vicarious masculinity via the symbolism of the strong, male grinder. There is no impetus to improve the technology of the winches so that all crew members could use them and there is no impetus to allow women to take on any position on the boat. As long as one position can be called masculine and only men are allowed aboard, all male sailors maintain vicarious masculinity.[33] Vicarious masculinity, then, is simply accountability to the male body, not athletic success or even individual skill of any kind.

Ex-athletes gain vicarious masculinity, regardless of how old or out of shape they have become, by citing their own, however ancient, successes. Beneke (1997) calls this phenomenon BIRGing—basking in reflected glory. Simply recalling past successes uses the power of masculine sporting accomplishment to bolster an ex-athlete's masculinity. One of the impacts of recording sports statistics is that athletes' selves can be "immortalized" through sport (Schmitt and Leonard 1986). The ongoing recognition of old sports glory allows former athletes to maintain vicarious masculinity through the performance of their former selves.

But how can nonathletic men gain vicarious masculinity? Think of the paradigm of the middle-aged armchair quarterback sitting in a recliner with a bag of chips, an order of wings, and half a case of beer, perhaps with a room full of buddies or even alone in front of the TV. This clearly unathletic practice can be symbolically aligned with masculinity simply via fanship. So simply by having a male body and knowing all the pertinent sports statistics, a male person can bank on positive accountability to masculinity.

Messner (1989) gives a very specific and illustrative example of this phenomenon, so we will quote it here at length:

> Sports as a mediated spectacle provides an important context in which traditional conceptions of masculine superiority are shored up. As a 32-year-old white professional-class man said of one of the most feared professional football players today:
>
> > A woman can do the same job as I can do—maybe even be my boss. But I'll be *damned* [emphasis in original] if she can go out on the football field and take a hit from Ronnie Lott.
>
> The statement above is clear identification with Ronnie Lott *as a man* [emphasis in original]. . . . Here men's [institutional] power over women becomes naturalized and linked to the social distribution of violence. . . . It is significant that the man who made the above statement about Ronnie Lott was quite aware that he (and probably perhaps 99 percent of the rest of the U.S. male population) was probably as incapable as most women of taking a "hit" from someone like Lott and living to tell about it. (79)

It is significant that any woman who may be just as proficient as any man at reciting team statistics while yelling out plays at the TV set (or at eating wings and drinking beer, for that matter) during the Saturday or Sunday afternoon ball game can never gain vicarious masculinity because of accountability to her female body. Perhaps she will gain respect for her knowledge, but not vicarious masculinity. Only men can attain it, and the need to draw that boundary seems pervasive. Indeed, when it was suggested in 2005 that the Vanderbilt University football team might purposely lose one midseason football game in order for two other Southeastern Conference (SEC) teams to receive a bowl bid, benefiting all SEC schools financially, a 1992 Vanderbilt graduate was quoted as saying, "What we are talking about is the manhood of every male that has ever gone to Vanderbilt" ("Quotable" 2005). Interestingly, it was not the "pride of all alums" that we were apparently talking about, nor the "honor of all students," it was the masculinity of all male students, and something apparently not significant to a single female alum.

This link between masculinity and sports is fully aided and abetted by the media, where gender surveillance is pervasive. It is common for televised and print media to play to the particular audience of male sports fans while de-emphasizing the athletic accomplishments of women. In analyzing hours of televised sports shows with a target audience of boys and men (e.g., football, basketball, baseball, extreme sports, and *SportsCenter*, a popular sports commentary show), Messner, Dunbar, and Hunt (2000) found a master narrative organizing the way sports are portrayed, which they call "The Televised Sports Manhood Formula." The "formula" includes 10 common themes orchestrated by the shows' producers and writers that emphasize a particular form of masculinity. These themes include the pre-eminence of sports as a "man's world," with white males in particular as the voice of authority, women as props or prizes for men, and competitive aggression and violence endorsed and encouraged. In short, sports shows are created to sell masculinity to males. The goal, of course, is to create boys and men as a market for the sale of all sorts of goods. Hence, the televised sports manhood formula works to benefit commercial interests, perhaps at the expense of women—and men. Messner, Dunbar, and Hunt (2000) write:

> The perpetuation of the entrenched commercial interests of the sports/media/ commercial complex appears to be predicated on boys accepting—indeed grat- ifying and celebrating—a set of bodily and relational practices that resist and oppose a view of women as fully human and place boys' and men's long-term health prospects in jeopardy. (391)

The resulting surveillance is that women's and men's sports are portrayed differently, suggesting to the viewer that men's sports should be seen as more important than women's. Throughout sports coverage, women are marked as "other" by naming conventions that refer to men's sports as *the* sport (e.g., "The Final Four" is assumed to be the men's basketball tourna- ment); whereas women's sports are of necessity marked as such (e.g., "The Women's Final Four") (Messner, Carlisle Duncan and Jensen 1993). Such gendered naming conventions are common for names of mascots of indi- vidual schools as well—the "Gators" are assumed to be the men's team, while the women's team will be called the "Lady Gators."

Commentators hold athletes accountable to gender messages by com- monly referring to female athletes as "girls" and "young ladies," whereas male athletes of all ages are referred to as "men" or "young men," but never as boys (Messner, Carlisle Duncan, and Jensen 1993). In addition, com- mentators tend to speak about female and male athletes' performances in very gendered ways. In a study of basketball commentating, descriptors commonly used to portray male athletes' play were "talent, intelligence, size, strength, quickness, hard work, and risk taking." But for female ath- letes, although "talent, enterprise, hard work, and intelligence" were com- mon, so were attributes like "emotion, luck, togetherness, and family" (Messner, Carlisle Duncan, and Wachs 1996).

Additionally, the technical production of media around women's and men's sports also plays into gendered messages by suggesting to the viewer the importance of the contest being viewed. Men's events are commonly supported with much more technical equipment and high-profile framing than women's sports (Carlisle Duncan et al. 1994). Multiple camera angles, use of high technology, increased use of special effects like slow-motion re- plays, increased use of statistics, and a greater number of commentators all work to increase tension for viewers and give the impression that men's games are of more value to watch.

Print media offer little improvement for gender surveillance and accountability. A 2004 article about Ellen MacArthur's attempt to circumnavigate the globe single-handedly in a 75-foot trimaran in pursuit of the around-the-world solo record was titled, "A Big Boat for a Small Skipper" (Todd 2004:20). Emphasizing her short stature, rather than her serious skill, this article does not predict her final triumph. MacArthur did beat the world record for circumnavigation by more than a day in February 2005. Upon her win, the same magazine proclaimed MacArthur "Sailing's Grand Dame," making her sound more like the queen's best buddy for tea rather than "Sailing's Grand Champion" or the "world record holder" that she is. Similarly, the America[3] women's team competing for the America's Cup in 1995 was described as too quiet to be competitive by many popular sailing magazines (Crawley 1998). In two separate studies of Olympic media coverage—of the 1992 Winter Games (Daddario 1994) and of the 1984 and 1988 games (Lee 1992)—and in coverage of sports in Finnish newspapers (Pirinen 1997), researchers found commentary that was specifically demeaning to women's sport, discussing women's sports as though they are secondary to and derivative of men's sports.

Even college media guides, glossy magazines produced by universities to promote their athletic departments, construct gendered messages about women's sports. Buysee and Embser-Herbert's (2004) analysis of college media guides showed that male players were more often pictured as athletes in the process of playing their sport (pictured in uniform, sweating, in action during play), whereas women's teams were more frequently pictured as though they are not athletes (out of uniform, dressed in feminine ways, and not near or holding athletic equipment). This suggests to the reader that men play sport and women simply have sports clubs in college.

This differential portrayal leads viewers, both women and men, to understand women's sports and female athletes as less serious and less competent than their male counterparts. Men's sports are serious, manly pursuits with which all men can align. Women's sports, we are told, are less important, playful, something to be taken lightly. The result of this gender surveillance allows all men, even nonathletes, positive accountability to the male body, whereas gender accountability is a serious image problem for women in sport.

Lesbian Baiting and the Participation of Women in Sports

If our messages of gender suggest that athletics build masculinity and masculine bodies, what happens when women play? Do they become masculine? And, what of their well-developed, muscled bodies? "Unladylike" is the notion that has been used for over a century to hold women accountable to behavior that is considered "inappropriate" for women with some class status (Cashmore 2005). More recently, it has become a commonsense concept used to curb women's and girls' full participation in sports. Have you seen (or been?) a young girl admonished by an adult like this? "Oh honey, that's not very ladylike!" is used to discourage a girl from physical activity (climbing a tree, fighting, sweating too much in a "pretty" dress).

According to Messner (1988), female athletes in our culture are "contested ideological terrain." While women's participation in sports has been increasing substantially over the last 30 years (primarily from an increase in sporting opportunities resulting from Title IX) and elite women's athletic performances have begun exceeding that of most so-called average men (and some elite men), the seeming tenuousness of femininity for the female athlete still makes many in our culture uncomfortable, and individual women are held accountable to femininity in all forms of sports. This surveillance of the feminine body can lead to extremely muscular female athletes (or even simply female athletes who can beat male competitors) having their sexuality called into question—that is, being called lesbians. Consistent with the gender box structure, if a woman becomes too good an athlete her status as (heterosexual) woman might be questioned. Should she fall outside the box on one measure (gender), her other identities (sexuality and, ultimately, sex itself) become suspect. *Lesbian baiting* is the term used to describe the phenomenon of women athletes, especially elite athletes, being called out as not meeting the heterosexual standard of feminine body appearance (Griffin1998; Hargreaves 1994; Lenskyj 1986; Pharr 1988). Heterosexuality is a significant component of gender accountability, and the patrolling of heterosexuality and heteronormative images is pervasive in women's sport (Birrell 1988; Blinde and Taub 1992a, 1992b; Cahn 1993, 1994, 1996; Caudwell 1999; Cox and Thompson 2000; Crawley 1998; Galst 1998; George 2005; Griffin 1998; Harris 2005; Lenskyj 1986; Levin 1998; Peper 1994; Plymire and Forman 2001; Sykes 1998). Women athletes are expected to present a (feminine) heterosexual image and those that do not are held accountable in myriad ways. Not only does "masculine" appearance call "appropriate" femininity into question, but sporting accomplishment has long been associated with sexual virility. Hence, women who are skillful at sport are often assumed to be inappropriately sexual (Cahn 1996; Hargreaves 1994; Jefferson Lenskyj 1994; Lenskyj 1986), shoring up the notion that a good female athlete must be a lesbian. Consequently, when any woman is particularly skilled at any given sport or particularly muscled as a result of sports participation, the boundaries of femininity can be patrolled by calling her a lesbian. Importantly, this surveillance and instances of individual accountability are relatively unrelated to any actual evidence of sexuality. A woman may be called a lesbian simply for being a good athlete, or perhaps for too closely challenging the accomplishments of men.

Cahn (1993) argues that during the development of women's sport in the twentieth century perhaps some lesbians were drawn to sport because sport was a public space in which women could exercise qualities—"aggressiveness, toughness, passionate intensity, expanded use of motion and space, strength, and competitiveness"—that were previously viewed as manifestations of homosexual deviance. In other words, it was a space to escape being ladylike. Cahn writes: "With such qualities defined as athletic attributes rather than psychological abnormalities, the culture of sport permitted lesbians to express the full range of their gendered sensibilities while sidestepping the stigma of psychological deviance" (362). As such we argue that lesbian baiting may have had (and continues to have) a much greater impact on heterosexual women's sports participation than lesbians' participation. Ironically, and sadly, the cumulative chilling effect of lesbian baiting—discouraging women from becoming strong, independent, self-competent people—is more likely to influence women who plan to date men than to influence lesbians.

Making Gender "Real": Gendering and the Development of Bodies

Sex segregation in sports is not simply a matter of who has access and who does not. Gendered messages that structure sport also structure and dichotomize bodies. That is, not only do gendered sports provide for gender-appropriate performances of participants, *gendered sports performances build gendered bodies* (Cashmore 2005; Dworkin 2001; George 2005; Hargreaves 1994; Lorber 1993, 1996). As Cashmore (2005) writes, "The body is a process, not a thing: it is constantly changing physically and culturally" (157). The surveillance of femininity and masculinity surrounding sports, or the lack of exposure to sports, literally builds the "lady" or the "man." Not only is football the paradigm of masculine embodiment, it actually builds large bodies that take up space and control a field with power and skill—as do weightlifting, boxing, and hockey. A woman gymnast is poised, graceful, toned, and "tight." She controls her own body (including maintaining its smallness), not other bodies or the spaces they occupy. And gymnastics builds the toned, small (although incredibly muscled), lithe body— as do aerobics and figure skating. In short, masculine sports are designed to build and highlight large bodies with upper-body strength, whereas feminine sports build smaller, toned, lithe bodies, concentrating on cardio training and size reduction rather than muscle building. In short, gendered (surveillance in) sports and gender movement (from gendered selves) build gendered bodies.

Gender is part of the structure of sport. Quite literally, the structure of each sport shapes athletes' bodies. Gymnastics is the classic example. No one looks like a gymnast unless they train as a gymnast. Elite gymnasts develop finely tuned muscular bodies that appear to display the "natural" archetypes of female and male bodies. Yet, none of them could have such a body without specific and well-practiced development, and the events that each sex is encouraged to pursue are specifically structured to point out femininity and masculinity of movement, as well as of the developed body itself. While the events in women's and men's gymnastics make it appear as though "natural" disparity exists between the sexes, only two events, the vault and the floor exercise, are shared by women and men. In addition, these events are designed to demonstrate femininity and masculinity, which in turn create feminine-appearing (small, toned, emphasis on lower-body strength) and masculine-appearing (large, toned, emphasis on upper-body strength) bodies. While women work on the balance beam (grace and balance), men work on the pommel horse (upper-body strength and control). Both work on bars, but women's uneven parallel bar routines are slower and use the lower body more effectively, while men's high bar routines are faster and emphasize primarily the upper body.[34] In particular, men have an event called rings (in which women do not compete) that emphasizes overdeveloped upper-body strength almost entirely. Notice that women's floor exercise routines are done to music as a kind of graceful dance routine in which the absolute strength of the trained female body is supposed to be hidden, whereas the men's routines are not set to music, not punctuated by flowing dance moves, and intentionally show off the development of muscles, especially upper-body strength. As Foucault would argue, this is a clear example of bodies being disciplined by institutions—in this case gendered sports. The athletes literally become the gendered bodies that surveillance requires—via rules, gendered practices, and gender accountabilities to not become the "wrong" body.

The aerobics craze that began in the 1980s and continues in various forms to this day suggests that for many women "working out" is nothing more than the pursuit of a specifically gender-appropriate, thin, toned body. While the paradigm of the Jane Fonda workout began primarily as a means to slim down for women, paradoxically this movement toward thinness has catalyzed the fitness industry for both women and men. Though aerobics was begun (and in many ways continues) as a means to shape thin bodies, it became clear that the cardio and strength-building benefits of this exercise also greatly increased athleticism in general (albeit without building muscle). In the late 1990s, the standard became one that demands some athleticism, not just weight loss. Hence, it is a contradictory standard that suggests women be "firm but shapely, fit but sexy, strong but thin" (Markula 1995). Shortly after women began the aerobics craze, many trainers began to use it to increase the athleticism of male athletic teams such as football teams. For many male teams, it is still common to engage in aerobic exercises to increase cardio abilities, flexibility, and tendon-muscle strength. But, because of gender surveillance, rather than call these exercises "aerobics," which connotes femininity, the same kinds of exercises for men are called "strength training" or "cardio work."

For many women athletes, the femininity that is required of all women— in particular an obsession with thinness—can actually affect body development and athletic performance (Dworkin 2001; George 2005; Hargreaves

1994; Markula 1995). Increasingly, "fitness" for women has become an ath-leticized goal, but it is still a goal with an upper limit for body size and mus-cular strength for women (Dworkin 2001; George 2005; Hargreaves 1994; Markula 1995). Dworkin's (2001) research on women's workout regimens in two different urban gyms argues that women's muscular strength is in-hibited by a "glass ceiling" of ideologies. She argues that it is emphasized femininity, rather than biology, that "structure[s] the upper limit of women's bodily strength and musculature" (337). That is, because of gender surveil-lance and individual accountability, there is an upper limit in the quest for strength that constrains women's muscularity, more so than an upper limit in biological possibilities. Many women in Dworkin's study specifically concentrated on cardiovascular exercise and avoided weight lifting to avoid becoming "bulky." Alternatively, some lifters would "lift light" (or not push themselves with weight lifting) or keep the weights the same over time. Many spoke of it as "holding back" (343) to meet gendered messages of femininity.

As a result of gender surveillance, many women athletes voice ambiguous understandings of their sporting experiences (Cox and Thompson 2000; George 2005). While they find a sense of strength and competence from their well-honed skills and developed musculature, they are also careful to be very aware of the ways in which they may be judged as unfeminine. Un-like male athletes, whose sporting experiences and developed bodies shore up their masculinity and relative worth as men, women athletes often expe-rience multiple understandings of the body—some that are positive and others that are negative. In interviewing elite female soccer players at a competitive Division I school, George (2005) notes a difference between their perceptions of the "performance body" and the "appearance body." The performance body is usually a very positive understanding of the phys-ical self as competent and strong, whereas the appearance body may suffer "flaws" developed directly from athletics, such as "overdeveloped" leg mus-cles that do not match expectations of feminine bodies. Incredibly, even for these elite athletes, many express the same type of surveillance of body fat that nonathletic women express. Many of these athletes are obsessed with any excess fat on the stomach, butt, or thighs, to the point of extending workouts, not for the purpose of improving soccer skills, but for weight loss to meet the feminine body ideal. Cox and Thompson (2000) relate similar findings from soccer players in New Zealand. For female athletes, especially those that do not expect to turn pro, the goal of athletic effort is always tem-pered with the need to maintain a feminine body. While an athletic body is generally received positively in our culture, and the ideal body image for women beginning in the 1990s has included not just thinness but some measure of muscle tone, a female body can be deemed too big or bulky. George's respondents worry about "getting huge" and how that might affect their nonsporting relationships, especially those with men. (George's sample suggests a strong expectation of compulsory heterosexuality and significant lesbian baiting.) Hence, female athletes experience a pull to athletic performance but also a counter pull toward meeting the feminine (small, lithe, toned, not muscular) "appearance body." Importantly, George's respondents relate that a number of audiences hold them accountable to the (feminine) appearance body, including male potential relationship interests, male coaches, female and male parents, and female teammates.

Dieting can inhibit athletic training and athletic ability. In "Creating 'Uniformity'," Ransom (1999) writes about female cross-country runners literally attempting to "run" into their uniforms. She notes the fashion trend of women's running uniforms becoming smaller and smaller in size, unlike men's uniforms, which have stayed relatively the same. As a result, the female athletes were dieting to look good in their skimpy uniforms rather than eating to maximize their athletic performances.

In sum, the argument we are making is not that women and men elect to participate in messages of femininity and masculinity. Rather, these messages are powerfully deployed as surveillance of each of our bodies. We have a sense of being *expected to* achieve specific body types that are nearly impossible to achieve (and certainly a labor-intensive pursuit). In our culture, there is a nagging pull toward fitting into these expectations, whether or not one ever achieves that ideal. Further, the ideal is not a flexible range of possibilities; it is very narrowly limiting. For male-bodied people, the appropriate body is large, tall, imposing, hard, strong, and capable. For female-bodied people, just the opposite—petite, thin, attractive, soft, and nonthreatening. Notably, the standard is also a heterosexual one that shores up the dichotomous gender box structure. The power of heteronormativity disciplines us into gendered bodies.

CONCLUSION

Notice that this discussion is not just about sports (although sports is a particularly glaring example). A parallel argument may be made about sex segregation at work and even in messages about the appropriate uses of the sexual body. If one works a hard-labor job, for example, in construction, one builds a stronger body. If one works a sedentary job, for example, secretarial work, one's muscles atrophy. While it is true that the world of work is not nearly as sex segregated as in the past—many more sedentary jobs in the service sector, for example, computer professionals, are populated by both men and women—it is still true that most heavy-labor jobs are predominantly filled by male workers, even where tools (e.g., dump trucks, forklifts, pneumatic hammers) have commonly replaced the need for brute force. So, among the entire population, we might expect the people in heavy-labor jobs (predominantly men) to have more developed musculature. However, even short of changes in body size, the use of the body affects the self. How I use my body affects how I think about myself. Gendered messages lead to gendered selves, lead to gendered bodies, each step having its own feedback loop (see figure 3.2). If I am told I should be strong, I see myself as potentially strong, I act in ways to become strong, people comment on my strength, and I feel even more like a strong person. I have become strong. And, of course, the opposite phenomenon is true.

This concept works for the sexual self as well. If I am supposed to be actively sexual and virile, I play out that self through the body. If I am told I am always potentially pregnant, I play out that self through the body.

Ultimately, we argue not that female and male bodies are the same, but rather that people recognized as male-bodied (athletes and nonathletes) are encouraged to fully develop their bodies, even push themselves physically, whereas people recognized as female-bodied are discouraged from developing strength and speed in many ways. In other words, the characteristics we tend to attribute to "natural" female bodies (e.g., smaller musculature, lesser strength and speed, general expectation of lesser physical abilities) and "natural" male bodies (e.g., larger musculature, greater strength and speed, general expectation of greater physical abilities) are, in part, if not significantly, a result of gender surveillance and individual accountability encouraging people to develop their bodies to meet their genders. Consistent with West and Zimmerman (1987) and our earlier argument, we see so-called biological sex as far more fluid and diverse than consisting of only two categories, especially if one considers the existence in fact of a wide variety of intersexed and transsexual bodies. Nonetheless, socially, our culture only recognizes two sex categories, falsely dichotomizing between "women" and "men," and narrowly assumes similar characteristics among all "women" and among all "men." In other words, it is the false category system that makes us think there are only males and females and that all males and all females should have similar body structures. It may be as nonsensical to argue that female bodies are the same as male bodies (different reproductive capacities and different hormonal and chromosomal compositions do exist, although varying widely and unpredictably from one individual to the next), as it is to argue that all female-appearing people are the same and that all male-appearing people are the same. Nonetheless, once we think we know the sex category of a person, we tend to hold them accountable to femininity or masculinity, with specifically different likelihoods of body development. This gender accountability and body surveillance results in real physical bodily differences. Female-bodied people could be larger than they are and male-bodied people might not be as large as they are, if gender encouragements were not as actively and consistently engaged. Many men (participants and even observers of "masculine" sports) benefit from this surveillance, because the everyday confirmations of men's sports participation add to the belief in naturally physically superior bodies, which gets read into the self as well. Most women, even female athletes (and some men who prefer to participate in "feminine" sports), do not benefit from these gendered messages, either because of total discouragement (and ultimately lack of access to sport), because they impede full athletic development, or because they create unnecessarily ambiguous feelings about the self ("Just because I'm a really good athlete, doesn't mean I'm a bad woman!"). Our point here is simply this: there is no need for this surveillance. Why not hold all people accountable to their efforts and work ethic in sports, not to their body types? Accountability to work ethic seems much more consistent with the use of sport to encourage good citizenship than constant accountability to maleness or femaleness.

To conclude, gender is not just what you do; it is also what others do to you. In our everyday lives, practices of surveillance (by self and others) and everyday accountabilities to a system of dichotomous gendered expectations encourage us to curb our behaviors and become the realization of the gender box structure. The results of our behaviors are usually consistent with the gender box structure and so become the everyday confirmations of the "naturalness" of gender. As Butler (1996) has described, the result is confused with the origin. Our everyday practices that are compelled by gendered cultural expectations produce the reality that confirms to us that gender is "real." It is a big feedback loop. People do behave in gendered ways and gendered bodies seem to confirm our suspicions. ("Of course, it must be natural because I can see it!") Body practices, compelled by others, confirm our gendered selves ("I'm strong." "I'm pretty."). First, we "know" the gender box structure is true, then we produce it (Lorber 1993) and we are all complicit in holding each other accountable to it.

In the next chapter we explore how surveillance and accountability in work, leisure/sports, and intimate relationships have created gendered inequalities in our worlds and everyday lives. Although "second wave" feminism[35] began over 30 years ago and many attitudes and practices have changed to make gender differences less apparent, gender does still have an impact on our lives. In the next chapter, we explore how gendered we remain.

NOTES

1. We did attempt to follow up on Aurora/Zachary's case and were unsuccessful, and so have no further detail about the origins or outcomes of this case. Nonetheless, our goal with this case is to illustrate that gender difference seemed to make this case newsworthy in the public media more so than alleged child abuse.

2. Foucault's ideas about knowledge/discipline are similar in many ways to what Dorothy Smith (1987) refers to as "relations of ruling" and what Judith Butler (1993) refers to as "regulatory regimes."

3. However, some states in the United States do still exercise retribution on the body by sentencing perpetrators of certain crimes to death.

4. Kimmel does not rely on Foucault's theory in this article, as his argument relies more on psychoanalytic theory and gender performance theory. But we believe it fits very well with Foucault's notion of panoptical surveillance.

5. Interestingly, the inverse is not true. Both women and men can comment on a woman's performance of femininity but it is perhaps men's assessment in terms of erotic interest ("He likes me!") that counts most.

6. Here we want to be clear that neither Kimmel nor the authors of this book endorse this discourse or practice. We simply note an ongoing social phenomenon that men experience as surveillance.

7. We offer special thanks to Tiffany Lukasik for this insight.

8. Given the current-day international sex trade and sexual trafficking across national boundaries, there are parallels with notions of citizenship and sexual access today, and clearly we are not endorsing those practices. We only use this discussion as an example that societies can organize notions of sexuality differently than ours does.

9. Indeed, in an anecdotal account from a lesbian friend, no amount of pleading by the lesbian patient could deter hospital staff from administering the pregnancy test, even though she had not had sex with any man in several years. Of course, all tests must be paid for by the patient.

10. The state has dropped the murder charge in exchange for a plea to two counts of child endangerment due to drug use during pregnancy.

11. 532 U.S. 67 (2001).

12. 577 S.E. 2nd 456 (S.C. 2003).

13. This type of scenario is satirically depicted in the film *Citizen Ruth*, starring Laura Dern, Swoozie Kurtz, and Mary Kay Place.

14. *Victoria W. v. Larpenter*, 369 F. 3d 475, 487 (5th Cir. 2004).

15. For an interesting analysis of masculinity and the marketing of erectile dysfunction drugs, see Wienke (2006). He traces the shift from impotence as a psychological concern to erectile dysfunction as a physiological disorder to the current designation of "erectile quality," a marketing construction designed to appeal to a wider (younger, healthier) consumer base.

16. 450 U.S. 464 (1981).

17. We use the term "Latin" here to denote people in the United States who self-identify as such on cultural bases. We view this term as preferable to "Hispanic," which we view as having implications for race and genetics that we do not imply in any sense.

18. The 2004 Unborn Victims of Violence Act makes it a punishable offense to cause death or bodily harm to a child in utero. The law does not require that the perpetrator had prior knowledge of the pregnancy or intended to harm or kill the fetus. The law does not allow prosecution of health care providers or pregnant women.

19. While it has been common for the media to present scientific "findings" suggesting that chances of harm to a fetus increase with the mother's age, it is has been much less common for men to be subject to this type of surveillance. However, some studies do show an increased risk of autism and schizophrenia in children fathered by men in their 40s (Fisch 2005).

20. Reissman (2000) noted the various ways in which women in her study resisted the stigma of childlessness. Some women used *strategic avoidance*, purposefully avoiding situations in which they might be judged negatively. Another strategy in-

cluded *resistant thinking,* or refusing to see themselves as deviant. A third strategy was *speaking out and acting up* in interactions with others. And finally, some women actively rejected motherhood.

21. It is a myth that men have testosterone while women do not. What is more accurate is that all human bodies have testosterone and estrogen, although males tend to have comparatively more testosterone whereas females tend to have comparatively more estrogen, although that is not true for all individuals (Strong et al. 2005). Hence the notion that testosterone rules men's behavior and is absent from women's bodies is more a public myth than a scientific reality.

22. The discussion of testing reflects Carole Tavris's (1993) argument that women's skills and characteristics are mis-measured because they are compared to men, who are assumed to be the "real" or "normal" human being. If women are different, they are judged unequal from men.

23. 499 US. 187 (1991).

24. The experiences of "the Mercury 7" were depicted in the Tom Wolfe novel (and the Ron Howard film) called *The Right Stuff.* The men who were chosen became heroes. Their names were Scott Carpenter, Leroy Cooper, John Glenn, Gus Grissom, Walter Schirra, Alan Shepard, and Deke Slayton.

25. Not all female pilots supported the efforts of the Mercury 13 to go into space. Jackie Cochran, founder of the Women Airforce Service Pilots (WASP), who selected and trained more than 1,000 women to serve as pilots assisting the U.S. Army and Air Force during World War II, opposed the entrance of women into the Mercury space program (Ackmann 2003).

26. At the time he was selected, Glenn did not have the required degree in engineering. He later completed the degree through correspondence study.

27. In 1998, the National Center for Women and Policing (NCWP) conducted a survey of the 176 largest law enforcement agencies in the United States. The survey revealed that women held only 13.8 percent of all sworn law enforcement positions. Many women got their jobs only after lawsuits were filed or court orders were issued. Penny Harrington, director of the NCWP, believes the biggest barrier to women in policing is the attitudes and behaviors of male colleagues.

28. Some researchers have argued that there are "inherent" differences between the abilities of the sexes beyond size and strength—e.g., eye-hand coordination, aggressiveness, facility with spatial relations or mechanics—that might favor either women or men for something like race car driving. We specifically do not want to engage these arguments because they assume that sex is the determinant of the "advantage" rather than the likelihood of the advantage being developed as a part of the gendering process. As this book argues throughout, not only is correlation not causation, but most of these approaches cannot imagine that our gendered, lived experiences have impacts on the body that produce this appearance of sex difference. Also, these causal sex approaches once again engage the all-women vs. all-men approach, ignoring great variation among female populations and among male populations. Both these approaches are flawed, as we argue throughout this book.

29. All data in this section are taken from the Official Website of the Olympic Movement, http://www.olympic.org (retrieved May 24, 2005).

30. Regardless of the nonsensical reasons for reifying differences in these sports, we, the authors, are not necessarily in favor of immediately merging the female-

male divisions. Given the argument throughout this book, we feel males may have advantages of encouragement to participate and in having their endeavors taken seriously, even in the absence of physical advantage. Hence, combining the sports may only serve to hamper even further the recent hard-won entrée of women into sport.

31. Here we assert that this use of the term *vicarious masculinity* is our own. This idea has been examined by others but not defined specifically in this way. Conversely, these words have been used to describe different ideas. For example, some psychoanalytic approaches suggest women gain masculinity (the symbol of the penis) vicariously through men (McCord, Norbeck, and Price-Williams 1968: 77–78)—an idea we find deeply flawed and do not intend here. Media studies scholars have suggested that men learn to experience pleasure visually by watching film and playing video games with hypermasculinized characters (Alloway and Gilbert 1998:103; Shackleford 2001:245). While these uses are quite similar to our notion of vicarious masculinity, we emphasize how men intentionally and actively align themselves with images of the strong male body, and do not just passively enjoy visual images (although perhaps visual pleasure is not so simply passive). Connell (1987) defines hegemonic masculinity as an intentional pursuit of dominance from which all men, not just those pursuing such dominance, still benefit. Nonetheless, she does not define vicarious masculinity specifically. Hartmann (2003) and Beneke (1997) both write about men's love of sport and particular sports figures as a kind of vicarious masculinity, but neither uses this term. So, they both introduced this notion, but without using this term. Only Candell (1974:16) both explains the concept and uses the term vicarious masculinity as we do, yet he does so in a short biography somewhat in passing rather than by way of writing theory. Our point here is not so much to take credit for this term as to describe this phenomenon more clearly than any of the literature has before.

32. According to one source, the America[3] website ("Women in the America's Cup" 2000), several women had participated in previous America's Cup teams. However, all but one appear to have been in support roles such as timekeepers (which were used in the 1850s for this sport but have long since ceased to exist on the vessels themselves in favor of more accurate timekeeping technology) and as backup navigators rather than original team members. In one case, Dawn Riley did participate in the crew of Bill Koch's 1992 America[3] team, which also boasted the first African American man aboard a vessel in this race. Riley later competed as captain of the 1995 Women's Team and then in 2000 as head of an America's Cup syndicate mixed-sex crew, America True. Still, aside from Riley's obvious skill, her appearance on the 1992 team seems to have been a specific response by Bill Koch to the sport's history of keeping women from accessing crew positions previously on vessels in this race.

33. In case you are wondering how the America[3] team fared against the men's teams, the women's team's grinders (who were capable of bench-pressing 200+ lbs.) were judged competent and competitive in pre-race grinding competitions, outgrinding many of the male competitors. In the actual match of sprint races that determined who would represent the United States to defend the cup, the women's team won several heats and Dennis Conner's team would have been eliminated from competition if the rules had not been changed during the competition. In the

end, an unprecedented three boats (rather than the traditional two) raced to determine the winner and America[3] lost to Dennis Conner's team in the last race.

34. However, since the 1970s the women's uneven parallel bars have had to be moved farther and farther apart to accommodate the more difficult giant swings and release moves (requiring a great deal of upper-body strength) that women are performing in competition.

35. Second wave feminism is the common term for the feminist movement of the 1960s and 1970s and beyond, which produced such things as rape crisis centers, domestic violence shelters, and Women's Studies programs across the United States. The term second wave is understood to contrast this historical period with the period of first wave feminism, which is more or less defined as the suffrage movement of the late 1800s and early 1900s, which culminated in women gaining the right to vote in the United States in 1920.

4

But Gender Is Real

Measurable Inequalities and Their Effects on Bodies

Sport and Violence

It was not until I was about 11 that I began to fear the world around me. As a girl that developed quickly, and well ahead of my peers, I faced attention that I was not equipped to deal with. Men, the age of my father, leering at me in the store; catcalls from moving cars; my brother's high school friends telling me how good I was looking; these were all situations that came about abruptly and I attributed them directly to my changing body. All of a sudden, the body that brought me so much joy with its ability to dance, play sports, and beat my big brother at leg wrestling came to be, in my opinion, a target that I wanted to shrink as small as I could so as not to be noticed (or hit).

Collette Dowling (2000:125) writes about this very phenomenon and talks about the bodily reactions, such as rapid heart rate, elevated blood pressure, and increased adrenaline, when faced with this type of attention. This is a stressful way to live and Dowling also connects the "diet-triggered epidemic of eating disorders in girls and their anxiety about living in a world that, clearly, becomes more and more dangerous for them the older they get" (123). This was true for myself. I began starving myself severely at the age of 15, after experiencing sexual victimization at the hands of a few males (who happened to be accomplished, college-aged rugby athletes). While I had body-image problems prior to that, this was the catalyst for a long, uphill battle with eating disorders. My body became something to loathe and it went from being something I had to control to an enemy that I wished to destroy. The anger that should have been directed at those responsible instead was turned inward. So there I was, at war with myself, mind against body, thinking the smaller I got, the less attention I would receive.

There is this sense of always needing to be aware of what women do every day to avoid sexual assault. The steps that we take every day to protect us from sexual assault are so ingrained that most are unconscious activities (e.g., avoiding walking alone at night, locking car doors immediately after getting in the car, carrying keys like a weapon in a dark parking lot, covering our drinks when we are out at a bar, etc.), yet, when something happens because we happen to "forget" to do one of those things, we are held accountable by other women, men, and the legal system (Dowling 2000:229–30). It really turns into a "me vs. the world" situation. In my own personal case, some of the first questions asked by detectives were in regard to how I was dressed, if I had anything to drink (the entire day), and how friendly I had been to my perpetrators (at any time in the past). Apparently, this was in order to establish my credibility before they moved forward. If I had not been injured to the extent that I was, I would have never said a word (at that time).

Michael Messner (2002:31–32) talks about the dynamics of gang rape and, looking back, I can see those dynamics in my own case. Looking back, the dominance bonding of the athletic peer group, luring girls into places where others may participate, the obvious suppression of empathy, and the "culture of silence" are all things that were present. In fact, there was one male involved that exhibited strong remorse, but the fear of "rolling over" on one of his comrades was greater than the remorse.

I feel happy that I have learned more about the dynamics of violence against women and can step back and look objectively at my own experience. It is empowering to be able to realize that it is not me (or my body) that is the problem, though it took a long time to realize that. I take no blame for the actions [of my attackers], yet it is a situation that I only share when it seems relevant. I guess there is a fear of judgment by others who I feel "don't get it."

—Erin, undergraduate student

The above inset, written by one of our students, demonstrates the premise of this chapter—that our ideas shaped in the social world play out as real consequences in our lives that have real impacts on our bodies. The gender feedback loop (see figure 4.1) starts with social messages about bodies but, as we take these messages into our selves and enact them in our everyday practices and performances, they become real inequalities and real bodily

Figure 4.1. Gender Feedback Loop: Performance / Surveillance. Through gender performance and gender surveillance, we become gendered people and experience inequalities.

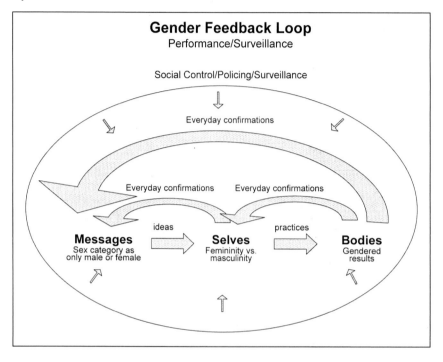

differences. Through the gender feedback loop (including the surveillance and accountability of gendered behavior), gendered messages develop gendered consequences. Further, these consequences become everyday confirmations that shore up our (inaccurate) notions that gender is innate. That is, we see these real consequences and use them as confirmations of the gendered messages that instructed us to behave differently in the first place. In this chapter, we talk about the different and often unequal experiences that women and men have as a result of gendering bodies.

"WHAT ONE BELIEVES TO BE REAL IS REAL IN ITS CONSEQUENCES"

While cultural messages about bodies may seem ethereal, their effects are real to the extent that they change actual bodies and impact our everyday lives and selves. In 1928, Thomas and Thomas famously wrote, "What one believes to be real is real in its consequences" (572). This means that what one believes to be true, one will put into action, which essentially makes that belief come into being. Regardless of the basis of one's beliefs, one's actions ultimately end in real consequences for one's self, interactions with others, and notions about and uses of the body.

In our society, women and men are not only different but, in many respects, unequal. Such fundamental aspects of life as education, employment, income, physical health, susceptibility to disease, and life expectancy are influenced by sex and gender. In this chapter, we focus on the ways in which our lives and bodies are changed through social interaction. We emphasize how treating women and men as categorically different can have an impact on the self and the body and the opportunities any individual has in everyday life. That is, we focus on the inequalities between women and men that result from gendering bodies. We also explore inequalities among women and among men.

Social Factors in Health, Illness, and Life Expectancy

We tend to see health as a biological issue unrelated to social factors, yet social processes affect risky behaviors and access to medical care. In this section we will touch on just a few examples of social factors affecting the body in the areas of health, illness, and life expectancy. We should note that health-related inequality is deeply intertwined with inequalities related to education, employment, and income. People living in poverty are at a higher risk for being in poor health for a number of reasons, including hazardous and physically demanding work conditions, inadequate or unsafe housing, low-quality diets (because of the high cost of fresh, healthy food), and lack of health insurance or adequate health care. So, while health has physiological components, these components are greatly complicated by gender-, class-, and race-based inequalities.

While people tend to think of women as fragile and men as tough or resilient, when we examine vital statistics (e.g., information about birth, death, illness, marriage, divorce, and other major behavioral events) we see a somewhat different picture. Some biologists estimate that 130 male fetuses develop for every 100 female fetuses and 105 male babies are born for every 100 female babies, yet in the United States there are only 95 men for every 100 women. Genetic abnormalities that plague male babies more often than female babies result in a greater spontaneous abortion rate among unborn males and also cause earlier death after birth. Also, the presence of two X chromosomes in females helps protect them against diseases such as muscular dystrophy (Stillion 1995). Additionally, for the past 100 years in the United States and all other industrialized nations, women, especially white women, have had a longer life expectancy (the average number of years a person can expect to live from birth or from a given age) than men. In fact, the gap is larger today than it was in 1900 (Lorber and Moore 2002).

Life expectancy also varies by race and social class. Black men have the lowest average life expectancy, 69.2 years, while white women have the highest average life expectancy at 80.5 years (Hoyert, Kung, and Smith 2005). White men and black women can expect to live to about age 76, on average. The gender differences in life expectancy result, in turn, in an unbalanced sex ratio (the number of men in the population for every 100 women).

Despite the fact that women have longer life expectancies and lower mortality rates than men, they have higher morbidity (illness) rates. For instance, women report more symptoms than men and are somewhat more likely to report that their health is only fair or poor (Waldron 1995). They also report more days of restricted activity, including bed rest, than men, and visit doctors and hospitals more often than men. Once in the hospital, though, men tend to stay longer than women. Part of the difference in medical visits may be due to women's lower likelihood of ignoring symptoms and greater likelihood of using preventative health measures (Waldron 1995).

Behavioral differences between women and men also contribute to sex differences in health and illness. There seems to be an association between life expectancy and traditional gender stereotypes. A large part of the difference in the death rate between women and men can be accounted for by men's greater susceptibility to heart disease, stroke, arteriosclerosis, and related problems (Lorber and Moore 2002; Waldron 1995). One of the major reasons that men are more likely to have these problems is cigarette smoking. Men are not only more likely than women to smoke, they also begin smoking at earlier ages, inhale more deeply, and smoke more of each cigarette they light (Waldron 1995). Women's rate of smoking increased significantly during the 1980s and rose among teenage girls during the 1990s, so this gender difference may soon disappear.[1] However, even among nonsmokers, the death rate from coronary heart disease for men exceeds that for women. Clearly, other factors play a role. One such factor is that men are more likely to exhibit what medical professionals refer to as the *coronary-prone behavior pattern* (also called "type A personality" by laypeople). The characteristics of this type of personality or behavior pattern resemble those considered masculine in our society—competitive, impatient, ambitious, and aggressive (Helgesen 1995).

While men are more likely to suffer from heart disease, heart disease in women has recently been recognized as a leading cause of female mortality. For many years, women's heart disease was misdiagnosed or went undiagnosed, partly due to sexism in medical research and medical treatment. Women have often been excluded from medical research out of concern for reproductive functioning (remember, women are thought to be "always potentially pregnant"). In 1948, the National Institutes of Health (NIH) began a major longitudinal study, the Framingham study, that included both men and women. The results of this study suggested that men who showed early signs of heart problems were likely to develop heart disease, while women were not. This influenced much future research, including drug trials, and clinical practice. The problem with this study was that it did not follow the subjects long enough. It turns out that women experience the most fatal types of heart disease later in life (often after menopause) than men do (Healy 1995). Women's complaints of chest pain continue to be taken less seriously than men's, resulting in less aggressive treatment, and black women's complaints are likely to be taken less seriously than white women's (Schulman et al. 1999).

A major public health issue that reflects gender inequality is interpersonal violence. While men are more likely than women to be victims of reported violence in our society (and men's violence toward other men is considerable in the United States), men are considerably less likely to be victims of intimate partner violence. If women are violently assaulted, their assailant is most likely a husband or boyfriend. When women are assaulted, they are more likely to be injured if they have an intimate relationship with the perpetrator. Feminist scholars argue that gender inequality and the oppression of women are the central features of violence in families. Historically, there have been norms and laws that condone violence against women. In the nineteenth century, for example, many states had laws specifically approving of wife beating. Battering is a reflection of the inequality between women and men and is a conscious strategy used by men to control women and to maintain the system of gender inequality. While services for victims of intimate violence and sexual assault have come a long way since their inception in the 1970s, many organizations still lack the ability to meet the needs of all victims, especially women of color; immigrants; heterosexual men; and the lesbian, gay, bisexual, and transgender communities (Donnelly et al. 2005; Martin 2006; Renzetti 1992).

So while there may be physiological differences between females and males, social factors such as gender, race, and class have a huge impact on health and the body. In the next section, we discuss some further gendered consequences for bodies and selves.

GENDERING BODIES IN ACTION

As in the previous chapter, we use the following section to present specific instances of how gender works in the context of sex and reproduction, at work, and in sports. In this chapter, we focus on the results of a gendered society. We point out how gendered processes result in inequalities. The entire literature of feminist theories works to demonstrate how and where gender inequality exists. In particular, a large literature shows that women still earn less than men as a result of gendered messages in our world. Here we show some further inequalities that result from gendering bodies.

Work

Nowhere is inequality more evident and more measurable than in the field of work. In the capitalist United States (and the increasingly capitalist world), work is a high-profile everyday activity that yields very measurable results. Income and wealth inequality has been the target of feminist investigations for decades and continues to be relevant to our everyday lives, selves, and bodies.

Because overt sexism is not generally popular and because many of us take gender messages to be a kind of truth or reality, it is often difficult for us to see gendered behavior at work as intentional inequality (Martin 2003). But gender performances and especially gender accountability often lead to differential opportunities and rewards at work.

Schilt's (2006) study of female-to-male (FTM) transgendered men sheds some light on this issue. Schilt's interviews with 29 transmen found that several reported more positive work experiences after transitioning to male than they experienced as female. They reported being granted more authority and competency by others (i.e., having their knowledge respected, not dismissed), getting greater recognition for hard work, having more personal space and less sexual harassment, and receiving expanded economic opportunities, or at least lack of restraint on their careers, after transitioning. Most of Schilt's interviewees were clear that they recognized these effects readily and some even claimed to become more feminist after having witnessed firsthand the differences between the treatment of women and men at work. Interestingly, among her sample, tall, white FTMs experienced the most advantages in the workplace.

In another study of women entrepreneurs in American harness (horse) racing, Larsen (2006) found that women have a particularly difficult time breaking into this field. Larsen writes:

> I found that women who run their own racing businesses lack certain resources necessary to become visible and successful in the eyes of customers (racehorse owners) and colleagues (male peers). Moreover, no matter what strategies these women employed to remain visible and viable in harness racing, their efforts did nothing to disrupt existing structures of segregation in this male-dominated industry. In fact, many women ended up "erasing" their gender—in effect, self-identifying with the dominant masculine culture—in order to remain in the industry. (120)

So, having a female body at work has real consequences. In this section we outline some further effects of gender differentiation at work.

Big Bellies, Talking Heads, and Pretty Faces: Discrimination in Employment

Because women are viewed as "always potentially pregnant" and sometimes do become pregnant, women often face differential treatment in the workforce. One example comes from the entertainment industry. In the late 1990s, Hunter Tylo, a star of the daytime soap opera *The Bold and the Beautiful*, was hired by television producer Aaron Spelling to join the cast of the nighttime show *Melrose Place* in the role of a "vixen" or "seductress." Her contract emphasized her appearance and stated that if her looks changed she could be fired. Before Tylo actually appeared on the show she became pregnant with her fourth child and was fired. Spelling said that a pregnant woman could not convincingly portray a sex symbol on television, and thus, he was justified in firing her. Moreover, he said, he could do this legally without violating federal laws against sex discrimination because "sexiness" was a *bona fide occupational qualification* (BFOQ) for the job and the pregnant Tylo no longer possessed the trait.[2] Tylo sued Spelling for breach of contract and pregnancy discrimination. She won a multi-million-dollar settlement. A jury in Los Angeles awarded her $4 million for emotional distress and nearly another $1 million for economic loss ("Revenge of a Vixen" 1997).

In 1978, the Pregnancy Discrimination Act was passed as an amendment to Title VII of the Civil Rights Act of 1964. The act states that "women affected by pregnancy, childbirth, or related medical conditions shall be treated the same for all employment-related purposes, including receipt of benefits under fringe benefit programs, as other persons not so affected but similar in their ability or inability to work." Thus, discrimination on the basis of pregnancy, childbirth, or related medical conditions constitutes unlawful sex discrimination. Prejudices against pregnant workers (among employers, co-workers, clients, or customers) cannot be used to justify refusal of employment to an otherwise qualified woman. An employer cannot refuse to hire a woman because of her pregnancy-related condition as long as she is able to perform the major functions of her job. In fact, an employer cannot ask a woman who is interviewing for a job if she is pregnant or if she plans to have children. Pregnant women must be allowed to work as long as they are able to perform their jobs. If they are temporarily unable to complete their responsibilities, their employer must treat them in the same way he or she would treat any other "disabled" employee. Pregnant women must not be discriminated against in terms of seniority, vacations, pay increases, or temporary disability benefits. Regardless of these laws, individual women deal with differential treatment in everyday life and often must answer to perceptions about pregnancy or being seen as "always potentially pregnant" by employers and co-workers.

Pregnancy is just one form of employment discrimination related to gendered bodies. The aging of gendered bodies is another area where employment discrimination is apparent. Christine Craft is a broadcast journalist who became the subject of numerous news reports herself when she filed a lawsuit against KMBC-TV in Kansas City for breach of contract. She had been hired by the ABC affiliate in the late 1980s to be the co-anchor of the station's nightly news. In spite of signing a two-year contract with KMBC, Craft was fired just eight months after she began, because the station's focus group research found that the audience thought she was "too old, too ugly, and not deferential to men." Ironically, Craft had cautioned the station when they approached her about interviewing for the anchor job that she was not willing to be "made over" for her on-air appearance. She had had a negative experience when she worked with the CBS television network's *Sports Spectacular* show and producers demanded that she undergo wardrobe consultation, a cosmetic makeover, and a drastic bleaching and restyling of her hair. When she was fired by KMBC, she filed a breach of contract suit. Twice she was awarded monetary verdicts against the station and twice judges overturned them. The U.S. Supreme Court refused to hear the case, so Craft's attempts to win legal sanction ended. She subsequently attended law school and reentered broadcast journalism after completing her degree.[3]

The United States has had federal legislation protecting workers against age discrimination since 1967, when the Age Discrimination in Employment Act (ADEA) was passed. The law came about in large part because of lobbying by groups whose members suffer the effects of discrimination, such as the Association for the Advancement of Retired Persons (AARP) and the Gray Panthers. This law protects individuals who are 40 years of age and older. It applies to persons who are already employed as well as to those who are applying for work. It pertains to hiring, firing, promotion, layoffs, compensation, benefits, job assignments, and training. It applies to all employers with 20 or more employees, including state and local governments, and is enforced by the Equal Employment Opportunity Commission (EEOC).

Now, nearly three decades after Christine Craft was involuntarily subjected to a radical makeover in order to meet the standards of broadcast journalism, appearance still seems to reign supreme in this field of work. In 2002, for instance, Greta Van Susteren, a legal analyst and interviewer on CNN, took a new job at Fox News and underwent a "surgical makeover" allegedly of her own volition. Van Susteren was trained as a lawyer at Georgetown Law Center and had built a reputation as a tough litigator in Washington when she was hired by a local CBS affiliate to provide legal analysis of then mayor Marion Barry's drug and perjury trial in 1991. After joining CNN full time in 1991, Van Susteren became highly visible during her analysis of the O. J. Simpson trial. Her look before the surgery was decidedly "nonglamorous" according to the apparent consensus of the media, who gave a great deal of attention to her appearance after the surgery. Van Susteren explained her decision to have surgery as one that was prompted by concerns about looking younger for her 30th high school reunion. She denies that Fox News pressured her to have the surgery as a condition of her employment. At about the same time that Van Susteren was hired by the news network, Paula Zahn was also hired. Her arrival at Fox News was announced with advertisements that called attention to her beauty and sex appeal.

In addition to discrimination based on pregnant bodies and aging bodies, there is a great deal of evidence to show that employers discriminate against overweight bodies in terms of hiring, compensation, promotions, and firing. Some experts say that size discrimination is even more rampant than sex or race discrimination, although it is a particular problem for women (Roehling 1990, 2002). There is very little protection or recourse for overweight persons against discrimination in the labor force.[4] The Civil Rights Amendment does not offer protection against weight discrimination and the Americans with Disabilities Act applies only in cases of extreme obesity.[5] Michigan is the only state that offers protection under its fair employment law.

Studies conducted in the 1990s found that there is a significant wage penalty associated with obesity (Hammermesh and Biddle 1994; Register and Williams 1990; Sargent and Blanchflower 1994). For example, one study that focused on younger workers (those ages 18 to 25) found that obese women are paid 12 percent less than their female peers of "normal" weight, while obese men were paid 5 percent less than male workers in the normal weight range. Furthermore, some research has shown that being obese at an early age can have long-term economic effects (Averett and Korenmann 1996). Men generally are not penalized for obesity until they are at least 100 pounds over the recommended weight for persons of their height and body frame. Women, on the other hand, are judged according to more subjective size criteria. For women, the economic impact of being overweight can be indirect, as well as direct, in that it reduces their likelihood of being married and, thus, deprives them of the cost-effectiveness of a dual-career household (Hammermesh and Biddle 1994).

Some managers have explained hiring decisions that work against obese individuals in health-related terms. They argue that millions of workdays are lost to obesity-related illnesses each year, costing them more than $47 billion annually (Meece 2000). But research that has examined the economic impact of obesity has shown that it is not health problems or lesser ability that causes overweight workers to earn less money. It is discrimination against overweight people that appears to be responsible (Averett and Korenmann 1996). There is also a large and significant race difference in the economic penalty associated with obesity. The stigma of obesity seems to affect white women more severely than other groups. Black workers tend to experience a smaller penalty than whites. In fact, white women who are mildly overweight (i.e., 20% over the recommended weight) experience greater wage penalties than black men who are obese (i.e., 100% over the recommended weight) (Maranto and Stenoien 2000).

A number of lawsuits have been filed by employees who have been penalized in some way because of their weight. One case that was settled involved flight attendants who were disciplined and/or terminated by United

Airlines for failing to comply with maximum weight requirements the airlines had in place from 1980 to 1994. United had weight requirements for both male and female flight attendants based on height and age, but the restrictions were more severe for women. The maximum allowable weight for men was greater than for women of the same age and height. In 1992, 13 female flight attendants filed a class-action lawsuit against United Airlines for sex discrimination. While they had all attempted to lose weight in order to comply with the requirements, every one was fined or terminated. After going through a complicated legal process, the case ended up in 2000 in the Ninth Circuit Court of Appeals,[6] which found that United's weight policy discriminated against female flight attendants.[7]

Dangerous Jobs: Occupational Safety Issues for Women and Men

Employment discrimination is not the only work-related issue where we see inequality based on gendered bodies. Occupational health and safety also plays out differently for men and women. However, in this arena, social class may be even more important than gender in explaining unequal bodily experiences.

Men are considerably more likely than women to sustain fatal injuries on the job. This can be explained in part because of the types of jobs in which they are employed, coupled with the risk taking encouraged by traditional male roles. In 2002, 92 percent of all workplace fatalities involved male workers. The Bureau of Labor Statistics has been collecting data about dangerous jobs since 1992. Each year, they conduct the *Census of Fatal Occupational Injuries* (which attempts to be a complete count of all mishaps that occur in workplaces) and the *Survey of Occupational Injuries and Illnesses* (which randomly surveys 250,000 establishments). From these data, jobs can be ranked in terms of the total number of persons who are killed each year in each occupation and the fatality *rate* experienced in each occupation (i.e., the number of workers in the occupation who are killed while working for every 100,000 persons employed in the occupation). The latter figure controls for differences in the numbers of persons employed across occupations.

In 2005, more than 5,700 American workers were killed on the job (Bureau of Labor Statistics 2005). Workers who are in the riskiest jobs do not work in factories or offices. They are employed outside or on the road (or in the skies). Typically the most dangerous jobs (defined in terms of the fatality rate in each occupation) included the following: timber cutters (loggers); fishers; pilots and navigators; structural metal workers; drivers in retail sales; roofers; electric power installers; farmworkers; construction laborers; and truck drivers. All of these jobs are male-dominated—that is, the workforce is at least 75 percent male. In fact, all of the jobs on this list, except farmworker, have more than 95 percent male workers. The combination of dangerous jobs being reserved for males and the performance of masculinity on the job (i.e., risk taking, aggressive behavior) may explain why men are more likely to die at work than women.

Nonetheless, many working-class female-dominated jobs, especially in factories, have been dangerous or fatal for employees. The first factories in North America were textile mills staffed primarily by young, single women. The working conditions of many factories in which women have worked since the early days of industrialization (particularly textile mills and garment factories) fit the definition of sweatshop (i.e., workplaces in which wages are so low that workers cannot meet their basic needs, conditions are dangerous and unsanitary, and intimidation occurs when workers try to improve their work conditions through unionization [von Drehle 2003]).

Although much legislation has been passed in the United States to improve working conditions, many workers still experience less-than-ideal situations at work, many of which take a toll on the body.[8] Indeed, recent estimates from the federal government suggest that sweatshops are still common in the United States. The largest concentration of garment industry sweatshops in the country (possibly even the world) is found in a 20-block area in the southern end of downtown Los Angeles. Approximately 160,000 workers are employed in the garment factories there. A government survey published in 2000 estimated that two-thirds of these factories violated minimum-wage laws and 98 percent violated health and safety laws. Many of the workers in these shops are undocumented immigrant women who are afraid to protest working conditions because they do not want to lose their jobs. In the late 1990s, factories in Los Angeles that produced garments for stores such as Macy's and Mervyn's were discovered to be subjecting Thai women workers to 17-hour workdays at wages of less than $2 per day. Because of steep competition and the need to cut production costs, garment factories in southern California are returning to labor conditions similar to those found in sweatshops in the early 1900s (Bonacich and Appelbaum 2000).

Sweatshops are not confined to Los Angeles, however. They can be found anywhere there is a supply of "cheap labor."[9] One such place is Beattyville, Kentucky, in the foothills of the Appalachian Mountains, where the Lion Apparel company makes uniforms for the U.S. military under sweatshop conditions. One former employee of Lion, when interviewed in an article that appeared in *Mother Jones* magazine, said that she would go home from work every day exhausted, her hands swollen (Boal 1999). She had constant back pain from hunching over an old, broken-down sewing machine for many hours every day. Fumes from formaldehyde, which is used to stiffen the fabric, gave her headaches and made it hard for her to breathe. It also caused her arms to break out in a rash. The plant had no air conditioning, so it was sweltering in the summertime. On the other hand, it was so cold in the winter that water in the toilets would freeze. After working at the plant for nine years, this woman was fired because she refused to perform a job that she thought would hurt her back. Other workers apparently had similar experiences, as Lion Apparel was cited and fined on numerous occasions for violations of occupational safety and health regulations, including failure to provide workers with proper face protection and failure to train them to handle hazardous chemicals. The federal government, however, lauded the company for being a success story because it saved the Department of Defense millions of dollars in uniform costs (Boal 1999).

Sexual Harassment in the Workplace

Another workplace safety issue is sexual harassment. In cases of sexual harassment, bodies are often targeted or more subtly implicated. Women are more often the victims of sexual harassment and men are more often the perpetrators. However, even when men are the victims of sexual harassment, men are still likely to be the perpetrators (Murphy-Geiss 2007; Waldo et al. 1998). All forms of sexual harassment are illegal, regardless of the gender of the victim or the perpetrator.[10]

Sexual harassment is defined by law as unwanted sexual attention at work, which is prohibited by the Civil Rights Act. It is a pervasive, serious, and injurious form of violation of a person's right to a safe workplace (Sev'er 1999). Some people assume that harassment only involves situations in which a woman worker is forced by a supervisor to engage in sexual acts in order to keep her job (or get a raise or promotion). Sexual harassment actually takes several forms. The situation just described is referred to as quid pro quo harassment by the Equal Employment Opportunity Commission (EEOC), the federal agency responsible for enforcing laws about discrimination in the labor force.[11] Another form of sexual harassment, which may now be more common than quid pro quo, consists of actions that create a hostile environment. This can include any unwelcome sexualized behavior such as jokes, cartoons, posters or calendars, banter, repeated requests for dates or sexual favors, references to body parts, or physical touching that creates an intimidating, hostile, or offensive work environment that interferes with an individual's work performance. The contributing acts must be severe and must be repeated in order to fit the definition of sexual harassment. The courts also recognize a third type of unlawful harassment in the workplace that is not sexualized per se but is based on gender stereotypes that demean women. The incident mentioned in the last chapter in which firefighters referred to their female colleagues as "sisters without backbone," "little girls playing firemen," and "job thieves" are examples of gender harassment.

Other types of jobs and workplaces are not immune to these forms of sexual harassment. Even prestigious professions like medicine and elite institutions such as Stanford Medical School have been the site of numerous incidents of sexual and gender harassment. At Stanford, these practices came to public attention in the early 1990s when Frances Conley, one of the nation's first female neurosurgeons, resigned from the medical school faculty because of concerns about rampant sexist attitudes and behaviors,[12] including male colleagues who showed slides of *Playboy* centerfolds during lectures to "spice them up." While some investigation into the matter followed Conley's resignation, sexual harassment apparently continued at the institution. In the late 1990s, dozens of female scholars from Stanford filed a 400-page complaint of gender discrimination against the university with the U.S. Department of Labor.[13]

Of course, in practice if not in law, each local work culture constructs its own boundaries around what is and what is not considered sexual harassment (Dellinger and Williams 2002). An interesting twist in the role of sexual harassment in creating inequality in the workplace is described by Dana Britton (2003) in her study of prison guards. Male prison guards expressed their opinion that a male prison was not an appropriate place for women to work (as guards). They seemed to cloak this attitude as a *protective concern* that female guards should not be put in a position to have to deal with sexual behaviors and comments from male inmates. Tellingly, the women guards reported that the inmates' sexual behavior and comments were a "minor irritation" (179) compared to their experiences with co-workers and supervisors. At the same time that the male prison guards expressed a *protective concern* about female guards, there was also an atmosphere of rumor and innuendo surrounding female guards' sexuality. Using a heteronormative framework, male guards seemed to assume that any female guard was at risk of succumbing to the seductions of a male inmate. This attitude led female guards to be extra careful about how they interacted with inmates, for fear that their actions would be misperceived.

Sexuality and Reproduction

Inequality starts early for gendered bodies and continues throughout the life course. Inequality can be measured among women or between women and men. Here we look at inequality in various experiences related to sexuality and reproduction—sexual experiences, sexual and reproductive health care, and reproductive technologies.

Frat Feminism: A Layered Account

My fraternity voice is hoarse today—like when you wake up mute and hungover, aware you've been dry heaving all night but not quite sure why you were yelling. Though it's faint and muffled, I can't ignore the misogyny that echoes through my inner dialogues. My dual identity, as an ex-fraternity member and developing feminist sociologist, helps mediate the tensions between all-male subcultures and egalitarian ideals. This layered account breaks the fraternity silence. The focus of this narrative is to trace my journey toward fraternity masculinity and to pinpoint the barriers that divided feminism and my former, undergraduate self.

* * *

This feminist moderator is a fucking idiot! Like all feminists he can't speak my language and doesn't want to. He telegraphs his ignorance with the stupid shit he says: *Sex is all about male hostility and power? Guys objectify and subjugate girls? Drunk chicks can't consent??* Bullshit.

Sex is rarely about the girl. If ever it's fueled by anger or sadism I'm not cognizant of that now. Sexual conquest is how I exert power—not over girls but over other guys. Women aren't sex objects; they're props that let me *not* feel powerless.

Feminists have no clue about any of that, though. They can't feel what I've been through. How can they demand I empathize with everyone else, while they make no attempt to empathize with me? Is my pain less valid because I have a penis?

* * *

Social hierarchies were born and raised in the high school lunchroom; it was there I first felt like I didn't belong. An awkward tenth grader, I knew better than to try to sit with the popular crowd. I would have settled for any "crowd" at all. But I was a social tumor in those days; my mere presence in a clique's vicinity ate away at its social status.

When all my acquaintances found creative excuses to ditch me, I gave up trying to sit with others. I retreated to the back corner of the cafeteria where I found a table next to a large plant that shielded me partially from the potshots of my peers. I turned up the silence until their insults sounded fuzzy—radio stations with bad reception. But one insult always out-blared the static in my head: "I bet you'll never get a girl." For the rest of tenth grade I ate with my plant, shrinking further inside myself, angry energy gurgling like a dormant volcano.

* * *

Almost overnight I erupted into an adolescent, testosterone frenzy. I hit the weight room instead of the books, made varsity, showed up at keg parties to which I hadn't been invited, and picked fistfights until fighting became my forte. It no longer mattered what I had to sacrifice to be seen as cool.

And today, ten years later, I still carry coolness around with me. Stretch marks curl around biceps that grew too fast. The glass shards in my forearm are easier to live around than to remove. My nose was stitched back together after surgery, but bruised knuckles stand out on permanently disfigured fists. Was my self-doubt ever as transparent as all the scars I got trying to erase it?

* * *

Comfortable in my new skin, I convinced myself my altered shell accurately reflects who I am inside. Females find me more appealing as a hard-ass than they ever did when I was a sensitive wuss. I point and laugh, from a crowded lunch table of beautiful people, at all the freaks and nerds who have no friends.

By high school graduation I'm doing a fairly convincing, if hyper-masculine, rendition of a popular boy. Joining a fraternity becomes the logical next step for the new me upon entering college. My newly recycled persona—narcissistic yet insecure, radiant though terrified of being outshined—meshes well with the fraternity model.

* * *

The hottest girl from last night's mixer departs timidly down our narrow hall, adorned in my sweats and baggy T-shirt, her makeup smeared and fading, my fake number scribbled on her hand. I hear my jealous frat brothers howl at her from the breakfast area. Rolling out of bed, I let the catcalls subside before emerging in my boxers to accept their praise:

"Dude... Van Voorhis! You get more ass than a toilet seat!"
"You're the fuckin' *man*, man!"
"You bang the hottest bitches I know, bro!"

It doesn't matter that I *didn't* bang her. The ecstasy of peer approval feels better and lasts longer than any orgasm ever could. I say nothing, but flash my signature grin—that cocky, asshole smirk it took me years to perfect—then dish up my scrambled eggs and disappear, knowing here is not the place for stimulating conversation.

* * *

This layered account does not hypothesize or force conclusions. Indeed, the issue itself remains very much unresolved, and I believe an autoethnographic project must reflect that. If I gloss over my past by emphasizing my more progressive, contemporary views, I risk insinuating that feminism ultimately had some positive effect on me as an undergrad. In fact, my shift toward a feminist orientation came only after I'd moved out of the frat house; by then it was too late for me to utilize my leadership positions within the fraternity as means to bring about social change.

—Matthew Van Voorhis, graduate student

Sexual Experiences

In the preceding account, the young man receives praise and acceptance for his perceived heterosexual adventures. Gendered messages encourage boys and men to engage in rampant sexual behavior that may be detrimental to their sense of self, physical well-being (e.g., if risky sex leads to sexually transmitted disease), and potentially to their partners' psychological well-being, if sex becomes coercive. As Matt describes, this behavior may come with its own form of pain for men. But how would the story sound if the narrator were a young woman? Despite the "sexual revolution," the meanings attached to men's and women's sexual experiences, especially *young* men's and women's experiences, are still different and often unequal.

Recall from chapter 3 our discussion of the term "slut" as a powerful social control mechanism. Not only are women less free than men to voluntarily choose to have pleasurable sexual experiences, they are also more likely to experience unwanted sexual encounters. While men certainly can be victims of sexual assault (and are probably even less likely than women to report the assault to authorities), women make up more than three-quarters of sexual assault victims. Social norms regarding rape and sexual assault have changed over time. Today sexual assault is seen as a crime and is generally frowned upon by society, but there are still questions as to what constitutes sexual assault. As recently as the early 1990s, there were some states whose laws did not recognize that rape could occur within marriage. Today, even though all states have laws prohibiting marital rape, it is often still difficult to prosecute.

In addition to more often being victims of sexual assault, women may also, at times, voluntarily engage in unwanted sex (Basile 1999; Houts 2005). In Houts's (2005) study of more than 10,000 young women's first voluntary sexual experiences, she found that approximately 28 percent did not really want to have sex and approximately 27 percent were somewhat ambivalent as to whether they really wanted to or not. On a scale of 1 (least wanted) to 10 (very wanted), the most common response was a 5. All this suggests that sometimes when women say "yes" to sex it may be because they acquiesce, more than a specific want or desire to have sex. In a qualitative study of women who had acquiesced to unwanted sex with a long-term male partner, Basile (1999) found several different categories of acquiescence. Some of the women in this study reported that sex was initially unwanted, but that they eventually enjoyed it. Other women claimed that they felt it was their "wifely duty" to have sex with their husbands. Still others reported that it was simply easier to give in to sex than to argue about it. And finally, some of the women acquiesced out of fear of what might happen if they did not. Interestingly, studies of this sort have not explored to what extent men have unwanted sex. It is likely that researchers have been limited by the cultural stereotype that depicts men as always thinking about and always wanting sex.

Even when sex is voluntary and wanted, there remains a certain double standard for men and women in the United States. Laura Carpenter's (2006) study of virginity loss demonstrates some of the different expectations for men and women in relation to sexuality. In interviews with 61 young adults about their understandings of their own virginity, Carpenter shows three interpretive themes: virginity as a special gift, virginity as a stigma, and virginity loss as a step in the process of becoming an adult and learning about sexuality. Heterosexual women were more likely than any other group to interpret their virginity as a gift, something they were saving for someone special, while heterosexual men were more likely than any other group to interpret their virginity as a stigma, or something they experienced as shameful. This re-emphasizes the gendered sexual double standard in U.S. culture, that women are expected to wait to have sex and to have fewer partners than men.[14] Gay men and lesbians were somewhat more likely than heterosexual men and women to interpret virginity as a step in a process, often intertwined with the coming-out process.

Sexual and Reproductive Health and Health Care

Inequalities related to sexual and reproductive health often begin much earlier than first sexual experiences. The average age of menarche, or first menstrual period, is about 12 years old for girls in the United States (Graber and Brooks-Gunn 2002), but may range from 9 to 17 years of age (Anderson and Must 2005). Menstruation has been used to justify the belief that women's bodies are inferior to men's and to keep women from full participation in society. Some cultures have considered menstruation taboo and thus have created laws to physically segregate menstruating women from the rest of the community, or to forbid them from handling food or having sex during menstruation (Delaney, Lupton, and Toth 1988; Golub 1992). Physicians, gym teachers, and popular advice manuals of the early to mid-1900s advised women to forego strenuous exercise or athletic competition during menstruation (Brumberg 1993; Lenskyj 1986; Verbrugge 2000).

When social messages about menstruation are negative, individual women have a difficult time understanding themselves and the female body as anything but negative. Janet Lee (1994) documents some of the ways that individual women experience their first menstrual period. In this study, many women reported feeling "ambivalent about their bodies" and expressing fear, shame, and embarrassment, particularly around boys. In their talk about their first menstrual periods, these women also felt alienated from their bodies, as if something were happening *to* them. In interviews with 26 girls ranging in age from 13 to 18, Laura Fingerson (2006) shows the extensive lengths girls go to in order to conceal menstruation, for example, planning for possible leaks, hiding supplies, and inventing metaphors such as "monthly visitor," "Aunt Flo," "flooding," and "flag day" (referring to the Japanese flag, which has a white background with a red circle). Fingerson (2006) also interviewed 11 boys, ages 14 through 19. Interviews with both boys and girls revealed that often boys have limited knowledge of menstruation, that they find it "gross," that they tell jokes about it, and that they use it to explain any part of girls' behavior that they do not like. One respondent, when asked how he would explain menstruation to a younger boy said, "it's when girls get really mean and they bleed everywhere" (116).

Many girls and even some boys in Fingerson's study seemed aware of the inequality that society creates around the physical experience of menstruation. In the classic essay, "If Men Could Menstruate," Gloria Steinem (1978:110) points out the inequality inherent in the way that menstruation is socially constructed. She writes that if menstruation were part of male body function:

> Men would brag about how long and how much.
>
> Boys would mark the onset of menses, that longed-for proof of manhood, with religious ritual and stag parties.
>
> Congress would fund a National Institute of Dysmenorrhea to help stamp out monthly discomforts.
>
> Sanitary supplies would be federally funded and free. (Of course, some men would still pay for the prestige of commercial brands such as John Wayne Tampons, Muhammad Ali's Rope-a-dope Pads, Joe Namath Jock Shields—"For Those Light Bachelor Days," and Robert "Baretta" Blake Maxi-Pads.)
>
> Military men, right-wing politicians, and religious fundamentalists would cite menstruation ("*men*-struation") as proof that only men could serve in the Army ("you have to give blood to take blood"), occupy political office ("can women be aggressive without that steadfast cycle governed by the planet Mars?"), be priests and ministers ("how could a woman give her blood for our sins?") or rabbis ("without the monthly loss of impurities, women remain unclean").

While Steinem is being satirical here, her point is clear. Menstruation could be constructed differently and in more favorable terms than it is in our culture.

Similarly to menstruation, menopause, or the cessation of menstruation, is also often constructed in a negative way. Some doctors and scientists call it a "deficiency disease" and certainly it is often thought of as a *crisis*, something pathological that must be treated by medicine and science. However, some women resist this definition of menopause and see it as a natural part of women's lives. There has been much debate over the years about the use of hormone replacement therapy (HRT) to "treat" menopausal women. In the 1960s, Robert Wilson wrote a book entitled *Feminine Forever* (1966) in which he argued that HRT would "cure" menopause and that women could maintain their physical and emotional femininity forever (Barbre 2003; Hunter and O'Dea 1997). More recently, in June 2002, the National Institutes of Health canceled a well-regarded research study, part of the Women's Health

Initiative, because the negative effects of HRT seemed to be outweighing the positive effects.

Counter to the medical model of menopause as a deficiency disease, some studies suggest that the majority of women experience few or no negative bodily experiences during menopause (Hunter and O'Dea 1997; Kaufert, Gilbert, and Tate 1992; also see Lorber and Moore 2002). In Hunter and O'Dea's (1997) qualitative study of 45 menopausal women, respondents' accounts defined menopause as *both* disease and deficiency *and* a natural part of life. For some women in this study, menopause was inextricably linked to aging. Because women's aging bodies have been culturally defined as unattractive and asexual, it is hard to decipher whether women actually experience menopause in a negative way or if it is really aging that they experience negatively (because of cultural stereotypes of aging). While menopause receives a great deal of attention from scientists, physicians, psychologists, and the popular press, men's changing hormone levels during the aging process are rarely discussed. Men in their 40s and 50s can experience andropause, which can include a drop in testosterone levels, leading to weight gain, loss of bone density, and fatigue (Fisch 2005; Szymczak and Conrad 2006).

Images of aging and sexuality are also different for men and women. Men (especially with the advent of erectile dysfunction drugs) often continue to be seen as sexual and fertile. Research on women's sex lives during and after menopause tends to focus on the negative bodily experiences: vaginal dryness, declining sexual activity, and decreases in sexual desire and quality of orgasm. One interesting study changed the focus by talking to heterosexual and lesbian women about if and how menopause had changed their sex lives (Winterich 2003). Of the 30 women in this study, many reported satisfying and active sex lives despite menopausal symptoms, often attributing this to good communication with their partners. Problems arose for some women, more so for heterosexual women. Winterich (2003) explains this difference by acknowledging traditional gender socialization in which women in heterosexual relationships may learn to defer to men. The author further points to problems with heterosexual definitions of sex. Sex is often equated with intercourse, which may be painful for women experiencing vaginal dryness, which in turn could lead to decreased desire and then to decreased activity. So, the heterosexual women in this study who reported problems, often spoke of male partners who refused to talk about sex or complained about their own lack of sexual pleasure, seemingly without concern for her sexual pleasure. When lesbians in this study encountered sexual difficulty, they seemed to be able to handle it more effectively, in part due to broader definitions of sex, more flexible sexual practices, and keeping open communication with their partners about sexual preferences.

Prior to menopause, all heterosexually active men and women must make decisions about controlling fertility. Although female and male bodies have different reproductive capacities, gendered messages have a significant impact on the ways we imagine and enact reproduction and sexual health, safety, and responsibility. For example, although it is clearly physiologically the case that two people must contribute equally to conception, culturally we make women much more responsible for the outcome of pregnancy simply because of the reality (at least at this point in history) that female-bodied people gestate developing fetuses. Nonetheless, there is no biological imperative for women to be held almost solely responsible for birth control and for child care after birth. Yet culturally, women are still assumed to be mostly, if not entirely, responsible for birth control and for decisions in the event of a pregnancy, and many insurance plans either do not cover contraception (although many do cover erectile dysfunction drugs) or do not cover a full range of contraceptive options.

People have attempted to control their fertility since prehistoric times. The methods that have been used include the use of herbs to induce abortions, condoms made of linen, douches, breastfeeding, magic, and objects such as lemon halves to cover the cervix. In the United States in the late 1950s, a rising demand for new contraceptive methods led to what some have referred to as the "contraceptive revolution." But this recent history of birth control has been as much about social control of information and legal control of access as it has been about individual ability to control fertility.

The U.S. Food and Drug Administration approved the first contraceptive pill in 1960. Nonetheless, the side effects of using this drug were not initially fully disclosed to the public. By 1962 there had been over 100 cases of circulatory disorders (blood clotting) associated with early versions of the pill, resulting in 11 deaths. In the 1970s U.S. feminists began to expose how little information was available to the public concerning the risks associated with the pill. They were eventually successful in forcing the Food and Drug Administration to list possible adverse effects in a direct patient package insert (Tone 1997, 2001) so that patients might work with their doctors to fully understand and deal with unwanted effects of the drugs. Contraceptive technology has improved immensely in the last 40 years.

Meanwhile, access to the pill was still restricted. While the pill has long been available by prescription, it has not always been available upon request.[15] It was not until 1965 that the U.S. Supreme Court ruled in *Griswold v. Connecticut*[16] that married couples could legally obtain contraception. These rights were extended to single women in 1972 (*Eisenstadt v. Baird*)[17] and to minors in 1977 (*Carey v. Population Services International*).[18] Hence, throughout the history of the emergence of effective birth control, access to and information about such methods has been an ongoing issue.

Historically contraception has been something that has put female bodies at risk to a much greater degree than male bodies. So, one might ask, why is there no male contraceptive pill? The answer to this question is complex and encompasses science, medical structures, the media, and the social construction of gender. For example, while scientists might easily recruit women for drug trials through gynecologists' offices and family planning clinics, there is no parallel medical structure for recruiting male subjects. Female methods of contraception (the pill, the patch, injections, IUDs) typically have to be administered by a health care provider; however, common male methods of birth control (withdrawal and condoms) have no need for a family planning context. And vasectomies are typically performed by physicians outside the family planning clinic context (Oudshoorn 2003).

Although scientists began to call attention to men's reproductive health in the 1960s, it was not until the late 1980s and 1990s that men became more of a focus in the family planning literature. The women's health movement drew attention to male responsibility, gender equity, and power relations in the family. Despite this call for attention to men's reproductive health and responsibility, the organizational structure of family planning clinics has been slow to respond. Waiting rooms, clinic facilities, patient literature, and even intake forms have not included space for men (Lichtenstein 2004; Raine et al. 2003). Making a space for men as clients of family planning has involved shifting definitions of masculinity. Under our culture's traditional conception of masculinity, men are stereotypically seen as wanting more children (proving virility) and thus being opposed to family planning. Therefore, family planning is relegated to the woman's realm. Encouraging men to take responsibility for family planning, a necessary step toward making men family planning clients, involves changing people's minds about the definition of masculinity (Oudshoorn 2003).

To recruit participants for a clinical trial of male hormonal contraception in Edinburgh, Scotland, researchers relied on hegemonic notions of masculinity. Using a poster with the words "First Man on the Pill" and a picture of an astronaut on the moon to recruit participants, researchers drew on notions of traditional masculinity such as bravery, exploration, and so forth. While the scientific community has painted a picture of brave, heroic men exploring the frontier of new contraceptive technology, the media instead focuses on men's inability to take responsibility and on issues of side effects and pain, portraying men as victims. Again these portrayals rely on stereotypical images of men as irresponsible and uninterested in contraception, but they also rely on less stereotypical images of men as oversensitive and weak (Oudshoorn 2003).

Although women have been held primarily responsible for birth control, childbearing, and child rearing, control of women's fertility has not always been up to women. Abortion became illegal in the United States in the mid-1800s. Even after it became illegal, women continued to seek out abortion providers and to attempt to self-induce abortions. Underground networks developed in an effort to provide women with information about where and how to terminate a pregnancy. In concert with the women's health movement of the 1960s, clinics such as JANE in Chicago provided women with safe, illegal abortions. Some states began to legalize abortion, but that did not help women who lived in states where abortion was illegal and who could not afford to travel to obtain a safe, legal abortion. In 1973, the Supreme Court decided the landmark *Roe v. Wade*[19] case, supporting a woman's right to privacy. Abortion was legalized. In the 30 years since *Roe v. Wade*, those opposed to abortion and those in support of a woman's right to choose have battled over this issue. The body has figured prominently, particularly in the pro-choice movement's slogans, for example, "get your laws off my body" and "my body, my choice."

Although the right to choose remains a legal right, many restrictions have been placed on women's access to abortion. Low-income women are especially affected by these restrictions, in part because federal funds cannot be used for abortions. But low-income women are also disproportionately affected by mandatory delays, which require that a woman seeking an abortion wait 24 hours after being counseled before obtaining an abortion. This forces two visits to a clinic, which again disproportionately affects low-income women, who may not be able to afford to take the time off work or to afford child care or transportation to the clinic.

Young women's access to abortion has also been restricted. As of 2006, 34 states required parental notification or consent for women under 18 seeking an abortion (Guttmacher Institute 2006). It is often the case that young women who are unable or unwilling to obtain their parents' consent have the option of going before a judge, who retains the power to decide whether the young woman may or may not have an abortion. The unanticipated consequences of these laws have included young women seeking illegal abortions. In 1988, Becky Bell, a teenager from Indiana, died from an infection after receiving an illegal abortion because she did not want to involve her parents. Most minors do involve one or both parents in abortion decisions (Henshaw and Kost 1992), and those who do not involve parents typically have a valid reason, such as fear of violence.

Historically, while a predominantly white, middle-class reproductive rights movement was focusing on maintaining a right to choose *not* to have a child, women of color and women with disabilities argued that true reproductive freedom also includes the right to choose *to* have children. African American, Latin, and Native American women in the United States have endured involuntary sterilization and other disincentives to reproduction (Davis 1981; Lopez 1997; Nelson 2003; Roberts 1997). Sterilization has been coercively linked to receiving government benefits. On other occasions, doctors have performed hysterectomies on minority and low-income women without obtaining their consent. Today, involuntary sterilization has taken on a new guise. Temporary sterilization, in the form of Norplant and Depo Provera, has been pushed on women and teens in low-income, particularly African American neighborhoods (Roberts 1997). These long-lasting contraceptive drugs have been offered in inner-city public schools and some states have attempted to make use of these contraceptive methods as a prerequisite for receiving welfare benefits. Further, women in the criminal justice system have been offered reduced sentences on the condition that they have Norplant implanted or receive regular Depo Provera shots.

Women with disabilities have also argued that the mainstream reproductive rights movement has ignored the needs and rights of women with disabilities. Historically, laws have existed that prohibited people with disabilities from marrying or discouraged them from reproducing. In addition, there is a concern with prenatal diagnosis to determine whether a fetus is "defective" or "disabled." Often women in these situations are counseled to terminate the pregnancy. The disabilities rights movement asks us to think about the social construction of "ability/disability" and what resources are available to help mothers in this situation to care for the children they may choose to have. In other words, what kinds of conditions would need to exist or change for women to be able to "freely choose" whether to continue a pregnancy where disability had been diagnosed? There would need to be affordable and accessible medical care and social support for help with special needs child care (Saxton 1998).

Control of men's reproductive capacities has its own set of issues. Because *Roe v. Wade* is based on the premise of a woman's right to privacy, men do not have a legally binding say in abortion decisions. Some men accept this as reasonable, while others wish they had more of a voice. Some men's rights organizations such as the National Center for Men (http://www .nationalcenterformen.org/) are pushing for more rights in connection with fatherhood. The courts have been pretty clear on this issue, striking down spousal consent laws in *Planned Parenthood v. Danforth* (1976)[20] and spousal notification laws in *Planned Parenthood v. Casey* (1992).[21] Social scientists have paid very little attention to the issue of men and abortion. The only extensive sociological study of men and abortion is the topic of the 1984 book, *Men and Abortion: Lessons, Losses and Love* by Arthur Shostak and Gary McLouth. The authors surveyed 1,000 men who accompanied partners to the clinic to terminate a pregnancy. Eighty-four percent of the men reported that they had reached a mutual agreement with their partner about terminating the pregnancy. Much has changed since 1984, yet very little attention has been paid to men's experiences with abortion.

Similar to research on male contraception, much less has been written about men's reproductive rights than about women's bodies and reproductive rights. However, in the late 1990s and early 2000s, three courts considered the reproductive rights of males within the criminal justice system. While the Supreme Court ruled in 1942 that prisoners have the right not to be sterilized (*Skinner v. Oklahoma*)[22] and in 1987 that they have the right to marry (*Turner v. Safley*),[23] new issues of reproductive rights for prisoners have emerged in recent years. In 1998, Tad Kline was arrested on child abuse charges. The court sentenced Kline to probation and added the condition that he abstain from fathering any children. Kline appealed, arguing that his procreative rights were being violated. The appellate court upheld the lower court's decision, arguing that Kline's potential victims were being protected and that his procreative rights were interfered with to "a permissible degree" (Miles 2002).[24] In 2001, the Wisconsin Supreme Court upheld the sentence of David Oakley, a man sentenced to three years' jail time and five years' probation for failure to pay child-support. The twist in his sentence was that he was ordered by a trial judge not to father any additional children during his probation period (Miles 2002).[25]

While the two cases described above restrict the procreative rights of men on probation within the criminal justice system, a 2002 case, *Gerber v. Hickman*,[26] protected the procreative rights of a man in prison for 55 to 111 years under California's "three-strikes" law. In 1997, William Gerber was sentenced to prison after a drug-induced shooting spree. Although his wife is the one who called the police, she decided that she wanted to have a child with her husband. California penal code does not allow for conjugal visits for inmates serving life sentences, so the Gerbers arranged to conceive through artificial insemination. The prison guard refused to facilitate the transportation of Gerber's sperm and the Gerbers sued. A Ninth Circuit Court of Appeals decided that "the fundamental right to procreate survives incarceration" (Miles 2002).

Reproductive Technologies and Inequality

In previous sections of this chapter we've discussed gender-based inequality and race- and class-based inequality at work. A discussion of reproductive technology continues the story of race and class inequalities and also adds inequalities based on sexuality. Various reproductive technologies, such as alternative insemination and in vitro fertilization (IVF), have given many people who are not able to conceive the "old-fashioned" way new hope.[27] Some segments of society hoped that these new technologies might make room for all kinds of alternative family forms. However, some would argue that in practice, reproductive technologies have been most successfully used to perpetuate the traditional heterosexual nuclear family and are promoted as a means of helping infertile, married, heterosexual couples conceive (Roberts 1997). The high cost of much of this technology keeps it out of reach for low-income individuals and families. Further, although reproductive technologies have allowed many lesbian women as well as heterosexual single women to conceive and build families, many others have been turned away from infertility clinics because they do not fit a heteronormative model (Agigian 2004). For example, in 1998, Melinda Millsaps, a 39-year-old single woman in Florida, was turned away from a university-based infertility clinic. The clinic claimed that its policy of only treating heterosexual couples should not be seen as a moral judgment. One doctor told a reporter, "We treat medical conditions. Biologically, you have to have a heterosexual couple to achieve pregnancy. Not having a male partner is not a medical condition" (Miller 2000:13A).

Journalists have been referencing a "gay baby boom" since the late 1970s. Gay men and lesbians have always been parents. In the past, children were products of previous heterosexual partnerships. Today, various technologies exist that allow for same-sex couples to create biological children of their own, separate from the act of sexual intercourse. For lesbians, one of the most popular methods is artificial insemination. Obtaining sperm for insemination can be a tricky procedure. Frozen sperm, purchased from a sperm bank, may be the safest and most efficient option. However, some sperm banks or clinics that contract with sperm banks refuse to inseminate lesbians and single, heterosexual women. Further, the cost of purchasing sperm may be prohibitive for some women. Lesbians may also seek donations of sperm from a known donor, in which case the sperm would not need to be frozen. Because of concerns about protecting donor identity and facing obstacles in obtaining frozen sperm, lesbian networks have emerged in which a third party arranges the donor and delivers the sperm so that donor and recipient do not need to be known to each other (Harrison 1995).

While alternative insemination has allowed some single women and lesbians to create families, an option for gay men and infertile heterosexual couples (and possibly single, heterosexual men) to create families has been surrogacy. Issues of inequality that surround surrogacy include negotiating the rights of surrogate mothers versus rights of contracting parents. Traditional modes of surrogacy involve using the sperm of a contracting father to impregnate a surrogate mother. Newer forms of surrogacy make use of more advanced technology to produce an embryo using a contracting mother's egg (or a donor egg) and a contracting father's sperm (or donor sperm) and then implanting the resulting embryo in the surrogate mother's uterus. Some feminists have framed surrogacy as the exploitation of low-income women's bodies (Blakely 1983; Oliver 1989; Singer 1993). How can one put a price on being pregnant 24 hours per day for 9 months? And what about the bonds that may be formed between a surrogate mother and the child to whom she gives birth? Other feminists have written about the agency that surrogates possess—particularly, that surrogates freely choose to contract their services. In one study of surrogate mothers, many enthusiastically saw themselves as a "host" body, an incubator, or used other metaphors of themselves as containers or receptacles for the children they carried (Roberts 1998).

Sports

The gendered messages throughout the practice of sport in our everyday worlds that we described in previous chapters result in considerable inequality between women and men. The consequences of the gender feed-back loop are particularly apparent in sporting opportunities, fanship, funding, and especially professional opportunities.

Title IX and Sporting Opportunities

Prior to 1972, it was quite common practice to treat women's and men's sports differentially. Indeed, it was the norm for women's sports to be completely unrecognized as sport or to be treated as quaint sideshows to men's "real" events. Cashmore (2005) gives the example that when Billie Jean King won her first Wimbledon title in 1966, her prize money was a £45 (about US$30) gift certificate to Harrods department store. In addition, very few sporting opportunities existed for women in earlier eras.

The passing of Title IX of the Education Amendments in 1972 changed much of that landscape in the United States in terms of women's access to amateur sport, which has likely had reverberations around the globe in terms of quality of play, competitiveness, and the quantity of available women's sport. Title IX is a federal law prohibiting sex discrimination in public education programs that receive federal funds, including the funding of and participation in sports. School sports in the early 1970s were very clearly out of compliance with the concept of sex equity. According to the Women's Sports Foundation, "In 1971, 1 in 27 high school girls participated in high school sports. Today, that figure is 1 in 2.5, an 800% increase from 1971. For boys, the figure has remained constant at 1 in 2."[28] Compliance with Title IX has greatly improved girls' and women's access to sporting opportunities, including making sports scholarships available to many women. Yet, 30 years after its passage, Title IX has yet to achieve the goal of equality, primarily because there is no system in place to enforce compliance (although there are instances of certain states attempting to enact such programs [Fish 1999]). Instead, individuals must bring a complaint with supporting evidence to the Office of Civil Rights of the Department of Education. Compliance with Title IX is assessed in response to lawsuits and is pursued by most institutions in order to avoid such lawsuits. Countless lawsuits have been filed on the premise of noncompliance with Title IX, yet Title IX remains a contested legal initiative and changes in political attitudes and political administrations foster arguments for weakening its impact.[29]

Currently many more girls have sports opportunities in high schools and colleges, but there are still subtle differences that have a large impact on individual experience and achievement. A significant number of Title IX lawsuits at the high school level have alleged inequality in facilities like ball fields (e.g., girls' fields needing lights, girls having to change in a tin shed rather than a locker room, girls having to use city fields that are not reserved for them instead of the high school's field), poor access to shared resources (e.g., inaccessibility of shared fields, receiving the worst training times, inequitable access to equivalent training staff and weight rooms), and that money that is given by the public for even distribution is often allocated to one specific sport (Pennington 2004a).

Still, athletic opportunities for women have increased dramatically since the inception of Title IX. Carpenter and Acosta (2006) have undertaken perhaps the most comprehensive review of the effects of Title IX on women's collegiate sports with a 29-year-long (and ongoing) study. They report "the highest ever participation by female athletes," with an average of 8.45 teams per school in 2006 as opposed to a little over two teams per school in 1972 (2). The level of women's sports participation has increased exponentially. High school girls' participation increased from 300,000 in 1972 to 2.78 million in 2001. For college students the difference is even more striking. While men's participation in college sports increased from 170,384 in 1972 to 208,866 in 2001, women's participation in college sports increased from 31,852 in 1972 to 150,916 in 2001.[30]

Women's Progress in Athletic Performance

Perhaps more importantly, it is significant to note how our changing attitudes toward greater sporting opportunities for women have already greatly changed minds *and bodies.* As the messages about women have changed to recognize the importance of physicality for all bodies and women have come to be seen as participants, not just audience members, women's athletic performances have increased and improved.

Studying women's and men's marathon records, Cashmore (2005) makes a compelling case that women's access to sports has made the greatest impact on women's actual bodies and performances. In comparing women's and men's marathon records from 1925 to 2004, Cashmore notes, "Women are nearly 92.25 percent as fast as men over the distance today, compared to 1925 when they were only 67.6 percent as fast as men"(153). From the 1920s to the late 1960s, women's marathon times were largely not recorded and many events specifically excluded women. (Marathon was not available as an Olympic event for women until 1984.) In 1925, the men's record was 2 hours 29 minutes, whereas the women's was 3 hours 40 minutes. In 2004, after over 20 years of competitive marathon events for women, the women's records are at about 2 hours 15 minutes and men's about 2 hours 4 minutes. Not only has the gap between women's and men's record times decreased considerably, but women's times today are better than the men's times of 1925. Cashmore goes on to speculate that the gap between women's and men's times would narrow further if women and men competed against each other in the same events. We discuss this possibility further in the chapter conclusion.

Another example comes from Alaska in the form of the Iditarod, an endurance dogsled race over a 1,150-mile course from Anchorage to Nome.

Taking anywhere from 10 to 17 days to complete, the race is a test of endurance of "musher" and dog team through dangerous and frigid terrain. The race has been run every year from 1973 to the present and was first won by a woman, Libby Riddles, in 1985. Winning four of the next five annual races, Susan Butcher dominated the field and the race became known for the impact women could have in the sport.[31] If you are thinking, "Sure she won, but the dogs are doing all the work," consider how that might sound to the men who finished behind her.

Women have achieved a number of other firsts when competing with and against men. In 1977, Janet Guthrie was the first woman to compete in the Indy 500 and Shirley Muldowney became the first woman to win a National Hot Rod Association Top Fuel Championship. She also won in 1980 and 1982, to make her the first person, woman or man, to win three championships. Nancy Lieberman became the first woman to play in a men's professional basketball game in 1986 and Ila Borders became the first woman to pitch a winning men's (minor league) professional baseball game in 1998, in which she pitched a shutout for the first six innings. Julie Krone was the first to win a Triple Crown horse race in 1993. In 2002, Katie Hnida was the first to play Division I football as a kicker for the University of Colorado, and Hayley Wickenheiser was the first to score a goal in a men's professional hockey game in 2003 (Lowitt 2003). In 2005, at the Indianapolis 500, Danica Patrick nearly won, leading the field for 19 laps, running low on fuel in the last seven, and ultimately finishing fourth—4.5515 seconds behind the leader. She also won rookie of the year in 2005 for being the highest-ranking rookie in the points standings at 12th overall.[32] In 2006, Kelly Kulick became the first woman to qualify to compete in the full season of the (men's) Professional Bowlers Association (PBA) tour.[33] Also in 2006, Michaela Hutchison became the first female wrestler in the United States to beat a male wrestler for a high school state title ("Short Takes" 2006).

In terms of actual differences in male and female body development, looking at male and female performance in the 100-meter sprint provides some interesting insights. In absolute measurements, it appears elite men are faster than elite women. But this fails to take height into account. Height (length of stride) is an advantage in sprinting. If sprinters were classed by height in the way boxers are classed by weight, we might get a more complete picture of women's achievements. Hudson (as cited in Dowling 2000) provides a different measure that takes height into account. Comparing Carl Lewis to Florence Griffith Joyner, Hudson says:

> A runner of the 100-meter dash, Lewis, who stood 6 feet 2 inches tall and held the men's world record of 9.92 seconds, had a relative velocity of 5.36 heights per second. But was he faster than Flo-Jo at 100 meters? You probably have guessed the biomechanical answer. Joyner, who was 5 feet 6½ inches tall, ran

the 100-meter dash in 10.49 seconds and thus had a relative velocity of 5.64 heights per second. "In other words," says Hudson exultantly, "the fastest woman is 5.3 percent faster than the fastest man!"(205)

Readers might point out, "but Carl Lewis still runs a shorter time." True. But it is also likely that if Mike Tyson and Sugar Ray Leonard, both boxing icons, were pitted against each other when both were in peak condition, Tyson would likely have knocked Leonard out with little difficulty because Tyson's sheer size gives him an ultimate advantage. Does that mean we should not appreciate the skills of Sugar Ray Leonard? Is Leonard less of an athlete? Perhaps height and weight categories make a great deal of sense.

Further, and most compelling, Hudson (cited in Dowling 2000) notes that, "the difference between elite and ordinary female athletes is greater than the difference between elite and ordinary male athletes" (206). This suggests that "average" men (men at less elite levels of athletic ability) tend to train more seriously than "average" women. Hence, gender performance and accountability to masculine and feminine gender messages has gendered results.

The point to be made here is that women's athletic achievements have increased considerably with athletic opportunities and, of course, with training. The change in gendered messages about what women can do has affected what women's bodies, especially those of elite women athletes, can do. What we have come to believe to be real, that women are very fine athletes, has come to be real. What would happen if we stopped believing that female bodies are innately less able than male bodies? We do not propose to know the answer to this question and we are not suggesting that some differences between femaleness and maleness (including wide ranges of variation within the group we call men and the group we call women) have no effect. What we are suggesting is that, as a society, we simply cannot know what women's bodies can do until we start to first believe in female bodies as capable and send messages of that capability. We have evidence that female bodies tend to sweat more efficiently (Kennedy et al. cited in Dowling 2000), which suggests that female bodies may have an advantage at retaining a cooler body temperature over athletic performance. So, perhaps females have a physiological *advantage* at endurance sports such as 100-mile ultra-marathons and long-distance swimming. In other words, we simply will not know what women's bodies can do until we change the gendered messages, especially the dichotomizing ones, that encourage boys and discourage girls from playing sports.

Remaining Inequalities: Opportunity, Money, and Fanship

So what inequalities remain to keep gendered bodies behaving according to gendered messages? With all the advances made by Title IX, there are still serious differences in sporting opportunities between women and men, in particular, discrepancies between outlets for elite female and male athletes. Ambitious athletes will only take their sport seriously if they have a serious goal—national or international competition at the amateur or professional level. To develop as an elite athlete, one must be able to have an elite goal. The existence of an elite level for any sport changes how all of us (kids, parents, coaches, school systems) orient to the introductory, amateur, and collegiate levels of play. We think differently about the seriousness of say, Little League, if we imagine "little Johnnie might have a shot at the pros," than we might if say, "little Suzie is playing city league softball with her friends." While both activities are perfectly healthy, fun enterprises for kids, we certainly take one more seriously and see it as more deserving of our attention and more important in terms of skills training, than the other.

Clearly, the Olympics stand out as one such elite type of competition where equity of opportunity is meaningful. Women have always had fewer sporting opportunities at the Olympics than men (that is, men have more events in which to compete) and this is still true as of this writing.[34] The modern Olympic Games, like their ancient predecessor, were originally envisioned as a male-only event. Pierre de Coubertin, an original organizer, argued the Olympics should "exult male athleticism . . . with female applause as reward" (Cashmore 2005:147, citing Snyder and Spreitzer 1983). In 1896, when the modern Olympic Games began, no women participated. Four events (tennis, croquet, golf, and yachting) were opened to women in 1900 but by 1921 still only 4 percent of competitors were women. By the 2000 Summer Games in Sydney, that percentage increased to 38 percent, with some countries entering teams with more than 55 percent women. However, other countries still maintained entirely male teams (Seager 2003).

While the inequity of number of available events has diminished considerably in the past few decades, many women's competitions have been added only very recently. Some examples of this include women's ice hockey (debuted in Nagano 1998), women's water polo (began in Sydney 2000), women's soccer (began in Atlanta 1996 to a record fan attendance of 76,000), women's weightlifting (began in Sydney 2000), women's pole vault and hammer throw (began in Sydney 2000), and women's freestyle wrestling (began in Athens 2004, although women have only four events, whereas the men have seven).

Recall from table 3.1 of the previous chapter that there are several competitions in which women are not allowed to compete at the same lengths as men, thereby hampering the possibility that women will be seen as competitive with men. However, most egregious are those sports in which women have no opportunity to compete at all—and, as of 2005, there were still a number of such events.[35] In the realm of winter sports, the event of ski jumping and Nordic combined (ski jumping and cross-country skiing) has no female equivalent events and bobsled has no "four-man" events available for women athletes (although a "two-man" event is available). In summer sports, there are a number of events that are unavailable to women. Boxing, Greco-Roman wrestling, and all forms of canoeing have no women's events or women's equivalent sports (although there are events for women in kayaking). For cycling, there are a number of women's events, but women do not compete in certain styles of cycling called Keirin, Madison, Olympic sprint, points race, and team pursuit (4,000 meters). Similarly, there are a number of women's and men's rowing events, including singles, doubles, and "eights" (eight-person events) but only men row in "fours without coxswain" (in which each rower has one oar and the boat has no one dedicated only to steering), even though women row in "quadruple sculls" (in which each rower has two oars and the boat has no one dedicated only to steering). "Athletics" (track and field) has its own men-only events: 3,000-meter steeplechase and 50-kilometer race walk.

What about the women-only events, you might ask? By our count, there are only two—rhythmic gymnastics and synchronized swimming. Note that both of these sports are very femininized in terms of sport typing. Would men choose to participate in such sports, or do the rigors of masculinity discourage such participation? (Actually, one man has participated. Bill May is famed throughout synchronized swimming for his successes in national and international competitions and because he is known as the only elite male synchronized swimmer. We discuss May further in chapter 5.)

What about college participation? The average undergraduate enrollment for colleges and universities overall in the United States is 53.4 percent women and 46.6 percent men (with a slightly higher percentage of women at Division III schools and slightly lower percentage of women at Division I schools).[36] However, the average number of female athletes at an institution is 210.0 (44.1%), whereas the average number of male athletes is 266.1 (55.9%). Over the last few years, this represents an increase in women's college enrollment but not a significant increase in women's athletic participation.[37]

What kinds of sports are college students playing? There are 24 major sports reported on in the National Collegiate Athletic Association (NCAA) survey, although not all 24 sports are open to women or to men. The most common sports teams for women (most schools reporting this kind of team) are, in descending order, basketball, cross-country, tennis, volleyball, track and field (indoor and outdoor combined), soccer, and softball. The most common for men are, in descending order, basketball, cross-country, golf, baseball, tennis, track and field (indoor and outdoor combined), and football. There are three sports for which no school had a female equivalent—football, baseball, and wrestling—and three sports for which no school had a male equivalent—softball, field hockey, and synchronized swimming (NCAA 2004:14). Nonetheless, it appears women have made great inroads into collegiate athletics in terms of participation relative to the pre–Title IX era.

While "women" in a generic sense have been helped by Title IX, women of color remain underrepresented in certain college sports while being overrepresented in others. As of 2001, Latin female college athletes at the Division I level were greatly underrepresented at only 3 percent of the female athletes, compared to 10.5 percent of all female college students being Latin/Hispanic (National Center for Education Statistics 2005). Although black female athletes comprise 11 percent of the female population in Division I sports, they are greatly overrepresented in certain sports, making up 35 percent of female basketball players and 25 percent of female track athletes. But black female athletes represent only 3 percent of female participants in all other Division I sports. So while some women of color are accessing certain sports with great success, many women's sports are not yet permeated by racial diversity (Suggs 2001).

A significant measure of parity, though, is not just number of participants but amount of resources (money!!) spent on team expenses and student scholarships. Division I schools are considered to be the highest level of competition in college athletics, so we will look more closely at the averages among Division I (A, AA, and AAA) schools. On average, for Division I schools, an institution spends over $3.4 million (34%) on women's teams and $6.5 million (66%) on men's teams, a wider disparity than one would expect based on participation rates (NCAA 2004:17). This difference is an average *per school*. If multiplied by the 305 Division I schools reporting, that's more than a $945 million difference nationwide, just among Division I schools. What sports comprise the difference? Some women's sports have significantly higher average overall expenses than some men's sports (e.g., gymnastics, rowing, and volleyball). But the most expensive women's team to support, basketball, averages just under $900,000 annual overall expenses per school, whereas three men's sports average considerably higher—ice hockey at $1.0 million, basketball at $1.4 million, and football at a whopping $4.3 million. What kinds of expenditures comprise the difference? Salaries and benefits for coaches and staff are fully double for men's teams; "guarantees and options paid" are over 13 times more for men's teams than women's; and a nondescript "other" category of expenses is three times more for men's than women's teams. So, men's sports are still getting a much greater proportion of the pie.

Another measure of monetary equity (of great importance to the athletes themselves) is scholarships. On average for Division I schools, male student-athletes receive more scholarships than women (91.4 athletes per school to 72.1), make up a greater number of students receiving any kind of athletic aid (145.5 male athletes to 116.7 female athletes), and receive a higher total dollar expenditure on scholarships and aid than women ($1.7 million to $1.38 million). The greatest disparity is between sports where there is no gender equivalent team. Scholarships for men's sports where there are no women's alternatives (football = $1,186,000 per school and wrestling = $132,550) total $1,318,500 (NCAA 2004:19). Scholarships for women's sports where there are no men's alternatives (field hockey = $198,100 and synchronized swimming = $109,000) total $307,100. (Scholarships for baseball and softball are nearly equivalent.) Hence, the significant difference is over a million dollar average *per school*, mostly attributable to football![38]

With all the hoopla over gender parity in sports over the last 30 years, football remains the symbolic and real absence of women's participation in sport. Supporting a football team costs far more than supporting any other sports team. Because of the size of the team required for football, it offers more opportunities to play and to get scholarships and aid for athletes. It pays, by far, the highest amounts for head coaches' salaries, among other costs (NCAA 2004:20). Perhaps you are thinking that we, the authors, must hate football. Not true! Having attended large state universities ourselves, we all count ourselves as fans. We think it is more relevant to ask: With all the interest in gender parity over the last 30 years, why don't girls and women play football (even if on a "women's" team)?

Nationwide, there are very few opportunities for girls and women to seriously play football. College intramural sports commonly include women's and co-ed flag football tournaments, and some high schools have a tradition of hosting one women's "powder-puff" football game each year (essentially as a parody of gender in which boys dress up as cheerleaders and make fun of the female football players). But there exists no serious, systematic organization through which girls and women can learn and play tackle football (the standard for boys and men) throughout the United States.[39] The question is: Why teach a sport so systematically to boys and not to girls?

This, we believe, is the significant symbolic inequality remaining around sports in terms of gendered messages. This lack of systemwide opportunity for girls to play football is the crux of the lingering gender box structure. Usually when boys begin playing football, girls are funneled toward cheerleading. Not only does this fully shore up the gender box structure with all its overt and covert gendered messages, but it creates fewer real opportunities for girls and women. Most cheerleading teams (on which men can compete) are smaller than football teams, hence, allowing fewer opportunities to participate. While cheerleaders are present at football games, the focus of each Friday night high school event, Saturday college event, and Sunday professional event (all weekend long!) is on football as the central festivity, to which the cheerleaders are window dressing. Although there are opportunities to participate in cheerleading for pay—as a coach, an employee of one of the many organizations that offer summer camps and competitions for cheerleading teams,[40] or as a cheerleader (or dancer) for professional sports teams[41]—the pay is very minimal. The difference between football and cheerleading is real and complete.[42] "But football draws in more money than other sports too," you may be saying. Hold that thought. We will return to it in a moment.

There are fewer professional opportunities in sports in the United States for women than men, and those generally pay much less than male equivalents. However, professional sports opportunities do exist for women in the United States.[43] Women have made a rather lucrative living at golf and tennis for at least three decades. However, "Ladies Professional Golf Association (LPGA) 1998 Player of the Year Annika Sorenstam won four tournaments and a then-record $1,092,748 in 1998. If she had been on the men's PGA tour, that would have put her in 24th place for earnings" (Gettings 2000–2007). The highest-ranked tennis players similarly make in the millions, and some tournaments, such as the U.S. Open and the Australian Open offer equal prize money for women's and men's events, yet Wimbledon did not offer equivalent prize money until 2007 ("Pay Inequity in Athletics" 2001–2007; "Wimbledon to Offer Equal Prize Money" 2006). In terms of team sports, one professional success story for women's sports has been the Women's National Basketball Association (WNBA). However, salaries still remain significantly lower than professional men's salaries. In 2004, the minimum salary for a WNBA player with zero to three years' experience was $30,600 ("WNBA Salaries" 2005). The minimum salary for an NBA player with zero years' experience in 2003–2004 was $366,931. In the same year, the minimum salary for an NBA player with three years' experience was $638,679 ("NBA Minimum Salary" 2005). Unlike women's basketball, women's professional soccer has had difficulty remaining solvent. Although the 1996 Atlanta Olympics featured the U.S. women winning gold in soccer, and the wildly popular 1999 Women's World Cup broke attendance records in the United States for women's sports with more than 90,000 in the stands (Starr and Brant 1999), the Women's United Soccer Association (WUSA) that was established in 2001 was unable to remain financially solvent and closed operations on September 15, 2003.[44] Nonetheless, the U.S. women's national soccer team has been wildly successful and wildly popular, but not well paid. The Women's Sports Foundation reports that, "For finishing in third place in the 2003 Women's World Cup, each U.S. women's national soccer team member was awarded $25,000. They would have received $58,000 if they had won the Cup. For reaching the quarterfinal of the World Cup in 2002, the U.S. men's national soccer team received $200,000 each" ("Pay Inequity in Athletics" 2001–2007).

Beyond elite forums for competition, coaching and administrative positions provide a major professional route for former players to organize a career. If accountability to bodies affects women at work, this is even more the case for women who work in sports. In 1972, when Title IX was enacted, more than 90 percent of women's teams were coached by women. Hence, although there were relatively few sporting opportunities, the women's teams that did exist offered employment opportunities for female coaches. As of

2006, only 42.4 percent of the coaches of intercollegiate women's teams are women. So, while women's sport is taken more seriously, coaching jobs of women's teams have become more competitive for women and men (Carpenter and Acosta 2006). Perhaps this is good news for women athletes—that coaching women's teams is understood as a competitive, serious career path. But the news is not as good for women seeking such positions. Of the new coaching jobs available between 2004 and 2006 (Carpenter and Acosta 2006), more men than women filled them.[45] Further, only 2 percent of head coaches of men's teams are women, a figure that has not changed since the passage of Title IX (Carpenter and Acosta 2006). And, while coaching positions for women's teams are now taken more seriously than in previous decades, these coaches are still paid far less than those for men's teams. Average annual head coaches' (whether male or female) salaries for all Division I men's teams in the NCAA stand at an impressive $660,500. The average salary for coaches of women's teams falls far below, at $410,200, a difference of $250,300 per school (or an over $76-million difference nationwide for all Division I schools reporting) (NCAA 2004:20). That is, head coaches for women's teams in Division I schools average 62 percent of the salaries of head coaches for men's teams.

If you argued earlier that football brings in more revenue than women's sports, now is your time for vengeance. You are right. Football for Division I schools averages more than $5.2 million in annual revenues per school, whereas all women's sports average just over $1.5 million in revenue per school (NCAA 2004:22). This brings us to our next issue. *Men's sports and sporting experiences are far more celebrated than women's.* We have regularly heard students argue, "Men's sports are more fun to watch. I just like watching them more." We ask: At what level? Is Little League more interesting than women's professional sports? Is little Johnnie playing Japan in the Little League World Series more exciting than Mia Hamm and company playing China for the Women's World Cup? If so, why? What causes us to choose what we watch? Is this really about celebrating the best physical accomplishment? Or is it about the gendered messages we receive regarding what is important to celebrate?

The celebration of sport (fan attendance, media reporting, remuneration of professional athletes, and so forth) is specifically gendered such that male athletics are culturally supported more than female athletics *at every level.* Indeed, in those few instances where women's sports are understood as superseding men's sports (perhaps gymnastics or figure skating) it is only so because those sports are structured as gender appropriate for women (feminine) and therefore questionable activities for (heterosexual) men. Indeed, sport celebration has everything to do with the gender box structure. Consistent with the gender box structure, it is not surprising that football is heralded as *the* sport deserving of celebration (Kidd 1990; Sabo and Panepinto 1990).

Indeed, Superbowl Sunday may be the largest nonreligious holiday of the year in the United States. In 2006, the Superbowl, which is not an international competition, although it is billed as a world championship, had coverage on three channels. ESPN dedicated six hours (11 a.m. to 5 p.m.) to pregame commentary with four of the game's hosts. ESPN2 played at least 13 hours (5 a.m. to 6 p.m.) of half-hour "classic" shows revisiting past games, one year at a time. Neither of these channels showed the actual game. The game aired on ABC after four hours (2:30 p.m. to 6:30 p.m.) of pregame commentary and celebration ending in a performance by Stevie Wonder. Finally, the game began and lasted another three-and-a-half hours, interrupted for about 45 minutes by a half-time show featuring the Rolling Stones. Postgame commentary lasted about another half hour. Whew. Clearly the fanfare far exceeds the game itself and, although only 22 people will be on the field at any one time to play the game, viewership polls showed the expected television audience to be between 80 and 100 million fans. Hence, we argue that fanship (and vicarious masculinity) has far greater gendered implications than actual play. The real inequalities of fanship are staggering.

Based in southern California, Carlisle Duncan, Messner, Willms, and Wilson (2005) recently completed a 15-year study of gender bias in national and local sports broadcasting by reviewing programming on three major networks (ABC, NBC, and CBS) and two major sports cable shows (ESPN's *SportsCenter* and Fox's local *Southern California Sports Report*). The results were staggeringly in favor of men's sports, with 91.4 percent of airtime on average dedicated to men's sports, only 6.3 percent to women's sports, and 2.4 percent to neutral topics. This represents a *decline* in coverage for women's sports from a high of 8.7 percent in 1999. The coverage of women's sports was worst for Fox (3.0%) and *SportsCenter* (2.1%). Additionally, lead stories were almost completely dominated by men's sports. On average, more than half of all broadcasts covered no women's sports. Tellingly, one little spike on programming on women during the analysis period was due to coverage of the 2004 Olympic Games. Further, women sports anchors were nearly nonexistent, with 94.4 percent of anchors being men. Not a single woman of color appeared as a news anchor during the period studied.

The evidence of the importance of men's sports is also measured in various subtle ways. The resources expended on men's sports as significant allows for much better coverage that encourages more fan excitement. For example, Carlisle Duncan et al. (1994) cite in the 1990 version of the same report that a free throw in a men's televised event will often use up to seven camera angles, whereas a women's game will have only two cameras dedicated to the entire event. Changing angles, close-up shots, slow-motion replays, calculation of statistics, and emotional reactions by other viewers are all filmic techniques to suggest to a viewer the emotionality of the event. In short, less money spent on the event translates into a less-exciting show.

Additionally, Carlisle Duncan et al. (1994) outline the gendered messages used by sportscasters such as calling women by their first names or referring to them as "girls," whereas men are called by their last names or the more adult terms "men" or "young men." (Think this is no big deal? Imagine anchors referring to adult male African American athletes as "boys.") Strong characteristics ("confident," "powerful," "gutsy") were regularly attributed to male athletes, whereas characteristics associated with weakness ("frustrated," "jittery," "mental mistake") more commonly were attributed to women.

Further, when women's actual accomplishments do get press coverage, it is often accompanied by sexualization of the athletes. In the newer sports show format, like *SportsCenter*, sportscasters become loud-talking personalities who use humor to spice up the broadcast. Often women athletes then become the targets of these sportscasters' humor such that their athletic accomplishments receive coverage but rarely without sexualization of the athletes as well. According to Carlisle Duncan, Messner, Willms, and Wilson (2005), in their previous report, Anna Kournikova, who rather famously has capitalized on her sexy image without winning any major tournaments, had been the target of many sexualized jokes. Maria Sharapova had become the new target in 2004 broadcasts. They report that Sharapova had won Wimbledon that year and was deserving of coverage, but rarely received it without also receiving some form of sexualized commentary.

Worse, many women's athletic feats are ignored altogether (Bryson 1987, 1990). What women do accomplish is often not understood as sport. For example, Bryson reports that women regularly beat men at endurance events such as ultramarathons and long-distance swimming. Indeed, most world records for swimming from one continent to another are held by women. Yet, this is largely ignored by the sports press as simply not sports. For example, only one person in recorded history has finished the 90-mile swim from Cuba to the United States (the Florida Keys). Do you know her name? Why not? Her name is Suzie Maroney. She finished the swim in 1997 at the age of 22. It was largely reported as a "human-interest" story in the media, not a sporting accomplishment. In 1998, she became the first person to swim from Mexico to Cuba (122 miles from Isla Mujeres near Cancun to Las Tumbas, Cuba). Many news sources reported her (in the "foreign desk" section) as the "first woman" to swim the distance (*Times* Wire Reports 1998), which while technically correct implies incorrectly that there had been men who previously did the same. Similarly, 36-year-old Tori Murden got little fanfare for being the first American to row a boat 3,000-plus miles across the Atlantic Ocean in 1999, although the *Tampa Tribune* did report her as the "first American—and first woman—to row across the Atlantic alone" (Faul 1999). Rowing as much as 95 miles in one day, her feat was billed more as a human-interest story than an athletic feat. More recently, Ellen MacArthur became a household icon in England but gained very little press in the United States for becoming the reigning record holder for solo circumnavigation of the globe in a 75-foot trimaran sailboat, beating the previous record by an entire day (at 71 days, 14 hours, 18 minutes, 33 seconds). The *St. Petersburg Times* afforded this feat a three-inch-by-three-inch picture and a one-paragraph article with no byline on the second page of the sports section with the headline, "Smell of Land Greets Sailor after Trip around World" (AP Wire 2005). One has to read into the article to know exactly what she did. *Sailing* magazine seemed to think her chances of setting the record slim when they reported in 2004 about her then upcoming trip with the headline, "A Big Boat for a Small Skipper" (Todd 2004).

The Results of Inequality outside Sport: Violence and Sexual Harassment

"Well, so what?" you may be asking. Why does this inequality in sport really matter? Are there effects from sports' inequality on life outside sport? One serious and real effect may be men learning violent or demeaning ideas about women that affect women's relationships with men. Men's sport and the masculinity it teaches has a propensity to aggrandize violence (Messner 1992; Sabo and Panepinto 1990; Schacht 1996). Because masculinity tends to involve notions of aggression, dominance, and control (recall hegemonic masculinity from chapter 2 and marketplace masculinity from chapter 3), tests of masculinity through sport often involve men exacting violence against each other as part of play, especially in certain sports like football (Messner 1992; Sabo and Panepinto 1990). Recall also that iconic masculinity involves hyper-(hetero)sexuality in men. As such, Messner (1992) argues that part of the masculine culture of sport includes learning to control women as sexual conquests. Male athletes can gain stature if presumed to be enjoying many sexual conquests. Similarly, in a study of the culture of men's rugby, Schacht (1996) demonstrates how rugby songs and the names of particular plays within the game aggrandize raping (presumably jokingly?) other men's girlfriends and mothers.

One of the first effects of these gendered messages may be on women athletes. Heywood (1999) cites cases of female athletes being sexually harassed by coaches and male athletes. Other findings suggest that male athletes may engage in partner violence at many levels. Crossett et al. (1996) report statistically significant findings that male student-athletes are overrepresented in reported cases of battering and sexual assault of women on campus in Division I schools. Similarly, Welch (1997) finds evidence to suggest that National Football League (NFL) players in prestigious roles as scorers (e.g., running backs, receivers) are overrepresented in domestic violence and sexual assaults committed against women.

But violence extends beyond male athletes who learn it on the field. Perhaps even more pervasive is the potential effect of vicarious masculinity on violence against women. White, Katz, and Scarborough (1992) show how admissions to emergency rooms in the Washington, D.C., area (where their study was conducted) are related to outcomes for Washington Redskins' football games. They write, "controlling for days of the week, months, years and special holidays for 1988-89, the results indicate that the frequency of admissions of women victims of gun shots, stabbings, assaults, falls, lacerations and being struck by objects increases *when the team wins*" (157, emphasis added). Hence, they theorize that the vicarious masculinity of fanship, in some cases, may lead to emboldened egos and intimate violence.

Are women the only victims of men's sports violence? Certainly not. Messner (1992) argues that, in learning "body as weapon," male athletes are also often hurt by the gendered messages in sport. He argues that boxers and participants in violent team sports often suffer "very high incidence of permanent injuries, disabilities, alcoholism, drug abuse, obesity and heart problems" (71). They may be encouraged to "play hurt," causing damage with long-term effects. Working-class men and men of color may be especially susceptible to this kind of physical damage because they perceive fewer options for success outside sport. Sabo and Panepinto (1990) offer a similar argument and suggest male sport ritual teaches conformity, social isolation, and aggrandizes inflicting pain, all of which they argue is damaging to players' psyches.

A newer trend is toward male athletes developing eating disorders. In particular, sports that encourage "making weight" (i.e., fitting into particular weight classes in order to compete), such as wrestling and boxing, may be at risk for teaching disordered eating. A brief discussion emerged during the 2000 Winter Olympics with regard to men's ski jumping. With athletes making statements that "Fat don't fly," sportscasters commented that eating disorders may be on the climb for competitive ski jumpers.

Psychological and Psychosocial Effects of Inequalities on Girls and Women

Although sports are not a cure-all for self-esteem or eating disorders in every case (as we discussed in chapter 3), access to sports in general seems to have many positive effects for women and for men. Many women athletes do report positive effects on their feelings about their bodies in terms of fitness (Blinde, Taub and Han 1993; George 2005). Additionally, there is evidence that sports foster "such contributors to self-esteem as physical competence, a favorable body image, and more flexible attitudes about what it means to be female" (Richman and Shaffer 2000:198). Some researchers have demonstrated a positive relationship between physical activity and self-esteem (Jaffee and Manzer 1992; Jaffee and Ricker 1993), including some effects across ethnic groups, for example, increased self-esteem among Mexican American and Puerto Rican girls (Erkut and Tracy 2002). In interviews with female college athletes, Blinde, Taub, and Han (1993) demonstrate that female athletes report that "sport participation related to the development of three empowering qualities women traditionally lack: (a) bodily competence, (b) perceptions of a competent self, and (c) a proactive approach to life" (47). So, athletics for women provided experiences that traditional femininity lacked. Also, male college students with physical or sensory disabilities also report feeling empowered by sports access (Blinde and Taub 1999; Taub, Blinde, and Greer 1999).

Additionally, there appear to be other positive sexual health outcomes from sport participation. Those girls involved in high school sports were less likely to have engaged in sexual risk-taking behaviors and more likely to have greater sexual and reproductive health, including being less likely to have been pregnant and less likely to have been treated for an STD (Jacobs Lehman and Silverberg Koerner 2004). As for long-term health benefits, high school sports participation seems to help prevent osteoporosis in women later in life (Teegarden et al. 1996).

CONCLUSION

Our beliefs about bodies do translate into inequalities and, at times, even physical bodily differences across gender. As we noted in the opening to this chapter, Thomas and Thomas's (1928) famous quote, "What one believes to be real is real in its consequences" (572) is as useful today as when they wrote it. What one believes to be true, one will put into action, which essentially makes that belief come into being. Regardless of the basis of one's beliefs, one's actions ultimately end in real consequences for one's self, interactions with others, and notions about and uses of the body. Given that gendered messages define gender as unequal, it is not surprising that we find gendered inequality in the world as a result. In "doing" gender at work, in sports, and even during sexual interactions, the gender we take to be natural actually comes to exist and makes its mark on the physical body and on the selves we develop and display for ourselves and each other.

Perhaps sports provide the clearest example of how bodies may be altered by repetitive performances and surveillance of gender. Our continual segregation of women's and men's sports into fully separate arenas in which women and men are trained differently, play different sports, use separate facilities, and are understood as pursuing different "natural" abilities creates different, and unequal, results for women and men. The practice of sports clearly can have both positive benefits (better health, stronger bodies, greater likelihood of positive self-image) and negative consequences (physical injury, emotional consequences from being labeled a "loser," development of a violent aggressiveness) for any individual, but full gender segregation ensures that the positives and the negatives are disproportionately spread on the basis of presumptions about bodies, rather than on the merit of individual performance. Sports also clearly build (gendered) physical bodies; if one lifts free weights, one builds bulk muscle, whereas if one engages in slimming cardio exercises, one tones a smaller,

more lithe body. And yet, there is no necessary reason for this enforced segregation of sports participation. It is entirely possible that sports might be
organized by body size (height and weight class) rather than presumptions
about sex. Of course this would require a major overhaul of the institution
of sport and the way we engage gendered messages throughout it. We are
not suggesting this happen overnight. A policy of eliminating women's sports
in favor of full and direct competition against men in the short term would
fail to recognize how women's current differential treatment has already
handicapped female athletes (and "average" women in everyday life as
well) from reaching their full potential. Perhaps there is some usefulness
to retaining "women's" leagues for the foreseeable future. But there seems
to be no serious affront to reason by allowing women and men to compete with and against each other where individuals' merits suggest this
makes sense.

This same premise might be applied to work settings and even intimate
relationships. If we as a culture were to avoid presuming strict gendered expectations for each individual (as we have begun to do to some degree), we
might expect to see individuals being placed in jobs based on their actual
skills and potentials, rather than on some presumed natural ability. While
intimate relationships have changed significantly over the last three decades,
female- and male-bodied people are still not understood as equally sexual,
equally involved in reproduction, and equally responsible for all forms of
housework and home maintenance. If we were to imagine a world without
strict gender expectations, that is, if we change the gendered messages, perhaps the inequality that continues to exist would diminish significantly, if
not entirely.

NOTES

1. For statistics on the prevalence of smoking among men and women from different age and race categories, see the Centers for Disease Control and Prevention
website: http://www.cdc.gov/tobacco/.

2. A similar case that invoked the BFOQ and contended that women's sex appeal was necessary for business involved the Hooters restaurant chain. In 1997, a
class-action lawsuit was brought against Hooters by a group of seven men who
claimed that they had endured sexual discrimination when they were denied employment as waiters. The case was settled out of court. Hooters was allowed to continue to hire only women as "Hooters Girls" but they had to pay $3.75 million to
the seven male plaintiffs and other men who could prove they were denied the
serving jobs reserved for women. Hooters executives did not argue that *femininity*
was essential for serving food at their restaurants. Their defense was based on the
claim that their business is *female* sex appeal. They also claimed to employ 3,000
men nationwide in back-of-the restaurant jobs. Part of their settlement was also an
agreement to consider men on an equal basis for more visible jobs (e.g., bar-

tenders, busboys, and managers) other than food servers. They created a new gender-neutral serving position to be called a "Hooters Person" whose duties include assisting Hooters Girls.

3. Christine Craft has written two books about her experiences, *Christine Craft: An Anchorwoman's Story* (1986) and *Too Old, Too Ugly, and Not Deferential to Men* (1991).

4. The National Association to Advance Fat Acceptance (NAAFA) demands the inclusion of height and weight as a protected category in existing local, state, and federal civil rights statutes and the enactment of additional laws as necessary to ensure protection against size discrimination. See their website at http://www.naafa.org.

5. According to the EEOC, the standard overweight person is not considered disabled under the Americans with Disabilities Act (ADA). Only severe obesity (more than 100 percent above the weight guidelines for one's height) qualifies as an impairment. Only disabilities that substantially limit a major life activity (e.g., breathing, learning, interacting with others) are covered under the ADA.

6. *Frank v. United Airlines, Inc.* 216 F.3d 845, 859 (9th Cir. 2000)

7. A similar case involving female flight attendants against Delta Airlines in the 1990s found for the airline.

8. Visit the website of UNITE (the Union of Needletrades, Industrial, and Textile Employees), which has an ongoing campaign to improve work conditions called STOP Sweatshops: http://www.unitehere.org/.

9. Sweatshops with inhumane working conditions continue to exist around the globe. The Clean Clothes Campaign (http://www.cleanclothes.org/), an international organization devoted to improving working conditions in the garment and sportswear industries, publishes a newsletter that reports on various situations around the world. They have reported, for instance, about factories in Indonesia that make apparel for companies such as the Gap, Old Navy, Tommy Hilfiger, Adidas, Nike, Fila, Reebok, and Polo, which deny women workers their constitutional right to two days of "menstrual leave" each month, forcing them to prove they are menstruating before granting the leave. In developing countries where women have little or no access to "sanitary" products or pain-relief medication, menstruation can become a very difficult situation to cope with while working long hours with little or no opportunity to take bathroom breaks. Such conditions violate the United Nation's guidelines for human rights and for the elimination of discrimination against women.

10. See *Oncale v. Sundowner Offshore Services, Inc.* 523 U.S. 75 (1998).

11. Ironically, it was the testimony of University of Oklahoma law professor Anita Hill in the 1991 Senate confirmation hearings for Clarence Thomas's nomination to the Supreme Court that called the nation's attention to this problem. Hill alleged that while she worked at the EEOC when Thomas was head of the organization, he repeatedly engaged in inappropriate discussion of sexual acts and pornographic films after she refused his requests for dates. Thomas's appointment was confirmed in spite of considerable opposition around the country. For an articulate discussion of the broader context of racism and sexism in the Hill-Thomas case, see Jill Niebrugge-Brantley's essay, "A Feminist Writes about the Anita Hill-Clarence Thomas Conflict," which is available online at http://chnm.gmu.edu/courses/122/hill/brantley.htm.

12. Conley describes her experiences and observations in her book, *Walking Out on the Boys* (1998).

13. Colleen Crangle, a medical student at Stanford in the 1990s, won an undisclosed amount of money from the school when she successfully established that the university had retaliated against her for making a sex discrimination charge.

14. Carpenter (2006) noted that feminism, HIV/AIDS activism, and religious conservatism have all influenced young people's ideas about virginity in interesting ways. Among her respondents, there were men who thought of virginity as a gift and planned to wait to share their virginity loss with "someone special." She also talked to women who felt stigmatized by their virginity and sought to change their status by having sex with a friend or casual acquaintance rather than waiting for "someone special."

15. In the late 1990s, emergency contraception (EC) came onto the scene as a way to prevent conception after intercourse. Technically, emergency contraception works either by preventing fertilization or by preventing implantation of a fertilized egg. However, many people, including some consumers of EC (Simonds and Ellertson 2004) often confuse EC with abortion. The confusion stems in part from seeing EC as the same as a medical abortion pill. The abortion pill was developed in France in the 1980s and originally named RU-486. In 2000, RU-486 was approved for use in the United States, where it is referred to as mifepristone. In the early 2000s, a roadblock for women seeking to control reproduction emerged in the form of pharmacists who refuse to fill prescriptions for EC (and in the most extreme cases for any type of contraception). In 2006, the FDA approved the sale of EC without a prescription for women 18 years and older. Women under 18, however, will still be at the mercy of pharmacists. This issue has yet to be adequately addressed in the legal arena, but some states are beginning to create laws that focus on the right of the patient to receive contraception with a legal prescription. Most states, however, have not addressed the issue. The ongoing tension is likely to center around a conscience clause for pharmacists and patients' rights to access legally prescribed medications.

16. 381 U.S. 479 (1965).

17. 405 U.S. 438 (1972).

18. 431 U.S. 678 (1977).

19. 410 U.S. 113 (1973).

20. 428 U.S. 52 (1976).

21. 505 U.S. 833 (1992).

22. 316 U.S. 535, 541 (1942).

23. 482 U.S. 78 (1987).

24. *State v. Kline*, 963 P.2nd 697, 698–99 (Or. Ct. App. 1998).

25. *State v. Oakley*, 629 N.W. 2d 200, 208–09 (Wis. 2001).

26. 291 F.3d 617 (9th Cir. 2002).

27. Other reproductive technologies, such as ultrasound, electronic fetal monitoring, amniocentesis, and fetal surgery have allowed for monitoring of the fetus in utero.

28. From http://www.womenssportsfoundation.org, accessed May 26, 2005. See "Women's Sports & Fitness Facts & Statistics, (updated 6/1/04)" from WSF fact sheet.pdf.

29. Early in 2001, a presidential commission established by George W. Bush revisited Title IX. The commission was arguably in favor of less stringent means of compliance and a public discussion ensued about whether to make changes that might weaken the law (Sanders 2002; Shalala 2002). Recent challenges that may weaken the effects of Title IX include a 2005 proposal by the U.S. Department of Education to gauge compliance with Title IX by administering e-mail surveys (Brennan

2005). Presumably the survey would ask girls about their interest in pursuing sports opportunities other than those currently provided by their schools. (It is unclear if the survey would ask boys if they would like to participate in additional sports such as gymnastics or figure skating.) These surveys would be used to shore up arguments that funds for sports were or were not allocated fairly based on gender. At least one commissioner argued that a similar survey used many years ago in Illinois found little support for adding girls' volleyball. Nonetheless, school officials instituted girls' volleyball programs anyway. Now volleyball is one of the most popular sports for girls in that state. How, they argue, can girls assess what sports they might like to play if they have never had exposure to those sports?

30. From the National Association for Women and Girls in Sport website, http://www.aahperd.org/nagws/template.cfm?template=titleix/facts.html, accessed June 21, 2005. See National Collegiate Athletic Association (2004) for slightly updated statistics.

31. Indeed, only two other people have won the race four times and only one has won it five times, so Susan Butcher stands near the top of the record books in the race. For the 2006 race, 18 of 94 mushers registered were women (from www.iditarod.com, accessed January 24, 2006).

32. From www.indyracing.com, accessed January 27, 2006.

33. Women have only been allowed membership in the PBA since 2004 because the Professional Women's Bowling Association Tour ran out of funds and became defunct (Allushuski 2006).

34. Farhi (2006) argues that the Winter Olympic Games is also exclusionary on the basis of social class. He argues that climate and terrain are not the major indicators of the likelihood that athletes and countries will be represented at the games. Instead, he argues wealth is necessary to train for such sports where, for example, bobsleds cost $35,000 and bobsled runs are even more expensive. Hence, countries like Peru, Chile, Nepal, Morocco, Afghanistan, and Ethiopia that have mountainous and cold regions are not represented at the Winter Games. Further, he cites that lack of funds is the reason the popular Jamaican bobsled team of the 1988 Games could not compete in Salt Lake City in the 2002 Games.

35. All the following data is taken from an analysis of the official website of the Olympic Games (www.olympic.org, accessed May 24, 2005). While the website was a wealth of information, the official rules for each sport are not published there. Hence, the data provided are the best available on that public site for the date of the analysis.

36. The National Collegiate Athletic Association (NCAA) collects this data via their Gender Equity Report, which we cite here for all college participation data. This data comes from their 2002–2003 report. It represents an 82.5 percent response rate from over 1,000 institutions surveyed (National Collegiate Athletic Association 2004).

37. While women's athletic participation increased significantly from the early 1990s to about 2001 (from 31% to 44%), it has held steady since. Interestingly, Division I-AAA schools (that, by definition, do not have football teams) have the greatest parity between women and men athletes at an average of 151.0 (50.2%) women to 149.7 (49.8%) men per school. Noticeably, there are a greater proportion of women to men athletes at Division I-AAA schools, but this still does not

fully represent women's enrollment, since Division I-AAA enrollment is 57.4 percent women to 42.6 percent men. Let it not be said that we are complaining. It certainly seems to be a trend toward relative parity.

38. Here, we mean so-called American football, not European football, which is called soccer in the United States.

39. As of 2006, there were more than 1,200 girls playing high school football in the United States, primarily on boys' teams (National Federation of High Schools 2006). As of this writing, there are three major professional football outlets for women—the Women's Professional Football League, Independent Women's Football League, and the National Women's Football Association (see www.womenssportsnet.com, accessed February 3, 2006). Usually teams are so meagerly funded that the players receive only token payment, certainly not enough income to forge a career. The teams do travel regionally or nationally to play their schedules, although generally at some expense to the players themselves. But these types of teams are more of a grassroots social movement than a publicly organized and supported sport. They are more the results of individual efforts to play than a systematic way to teach sports as fundamental to students' education.

40. Opportunities exist to work as an instructor for many different cheerleading organizations that host summer camps and competitions for youth, high school, and college cheerleading teams. See for example, America's Best Cheer and Dance, Inc. http://www.americasbestcheer.com/ or American Cheerleaders Association http://www.varsity.com/. However, these jobs are typically summer jobs for college students and pay a minimum salary and room and board for the summer.

41. Cheerleaders for professional sports teams, such as the Dallas Cowboys football cheerleaders, are paid minimally. According to the Dallas Cowboys Cheerleaders' website (accessed April 7, 2007, http://www.dallascowboys.com/cheerleaders/auditions_rules.cfm), "Cheerleaders are paid $50.00 per home game. Cheerleaders are not compensated for rehearsals. Opportunities for paid appearances and shows are available!" While the opportunities for paid appearances are likely quite lucrative, cheerleaders are not being paid as athletes, but as performers and entertainers.

42. While cheerleading remains secondary to sports like football, there have been major changes in the sport of cheerleading over the last 10 to 15 years. Cheerleading has become much more athletic and opportunities for teams to compete have expanded. City leagues have emerged that are completely independent from schools or football or basketball teams. And even many school-based squads consider their main priority to be competing as athletes. While school spirit and supporting another team are typically still a requirement of school-based squads, for many it merely serves as a means to an end. For an interesting study of cheerleading see Adams and Bettis (2003).

43. Professional opportunities exist in basketball, softball, tennis, golf, bowling, and pool; and there are some opportunities for prize money in running, cycling, surfing, windsurfing, waterskiing, sailing, snow skiing, and snowboarding (see www.womenssportsnet.com, accessed February 3, 2006).

44. A group of players tried to revive it for the 2004 season but there are no signs of solvency and, as of this writing, there remains no contact information on their website (www.wusa.com, accessed February 3, 2006).

45. Men occupy a significant percentage of coaching positions for women's teams in prominent women's sports in Division I schools: basketball—31.6 percent head and 38.9 percent assistant coaches; soccer—65.5 percent head and 47.8 percent assistant coaches; softball—28.7 percent head and 29 percent assistant coaches; and volleyball—45.2 percent head and 46 percent assistant coaches (NCAA 2004:17–18). Yet, among all head and assistant coaches reported for men's Division I baseball, basketball, football, ice hockey, and wrestling teams, there is only one female, full-time assistant ice hockey coach. There were no female head coaches reported for any of the above sports. Similarly, at its inception in 1997, only one head coach in the WNBA was male, but as of the 2006 preseason only 4 of 14 head coaches are women. Men are using the WNBA as a stepping-stone to NBA coaching (as did Michael Cooper in moving from the L.A. Sparks to the Denver Nuggets) and some men have moved from coaching positions in the NBA to coaching in the WNBA (as did Ron Rothstein), but women have no reciprocal access to coaching in the NBA. Other administrative employment opportunities for women seem equally unattainable. In 1972, more than 90 percent of women's programs were directed by female head administrators. In 2006, only 18.6 percent of women's programs have female directors (Carpenter and Acosta 2006).

5

Undisciplining Gender

Gender Agency and Resistance

Changing Women

In the words of Shari Dworkin, "I am living third wave" (Heywood and Dworkin 2003:70). Of course, I was not aware that I was part of the third wave of feminism when I was a child. However, I was aware, at least subconsciously, that I valued "the masculine as well as feminine parts" of myself (Heywood and Dworkin 2003:70). At a very young age, I was defying the socially constructed dichotomy of gender.

From the age at which I walked to about age 11, I participated in a vast array of activities, from tree climbing to playing with Barbie dolls. Back then, I had no concept of either of these activities as gendered— I just enjoyed them. Once I left elementary school behind, though, I became a very gendered being and all but forgot the joy and pleasure I had received from participating in traditionally masculine activities. I had succumbed to the socialization process and had accepted the binary roles of gender as "natural." I became inactive, passive, frail.

Fast-forward 20 years to an event called the MS-150 (a 150-mile bike ride to benefit multiple sclerosis charities). I signed on. After all, I had always loved cycling. I participated in my first event and barely finished. I had not taken it seriously and had severely undertrained. I vowed to do better the next year, so I signed on a training partner— Lois, whose mom has MS—and the "journey" was underway.

Lois and I soon discovered two important things outlined in Colette Dowling's *The Frailty Myth*: first, that one's body "is an instrument of power," and second, that "the potential for improvement has nothing to do with gender and everything to do with know-how" (Dowling 2000:192, 208). We learned tips and techniques from people of every size, age, and gender and implemented the good ones through a process of trial and error. Further, we found that our "instruments of power" could breeze by some cyclists and be "dropped" (a cycling term for getting left behind) by others. Thinking back, I imagine that feeling we experienced when we did the "dropping" to be the prize that every athlete strives for (on a larger scale, of course).

My greatest epiphany came one day when we were out riding and a bug flew into my mouth—a hazard common to cyclists. I promptly "hocked a loogey" and spit it out as far to my right as I could. Lois, riding behind me, caught up on my left and stared at me in disbelief. "I can't believe you just spit . . . like a baseball player," she said. I laughed and shrugged but I had discovered something that I hope future generations of women find liberating—"masculinity is not at all the property of men" (Heywood and Dworkin 2003:98). What's more, I found the act of spitting *so* liberating that I continued to do it—even without the presence of an offending bug.

Lois and I also discovered the joy of the "V" that cyclists (almost exclusively) enjoy. The "V" is the shape that the back of the calf eventually resembles after months and months of training. We elatedly pointed out the "V" as well as other changes in each other's bodies as soon as we noticed them and with no trace whatsoever of homophobia. We each appreciated the beauty of the other's new athletic physique and increasingly stronger body. We had discovered the joy of what Heywood and Dworkin refer to as the "postmodern notion . . . that you can construct your own identity and body however you might like . . ." (Heywood and Dworkin 2003:92). In fact, with the changes in our bodies came an increase in self-confidence and gregariousness.

It is important to note that the "V" is gender-blind. In fact, a past issue of *Bicycling* magazine featured several pictures of "V-ed" legs and it was virtually impossible to tell the men from the women, especially since male cyclists often shave their legs to curb wind resistance. This proof of the ability of men and women to attain similar physiques flies in the face of the attempt of the modern sports regime to deflect "attention from just how physically similar males and females actually are" (Heywood and Dworkin 2003:192).

My hope is that every woman, at some point in life, will have the pleasure of experiencing that thrill I experienced when I did something as simple as spit. And, I hope that every woman will one day participate in an activity earnestly enough to recognize the "artificial construct of what is masculine and feminine in sports" (Heywood and

Dworkin 2003: 221). Women are capable. Women are strong. "Female physical frailty is not a reality but a myth with an agenda" (Heywood and Dworkin 2003:213).
Most importantly, the frailty myth is just that—a myth!

—Jennifer Wood, former undergraduate student

Gendered messages are powerful. We spend much of our lives responding to the messages we receive about our gender performances from friends, parents, churches, schools, governments, co-workers, employers, peers, partners, and various sources in the mass media. But we do not always comply with those demands for conformity. Sometimes as individuals and in groups, people resist gendered messages. Although bodies are defined, constructed, manipulated, disciplined, and surveyed by individuals and institutions, individuals do participate in how they respond to gendered messages—often conforming but sometimes resisting gendered messages depending on the social context or personal need. This balancing of the structural world and human agency is a classic tension for sociologists (see, e.g., Archer 1988; Bourdieu 1980; Giddens 1984). In this chapter, we discuss how people exert agency and engage in resistance against gendered imperatives.

Agency is the term commonly used by theorists who debate the degree to which each person actually makes a decision about self-presentation and bodily practices, as opposed to simply conforming. Agency means acting as an agent on one's own behalf, or acting for one's own benefit. When one acts in agentic ways, one makes active decisions about how to regard gendered messages. Although one may choose to go along with the pressures of any set of messages because it is beneficial to do so, one may also decide to resist the public messages in favor of another choice, especially if public messages are inconsistent with experiences of one's own body.

As an example, in today's world, pregnant women are inundated with information and behavioral mandates (Browner and Press 1997; Chase and Rogers 2001; Copelton 2004; Klassen 2001; Root and Browner 2001). These come from doctors, nurses, childbirth educators, self-help books and websites, mothers, fathers, children, friends, co-workers, and strangers. Women must figure out a way to negotiate all these messages along with their own experiences of their bodies. Based on interviews with 45 home-birthing women, Klassen (2001) argues that pregnant and birthing women today may not always view conventional medicine as the best or only alternative available to them. While they might accept some things that conventional medicine has to offer, they are likely to give equal or greater weight to alternative systems of knowledge such as religion, folk healing, and/or their own bodily knowledge. Root and Browner's (2001) study of pregnant women's compliance and resistance to prenatal norms illustrates this point:

Cathy Delgado, for example, was encouraged by four different sources to change her dietary and other health-related habits. From her prenatal care courses, she learned to decrease the amount of red meat she ingested, from her mother to consume more fruit, from her five year old daughter to quit smoking, and from her father to have an occasional glass of beer. [Delgado said:]. . ."I take my mother's advice [such as increasing her fruit consumption] because she had ten kids and went through ten pregnancies, so I believe her a lot of the times more than I do some of the nurses and doctors." (Root and Browner 2001:207)

Browner and Press (1997) interviewed 158 women enrolled in prenatal care courses. They found that women often resisted what they were told by the medical establishment and relied on embodied knowledge (or their own bodily experiences) to determine whether or not to follow the advice of their physicians. For example, one woman who had not stopped drinking caffeine initially, did stop after she felt her baby kicking each time she drank coffee. Other women rejected medical advice if it did not fit with their experiences during previous pregnancies or if the advice was difficult or impossible to incorporate into their everyday routines. For example, a woman with three children was restricted to bed rest for two months and could not comply because she had to take care of her children.[1]

The point we make here is that gendered messages do have a large impact on the ways we perform gender and the kinds of surveillances and accountabilities we endure, but they are not deterministic or absolute. When mass-media sources, political institutions, religions, educational systems, and other organizations and institutions circulate consistent messages about the "rights" and "wrongs" of the practices of female and male bodies, they can be hard to resist. Nonetheless, gender resistance does happen in interaction by individuals alone and sometimes among community participants. Recall from the Foucauldian model that gendered messages are swirling through institutions and individual selves and on bodies (as in the example of the gender feedback loop) but there is no specific origin, and each individual has opportunities to respond to these compulsions to participate or to resist or change the messages they receive from others. An important part of Mead's model of the internal conversation that comprises the self (i.e., "the I" and "the Me") is that "the I" portion of the internal conversation includes some degree of agency or decision-making capacity, although it will always be in reaction to a pre-existing process or idea, according to Mead ([1934]1964). We can decide to resist the gendered messages.

In this chapter, we define three categories of agency with regard to gender—gender emphasis, gender disruptions, and gender combinations. We define and use these three categories as descriptors of how agency and resistance could change gendered messages, and in some cases, how agency shores up these messages. Created only for analytic purposes, the categories are not intended to be mutually exclusive, exhaustive, or predictive of behavior or social change. They simply help us illustrate how everyday disruptions and everyday confirmations might look in action.

Gender emphasis is the use of gendered expectations to achieve some particular goal. A common example is women who are accomplished at something (other than modeling) posing nude for a magazine feature in order to promote the other accomplishment. Brandi Chastain did this after winning the Women's World Cup in soccer in 1999. While her fame and accomplishment came from soccer, she could achieve additional promotion from posing nude. Similarly, in 2004, the women from the hit television show *The Apprentice* posed in lingerie for *FHM* magazine. These women garnered fame (if only 15 minutes' worth) because they were smart businesswomen who beat out millions of other candidates for a televised interview with Donald Trump. This particular kind of agency may support the gender box structure more than work to resist it, but it is worthy of note as gendered agency. As another example, if a woman bats her eyelashes to get what she wants or purposefully cries to attempt to get out of a speeding ticket, she is playing into gender messages yet still acting on her own behalf. Men also use gender as agency when they make claims to knowledge "as a man" (e.g., "As a man, I naturally prefer grilling outside to cooking on the stove"), or pretend to like sports or hunting (even if they don't) in order to impress their bosses or to avoid having their masculinity questioned. These are everyday confirmations of gender rather than resistance, yet they are still agency.

Both gender disruptions and gender combinations (as we discuss them here) can be forms of resistance to gendered messages. *Gender disruptions* involve accomplishing the opposite of gendered expectations for the purpose of resisting gender or simply presenting gender "wrong" in ways that disrupt binaries. Butler (1990, 1993) argues for gender disruptions and suggests that the possibility of opposing the "regulatory apparatus" of gender exists only in performing normative categories in nonnormative ways—what we call everyday disruptions below. Butler suggests that consciously performing gender in ways that should be culturally impossible (e.g., male drag, female masculinity) subverts dominant notions of gender and exposes the impossibility of a so-called natural gender binary. Important to her argument is that gender must be recognizable while it is being resisted. After all, dressing like a clown or wearing a tent to avoid dressing in dominant gendered patterns may be avoiding complicity with gender but it is not a critique of gender because it is not recognizable as gender. It is not coherent (Gubrium and Holstein 1997, 1998)—that is, it is not addressing and participating in the cultural messages. When dressed as a clown, you may be seen as playing or having fun, but not as making a comment on gender. Wearing a tent may be interpreted as insanity but is not seen as a critique of gender. Hence, only doing gender "wrong" or doing the "wrong" gender well disrupts the dominant gender messages.

The last form we discuss we call *gender combinations*—or women and men working together in combination, not under the premise of masculine and feminine dichotomous division of labor, but rather as interchangeable equals working to achieve a common goal. For example, through the gender box structure, we commonly think of "mothering" as nurturing and caring for children, whereas "fathering" is enforcing discipline and being the provider. Instead of dividing parenting into gendered roles, we might envision it as an equal division of labor in which both parents nurture, discipline, play, provide, and mentor equally and interchangeably. In this scenario, the common goal of working together diminishes the need for a rolebound division of labor.

Throughout this chapter, we will provide examples of gender emphasis, gender disruptions, and gender combinations as forms of agency. We want to be clear that gender emphasis may be agency but is often not resistance to gender messages because it provides everyday confirmations of gendered messages to others. Because we have focused on gender conformity and gender confirmations up to this point in the book, we will focus most of this chapter on gender disruptions and gender combination as forms of resistance against heteronormative gender messages. Hence, here we will take care to explain in some detail how gender can be utilized as resistance, not just confirmation.

GENDER RESISTANCE AND EVERYDAY DISRUPTIONS

In the gender feedback loop that we have been completing throughout this book (see figure 5.1), there is room for resistance to the gendered messages we receive on an everyday basis. Recall we started by arguing that gender performance flows from gendered messages in social settings that each of us takes into the self and uses the body to perform (i.e., the messages → selves → bodies section of the feedback loop). If conformity to gendered messages were imminent and uncontested, there would be no need for arrows on our diagram that circle back from selves → messages, from bodies → selves, and from bodies → messages. What we feel through our bodies may or may not confirm the messages we are expected to follow. If, for example, playing sport gives one the feeling of having a strong body, a woman playing sport may hear the message that men are supposed to be strong and women to be weaker and experience that idea as inconsistent with her own feelings, hence, modifying her sense of self. If she demonstrates her strength to others, perhaps that example will alter the notion of female bodies as weak for those who observe her prowess. The messages pass back from bodies → selves → gendered cultural messages in feedback loops that disrupt the box structure. Of course, if this woman has been taught to be "ladylike" and spends most of her life not engaging athletics, then tries at 25 years old to start to learn sports, she may experience the messages as "accurate" because of her lack of

Figure 5.1. Gender Feedback Loop: Resistance. Because gender surveillance and accountability are often stifling, some of us at times attempt to resist gender messages in large and small ways.

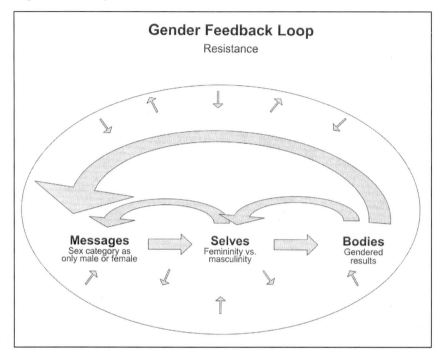

training, thereby confirming the messages, rather than disrupting them. Similar processes could also happen for men and masculinity. If the rules of masculinity are experienced as pleasing, they may be confirmed. If not, they may be disrupted. Intersexed and transgendered people constantly come up against this feedback loop in ways that disrupt or confirm self and messages about bodies for others.

Also, recall that we added a circle around the entire diagram with small arrows pointing in toward the messages → selves → bodies loop to demonstrate the boundaries and pressures established by social control. In this section we add arrows from the messages → selves → bodies loop pointing outward toward the social control oval as though they are pushing against those social control boundaries. The little arrows pointing outward and the feedback arrows looping from selves and bodies backward toward messages map out the ways in which each of us exerts agency in resistance to gendered messages and the everyday disruptions we might accomplish resisting the gender box structure (see figure 5.2).

In chapter 3, we discussed everyday confirmations of gender messages in the form of gender accountability. The opposite of those might be termed everyday disruptions. If each of us is subject to surveillance and everyday

Figure 5.2. Gender Feedback Loop: Resistance. In everyday life, we may engage in everyday disruptions—intentional practices that attempt to change gender messages or show the gender box structure to be false.

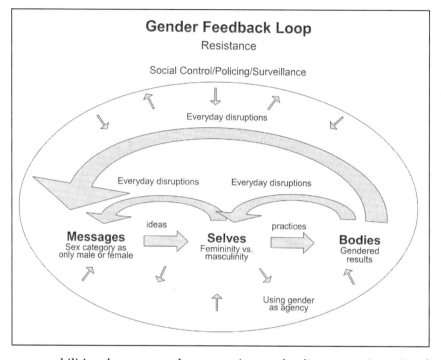

accountabilities, then we can also engage in *everyday disruptions*—intentional practices on a day-to-day basis to attempt to change gendered messages or show the gender box structure to be false. These are simple everyday actions intended to disrupt the consistency of the gender box structure. Here's an example. Cigar smoking is often considered a masculine pastime—perhaps unladylike. It is also seen as a sign of success, and can be a so-called male-bonding activity among businessmen. If a woman were to "join the boys" by smoking with business associates simply to demonstrate that she knows how to engage in these rituals, that might be a type of everyday disruption to those who witness it. Of course, either women or men may enjoy smoking cigars (or not) as a matter of personal choice, but if it is done in such a way as to participate in and disrupt a specifically gendered context, it is understood as an everyday disruption. For men, perhaps an example is talking about hair care products. If men are supposed to be ignorant of beauty in self-presentation, making a conscious effort to step outside those boundaries marks a disruption to the consistency of the gender box structure.

At times people resist conformity to bring about change. At other times resistance serves as a survival mechanism for living under unfair or oppressive conditions. Either way, though, people are actively making choices about how to live in a world that discriminates based on race, gender, age, sexuality, and physical ability and that encourages conformity rather than diversity and individual difference.

GENDER RESISTANCE IN COLLECTIVE ACTION

Gender resistance in collective action (people working in groups) has a long history. Interestingly, we cannot find many examples of heterosexual, able-bodied white men acting collectively to resist constructions of the masculine body. One possible exception might be the countercultural movements of the 1960s and 1970s in which many men grew their hair long. While these men were clearly resisting the appearance norms of mainstream culture, it is not clear to what extent they were deliberately resisting gender norms.[2] This lack of resistance makes sense because traditional conceptions of masculine bodies are the norm—the standard, and heterosexual, able-bodied white men tend to be the ones who have most benefited from traditional constructions of bodies. However, others have attempted to resist or change the expectations of the gender box structure.

An example of gender combinations engaging in resistance involves the women and men who were part of the nineteenth-century women's dress reform movement. These activists challenged the restrictive fashions of the times, including corsets and petticoats, arguing that these fashions not only endangered women's health, but also restricted movement in such a way as to keep women from participating in various activities such as bicycling (Fischer 2001; Kesselman 1991).

A more recent example of men and women working together to change messages about bodies is the work of the National Association for the Advancement of Fat Acceptance (NAAFA).[3] This group works to dispel myths about and fight discrimination against people who are overweight and to encourage people to accept their bodies no matter what their size. In her sociological memoir, *Taking Up Space* (2005), Pattie Thomas (along with her coauthors) points out that the "war on obesity" is a socially constructed war engaged in by a variety of institutions (including medicine, government, media, and workplaces) with a variety of surveillance tools at their disposal, holding people accountable to an arbitrary standard for body size. Thomas reiterates throughout the memoir "we find ourselves reluctant warriors in a war we do not want to fight" (39).

Like the dress reform movement and the NAAFA, the movement toward recognizing intersexual rights also challenges the notion of fixed body essences (Kessler 1998; Preves 2003). Organized by Cheryl Chase, herself an intersexed person (i.e., a person not readily classified by medical standards as male or female), the Intersex Society of North America (ISNA) advocates for the visibility of intersexed persons and for the right of personal choice to live in the sex of choice or without a need to choose one or the other. The primary advocacy for this group is to address medical doctors in an attempt to convince the medical establishment to stop engaging in surgical procedures on intersexed babies, arguing instead for allowing intersexed people to make their own decisions about surgeries and bodily choice later in life.

Sometimes, resistance is collective, but perhaps not as intentionally organized as the dress reform movement, the NAAFA, or the ISNA. For example, during slavery, there were loose networks of slave women who would secretly perform abortions, knowing that if they continued to produce children for the benefit of the slave owners, not only would their health suffer, but their children would be born into slavery (Fox-Genovese 1988; Ross 1998). Black midwives in the South were in a special position to be able to travel from plantation to plantation to deliver babies. In their travels they were also able to secretly spread the word about ways to terminate a pregnancy, thus creating opportunities for women to resist using their bodies in ways that were expected or demanded of them.

The feminist movement and civil rights movements of the mid- to late-twentieth century are examples of collective resistance to gendered (and racialized) messages that tended to benefit men and white people. The goals of both movements were to change social structures like work and to allow for greater accessibility of high-paying jobs to women and people of color. But both movements also worked to change the social messages about what it meant to be a woman or a person of color. While it is important to change laws to reduce physical barriers to entry, it is also essential to change minds regarding what it means to be a woman or to be a member of a minority group—in other words, to change the gendered and racialized messages. In terms of gender, much of second wave feminism (the movement that took place in the late 1960s and 1970s) worked to change ideas about what women can accomplish, to question the usefulness of dividing relationships on the basis of unequal power differences, and to imagine women as fully capable participants in social institutions like work, family, religions, and so forth.

Newer forms of feminism that emerged during the 1990s and beyond, often called third wave feminism, focus much more on gender as performance and the ways women and men can work to resist social messages that encourage them to conform by engaging protest with the body through disruptive gender performance (Findlen 1995; Heywood and Drake 1997). Interestingly, third wave feminism, informed by black feminist thought, also focuses more on resisting both gendered and racialized messages, rather than concentrating on critiquing each separately. Some examples of third wave collective activism are the riot grrl music movement of the 1990s, the radical cheerleaders, and the 'zine movement.

Begun in the Pacific Northwest, especially Seattle and Olympia, Washington, concurrent with the "grunge" music scene of the early 1990s (and centered in other major cities like Washington, D.C., and New York), the riot grrl movement was and is a movement among young women musicians who resist the male-centered, capitalist music industry that has traditionally encouraged women in music to play into heteronormative performances of femininity and sexiness. Countering highly feminized Madonna-like images, riot grrl bands like Bikini Kill, Bratmobile, Sleater-Kinney, and Tribe 8 were organized by mostly female musicians playing slasher-style, punk rock music, who dressed in the opposite of heteronormative femininity (e.g., old, torn-up jeans; messy hair; piercings and tattoos) and sang lyrics that critiqued traditional heteronormativity; violence against women; and the capitalist music industry, which squelches messages about strong women, among other messages (Klein 1997).

Also based on performance, the radical cheerleaders is a social protest group with small but active groups around the country. To protest, female and male radical cheerleaders dress in mocking mismatched cheerleader "uniforms" and, with pom-poms in hand and little coordination, chant lyrics that offer similar critiques to the riot grrl movement. Written as a call to action, their website describes the radical cheerleaders:

> Radical Cheerleading is Protest+Performance. It's activism with pom poms and middle fingers extended. It's screaming FUCK CAPITALISM while doing a split. The Radical Cheerleaders started when once upon a time, two magical sisters from the land of Florida named Cara and Aimee decided that regular old protests on street corners holding signs and waving at oncoming traffic was just not RADICAL enough. (Radical Cheerleaders 2006)

Their website offers "girl positive cheers, queer/sex-positive cheers, environmental cheers, and anti-authority cheers," among others.

Emerging about the same time through the third wave movement, an active, underground community of writers began producing homemade magazines called 'zines. Similarly countering the capitalist, high-cost, and generally exclusive magazine industry, 'zines gave voice to individuals with all sorts of messages of social critique. Following the 'zine movement of the 1990s, several glossy magazines have emerged that specifically resist gendered messages and attempt to change magazine publishing standards by selectively accepting advertising from socially conscious companies. *Bitch*, *Bust*, and *HUES* magazines are specific examples of this genre. Billed as "feminist response to pop culture," *Bitch* magazine updates the feminist tradition of *Ms.* magazine (which focuses primarily on traditional politics as it happens in Washington, D.C., and in local state capitals) by commenting primarily on pop culture and gendered media images in everyday life. Perhaps somewhat more oriented toward encouraging women's sexuality, *Bust* magazine sells itself as a magazine "for women with something to get off their chests." Countering the *Cosmo* paradigm, *Bust* engages discussions of sexuality openly but with an orientation to pleasing women, rather than women making themselves pleasing to men. Another similar style of magazine that bills itself to girls and young women as countering racialized messages, *HUES* (Hear Us Emerging Sisters) magazine orients to women of various cultural backgrounds. Published by New Moon publishing, their mission statement reads:

> HUES began and lives on today because we are tired of women's magazines that patronize women—magazines that teach women to hate their bodies, that ignore culture and identities, that encourage women to fade into the background instead of showing their true colors. HUES is an antidote to all this. It's a forum where women of all colors, sizes, and identities can share experiences, insights, and recipes for power and attitude. (HUES 1999:2)

Each of the magazines listed above focuses on body image and media; in particular they focus on changing gendered messages.

GENDER RESISTANCE AS INDIVIDUAL ACTION

In addition to collective action, individuals may also engage in behaviors that resist or challenge gender norms.[4] Individual resistance usually occurs when the gendered or racialized messages leave little option for some individuals to comply and when no collective movement is available. While we have not delved much into social class issues thus far, individual resistance to gender and racialized messages is a fine example of social class issues and the body because often people with little means have no resources to form resistance other than with the body itself. People with means and political access might choose other avenues for agency. But those marginalized groups with few resources often use the body itself to display messages of social protest. Some examples here might be hairstyles, "cool poses" and performances of resistance, and transgendered people's performances of ambiguity.

In her book *Rapunzel's Daughters*, Rose Weitz (2004) describes how women have used hairstyles to try out new identities and to resist narrow standards of femininity. Weitz describes women who have used their hair to both downplay femininity and to emphasize femininity, depending on the situation. Hair is often an important marker in creating gendered ethnic and social class identities (Banks 2000; Bettie 2000; Chambers 2004; Craig 2002; hooks 1999). Weitz (2004) writes:

> As girls learn to consider hair an important marker of their identity, hair also can give girls a comforting sense of belonging to a larger ethnic community. While she was growing up in England, Pratibha's long black hair, kept in the oiled braids of her native India, gave her a welcome sense of belonging to the emigrant Indian community. Mexican-American girls growing up in the United

States tell how, within their communities, their tight braids signaled not only that they were pretty, but that they were pretty *Mexican* girls . . . .(55–56)

In recent U.S. history, hairstyles and the question of whether or not to straighten hair have been a significant issue of beauty, ethnic pride, and race politics for African American women in ways that have not been paralleled for women of other ethnic subgroups in the United States.

At times, some men also resist gendered bodily norms and stereotypes. Gerschick and Miller (1995) write about how men with physical disabilities relate to traditional norms of masculinity. Some of the men they interviewed continued to adhere to these traditional norms, emphasizing their physical strength, athleticism, and sexual prowess. Other men reformulated their sense of masculinity, shaping it to fit their own abilities and perceptions. A few men in this study resisted traditional ideals altogether and instead created alternative definitions of masculinity.

Describing what he calls "cool pose (i.e., a set of expressive lifestyle behaviors)," Richard Majors (1990:109) writes on the ways black men resist traditional notions of masculinity with their bodily performances. He writes that black men, who traditionally lacked access to powerful institutions like higher education and corporate and political institutions, instead focus their presentation of self in ways to command respect from others:

> Black men often cope with their frustration, embitterment, alienation, and social impotence by channeling their styles of demeanor, speech, gesture, clothing, hairstyle, walk, stance, and handshake. For the black male, these expressive behaviors . . . offset an externally imposed invisibility, and provide a means to show the dominant culture (and the black male's peers) that the black male is strong, proud and can survive, regardless of what may have been done to harm or limit him. . . . In that sense, then, cool pose is an attempt to carve out an alternative path to achieve the goals of dominant masculinity. (111)

While the "cool pose" illustrates gender emphasis, Brent Staples (1997) demonstrates gender and race disruption when he writes of resisting stereotypical messages of black masculinity. He recounts his realization of racist constructions of African Americans, noting that as a black man, people, especially white women, were afraid of him when they saw him walking down the streets of Chicago at night. He describes how he altered his physical presence by avoiding close contact with strangers and by whistling classical music to make himself appear less threatening to white people. He writes that his goal was to change racist public perceptions about black men by presenting himself as nonthreatening.

Another example of individual resistance among heterosexual men in the early 2000s is the emergence of "metrosexual" identities. A slang word that is used playfully in everyday language, "metrosexual" is defined by the website Word Spy[5] as:

metrosexual (met.roh.SEK.shoo.ul) *n*. An urban male with a strong aesthetic sense who spends a great deal of time and money on his appearance and lifestyle.

They go on to cite a usage in the *Washington Post* as follows:

> . . . A *metrosexual* . . . is a straight man who styles his hair using three different products (and actually calls them "products"), loves clothes and the very act of shopping for them, and describes himself as sensitive and romantic. In other words, he is a man who seems stereotypically gay except when it comes to sexual orientation.

Presumably, then, metrosexuality is the consumerist emphasis on body image that has traditionally been understood as a part of femininity, not masculinity. While metrosexuality is certainly not a critique of capitalism or the system of competitive body image that women have traditionally engaged, it is a bit of a challenge to traditional masculinity in terms of engaging heterosexual men in the kinds of body surveillance that women have traditionally endured and enacted.

As we described in chapter 1, transgendered people resist gender messages altogether by refusing to be labeled as a particular gender. Perhaps this is the most extreme instance of everyday disruptions in which the goal is to make gender so fluid that sex category cannot be assigned. Many trans people practice their gender resistance just by living their everyday lives in a form that is difficult to place in a sex category (Bornstein 1994; Crawley 2002a; Stone 1991; Wilchins 1997, 2004). Others actively engage gender disruption through art forms that seek to make sex and gender difficult to read. In the pictures included in the inset, is this person female or male? Can you tell? Can you tell her/his race? Lewis plays with gender ambiguity in everyday life and in art such as these photos. He was born female-bodied.

Art Is Performance; Performance Is Art

Embodying the ambiguous is performance in itself—conscious or unconscious. For me it is the combination of the two. Some days I wake up and wonder if my gender presentation will stir questioning from a passerby. Most days I imagine that it is just another day and my gender presentation never even crosses my mind, although in the past I have experienced physical harm due to my ambiguous gender. Living the "in-between" of male and female, lesbian and trans, black and white makes my life an undulating shape-shifting form of art that necessitates courage and patience in the faces of a slowly changing society. Art prescribes emotion and emotion dictates creativity. For me, an

African American and German ambiguous trans-identified individual, art allows me to create a voice and a space that is otherwise silenced, seen as disruptive, misunderstood, or not even acknowledged to exist.

Stepping in the frame of any photograph allows for there to be an open interpretation from the viewer of the photo. In these photos, sex is not clearly "marked." There are no physical markers that would indicate my sex. This is not done on purpose. This is me, Lewis, in my truest and most comfortable form. This is me within the only form that I know to exist. I am comfortable and yet I challenge many of the norms that exist because of the socially constructed notions of what is expected

of gender presentations. It is left up to the reader/viewer to assign a gender that is molded out of their conceived understandings of two and
only two legitimated sex categories. I do not fit either. I am female-born
but male-identified. I desire women; however, my desire for women has
not molded me into the individual in these photos. I embrace queer-
ness. I am just me. I am . . . trans-formation embodied in process.

—Lewis, graduate student

Since the early 1990s, an academic literature called queer theory has
emerged, somewhat similar to feminism, but concentrating on sexual orientation's relationship to so-called biological sex and gender. Queer theorists
work to undo heteronormative gender messages by separating the expectation
that physiology (sex) is related to gender performances or sexual orientation
(Butler 1990, 1993; Halperin 1989; West and Zimmerman 1987). In terms of
gender disruption, they argue that one can resist heteronormative gender
messages by performing the "wrong" gender well or unrecognizably (Bornstein 1994; Butler 1990, 1993; Wilchins 1997, 2004). An example of this
might be the ways that "butch" and "femme," identity categories in lesbian
communities, disrupt dominant gender messages by challenging the naturalness of gender performance and male-female coupling (Butler 1990, 1993;
Case 1989; Crawley 2002a, 2002b, 2002c; Lapovsky Kennedy and Davis 1993).
Butch and femme clothing styles illustrate that female-bodied people can perform either masculinity or femininity. In a study of working-class bar culture
in Buffalo, New York, in the 1940s, 1950s, and 1960s, Lapovsky Kennedy and
Davis (1993) suggest that one reason that butches developed their personas
was as a necessary means of gaining respect from heterosexual men. In this
way, female masculinity demonstrated the falseness of the so-called natural
link between maleness and masculinity (Halberstam 1998).

While perhaps more contested, male drag may also provide some resistance to gender messages (Hennen 2004; Newton 1972; Rupp and Taylor
2003; Schacht 2002). The campiness of gay male drag has a long history of
social critique. While many have argued that gay male camp is more a
misogynist parody of women than a social critique (Schacht 2002), others
have argued for some value of the everyday disruption of seeing male bodies do femininity well (Hennen 2004; Newton 1972; Rupp and Taylor
2003). Hennen (2004) describes a community made up primarily of men
called the Radical Faeries, who are statedly devoted to resistance to hegemonic masculinity by engaging in satire through drag.

Transgendered and transsexual people may transform their bodies to perform gender in ways that resist the idea that biological sex determines gender (Crawley 2002a; Dozier 2005; Halberstam 1994; Monro and Warren
2004; Schliefer 2006; Schrock, Reid and Boyd 2005). While some have cri-

tiqued transsexualism as the ultimate in gender conformity (Raymond 1979), other queer theorists analyze the ways that trans people use their bodies as an instrument of resisting the gender box structure, which presumes that biological sex (genital appearance) defines both gender and sexual orientation (Dozier 2005; Green 2004; Halberstam 1994; Monro and Warren 2004; Schliefer 2006; Schrock, Reid and Boyd 2005; Rubin 2003). Trans people challenge the notion that bodies are the basis of personhood and disrupt the notion that sex is fixed. Many transsexual people argue that their gender is more fixed than their biological sex, hence it is easier to change sex than change gender. Some of these people perhaps align more with the gender box structure ultimately by hoping to make their bodies fit specifically into one of the two normative "boxes" and disclaiming or hiding their histories of having been born in a different body. However, many transsexuals do not hide their histories of having transgressed bodily sex and remain quite open about having changed their bodies—perhaps the most radical disruption of the gender box structure. Pushing the everyday disruption to its fullest, some transgendered people argue for living in a state of being permanently trans, not choosing to live in a recognizable sex (i.e., having some bodily modification but not necessarily fully "transitioning" to the "other sex") as a specific critique to the fixity of the body (Bornstein 1994; Wilchins 1997, 2004).

GENDERING BODIES IN ACTION

We use these three concepts—gender emphasis, gender disruptions, and gender combinations—to discuss the ways gendered messages are both supported and resisted using agency. As in previous chapters, we use this section to present how specific instances of these theories have played out at work, in sex and reproduction, and in sports.

Work

Joan Acker (1990) was one of the first sociologists to point out that workers have bodies and that sex and gender matter at work. Throughout this book we have given examples of how bodies are gendered by the messages we receive about work and by the actual work we do. Here we give examples of gender emphasis, gender disruptions, and gender combinations in the workplace.

Gender Emphasis

Women in the workplace can use gender emphasis by highlighting their bodily femininity to achieve a desired end. We discussed an example of this in chapter 4. Actress Hunter Tylo filed a lawsuit against Aaron Spelling for firing her from *Melrose Place* because she became pregnant shortly before shooting the first of her appearances on the show. As we reported, Tylo won a considerable amount of money in the case, in large part because she demonstrated her "sex appeal" (i.e., her bodily femininity) in court, day after day, as she appeared in miniskirts and tight-fitting clothing, shortly after giving birth. Clearly, this was a way in which she could use her svelte, womanly physique to plead a case in court against an employer who tried to use conventional notions of gendered bodies to justify breaking a contract.

While Hunter Tylo relied on traditional notions of a "sexy," feminine body, midwives often rely on conventional notions of feminine, maternal bodies in an effort to legitimize their occupation (Foley 2005b, 2006). While there are a handful of male midwives, this is an occupation that is overwhelmingly female. It is not uncommon to hear midwives emphasize gendered bodies to contrast themselves to male obstetricians, in other words making the point that as women they can better relate to birthing women than a man could. For example, one midwife claims, "I just think it's obscene for anyone to deliver a child who hasn't given birth. I don't see how anybody would want to have a male doctor that hasn't had a kid, that hasn't been there you know vomiting and pooping on the table" (Foley 2005b:6).

While midwives use gender emphasis to suggest they provide the best care for their clients, female clergy employ gender emphasis to demonstrate caring for their congregation. Shehan, Schultz, and Wiggins-Frame (1999) (Wiggins-Frame is herself an ordained United Methodist clergywoman) focus on the challenges faced by female clergy—and the coping strategies they use. With the exception of a few specific denominations such as Reform Judaism and Unitarian Universalists, the clergy remains among the most male-dominated of the professions. Gendered messages about the ministry suggest clergy are understood as needing "masculine" qualities in terms of leadership and authority, and in many Protestant denominations, needing to be "fatherly." Female ministers often report feeling resistance to their positions not only among their parishioners but also among the hierarchies of their churches. They report exaggerating their "feminine" qualities—nurturance, in particular—and dressing in traditionally feminine ways to diminish the resistance they feel. Rather than adopting masculine performances (e.g., exerting authority), clergywomen try to win acceptance by appealing to traditional notions of femininity, using their bodies to perform femininity. One 51-year-old married clergywoman described her job in terms of "birthing," "bathing," "feeding," and "nurturing."

A similar gender emphasis strategy was used by women in dual-career couples in the late 1960s (Rapoport and Rapoport 1971), but in this case, the gendered messages that wives with their own professional careers were encountering were being enforced by their parents, in-laws, neighbors, and friends. Because married women in the professions were relatively rare in the 1960s, those who held these positions felt considerable social disapproval. To deal with this, many resorted to exaggerating their "normalcy" in other areas of life; they compensated by being ultrafeminine in their family lives and doing all of the "wifely" and "motherly" tasks traditional wives were expected to do (e.g., baking cupcakes for their children's school functions, preparing gourmet meals for their families, and dressing in traditionally feminine ways).

Men, too, use this strategy of emphasizing traditional gendered behaviors and/or characteristics in the workplace. This can most easily be seen among men who are employed in "feminine" occupations. Christine Williams (1995) studied men employed in nursing, elementary school teaching, librarianship, and social work to uncover the strategies men use to assert and maintain their masculinity in situations where it is challenged. As Williams observed, men who enter predominantly female professions "do not abandon their gender identity (despite stereotypes about them) nor do they lose their interest in sustaining male privilege" (17). She identified several different strategies that men employed in female-dominated occupations use to maintain hegemonic masculinity. They distinguish themselves from the women in their workplaces by segregating themselves into certain masculine specialties. Additionally, men in Williams's study often highlighted the masculine aspects of their work in their attempts to maintain a sense of themselves as "real men." Those who worked as librarians highlighted the computer technology involved in their work. Other men emphasized the physical aspects of their work. Recall from chapter 2 the man who had previously worked as a teacher at a school for autistic children who said "men were needed for restraining the children, some of whom were very, very violent" (127). A final strategy is to dissociate from their work. This can involve condemning or deriding others who are in the profession, such as the public librarian who described his male co-workers as "a bit old ladyish because they've worked in reference a long time" (139). By condemning the entire field or the other men in it, they can preserve a sense of themselves as different, more masculine, and better than their co-workers.

Other studies have discussed gender emphasis as agency for men in female-dominated professions. Rosemary Pringle (1993), who studied secretaries, found that men in this type of work are often given different job titles (e.g., administrative assistant, information officer, or computer operator). Male workers collude with their employers in this renaming process, obscuring the actual similarity between men's and women's work and justifying men's greater rate of pay. Additionally, Benokraitis has written about several forms of what she calls subtle sexism in the workplace, which are essentially forms of sexual harassment by men (e.g., telling hostile jokes) intended to keep women in the workplace from seeking jobs that might have power over the men (Benokraitis 1997; Benokraitis and Feagin 1995).

As Williams (1995) argues, men who work in these female-dominated fields once referred to as "semi-professions" have a lot at stake in maintaining their masculinity, not the least of which is the economic and status benefits that accrue to those who can successfully convince others that they are different from and better than their female colleagues. But for many men, the challenge also includes persuading themselves that they can still be "real men" when they are spending their lives doing work that is regarded by others as only appropriate for persons of "the other" sex/gender.

Gender Disruptions

The transition of women into traditionally male-dominated jobs is a form of gender disruption, causing us to rethink gender messages about work and questioning the alignment of masculine performance with certain jobs. The 2005 film *North Country* is based on a true story about women in the mining industry in the 1970s. Lois Jensen, the real name of the woman played by Charlize Theron, was at the center of the first-ever class action sexual harassment suit. She was one of the first women to be hired to work in the iron mines in Minnesota. Lois and her female co-workers' experiences illustrate clearly that women who sought jobs in mines (as well as in other male-dominated jobs) by their very presence challenged long-standing notions about a "woman's place." Simply by seeking jobs in the mining industry, Lois and her female co-workers disrupted the fiercely held ideas about women that were characteristic at the time.

Perhaps the most striking example of gender disruption at work has been the full integration of women into the military, especially the Marine Corps. Even today, 30 years after active integration of women into the military, the notion of a female marine may in itself be a gender disruption. Although women have been serving in or actively aiding the military since the Revolutionary War (Jones 2000) and women's participation in World War II is commonly known today, the idea of women in a military unit and in combat is still contested terrain.

In a study of female marines, Williams (1989) discusses the ways in which gendered messages are disrupted simply by women's presence in the Marine Corps. Of all the military branches, the Marines prides itself on representing the most masculine embodiment of the warrior. Female marines, then, by their very existence, disrupt this very gendered image. As part of the surveillance mechanisms of the Marines, the official uniform for female marines included wearing makeup and dressing in a skirted uniform. Still, the women who enlisted did so for their own agentic purposes, including seeking job security, personal discipline, and career building.

Men who work in nontraditional occupations can also disrupt the gender box structure. While some men emphasize masculinity in these jobs, others do not. Further, the fact that men who work in jobs typically associated with women ride a "glass escalator" to promotions within the organization or the profession (Williams 1992) might say more about the structure of the job or the organization than about the workers themselves. In her study of paid careworkers, Julia Twigg (2000) argues that the job of carework is designed and structured around assumptions about women and traditional notions of femininity, yet "it is the job that is gendered and this can be at odds with the person who occupies it" (129). Several studies of paid and unpaid carework (work that is often very physical) show that many of the men who do this work do it well and find it rewarding (Kaye and Applegate 1995; Stacey 2004; Twigg 2000). The image of a man using his body to bathe a cancer patient, help an elderly woman use the toilet, or change the clothes of an elderly man certainly disrupts the norm of gendered bodies.

Gender Combinations

Because traditionally male-dominated jobs tend to be better paid than female-dominated jobs and men risk accountability to being chided as feminine, it has been much more common for women to seek access to male-dominated jobs than for men to seek access to female-dominated jobs. But significant shifts in the economy of a country (e.g., a recession with high unemployment) or in technology always shake up the social organization of jobs and at times lure women and men to work together in ways they traditionally have not (Bradley 1993). While women and men may rely on gender emphasis as agency as these transitions occur, over time the polarity of gendered messages about jobs can diminish if we simply see women and men working interchangeably in those positions.

One interesting demonstration of gender combinations at work is described by Patricia Yancey Martin (2006) in her book

Photo 5.1. Gender combinations: This National Geographic *photo of firefighters taken in 2002 shows how gendered images might change gendered messages if women and men are seen working together in jobs we call masculine or feminine.*

Rape Work. Martin argues that while some people whose jobs involve work-ing with victims of sexual assault (health care professionals, law enforcement officers, rape crisis workers) continue to believe that women are better than men at this kind of work, often these workers claim that "gender is irrele-vant" and that with the right kind of training, men and women can both be good at this work. On the flip side, without the right kind of training, men and women can be equally inept at this work.

In Foley's (2006) study of Sexual Assault Nurse Examiners (SANE), a male nurse uses a dual strategy of gender emphasis (emphasizing a masculine per-formance) and then gender disruption (drawing on nontraditional aspects of masculinity) in his work with women who have been sexually assaulted:

> The truth of the matter is, I think that the patients when they are in that mode, they're worried about a hundred thousand other things other than my gender, number one, number two, some of the women are still socialized and see men as doctors and so they don't really, in the healthcare setting, you know I've got a lab coat on and dressed professionally. The other thing that I like to stress in con-versations about that however is that in most situations, the woman has had her power and control ripped away by a male. When I talk to law enforcement offi-cers or EMTs and paramedics, I talk about the fact that having a male, number one ask for their consent before they touch them or talk to them or whatever and also show them a caring attitude and even a caring touch is therapeutic. I mean, have we studied that, I don't know, but inherently it seems like it would be help-ful and therapeutic to them in their process. So maybe strike out some of those fears that they have to be scared of all men because of what's happened to them.

Ultimately, this male nurse is arguing for the inclusion of both women and men in the process of sexual assault recovery—that working in combination may help rather than hinder the recovery of assault victims.

Sexuality and Reproduction

Gender messages are nowhere more present than in issues of sex, sexual-ity, and reproduction. Given the pervasiveness of the belief in the "natural-ness" of gender, it should be no surprise that people use and resist these messages about sexuality.

Gender Emphasis

The examples we provide here differ in some ways from the examples of gender emphasis in the workplace. Whereas before we showed gender em-phasis for personal gain or to maintain the status quo, here we show examples of gender emphasis employed for social change. One of the earliest examples of gender emphasis using the body as resistance comes from Sojourner Truth, an outspoken slave and activist, speaking out publicly in opposition to sexism and racism simultaneously in the 1850s. bell hooks (1981) records an instance of Truth speaking against slavery to a crowd of white men in Indiana in which she responded to one man's disbelief that she was as much a woman as white women by baring her breasts to prove her body was not different than a white woman's. On another occasion in 1852 in Akron, Ohio, Truth spoke out against racism to a crowd of white feminists and rather famously argued for black women's inclusion in the feminist movement by asserting, "Ain't I a Woman?" hooks quotes Truth's famous speech as follows:

> Dat man ober dar say dat women needs to be helped into carriages, and lifted ober ditches, and to ha de best places . . . and ain't I a woman? Look at me! Look at my arm! . . . I have plowed, and planted, and gathered into barns, and no man could head me—and ain't I a woman? I could work as much as any man (when I could get it), and bear de lash as well—and ain't I a woman? I have borne five children and I seen mos all sold off into slavery, and when I cried out with a mother's grief, none but Jesus hear—and ain't I a woman? (160)

Simultaneously critiquing the notion that women are frail as well as the notion that black women are deserving of different treatment from white women, Sojourner Truth used the emphasis of her physical and reproductive body to change notions about what it meant to be a women and to be black. Here she both emphasizes gender (e.g., Shouldn't she be treated with the same respect as a white woman?) and disrupts it (e.g., Isn't her hard work the same as a man's?) simultaneously. She uses the "truth" of her bodily physiology (having breasts as well as strong arms) and body practices (demonstrating hard work and her reproductive capacities) at the same time to resist the dominant messages that her sex and race are inferior.

More recently women have actively engaged their sexual bodies in order to resist lack of knowledge in women's health care provision. In the past, medical students have learned and practiced pelvic exams on dolls and cadavers (dead bodies) and even on anesthetized women without their consent. Prostitutes have also been hired as "teaching material" in medical schools. As part of the women's health movement of the 1960s and 1970s, women began volunteering as Gynecological Teaching Assistants (GTAs). In this role, women would actually talk back to the medical students, telling them what hurt and suggesting how they could make the procedure more comfortable (Kapsalis 1997). We see a move from women as passive objects (cadavers) or commodities (prostitutes) to women as active participants in their own health care. Beginning in the 1980s, groups of mostly women menstrual activists[6] began to pressure the makers of sanitary products to improve the safety of their products. These groups try to raise awareness, remove the stigma surrounding menstruation, and educate about health and environmental concerns related to mainstream menstrual products. These activists emphasize gender in order to resist both gender surveillance and gender inequality (see Bobel 2006 for an analysis of menstrual activism).

Mothers may engage in political action based on their identities as mothers. Sometimes this is done out of the sincere belief that motherhood confers special insights and responsibilities to solve the problems plaguing families and communities (clearly an everyday confirmation of gender messages). Mothers may be drawn into activism beginning with a concern for their own children. As they become active in trying to create social change for their children, they may then develop a concern for all mothers and children and seek social and political change through collective action. Other folks might use motherhood strategically, believing that speaking out as mothers would give them more credibility in sexist societies than speaking out as women. Consider the use of the maternal body in the following stories (from Jetter, Orleck, and Taylor 1997). In the early 1980s, Dollie Burwell, a mother and an environmental activist in North Carolina, along with other mothers literally laid her body in front of trucks filled with contaminated soil that was meant to be dumped in her neighborhood. In yet another instance, Wangari Maathai (the 2004 Nobel Peace Prize recipient) and the women of the Greenbelt Movement in Kenya staged a hunger strike to demand that their sons, political prisoners, be released. Maathai describes the events: "Then the authorities turned on the women with beatings and tear gas, the women used an old tradition to ward off attackers: some of them stripped naked and shocked the oppressors and onlookers alike! Women decided to use their bodies to fight the injustices against their children" (Jetter, Orleck, and Taylor 1997:75).

Another example of emphasizing the normative, but in nonnormative ways, is the "gay baby boom"—the incidence of lesbians and gay men having babies and arranging their families to include small children. The goal of much of this new movement is not to disrupt the notion of families per se, but usually to replicate the very standard, nuclear family form that readily reemphasizes the normative family style, albeit with two parents of the same sex. While establishing families with two parents who support children may appear to be normative, being a same-sex couple who establishes this family uses the emphasis of the normative to challenge commonly gendered messages about reproduction and the family. Stacey (2006) argues that the gay men she interviewed expressed a continuum of responses in terms of a "passion for parenthood" that both shore up and question the common parenting desires of men. Ultimately she argues that gay male parenthood may help to reconfigure heteronormative expectations about parenthood.

Gender Disruptions

If you enjoy the notion of having sex for pleasure and not just for reproduction, thank a feminist. In the nineteenth century, the voluntary motherhood movement (part of the birth control movement) was fighting for women to take control of their reproductive bodies. To do so they disrupted common gender norms of the day by emphasizing women as sexual beings. They believed that by controlling reproduction, motherhood would become a more valued social status. Unlike modern feminists who support women's rights to access contraception and abortion, the women in the voluntary motherhood movement were opposed to contraception and abortion. Instead, they advocated periodic abstinence as a way of preventing unwanted pregnancy. This was actually a fairly radical stance at the time because husbands had absolute rights to their wives' bodies and could demand sex at any time. Women in the voluntary motherhood movement were fighting for the right to refuse sex or to have some agency in the matter (Gordon 1974).

In 1873, the Comstock Laws made it a federal crime to send obscene material, including information about birth control and abortion, through the mail. Violators could be punished with a six-month to five-year prison term, hard labor, or a substantial fine. These kinds of laws lasted until after World War II. Margaret Sanger (a nurse and activist who coined the phrase birth control) and Emma Goldman (a leader in the socialist movement) disrupted the notion of women as naturally always pregnant and as passive sexual objects by working to provide information about contraception and actual contraceptive devices particularly to poor, working-class, and immigrant women.

One of the original premises of second wave feminism is that women should claim their sexuality, taking control of sex so that women's bodies are not just about reproduction (Firestone 1970; Frye 1983; Rich 1986). Women, then, should be seen as human more generally and not just "always potentially pregnant." Of course, women's sexual freedom means further sexual freedom for heterosexual men as well because sexuality can now be understood as being about pleasure, not just reproduction (Seidman 1991). The gay rights movement of the late 1960s and 1970s was also about sexual freedom, gender disruption, and the separation of female and male bodies from expectations of heterosexuality. Articulating a sexuality that is not about male-female couples or about reproduction was a form of resistance to limiting notions of sexual possibilities (Adam 1987; Frye 1983, 1992). The movement broadcast a message that individual people with same-sex sexual interests should be allowed to narrate a self that works to resist the gender box structure; it worked to create a social space for lesbians and gay men (Plummer 1995).

Queer theorists argue that sexual orientation (both heterosexuality and homosexuality) is a concept that was invented in a specific historical period and is no more a part of the body than is gender. Rather, sexual orientation, especially the notion of strict heterosexuality, is something that is shaped and disciplined into the body by a culture that forbids other options beyond marriage-based, legally sanctioned sex between apparent biological opposites (Foucault 1978; Katz 1995; Sedgwick 1990). In other words, each person might express a greater range of sexuality and gender if not for cultural surveillance that encourages and sanctions only one form of so-called appropriate sexuality.

A key argument among queer theorists is that all binaries, like the gender box structure, are false. Sedgwick (1990) asserts rather persuasively that sexual orientation is a social, not innate concept. She argues that the heterosexual/homosexual binary exists only because these supposed fixed sexualities are enforced through the metaphor of "the closet." She argues that "the closet"—that is, the idea that homosexuality is a spoiled identity and homosexual people are encouraged to hide their interests—has equal impact on heterosexual-identified people, in that admitting any minute feeling of same-sex interest will taint that individual's reputation. Thus, forcing people with same-sex interests to hide those interests or face public ridicule not only affects lesbians and gay men, but also encourages straight-identified people to be very straight in public, never admitting to even a momentary digression—a same-sex dream or fond feeling toward someone of the same sex. Given that all people are under surveillance that they should tell the "truth" of their sexuality (i.e., admit and feel ashamed of any sexual or intimate feelings toward a person of the same sex), the power of "the closet" to encourage people to "become 100% straight" (Messner 2000) or hide their same-sex feelings constantly creates the very binary of sexuality that is assumed to reside in the body.

It has been argued that even when "out of the closet," same-sex couples at times mirror heterosexual gender norms. However, proponents of "butch and femme as sexual identities" address the implicit critique of active/passive sexual practices as potentially imitative of heterosexuality. In their study of Buffalo, New York, in the 1940s, 1950s, and 1960s, Lapovsky Kennedy and Davis (1993) are quick to point out that, although butches were the "doers" and femmes the recipients, the purpose was for butches to *give* pleasure, not to take it, as a heterosexual model suggests. Further, the notion that women can receive pleasure from women, without the need for a penis, disrupts the notion that heterosexual sex is the only or most natural form of sexual enjoyment. Case (1989) offers an interpretation that butch/femme, when taken together, present a critique to dominant messages of the naturalness of heterosexuality. Case suggests that the notion that two women can create an erotic sexuality without men falsifies the heterosexist ideal that sexuality is and must be about men.

Perhaps even a greater challenge to heteronormativity and a means to breaking down binaries are movements arguing for sexual fluidity. Open bisexuality, whether monogamous or nonmonogamous, challenges the binary of hetero/homo sexuality (Rust 1995). The notion of an open sexual orientation in which the sexual object choice of any given person is not based on bodily sex is a significant challenge and source of discomfort to heterosexuality and homosexuality alike. How can the concept of sexual orientation exist if the sex of one's partner is not the primary dividing mechanism for identities? Sheff (2005) writes about people who advocate for polyamory—having significant sexual relationships with more than one person at a time. Sheff argues that these people are clear that they are not "swinging"—switching partners for only one instance of sexual gratification—but are pursuing several simultaneous relationships. Clearly this idea of multiplicity questions heteronormative notions of monogamy. Adam (2006) also argues that his respondents—gay male couples in the Toronto area—developed new ideas about sexuality in gay male relationships that challenge the norms of monogamy often in favor of sexual autonomy.

Gender Combinations

In the 1970s and 1980s, radical feminists argued that reproductive technologies gave male doctors increasing control over women's bodies (Corea 1985; O'Brien 1983). More recent discussions of gender and reproductive technologies and reproductive decision making show we are moving in a de-gendered, out-of-the-box direction. In a study of men's roles in reproductive decision making, Markens, Browner, and Preloran (2003) discuss how both "women and men simultaneously reproduce and challenge norms about gender and parenting" (479). In this study, which looked specifically at Latin couples and fetal diagnosis, the authors show how reproductive decision making was often shared equally between male and female partners. As men have become more involved in pregnancies and birth, the cultural messages have changed. Many men today expect to attend childbirth classes and prenatal visits, to be in the labor and delivery room and possibly even to cut the umbilical cord, things that their fathers probably didn't do and their grandfathers wouldn't have even dreamed of doing (Marsiglio 1998; Marsiglio et al. 2001; Reed 2005).[7]

When we think of mothering a child, we think of nurturance and child rearing. When we think of fathering a child, it usually has a connotation that does not go past conception. How then could we think about uses of paternal bodies if we think about "fathering" as disconnected from physical contact with children? Barbara Katz Rothman ([1989] 2000) gives us an interesting idea to think about. She describes in detail a famous experiment conducted by Harry Harlow in which baby monkeys were given the choice between two fake mothers. One was covered in soft cloth, one was made out of wire. A milk bottle was randomly placed sometimes with the soft cloth mother and sometimes with the wire mother. Harlow found that regardless of where their food source was, the baby monkeys became attached to the soft cloth mother. Rothman turns this research question around and asks:

> But what if I wanted to run a study on the question: do infant monkeys necessarily love their mothers, or could they just as well love their fathers? I might

set up each monkey in a cage with two parent dolls. One would give milk, and I would call that the mother doll. The other would give no milk and I would call that the father doll. In half the cages the father would be wire and the mother cloth, and in the other half the mother would be wire and the father cloth. I would learn that monkeys can love whichever parent, mother or father, offers them contact comfort. (Rothman [1989] 2000:149)

For years now, feminists have advocated for fathering to be more than just a genetic relationship, but to also be a social one (see, e.g., Coltrane 1996; Lorber 2005; Risman 1998; Rothman [1989] 2000).[8]

Sports

Given that sport was designed as a male preserve in order to teach masculinity to boys, one could argue that all women's participation in sport is a form of gender resistance and disruption. If sports have been understood as *the* means for men to demonstrate masculinity, then all girls and women who show interest and proficiency in sport are breaking down the gender binaries. But there are men (and women and men together) engaging in gender resistance as well.

In *Built to Win*, Heywood and Dworkin (2003) argue that sport is the feminism of the third wave. They write, "The athletic female body: a body for herself, for her own strength and breath, her own use. A new multicultural, multiracial, perhaps even multisexual image, a new ideal for the millennium" (xxix). Their overarching premise is that women who are experiencing their athletic bodies as powerful are rejecting notions of passivity in other parts of their lives as well. This may also be true of men in traditionally female-dominated sports.

The year 1996, in particular the 1996 Summer Olympic Games, marked a significant shift in the popularity and attentiveness to women's sport in the United States (Heywood and Dworkin 2003; Messner 2002). Along with a general growth in girls' and women's sports participation, this change was largely the result of several U.S. women's teams dominating their sports at the Atlanta games, all while taking place in front of a very patriotic, "home" crowd. U.S. women's teams won gold in basketball, gymnastics, soccer, and softball in the Atlanta games, which was especially significant since both women's soccer and softball were introduced in those games. In 1999, the U.S. women's soccer team won the Women's World Cup, often understood as *the* international soccer competition. With such high-profile successes, women's sport gained attention and many women's sports spun off professional leagues (e.g., the Women's National Basketball Association, Women's United Soccer Association), while existing leagues (National Pro Fastpitch) gained some prominence as a result. While not all of these leagues have survived, women's participation in sports at many levels had never been higher and many argue that the gendered messages surrounding athletics for women has changed as a result (Heywood and Dworkin 2003; Messner 2002).

While traditional male-centered sports are still very popular, nontraditional sports for women and men are also gaining popularity and changing gender messages in the process. Messner (2002) demonstrates that football, men's basketball, and baseball still maintain the institutional and cultural "center" of sport today in terms of money expended and fan and media celebration. However, women's sports and peripheral men's sports are changing and continue to provide resistance to the model that sport is the preserve of hegemonic masculinity (Birrell and Richter 1994; Crossett 1995; Kane 1995; Theberge 1986). Below we give examples of how women's and men's sports are changing to resist gender messages that keep us in our boxes.

Gender Emphasis

One way in which women's sports figures have attempted to gain attention for their sports or gain financially through promotions is by using what Griffin (1998) calls a "heterosexy" image—posing for ads or articles, not in a way to show off athletics, but rather in feminized and sexualized ways (e.g., nude or in evening wear, with clearly feminized face makeup, in poses that imply sexuality, or in sexualizing contexts like *Playboy* magazine). Griffin argues that the Ladies Professional Golf Association and the Women's Tennis Association have both used feminized, sexualized images of players to promote their sports associations. Likewise, Messner (2002) reports that the Women's National Basketball Association has feminized its players to promote the women's version of this professional sport. Similarly, individual athletes have marketed their images in ways that specifically promote heterosexual attractiveness. Examples include Jeannette Lee, a champion of the Women's Professional Billiards Association, posing in an off-the-shoulder evening dress; swimmer Jenny Thompson posing for *Sports Illustrated* in tight-fitting swim shorts and red boots and nothing else; high jumper Amy Acuff posing for *Esquire's* "Girls of Summer" issue; soccer champion Brandi Chastain posing for *Gear* magazine nude and crouching behind a soccer ball (Heywood and Dworkin 2003); and, most famously, tennis player Anna Kournikova who, regardless of never winning a major tennis tournament, parlayed her image into a $10-million-a-year enterprise by 2002 (Messner 2002).

Some of these athletes are quite open about simply wanting to pose for their own financial gain. Others argue that the use of their heterosexy images helps to promote women's sport. Still others, like Jenny Thompson, argue that their nearly nude but powerfully muscled bodies make a statement about the power of women's bodies that might be considered feminist (Heywood and Dworkin 2003). While it may be understandable that athletes want to promote their sport through various media outlets in ways that get public attention, the intentional use of heterosexy images may emphasize gendered messages more than disrupting them. Messner (2002) argues that it is not just the images themselves that may be damaging to women's pursuit of serious sport, but when these images are placed against a backdrop of sexualizing humor in sports media commentary and the general lack of reporting on women's accomplishments, they do little to change attitudes so that women's sports could be considered serious, important, and worthy of attention on the basis of sporting merit. In other words, these images do not popularize women's sports *as athletics*, but rather continue to promote the message that women's bodies are sex objects to be viewed.[9]

Do all athletes playing "gender-appropriate" sports buy into heteronormativity and confirm gendered messages? Yes and no. Markula (2003) shows how aerobics enthusiasts have a contradictory experience of their sport—that aerobics is always perceived as both "feminine" and good training for "real" sport. Markula reports that her respondents stopped buying workout magazines and videos that promote only the heterosexy model without good athletic, aerobic content, and that many aerobics enthusiasts experience the change in bodily power with aerobic practice and some see themselves differently as a result.

Interestingly, Wachs (2005) describes one instance in which gender messages and the underestimation of women's abilities offered a competitive advantage in co-ed recreational softball. In this sport, it is assumed in the rule structure that women will not be able to hit as far as men (an instance of surveillance described in chapter 3). Hence, all outfielders must stand behind a line about halfway out in the outfield demarcating a certain distance from the infield so that outfielders do not crowd the infield and allow for an "easy out." Wachs describes an instance of a female player hitting a home run because an outfielder charged toward the infield assuming she could not hit far. Instead, she hit the ball far over his head and he needed to turn around and run farther into the outfield to retrieve the ball. She reports that several players she observed used that as a tactic to create an advantage and then continued to place hits strategically to keep outfielders off guard. The players allowed competitors to assume their inferiority, ultimately demonstrating their batting skill to their opponents.

Some individual gay male athletes do offer examples of emphasizing masculinity as protection from homophobia. Anderson (2005a) writes about gay athletes who emphasize masculinity to alleviate some of the stigma of being gay. In essence, these gay male athletes simply perform masculinity well by playing hard, demonstrating physical abilities, and winning, in the same way straight men gain masculine capital from winning at sports. While this may provide some critique of the link between masculinity and heteronormativity (an everyday disruption?), this kind of gender emphasis does not do much to critique the hierarchical box structure that expects men to be tough and women to be weak and passive.

Indeed gender emphasis works to recreate gendered messages and seems to have limited potential to create serious change, since conformity, regardless of whether it is actively intended, in some way always shores up the gender box structure. To radically change or disrupt the box structure requires resisting gender messages.

Gender Disruptions

In January 2006, the *Christian Science Monitor* reported on the second annual Lahore (Pakistan) Marathon (Montero 2006). Newsworthy in the West because it was the first Pakistani marathon to allow women and men to run together, it was reportedly protected by 6,000 armed police and more than 400 people were arrested when protests against the co-ed race turned violent. The protests did not stop the race and women competitors took part while wearing robes that draped their full bodies with the exception of their faces. The marathon was reportedly hailed by President Pervez Musharraf as advancing Pakistan's commitment to "enlightened moderation." The race was significant for showing both the ways in which gendered messages about women's bodies and sport have changed and also for showing how far there is to go (i.e., why are there still violent protests over women's participation in games?).

The argument we make throughout this chapter is that certainly bodily experiences that contradict gender messages may encourage each of us to agentically redefine our own understandings of ourselves, or that witnessing the bodily performances of others that do not neatly fit the gender box structure may cause everyday disruptions of gender messages for viewers. Stories like the one from a student that opens this chapter demonstrate how our body experiences can invert our notions about the innateness of femininity and masculinity. Gender nonconformity is perhaps the most compelling of examples of this transformation of gender messages. Experiencing or performing women's bodies as powerful or men's bodies as graceful can be instrumental in resisting stereotypes.[10]

Women playing traditionally male-dominated sports give common examples of this resistance. Leslie Heywood talks about her own experience of changing her understanding of self through weight lifting, especially through the social experience of succeeding at bench press with a group of male workout buddies watching (Heywood and Dworkin 2003). She writes about the acceptance of the men who watched her and her own response to her achievement and the playful name transition she and her friends used to mark the acceptance of her weight-lifting successes. She writes:

Lester was officially named the day I broke the 200-pound barrier on the bench, 200 and then 225. Two hundred is one of those turning points that clearly separates one class of lifter from the next, the men from the boys and certainly the women from the men. It was the day I went from being "strong for a girl" to just plain strong, seen no differently from "them." . . . I'd always faltered on this weight, getting it only an inch or so off my chest, like some biological limitation I'd never transgress. But today was different, I could feel it going down. I could feel the bar, the weight on it, but there was the sensation of not feeling it, too. This time, there was no sticking. This time, the weight flew up like it wasn't there, and as I racked it at the top, Billy and Chris roared with joy, jumping up in the air shouting, "Lester! Lester! She's with the big dogs now!" Everyone around us was staring, and I felt years of frustration drop away. It was a small thing, the shift form Leslie to Lester. A single bench press in a single gym, lost in the backwoods of an upstate New York town. It didn't change the world. It surprised a few people, maybe . . . But I felt something, part of something. An acceptance I've never felt in any other place. (56–57)

Even in newer sports such as skateboarding, women experience a sense of achievement in becoming "one of the guys" when they skate well (Beal 1996). After interviewing both male and female skateboarders, Beal offers this insight into the organization of gender in skateboarding:

For Shelley, this meant that she actually split her personality into two parts: masculine and feminine. When she skates she "stops thinking like a girl" and then she can do better. While she skates she wants to be treated like "one of the guys"; she doesn't want to be "scammed on." Then she stated, after she skates she can get "dressed up." (217)

For Shelley, although the male skaters treated her with some disrespect for being female, she adapted her own understanding of self as accomplished at skating regardless of her interests in feminizing when not skating.

Women involved in sports that have traditionally been seen as gender inappropriate regularly report how sporting experiences alter the gender messages they take into their sense of selves. Many other athletes have written about the experiences of play and/or the forms of interaction they witness as acts of resistance to gender messages (Bolin and Granskog 2003; Cox and Thompson 2000; George 2005; Granskog 2003).

For women, playing ice hockey—with its imagery of toothless male players who fight as part of the strategy of the game—clearly conflicts with gender messages of women as passive, weak, and overly concerned with attractive, feminine appearance. In Theberge's research (1997, 2000) with female ice hockey players, she finds that players commonly express their satisfaction with expressing aggression that hockey allows. The players talk about enjoying the physicality of the game and "fighting for the puck" (2000:113), arguing that they feel empowered by the sense of being stronger than another player.

Similarly, women who play rugby speak about their experiences as shoring up a sense of possibility for women. Rugby has long been recognized for its violent play and its postgame culture of hard drinking replete with highly sexualized and sexist pub songs (Broad 2001; Howe 2003). How might this culture be transformed when women play? Broad argues that women who play rugby, rather than engaging a feminine apologetic as we described in chapter 2, instead engage a "gendered unapologetic," or specific attempts at "transgressing gender, destabilizing the heterosexual/homosexual binary, and 'in your face' confrontations of stigma" (182) of women playing masculinized sports. Broad quotes a player who comments on enjoying challenging gender messages as follows:

> My grandmother . . . goes off, "Oh my god, I don't know why you play that. You're going to hurt yourself. You're going to kill yourself. You're going to maim yourself. No one is going to want to date you." And I just nod my head. You're a badass to them. Everyone thinks you are a badass. (188)

Broad goes on to explain:

> Instead of listening to doctors, boyfriends, and family, women who played rugby continued to go out every weekend and get bruises and broken noses. . . . Rather than defensively curling their hair and applying make-up to apologize for their masculine athletic pursuits, rugby players resisted and challenged beauty standards. (189)

Similarly, in response to lesbian baiting or questioning about their sexuality, Broad reports the rugby players in her study, both heterosexual and lesbian-identified, worked to destabilize notions of sexual passivity by sexualizing themselves. The sexist and objectifying rugby songs common among men's rugby were amended to be less sexist, or new songs were created that were equally raunchy but allowed women more agency.[11] Broad's point is that women rugby players are actively working to change restrictive notions of gender and sexuality "unapologetic"-ly and hence changing women's notion of self and causing everyday disruptions for others.

While many of these experiences involve transitions in self for women as a result of social embodiment and their own physical experiences, others can witness women's athletics as an everyday disruption of gender messages. Perhaps the pinnacle of this kind of disruption is women in competitive bodybuilding. Quite commonly when viewing pictures of female bodybuilders, our own students react with distaste ("Yuck!"), or distrust that female bodies could be built as large without some chemical alteration ("That's steroids!"). Heywood and Dworkin (2003) report in their study of elementary and high school students' reactions to athletic images that in response to images of female bodybuilders, "students overwhelmingly offered the terms ugly, nasty, grotesque, gross, strange, manly, a man, unnatural, unacceptable, too strong, inappropriate, and they clearly stated why—'too much' muscle" (147).

Women's bodybuilding threatens at its deepest core the notion that the gender box structure is natural and innate (Bolin 2003; Cole 1994; Fisher 1997; Frueh 1999; Hall 1996; Heywood 1998; Lowe 1998; Mansfield and McGinn 1993; Moore 1997; Shea 2001; Wesely 2001). Mansfield and McGinn (1993) argue that, "Because muscularity has been coded as a fundamentally masculine attribute, its adoption by women has offered a threat and a challenge to notions of both the feminine AND the masculine" (65, emphasis in original). Hence, the challenge is not just to the perceived natural link between femininity and the female body, but also the link between muscularity and the male body. Women's bodybuilding threatens both (Cole 1994). It makes us uncomfortable because it gives us very real images that counter our gender messages. Bolin (2003) refers to our cultural discomfort with women's bodybuilding as a confrontation of "beauty or the beast." We cannot tell who we see in the form. Is she a strong masculine person or a beautiful fit female body?[12]

The image in photo 5.2 offers a glimpse into this kind of everyday disruption. Here, Marion Jones, a runner and former college basketball player, not a bodybuilder, accepts an award at the 2001 ESPYs (ESPN's annual awards show) in a traditionally feminine dress. The gender disruption of her massive biceps and shoulders juxtaposed against a spaghetti-strapped evening gown offers the viewer a new message about muscularity, women's bodies, and the assumption of femininity.

Men playing confidently and competitively, recognizing the social embodiment of power and strength learned through sport, hardly represent a disruption of masculinity. As we argued earlier, sport is more than consistent with masculinity. So,

Photo 5.2. Track-and-field star Marion Jones accepts her ESPY for U.S. Female Olympian of the Year in 2001. Her bulging biceps and square shoulders offset the high-fashion dress that is seemingly required of women attending national awards shows and create an example of everyday gender disruptions—strong body in supermodel attire.

in what ways can sporting participation for men be a gender disruption? Well, generally it is not, except where male athletes are playing against dominant performances of masculinity through sport. Whitson (1994) argues hopefully that perhaps newer sports and fitness pastimes such as running, mountain biking, triathlon, cross-country skiing, and skateboarding will be less culturally loaded with gender stereotypes and, hence, will challenge the gender binary. Wheaton (2000) finds some small support for the idea of ambivalent masculinities in windsurfing in England, but also finds strong support for gender lines being drawn in this largely noncompetitive pastime. However, perhaps some gender disruption is happening in "gender-inappropriate" sports for men.

In the 2006 Winter Olympics in Turin, Italy, male figure skater Johnny Weir became the best hope for U.S. success in individual figure skating as an unapologetically expressive and graceful man. Regardless of his over-the-top personality, his playful flirting with hints about his sexual orientation, his arguably feminine routines, and outspokenness against institutional skating, Weir received support from masculine-talking sportswriters as the patriotic choice for U.S. fans (Shelton 2006a, 2006b). Instead of ridicule for his behavior, Weir's successes garnered a change in tone from sportswriters who commonly pick fun at the feminine in sport. Commending Weir for his successes over much more masculine but unsuccessful athletes like Bode Miller, one writer (Shelton 2006a) put it this way:

> Here is Weir, the guy who answers to the nickname "Tinkerbell." The guy who admits he is "princessy." The guy who referred to himself as "the prettiest flower in the pond." . . . There is something to be said for being comfortable in your own skin, isn't there? Weir has that gripped with both hands. Although the trend in men's figure skating costumes has become more conservative over the years. . . . Weir has remained loyal to his lace. He even names his costumes. . . . In other words, Weir is a hoot. . . . The thing is, Weir can also skate.

And so, the writer rewrites the gendered messages about men's sport in support of gender-bending when there is an opportunity to win for the patriotic cause. Surely that is an example of everyday disruptions that affect gender messages.

Similarly, the sole male in synchronized swimming makes waves. (Ouch!) Bill May is the only male member of the Santa Clara (California) Aquamaids, a competitive synchronized swimming team that trains 8–10 hours a day, six days a week (CBS News 2003). His coach calls him one of the top five competitors in synchronized swimming in the United States. He has won national solo competitions and is recognized as one of the best in the world, but he cannot compete in the Olympic Games because there is no accommodation for male swimmers in that sport in the Olympics (Grudowski 1997). In 2003, May and his partner Cristina Lum petitioned the International Olympic

Committee to be able to do a mixed pairs exhibition in the 2004 Games and were rejected in that effort (CBS News 2003).[13]

Other movements in sport work to break down the requisite heteronormativity of athletics, especially among male athletes. The Gay Games is an example of a collective movement to resist heterosexism.[14] The Federation of Gay Games website describes the initiative to hold athletic competitions for gay and lesbian competitors as follows: "Built upon the principles of Participation, Inclusion and Personal Best™, for more than 20 years the Gay Games have empowered tens of thousands of lesbian, gay, bisexual and transgender athletes through fellowship and friendly competition" (Federation of the Gay Games 2006).

Originated in 1980 by former Olympic decathlete Tom Waddell, the Gay Games are now held every four years in cities around the world and are supported by athletic organizations of four continents. Working from traditional sports rules but expanding opportunities to include gender nontraditional sports (e.g., women's football) and same-sex doubles competitions (e.g., same-sex figure skating pairs), they foreground competition and athletic achievement in an environment in which all people are welcome.

Gender Combinations

Every year during "March Madness," the annual pursuit of the NCAA college basketball tournament, a familiar scene takes place all over the country. As teams are winning their conference tournaments, guaranteeing a seed in the prestigious college play-off tournament, hundreds of fans stream onto the court, creating an undulating mass of celebrants hugging players, high-fiving each other, hoisting the coach on their collective shoulders, and celebrating long into the night. The same scene played out in 2006 on an ESPN broadcast when Army's Black Knights won their first-ever Patriot conference championship.[15] What makes this particular event unique is that the team being cheered by student-soldiers, both male and female, who streamed onto the court in raucous celebration, was the *women's* basketball team, and the coach they hoisted on their shoulders in wild appreciation was first-year head coach Maggie Dixon.[16] Coincidentally, in 2006, West Point celebrated the 30th anniversary of women's admission into the academy. What a difference 30 years makes. In 1975, women were specifically discriminated against by not being allowed into West Point, the elite institution that trains the Army's top military officers. In 2006, a crowd of predominantly male soldiers ran onto the court of their winning team, the women's basketball team. This case provides an example of the power of gender combinations—women and men working together toward a common goal—to change gendered messages. Among the celebrating fans, the sex of the players of "their" team did not appear to matter in their expression of pride.

Another form of gender combinations is the emerging advocacy of fathers on behalf of daughters' sports opportunities. A new twist to the gains of Title IX is men filing suits against noncompliant educational institutions on behalf of girls' sports (Pennington 2004a). Instigating lawsuits in several states, angry dads, in particular, are now contributing to the push for equal resources and facilities for high school players, especially in softball, where facilities may not be shared by female and male students. A Title IX lawyer[17] is quoted as saying, "The fathers tend to get more riled up . . . The fathers have already experienced the benefits of a full high school athletic experience. Then they have a daughter and she goes to high school and they can't believe she isn't being treated like they were" (Pennington 2004a:2). Resulting from the successes of Title IX, the new gender message that girls should have access to good facilities seems to have pervaded parents' consciousness such that there are now higher expectations for girls' sports facilities. Occurring in other sports as well, such as soccer, field hockey, gymnastics, and pole vault, dads and male coaches in particular are taking seriously the differential in facilities and equipment and advocating for girls as athletes. This powerful gender combination adds important influence to the push for serious athletic opportunities for all students.

Another interesting phenomenon among Top-10 college women's basketball teams such as Rutgers is the use of male practice players to train with the women's teams (Finley 2006; Pennington 2004b). Combining women and men during practice allows the women to train with male students who may not be proficient enough or tall enough to play on men's teams at the Division I level. (Pennington argues that these men are usually at the men's Division II level of play.) Yet the elite female players are able to train against classmates who are of a height and strength usually not found throughout the school's student body of women. Already basketball enthusiasts who have likely trained through high school systems that afford men serious facilities, equipment, and training, these male practice players provide the size and competition to improve the varsity women's teams. Also, the male practice players develop a respect for and rapport with female team members and therefore celebrate team accomplishments with them and get to feel as if they are a part of the Division I sports for which they themselves cannot qualify. Working in combination, the female team members and male practice players support the school's goal of producing a competitive team.

Gender combinations make an important point. If sports can be used as resistance to the gender box structure that dichotomizes the great diversity of human existence into two narrowly envisioned "boxes"—men vs. women—we must envision a world of sports that refuses to dichotomize them into women's sport and men's sport. The work cited in this book demonstrates that women and men are resisting gender messages in sport.[18] While it may still be practical to segregate women's sport in many instances because women's lack of traditional opportunities may have hindered some women's full potential, in order to transform sport it will be important to begin taking advantage of gender combinations where practical and applicable (Kane 1995).

Until men are interested in women's sport as a serious venture and women and men are supported in pursuing all kinds of sports, not just gender-appropriate sports, sports will continue to reinforce the binary of the gender box structure. To step outside that binary, we need to imagine the possibility of competitions between women and men as well as encourage and support competitions at all levels for the sake of encouraging body knowledge for all people (Hargreaves 1994; Jefferson Lenskyj 1994; Messner 2002). We need to begin to envision structural changes to sport that allow women and men to work together, such as using weight and height to determine competitive classes rather than simply assuming sex should be the basis of all sport divisions. Watching elite competitions is thrilling and fun, but the greater good of sport comes in what each of us of all body types can learn as players about our various forms of ableness, and about what each of us as coaches, supporters, and fans can teach others about equity, fair play, and the pursuit of excellence in all segments of life, not just the playing field.

CONCLUSION

Throughout this chapter we have illustrated the ways in which gender agency may be enacted. At times working to re-create the gender box structure and at times working to disrupt it, people do make tactical decisions about how to leverage the ever-present existence of gender in their lives. While we have discussed in detail throughout this book the pervasive and sometimes oppressive forces in interaction encouraging individuals to play along with binary gender messages (i.e., surveillance and accountability), each of us can make choices about our gender performances if we are actively aware of the ways gender messages influence our lives. Indeed, we contend it is possible to more actively increase one's agency only if each of us is aware of the interactive practices of gender that we outline in this book. When you understand the process of how bodies and selves become gendered, only then can you make conscious, aware decisions about the components of gender that you will employ and those that you seek to avoid. Further, we argue that by moving beyond uninformed, binary gender performance we create greater opportunity for all people to become the infinitely diverse individuals we imagine ourselves to be.

NOTES

1. Birthing women are not alone in having to negotiate the world of medicine and the world of experience. Although an oppositional model with medicine at one end and midwifery at the other end has been common in social science and femi-

nist writing for some time, scholars are now beginning to argue for less polarization. Rather, the focus might be on the way the two worlds interact (Annandale and Clark 1996, 1997; Davis-Floyd, Pigg, and Cosminsky 2001; Foley and Faircloth 2003; Foley 2005a). Like birthing women, childbirth practitioners have begun to make use of a range of messages and practices, speaking in medical terminology one moment and midwifery or self-help terminology in another moment.

2. Although not necessarily working to change ideas about the construction of bodies, the National Organization of Men Against Sexism (NOMAS) is an organization of men whose stated mission is to change men. However, the size of their membership is not clear and the organization appears to have only eight chapters nationwide as of this writing.

3. See NAAFA's website for more information: http://www.naafa.org.

4. Mindy Stombler and Irene Padavic (1997) argue that structural and cultural factors influence the feasibility of collective resistance versus individual resistance. Their research demonstrates that white women who are little sisters in predominantly white fraternities are more likely to use individual strategies to resist men's exploitation, while black women who are little sisters in predominantly black fraternities are more likely to engage in confrontational and collective resistance to exploitation. In their research, these differences were influenced by the organizational autonomy and programs for group bonding of the black little sister programs compared to a lack of autonomy and bonding in the white little sister programs.

5. Word Spy is "devoted to *lexpionage*, the sleuthing of new words and phrases. These aren't 'stunt words' or 'sniglets,' but new terms that have appeared multiple times in newspapers, magazines, books, Web sites, and other recorded sources" (http://www.wordspy.com/words/metrosexual.asp, accessed March 10, 2006).

6. See the Blood Sisters Project http://bloodsisters.org/bloodsisters/ and Tampaction http://seac.org/tampons/.

7. LaRossa (1997) argues that the cultural notions and expectations of "new fatherhood" are somewhat removed from the actual practices of men as fathers.

8. The idea of fatherhood as embodied practice is only just beginning to be explored. Doucet (2006) argues that "male embodiment constantly shifts in the weight of its salience in the identities and practices of fathers and caregiving" (696).

9. While one might argue that all sports are sexualizing and that one (perhaps positive) effect of playing sport is that athletics tends to build culturally beautiful bodies, Messner (2002) argues that, for men's sports, even if male athletes are periodically sexualized, the actual accomplishments of athletes are prioritized in the media. However, for women's sports, there remains very little recognition of women as athletes without the feminizing and sexualizing that comes with gender messages.

10. Experiencing bodies as powerful can happen in pastimes as well as in competitive sports. DeWelde (2003) demonstrates how it does not require a lifetime of athletic participation to change women's minds about their bodies and bodily capacities. Something as relatively simple as taking two five-hour self-defense classes over the course of a weekend can have a similar effect. Using both physical techniques and narratives that DeWelde calls "enabling the body," women learned to think of themselves as strong and physically able to react to the possibility of sexual victimization. She writes, "Women seemed to embrace their bodies as strong weapons, where they had not before" (268).

Joans (2003) writes about the explosion of women riding motorcycles and their transformed experiences of self as differently feminine as a result. Women used to be relegated to riding on the backs of men's motorcycles, spawning the very degrading but common term of women riders as the "bitch in the back." In interviewing women who ride their bikes, Joans proclaims "the bitch in the back is dead." Women are transforming their bodily experience of femininity and ableness by riding on their own motorcycles, and they are changing the gendered messages of women's bodies as others watch them ride competently on their own.

11. An example of one such new creation began with the following: "I don't want to be a housewife. I'd much rather be a whore. I'd rather turn some tricks involving foot long pricks, housework's such a bore—Oh Blimey!" (continues for several verses). A female rugby player recognized the sexualized implications but explained how the reversal of agency changes the meaning for women players. She stated, "It says how I feel and it shows that we are tough. It's totally fun, plus it is inclusive of all sexual preferences so we can all be united instead of seeing each other as straight or gay or whatever. It reminds me of what women can do. . . ANYTHING!" (Broad 2001:193).

12. Increasingly, competitive bodybuilding for women is gendered terrain. Whereas successful bodybuilding for men is judged on the basis of who is biggest, most muscular, and most "ripped," women are judged for muscularity but also for compliance with appropriate femininity, so that a competitor can be judged to be too large or not appropriately proportioned in women's bodybuilding (Bolin 2003; Lowe 1998). The feminine apologetic is cut through and through in women's competitive bodybuilding, as competitors feminize their hairstyles, wear significant quantities of makeup and jewelry, and tend to wear feminizing outfits such as skimpy bathing suits or miniskirts. Increasingly, the routines of women's bodybuilding have transitioned from a series of still poses like those used by men to demonstrate muscle, to routines set to music that show grace, fluidity, and poise in addition to muscularity. In short, women's competitive bodybuilding is becoming more "gender appropriate" to resemble women's gymnastics or aerobics. So bodybuilding as a sport is not impervious to pressures to fit the gender box structure. Nevertheless, the built female body does seem to cause everyday disruptions.

13. May is advertised as part of the synchronized swimming troupe for Cirque du Soleil (Cirque du Soleil 2006). He is still recognized as a premier swimmer and strong competitor.

14. The Gay and Lesbian International Sport Association (GLISA) sponsored a similar event in 2006 with the first World OutGames in Montreal, Canada. The second World OutGames are scheduled to take place in Copenhagen, Denmark, in 2009. See the GLISA website for more information: http://www.glisa.org.

15. The scene described was replayed on ESPN's *NCAA Selection Show* on March 13, 2006, at 7 p.m. EST.

16. From http://goarmysports.collegesports.com/sports/w-baskbl/spec-rel/031006aaa .html, "NCAA Women's Basketball Selection Show Monday" (accessed March 14, 2006).

17. Tennessee lawyer Sam Schiller and University of Tulsa law professor Ray Yasser together have been involved in more than 30 Title IX cases. Yasser is a coauthor of one of the premier sports law textbooks, *Sports Law: Cases and Materials* (2003).

18. Other work shows the ways women around the world—in Eastern Europe, Cuba, and China (Riordan 1985) and in South Africa, Muslim-dominated countries, and in Aboriginal communities in Canada and Australia (Hargreaves 2000)— are making gender change through sport.

6

A World without Dichotomies?

"What Are You?"

I have two identity problems. What I really mean is, there are two identities that I just do not know how to have in socially acceptable ways and still feel true to myself. One is gender. I can talk about gender: tell stories, articulate theories, apply them to my life, write page after page about gender dysphoria. I am conscious of disrupting the gender binary. There is agency in the decision to disrupt gender. The other identity problem is race. My racial ambiguity is written on my body. I have not found a way to theorize race that feels empowering.

Goffman (1967) argues that people observe others' appearance and use it to put them into person categories that provide guidelines for how to act toward different people. I decided to perform gender ambiguously, but I had racial ambiguity written on my body. I do not find it empowering when someone asks me if Spanish was my first language. There is one question that I have been asked my whole life and it still jars me no matter how many times I hear it: "What are you?"— as if there were one answer that would satisfy the question. These three words demonstrate Goffman's argument and illustrate the social dilemmas that ensue when a category cannot be quickly assigned. To be honest I think I've heard it so many times that my first thought is, "I can't believe this is happening again," then I promptly give them any correct answer that does not tell them what they want to know. What I want to tell them is some variation of B-horror-movie villains. They ask, "What are you?" I answer, "A pod person from Mars here to eat

your appendages and make jerky out of your pets which I will package in pink foil wrappers and sell for 49 cents a piece at Wal-Mart."

This question is referring to my nationality or ethnicity or where I
come from or some combination of the three that people seem to
stumble over or mumble, making it clear that they are not comfortable asking directly for the information that they want. What they
want to know is which well-defined racial category to put me in so
that I can be treated accordingly. I hate that this bothers me, that I
haven't found a way to turn it around and claim it. It is not that I wish
that I never had these interactions; they are productive in their own
way, but they reduce me to my body and make me feel objectified.

When I was very little and my family was Christian fundamentalist,
a man from our church said to my mother, "I feel bad for your children; they'll never know what they are." He said this because my parents are racially different from each other. If I was present at the time,
I was too young to remember but I imagine the scene every time
someone asks "What are you?"

Most people who ask this question do not know me very well and are
interested in my ethnicity because my race is not immediately obvious
to them. The answer I give depends on who is asking and my mood at
the time, but the truth is I cannot answer this question with certainty.
There are a series of more involved responses I have developed over the
years, but at the deepest level I simply do not know. The first response
is that I am biracial; one black and one white parent. My mother is Cape
Verdean and my father is Portuguese, English, and Irish. To simply give
this answer would not tell the whole story, even if the questioner knows
what or where Cape Verde is. Still there is a problem of what it means
to be Cape Verdean. Cape Verde is an archipelago off the northwest
coast of Africa. It was uninhabited until the Portuguese used it as a center for the slave trade. Decades of slave trading, raping, and colonizing
by Europeans left a fairly small collection of people whose racial and
ethnic makeup was mixed, ambiguous. It is not unheard of for Cape
Verdeans to be born with blue eyes or red hair or dark brown skin.

My racial ambiguity was a visual cue that set me apart from my
peers throughout my education in predominantly white and middle-
to upper-class schools where I constantly felt put in the position of
speaking up for people of color. As early as fourth grade I can specifically remember moments when racial markers of identity set me apart
from my classmates. If nothing else, such experiences taught me to
think more critically about the world in which I live.

Howard Winant argues, in *The World Is a Ghetto*, that "race is not
'natural' but sociohistorical" (2002: 290). He traces racism back to the

historical imperative to see some groups as inferior in order for colonialism and slavery to operate. The ideology that once provided the justification for domination became the basis for examining the "other" for differences in order to build an idea of the white, European self that was distinct from subordinate groups. The dominant self became what the other was not, with the result of establishing a "racial classification [that] became an indispensable indicator of social location" (Winant 2002:297).

For me all this means that the color of my skin defines me as *not white* and locates me socially despite the fact that my father is white and I am not what would be considered underprivileged. Even as I am writing this I feel as if I am outing myself, revealing some family secret, or declaring myself a victim of some unnameable offense. As I sit in my apartment with central air, cable, Internet, a car parked outside, family and friends that care about me, and time to think about my identity, I am struck by the countless ways in which I am incredibly privileged. The outcome of years of being asked what I am has not only led me to question what I am, but to question race, gender, and categorization of people in general. I have come to understand simple experiences, such as filling out institutional documents where I have to check a race box, as examples of a subtle form of racism and social control. There is no box labeled "I do not fully know how to answer this question."

If I am to understand the lack of a box to check and the repeated questioning of what I am from a Foucauldian framework then I would have to see that I am discursively told that I occupy a social space that should not exist. It is significant that there is no box marked "multiracial" or "prefer not to answer." I am told that I must pick from a small list of possible racial orientations because those are the only options available to me. I am called to account for my ambiguous appearance in my interactions when I am asked what I am.

Being unable to answer the question "What are you?" would cause my competence as a social actor to be doubted. Perhaps this is my lack of creativity showing, but I cannot imagine feeling empowered by an interaction in which I tell someone that I do not know what I am. My refusal to answer "I don't know" is also indicative of the discursive power of racial identity categories. Everyone is expected to belong to a clear racial group and to identify with that group. If I were to say "I don't know" I would likely find myself confronted with a further question about where my parents are from and so on until the opportunity to self-define my race had been taken away from me.

Despite a lifetime of being confronted with this question I have not found a way to get through these interactions without feeling objectified and reduced simply to my body and its excesses and deficiencies. I value these experiences for the questions they have led me to ask and the skills they have taught me, but they are a source of ongoing personal conflict.

—Sharla Alegria, graduate student

Our goal with this book is to shift your understanding of gender and bodies and the processes by which we become gendered people. To conclude, we would like to revisit the problem of the gender box structure, explain our intent in defining the gender feedback loop, and propose some new directions for both research and personal ethics.

WHY LOOPS ARE BETTER THAN BOXES

The commonly used set of gender messages in Western cultures that we call the gender box structure (figure 6.1) far too readily makes assumptions about an essential, natural self. It is a comfortable idea, that we are naturally just a certain type of thing, but it is far too simplistic to describe the vast diversity of people in the world and the multiple inputs involved in producing each person.

Figure 6.1. Gender Box Structure. The Gender Box Structure is the ruling message that instructs us to believe that there are only two kinds of "natural" bodies and that gender and sexuality are determined by these two distinct kinds of bodies.

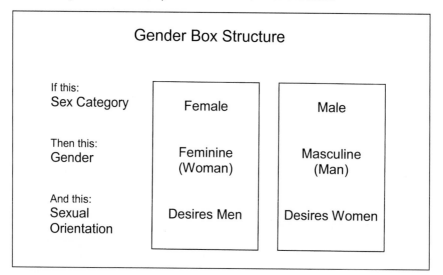

Our belief in a natural sex, which results from actively applying messages of the gender box structure constantly in our everyday interactions, is not natural at all. As West and Zimmerman (1987) describe, we do not use some real, measurable sense of physiology to gender others. Rather, in everyday life we use *sex category* as a proxy for biology. Sex category mobilizes the belief in a dichotomous, definable difference between the categories of male and female that we apply based, not on bodies, but on assumptions about what lies under our clothes. In everyday life, we don't actually see genitals or measure hormone levels or determine chromosome structure before we make an assignment of male or female for the others we interact with every day. The appearance of facial hair is assumed to mean a certain genital structure and a consistent level of hormones and chromosomal structure. The size of one's hands or prominence of the larynx or bulges (or lack of bulges) in pants or under shirts are used to presume a consistent and mutually exclusive "nature" about each person. We know this exclusivity to be false. Fausto-Sterling (2000) outlines for us that even if we did measure genitals or hormones or chromosomes we would find such a range of differences among members of the group we call female and the group we call male that the notion of a truly definable sex falls apart. Unlike the gendered messages we receive from the gender box structure, there is considerable overlap between the groups male and female, and there are people who cannot be readily defined as fitting in either. As Fausto-Sterling demonstrates, *there is no single measure that truly, accurately, and consistently determines so-called biological sex for every person.* If there were, intersexed people would not exist. But intersexed people are a biological reality that our culture has tried very hard (and quite disrespectfully) to ignore, erase, or change through the use of surgery and hormonal control. Sadly, their unfortunate treatment highlights our absolute discomfort with difference and fluidity and our need to socially construct a "truth" of nature. It is time to lose this symbolic and practical reliance on binaries and begin showing respect for all our natural, colorful differences.

The use of a dichotomous sex category, then, as a substitute for some measure of presumed actual biology is not only risky, it hides a great deal of human variety of bodies, experiences, and identities. Nonetheless, on an everyday basis, we hold people accountable to our expectations of their place in the box structure. Female is assumed to mean feminine and desires men and a whole host of other preferences; similarly, male is assumed to mean all sorts of consistent characteristics, from body size and strength to emotional preference to thought patterns.

Although the commonly understood gender box structure pins sex, gender, and sexuality together based on ideas about "natural" bodies, it is much more descriptive of the world of human experience not to make such a correlation. So, rather than fitting each individual into a dichotomous box structure, we suggest seeing sex, gender, and sexuality as (at least analytically) separate attributes, and as a vast set of possibilities for each person. That is, we suggest that in looking beyond the boxes we come closer to understanding the diversity of bodies, experiences, practices, and wants in the world of lived human experience.

Instead of looking for natural boxes, we suggest seeing *everyday processes* of bodies, meanings, interactions, and practices that determine who we are as people and how we live in the world. We propose the gender feedback loop (figure 6.2) as a more descriptive process by which humans are made. As a process, rather than a fixed set of boxes, the gender feedback loop recognizes change and fluidity within each person's life and that gender is an everyday accomplishment, not an initially conferred category (Butler 1990, 1993; Lorber 1994; West and Zimmerman 1987). The gender feedback loop also recognizes the swirling pressures of surveillance (Foucault 1977) and accountability (West and Zimmerman 1987), as well as the constant responsiveness each of us must attend to in order to make our worlds a reality (Mead [1934]1964).

Figure 6.2. Gender Feedback Loop: Performance / Surveillance / Resistance. More accurate than the Gender Box Structure, the Gender Feedback Loop describes how gender messages affect our thoughts about selves and our practices of the body in everyday life, which actually creates the conformity that we tend to believe exists in natural bodies originally.

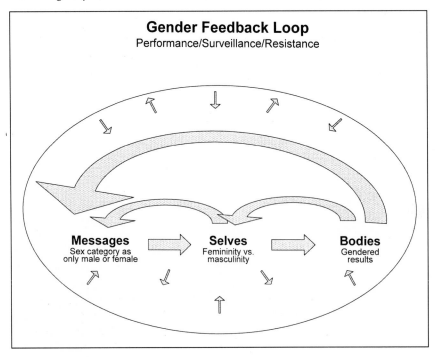

Each of us emerges into this world with cultures, languages, and gendered messages already preceding us. As much as our strongly held belief in individualism suggests otherwise, these preexisting messages in our worlds shape our selves, which in turn encourage us to use our bodies in specific ways (e.g., practices of femininity and masculinity). What Thomas and Thomas (1928) so profoundly wrote is very applicable here: "What one believes to be real is real in its consequences." The selves we develop in everyday life shape our everyday practices, which, over time, actually shape our bodies and our experiences of embodiment. Certainly each of us is given physiological limits (e.g., you can't make yourself grow taller regardless of what you want to believe—although with advances in medical technology that could change someday), but we affect our physiologies through nutrition, exercise (or lack of exercise), and physiological exposure to chemicals and weather in thousands of minute ways each day. Over time, the chivalry that suggests men do all the lifting and women demurely allow the work to be done for them affects each person's future physical capabilities. On average, men's workout patterns and diet routines (free weights and protein supplements) build different bodies than women's (aerobics and dieting). We do not always comply with these surveillances and accountabilities. In many ways, individuals and collectivities acting in social movements resist and work to make changes in gendered messages. It is an interactive, swirling, everyday process of social inputs and body practices that builds humans and societies.

Masculine Knitters of the World, Unite!

Although they did not laugh (in my presence), there was no mistaking the amusement in the air. I was not looking for someone, I simply wanted to knit a sweater for my child; it would be getting cold soon.

The quaint little yarn shop was discovered by my stepmother, right next to the grocery store my partner and I frequented. My stepmother was in there forever, it seemed, and afterwards went on and on about . . . well, I couldn't really say. I tuned out the exuberant monologue somewhere around the word "cute." Cute and yarn did not exactly boil the blood—that is, my blood. Times have changed.

Later that evening, watching my son crawl around on the floor of her hotel room, my stepmother looked up from her crochet, seemingly out of the blue, and suggested I might enjoy learning. "You might make something for the baby," she said, with frightening seriousness. It was frightening because I was offended, chastened, and challenged at the same time. Offended because I felt my masculinity was being affronted, chastened because I knew masculinity was socially constructed, and challenged because the only masculine thing left for my "possible selves" to do was conquer the problem of knitting.

You may have noticed that I said "knitting" as opposed to "crochet." This was a very deliberate choice in bargaining with myself. First, knitting sounded more masculine, "tougher" if you will. I was not about to listen to my brothers gibe me about my latest crochet project. It's a subtle difference, but one which, I assure you, played more of a role than I'd care to admit. Second, I read somewhere that male anglers have knit for centuries in order to mend their nets, and so forth. This might have been purely fictional, but it served its purpose to bolster my shaky sense of manhood.

In the end, it was not a very dramatic event. While amused, a very knowledgeable person named Rosemary tutored me through my son's first scarf, hat, socks, mittens, and then, one year later, when I was "ready," a shawl-collared button-up sweater with pockets and hand-carved wood buttons.

When one knits, one begins to tie in with the singular thread with which one works. So long as one's skein is large enough, an entire garment may be composed of one united strand. Your hands become very strong, nimble, and fully in your control. They dance a spider's dance.

The needles—I came to prefer bamboo—warm up with your hands. They mark your pace with their low, metronomic tap. The heart begins to beat with their rhythm, the breathing comes in line; you are tied in. This is a very pleasurable experience. Like many performances, when knitting one can become bewitched, and to be bewitched in this case is to be free. Your body is no longer a male or female, masculine or feminine: it is human, and it is your own. That is, until a horn honks outside and you realize you are the only one knitting at Starbucks and your coffee's gotten cold.

The most important and profound part of the whole experience, what truly affects me to this day, is how so trivial an example can lay bare the difficulty of seeing our own personal attachments to gender categories, how doggedly we expend energy on their maintenance, and how our very nearly narcissistic practice of identity construction distracts us from what is to be had in the experience of human life, sexuality, reproduction, and the parenting of children.

In this case, might it have been simple enough to hear a person speak about their affinity for a craft, see that such a skill might allow you to contribute something interesting to the life of your child, and then simply accept the offer to take it up? Instead, bargaining takes place (at least in my experience it does). Would a "real man" do this? Will my partner still find me attractive? Will my child laugh hysterically some day? (Surely!) If I grow a beard, dress like a lumberjack, and use rugged wooden needles, will other people understand that I am a man and not a woman? Silly isn't it, the things we do to knit our children sweaters?

These days I am working on a teddy bear (my first), and occasionally attend a knitting group that meets at a local sports bar on Friday nights.

—Rob Tolliver, graduate student

RECOGNIZING GENDERED PROCESSES IN WORK, SPORTS, AND SEX

We chose to give examples of the gender feedback loop in everyday processes at work, in sports, and with regard to sexuality, because we see these as three very significant parts of lived experience. Work and leisure activities take up the largest proportion of most people's everyday waking hours and sexuality is perhaps the most intimate part of self for each of us. Much of the self is interpreted through these three aspects of life. Here we return very briefly to consider the implications of the gender feedback loop for each aspect.

In terms of sexuality, the general sex negativity in our culture prevents us from talking openly and honestly about sex as well as treating it analytically in academic study (Myerson et al. 2007). The diversity of sex practices and interests in the United States is clearly not represented by the gender box structure. Increasingly, sexuality is becoming a site for resistance to outdated moralities based on Victorian standards and religious doctrines that have trouble adjusting to new fertility and fertility control technologies (e.g., birth control). The notion that sex is a natural phenomenon based largely on presumed reproductive capacity is a remnant of moral surveillance of earlier times. Sexuality has evolved considerably in the last century such that the vast majority of sexual interactions over the course of one's life are not intended to result in reproduction. The sexual self for most of us is only very minutely an actual reproductive being, yet our assumptions about sex rest so heavily on expectations of reproduction that we are blinded to sexual fluidity and diversity.

Even our notions of reproduction are gendered more than nature would require. Gendered norms influence the performance of pregnancy and even labor and birth, mostly for women, but also for men in the case of couvades syndrome. In a "degendered" world, women would not need to worry about being nice and polite while giving birth and fathers who wanted to participate in the pregnancy and birth experience as fully as possible would not be labeled with a psychosomatic syndrome. Furthermore, Lorber (2005) argues that in a "degendered society . . . biological procreation may be more commonly separated from parenting" (174) and that "degendering kinship will necessitate some way in which to regularize responsibility for dependents—legalized civil unions, household contracts. It is hoped that a structure of equality for the adults involved and shared care for dependents will be part of these contracts" (172).

If family structures are degendered, workplaces will have to change as well. There will need to be a recognition that all workers (not just women) may be parents and thus have family responsibilities (Lorber 2005) and that hazardous conditions in the workplace can affect the reproductive capabilities of both men and women. So, flexible workplace polices would need to become gender neutral (not just officially, as many are, but in practice as well) and companies would need to provide safe workplaces for *all* their employees, rather than discriminate based on presumed reproductive capacity and desire. A restructuring of this sort in the workplace would allow for people to choose jobs based on their interests and skills rather than as a result of gendered surveillance and accountability.

Last, if athletics are good for human bodies (and we believe they tend to be), then they are good for *all* human bodies. We advocate removal of the significant social and interactional discouragements on women's active sporting participation (and also discouragements that keep men from engaging in "feminine" sports where individuals prefer to do so) in order to see what a diverse human "body" might produce. We also encourage competition between women and men (and intersexed and transgendered people) or on mixed-sex teams in the interest of reducing the surveillance of the categories "female" and "male" so that all people have greater access to play, sport, and fitness.

THE JOHN/JOAN CONTROVERSY, OR,
WILL NATURE OR NURTURE EVER WIN?

Usually at this juncture in our argument the reader will still harbor at least some sneaking suspicion that nature must really play a bigger role in the human equation than sociologists are willing to admit. Having followed us this far, many people will respond to our argument for the gender feedback loop by bringing up the John/Joan case. The argument usually goes something like this:

> But I learned on the Discovery Channel about this set of identical twins and during circumcision one of them had his penis cut off so the doctors turned him into a girl. They said they could just make him a girl. And they were identical twins so it should have been a good test of whether gender is constructed. But later in his life, the twin who lost his penis wanted to transition back to being a boy. So doesn't that prove that gender really is innate?

The so-called John/Joan case is an actual case of real people but it has been so mythologized in the public imagination and it has had such an important impact on gender studies that we feel it necessary to address it here at least briefly. The twin's name was David Reimer, an important point, we think, because sadly his identity as a real person has been largely lost in this public discussion. The pseudonym John/Joan was used presumably to protect his identity and that of his family while he was growing up. The actual events of David's life are probably best logged in the biography that he himself approved and narrated to a journalist (Colapinto 2000). The events of his life described in his biography are briefly outlined as follows: Bruce (who later changed his name to David) and twin brother Brian Reimer were born on August 22, 1965, in Canada. On April 22, 1966, both boys were scheduled for circumcision. Bruce was the first to undergo the procedure, and through what appears to be a series of mishaps, Bruce's penis was accidentally cauterized badly with equipment not meant for use in circumcision. Brian's circumcision was pre-empted as a result. Within a few days of healing, it became clear that Bruce no longer had any flesh left for a penis. In 1967, having exhausted all options offered by medical doctors for reconstruction, Bruce's parents saw Dr. John Money appear on a talk show about the possibility of sex reassignment and subsequently contacted him. Apparently Money took Bruce's case, assuring his parents that Bruce could be raised as Brenda and could live a full life as a female. Thus began the long process of physical and social transition to change Bruce to Brenda. In the biography, David remembers the process as very invasive, perhaps abusive, in that "Brenda" was always being instructed how to be the girl she was to become, rather than being asked what kind of person he might like to become. David also reports feeling sexually abused by the medical establishment, especially John Money, by being poked and prodded and having his genitalia constantly photographed for research purposes at regular intervals throughout his young life as Brenda. But Brenda was apparently never comfortable with her life as a girl, as David describes it, expressing discomfort with feminine clothing and the mandate to act "ladylike" from her parents. In 1980 and in his mid-teens, Brenda transitioned back to boyhood, becoming David. He eventually had his breasts removed and engaged in testosterone treatments to transition back to maleness. He eventually married a woman who had a child from a previous relationship and they attempted to create what appeared to be a nuclear family.

The entire process of David's two transitions exacted a toll. David's parents divorced and David became distant from them. He describes a series of family moves that left each of the family members isolated and depressed. David's brother Brian also dealt badly with the revelations of Brenda's origins as Bruce and his eventual transition to David. It is unclear to what degree other problems (such as abuse, his mother's alleged mental illness, or brother Brian's schizophrenia) were also involved, but David describes his life as a sad one filled with disruption. Eventually, Brian committed suicide and, two years later, on May 4, 2004, David took his own life at age 38 (Chalmers 2004).

In the biography, David himself interpreted his return to masculine interests as an innate gender. He felt himself a boy. Many pronounced Money's experiments an absolute failure and use this case as evidence that social constructionism is demonstrably false. Although this case is truly sad, does it alone sensibly challenge a social constructionist argument? While it is easy to suppose that this case demonstrates the primacy of nature over nurture, no truly analytic approach could ever be resolved by the evidence of one case. There are ways in which to argue the strict social constructionist side of the debate as well. Perhaps one might argue that growing up with a twin brother is exactly the social reason why Bruce could never become Brenda. Femininity is a much more restricting practice than masculinity. Brenda would have been jealous to watch Brian, her identical twin in every respect, be allowed to act out physically, dress comfortably, and enjoy the privileges accorded males when girls are expected to "act ladylike," so the argument would go. All sisters in that position would logically be jealous of brothers not subject to the restrictions of femininity. Certainly many girls have voiced this argument—including at least one author of this book (Crawley 2002b)—opting in favor of tomboyism over femininity as resistance to being told that looking pretty is preferable to enjoying the pleasures of rough-and-tumble play.

Rather than attempting to fall on either side of this endless debate, we would like to offer another argument. We argue that John Money's contention that he could "create" a girl was more likely the problem than the recognition that each of us is impacted by social gender messages.

So, then, what was wrong with John Money's approach? Arrogance was the problem here. We argue that this case is an example of science gone bad more than support for either side of the so-called nature/nurture debate. This is a case of bad ethics, not the resolution of a long-standing (and ultimately pointless) debate. The kind of science that presumes to predict and control for another person who they will be was the downfall of David and his family. Much like the surgical alteration of intersexed infants, the alteration of any child is dangerously arrogant. How is it possible to predict for another person what they will prefer to feel emotionally, sexually, or intellectually about their bodies? How much different is this kind of positivism run amuck than the eugenic experiments of the Nazis? Money's mistake, as we see it, was not so much a willingness to see social impacts in the development of self as the arrogance to believe that he should or could be the person to put those social constructs into David's person. The gender feedback loop surely demonstrates that thousands of inputs go into the development of self and that no one person, not even ourselves, has absolute control to choose how we turn out. It is a long and ongoing process for each of us, not a particular choice made at any given time.

The nature vs. nurture argument is both silly and persistent. Clearly, a human life is composed of physiology and social interaction at every point in that life (Fausto-Sterling 2000). The notion that a person is made up of nature *or* nurture is simply untenable. Each of us is both physiology and mind at all times in our lives. We are always both nature *and* nurture.

Recent academic discussion seems to have recognized this, but the debate remains persistent. Now it seems the nature/nurture algorithm is debated in terms of how much of the person is controlled by each. Is nature more controlling? Is nurture? Is it 50 percent nature and 50 percent nurture? Eighty percent nature and 20 percent nurture? Or 10 percent nature and 90 percent nurture? Why is there still a persistent need to argue for disciplinary control of the human subject? We argue that the only reason either side—biologists or confirmed social constructionists—want to pinpoint exactly from whence gender or sexual orientation comes is to create a sense of predictability. Both sides of this debate are following a scientific ethic—trying to "get it right"—by creating the correct theory to explain how the person works. Like dissecting a scrumptious dish into the components found in a recipe, now we will know how to build a person. Just like with the scrumptious dish, the recipe never truly helps us understand the flavorful complexity of the tasty dish. Much like the scientific interest in classification, the notion that we need to know an origin stems from an interest in knowing and, hence, controlling the production process. If it is in the biology, we will manipulate the genes. If it is in behavior, we will sanction your acts. Under the scientific ethic, Westerners as a culture cannot seem to stand the possibility that person production is actually out of our control. Much like overbearing parents trying to sculpt a doctor or a lawyer out of a small child and then freaking out when what they get is a counterculture punk-rocker, scientists want to make the world feel predictable and logical.

Science also gives us the notion that there is one best, right answer. Imbued through science is the Western competitive ideal of a best option. This sense of a hierarchical arrangement in the world and in nature is pervasive throughout our cultural understanding of reality. It engages us to look for only one right answer or one "best" option. We are afraid to imagine several concurrent right answers or none at all. We presuppose that people must work toward and conform to a goal. The notion that there is one best way to be encourages us to look for icons and emulate them to our "best" abilities. It encourages each of us to pursue the goal of one, best gendered body, as though there should be one best masculinity or femininity and each should be attached to a particular set of ("perfect") genitals.

We propose a shift away from the nature/nurture argument. This shift has two components: one for academic analysis and one for personal ethics. In terms of academic analysis, we endorse Fausto-Sterling's (2000) gender systems theory and her call for greater interdisciplinary analysis. The nature/nurture debate persists as a result of our discipline-bound academy. Our need to determine whether the biologists or the social scientists "win" this debate keeps it going more than is useful for true scientific description. Fausto-Sterling advocates for interdisciplinary theorizing, rather than rehashing tired debates over disciplinary boundaries. A biologist and feminist theorist, she gives many examples of biological adaptation to environmental stimuli to counter the idea that the body is primary and more effective than social inputs in the physical system. Yet, she remains impressed by

insights of biologists that bodies are physical processes, not just social, linguistic responses to stimuli. She offers an approach called gender systems
theory—an analytic that presumes both biology and environmental inputs
as a system and process of adaptation. We concur with her interest in interdisciplinary approaches over maintaining disciplinary boundaries and believe the best future research will open theories to cross these boundaries.

As for personal ethics, we propose a shift from the scientific ethic to what
might be called the Beatles' ethic (yes, we mean the band)—why not "let it
be" and be comfortable that various factors contribute to the person? Rather
than focusing on dissecting the body, why not focus on the social possibilities of a world that accepts what each of us brings to the party and work toward making a world in which each us can express ourselves free of boxes
that limit our differences? We believe that David Reimer, whose name and
personhood gets lost in the "John/Joan" debate, might be alive today if all
of us focused less on pinpointing origins of urges and more on creating opportunities for differences. Certainly this is true for the lives of so many
transgendered people, gay men and lesbians, people of color, and domestic
violence victims who lost their lives to messages of conformity. Perhaps it
is also true for each one of us—for that creative, funky, individualistic part
of us that we hide or repress in order to fit some surveillance standard or
social message intended to make us conform. Perhaps if we get comfortable
with the notion that we will never "know," that life is not really that predictable, that diversity and unpredictability increase our humanity, that we
can "let it be," then perhaps we can start to truly imagine a world of individualism and conventionality, sameness and difference—both/and, rather
than either/or. That world would surely be more interesting and colorful.

Through this personal ethic we are not calling for an end to academic study
(or suggesting a kind of moral relativism in academics). It is possible to approach the social world and the physical world with a fascination to know
more without that study implying a strict, predictive classificatory system. Instead we join with Judith Lorber's call for a *degendering* of the social world.
Lorber (2005) imagines "societies where people come in all colors, shapes,
and sizes and where body characteristics are not markers for status identification or for predetermined allocation to any kind of activity" (166). Perhaps
an ethic of multiplicity will allow us to develop even more interesting theories. We could still agree that social systems run better when merits are recognized over body types. (Indeed, perhaps it makes that system possible for the
first time!) Our call to shift ethics is not a call to end academics and social organization altogether. Instead, it is a call to *describe* rather than *predict* and to
defend difference rather than expect conformity—to find fascination with
the diversity that exists, rather than finding a need to control a diverse world.
Perhaps with that ethic, the shape of the future will be much more fascinat-
ing and that future will bring many intriguing human possibilities.

References

Acker, Joan. 1990. "Hierarchies, Jobs, Bodies: A Theory of Gendered Organizations." *Gender and Society* 4:139–58.

Ackmann, Martha, and Lynn Sherr. 2003. *The Mercury 13: The Untold Story of Thirteen American Women and the Dream of Space Flight*. New York: Random House.

Adam, Barry D. 1987. *The Rise of a Gay and Lesbian Movement*. Boston, MA: Twayne Publishers.

———. 2006. "Relationship Innovation in Male Couples." *Sexualities* 9:5–26.

Adams, Natalie Guice, and Pamela J. Bettis. 2003. *Cheerleader: An American Icon*. New York: Palgrave.

Agigian, Amy. 2004. *Baby Steps: How Lesbian Alternative Insemination Is Changing the World*. Middletown, CT: Wesleyan University Press.

Alloway, Nola, and Pam Gilbert. 1998. "Video Game Culture: Playing with Masculinity, Violence, and Pleasure." In *Wired Up: Young People and the Electronic Media*, edited by S. Howard, 95–114. London, England: Routledge.

Allushuski, Ty. 2006. "NJ Woman Bowls over Barriers, Lands Full-Time Spot on Men's Tour." *USA Today*, June 5. Retrieved July 3, 2006 (http://usatoday.com/sports/bowling/2006-06-05-kulik_x.htm).

Almaguer, Thomas. 1993. "Chicano Men: A Cartography of Homosexual Identity and Behavior." In *The Lesbian and Gay Studies Reader*, edited by H. Abelove, M. A. Barale, and D. M. Halperin, 255–73. New York: Routledge.

Andersen, A. E., and L. Didomenico. 1992. "Diet vs. Shape Content of Popular Male and Female Magazines: A Dose-Response Relationship to the Incidence of Eating Disorders." *The International Journal of Eating Disorders* 11:283–87.

Anderson, Eric. 2005a. *In the Game: Gay Athletes and the Cult of Masculinity*. Albany: State University of New York Press.

———. 2005b. "Orthodox and Inclusive Masculinity: Competing Masculinities among Heterosexual Men in a Feminized Terrain." *Sociological Perspectives* 48:337–55.

Anderson, S. E., and A. Must. 2005. "Interpreting the Continued Decline in the Average Age at Menarche: Results from Two Nationally Representative Surveys of U.S. Girls Studied 10 Years Apart." *Journal of Pediatrics* 147:1739–48.

Annandale, Ellen, and Judith Clark. 1996. "What Is Gender? Feminist Theory and the Sociology of Human Reproduction." *Sociology of Health and Illness* 18:17–44.

————. 1997. "A Reply to Rona Campbell and Sam Porter." *Sociology of Health and Illness* 19:521–32.

AP Wire. 2005. "Smell of Land Greets Sailor after Trip around World." *St. Petersburg Times*, February 9, p. 2C.

Archer, Margaret S. 1988. *Culture and Agency: The Place of Culture in Social Theory.* Cambridge, England: Cambridge University Press.

Averett, Susan, and Sanders Korenmann. 1996. "The Economic Reality of the Beauty Myth." *The Journal of Human Resources* 31:304–30.

Baglia, Jay. 2003. "Building Masculinity: Viagra and the Performance of Sexual Health." Ph.D. dissertation, Department of Communication, University of South Florida, Tampa, FL.

Bailey, Lucy. 2001. "Gender Shows: First-Time Mothers and Embodied Selves." *Gender and Society* 15:110–29.

Balsamo, Anne. 1999. "Public Pregnancies and Cultural Narratives of Surveillance." In *Revisioning Women, Health and Healing: Feminist, Cultural, and Technoscience Perspectives*, edited by A. E. Clarke and V. L. Olsen, 231–53. New York: Routledge.

Banks, Ingrid. 2000. *Hair Matters: Beauty, Power, and Black Women's Consciousness.* New York: New York University Press.

Barbre, Joy Webster. 2003. "Meno-Boomers and Moral Guardians: An Exploration of the Cultural Construction of Menopause." In *The Politics of Women's Bodies: Sexuality, Appearance, and Behavior*, edited by R. Weitz, 271–81. New York: Oxford University Press.

Bartky, Sandra Lee. 1990. *Femininity and Domination.* New York: Routledge.

Basile, Kathleen. 1999. "Rape by Acquiescence: The Ways in Which Women 'Give In' to Unwanted Sex with Their Husbands." *Violence against Women* 5:1036–58.

Baudrillard, Jean. 1983. *Simulations.* New York: Semiotext(e).

Beal, Becky. 1996. "Alternative Masculinity and Its Effects on Gender Relations in the Subculture of Skateboarding." *Journal of Sport Behavior* 19:204–20.

Beauvoir, Simone de. 1952. *The Second Sex.* New York: Alfred A. Knopf, Inc.

Becker, Gay. 1994. "Metaphors in Disrupted Lives: Infertility and Cultural Constructions of Continuity." *Medical Anthropology Quarterly* 8:383–410.

Bem, Sandra Lipsitz. 1993. *The Lenses of Gender.* New Haven, CT: Yale University Press.

Beneke, Timothy. 1997. *Proving Manhood.* Berkeley: University of California Press.

Benokraitis, Nijole V. (ed.). 1997. *Subtle Sexism: Current Practice and Prospects for Change.* Thousand Oaks, CA: Sage Publications.

Benokraitis, Nijole V., and Joe R. Feagin. 1995. *Modern Sexism: Blatant, Subtle, and Covert Discrimination.* 2nd ed. Englewood Cliffs, NJ: Prentice Hall.

Berkowitz, Dana, Linda Belgrave, and Robert Halberstein. Forthcoming 2007. "The Interaction of Drag Queens and Gay Men in Public and Private Spaces." *The Journal of Homosexuality* 52.

Bettie, Julie. 2000. "Women without Class: Chicas, Cholas, Trash and the Presence/Absence of Class Identity." *Signs* 26:1–35.

Bird, Sharon R. 1996. "Welcome to the Men's Club: Homosociality and the Maintenance of Hegemonic Masculinity." *Gender and Society* 10:120–32.

Birrell, Susan. 1988. "Discourses on the Gender/Sport Relationship: From Women in Sport to Gender Relations." *Exercise and Sport Sciences Reviews* 16:459–502.

Birrell, Susan, and Cheryl Cole. 1994. "Double Fault: Renée Richards and the Construction and Naturalization of Difference." In *Women, Sport, and Culture*, edited by S. Birrell and C. Cole, 373–97. Champaign, IL: Human Kinetics Books.

Birrell, Susan, and Diana M. Richter. 1994. "Is a Diamond Forever? Feminist Transformations of Sport." In *Women, Sport, and Culture*, edited by S. Birrell and C. Cole, 221–44. Champaign, IL: Human Kinetics Books.

Blackless, Melanie, Anthony Charuvastra, Amanda Derryck, Anne Fausto-Sterling, Karl Lauzanne, and Ellen Lee. 2000. "How Sexually Dimorphic Are We? Review and Synthesis." *American Journal of Human Biology* 12:151–266.

Blakely, Mary Kay. 1983. "Surrogate Mothers: For Whom Are They Working?" *Ms.*, March, 18–20.

Blinde, Elaine M., and Diane E. Taub. 1992a. "Women Athletes as Falsely Accused Deviants: Managing the Lesbian Stigma." *The Sociological Quarterly* 33:521–33.

———. 1992b. "Homophobia and Women's Sport: The Disempowerment of Athletes." *Sociological Focus* 25:151–66.

———. 1999. "Personal Empowerment through Sport and Physical Fitness Activity: Perspectives from Male College Students with Physical and Sensory Disabilities." *Journal of Sport Behavior* 22:181–202.

Blinde, Elaine M., Diane E. Taub, and Linling Han. 1993. "Sport Participation and Women's Personal Empowerment: Experiences of the College Athlete." *Journal of Sport and Social Issues* 17:47–60.

Boal, Mark. 1999. "An American Sweatshop." *Mother Jones*, May/June. Retrieved November 21, 2006 (http://www.motherjones.com/news/feature/1999/05/boal.html).

Bobel, Christina G. 2006. "'Our Revolution Has Style': Menstrual Product Activists 'Doing Feminism' in the Third Wave." *Sex Roles: A Journal of Research* 54:331–45.

Bolin, Anne. 2003. "Beauty or the Beast: The Subversive Soma." In *Athletic Intruders*, edited by A. Bolin and J. Granskog, 107–30. Albany: State University of New York Press.

Bolin, Anne, and Jane Granskog (eds.). 2003. *Athletic Intruders: Ethnographic Research on Women, Culture, and Exercise.* Albany: State University of New York Press.

Bonacich, Edna, and Richard P. Appelbaum. 2000. *Behind the Label: Inequality in the Los Angeles Apparel Industry.* Berkeley: University of California Press.

Bordo, Susan. 1986. "The Cartesian Masculinization of Thought." *Signs* 11:439–56.

———. 1993. *Unbearable Weight: Feminism, Western Culture, and the Body.* Berkeley: University of California Press.

———. 1998. "Pills and Power Tools." *Men and Masculinities* 1:87–90.

———. 1999. *The Male Body.* New York: Farrar, Straus and Giroux.

Bornstein, Kate. 1994. *Gender Outlaw: On Men, Women, and the Rest of Us.* New York: Routledge.

Bourdieu, Pierre. 1980. *The Logic of Practice.* Palo Alto, CA: Stanford University Press.

Bradley, Harriet. 1993. "Across the Great Divide: The Entry of Men into 'Women's Jobs.'" In *Doing "Women's Work": Men in Nontraditional Occupations*, edited by C. L. Williams, 10–27. Newbury Park, CA: Sage.

Brady, Teresa. 1994. "The Legal Status of Sex-Specific Fetal Protection Policies." *NWSA Journal* 6:468–74.

Branaman, Anne (ed.). 2001. *Self and Society.* Malden, MA: Blackwell Publishers.

Brandth, Berit, and Marit S. Haugen. 2000. "From Lumberjack to Business Manager: Masculinity in the Norwegian Forestry Press." *Journal of Rural Studies* 16:343–55.

———. 2005. "Text, Body, and Tools: Changing Mediations of Rural Masculinity." *Men and Masculinities* 8:148–63.

Brennan, Christine. 2005. "E-mail Surveys May Be First Step in Effort to Cripple Progress of Title IX." *USA Today*, March 24, 8C.

Britton, Dana. 2003. *At Work in the Iron Cage: The Prison as Gendered Organization.* New York: New York University Press.

Broad, K. L. 2001. "The Gendered Unapologetic: Queer Resistance in Women's Sport." *Sociology of Sport Journal* 18:181–204.

Bromley, Dorothy D., and Florence H. Britten. 1938. *Youth and Sex: A Study of 1300 College Students.* 3rd ed. New York: Harper and Brothers.

Brown, Lester. 1997. *Two Spirit People: American Indian Lesbian Women and Gay Men.* New York: Haworth Press.

Browner, Carol H., and Nancy Press. 1997. "The Production of Authoritative Knowledge in American Prenatal Care." In *Childbirth and Authoritative Knowledge: Cross-Cultural Perspectives*, edited by R. E. Davis-Floyd and C. F. Sargent, 113–31. Berkeley: University of California Press.

Brumberg, Joan Jacobs. 1993. "'Something Happens to Girls': Menarche and the Emergence of the Modern American Hygienic Imperative." *Journal of the History of Sexuality* 4:99–127.

Bryson, Lois. 1987. "Sport and the Maintenance of Masculine Hegemony." *Women's Studies International Forum* 10:349–60.

———. 1990. "Challenges to Male Hegemony in Sport." In *Sport, Men, and the Gender Order*, edited by M. A. Messner and D. F. Sabo, 173–84. Champaign, IL: Human Kinetics Books.

Bureau of Labor Statistics. 2005. "Census of Fatal Occupational Injuries Summary, 2005." Retrieved November 28, 2006 (http://www.bls.gov/news.release/cfoi.nr0.htm).

Burton Nelson, Mariah. 1994. *The Stronger Women Get, the More Men Love Football: Sexism and the American Culture of Sports*. New York: Harcourt Brace & Co.

Butler, Judith. 1990. *Gender Trouble: Feminism and the Subversion of Identity*. New York: Routledge.

———. 1993. *Bodies That Matter: On the Discursive Limits of "Sex."* New York and London: Routledge.

———. 1996. "Imitation and Gender Insubordination." In *The Material Queer*, edited by D. Morton, 180–92. Boulder, CO: Westview Press.

Buysee, Jo, and Melissa S. Embser-Herbert. 2004. "Constructions of Gender in Sport: An Analysis of Intercollegiate Media Guide Cover Photographs." *Gender and Society* 18:66–81.

"Caesarean Refusal Leads to Murder Charge." 2004. *CNN.com*, March 12. Retrieved March 25, 2004 (http://www.cnn.com/2004/US/West/03/11/mother.charged.ap).

Cahill, Spencer E., William Distler, Cynthia Lachowetz, Andrea Meaney, Robyn Tarallo, and Teena Willard. 1985. "Meanwhile Backstage: Public Bathrooms and the Interaction Order." *Journal of Contemporary Ethnography* 14:33–58.

———. 1986. "Language Practices and Self-Definition: The Case of Gender Identity Acquisition." *The Sociological Quarterly* 27:295–311.

———. 1989. "Fashioning Males and Females: Appearance Management and the Social Reproduction of Gender." *Symbolic Interaction* 12:281–98.

———. 1998. "Towards a Sociology of the Person." *Sociological Theory* 16:131–48.

Cahn, Susan K. 1993. "From the 'Muscle Moll' to the 'Butch' Ballplayer: Mannishness, Lesbianism, and Homophobia in U.S. Women's Sport." *Feminist Studies* 19:343–68.

———. 1994. "Crushes, Competition, and Closets: The Emergence of Homophobia in Women's Physical Education." In *Women, Sport, and Culture*, edited by S. Birrell and C. L. Cole, 327–38. Champaign, IL: Human Kinetics Books.

———. 1996. "'So Far Back in the Closet We Can't See the Keyhole': Lesbianism, Homophobia, and Sexual Politics in Collegiate Women's Athletics." In *The New Lesbian Studies: Into the Twenty-First Century*, edited by B. Zimmerman and T. A. H. McNaron, 215–22. New York: The Feminist Press.

Cameron, Loren. 1996. *Body Alchemy: Transsexual Portraits*. San Francisco, CA: Cleis Press.

Candell, Peter. 1974. "When I Was about Fourteen. . . ." In *Men and Masculinity*, edited by J. H. Pleck and J. Sawyer, 14–17. Englewood Cliffs, NJ: Prentice Hall.

Carlisle Duncan, Margaret. 1994. "The Politics of Women's Body Images and Practices: Foucault, the Panopticon, and *Shape* Magazine." *Journal of Sport and Social Issues* 18:48–65.

Carlisle Duncan, Margaret, Michael A. Messner, Linda Williams, Kerry Jensen, and Wayne Wilson. 1990 [1994]. "Gender Stereotyping in Televised Sports." In *Women, Sport, and Culture*, edited by S. Birrell and C. Cole, 249–72. Champaign, IL: Human Kinetics Books.

Carlisle Duncan, Margaret, Michael A. Messner, Nicole Willms, and Wayne Wilson. 2005. "Gender in Televised Sports: News and Highlights Shows, 1989–2004." Research report commissioned by the Amateur Athletic Foundation of Los Angeles. Retrieved February 5, 2006 (http://www.aafla.org/9arr/ResearchReports/tv2004.pdf).

Carpenter, Laura M. 2006. *Virginity Lost: An Intimate Portrait of First Sexual Experiences*. New York: New York University Press.

Carpenter, Linda Jean, and R. Vivian Acosta. 2006. "Women in Intercollegiate Sport: A Longitudinal, National Study, Twenty Nine Year Update, 1977–2006." Retrieved November 21, 2006 (http://www.aahperd.org/nagws/pdf_files/logitudinal29.pdf).

Cartwright, Elizabeth. 1998. "The Logic of Heartbeats: Electronic Fetal Monitoring and Bio-medically Constructed Birth." In *Cyborg Babies: From Techno-Sex to Techno-Tots,* edited by R. Davis-Floyd and J. Dumit, 240–54. New York: Routledge.

Case, Sue-Ellen. 1989. "Toward a Butch-Femme Aesthetic." In *Making A Spectacle,* edited by L. Hart, 282–98. Ann Arbor: University of Michigan Press.

Cashmore, Ellis. 2005. *Making Sense of Sports.* 4th ed. London, England: Routledge.

Caudwell, Jayne. 1999. "Women's Football in the United Kingdom: Theorizing Gender and Unpacking the Butch Lesbian Image." *Journal of Sport and Social Issues* 23:390–402.

CBS News. 2003. "Blood, Tears of Synchronized Swimming." *CBS News* online. Retrieved March 15, 2006 (http://www.cbsnews.com/stories/2003/04/25/sunday/main551123.shtml).

Centers for Disease Control and Prevention. 2006. "Recommendations to Improve Preconception Health and Health Care—United States: A Report of the CDC/ATSDR Preconception Care Work Group and the Select Panel on Preconception Care." MMWR April 21: 55 (No. RR-6):1–23. Retrieved June 15, 2006 (http://www.cdc.gov/MMWR/preview/mmwrhtml/rr5506a1.htm).

Chalmers, Katie. 2004. "Sad End to Boy/Girl Life: Subject of Gender Experiment." *Winnipeg Sun.* Retrieved May 19, 2004 (http://www.canoe.ca/NewsStand/WinnipegSun/News/2004/05/10/pf-453481.html).

Chambers, Veronica. 2004. "Dreadlocked." In *Women's Voices, Feminist Visions: Classic and Contemporary Readings,* edited by S. M. Shaw and J. Lee, 228–30. Boston, MA: McGraw-Hill.

Chase, Susan E., and Mary F. Rogers. 2001. *Mothers and Children: Feminist Analyses and Personal Narratives.* New Brunswick, NJ: Rutgers University Press.

Chetkovich, Carol. 1997. *Real Heat: Gender and Race in the Urban Fire Service.* New Brunswick, NJ: Rutgers University Press.

Cirque du Soleil. 2006. "The Acts." Retrieved March 15, 2006 (http://www.cirquedusoleil.com/CirqueDuSoleil/en/showstickets/o/O-acts2.htm).

Clasen, Patricia R. W. 2001. "The Female Athlete: Dualisms and Paradoxes in Practice." *Women and Language* 24:36–41.

Clean Clothes Campaign Newsletter. 2000. November, 13. Retrieved on May 1, 2002 (http://www.cleanclothes.org/news/newsletter13-indon.htm).

Cloud, John. 2000. "His Name Is Aurora." *Time Magazine,* September 25. Retrieved November 20, 2006 (http://www.time.com/time/magazine/article/0,9171,998007,00.html).

Coakley, Jay. 2001. *Sport in Society.* 7th ed. Boston, MA: McGraw-Hill.

Cockburn, Cynthia. 1981. "The Material of Male Power." *Feminist Review* 9:41–58.

Colapinto, John. 2000. *As Nature Made Him.* New York: HarperCollins.

Cole, Cheryl L. 1994. "Resisting the Canon: Feminist Cultural Studies, Sport and Technologies of the Body." In *Women, Sport, and Culture,* edited by S. Birrell and C. L. Cole, 5–30. Champaign, IL.: Human Kinetics.

Collins, Patricia Hill. 1990. *Black Feminist Thought.* Boston, MA: Unwin.

———. 2004. *Black Sexual Politics: African Americans, Gender, and the New Racism.* New York: Routledge.

Coltrane, Scott. 1996. *Family Man: Fatherhood, Housework, and Gender Equity.* New York: Oxford University Press.

Combs-Jones, Yvonne. 2004. "African-American Women at Midlife: The Social Construction of Health and Aging." Ph.D. dissertation, Department of Sociology, University of Florida, Gainesville, FL.

Conley, Frances. 1999. *Walking Out on the Boys.* New York: Farrar, Straus and Giroux.

Connell, R. W. 1983. *Which Way Is Up? Essays on Sex, Class and Culture.* Sydney, Australia: George Allen and Unwin.

———. 1987. *Gender and Power.* Palo Alto, CA: Stanford University Press.

———. 1990. "An Iron Man: The Body and Some Contradictions of Hegemonic Masculinity." In *Sport, Men, and the Gender Order,* edited by M. A. Messner and D. F. Sabo, 83–96. Champaign, IL: Human Kinetics Books.

———. 1995. *Masculinities.* Berkeley: University of California Press.

———. 2002. *Gender: Short Introductions.* Cambridge, MA: Polity.

Coontz, Stephanie. 1992. *The Way We Never Were: American Families and the Nostalgia Trap.* New York: Basic Books.

Copelton, Denise. 2004. "Reading Pregnancy Advice: An Exploration of How and Why Women Consult Popular Pregnancy Advice Books." Presented at the annual meeting of the American Sociological Association, August, San Francisco, CA.

Corea, Gena. 1985. *The Mother Machine: Reproductive Technologies from Artificial Insemination to Artificial Wombs.* New York: Harper and Row.

Cox, Barbara, and Shona Thompson. 2000. "Multiple Bodies: Sportswomen, Soccer, and Sexuality." *International Review for the Sociology of Sport* 35:5–20.

Craft, Christine. 1986. *Christine Craft: An Anchorwoman's Story.* Santa Barbara, CA: Capra Press.

———. 1991. *Too Old, Too Ugly, and Not Deferential to Men: An Anchorwoman's Courageous Battle against Sex Discrimination.* New York: Prima Lifestyles Press.

Craig, Maxine. 2002. *Ain't I a Beauty Queen? Black Women, Beauty, and the Politics of Race.* Berkeley: University of California Press.

Crawley, Sara L. 1998. "Gender, Class and the Construction of Masculinity in Professional Sailing: A Case Study of the America³ Women's Team." *International Review for the Sociology of Sport* 33:33–42.

———. 2002a. "Prioritizing Audiences: Exploring the Differences Between Stone Butch and Transgender Identifications." *Journal of Lesbian Studies* 6:11–24.

———. 2002b. "'They *still* don't understand why I hate wearing dresses': An Autoethnographic Rant on Dresses, Boats and Butchness." *Cultural Studies<=>Critical Methodologies* 2:69–92.

———. 2002c. "Narrating and Negotiating Butch and Femme: Storying Lesbian Selves in a Heteronormative World." Ph.D. dissertation, Department of Sociology, University of Florida, Gainesville, FL.

Crawley, Sara L., and K. L. Broad. 2004. "'Be Your[Real Lesbian]Self': Mobilizing Sexual Formula Stories through Personal (and Political) Storytelling." *Journal of Contemporary Ethnography* 33:39–71.

Croissant, Jennifer. 2006. "The New Sexual Technology: Viagra in the Hyperreal World." *Sexualities* 9:333–44.

Crossett, Todd. 1990. "Masculinity, Sexuality, and the Development of Early Modern Sport." In *Sport, Men, and the Gender Order*, edited by M. A. Messner and D. F. Sabo, 45–54. Champaign, IL: Human Kinetics Books.

———. 1995. *Outsiders in the Clubhouse.* Albany: State University of New York Press.

Crossett, Todd W., James Ptacek, Mark A. McDonald, and Jeffrey R. Benedict. 1996. "Male Student-Athletes and Violence against Women." *Violence against Women* 2:163–79.

Daddario, Gina. 1994. "Chilly Scenes of the 1992 Winter Games: The Mass Media and the Marginalization of Female Athletes." *Sociology of Sport Journal* 11:275–88.

Daniels, Cynthia R. 1997. "Between Fathers and Fetuses: The Social Construction of Male Reproduction and the Politics of Fetal Harm." *Signs* 22:579–616.

Davis, Angela. 1981. *Women, Race and Class.* New York: Random House.

Davis, Ian. 1999. *My Boys Can Swim! The Official Guy's Guide to Pregnancy.* New York: Prima Publishing.

Davis-Floyd, Robbie. 1992. *Birth as an American Rite of Passage.* Berkeley: University of California Press.

Davis-Floyd, Robbie, Stacey Leigh Pigg, and Sheila Cosminsky (eds.). 2001. "Daughters of Time: The Shifting Identities of Postmodern Midwives." *Medical Anthropology* 20:105–39.

Delany, Janice, Mary Jane Lupton, and Emily Toth. 1988. *The Curse: A Cultural History of Menstruation.* Urbana and Chicago, IL: University of Illinois Press.

Dellinger, Kirsten, and Christine L. Williams. 1997. "Makeup at Work: Negotiating Appearance Rules in the Workplace." *Gender & Society* 11:151–77.

———. 2002. "The Locker Room and the Dorm Room: Workplace Norms and the Boundaries of Sexual Harassment in Magazine Editing." *Social Problems* 49:242–57.

Denzin, Norman. 1991. *Images of Postmodern Society.* London, England: Sage Publications.

DeWelde, Kristine. 2003. "Getting Physical: Subverting Gender through Self-Defense." *Journal of Contemporary Ethnography* 32:247–78.

Diagnostic and Statistic Manual of Mental Disorders IV-TR. 4th ed. 2000. Arlington, VA: American Psychiatric Publishing.

Donnelly, Denise, Kimberly J. Cook, Debra VanAusdale, and Lara Foley. 2005. "White Privilege, Color Blindness, and Services to Battered Women." *Violence against Women* 11:6–37.

Doucet, Andrea. 2006. "'Estrogen-Filled Worlds': Fathers as Primary Caregivers and Embodiment." *The Sociological Review* 54:696–715.

Dowling, Collette. 2000. *The Frailty Myth.* New York: Random House.

Dozier, Raine. 2005. "Beards, Breasts, and Bodies: Doing Sex in a Gendered World." *Gender and Society* 19:297–316.

Draper, Jan. 2002a. "'It Was a Real Good Show': The Ultrasound Scan, Fathers and the Power of Visual Knowledge." *Sociology of Health and Illness* 24:771–95.

———. 2002b. "'It's the First Scientific Evidence': Men's Experience of Pregnancy Confirmation." *Journal of Advanced Nursing* 39:563–70.

———. 2003. "Blurring, Moving and Broken Boundaries: Men's Encounters with the Pregnant Body." *Sociology of Health and Illness* 25:743–67.

Dunden, Barbara. 1992. "Quick with Child: An Experience That Has Lost Its Status." *Technology in Society* 14:335–44.

Dunn, Robert G. 1997. "Self, Identity, and Difference: Mead and the Poststructuralists." *The Sociological Quarterly* 38:687–705.

Dunning, Eric. 1986. "Sport as a Male Preserve: Notes on the Social Sources of Masculine Identity and Its Transformations." *Theory, Culture, and Society* 3:79–90.

Dworkin, Shari L. 2001. "'Holding Back': Negotiating a Glass Ceiling on Women's Strength." *Sociological Perspectives* 44:333–50.

Dworkin, Shari L., and Faye Linda Wachs. 2004. "'Getting Your Body Back': Postindustrial Fit Motherhood in *Shape Fit Pregnancy* Magazine." *Gender and Society* 18:610–24.

Eitzen, D. Stanley. 1999. *Fair and Foul.* Lanham, MD: Rowman & Littlefield.

Emery, Kim. 2002. *The Lesbian Index: Pragmatism and Lesbian Subjectivity in the Twentieth-Century United States.* Albany: State University of New York Press.

Ensler, Eve. 1998. *The Vagina Monologues.* New York: Villard.

Erickson, Frederick. 2004. *Talk and Social Theory.* Malden, MA: Polity.

Erkut, Sumru, and Allison J. Tracy. 2002. "Predicting Adolescent Self-Esteem from Participation in School Sports among Latino Subgroups." *Hispanic Journal of Behavioral Sciences* 24:409–29.

Espiritu, Yen Le. 1997. *Asian American Women and Men: Labor, Laws and Love.* Thousand Oaks, CA: Sage.

Evans, Arthur S., Jr. 1997. "Blacks as Key Functionaries: A Study of Racial Stratification in Professional Sport." *Journal of Black Studies* 28:43–59.

Farhi, Paul. 2006. "Where the Rich and Elite Meet to Compete." *Washington Post*, February 5, B01.

Faul, Michelle. 1999. "Woman Rows Atlantic." *Tampa Tribune*, December 4, 1A.

Fausto-Sterling, Anne. 1986. *Myths of Gender: Biological Theories about Women and Men.* New York: Basic Books.

———. 1995. "How to Build a Man." In *Constructing Masculinity*, edited by M. Berger, B. Wallace, and S. Watson, 127–35. New York: Routledge.

———. 2000. *Sexing the Body: Gender Politics and the Construction of Sexuality.* New York: Basic Books.

Federation of the Gay Games. 2006. "Welcome to the Gay Games." Retrieved March 15, 2006 (www.gaygames.com/en).

Feinberg, Leslie. 1996. *Transgender Warriors: Making History from Joan of Arc to Dennis Rodman.* Boston, MA: Beacon Press.

Findlen, Barbara (ed.). 1995. *Listen Up: Voices from the Next Feminist Generation.* Seattle, WA: Seal Press.

Fingerson, Laura. 2006. *Girls in Power: Gender, Body, and Menstruation in Adolescence.* Albany: State University of New York Press.

Finley, Bill. 2006. "Where the Boys Are." *New York Times,* January 29, section 14NJ, 4.

Firestone, Shulamith. 1970. *The Dialectic of Sex: The Case for Feminist Revolution.* New York: Morrow.

Fisch, Harry. 2005. *The Male Biological Clock.* New York: Free Press.

Fischer, Gayle V. 2001. *Pantaloons and Power: A Nineteenth-Century Dress Reform in the United States.* Kent, OH: Kent State University Press.

Fish, Mike. 1999. "Equity Backers Stirring." *Atlanta Journal-Constitution,* December 19, 1E.

Fisher, Leslee A. 1997. "'Building One's Self Up': Bodybuilding and the Construction of Identity among Professional Female Bodybuilders." In *Building Bodies,* edited by P. L. Moore, 135–61. New Brunswick, NJ: Rutgers University Press.

Foley, Lara. 2005a. "Midwives, Marginality and Public Identity Work." *Symbolic Interaction* 28:183–203.

———. 2005b. "Midwives and Motherwork." Paper presented at the annual meeting of the Pacific Sociological Association, April 7, Portland, OR.

———. 2006. "Gender Narratives in the Work of Sexual Assault Nurse Examiners." Unpublished manuscript.

Foley, Lara, and Christopher Faircloth. 2003. "Medicine as a Discursive Resource: Legitimation in the Work Narratives of Midwives." *Sociology of Health and Illness* 25:165–84.

Foucault, Michel. 1973. *The Birth of the Clinic.* London: Tavistock.

———. 1977. *Discipline and Punish: The Birth of a Prison.* New York: Random House.

———. 1978. *The History of Sexuality: An Introduction, Volume 1.* New York: Vintage Books.

———. 1980. *Power/Knowledge: Selected Interviews and Other Writings 1972–1977,* edited by C. Gordon. New York: Pantheon.

Fox-Genovese, Elizabeth. 1988. *Within the Plantation Household: Black and White Women in the Old South.* Chapel Hill: University of North Carolina Press.

Frank, Arthur. 1991. "For a Sociology of the Body: An Analytical Review." In *The Body: Social Process and Cultural Theory,* edited by M. Featherstone, M. Hepworth, and B. S. Turner, 36–102. London, England: Sage.

Freud, Sigmund. 1949. *An Outline of Psychoanalysis,* translated by James Strachey. New York: W. W. Norton.

Frueh, Joanna. 1999. "Monster/Beauty: Midlife Bodybuilding as Aesthetic Discipline." In *Figuring Age: Women, Bodies, Generations,* edited by K. Woodward, 212–26. Bloomington: Indiana University Press.

Frye, Marilyn. 1983. *The Politics of Reality: Essays in Feminist Theory.* Freedom, CA: The Crossing Press.

———. 1992. "Lesbian 'Sex.'" In *Willful Virgin: Essays in Feminism,* 109–19. Freedom, CA: The Crossing Press.

Gagnon, John. 1977. *Human Sexualities.* New York: Scott, Foresman.

Gagnon, John H., and William Simon. [1973] 2005. *Sexual Conduct.* New Brunswick, NJ: AldineTransaction.

Galst, Liz. 1998. "The Sports Closet." *Ms.,* September/October, 75–78.

Garfinkel, Harold. 1967. *Studies in Ethnomethodology.* Englewood Cliffs, NJ: Prentice Hall.

George, Molly. 2005. "Making Sense of Muscle: The Body Experiences of Collegiate Women Athletes." *Sociological Inquiry* 75:317–45.

Gerber, E. W., J. Felshin, P. Berlin, and W. Wyrick. 1974. *The American Woman in Sport.* Reading, MA: Addison-Wesley Publishing Company.

Gerschick, Thomas J., and Adam Stephen Miller. 1995. "Coming to Terms: Masculinity and Physical Disability." In *Men's Health and Illness: Gender, Power and the Body,* edited by D. Sabo and D. F. Gordon, 183–204. Thousand Oaks, CA: Sage.

Gettings, John. 2000–2007. "The Wage Gap in Pro Sports." Pearson Education, publishing as Infoplease. Retrieved on April 7, 2007 (http://www.infoplease.com/spot/sptwagegap1.html).

Giddens, Anthony. 1984. *The Constitution of Society: Outline of the Theory of Structuration.* Berkeley: University of California Press.

Gissendanner, Cindy Himes. 1994. "African-American Women and Competitive Sport, 1920–1960." In *Women, Sport, and Culture,* edited by S. Birrell and C. L. Cole, 81–92. Champaign, IL: Human Kinetics.

Goffman, Erving. 1959. *The Presentation of Self in Everyday Life.* New York: Anchor Books.

———. 1963. *Stigma. Notes on the Management of Spoiled Identity.* Englewood Cliffs, NJ: Prentice Hall.

———. 1967. *Interaction Ritual.* New York: Anchor Books.

———. 1977. "The Arrangement between the Sexes." *Theory and Society* 4:301–31.

Golub, Sharon. 1992. *Periods: From Menarche to Menopause.* Newbury Park, CA: Sage Publications.

Gordon, Linda. 1974. *Women's Bodies, Women's Rights: A Social History of Birth Control in America.* New York: Penguin.

Graber, Julia, and Jeanne Brooks-Gunn. 2002. "Adolescent Girls' Development." In *Handbook of Women's Sexual and Reproductive Health,* edited by G. M. Wingood and R. J. DiClemente, 21–42. New York: Kluwer Academic/Plenum Publishers.

Grace, Victoria, Annie Potts, Nicola Gavey, and Tiina Vares. 2006. "The Discursive Condition of Viagra." *Sexualities* 9:295–314.

Granskog, Jane. 2003. "Just 'Tri' and 'Du' It: The Variable Impact of Female Involvement in the Triathlon/Duathlon Sport Culture." In *Athletic Intruders,* edited by A. Bolin and J. Granskog, 27–52. Albany, NY: State University of New York Press.

Green, Jamison. 2004. *Becoming a Visible Man.* Nashville, TN: Vanderbilt University Press.

Greil, Arthur L., Thomas A. Leitko, and Karen L. Porter. 1988. "Infertility: His and Hers." *Gender and Society* 2:172–99.

Griffin, Pat. 1998. *Strong Women, Deep Closets.* Champaign, IL: Human Kinetics.

Grint, Keith, and Steve Woolgar. 1995. "On Some Failures of Nerve in Constructivist and Feminist Analyses of Technology." *Science, Technology, & Human Values* 20:286–310.

Grudowski, Mike. 1997. "My Name Is Bill. I'm an Aquamaid." *Outside Magazine* online. Retrieved March 15, 2006 (http://outside.away.com/magazine/1297/9712aqua.html).

Gubrium, Jaber F., and James A. Holstein. 1997. *The New Language of Qualitative Method.* New York: Oxford University Press.

———. 1998. "Narrative Practice and the Coherence of Personal Stories." *The Sociological Quarterly* 39:163–87.

Guttmacher Institute. 2006. "State Policies in Brief: Parental Involvement in Minors' Abortion Decisions." Retrieved February 10, 2006 (http://www.guttmacher.org/statecenter/adolescents.html).

Halberstam, Judith. 1994. "F2M: The Making of Female Masculinity." In *The Lesbian Postmodern,* edited by L. Doan, 210–28. New York: Columbia University Press.

———. 1998. *Female Masculinity.* Durham, NC: Duke University Press.

Hall, M. Ann. 1996. *Feminism and Sporting Bodies.* Champaign, IL: Human Kinetics.

Halperin, David M. 1989. "Is There a History of Sexuality?" *History and Theory* 28:257–74.

Hammermesh, Daniel S., and Jeff E. Biddle. 1994. "Beauty and the Labor Market." *American Economic Review* 84:1174–94.

Hargreaves, Jennifer. 1994. *Sporting Females.* London, England: Routledge.

———. 2000. *Heroines of Sport: The Politics of Difference and Identity.* London, England: Routledge.

Harris, John. 2005. "The Image Problem in Women's Football." *Journal of Sport and Social Issues* 29:184–97.

Harrison, Kate. 1995. "Fresh or Frozen: Lesbian Mothers, Sperm Donors, and Limited Fathers." In *Mothers in Law: Feminist Theory and the Legal Regulation of Motherhood,* edited by M. A. Fineman and I. Karpin, 167–201. New York: Columbia University Press.

Hartley, Heather. 2006. "The 'Pinking' of Viagra Culture: Drug Industry Efforts to Create and Repackage Sex Drugs for Women." *Sexualities* 9:363–78.

Hartmann, Douglas. 2003. "The Sanctity of Sunday Football: Why Men Love Sports." *Contexts* 2:13–19.

Haubegger, Christy. 1994. "I'm Not Fat, I'm Latina." *Essence*, December, 8.

Healy, Bernadine. 1995. *A New Prescription for Women's Health*. New York: Penguin Books.

Helgesen, Sally. 1995. *The Female Advantage: Women's Ways of Leadership*. New York: Doubleday.

Hennen, Peter. 2004. "Fae Spirits and Gender Trouble: Resistance and Compliance among the Radical Faeries." *Journal of Contemporary Ethnography* 33:499–533.

Henshaw, Stanley K., and Kathryn Kost. 1992. "Parental Involvement in Minors' Abortion Decisions." *Family Planning Perspectives* 24:196–209.

Herbert, Melissa S. 1998. *Camouflage Isn't Only for Combat: Gender, Sexuality and Women in the Military*. New York: New York University Press.

Hesse-Biber, Sharlene Nagy. 1996. *Am I Thin Enough Yet? The Cult of Thinness and the Commercialization of Identity*. New York: Oxford University Press.

Heywood, Leslie. 1998. *Bodymakers: A Cultural Anatomy of Women's Body Building*. New Brunswick, NJ: Rutgers University Press.

———. 1999. "Despite the Positive Rhetoric about Women's Sports, Female Athletes Face a Culture of Sexual Harassment." *Chronicle of Higher Education*, January 8, B4–5.

Heywood, Leslie, and Jennifer Drake (eds.). 1997. *Third Wave Agenda: Being Feminist, Doing Feminism*. Minneapolis: University of Minnesota Press.

Heywood, Leslie, and Shari L. Dworkin. 2003. *Built to Win: The Female Athlete as Cultural Icon*. Minneapolis: University of Minnesota Press.

Hill, Thomas. 1993. *What to Expect When Your Wife Is Expanding*. Kansas City, MO: Cader Books.

Hochschild, Arlie Russell. 1983. *The Managed Heart: Commercialization of Human Feeling*. Berkeley: University of California Press.

Hohman, Leslie B., and Bertram Schaffner. 1947. "The Sex Lives of Unmarried Men." *The American Journal of Sociology* 52:501–7.

Holland, Janet, Caroline Ramazanoglu, and Rachel Thomson. [1996] 2002. "In the Same Boat?" In *Gender: A Sociological Reader*, edited by S. Jackson and S. Scott, 326–37. London, England: Routledge.

Hollander, Jocelyn A., and Judith Howard. 2000. "Social Psychological Theories on Social Inequality." *Social Psychology Quarterly* 63:338–51.

Holstein, James A., and Jaber F. Gubrium. 2000. *The Self We Live By: Narrative Identity in a Postmodern World*. New York: Oxford.

hooks, bell. 1981. *Ain't I a Woman: Black Women and Feminism*. Boston, MA: South End Press.

———. 1992. *Black Looks: Race and Representation*. Boston, MA: South End Press.

———. 1999. *Happy to Be Nappy*. Los Angeles, CA: Hyperion.

Houts, Leslie A. 2004. "Backstage, Frontstage Interactions: Everyday Racial Events and White College Students." Ph.D. dissertation, Department of Sociology, University of Florida, Gainesville, FL.

———. 2005. "Young Women's First Voluntary Sexual Intercourse." *Journal of Family Issues* 26:1082–1102.

Houvouras, Shannon. 2004. "Negotiated Concepts: Body, Mind, Emotions and Self in Women's Childbearing Narratives." Ph.D. dissertation, Department of Sociology, University of Florida, Gainesville, FL.

Howard, Judith, and Jocelyn Hollander. 1997. *Gendered Situations, Gendered Selves: A Gender Lens on Social Psychology*. Thousand Oaks, CA: Sage Publications.

Howe, P. David. 2003. "Kicking Stereotypes into Touch: An Ethnographic Account of Women's Rugby." In *Athletic Intruders*, edited by A. Bolin and J. Granskog, 227–46. Albany: State University of New York Press.

Hoyert, Donna L., Hsiang-Ching Kung, and Betty L. Smith. 2005. "Deaths: Preliminary Data for 2003." *National Vital Statistics Report* 53(15), February 28.

HUES. 1999. "Mission Statement." March/April, 2.

Humphreys, Laud. 1970. *Tearoom Trade: Impersonal Sex in Public Places.* Chicago, IL: Aldine Publishing Company.

Hunter, Myra S., and Irene O'Dea. 1997. "Menopause: Bodily Changes and Multiple Meanings." In *Body Talk: The Material and Discursive Regulation of Sexuality, Madness and Reproduction*, edited by J. M. Ussher, 199–222. London, England: Routledge.

Ingraham, Chrys. 1996. "The Heterosexual Imaginary: Feminist Sociology and Theories of Gender." In *QueerTheory/Sociology*, edited by S. Seidman, 168–93. Malden, MA: Blackwell.

"IOC Makes Gender Ruling." 2004. *BBC Sport*, May 21. Retrieved November 21, 2006 (http://news.bbc.co.uk/sport2/hi/olympics_2004/3496678.stm).

Jackson, Stevi, and Sue Scott. 2001. "Putting the Body's Feet on the Ground: Towards a Sociological Reconceptualization of Gendered and Sexual Embodiment." In *Constructing Gendered Bodies*, edited by K. Backett-Milburn and L. McKie, 9–24. New York: Palgrave.

Jacobs Lehman, Stephanie, and Susan Silverberg Koerner. 2004. "Adolescent Women's Sports Involvement and Sexual Behavior/Health: A Process-Level Investigation." *Journal of Youth and Adolescence* 33:443–55.

Jaffee, Lynn, and Rebecca Manzer. 1992. "Girls' Perspectives: Physical Activity and Self-Esteem." *Melpomene Journal* 11:14–23.

Jaffee, Lynn, and Sherri Ricker. 1993. "Physical Activity and Self-Esteem in Girls: The Teen Years." *Melpomene Journal* 12:19–26.

Jay, Nancy. 1981. "Gender and Dichotomy." *Feminist Studies* 7:38–56.

Jefferson Lenskyj, Helen. 1994. "Sexuality and Femininity in Sport Contexts: Issues and Alternatives." *Journal of Sport and Social Issues* 18:356–76.

Jetter, Alexis, Annelise Orleck, and Diana Taylor (eds.). 1997. *The Politics of Motherhood: Activist Voices from Left to Right.* Hanover, NH: University of New England Press.

Joans, Barbara. 2003. "Women Who Ride: The Bitch in the Back is Dead." In *Athletic Intruders*, edited by A. Bolin and J. Granskog, 159–76. Albany: State University of New York Press.

Jones, David E. 2000. *Women Warriors: A History.* Washington, DC: Brassey's.

Kane, Emily W. 2006. "'No Way My Boys Are Going to Be Like That!': Parents' Responses to Children's Gender Nonconformity." *Gender and Society* 20:149–76.

Kane, Mary Jo. 1995. "Resistance/Transformation of the Oppositional Binary: Exposing Sport as a Continuum." *Journal of Sport and Social Issues* 19:191–218.

Kane, Mary Jo, and Elaine Snyder. 1989. "Sport Typing: The Social 'Containment' of Women in Sport." *Arena Review* 13:77–96.

Kapsalis, Terry. 1997. *Public Privates: Performing Gynecology from Both Ends of the Speculum.* Durham, NC: Duke University Press.

Katz, Jonathon Ned. 1995. *The Invention of Heterosexuality.* New York: Dutton.

Kaufert, Patricia, Penny Gilbert, and Robert Tate. 1992. "The Manitoba Project: A Reexamination of the Relationship between Menopause and Depression." *Maturitas* 14:143–56.

Kaye, Lenard W., and Jeffrey S. Applegate. 1995. "Men's Style of Nurturing Elders." In *Men's Health and Illness: Gender, Power and the Body*, edited by D. Sabo and D. F. Gordon, 205–221. Thousand Oaks, CA: Sage.

Kesselman, Amy. 1991. "The 'Freedom Suit': Feminism and Dress Reform in the United States, 1848–1875." *Gender and Society* 5:495–510.

Kessler, Suzanne J. 1998. *Lessons from the Intersexed.* New Brunswick, NJ: Rutgers University Press.

Kessler, Suzanne J., and Wendy McKenna. 1978. *Gender: An Ethnomethodological Approach.* Chicago, IL: University of Chicago Press.

Kidd, Bruce. 1990. "The Men's Cultural Centre: Sports and the Dynamic of Women's Oppression/ Men's Repression." In *Sport, Men, and the Gender Order*, edited by M. A. Messner and D. F. Sabo, 31–44. Champaign, IL: Human Kinetics Books.

Kilbourne, Jean. 1999. *Deadly Persuasion.* New York: Free Press.

Kilvert, Gwen. 2002. "Missing the X Chromosome." *Sports Illustrated Women*, July/August, 20–22.

Kimmel, Michael. 1990. "Baseball and the Reconstitution of American Masculinity, 1880–1920." In *Sport, Men, and the Gender Order*, edited by M. A. Messner and D. Sabo, 55–66. Champaign, IL: Human Kinetics Books.

———. 1994. "Masculinity as Homophobia: Fear, Shame, and Silence in the Construction of Gender Identity." In *Theorizing Masculinities*, edited by H. Brod and M. Kaufman, 119–41. Newbury Park, CA: Sage.

King, J. L. 2005. *On the Down Low: A Journey into the Lives of "Straight" Black Men Who Sleep with Men*. New York: Harlem Moon.

Kinsey, Alfred C., Wardell B. Pomeroy, and Clyde E. Martin. 1948. *Sexual Behavior in the Human Male*. Philadelphia, PA: W. B. Saunders.

Kinsey, Alfred C., Wardell B. Pomeroy, Clyde E. Martin, and Paul Gebhard. 1953. *Sexual Behavior in the Human Female*. Philadelphia, PA: W. B. Saunders.

Klassen, Pamela. 2001. *Blessed Events: Religion and Home Birth in America*. Princeton, NJ: Princeton University Press.

Klein, Melissa. 1997. "Duality and Redefinition: Young Feminism and the Alternative Music Community." In *Third Wave Agenda: Being Feminist, Doing Feminism*, edited by L. Heywood and J. Drake, 207–25. Minneapolis: University of Minnesota Press.

Kotula, Dean. 2002. *The Phallus Palace: Female to Male Transsexuals*. Los Angeles, CA: Alyson Books.

Krasas Rogers, Jackie, and Kevin D. Henson. 1997. "'Hey, Why Don't You Wear a Shorter Skirt?': Structural Vulnerability and the Organization of Sexual Harassment in Temporary Clerical Employment." *Gender & Society* 11:215–37.

Kwolek-Folland, Angel. 1994. *Engendering Business: Men and Women in the Corporate Office, 1870–1930*. Baltimore, MD: The Johns Hopkins University Press.

Lane, Charles. 2005. "High Court Allows Inmate's Abortion." *Washington Post*, October 18, A18. Retrieved October 27, 2005 (http://www.washingtonpost.com/wp-dyn/content/article/2005/10/17/AR2005101700515).

LaPointe, Eleanor. 1992. "Relationships with Waitresses: Gendered Social Distance in Restaurant Hierarchies." *Qualitative Sociology* 15:377–93.

Lapovsky Kennedy, Elizabeth, and Madeline D. Davis. 1993. *Boots of Leather, Slippers of Gold: The History of a Lesbian Community*. New York: Routledge.

Laqueur, Thomas. 1990. *Making Sex: Body and Gender from the Greeks to Freud*. Cambridge, MA: Harvard University Press.

LaRossa, Ralph. 1997. *The Modernization of Fatherhood: A Social and Political History*. Chicago, IL: University of Chicago Press.

Larsen, Elizabeth A. 2006. "A Vicious Oval: Why Women Seldom Reach the Top in American Harness Racing." *Journal of Contemporary Ethnography* 35:119–47.

Lee, Janet. 1994. "Menarche and the (Hetero) Sexualization of the Female Body." *Gender and Society* 8:343–62.

Lee, Judy. 1992. "Media Portrayals of Male and Female Olympic Athletes: Analyses of Newspaper Accounts of the 1984 and the 1988 Summer Games." *International Review for the Sociology of Sport* 27:197–218.

Lenskyj, Helen. 1986. *Out of Bounds: Women, Sport and Sexuality*. Toronto, ON: Women's Press.

LeVay, Simon, and Sharon M. Valente. 2002. *Human Sexuality*. Sunderland, MA: Sinauer Associates.

Levin, Nancy. 1998. "Playing the Game: 'Passing' in Basketball." *Curve*, January 7(6), 30–31.

Levit, Nancy. 1998. *The Gender Line: Men, Women, and the Law*. New York: New York University Press.

Lichtenstein, Bronwen. 2004. "Caught at the Clinic: African American Men, Stigma, and STI Treatment in the Deep South." *Gender and Society* 18:369–388.

Lipka, Sara. 2005. "High Court Expands Protections of Title IX." *Chronicle of Higher Education*, April 8, 1.

Loe, Meika. 2004. *The Rise of Viagra: How the Little Blue Pill Changed Sex in America.* New York: New York University Press.

Lopez, Iris. 1997. "Agency and Reproductive Freedom among Puerto Rican Women in New York City." In *Situated Lives: Gender and Culture in Everyday Life,* edited by L. Lamphere, H. Ragone, and P. Zavella, 157–74. New York: Routledge.

Lorber, Judith. 1993. "Believing Is Seeing: Biology as Ideology." *Gender and Society* 4:568–81.

———. 1994. *Paradoxes of Gender.* New Haven, CT: Yale University Press.

———. 1996. "Beyond the Binaries: Depolarizing the Categories of Sex, Sexuality, and Gender." *Sociological Inquiry* 66:143–59.

———. 2001. *Gender Inequality: Feminist Theories and Politics.* 2nd ed. Los Angeles, CA: Roxbury.

———. 2005. *Breaking the Bowls: Degendering and Feminist Change.* New York: W. W. Norton & Company.

Lorber, Judith, and Patricia Yancey Martin. 1998. "The Socially Constructed Body: Insights from Feminist Theory." In *Illuminating Social Life: Classical and Contemporary Theory Revisited,* edited by P. Kivisto, 183–206. Thousand Oaks, CA: Pine Forge Press.

Lorber, Judith, and Lisa Jean Moore. 2002. *Gender and the Social Construction of Illness.* 2nd ed. Walnut Creek, CA: AltaMira Press.

Loseke, Donileen R. 1999. *Thinking about Social Problems: An Introduction to Constructionist Perspectives.* New York: Aldine de Gruyter.

Lowe, Maria R. 1998. *Women of Steel: Female Body Builders and the Struggle for Self-Definition.* New York: New York University Press.

Lowitt, Bruce. 2003. "Women Pioneers: Ten Who Broke Barriers in Sports." *St. Petersburg Times,* May 18, 8–9C.

Lucal, Betsy. 1999. "What It Means to Be Gendered Me: Life on the Boundaries of a Dichotomous Gender System." *Gender and Society* 13:781–97.

Majors, Richard. 1990. "Cool Pose: Black Masculinity and Sports." In *Sport, Men, and the Gender Order,* edited by M. A. Messner and D. F. Sabo, 109–26. Champaign, IL: Human Kinetics Books.

Mansfield, Alan, and Barbara McGinn. 1993. "Pumping Irony: The Muscular and the Feminine." In *Body Matters: Essays on the Sociology of the Body,* edited by S. Scott and D. Morgan, 49–68. London, England: The Falmer Press.

Marable, Manning. 2000. "The Black Male: Searching beyond Stereotypes." In *Gender through the Prism of Difference.* 2nd ed., edited by M. Baca Zinn, P. Hondagneu-Sotelo, and M. A. Messner, 251–57. Boston, MA: Allyn and Bacon.

Maranto, Cheryl L., and Ann F. Stenoien. 2000. "Weight Discrimination: A Multidisciplinary Analysis." *Employee Responsibilities and Rights Journals* 12:9–24.

Markens, Susan, C. H. Browner, and H. Mabel Preloran. 2003. "'I'm Not the One They're Sticking the Needle Into': Latino Couples, Fetal Diagnosis, and the Discourse of Reproductive Rights." *Gender and Society* 17:462–81.

Markula, Pirkko. 1995. "Firm but Shapely, Fit but Sexy, Strong but Thin: The Postmodern Aerobicizing Female Bodies." *Sociology of Sport Journal* 12:424–53.

———. 2003. "Postmodern Aerobics: Contradiction and Resistance." In *Athletic Intruders: Ethnographic Research on Women, Culture, and Exercise,* edited by A. Bolin and J. Granskog, 53–78. Albany: State University of New York Press.

Marshall, Barbara L. 2006. "The New Virility: Viagra, Male Aging and Sexual Function." *Sexualities* 9:345–62.

Marsiglio, William. 1998. *Procreative Man.* New York: New York University Press.

Marsiglio, William, Sally Hutchinson, and Mark Cohan. 2001. "Young Men's Procreative Identity: Becoming Aware, Being Aware, and Being Responsible." *Journal of Marriage and Family* 63:123–35.

Martin, Emily. 1987. *The Woman in the Body: A Cultural Analysis of Reproduction.* Boston, MA: Beacon Press.

———. 1991. "The Egg and the Sperm: How Science Has Constructed a Romance Based on Stereotypical Male-Female Roles." *Signs* 16:485–501.

Martin, Karin. 1998. "Becoming a Gendered Body: Practices of Preschools." *American Sociological Review* 63:494–511.

———. 2003. "Giving Birth Like a Girl." *Gender and Society* 17:54–72.

Martin, Patricia Yancey. 2003. "'Said and Done' versus 'Saying and Doing': Gendering Practices, Practicing Gender at Work." *Gender and Society* 17:342–66.

———. 2004. "Gender as Social Institution." *Social Forces* 82:1249–73.

———. 2006. *Rape Work: Victims, Gender and Emotions in Organization and Community Context.* New York: Routledge.

Martin, Susan. 1980. *Breaking and Entering: Policewomen on Patrol.* Berkeley: University of California Press.

———. 1994. "'Outsider Within' the Station House: The Impact of Race and Gender on Black Women Police." *Social Problems* 41:382–400.

Masters, William H., and Virginia E. Johnson. 1966. *Human Sexual Response.* Boston, MA: Little, Brown.

McCord, William Maxwell, Edward Norbeck, and Douglass Price-Williams. 1968. *The Study of Personality: An Interdisciplinary Appraisal.* New York: Holt, Rinehart and Winston.

McHoul, Alec, and Wendy Grace. 1993. *A Foucault Primer.* New York: New York University Press.

McKay, Jim, and Debbie Huber. 1992. "Anchoring Media Images of Technology in Sport." *Women's Studies International Forum* 15:205–18.

McLaughlin, Helen. 1994. *Footsteps in the Sky: A Pictorial History of Airline Inflight Service.* Denver, CO: State of the Art Book Publishing Company.

Mead, George Herbert. [1934] 1964. *Mind, Self, and Society,* edited by C. W. Morris. Chicago, IL: University of Chicago Press.

Meece, Mickey. 2000. "Mind-set: Only the Svelte Need Apply." *New York Times,* March 22, 1G.

Mellstrom, Ulf. 2004. "Machines and Masculine Subjectivity: Technology as an Integral Part of Men's Life Experiences." *Men and Masculinities* 6:368–82.

Messing, Karen, Katherine Lippel, Diane Demers, and Donna Mergler. 2000. "Equality and Difference in the Workplace: Physical Job Demands, Occupational Illnesses, and Sex Differences." *NWSA Journal* 12:21–49.

Messing, Karen, Carmen Sirianni, and Paula Rayman. 1998. *One-Eyed Science: Occupational Health and Women Workers.* Philadelphia, PA: Temple University Press.

Messner, Michael A. 1988. "Sports and Male Domination: The Female Athlete as Contested Ideological Terrain." *Sociology of Sport Journal* 5:197–211.

———. 1989. "Masculinities and Athletic Careers." *Gender and Society* 3:71–88.

———. 1990. "When Bodies Are Weapons: Masculinity and Violence in Sport." *International Review for the Sociology of Sport* 25: 203–20.

———. 1992. *Power at Play.* Boston, MA: Beacon Press.

———. 2000. "Becoming 100% Straight." In *Gender through the Prism of Difference,* edited by M. Baca-Zinn, P. Hondagneu-Sotelo, and M. A. Messner, 205–210. Boston, MA: Allyn and Bacon.

———. 2002. *Taking the Field.* Minneapolis: University of Minnesota Press.

Messner, Michael A., Michele Dunbar, and Darnell Hunt. 2000. "The Televised Sports Manhood Formula." *Journal of Sport and Social Issues* 24:380–94.

Messner, Michael A., Margaret Carlisle Duncan, and Kerry Jensen. 1993. "Separating the Men from the Girls: The Gendered Language of Televised Sports." *Gender and Society* 7:121–37.

Messner, Michael A., Margaret Carlisle Duncan, and Faye Linda Wachs. 1996. "The Gender of Audience Building: Televised Coverage of Women's and Men's NCAA Basketball." *Sociological Inquiry* 66:422–39.

Messner, Michael A., and Don F. Sabo. 1990. "Introduction: Toward a Critical Feminist Reappraisal of Sport, Men, and the Gender Order." In *Sport, Men, and the Gender Order,* edited by M. A. Messner and D. F. Sabo, 1–16. Champaign, IL: Human Kinetics Books.

Miles, Rebecca. 2002. "Criminal Consequences for Making Babies: Probation Conditions that Restrict Procreation." *Washington and Lee Law Review* 59:1545–84.

Miller, Carrie. 2000. "Single Woman Wants Baby; UF Clinic Says No." *Gainesville Sun,* October 31,1A, 13A.

Mills, Albert J. 1998. "Cockpits, Hangars, Boys and Galleys: Corporate Masculinities and the Development of British Airways." *Gender, Work, and Organization* 5:172–88.

"Minimum Qualifications to Become a Flight Attendant." Cabincrewjobs.com. Retrieved March 15, 2006 (http://www.cabincrewjobs.com/flight-attendant-qualifications.html).

Mitchell, Lisa M. 2001. *Baby's First Picture: Ultrasound and the Politics of Fetal Subjects.* Toronto, ON: University of Toronto Press.

Monro, Surya, and Lorna Warren. 2004. "Transgender Citizenship." *Sexualities* 7:345–62.

Montero, David. 2006. "Pakistani Women Defy Threats, Run Mixed Marathon." *Christian Science Monitor,* January 30. Retrieved on June 15, 2006 (http://www.csmonitor.com/2006/0130/p01s03-wosc.html?s=hns).

Moore, Lisa Jean. 2003. "'Billy, the Sad Sperm with No Tail': Representations of Sperm in Children's Books." *Sexualities* 6:277–300.

Moore, Pamela L. 1997. "Feminist Bodybuilding, Sex, and the Interruption of Investigative Knowledge." In *Building Bodies,* edited by P. L. Moore, 74–86. New Brunswick, NJ: Rutgers University Press.

Murkoff, Heidi. 2002. *What to Expect When You're Expecting.* 3rd ed. New York: Workman Publishing Company, Inc.

Murphy-Geiss, Gail. Forthcoming 2007. "Hospitable or Hostile Environment: Sexual Harassment in the United Methodist Church." *The Review of Religious Research* 47.

Myerson, Marilyn, Sara L. Crawley, Erica Hesch Anstey, Justine Kessler, and Cara Okopny. 2007. "Who's Zoomin' Who? A Feminist, Queer Content Analysis of 'Interdisciplinary' Human Sexuality Textbooks." *Hypatia* 22:92–113.

Nagel, Joane. 2000. "Ethnicity and Sexuality." *Annual Review of Sociology* 26:107–33.

National Center for Education Statistics. 2005. "Table 205. Total Fall Enrollment in Degree Granting Institutions by Race/Ethnicity, Sex, Attendance Status and Level of Student. Selected Years: 1976-2004." U.S. Department of Education. Retrieved on June 12, 2006 (http://nces.ed.gov/programs/digest/d05/tables/dt05_205.asp).

National Collegiate Athletic Association. 2004. "2002–03 NCAA Gender-Equity Report." Retrieved November 21, 2006 (http://www.ncaa.org/library/research/gender_equity_study/2002-03/2002-03_gender_equity_report.pdf).

National Federation of High Schools. 2006. "Participation in High School Sports Increases Again: Confirms NFHS Commitment to Strong Leadership." Retrieved November 22, 2006 (http://www.nfhs.org/web/2006/09/participation_in_high_school_sports_increases_again_confirms_nf.aspx).

"NBA Minimum Salary." 2005. InsideHoops. August 10. Retrieved April 7, 2007 (http://www.insidehoops.com/minimum-nba-salary.shtml).

Negron-Mutaner, Frances. 1997. "Jennifer's Butt." *Aztlan,* 22:181–94.

Nelson, Jennifer. 2003. *Women of Color and the Reproductive Rights Movement.* New York: New York University Press.

Nestle, Joan, Clare Howell, and Riki Wilchins. 2002. *Genderqueer: Voices from Beyond the Sexual Binary.* Los Angeles, CA: Alyson Books.

Newton, Esther. 1972. *MotherCamp: Female Impersonators in America.* Englewood Cliffs, NJ: Prentice Hall.

O'Brien, Mary. 1983. *The Politics of Reproduction.* London, England: Routledge and Kegan Paul.

Official Website of the Olympic Movement. 2006a. "Softball." Retrieved November 26, 2006 (http://www.olympic.org/uk/sports/programme/index_uk.asp?SportCode=SO).

———. 2006b. "Shan Zhang: The Woman Who Outshot the Men." Retrieved November 26, 2006 (http://www.olympic.org/uk/athletes/profiles/bio_uk.asp?SPO_S_CODE=SH&PAR_I_ID=68237).

Oliver, Kelly. 1989. "Marxism and Surrogacy." *Hypatia* 10:95–115.

Oudshoorn, Nelly. 2003. *The Male Pill: A Biography of a Technology in the Making.* Durham, NC: Duke University Press.

Paap, Kris. 2006. *Working Construction: Why White Working Class Men Put Themselves and the Labor Movement in Harm's Way.* Ithaca, NY: ILR Press.

Paechter, Carrie. 2003. "Masculinities and Femininities as Communities of Practice." *Women's Studies International Forum* 26:69–77.

———. 2006. "Power, Knowledge and Embodiment in Communities of Sex/Gender Practice." *Women's Studies International Forum* 29:13–26.

"Pay Inequity in Athletics." 2001–2007. Women's Sports Foundation. Retrieved April 7, 2007 (http://www.womenssportsfoundation.org/cgi-bin/iowa/issues/disc/article.html?record=1185).

Pennington, Bill. 2004a. "Title IX Trickles Down to Girls of Generation Z." *New York Times*, June 29. Retrieved on November 20, 2006 (http://www.nytimes.com/2004/06/29/sports/othersports/29title.html).

———. 2004b. "College Basketball: For These Men, Lots of Guts but Little Glory." *New York Times*, March 5, 1D.

Peper, Karen. 1994. "Female Athlete = Lesbian: A Myth Constructed from Gender Role Expectations and Lesbiphobia." In *Queer Words, Queer Images: Communication and the Construction of Homosexuality*, edited by R. J. Ringer, 193–208. New York: New York University Press.

Pharr, Suzanne. 1988. *Homophobia: A Weapon of Sexism.* Inverness, CA: Chardon.

Pierre, Robert E. 2002. "Girls (sic) Hockey Team Battles It Out in Court." *Miami Herald*, February 3, 27A.

Pirinen, Riitta. 1997. "Catching Up with Men?" *International Review for the Sociology of Sport* 32:239–49.

Plummer, Kenneth. 1995. *Telling Sexual Stories: Power, Change and Social Worlds.* London, England: Routledge.

Plymire, Darcy C., and Pamela J. Forman. 2001. "Speaking of Cheryl Miller: Interrogating the Lesbian Taboo on a Women's Basketball Newsgroup." *NWSA Journal* 13:1–21.

Potts, Annie, and Leonore Tiefer. 2006. "Special Issue on 'Viagra Culture': Introduction." *Sexualities* 9:267–72.

Preves, Sharon. 2003. *Intersex and Identity: The Contested Self.* New Brunswick, NJ: Rutgers.

Pringle, Rosemary. 1993. "Male Secretaries." In *Doing 'Women's Work': Men in Nontraditional Occupations*, edited by C. L. Williams, 128–51. Newbury Park, CA: Sage.

Professional Safety. 2000. "AFA Survey Reports 10 Percent of Flight Attendants Injured on Job." August, 21.

Prosser, Jay. 1995. "No Place like Home: The Transgendered Narrative of Leslie Feinberg's *Stone Butch Blues*." *Modern Fiction Studies* 41:483–514.

"Quotable." 2005. *St. Petersburg Times*, October 13, 1C.

Radical Cheerleaders. 2006. "Homepage." Retrieved March 10, 2006 (http://radcheers.tripod.com/RC/).

Raine, Tina, Arik Marcell, Corinne Rocca, and Cynthia Harper. 2003. "The Other Half of the Equation: Serving Young Men in a Young Women's Reproductive Health Clinic." *Perspectives on Sexual and Reproductive Health* 35:208–214.

Ransom, Elizabeth. 1999. "Creating 'Uniformity': The Construction of Bodies in Women's Collegiate Cross Country." In *Interpreting Weight: The Social Management of Fatness and Thinness*, edited by J. Sobal and D. Maurer, 183–208. New York: Aldine de Gruyter.

Rapoport, Rhonda, and Robert N. Rapoport. 1971. "Further Considerations on the Dual-Career Family." *Human Relations* 24:519–33.

Raymond, Janice. 1979. *The Transsexual Empire: The Making of the She-Male.* Boston, MA: Beacon.

Reed, Richard K. 2005. *Birthing Fathers: The Transformation of Men in American Rites of Birth.* New Brunswick, NJ: Rutgers University Press.

Register, Charles A., and Donald R. Williams. 1990. "The Wage Effects of Obesity." *Social Science Quarterly* 71:130–40.

Reissman, Catherine Kohler. 2000. "Stigma and Everyday Resistance Practices: Childless Women in South India." *Gender and Society* 14:111–35.

Renzetti, Claire M. 1992. *Violent Betrayal: Partner Abuse in Lesbian Relationships*. Newbury Park, CA: Sage Publications.

Reskin, Barbara, and Patricia Roos. 1987. "Status Hierarchies and Sex Segregation." In *Ingredients for Women's Employment Policy*, edited by C. Bose and G. Spitze, 3–21. Albany: State University of New York Press.

"Revenge of a Vixen." 1997. *New York Times*, December 24, 16A.

Rich, Adrienne. 1986. "Compulsory Heterosexuality and the Lesbian Existence." In *Blood, Bread and Poetry: Selected Prose, 1979–1986*, 23–76. New York: Norton.

Richman, Erin L., and David R. Shaffer. 2000. "'If You Let Me Play Sports': How Might Sport Participation Influence the Self-Esteem of Adolescent Females?" *Psychology of Women Quarterly* 24:189–99.

Riordan, James. 1985. "Some Comparisons of Women's Sport in East and West." *International Review for the Sociology of Sport* 20:117–25.

Risman, Barbara J. 1998. *Gender Vertigo: American Families in Transition*. New Haven, CT: Yale University Press.

———. 2004. "Gender as a Social Structure: Theory Wrestling with Activism." *Gender and Society* 18:429–50.

Ritzer, George. 1996. *The McDonaldization of Society*. Thousand Oaks, CA: Pine Forge Press.

Roberts, Dorothy. 1997. *Killing the Black Body: Race, Reproduction, and the Meaning of Liberty*. New York: Vintage Books.

Roberts, Elizabeth. 1998. "Native Narratives of Connectedness: Surrogate Motherhood and Technology." In *Cyborg Babies: From Techno-Sex to Techno-Tots*, edited by R. Davis-Floyd and J. Dumit, 193–211. New York: Routledge.

Roehling, Mark V. 1990. "Weight-Based Discrimination in Employment: Psychological and Legal Aspects." *Personnel Psychology* 52:969–1017.

———. 2002. "Weight Discrimination in the American Workplace: Ethical Issues and Analysis." *Journal of Business Ethics* 40:177–89.

Rohrbaugh, J. B. 1979. "Femininity on the Line." *Psychology Today*, August, 31–33.

Rooks, Noliwe M. 1996. *Hair Raising: Beauty, Culture, and African American Women*. New Brunswick, NJ: Rutgers University Press.

Root, Robin, and C. H. Browner. 2001. "Practices of the Pregnant Self: Compliance with and Resistance to Prenatal Norms." *Culture, Medicine, and Psychiatry* 25:195–223.

Ross, Loretta J. 1998. "African American Women and Abortion." In *Abortion Wars: A Half Century of Struggle, 1950–2000*, edited by R. Solinger, 161–207. Berkeley: University of California Press.

Roth, Rachel. 2004a. "'No New Babies?': Gender Inequality and Reproductive Control in the Criminal Justice and Prison Systems." *Journal of Gender, Social Policy and the Law* 12:391–425.

———. 2004b. "Searching for the State: Who Governs Prisoners' Reproductive Rights?" *Social Politics: International Studies in Gender, State, and Society* 11:411–38.

Rothman, Barbara Katz. [1989] 2000. *Recreating Motherhood*. New Brunswick, NJ: Rutgers University Press.

Ruane, Janet M., and Karen A. Cerulo. 2000. *Second Thoughts: Seeing Conventional Wisdom through the Sociological Eye*. Thousand Oaks, CA: Pine Forge Press.

Rubin, Gayle. 1984. "Thinking Sex: Notes for a Radical Theory of the Politics of Sexuality." In *Pleasure and Danger: Exploring Female Sexuality*, edited by C. S. Vance, 267–319. Boston, MA: Routledge & Kegan Paul.

Rubin, Harry. 2003. *Self-Made Men: Identity and Embodiment among Transsexual Men*. Nashville, TN: Vanderbilt University Press.

Rupp, Leila J., and Verta Taylor. 2003. *Drag Queens at the 801 Cabaret*. Chicago, IL: University of Chicago Press.

Rust, Paula C. 1995. *Bisexuality and the Challenge to Lesbian Politics: Sex, Loyalty, and Revolution*. New York: New York University Press.

Sabo, Donald F., and Joe Panepinto. 1990. "Football Ritual and the Social Reproduction of Masculinity." In *Sport, Men, and the Gender Order*, edited by M. A. Messner and D. F. Sabo, 115–26. Champaign, IL: Human Kinetics Books.

Sampson, Robert J., and Stephen W. Raudenbush. 2004. "The Social Structure of Seeing Disorder." *Social Psychology Quarterly* 67:319-42.

Sanders, Lynn. 2002. "Hardly Sporting: Don't Gut Title IX Until You Know What It Does." *Slate at MSN.com*, October 1. Retrieved November 21, 2006 (http://www.slate.com/?id=2071832).

Sargent, James D., and David G. Blanchflower. 1994. "Obesity and Stature in Adolescence and Earnings in Young Adulthood." *Archives of Pediatric Adolescent Medicine* 148:681-87.

Saxton, Marsha. 1998. "Disability Rights and Selective Abortions." In *Abortion Wars: A Half Century of Struggle, 1950–2000*, edited by R. Solinger, 374-99. Berkeley: University of California Press.

Schacht, Steven P. 1996. "Misogyny on and off the 'Pitch': The Gendered World of Male Rugby Players." *Gender and Society* 10:550-65.

———. 2002. "Four Renditions of Doing Female Drag: Feminine Appearing Conceptual Variations of a Masculine Theme." *Gendered Sexualities* 6:157-80.

Schiebinger, Londa. 1993. *Nature's Body*. Boston, MA: Beacon.

Schilt, Kristen. 2006. "Just One of the Guys? How Transmen Make Gender Visible at Work." *Gender and Society* 20:465-90.

Schleifer, David. 2006. "Make Me Feel Mighty Real: Gay Female-to-Male Transgenderists Negotiating Sex, Gender, and Sexuality." *Sexualities* 9:57-75.

Schmidt, Matthew, and Lisa Jean Moore. 1998. "Constructing a Good Catch: The Development of Technosemen and the Deconstruction of the Monolithic Male." In *Cyborg Babies: From Techno-Sex to Techno-Tots*, edited by R. Davis-Floyd and J. Dumit, 21–39. New York: Routledge.

Schmitt, Raymond L., and Wilbert M. Leonard II. 1986. "Immortalizing the Self through Sport." *American Journal of Sociology* 91:1088-1111.

Schrock, Douglas, Lori Reid, and Emily M. Boyd. 2005. "Transseuxals' Embodiment of Womanhood." *Gender and Society* 19:317-35.

Schulman, Kevin A., Jesse A. Berlin, William Harless, Jon F. Kerner, Shyrl Sistrunk, Bernard J. Gersh, Ross Dube, Christopher K. Taleghani, Jennifer E. Burke, Sankey Williams, John M. Eisenburg, Jose J. Escarse, and Willam Ayers. 1999. "The Effect of Race and Sex on Physicians' Recommendations for Cardiac Catheterization." *New England Journal of Medicine* 340:618-26.

Schutz, Alfred. 1970. *On Phenomenology and Social Relations: Selected Writings*. Chicago, IL: University of Chicago Press.

Schwartz, Pepper, and Virginia Rutter. 1998. *The Gender of Sexuality*. Thousand Oaks, CA: Pine Forge Press.

Seager, Joni. 2003. *The Penguin Atlas of Women in the World*. 3rd ed. New York: Penguin Books.

Sedgwick, Eve Kofsofsky. 1990. *Epistemology of the Closet*. Berkeley: University of California Press.

Seidman, Steven. 1991. *Romantic Longings*. New York: Routledge.

———. (ed.). 1996. *QueerTheory/Sociology*. Malden, MA: Blackwell.

Sev'er, Aysan. 1999. "Sexual Harassment: Where We Were, Where We Are and Prospects for the New Millennium." Introduction to the Special Issue. *The Canadian Review of Sociology and Anthropology* 36:469-97.

Shackleford, Ben A. 2001. "Masculinity, the Auto Racing Fraternity, and the Technological Sublime." In *Boys and Their Toys? Masculinity, Technology, and Class in America*, edited by R. Horowitz, 229–50. New York: Routledge.

Shalala, Donna. 2002. "30 Years of Leveling the Playing Field." *Miami Herald,* June 23, 1L.

Shapiro, Jerrold. 1987. "Expectant Father." *Psychology Today,* January (36), 9, 42.

Shea, B. Christine. 2001. "The Paradoxes of Pumping Iron: Female Bodybuilding as Resistance and Compliance." *Women and Language* 24:42–46.

Sheff, Elisabeth. 2005. "Polyamorous Women, Sexual Subjectivity and Power." *Journal of Contemporary Ethnography* 34:251–83.

Shehan, Constance, Jesse Schultz, and Marsha Wiggins-Frame. 1999. "Feeding the Flock and the Family." *Sociological Focus* 32:247–63.

Shelton, Gary. 2006a. "Give Him a Big Hug." *St. Petersburg Times,* February 15, 1C, 7C.

———. 2006b. "When His Big Moment Arrives, Weir Freezes." *St. Petersburg Times,* February 15, 1C, 9C.

Shilling, Chris. 1993. *The Body in Social Theory.* London, England: Sage.

"Short Takes." 2006. *Ms.,* Spring, 20–21.

Shostak, Arthur B., Gary McLouth, with Lynn Seng. 1984. *Men and Abortion: Lessons, Losses and Love.* New York: Praeger.

Simonds, Wendy, and Charlotte Ellertson. 2004. "Emergency Contraception and Morality: Reflections of Health Care Workers and Clients." *Social Science and Medicine* 58:1285–97.

Singer, Linda. 1993. *Erotic Welfare.* New York: Routledge.

Sir Mix-A-Lot. 1992. "Baby Got Back." *Mack Daddy.* American Recordings. Catalogue number: 586795.

Smith, Dorothy. 1987. *The Everyday World as Problematic: A Feminist Sociology.* Boston, MA: Northeastern University Press.

Smith, George W., and Dorothy E. Smith. 1998. "The Ideology of 'FAG': The School Experience of Gay Students." *The Sociological Quarterly* 39:309–36.

Snyder, E., and E. Spreitzer. 1983. *Social Aspects of Sport.* 2nd ed. Englewood Cliffs, NJ: Prentice Hall.

Somerville, Siobhan B. 2000. *Queering the Color Line.* Durham, NC: Duke University Press.

Sprague, Joey. 1997. "Holy Men and Big Guns: The Can[n]on in Social Theory." *Gender and Society* 11:88–107.

Stacey, Clare. 2004. "Justify My Love: Constructing Moral Boundaries in Carework." Paper presented at the annual meeting of the American Sociological Association, August, San Francisco, CA.

Stacey, Judith. 2006. "Gay Parenthood and the Decline of Paternity As We Knew It." *Sexualities* 9:27–55.

Staples, Brent. 1997. "Just Walk On By: A Black Man Ponders His Power to Alter Public Space." In *Reconstructing Gender: A Multicultural Anthology,* edited by E. Disch, 165–67. Mountain View, CA: Mayfield.

Staples, William G. 2000. *Everyday Surveillance: Vigilance and Visibility in Postmodern Life.* New York: Rowman & Littlefield.

Starr, Mark, and Martha Brant. 1999. "It Went Down to the Wire and Thrilled Us All." *Newsweek,* July 19, 46–54.

Steinem, Gloria. 1978. "If Men Could Menstruate." *Ms.,* October, 110.

Stern, Seth. 2001. "Women Firefighters Struggle for First Rung." *Christian Science Monitor,* December 3. Retrieved on November 20, 2006 (http://www.csmonitor.com/2001/1203/p18s1-wmwo.html).

Stillion, Judith. 1995. "Premature Death among Males: Extending the Bottom Line of Men's Health." In *Men's Health and Illness: Gender Power and the Body,* edited by D. Sabo and D. F. Gordon, 46–67. Thousand Oaks, CA: Sage.

Stoltenberg, John. 1990. *Refusing to Be a Man: Essays on Sex and Justice.* New York: Meridian.

Stombler, Mindy, and Irene Padavic. 1997. "Sister Acts: Resisting Men's Domination in Black and White Fraternity Little Sister Programs." *Social Problems* 44:257–75.

Stone, Sandy. 1991. "The Empire Strikes Back: A Posttranssexual Manifesto." In *Body Guards,* edited by J. Epstein and K. Straub, 280–304. New York: Routledge.

Strong, Bryan, Christine DeVault, Barbara W. Sayad, and William L. Yarber. 2005. *Human Sexuality.* 5th ed. Boston, MA: McGraw-Hill.

Suggs, Welch. 2001. "Left Behind." *Chronicle of Higher Education,* November 30, A35.

Sykes, Heather. 1998. "Turning the Closets Inside/Out: Towards a Queer-Feminist Theory in Women's Physical Education." *Sociology of Sport Journal* 15:154–73.

Szymczak, Julia, and Peter Conrad. 2006. "Medicalizing the Aging Male Body: Andropause and Baldness." In *Medicalized Masculinities,* edited by D. Rosenfeld and C. Faircloth, 89–111. Philadelphia, PA: Temple University Press.

Tanenbaum, Leora. 1999. *Slut! Growing Up Female with a Bad Reputation.* New York: Perennial.

Taub, Diane E., Elaine M. Blinde, and Kimberly R. Greer. 1999. "Stigma Management through Participation in Sport and Physical Activity: Experiences of Male College Students with Physical Disabilities." *Human Relations* 52:1469–84.

Tavris, Carol. 1993. *The Mismeasure of Woman.* New York: Simon and Schuster.

Teegarden, Dorothy, William R. Proulx, Mark Kern, Darlene Sedlock, Connie M. Weaver, Conrad C. Johnston, and Roseann M. Lyle. 1996. "Previous Physical Activity Relates to Bone Mineral Measures in Young Women." *Medicine and Science in Sports and Exercise* 28:105–12.

Teicher, Stacy A. 1999. "Fight to Diversify Fire Departments." *Christian Science Monitor.* Retrieved on August 2, 2004 (http://www.csmonitor.com/durable/1999/03/08/text/p2s1.html).

Theberge, Nancy. 1986. "Toward a Feminist Alternative to Sport as a Male Preserve." *Sociology of Sport Journal* 3:193–202.

———. 1991. "Reflections on the Body in the Sociology of Sport." *Quest* 43:123–34.

———. 1997. "'It's Part of the Game': Physicality and the Production of Gender in Women's Hockey." *Gender and Society* 11:69–87.

———. 2000. *Higher Goals.* Albany: State University of New York Press.

"Things I Never Anticipated." Cabincrewjobs.com. Retrieved on March 15, 2006 (http://www.cabincrewjobs.com/flight-attendant-things.html).

Thomas, Pattie, Paul Campos, and Carl Wilkerson. 2005. *Taking Up Space: How Eating Well and Exercising Regularly Changed My Life.* Nashville, TN: Pearlsong Press.

Thomas, William I., and Dorothy S. Thomas. 1928. *The Child in America: Behavior Problems and Programs.* New York: Knopf.

Thompson, Becky W. 1994. *A Hunger So Wide and Deep: A Multiracial View of Women's Eating Problems.* Minneapolis: University of Minnesota Press.

Thornton, Terry E., and Lynn Paltrow. 1991. "The Rights of Pregnant Patients: Carder Case Brings Bold Policy Initiatives." *HealthSpan* 8(5). Retrieved October 27, 2005 (http://advocatesforpregnantwomen.org/articles/angela.htm).

Tiefer, Leonore. 2004. *Sex Is Not a Natural Act and Other Essays.* Boulder, CO: Westview Press.

———. 2006. "The Viagra Phenomenon." *Sexualities* 9:273–94.

Times Wire Reports. 1998. "Woman Swims the Yucatan Channel." *Los Angeles Times,* June 2, 4A.

Todd, Paul. 2004. "A Big Boat for a Small Skipper." *Sailing* 38(April):20, 30.

Tone, Andrea (ed.). 1997. *Controlling Reproduction: An American History.* Wilmington, DE: Scholarly Resources Books.

———. 2001. *Devices and Desires: A History of Contraceptives in America.* New York: Hill and Wang.

Tripp, Laurel. 2003. "It's Great to Be a Florida Gator: Fans Negotiating Ideologies of Race, Gender, and Power." Ph.D. dissertation, Department of Sociology, University of Florida, Gainesville, FL.

Trumbach, Randolph. 1994. "The Origins and Development of Modern Lesbian Role in the Western Gender System: Northwestern Europe and the United States, 1750–1990." *Historical Reflections/Réflexions Historiques* 20:287–320.

Tuana, Nancy. 1989. "The Weaker Seed: The Sexist Bias of Reproductive Theory." In *Feminism and Science,* edited by N. Tuana, 147–71. Bloomington: Indiana University Press.

Tuller, David. 2004. "Gentlemen, Start Your Engines?" *New York Times,* NYTimes.com, June 21. Retrieved November 21, 2006 (http://query.nytimes.com/gst/fullpage.html?sec=health&res=9A07E0DE1239F932A15755C0A9629C8B63).

Turner, Bryan S. 1996. *The Body and Society*. 2nd ed. London, England: Sage.

Twigg, Julia. 2000. *Bathing, the Body and Community Care*. London, England: Routledge.

Tyler, Melissa, and Taylor, Steve. 1998. "The Exchange of Aesthetics: Women's Work and 'The Gift.'" *Gender, Work, and Organization* 5:165–71.

Upton, Rebecca, and Sallie Han. 2003. "Maternity and Its Discontents: 'Getting the Body Back' After Pregnancy." *Journal of Contemporary Ethnography* 32:670–92.

U.S. Department of Labor. Women's Bureau. 2003a. "Nontraditional Occupations for Women in 2003." Retrieved November 21, 2006 (http://www.dol.gov/wb/factsheets/nontra2003.htm).

———. 2003b. "20 Leading Occupations of Employed Women Full-Time Wage and Salary Workers." Retrieved November 21, 2006 (http://www.dol.gov/wb/factsheets/20lead2003.htm).

Vares, Tiina, and Virginia Braun. 2006. "Spreading the Word, But What Word Is That? Viagra and Male Sexuality in Popular Culture." *Sexualities* 9:315–32.

Verbrugge, Martha. 2000. "Gym Periods and Monthly Periods: Concepts of Menstruation in American Physical Education, 1900–1940." In *Body Talk: Rhetoric, Technology, Reproduction*, edited by M. M. Lay, L. J. Gurak, C. Gravon and C. Myntti, 67–97. Madison: The University of Wisconsin Press.

von Drehle, David. 2003. *Triangle: The Fire That Changed America*. New York: Atlantic Monthly Press.

Wachs, Faye Linda. 2003. "'I Was There. . .': Gendered Limitations, Expectations, and Strategic Assumptions in the World of Co-ed Softball." In *Athletic Intruders*, edited by A. Bolin and J. Granskog, 177–99. Albany: State University of New York Press.

———. 2005. "The Boundaries of Difference: Negotiating Gender in Recreational Sport." *Sociological Inquiry* 75:527–47.

Waldo, Craig R., Jennifer L. Berdahl, and Louise F. Fitzgerald. 1998. "Are Men Sexually Harassed? If So, by Whom?" *Law and Human Behavior* 22:59–79.

Waldron, Ingrid. 1995. "Contributions of Changing Gender Differences in Behavior and Social Roles to Changing Gender Differences in Mortality." In *Men's Health and Illness: Gender, Power and the Body*, edited by D. Sabo and D. Gordon, 22–45. Thousand Oaks, CA: Sage Publications.

Weeks, Jeffrey. 2003. *Sexuality*. 2nd ed. London, England: Routledge.

Weinberg, Martin S., and Colin J. Williams. 2005. "Fecal Matters: Habitus, Embodiments, and Deviance." *Social Problems* 52:315–36.

Weitz, Rose. 2004. *Rapunzel's Daughters: What Women's Hair Tells Us about Women's Lives*. New York: Farrar, Straus and Giroux.

Welch, Michael. 1997. "Violence against Women by Professional Football Players." *Journal of Sport and Social Issues* 21:392–411.

Welter, Barbara. 1978. "The Cult of True Womanhood, 1820–1860." In *The American Family in Social Historical Perspective*, 2nd edition, edited by M. Gordon, 313–33. New York: St. Martin's Press.

Wesely, Jennifer K. 2001. "Negotiating Gender: Bodybuilding and the Natural/Unnatural Continuum." *Sociology of Sport Journal* 18:162–80.

West, Candace, and Don Zimmerman. 1987. "Doing Gender." *Gender and Society* 1:125–51.

Wheaton, Belinda. 2000. "'New Lads?': Masculinities and the 'New Sport' Participant." *Men and Masculinities* 2:434–56.

White, Emily. 2002. *Fast Girls: Teenage Tribes and the Myth of the Slut*. New York: Scribner.

White, Garland F., Janet Katz, and Kathryn E. Scarborough. 1992. "The Impact of Professional Football Games upon Violent Assaults of Women." *Violence and Victims* 7:157–70.

White, Phillip G., and Anne B. Vagi. 1990. "Rugby in the 19th-Century British Boarding School System." In *Sport, Men, and the Gender Order*, edited by M. A. Messner and D. F. Sabo, 67–78. Champaign, IL: Human Kinetics Books.

Whitson, David. 1990. "Sport in the Social Construction of Masculinity." In *Sport, Men, and the Gender Order*, edited by M. A. Messner and D. F. Sabo, 19–32. Champaign, IL: Human Kinetics Books.

———. 1994. "The Embodiment of Gender: Discipline, Domination, and Empowerment." In *Women, Sport, and Culture*, edited by S. Birrell and C. Cole, 353–72. Champaign, IL: Human Kinetics Books.

Wienke, Chris. 2006. "Sex the Natural Way: The Marketing of Cialis and Levitra." In *Medicalized Masculinities*, edited by D. Rosenfeld and C. Faircloth, 45–64. Philadelphia, PA: Temple University Press.

Wilchins, Riki Anne. 1997. *Read My Lips: Sexual Subversion and the End of Gender*. Ithaca, NY: Firebrand Books.

———. 2004. *Queer Theory/Gender Theory: An Instant Primer*. Los Angeles, CA: Alyson Books.

Williams, Christine L. 1989. *Gender Differences at Work: Women and Men in Nontraditional Occupations*. Berkeley: University of California Press.

———. 1992. "The Glass Escalator: Hidden Advantages for Men in the Female Professions." *Social Problems* 39:253–67.

———. 1995. *Still a Man's World: Men Who Do "Women's Work."* Berkeley: University of California Press.

Willis, Paul. 1982. "Women in Sport in Ideology." In *Sport, Culture, and Ideology*, edited by J. Hargreaves, 117–35. London, England: Routledge and Kegan Paul.

Wilson, Robert A. 1966. *Feminine Forever*. New York: Evans.

"Wimbeldon to Offer Equal Prize Money." 2007. The Official Web Site of Wimbeldon. February 22. Retrieved April 7, 2007 (http://www.wimbledon.org/en_GB/news/pressreleases/prizemoney.html).

Winant, Howard. 2002. *The World Is a Ghetto*. New York: Basic Books.

Winterich, Julie A. 2003. "Sex, Menopause, and Culture: Sexual Orientation and the Meaning of Menopause for Women's Sex Lives." *Gender and Society* 17:627–42.

"WNBA Salaries." 2005. InsideHoops. May 28. Retrieved April 7, 2007 (http://www.insidehoops.com/wnba/salaries.shtml).

"Women in the America's Cup: A (Very) Brief History up to 1995." Updated 2000. Retrieved April 7, 2007 (http://www.a3.org/95_Press_Releases/A3_95_History_Women_AC.html).

Women in the Fire Services, Inc. 2006. "Status Report 2005." Retrieved November 21, 2006 (http://www.wfsi.org/women_and_firefighting/status_report.php).

Yasser, Ray, James R. McCurdy, C. Peter Goplerud, and Maureen A. Weston. 2003. *Sports Law: Cases and Materials*. 5th ed. Cincinnati, OH: Anderson Publishing Co.

Young, Antonia. 2000. *Women Who Became Men: Albanian Sworn Virgins*. Oxford: Berg.

Young, Iris Marion. 1979. "The Exclusion of Women from Sport: Conceptual and Existential Dimensions." *Philosophy in Context* 9:44–53.

———. 1980. "Throwing Like a Girl: A Phenomenology of Feminine Body Comportment, Motility and Spatiality." *Human Studies* 3:137–56.

———. 2005. *On Female Body Experience*. New York: Oxford.

Zerubavel, Eviatar. 1996. "Lumping and Splitting: Notes on Social Classification." *Sociological Forum* 11:421–33.

Index

About the Authors

Sara L. Crawley is assistant professor of Women's Studies at the University of South Florida. She received her Ph.D. from the University of Florida in sociology and Women's Studies in 2002. Her research centers around aspects of identity work among lesbian/gay/bisexual/transgendered people and performances of the gendered body. She has been published in such journals as *The Sociological Quarterly, Gender & Society, Hypatia, Journal of Lesbian Studies, International Review for the Sociology of Sport,* and *Journal of Contemporary Ethnography.* She teaches courses in gender, sexualities, queer theory, feminist theory, and feminist pedagogy. Engaging everyday disruptions as often as possible, she is also a sailor and U.S. Coast Guard–licensed boat captain, attempting to negotiate a self that lies somewhere between Ernest Hemingway and Marilyn Frye.

Lara J. Foley is associate professor of sociology and affiliated faculty in Women's Studies at the University of Tulsa. She received her Ph.D. in sociology and graduate certificate in Women's Studies from the University of Florida in 2001. The major themes of her work are individual and collective identity negotiation in interpersonal relationships and in organizational and occupational contexts. She has conducted research on midwives and Sexual Assault Nurse Examiners (SANEs). Foley has published in journals such as *Symbolic Interaction, Sociology of Health and Illness,* and *The Sociological Quarterly.* She teaches courses in sociology of medicine and sociology of law.

Constance L. Shehan is professor and chair of the Department of Sociology at the University of Florida. She also served as the director of UF's

Women's Studies program in the mid to late 1980s. Her research and teaching focus on the areas of gender, families, work, and aging. Much of her work has examined women's experiences in "work" (both paid labor and unpaid carework in the home), highlighting the relationship between women's work and health. She has examined the impact of the structural characteristics of jobs on personal and family well-being, focusing on women and men in the ministry. Her recent projects focus on gender and aging, particularly women's roles as caregivers and aging women's body images. She is the editor of the *Journal of Family Issues* and was recently recognized as a Fellow of the National Council on Family Relations.

Fr. Faye

Thank you for many inspiring & informative hours. Have a joyful Christmas.

Bro. John Barrett, C.P.M.

JOHN
The Different Gospel

J O H N
The Different Gospel

A Reflective Commentary

by

MICHAEL J. TAYLOR, S.J.

ALBA · HOUSE NEW · YORK

SOCIETY OF ST. PAUL, 2187 VICTORY BLVD., STATEN ISLAND, NEW YORK 10314

Library of Congress Cataloging in Publication Data

Taylor, Michael J.
  John, the different gospel.

  Bibliography: p.
  1. Bible. N.T. John—Commentaries. I. Title.
  BS2615.3.T34   1983   226'.507   83-15485
  ISBN 0-8189-0456-9 (pbk.)

Designed, printed and bound in the United States of
America by the Fathers and Brothers of the
Society of St. Paul, 2187 Victory Boulevard,
Staten Island, New York 10314, as part of their
communications apostolate.

1 2 3 4 5 6 7 8 9 (Current Printing: first digit)

CONTENTS

Introduction

The Different Gospel

Like the Synoptics before him, John proclaims the *good news* that the world finds salvation in the death and Resurrection of Jesus. With dramatic narrative he recounts this final chapter of Jesus' life. He records other events that precede this last hour, shedding interpretive light on it. He recounts episodes that show Jesus *fulfills* the meaning and purpose of God's covenant with Israel. His Jesus tells believers how they are to know and defend him, how they are to live and celebrate the saving life he shares with them. To be sure, John has his own way of doing this, but in doing all of the above, we see that he did what Matthew, Mark and Luke did before him—namely, he has put together a gospel.

And yet the central figure that emerges from John's telling is remarkably *different* from *theirs*, so much so that we wonder if John is talking about the same person. The Christ of the Synoptics, while drawing closer to God and ultimate exaltation through obedience and fidelity to his Messianic mission and the sufferings he endures, comes through, as the theologians say, very much the created, human, "low" Christ. John, however, gives us a Jesus who, through encased in human flesh, is exalted from the start. He is—again, as the theologians say— very much the "high" Christ, pre-existent, one with the Father, co-creator of the world, descended from above, an unextinguishable and eternal light come into the world. (*Granted Jesus in the Synoptics is given "high" titles, he does not enjoy them as consistently or as clearly as he does in John.*)

And if Jesus is "high" Christ, he speaks in high accents indeed. The earthy parables, homey moral aphorisms, much of the rabbinic sound of Jesus of Nazareth are gone. They are replaced by the longer more majestic discourses of the Son of God. His words and those about him contain rich multi-leveled symbolism. The gospel is heavy with dramatic irony and dualism. The works of power that indicate the "Reign of God" is at hand are not here. In their place we discover *seven* self-revealing "signs" performed by an *"ego-eimi"* figure from heaven. Rarely do we find mention of a "Kingdom Come" that sums up the principal work of Jesus in the Synoptics. More frequently we hear reference to symbolic abstractions like life, bread from heaven, living waters, light, truth, glory that Jesus brings from above and wishes to share with the world *now* and not in some Future Age. Yes, John is the gospel of the "high" Christ *par excellence*, the book whose Messiah offers *eternal life* and offers it now (realized eschatology). We might wonder if he arrived at such a Christ using the same sources, the same Jesus data available to the Synoptics. Or did he produce his picture from entirely different material? *Or* could he have fabricated his vision altogether?

Sources for the Gospel

The evidence is that John does not fabricate his "different" Christ, nor does he write his gospel from wholly new sources. He obviously uses *traditional* Jesus material, data remembered and compiled by the early Christian witnesses for kerygmatic, catechetical, pastoral and other reasons. In fact scholars find a good deal of the common (Synoptic) tradition about Jesus in John's gospel. He could have known one or more of the Synoptic gospels. If not, he seems to have had access to much of their data. If John's telling of the common data is different, it can be because he has, with the help of the Spirit (cf., cc's. 14-16), reached a deeper understanding of the identity of Jesus and seeks to show his insight by the way he narrates the traditional episodes and by the way he has Jesus speak. If the "low" Christ is now perceived to have been "high" Christ all along, some transposing, indeed some basic reinterpretation of the remembered sayings and deeds of Jesus is in order.

Material found in John that is new could well derive from a new source. Some scholars notice that John is more focused in the material that shows Jesus active in the Jerusalem area and suggest that he had access to data originating from Jesus' mission to Judea not available to previous evangelists. Others see John's seven *signs* deriving from a "signs source"; again, a source containing some but not all of Jesus' Synoptic miracles (and some new sayings as well), and thus in part material not available to the Synoptics. John's discourses could be *constructed* from Jesus' sayings found in these old and new sources. It is his insight into Jesus' identity as the "high" Christ that requires him to reinterpret and transpose the signs and sayings into a "higher key" as it were, not unlike the style and expression of contemporary Graeco-Roman revelation literature, resulting in richer, more symbolic narrative and a more exalted *sound* to Jesus' speech.

Also, parts of the gospel claim to be based on eyewitness testimony, the witness of one of Jesus' own followers (cf., 19:34-35; 21:24). This eyewitness seems to be a disciple of Jesus quite likely Judean and not one of the "twelve." This would account for still another source for the document, namely, the personal memory of a faithful non-Galilean disciple. Synoptic data—Judean mission material—a *signs* source— personal recollections—could account for much of the similarity and difference in John's gospel vis-à-vis the Synoptics. Insight and transposition could explain the different *persona* and *sound* of Jesus. Indeed the author claims God's Spirit helps him arrive at a fuller understanding of Jesus, allowing him to be bold and confident in the work of reinterpreting his own and the traditional data in light of his deeper insight (14:26; 16:13).

And there seem to be other factors that contribute to the "different Christ" that emerges from his gospel. The evangelist it appears comes from a different background than that which produced the Synoptic data (the background for the Synoptics could loosely be termed "main-stream" Judaism). It is difficult to discover exactly what the background of John was, but a growing number of scholars see it as distinctly "out of the mainstream," a sectarian Judaism that seems influenced by non-Jewish religious and philosophical currents circulating in Palestine and its environs in the century contemporary with Jesus and the early Church.

John writes in Greek. He would be at least casually familiar with the Graeco-Roman world and its cultural and religious values. He is not reluctant to use terms that even a non-Jewish hellenist of the time would find meaningful, as for example, when his Jesus claims to be the "way," the "truth," access to a new "life" and "light" for the world. And yet his work manifests an *insider's* knowledge of the Old Testament. Though he quotes it less than the other evangelists, he refers to various parts of it explicitly and by allusion. He can, for instance, use quotes from Isaiah like the "blinded eyes . . . hardened hearts" text (Jn 12:40; Is 6:10). He can use bold biblical imagery such as the bronze serpent on the staff to symbolize the crucified and exalted Christ (Jn 3:14; Nb 21:9). And the gospel is rich in Old Testament motifs: the Creation Story (1:1-18); Moses and the events of Exodus (c. 6); the Good Shepherd of Ezekiel (c. 10); Zechariah's donkey (c. 12), to mention a few. A number of scholars further detect in John many motifs from the OT Wisdom literature where he apparently finds biblical precedent and analogy for the divine "high" Christ he discovers in Jesus. And although he seems to manifest some bias against the Temple and the cult surrounding it, he is very knowledge-able of the festal and cultic life of Israel centered in Jerusalem. So there seems to be no question that John is from a Jewish background. The question is from what kind of Jewish background? More and more the evidence seems to suggest he is not from the "mainstream." It might be that many Jews would consider his Judaism "far out" or heterodox.

An example of a heterodox Jewish movement contemporary with Jesus and John is the Essene sect of Qumran, known to us through the now famous Dead Sea Scrolls. Though these documents antedate John's gospel by some years, there are striking similarities between the language of the Scrolls and key Johannine expressions: e.g., the use of strong dualist *light/darkness* categories, phrases such as "witnessing to the truth," "the Spirit of truth," "loving the brethren," "prince of dark-ness," and others which have close Johannine parallels. Qumran shows us closeup a first-century Judaism at odds with the mainstream, one that like John expresses its faith in strong dualistic terms. John need not have come from this particular, quite exclusivist Jewish group, but his Judaism seems to have an affinity with some of its religious categories and would thus be a bit outside the mainstream too (some have variously called it—an anti-Temple Judaism like that of Stephen the deacon [cf., Ac, cc's. 6-7], "hellenist-syncretist," a Judaism influenced by Samaritan theology, Moses-mystical, etc.). This could account for why the terminology he uses to draw his picture of Jesus is often different from that found in the Synoptics. He sees Judaism and Jesus in different categories from the mainstream. Incidentally Jesus, had he known of such Jewish "minorities," would have been as outgoing to them as to his brothers and sisters of the "mainstream" and could have won and retained faithful disciples among them.

The Johannine writings suggest that *hellenist* religious and philosophical forces of his time may have had some influence on the evangelist and the way he thought and expressed himself. Many scholars, for instance, detect in John a "gnostic" flavor and terminology. Gnosticism in its later more developed form is heavily dualistic, indeed ontologically so. It stresses certain souls are radically good but unaware of it because trapped in flesh. It is a mythological system that believes a *heavenly revealer* comes to save these good souls by communicating to them special *knowledge* (*gnosis*) of their psychic goodness and heavenly destiny. Similarities to Johannine thought and expression are impressive. Certainly Jesus for John is a *heavenly revealer* who brings spiritual knowledge of God to the world. In the last analysis John's dualism is not ontological, but in its heaviness it sounds at times not unlike the gnosticism of later centuries. Could there be some connecting link here that would account for John's occasional "gnostic" flavor?

Other scholars see in John a similarity to Stoicism in his use of the term *Logos* to describe Jesus in the opening lines of the gospel. *Logos* or *Word* is the uttered thought of God. The Stoic philosophers spoke of God as the *Logos* when he "thought" rationality into the universe, when he endowed creation with principles that gave *meaning* and *purpose* to nature. On inspection, John's gospel makes clear that the fullest *meaning* and *purpose* God gave the world was when he sent to it his Son, the *Word-made-flesh*. Again, something of a similarity of thought and possible source of influence.

Other commentators wonder if John had knowledge of the *Logos* speculations of the Jewish philosopher Philo. Philo it seems sought to tie in the Stoic concept of *Logos* with the divine mediating mystery of Wisdom in the OT. John seems to develop this theme also. However, he goes far beyond Philo. For John, Wisdom is not a divine "idea" but a divine person, Jesus, who becomes incarnate. The question of gnostic, Stoic, or Jewish philosophical influence on John is by no means clear. Still, he could have come from a form of Judaism that knew some sort of syncretist-philosophical influence. Once converted to Christ he would naturally explain Jesus in the "dualistic" terms normal to him and the particular milieu of his Judaism. As a believer, he could have circulated among syncretistic hellenist circles and sought to show these people that Jesus was the *Logos-meaning-giver* and the *heaven-sent-revealer* these systems supposed. Indeed he was *much more* than these systems supposed.

No one claims to be close to discovering the precise background of John. But there is a strong likelihood that he was *not from the mainstream* and this could account in part for his "different" Christ. All in all he has written a remarkable volume that finds so many resonant parallels with the different religious and philosophical movements of his day. John lived in a hellenistic world, greatly interested in religious syncretism and universalism. He seems well versed not only in the Bible, its various Jewish interpretations, and the new Christian tradition developing around Jesus as Messiah, but also in the religious tendencies and aspirations of other non-Jewish contemporaries near and beyond his own Jewish (minority) tradition. He seems to have chosen to present Jesus in an idiom somehow familiar to him that would reflect these many interests, especially to emphasize the appeal of Jesus for *all* human persons, both Jews and non-Jews. Such a reflection by no means answers all our questions about his Jesus, but it helps us realize his religious and cultural frame of reference seems to be *different* and this helps us understand why his Jesus in turn is different from the Synoptics. And if some find an evangelist from such background perhaps unsuited for the task of writing a *Christian* gospel, John would remind them that the Spirit of Jesus is very much in the picture directing his somewhat different cultural and religious mind-set, to a *correct reading* of all his data about Jesus.[1]

---

[1]We should, however, make it clear that the identity of the author of the Fourth Gospel is disputed and it seems must ever remain so. In the second century the anonymous work came to be attributed to "John" but it is only Irenaeus late in the century who identified the Apostle John with the evangelist. The arguments for or against Irenaeus' position cannot be restated here and are inconclusive in any case. It might be best to say we simply do not know for sure who the author is. Still, many scholars rule out the Apostle. And not a few seem to think the main authority behind the book is the figure referred to in the gospel itself, the anonymous "other disciple" (18:15-16; 21:2), sometimes called the "beloved disciple" (13:23; 19:26-27; 21:7, 20-23). This individual, they say, seems not to be one of the "twelve," but from another group of Jesus' followers as indicated above, a bit out of the Jewish mainstream, who remained faithful to Jesus even when he went to the Cross and who was one of the first to believe in his Resurrection. He became a respected figure in a Church that remained and developed for the most part separately from the "Great Church" of the "twelve Apostles" and Paul. This Church always considered itself authentically Christian, going back as it did to Jesus through its "beloved eyewitness disciple" who was also highly respected as a Spirit-filled prophet. In time, Christians generally came to accept the gospel as an *inspired reading* of Jesus' true identity. In this commentary the evangelist will simply be called *John*.

Purpose

The document is written mainly to strengthen the faith of members of John's own community (20:31); still, quiet mention is made of "others" (Jews and non-Jews) whom Jesus seeks as members of his flock and the gospel is put together in such a way that it has meaning and appeal for all sincere "outsiders" seeking answers to the quest for religious truth. But the polemical cast of much of the gospel indicates that the document has in mind the particular faith-needs of its own members, many of whom are in hostile debate with the "Jews" of a nearby Synagogue(s). It provides them with arguments that counteract the accusations being leveled against Jesus as Messiah, especially as "high" Messiah, a concept many Jews find blasphemously incompatible with Jewish monotheism. Quite recently Jewish members of John's Church have been "excluded from the Synagogue" because of their belief in Jesus (9:34; 16:1); they are experiencing persecution in one form or another. They must be given ways of dealing with this traumatic event that will safeguard and enhance their faith in Jesus. The gospel will show that Jesus provides for them (and all people) the full values of Judaism and indeed immeasurably more. To stay faithful to Jesus apart from official Judaism is not loss, but infinite gain.

Scholars see the document with its obvious editorial additions (and at times unique location of material) as evolving through a number of "unpublished" editions as problems and crises beset the Church (for example: the problem of a John the Baptist sect; the problem of the crypto-Christians; the difficulties Jews have with the "high" Christ; the time of possible dialogue with the "Great Church," etc.) before it reached its final form containing a redactor's appended chapter (21). Perhaps the main authority-figure behind the gospel—the "other" and "beloved disciple"—was involved in all but the last edition. Other disciple hands, however are in evidence, and the "beloved disciple" is dead before c. 21 is written.

Brief Overview of the Gospel

The "high" Christ is revealed at the outset in the prologue's Hymn (1:1-18). He comes from God with life, light and love from above. He comes in human flesh to reveal and share his and the Father's gifts with all who open themselves to him in faith. He gathers disciples around him who accept him as Messiah. Through his discourses and signs (cc's. 1-12, are often called the Book of Signs) he progressively reveals that he is the "high" Christ sent by the Father and thus one who fulfills and transcends the authentic expectations, values and blessings of Judaism. However, after two signs, Jesus meets a hostile response and enters into controversy with the "Jews" over his identity. They perceive little of his higher glory and the theme of Jesus as "light" opposed by non-believers as people of "darkness" develops and intensifies as the gospel proceeds. He speaks of a coming final sign, his "hour," when he will fully show the glory and light he has from the Father. With his raising of Lazarus and solemn entry into Jerusalem we see that the final "hour" is at hand.

The second part of the gospel (cc's. 13-20, often called the Book of Glory) dwells on Jesus' approaching "hour" when he is to return to the Father through death and Resurrection—the event that will render his *glory* communicable to believers. Chapters 13-17 contain Jesus' "Last Discourse" where he explains to his disciples the meaning, necessity and repercussions of his "hour." He reveals that upon Resurrection he will return to give them the Spirit. The Spirit will bring them his eternal gifts and be his presence with them always. With majestic resolve Jesus enters into his "hour." Once risen, he returns to the disciples and shows that the *glory* he has from the Father is now to be *theirs*. He gives them his Peace, breathing his Spirit upon them. They are to be the Spirit-indwelt agents of his *glory* to the world through time.

J O H N
The Different Gospel

Chapter 1

GENERAL COMMENTS (and reflections):

Mark's gospel begins with Jesus' baptism at the Jordan. Matthew and Luke begin their gospels near the birth of Jesus at Bethlehem. John begins his in heaven with Jesus identified as the Word of God. Though all, in their way, indicate the cosmic role of Jesus in the drama of salvation, John shows more profoundly why Jesus is cosmic redeemer. He will be more than a chosen instrument to mediate salvation and judgment (although he will be that), for John reveals Jesus as one sharing God's life in fullness at the start and who comes in human flesh to share God's love with all who open themselves to it . . . "God so loved the world that he gave it his only Son, so that all who believe in him may not perish but have eternal life" (3:16).

Prologue: 1:1-18

disagree some eg. Barrett with this observe

John begins his gospel with a prologue, mostly hymnic in form, revealing Jesus' divine origins. Like a musical overture, the Hymn introduces many of the themes that will be developed in the gospel . . . Jesus' role is to bring life, light and enduring love to a world that knows little life and much darkness, to persons who often prefer darkness to light. But he comes to a world that has the ability to recognize and accept him and thus be caught up in a personal relationship of love with him and the Father. As the Hymn says, human persons have the power to receive him and become "children of God" (v. 12).

But this is saying quite a bit. Does John know his hymnal claims for Jesus are true? Right away we realize that as one reads (or, more likely for John's people—hears) any passage in the gospel, he expects the reader to see it against the background of the whole book. The Jesus described in the Hymn is the Jesus who took on flesh, whose human words and actions were historically witnessed, whose heavenly gifts have been shared by many both before and after his Resurrection. The reader-hearer as well as John knows about the seven signs and the Resurrection and that *they* validate what the Hymn declares.

Scholars debate about the origin of the Hymn (interrupted four times by John or editors with what are felt to be necessary comments about John the Baptist's role vis-à-vis Jesus, vv. 6-9, 15; the mystery of the "new birth," v. 13; and a Jesus-Moses comparison, vv. 17-18). Did John write it as a fitting introduction for his gospel or find it already in use in the liturgy of his Church and incorporate it into his gospel because of its suitability? Whether written especially for or incorporated after an edition or two had already been written, it proves to be an exceptionally appropriate lead-in to the full gospel and indeed a fine hymnal summary of the high *persona* of Jesus and resumé of his historical years on earth. It has enjoyed a privileged place in the thoughts and prayers of Christians from the beginning.

The author of the Hymn was faced with a formidable task: how to state majestically and poetically the cosmic event—God's Son, his eternal Word becoming man. What categories, terms or comparisons could he use to describe it? Only one biblical event in any way compares to it . . . the event of the first creation, and so the primary motif of the Hymn is the *Creation Story* from the early verses of Genesis. Like Genesis the Hymn starts "In the beginning" . . . for in Jesus the world, after years of living apart from God in darkness, is to find a Second Creation, an unbelievably wonderful "new beginning." As Genesis finds God creating the world, so John depicts Jesus present at the creation as God's Word. As God discovers the earth in darkness and creates light, so Jesus as light from above comes to shine in the darkness. As God is living and gives life, so Jesus too has life to give. As God was rejectible in the beginning, so too Jesus will know rejection. At first, human creation reflected God's image; now it is to be born again of God, sharing in the fullness of Jesus' heavenly glory. So in the Creation Story the author has found a most apt biblical motif to reveal the divine identity and saving functions of Jesus.

The Hymn's term, *Logos* (Word), is a new way of identifying Jesus (unknown in the New Testament outside the so-called Johannine Writings) and the origin of the term as we saw could derive from several sources. It was the name Stoics gave to God when he put order and meaning into the universe. Philo uses the term in his syncretistic efforts to reconcile Stoicism and Judaism, it seems drawing his reflections on a mediating Logos between heaven and earth from the Wisdom literature of the Old Testament. And Jews generally use the term, Word, to indicate God as revealing himself. One *sees* God as he *speaks*. In the first creation he *spoke life* and *light* and they happened; God in that *speaking* thus revealed himself to be and have life and light. He *speaks* his law and message to Moses; he *speaks* his continuing words to the prophets, and one sees and knows him, his will, his plan for Israel. John could well have used the term *Logos* to indicate to Jews that God *speaks* the ultimate revelation and message about himself through Jesus; the Jewish God after all had so often revealed himself in *words*. And the gospel will bear this out: Jesus is depicted there in everything he does and says as *revealing* the Father. But perhaps not unlike Philo, John (because he moves in a partly Stoic syncretistic milieu) finds the Greek word *Logos* an apt translation for the OT mystery of *Wisdom*. Scholars see in the Hymn many motifs from the Wisdom literature. When the Bible spoke metaphorically of God's loving concern for creation under the term Wisdom, John could well have found the personified metaphor to be much more than figure of speech. God's Wisdom, he came to see, *is* a literal *person*, Jesus, and that person became flesh. Note how the "history" of Jesus and Wisdom coincides:

—Wisdom was pre-existent with God in the beginning,
   involved with creation (Pr 8:22; 27-31)

(Jn 1:1-5)

—Wisdom descends from heaven; dwells as
   in a tabernacle in Israel (Ws 9:10; Si 24:3ff)

(Jn 1:10-12, 14)

—Wisdom reflects God's light (Ws 7:26)

(Jn 1:4-5)

—Wisdom is rejected (Pr 1:24-25)

(Jn 1:10-11)

And certainly as the gospel proceeds beyond the prologue, John will depict Jesus in other Wisdom motifs: he like Wisdom will bring gifts from above (Ws 7:25; 8:4; 9:15-18); he will speak of himself in the symbolic words Wisdom uses of herself: for example, he invites people to "eat" and "drink" of himself (Si 24:19f); he offers them good wine and bread (Pr 9:2-5); like her, he will be the vine (Si 24:22f); like her, he will have "disciples" and call them "friends" (Ws 7:14, 27); as she cries out in discourses, so does Jesus. So scholars see the new term, *Logos*, reflecting rich associations from a wide assortment of different religious and cultural contexts that in consort help to identify Jesus . . . he is the one who gives a new, indeed an absolute *meaning* to the universe; he is the definitive *revelation of God*; he is in fact the descending and ascending Son of God, *Wisdom incarnate*. A bold claim indeed, but the upcoming gospel will illustrate that the claim is not without substance.

The Incarnation: 1:14

If another's psychic love can be known by human persons only when it is encased in a sensual humanly perceivable symbol, then God has established the depth of his love for the human family by encasing his eternal life, light and enduring love in the symbol of the human flesh of Jesus. Flesh seen and given is the normal symbol of human love. In the gospel Jesus will be seen in the flesh from Cana through to his death and Resurrection when that flesh as encasement of his love will be given in full measure. God has used symbols before to encase his loving presence: the fiery bush, the pillar of cloud and fire, tablets of stone, the tent, the temple, the altar, the sacrificial meal, but no more revealing symbol than this—the sensually perceivable human flesh of Jesus. Now one can understand in human terms the meaning of God's grace and truth. As the gospel unfolds in the human actions and words of Jesus one perceives not only *his* great love for the world, but the *Father's* limitless mercy, love and faithfulness as well (v. 18). As Jesus will say in 14:9 . . . "Philip, he who *sees me sees* the *Father*."

FURTHER PARTICULAR COMMENTS:

Vv. 6-9, 15 . . . These inserts into the Hymn about the Word seem to indicate that John's community is having problems with a sect of John the Baptist people. Do they understand the Baptist to have been the Messiah,

God's light and word-bearer? These inserts along with others later in the chapter and episodes in c. 3, clarify that the Baptist is none of these, but is sent to witness Jesus. His role is preparatory and subordinate. Note also the word *witness* is important to John; it comes up thirty times in the gospel. Christians whose faith is based on the witness of earlier Christians are no less recipients of Jesus and his grace than the witnesses themselves.

Additions and inserts of this sort often indicate the gospel underwent redactional evolution. As new problems beset the community, answers had to be appended to the document and the document itself had to be reshaped a bit to solve the problems—in this case, the problem of the John the Baptist sect. In the other insertions in vv. 13, 17-18, one detects pastoral and apologetical problems about baptism and about Jesus as a salvational mystery superior to the Moses-Exodus event. These additions bespeak further subordinate "purposes" the gospel has beyond its main early purpose stated in 20:31.

Vv. 10-11 . . . These verses speak in summary of what is to be narrated in cc's. 1-12 (often called the Book of Signs).

Vv. 12-13 . . . These verses speak in summary of what is to be found in cc's. 13-20 and the epilogue chapter 21 (often called the Book of Glory).

V. 13, "*begotten . . . by God*" . . . This will become clearer as one reads Jesus' words to Nicodemus in c. 3, and a related discourse with a Samaritan woman in c. 4. These words are inserted it seems because the need for *another birth* beyond that which Jews have from Abraham has been questioned or ridiculed.

V. 14 . . . That the Johannine Word becomes flesh indicates how radically John differs from developed gnosticism with *its* heavenly revealer. Jesus comes not to liberate people from the flesh, but to take it on and thus save them. God brings to human persons what he is; he does not rescue them from what they are. Humanists should note that Christians perceive humanity to be this good! It is capable of encasing God's love.

Vv. 16-18 . . . These verses and the earlier ones, 10-12, show that God's Word is not forced on anyone. In John's view there are two free responses (two options if you will) to the Word: one, acceptance, and this brings a new birth and eternal life; another, rejection, and this leaves one in darkness. People bring judgment on themselves by choosing darkness over light.

Vv. 16-18 . . . God's love in the Old Testament was especially manifest in his gift of the law to Moses. But Jesus is not just another prophet like Moses with a better law; he is the earthly encasement of God's life. Moses only saw the back of God (Ex 33:19-23); Jesus sees the face of God and reveals it to the world.

The Baptist's Witness to Jesus: 1:19-34

GENERAL COMMENTS (and reflections):

In earlier editions of his book John, like Mark, started his gospel with a Jesus-John the Baptist episode (the Baptist will hereafter be referred to as JB). John's interest, however, is not to identify JB as the prophetic moralizer of the other tradition. He reinterprets the data to make JB a witness to the Johannine Christology of Jesus. Two purposes will be served: a) Jesus will be early identified as the Messiah with JB's titles correcting popular misconceptions of what kind of a Messiah God sends Israel, and b) the reader will find out that JB is *not* the end-time Agent some mistook him to be, i.e., the Messiah, the Elijah-returned figure, or the Prophet-to-come of Moses. It seems the Johannine community is in dialogue with members of a JB sect who believe that he is all of these (it should be noted JB was accepted as the Messiah by many even into the third century). JB himself will contradict this view and settle the question. And since he encourages his own "followers" (the present JB sect) to follow Jesus (vv. 35-37), the JB episode here and in c. 3 could encourage these people to compare Jesus' life to JB's and possibly follow Jesus.

Scholars note the gospel proper begins and continues with the mood of a trial. *Prosecutorial questions* are asked about Jesus' identity; he and his disciples must give *answers defensively* about him; *witnesses testify* to Jesus' identity; reactions to Jesus are sometimes called *judgments*. It will be John's genius in this and coming "trials" to prove conclusively Jesus' "high" as well as "low" Messianic identity. And in the last analysis it will not be Jesus who is on trial so much as the "prosecution" (the "Jews"), for they reject the *evidence* (Jesus' seven signs and Resurrection). Rejecting him as both Messiahs, they will find in the end they are *judged* and *condemned* to live in darkness.

So priests and Levites (and later the Pharisees, all symbols of Jesus' non-believing "Prosecutors") come to ask JB point blank: is he the Messiah? JB replies that he is not. They ask in turn, is he Elijah or the Prophet? He says he is neither (vv. 19-21). The point: if JB is none of these, Jesus must clearly be all of them. The Jesus-identity process begins now historically. The first word, Messiah, is the prophets' term for the end-time Agent of God who is to inaugurate the New Age. The third word, Prophet, is the Mosaic term for this expected figure (Dt 18:15-18). The term Elijah for many is popularly associated with the end-time. Elijah, a ninth-century BC prophet, whose translation to heaven but not his death was recorded in the Scriptures (II K 2:11; II Ch 21:12), was, because of a passage attributed to Malachi (Ml 4:5-6), expected to return before the "Day of the Lord." Since an "Elijah who is to return" could confuse people over who is God's end-time Agent, it seems John removes the confusion by saying this "end-time" figure has returned for all practical purposes in Jesus. Did JB actually identify Jesus as all three? Little matter to John (although JB could well have recognized Jesus to be the Messiah). It is the Church of John that sees Jesus to be all three and so JB expresses *their* belief.

And if one inquires about JB's main role in relation to Jesus, it is to be found in Second-Isaiah 40:3 . . . "he is a voice crying in the wilderness; make straight the way of the Lord," assuming the angels' role of removing all obstacles for the Jews as they make their return to the homeland after the Babylonian captivity. By adapting the text JB seems to say his role is to prepare a way for Jesus (vv. 22-23). But again JB, because of his different, eschatological-type baptism and message (note, Mt 3:2 has JB preaching that the "Kingdom of heaven is at hand") could be mistaken for the Messiah. The nature and difference of his baptism, then, must be shown. Elsewhere in the New Testament JB's baptism is described as being one of repentance, confession and forgiveness of sins (Mt 3:6; Mk 1:4; Lk 3:3; Ac 19:4). Here in v. 26 and in v. 33, JB states that his baptism is "of water," doubtless meaning that received penitently it cleanses one from sin in the sense of Ezk 36:25 . . . "I will wash you with clean water and *make you clean* . . ."—a baptism of no inconsiderable value. But Jesus will baptize with the "Spirit," that is to say, his baptism will symbolically encase the Spirit who will generate believers to new life. This answer and JB's plea of unworthiness to tie

Jesus' shoes further help to clarify who is truly the Messiah in the ongoing debate between John's Church and the JB sect (v. 27).

With vv. 29-34, John continues to use JB as witness to Jesus' Christological identity. He will call Jesus in turn; Lamb of God, one who pre-exists him, one upon whom the Spirit descends and remains, the chosen one of God. JB could have understood Jesus to be all of these. More certainly after some sixty years of existence, John's Church has come to know Jesus as all these and the faith of this community is reflected in what JB says. The title, Lamb of God (one unique to John), not only identifies Jesus as Messiah; it theologically explains the functions of his Messianic office. The "Lamb" could have at least three meanings, all complementary. First, Jesus could be seen as the Lamb found in the Apocalyptic writings of the time. This literature often used animals as symbols for theological messages. God, for example, is referred to as one who sends a lamb who is to overcome stronger animals, symbols of the power of evil. This lamb overcomes the more powerful beasts, showing God's destructive power over sin. This lamb is also a judgment on the world (an example of this form of literature in the New Testament is the Book of Revelation). In the gospel John's Jesus is seen as one who destroys *moral evil* as he drives *physical evil* from believers; e.g. the cripple, the blind man, etc. And Jesus is also seen as a *judgment* on the world.

The expression "chosen one of God" in v. 34 alerts the reader to a second "Lamb" Jesus could be, for the phrase is found in the first verse of Second-Isaiah's suffering servant songs (Is 42:1). John and his Church doubtless see Jesus as the servant who saves them through suffering and death. Though the theme of suffering is subdued in John, it is there (cf., Is cc's. 52-53 especially). His Jesus like the servant is "lifted up"— "familiar with suffering"—"a lamb to be slaughtered"—who "offers his life"—and who, after death, will "see his heirs." Many Jews found such a fate unbelievable for a Messiah. JB and Isaiah help show the Jews such a Messiah was not unknown to God.

Thirdly, as the gospel will reveal, Jesus is also seen to be God's perfect and ultimate Paschal Lamb (Ex 12:7, 8). John in c. 19:14, 29, 36 will note paschal images associated with Jesus' death, indicating he sees Jesus' blood as fulfilling a function not unlike that of the blood of the first paschal lamb of Exodus. There the lamb's blood saved the Israelites from physical death; Jesus' blood (blood for Jews encased the mystery of human life) before and after death brings a new, even eternal life. In John's testimony, v. 30, one even finds hints that Jesus is "pre-existent" Messiah; at least if Jesus is said to be the Elijah-figure (a ninth century BC prophet), this would account for why Jesus is "older" than JB and "pre-exists" him. And John's community would realize that Jesus is a good deal "older" than that. In sum, JB's own disciples could have mistaken him for all three of these "lambs." The episode shows the error of such belief. Vv. 32-33, as stated earlier, show the difference in Jesus' baptism. God's Spirit not only comes to him, but *remains* with him and thus he is able to share the Spirit with believers. John's people would instinctively see the water of their baptisms as containing Jesus' Spirit.

Other Disciples Witness to Jesus' Identity: 1:35-51

In vv. 35-42, John presents others who witness to Jesus as Messiah. JB has given his witness and now two of his own disciples accept his testimony and follow Jesus. In this gospel all who hear true testimony about Jesus are *expected* to "follow him," i.e., they should believe in and become disciples of Jesus. Having done this, Jesus then will give them testimony of himself. Translated for John's people this would read: later members of John's Church should hear the true testimony of the earlier witnesses about Christ and "follow Jesus" where he now resides . . . in the community; once there, Jesus through his Spirit will give them testimony of himself. Belief through witnesses is no less a valid coming to and finding of Jesus than some ca. 27-30 AD one-on-one meeting would be.

In the question . . . "what are you looking for" (v. 38), the reader finds an example of what John is so good at: putting several layers of meaning into the Jesus data available to him. The question viewed superficially seems just polite conversation. Seen theologically, it asks a profound question: "what are you seeking out of life?" In John's view, what one should be looking for and seeking is the Jesus of the prologue. And the question . . . "where do you *live*?" (v. 38) has already been answered in the prologue where John said "Jesus *lives* in the flesh and dwells among us" (1:14). The invitation . . . "come and see" (v. 39) is not just "come over to my house," but an invitation to faith. Also it invites the reader to begin looking at Jesus' coming signs and Resurrection; if one is looking for God-with-us one will find him there. People cannot on their own find God, but in Jesus and his historical life God comes to them and can be "seen." And as the gospel will show "not to come and *see*" Jesus as Messiah and God-with-us is to know only darkness. "They went to *see* and stayed . . ." (v. 39). Again, John plays on the word *see* (he loves the meanings of words and the associations they stimulate). Jesus in the gospel will not try to hide his identity or make it difficult to perceive; as "light" he always tries to reveal himself. If some do not see, it is not because Jesus does not reveal. He cannot help but reveal; he is after all the "light."

Andrew, having come to Jesus, seeks to bring others and of course Jesus is again identified as Messiah. John's Jesus "knows all things" and sees the future mission of Andrew's brother, Simon. His name is changed to Peter, the Rock, to signify a special function he is to serve in the post-Resurrection community of believers——it seems a foundational-shepherd role (cf. c. 21, also). (*Biblical name-changing often served the purpose of giving one a new vocation, e.g., Abram-Abraham; Jacob-Israel.*)

In v. 43, Jesus calls Philip to belief in him and Philip responds in Johannine fashion by telling another person of Jesus' identity as Messiah. The other, in this case, Nathanael, helps John introduce a theme that occurs frequently in the gospel, the debate about Jesus' real origins. Is he Joseph's son and from Nazareth only, or could he have a more profound "beginning"? This also introduces the reader to John's keen appreciation for irony. The question . . . "can anything good come from Nazareth?" was doubtless a cynical remark attached to this backwater town in Galilee. John and his people knowing the divine origins of Jesus have their *own* deeper answer to that question (can we see them smiling?). The "come and see" is an invitation not only to faith in Jesus but also a challenge to look in on the whole gospel; there one can see if anything good comes from Nazareth. And since Nathanael comes "seeing" (i.e., open to what is to be revealed), his seeing is said to be genuine, without guile and truly Israelite (v. 48). He does not set conditions like the "Jews" often do. Jesus, finding Nathanael so open, reveals that he knows a bit about him; indeed it seems Nathanael thought only God knew he was under *that* "fig tree." If Jesus is so "all knowing" he *must* be Son of God . . . King of Israel (v. 49). These titles are Messianic for some at least. But John would want his own people to catch a deeper meaning to these titles, viz., that Jesus is Son of God in the sense of the prologue; that he is King not in the expected nationalistic sense, but a King who will rule through death and Resurrection, for his Jesus invites them to look ahead to these events in his words . . . "you will see *far greater things* than this" (v. 50).

In v. 51 (an editorially added verse), there seems to be another hint at the "greater things" that are to be discovered in Jesus, for he begins a further revelation of his identity with a double Amen (unique to John). This more properly describes the way *God* speaks. Man speaks hoping for an "Amen" from his audience. God always speaks truth and thus invites the listener to hear his truth. Further signs of the "greater" are seen as Jesus links the biblical symbols of "Jacob's ladder" (Gn 28:10, 12) and Daniel's "Son of Man" (Dn 7:13-14; also found in the apocryphal books of Enoch and 4 Esdras). The ladder on which angels descended and ascended seems a biblical device to permit the revelations of a transcendentally other and awesome God to come to people most unworthy of those revelations. No longer is it biblically necessary to protect God's transcendence against man's unworthiness. Jesus has bridged the gap between God and man. He is the absolute revelation about God and *locus* of his presence. The title Son of Man is used seventy times in the Synoptics; John will use it twelve times. It seems to be solidly in the data as a favorite self-description of Jesus (or at least it reflected well the early Church's way of perceiving him). In Daniel's vision the Man was seen as a mysterious figure who would come on the clouds of heaven; the non-canonical books say he is to "reveal hidden treasures"—to be agent of "God's judgment" (Enoch 46)—he is to "establish a new order" (4 Esdras 13). The title is more open-ended than others and less corruptible to a political, socio-economic or military understanding, perhaps accounting for why both traditions use it so frequently. Since it is a bit ambiguous it offers Jesus an opportunity to reveal who precisely the Son of Man is. The humanity, the sufferability of Jesus is implied in the title along with the "new dimension" Jesus brings to the Messianic agency—his "new order," his "hidden treasures." It is as Son of *Man* that human persons are able to "see" the Son of *God;* human beings can only see a transcendental divine mystery through the medium of a human symbol.

Looking back at vv. 19-51, the Messianic identity of Jesus was revealed in short dramatic scenes, in episodes where JB and the disciples gave many titles to Jesus, biblical images were alluded to, etc., and the process may seem to the modern reader quite hurried and contrived. But if we allow for the style of an ancient writer the point is well made: Jesus should be believed to be the Messiah, not so much that the immediate cast of characters in the time frame mentioned came to so mature a faith this early, as that the first Christians after living with the Risen Jesus for a time came then to this more mature Christological faith.

FURTHER PARTICULAR COMMENTS:

V. 21 . . . These three terms for the "end-time" figure and the others to be mentioned indicate there was no one standard way of identifying this expected person. In the matter of Elijah, it can be noted Mt. and Mk. identify JB as Elijah; this shows how evangelists variously interpret and adapt data to say the theological thing they think should be said. Some see John's gospel developing in part at least an Elijah-Jesus motif, for Jesus like the tradition surrounding Elijah, is an ascending to-descending from heaven figure who works similar miracles such as healing the blind, feeding the multitudes, etc. Jesus like Elijah is certainly an eschatological figure.

V. 29 . . . It should be noted also that *lambs* were common sacrifices offered by Jews to God for their sins, to show God their love, to ask for his grace. Jesus in the gospel is seen as a source of forgiveness, a bringer of love and grace.

V. 42 . . . *Cephas*, a nickname, Rocky. To some scholars a reference to Simon and the mission he is to fulfill for the brotherhood. It could be saying something about the communities of the "Great Church," the larger but separate Churches running "side by side" with John's Church (20:4), founded by the "twelve," Paul and their disciples. Since by the last edition of the gospel, the Johannine Church no longer has its shepherd, the beloved disciple, and seems to be falling into factionalism (cf., the Johannine Epistles), it could be looking for some kind of unity with the Great Church and its more structured, more strongly shepherded communities.

V. 45 . . . *Nathanael*, not a name that appears in various lists of the "twelve." Some wonder, could he be an example of another "group" of disciples (a non-mainstream group perhaps) that Jesus could also have attracted and who were faithful to him in this particular community?

V. 48 . . . Some scholars see "under the fig tree" as a rabbinic expression for "reading the Scriptures"; if so, with a little help, Nathanael could find Jesus foretold there.

Chapter 2

GENERAL COMMENTS (and reflections):

Jesus has chosen disciples who recognize him as Messiah (1:19-51). In the coming signs and related discourses Jesus will deepen their (and the reader's) awareness of this truth. But he has also hinted that there is "more" to his identity than that (1:50). In the *signs* the mystery of the "greater things" will be revealed too. Cana begins the public ministry of Jesus; it reveals that in him the Messianic Age has arrived. And as the disciples witness the sign Jesus works there, they will begin to see the deeper ("higher") mystery also . . . "there he revealed his *glory* and his disciples believed in him" (v. 11). As Messiah-purifier Jesus then will go to Jerusalem and cleanse the Temple and in the process reveal that he is to be a New Temple for Israel. And the chapter will indicate that all of Jesus' revealing signs must be seen in the context of the sign that is to happen at the close of the gospel, namely, Jesus' death and Resurrection. Thus Jesus "foretells" this Paschal happening in both episodes: he speaks of it under the term "hour" at Cana (v. 4), and on the occasion of the Temple-cleansing he speaks of it as the "sign" that validates his right to purify his Father's house (vv. 21-22). Ultimately it is the death/Resurrection that will help believers see Jesus is the Messiah and the possessor and sharer of the eternal, purifying *glory* of God.

As John narrates the first of Jesus' seven pre-Resurrection miracles we note that he does not call them "works of power" as the earlier tradition did (the "power"—"wonder"—"miraculous" elements in fact are played down in his gospel). He calls them *signs*. They are *revelations*, Christological "epiphanies" as the theologians say, meaning they reveal in a sensually understandable way the inner, spiritual, transcendental identity of Jesus—who he is in himself and who he is for believers. Jesus works signs not because he is in the entertainment or

problem-solving business. He is the world's Messiah and Savior and his
works must show this. Believers must "come and see" . . . give Jesus
their searching, open minds and hearts. If they do, then he reveals who he
is and the revelation draws them to a deeper "coming," to a deeper
belief. Jesus wants their "coming" to be to the real and total him and the
signs and Resurrection reveal the total Christ (both "low" *and* "high").

Scholars have found John's narration of Jesus' signs to be extremely
rich in their symbolic content. John, an obviously good catechist and
teacher, must have explained and schooled his people through homilies
and instructions in the symbolism of Jesus' words and actions to the point
where the mere oral recall of a scene would trigger in their minds the
deeper symbolic meaning of the event, which in turn would draw them to
renew and deepen their faith in Jesus. Modern readers who are not
recipients of John's personal schooling in symbolism will have to work a
little harder to discover the symbolism that was so "obvious" to his own
people.

Now, to Jesus' first sign, the Wedding at Cana. If Jesus' signs are
revelations of his Christological identity, what does this sign particularly
reveal? In chapter 1 Jesus had been identified as Messiah. Messiah is
God's Agent who inaugurates the New (Messianic) Age, the time when
God's covenant would become new, fuller and contain more abundant
blessings. The incident will, therefore, *contain* symbols of the present
covenant and Jesus' "coming" will add a *new*, *fuller*, more *abundant*
dimension to it. In the first instance Jesus comes to a *Wedding*. The OT
covenant was often referred to in *nuptial* images (e.g., Ho2; Is 54:4f; Jr
2:2, etc.) to indicate that God's relationship with Israel was one of
interpersonal love; with Jesus' coming that relationship is to continue and
be perfected. The present covenant was one of *purification*, meaning God
was trying to purify humanity from its selfishness; he was trying to make
his people more authentically human. And the symbols of OT purification are present—the "pots" (v. 6), six in number, probably indicating
the Mosaic "law" approach to purification is less than perfect. Jesus is to
bring to Israel a more perfect mode of purification. The covenant was
based on *faith*, and the scene has believers in it (the Wedding party,
especially Mary and the disciples); Jesus too appreciates the essential
element of faith. He will solicit people to a deeper, more personal, more
focused faith in God through him. As God has blessed Israel with many

provident gifts, the *water* would symbolize (in a very arid part of the world) the present blessings of Yahweh. Jesus comes to the water and will change it to wine.

So symbolically the OT is present at Cana. And Jesus as Messiah is seen as inaugurating the New Age because he brings to the "existing covenant" a *newness*, *fullness*, *abundance* it does not have. The scene itself is a festive Wedding *banquet*—this is the very biblical image many associated with the New Age. Recall especially that Isaiah, speaking of that time, said: "It will be on Mount Zion that the Lord Almighty will set up a *banquet* for all the world's nations . . . a *banquet* [at which they will drink the] . . . finest *wine* (Is 25:6). And Amos foresaw: "The days coming . . . when . . . grapes will grow faster than one can make *wine*. The mountains will flow with sweet *wine* . . . " (Am 9:13; cf. also, Ho 2: 24; 14:8; Jl 4:18; Jer 31:12). The earlier tradition contained a parable of Jesus that described the Kingdom of God as a Wedding Feast prepared by a king for his son to which all people, friends and strangers, would receive the invitation . . . "come to the *Wedding Feast*" (Mt 22:4). So the Wedding and banquet character of the episode symbolizes the New Age is happening. And note, the Wedding has a "supply problem." "They have no wine" (v. 3). They only have their present OT blessing—water. Jesus will take an *abundant* quantity (120-150 gallons) of that water and *change* it into his "Messianic wine." The *abundance*, *newness*, *fullness* expected, has arrived! The OT is not cast aside; it is changed for the better. The Messianic Age was to be the *last* and *best* of times; it was to come on God's *time-schedule*; it was to reveal his *glory* . . . and Jesus at Cana is seen as providing the "*last*" and "*best*" wine (v. 10) . . . the sign seems symbolically to say God's "*hour*" is very near (v. 4) . . . and the episode reveals God's "*glory*" (note, Jesus' disciples to a degree see that *glory* here, v. 11).

The gospel after Cana will show Jesus making other *changes* besides. It will reveal that Jesus contains within himself all the institutions, values, the meaning of the OT covenant encased in Israel's feasts . . . Jesus' covenant will contain all of these: it will still be interpersonal purification, built on faith, contain God's blessings . . . but will surpass all these values in "abundant" measure. No doubt about it, with Cana the Messianic Age is beginning to happen; it will fully happen when Jesus' "hour" arrives.

Jesus' mother appears in the scene and is called "Woman" (not as harsh a term as it sounds, but then not too filial either). With the same title she will appear in chapter 19 at the foot of the Cross. Many Christians find here reference to Mary's strong interceding power with Jesus. That may well be. But John, remember, is the teacher of meaning through symbol and it seems his mother appears here and in chapter 19 called "Woman" because he sees her actions symbolizing a truth that is important for his Church to realize. Her actions here (c. 2) are prophetic of what her role is to be later (c. 19). Here she leads people to Jesus who begins to reveal his inner ("higher") glory; later like a mother she will lead *disciples* to the Jesus who is to transcend death. Who in John's understanding leads believers to the transcendent Christ? It is mainly the Church, the early believing witnesses of Jesus and those who believe because of them. They are the ones who brought and bring believers to Jesus where they find his glory and drink of his new wine (now understood to be the symbolic encasement of the "blood" he shed for them on the Cross). The Church is the "Woman" who brings people to Christ and his blessings . . . and Mary symbolizes this mystery. Like Eve she too is called "Woman" (Gn 2:23) who after the Death of Jesus becomes the "*mother* of all the living" (Gn 3:20); it is in and through the Church that "generation into Christ" takes place.

The episode seems to contain a Wisdom motif as well. In Sirach (24:19, 21), Wisdom invites her hearers to "eat and drink" . . . she promises them a *banquet* where they can dine to contentment. In chapter 9 of Proverbs she invites them in fact to *drink* of her *wine*. In Jesus, then, Wisdom and her wine, now understood as a divine person become incarnate, is present. And some scholars, as implied above, detect also a Sacramental motif (not primary surely, but still perceivable to a community schooled in symbolism). John's people would have celebrated their sharing in Jesus' New Covenant as they drank the *wine* of the Eucharist (the Synoptics and Paul spoke of the Eucharist under the symbol of wine as the "blood of the New Covenant"; Mt 26:28; Mk 14:24; Lk 22:20; I Cor 11:25). There is in fact a painting in the catacombs which joins the Cana scene with the multiplication of the bread (a NT episode associated with the Eucharist).

The scene in its simple, dramatic narrative would be quite easy to remember. John, like all evangelists, fashions his scenes to make them memorable and thus easily memorizable (since few of his people could read). The genius of John is that the brief scene contains so rich a symbolism to reveal in depth Jesus' identity.

FURTHER PARTICULAR COMMENTS:

V. 1 . . . *"on the third day"* . . . Perhaps a Johannine clue for his audience to associate a "resurrectional motif" with this scene; the Resurrection is the presumed background to all Jesus' signs.

V. 9 . . . The headwaiter has no idea where the wine came from; this again reflects John's theme that many cannot *see* the "higher" origins of Jesus. By contrast, the disciples know something of those origins and begin to *see* "glory" in the sign.

V. 9 . . . the *"bridegroom"* . . . Some see him as symbolizing Jesus, in that in the New Covenant Jesus is related to all believers as groom (i.e. psychic lover) to a bride (i.e., the psychically loved and loving). Note, in c. 3:39, JB will refer to Jesus as the *bridegroom*; JB is only the best man.

Jesus Cleanses the Temple: 2:13-22

By his action of changing the purification waters to wine at Cana, Jesus in effect has "taken over" the purification function of the OT (others would put it: Jesus "replaced" or "fulfilled" this function). The ultimate basis of Jesus' purifying power will of course be his "hour"; Cana and the remaining signs will anticipate symbolically the power of that event.

Jesus' power is *purificational* and the OT is in need of purification and Jesus as Messiah begins that task. The Temple and abuses that surrounded it symbolize impurities that exist in Israel. But what particularly is wrong with Temple practice? How is it being abused? First, one should ask what do God and devout Jews think should be going on there? What are temples for?

Well, God's law is enshrined in that house; his reflected glory or *shekinah* is thought mysteriously to dwell there. Enshrining a revealed and reflected presence of God, it is thought, then, to be the perfect place of encounter with him. Feeling closer to God and gathering as a family,

Israelites can pray and converse with him more "naturally"; speak their love, ask for forgiveness of sin and their many other needs. Their sacrifices and vocal prayers offered there encase the inner feelings of their hearts. That's the theory anyhow.

But Jewish history showed only too often that theory was forgotten in practice. Prayers were said and sacrifices offered with little psychic content. The ritual, the gesture, the spoken words were often devoid of heart and conviction (Christians know well the abuse under the term "ritualism" or "formalism"). Yahweh knew the emptiness of his people's worship and sent prophets to speak his displeasure. Jeremiah reminded them that Yahweh was well aware they made his Temple a den of thieves and that he would destroy it if abuses continued (Jr 7:11-15). Others foretold that the Temple would be purified on the "day of God's coming" (Ml 3:1-5; Zc 14:21; Ps 69:8-10). Thus if the Temple has covenant "value" but is being abused, it *should* be the task of the Messiah to be God's Agent for its purification. And so the incident contains *symbols* of the formalism and commercialism that make Jewish worship "empty" in God's sight: the animals sold in the Temple precincts and the money-changers conducting business there (actions which more properly belong outside the Temple). Jesus confronts these *symbols* and "drives them out." So for a time at least the Temple is cleansed of those who abuse its purpose.

But one can object: the abuses will return in short order. So just how good is Jesus' purification? The answer will be given in a minute and it will be a most striking revelation. But of course Jesus does something here that only a Messiah or prophet of God would be permitted to do, and many see him as neither, and demand of him a "sign" (v. 18). As John at Cana had referred to Jesus' "hour" as being the time when the Messiah's saving functions become eternally efficacious, so Jesus here refers to his "hour" by referring to his humanity as a "Temple" to be destroyed. The sign that will show his power to purify is the purifying, cleansing moment of his death followed by Resurrection . . . "destroy this Temple and in three days I will build it up again" (v. 19). This temple of stone it is true can be sullied again and destroyed, but Jesus' humanity, now revealed as the proper *place* for valid encounter with God, cannot be sullied. And as will be seen soon enough, it cannot be *destroyed* either. John (or his editors) makes sure the reader sees the deeper symbolic meaning of the episode. Jesus cannot only legitimately purify temples; he himself is a Temple who is to become the one and only Temple of believers, the purest place and form of worship they will ever know (vv. 21-22)—and this pure and indestructible Temple will be theirs to enter come the Resurrection.

John's people in the years 90-95 AD, looking at the Temple scene in vv. 13-22, see much more than the "Jews" or indeed the early Christians, for as Jesus speaks of *his* Temple while standing before *theirs*, Johannine Christians know that the Jerusalem Temple, beautiful and clean as it is in the scene, has been destroyed utterly by the Romans in 70 AD. The Jewish Temple is gone; *but* the Christian Temple, namely Jesus, stands there and will last forever. After the Temple's destruction, the synagogue in time became the Jewish replacement for that holy place, but in John's time Christian Jews because of their faith in Jesus were even being excluded from the synagogue. Yet again, as the synagogue disappears from their lives, Johannine Christians can know from this scene that Jesus, the eternal Temple-Synagogue, can never disappear.

With vv. 23-25, John explains why some see glory in Jesus' signs (and in a sense the cleansing scene is a sign too) and others do not. Some perceive only the surface of Jesus' actions and come away with a sense of wonder, or power, or as in the case of the cleansing a certain indignation. The reader should, however, look more deeply into them and see them as revelatory of Jesus' true identity; they reveal his inner glory. And they should pay heed to the words he and others speak as the signs are worked; those words are part of the revelation of the work's meaning. Jesus knows how his works are perceived by others. Belief in signs alone without listening to Jesus' accompanying words is not the seeing or faith Jesus seeks. Nicodemus will be the classic example of this wrong reaction to signs, and of an imperfect form of faith that results from viewing them as only works of power, and these verses prepare for his meeting with Jesus in chapter 3.

FURTHER PARTICULAR COMMENTS:

V. 13 . . . the Jewish Passover. John's book with three Passover feasts presupposes a longer public ministry than the Synoptics who recount only one Passover. Most scholars find it improbable that Jesus cleansed the Temple this early, seeing the Synoptic timing (just before Jesus' arrest) more probable. It seems John moves the datum to this time for theological reasons. Indeed his words about the destruction of the Temple would doubtless have occurred later in Jesus' ministry but are moved here and joined with this episode to help the reader see the deeper meaning of the action (cf. Mk 15:58).

V. 14 . . . the reference to animals. Some scholars see the episode as indicating that the coming of Jesus brings an end to the era of worship through animal sacrifices. Christ is the "Lamb" God finds a suitable and perfect offering in and through which believers can come to him. Money-changers were needed to change "obscene" Roman coins for Hebrew money so that sacrificial animals could be purchased. Some unholy "profits" were made in the exchange.

Vv. 17, 22 . . . "the disciples *recalled*." In John this indicates a post-Resurrection understanding of the event in question. In the gospel the Spirit (14:26) will be described as helping believers penetrate the meaning of the data about Jesus. John and his Church aided by the Spirit *now* (at the time the gospel was being written) see the theological meaning of what was *really* going on ca. 27-30 AD and this deeper meaning is then structured back into the telling of the episode. E.g., this episode shows that Jesus identified himself as the pure and indestructible Temple since *now* disciples know he is indeed that. And in a post-Easter perspective Christians often recalled Scripture passages that helped explain an incident, as e.g., v. 17, the disciples "recall" Ps. 69:9 to explain Jesus' unprecedented action here, even changing the verb, *consume*, to the future tense since now they see Jesus' zeal as consuming him in full measure when he dies on the Cross.

V. 20 . . . An example of John's frequently used catechetical technique of *misunderstanding*. Jesus often says something that will be misunderstood, usually because his hearers take his words superficially, literally or without the insights of faith. This gives Jesus (or John and his editors) the opportunity to explain the deeper, truer meaning of his words and actions. In a sense this technique is not unlike the Synoptic parables. They too were frequently misunderstood and Jesus had to explain them more clearly to the Apostles (and so to the readers of those gospels).

V. 22 . . . *the Scriptures*: Ps 16:10; Ho 6:2-3; Jon 2:1.

Vs. 23-25 (along with vv. 13-22) . . . introduce the reader to conflicts

Jesus has with Jewish authorities and people who approve him with inadequate faith and misread his words and actions. Hostility will grow in intensity as the gospel works its way to the crucifixion—the theme of "light" coming to his own and his own not receiving him (1:10).

Chapter 3

First of Jesus' Discourses

Before discussing this chapter we should say a word about the discourses of Jesus in the Fourth Gospel. As noted in the Introduction Jesus "sounds" differently here from the way he speaks in the Synoptics. He does not talk in the manner of a first-century Palestinian rabbi (e.g., in earthy parables, in short pronouncements, moral aphorisms, etc.). He speaks in rather unified homilies a little like the "homily" known as the First Epistle of John. Since the author of this latter work is obviously not Jesus and yet "sounds" a lot like the Jesus of this gospel, one might wonder who is speaking in the Johannine discourses—Jesus or the theologian-evangelist (or a disciple-editor of the evangelist)? Is this the real Jesus or a theologian's interpretation? Christian scholars believe *gospels* give us the *real Jesus* as well as theological interpretations of Jesus. Evangelists always begin with his remembered words and actions. They are not, however, as cautious as modern writers in quoting his words or describing the events of his life exactly. They all adapt, adjust, transpose their material so that it will have the most meaning for the spiritual needs of their own communities (as some put it: gospels speak to the pastoral, catechetical, apologetical and liturgical needs of particular groups of Christians).

But even so, the Synoptics in their adaptation of material are generally considered to have captured more of the historical "sound" of Jesus than John. And the reason for John's different sound may be quite simple. He is for his time a sophisticated theologian-pastor who has lived with Jesus' words and deeds for many decades and has transposed their meaning into homilies and narrative that particularly suit his own people.

Without hardly knowing it, that data has become so much a part of his own life and meditative thoughts and preaching that in time Jesus came to "sound" like the evangelist. The words of Jesus are here but they are put forth in the speech patterns and vocabulary of John. Jesus' meaning for believers is more important than his "sound." And indeed if Jesus' origins are now understood to be "higher" than first recognized, the Jesus data must be looked at anew and reinterpreted in light of this new insight. The person who spoke these words and performed these deeds was and is God's eternal Word and the data must be transposed into a "higher key" so that it "sounds" as coming from God's Word. And if one should object that an evangelist could lose the historical Jesus altogether by engaging in such a transposition, John would remind such a one (cf., 14:26, again) that Jesus' own Spirit is with him to see to it that he rightly understands and interprets Jesus. At the end of these "general comments" we will indicate the "data" from which John seems to have drawn the material found in this chapter. He is the freest of all in the way he adapts material, but many Christians regard his "Spirit-guided" mode of transposition the most successful of all.

Jesus and Nicodemus

The reader has just heard John comment on improper attitudes, wrong reactions to Jesus' signs (2:23-25). Nicodemus as one drawn to Jesus because he performs powerful works will typify this attitude (he is affected by signs but does not understand them as revelations of Jesus' "from above" identity). He thus symbolizes a general negative attitude on the part of "Israel's teachers" (v. 10) who are unwilling to accept Jesus as Messiah because he ascends (and in the time-frame of the gospel, *has already ascended*) to glory through *crucifixion*. He also seems to represent people who cannot fit into their theological scheme of things a Messiah who comes from heaven. Jesus as a Messiah too "high" and, in another sense (since he dies through crucifixion) a Messiah too "low," causes special problems for "Jewish teachers." And since the discourse of Jesus speaks of a "new birth" (vv. 3, 5, 8) needed for Israel (and all peoples), Nicodemus symbolizes "Jews" who find that concept unacceptable, since they regard their present "birth from Abraham" (8:53) as sufficient foundation for the reception of all God's covenant privileges and promises. John's Jesus, however, is not a Messiah who carries on business as usual or as expected. He is establishing a fuller covenant, involving a more profound psychic relationship of interpersonal love than the OT understood, and thus present realities, present "birth" are not enough. God has come in Jesus to make this more profound relationship a reality.

We say Nicodemus is a symbol because the discourse begins addressed to him in the singular (vv. 3, 5, etc.) but it ends addressed to a plural, "you people" (v. 11 f).[1] We should bear in mind Jewish members of John's community at the time the gospel is being written are being excluded from Jewish synagogues precisely because of their faith in a Jesus who is seen as coming from heaven to establish a new God-humankind relationship; this Christian form of Judaism has been labeled "heretical" by the synagogues. And of course Jesus' "high origins," his insistence that in him is made possible a "new (birth) relationship" with God would mean that all existing authority in Judaism must now rest completely on him and his disciple-witnesses; many "teachers of Israel" (the present authorities in Judaism) are not ready for that to happen. And so Nicodemus' statements and Jesus' reply seem to reflect all these Johannine-Synagogue controversies.

And here it might be good to comment on what could be called the "Johannine presumption." As the chapter develops it seems to modern readers that Jesus will be too hard on Nicodemus (and "you people"). He should be drawing them to an awareness of his identity more gradually and patiently. There is no room for this patience in John's thinking, for he *presumes* every person (and the people and attitudes they represent) who appears in this gospel is also present at every other scene in the gospel. Not only is Nicodemus now talking with Jesus, he should have been at Cana, he should know about the coming six signs and the Resurrection. But the modern mind objects that this is not nor was it the case. Yes, says John, it *was* and *is* the case, for Nicodemus is a symbol of an attitude of people who have been told about Cana, the other signs and the Resurrection for forty-to-sixty years; they have "seen" all the events of this gospel many times in the preaching of this Christian community and in the debates it has carried on with the "Jews" and others. Jesus can be

---

[1] A further word on this and other literary problems in Chapter 3 is discussed in the "particular comments" at the close of the chapter.

very frank with Nicodemus because the "case for Jesus" is not first made here; it has been going on for a long time.

Nicodemus, then, comes to speak to Jesus but with the wrong attitude. Impressed with signs, he does not see them as symbols of the inner glory Jesus brings from heaven. His coming is "at night" (v. 2), the time of darkness, reflecting the inner status of his soul and its inadequate faith. Jesus insists that the Kingdom of the New Age can come only to those who are "born from above" (v. 3). The phrase has an obvious meaning to John's people. This must have been the way he spoke of the new relationship Christians have with God through Jesus. The newly-come relationship has two poles: God and believers. The disciple must come to him—this is faith. God must come to the disciple with heavenly life, light and enduring love—this is New Birth. Since the "mutual coming" or relationship initiates a new and deeper psychic union with God, he called it being "born into the life from above." Conception-to-birth is a life-giving process; what is perceived as happening "naturally" between humans is now known to be happening between God and the disciples. What better term to identify it than "birth"? The Kingdom is no longer seen as a further perfecting and heightening of what the disciples have . . . it is a breakthrough coming to them from heaven . . . the "kingdom" is *new birth into God* through Jesus and his Spirit. But Nicodemus, a man of inadequate faith, is incapable of understanding so startling a revelation and he "*misunderstands*" (v. 4) what Jesus is talking about. This as we saw is a Johannine device to inform the reader the "misunderstander" is not listening to Jesus with Christian faith, and it gives Jesus the opportunity to clarify his words—in this instance, what the New Birth is all about. Nicodemus cannot properly understand Jesus' words on his present level of understanding; he is thinking in human, earthly categories only. One should not do this with Jesus. He exists on two levels, the human *and* the divine, and Nicodemus should pay attention to both these levels. But he (like so many other non-believers in the gospel) will hear Jesus only on the human level. Jesus' actions, his words are human and have human meanings, but faith reveals a deeper, divine meaning contained there. Jesus has come from heaven with an offer of God's life; as sent by God he *can* initiate that life, that new heaven-to-earth relationship. Nicodemus cannot see this yet because he has not yet seen the *divine* in Jesus. Hearing the word "birth" he thinks in terms of human generation only.

But he and all Jews should know that divine birth is not the same as human birth. God "begets" differently than human beings; his begetting is a psychic surrender and sharing "from above." It is not visibly perceivable in itself; it is like "breath"—like the "wind" (vv. 6-8). "God *breathed* . . . and there was *life*" (Gn 2:7). One cannot see breath or the wind but one "knows" they are there; so it is with God's new "begetting." It is not seen as human begetting and birth can be, but it is known as happening because God in Jesus says it is happening (God is in Jesus and in his signs). New Birth is known in its effects. As believers give themselves to Christ, they are caught up in a new interpersonal relationship with God's psychic love and experience this "union." The Johannine gospel expression for this is "New Birth." Nicodemus, reflecting the earth-bound attitude of non-believers, objects: "how can such things happen?" (v. 9) God's continued and heightened provident care for his creation is one thing . . . this is understandable. But "psychic sharing" . . . "new birth into God" as Jesus puts it . . . this is too much! Well, Nicodemus, it is too much only if your perspective is limited to earthly understanding, only if you continue in your shallow understanding of Jesus. You must open your eyes to his "true origins." Then you can acquire a heavenly perspective (vv. 12-21) and know that a new birth—a new God-creation relationship is indeed possible. *Here we notice Nicodemus for all practical purposes disappears from the scene and Jesus continues to speak to the "mentality" typified by Nicodemus (those who refuse to see a divine dimension to Jesus' signs) and we should also notice Jesus becomes a "we" (v. 11) and is spoken of in the third person (vv. 13-21). This shows Jesus and the comprehension of Jesus by John and his community have become one and the same.*

For Jesus to speak so categorically about "new birth" to a people who think their present birth is almost a guarantee of God's provident care is the height of arrogance . . . *unless* Jesus' origins as described earlier were *truly* described (1:1-18). If Jesus originates from the divine pole of this "new birth" (relationship) then his words make sense and should be believed in. Thus John reminds believers and non-believers alike that Jesus knows what goes on with God, for he is one who not only ascended to heaven, but is one who first descended from there. The "Son of Man" . . . thought to mean so many different things to different Jewish theologies . . . is now *correctly* identified by John as meaning this: the *Son of Man* is the one who is the descended and ascended Word of God. Though "divine" he can also be called "man" because as God's Word he descended and became encased in human flesh and in that flesh ascended to God thus making all human flesh capable of sharing in the glory he always had as Word (vv. 13-16).

But to many Jews an ascension process involving the *crucifixion* of God's Messiah seems beyond belief (indeed Gentiles at first found the idea nearly incomprehensible). The early data of Christianity gives evidence that the crucifixion was indeed so "embarrassing" to Christians (Paul we remember called it a 'stupidity' to Gentiles and a 'stumbling block' to Jews, I Cor 1:23), they had to take refuge in Scripture to explain it, finding it foreseen there as part of God's plan to save the world. Later, atonement theories for this cruel act were developed. John, however, finds no "embarrassment" in the datum at all. He has discovered an image in the OT that beautifully and profoundly foretells and reveals the mystery that took place there. In the Book of Numbers (21:4-9) he sees the Israelites in the desert being smitten by serpents, saved and freed from their death-dealing bites as they beheld the "lifted up" figure of the bronze serpent. All who looked at the serpent were restored to health and life. For John this "lifted up" serpent is an OT type or foretelling of Jesus' death and its saving capacities. For John the crucifixion is not a horrible earthly tragedy . . . it is Jesus, God's Word, *giving* himself in love to the Father for the world. And the coming of the disciples to that event and gazing at it in faith gives them access to the eternal life and love that was *given* there. Jesus' "lifting up" action is his total surrendered love and life for the world. And as v. 16 says, it also reveals the totality of God's love for the world. The Father did not tell Jesus to go and get himself crucified. He said go and tell my people *how much* I love them. It just so happened the "telling" took the form of crucifixion, a "lifting up." To the cynical question of non-believers . . . "who can believe in a *crucified* Messiah?", John has answered with one of the most memorable lines in all the New Testament: "God so loved the world that he gave it his only Son so that everyone who believes in him may not perish but have eternal life" (v. 16). John's people know where Jesus' "lifting up" brought him. If Jesus is now with-the-Father as he was in the beginning, then his words about the necessity of "new birth" are not to be lightly dismissed by anyone.

And almost as a "knee-jerk" reaction, Jesus (and John's Church) must answer the often heard objection: if Jesus is as good as the gospel makes him out to be, why is it that so many reject him? John must deal with this enigma without the facile distinctions of philosophy, but he knows that the rejection of that which is good is a power endemic to all humankind. All human beings have—in John's thinking—two options vis-à-vis Jesus . . . they can follow him (variously spoken of in the gospel as . . . coming to, believing in, seeing, hearing, receiving, knowing him) and find salvation and eternal life . . .or . . . they can reject him and "know" only their limited world with all its darkness. In rejection they find their own condemnation and judgment. Judgment is not something imposed by God; it is something asked for by non-believers (vv. 17—20). The light that comes into the world does not force itself on anyone; it can be accepted or rejected.

In this discourse we are getting a strong taste of the heavy either/or dualism of John, indicating his background seems to have been from a form of Judaism that expressed its faith in strong, very heightened dualistic terms. John as a master of dramatic contrasts obviously loves the built-in drama his dualistic background provides him. In a "two-option" world he can draw his picture of Jesus in extremely attractive images *and* he can deter his people from pursuing non-Jesus options by painting them in most unappealing terms. But it is good to remember John is a "two-option" man and this makes his dualism, although strong at times, safely Jewish (i.e., it is moral dualism and not the ontological dualism of gnosticism; to the modern taste perhaps a little simplistic, but by the standards of his own mindset it allows him to reveal clearly the radical meaning of Jesus). Though John's main and fundamental "sin" is non-belief in Jesus, he does see other "sins" contributing to that wrong option, viz., "practices of wickedness" and "evil deeds"—biblical words for "breaking the commandments." It seems if people were not so free and easy with the commandments, they would not make the most fatal decision of all—rejecting God's light come into the world (vv. 19-21).

Skipping ahead for a moment, we find in vv. 31-36, a short discourse in the Johannine style that is very similar to what has already been said in vv. 12-21. It seems to belong more properly here, before the appearance of JB. And yet this later discourse is quite repetitious of what is here. True, there is a nuance or two that complements what has been said, but there would be no essential loss of meaning by its exclusion. Theories abound on how vv. 31-36 got there; to me an answer that makes sense is that it was added after the evangelist died. It may not add great meaning to vv. 12-21, but it was written by the now-dead "master" and a respectful editor-disciple does not want it to be lost. He found the place where it fits in thematically and included it. If John had a say in the final edition (which he didn't) he probably would have dropped it or included its additional nuances in vv. 12-21. With "near duplicate" discourses (as well as the many 'asides' the gospel contains) we should perhaps prefix the notice: "caution . . . editor-at-work."

Scholars agree that vv. 22-30, more logically and chronologically belong in chapter 1, but John's logic is often in the last analysis "theological" and the passage inserted here draws attention to the implied baptismal motif of the Nicodemus scene. Christians of John's time know that Jesus came after his Resurrection to the early disciples and "breathed" (20:23) his Spirit upon them; this was their "birth from above." The question Jesus must solve for them is how he *breathes* the new birth on them now, ca. 90-95 AD. They must know the "breathing of the Spirit's life on them" comes encased in the waters of Baptism (v. 22). And since some members of the Church were formerly JB sect people and a debate is going on between the Church and the sect, John in this scene underlines the importance of the Baptism into Jesus by having JB defer to Jesus (vv. 27-30). "Water" has been mentioned now twice; Baptism, four times. This does not seem incidental to the purpose of John. His people associate water with the Spirit surely, but they also associate water as the symbol that encases the Spirit, i.e., Christian Baptism. In the early Church we recall the words "born again" and "to become as a little child" were descriptive expressions for Baptism.

Scholars remind us that this discourse reveals John's eschatology to be mainly *realized*, as distinct from an earlier eschatology, called *future* or *final*. The effects of a faith response to Jesus' light do not await death and final judgment; they are in force *now* (cf. vv. 15, 16, 36; they speak of eternal life flowing to believers *now*. Also those who reject Jesus know condemnation *now*, vv. 18-21).

Earlier we spoke of John's freer, more creative transposition of the Jesus data and we wondered if he could be so free as to "miss the point" of the data. If one assumes the Synoptics work from Jesus data (transposing it less "freely" than John), is the data they worked with discernible in this chapter? Well, recall in Mt 18:3 (and correspondingly in Mk 10:15; Lk 18:17) there is the sentence: "unless one becomes like a little child he will not enter the kingdom of heaven." This is very close to . . . "you must be born from above." Luke speaks of Jesus' promise of the Spirit, corresponding to Jesus' declaration in John of the new birth as being "of the Spirit." All of the Synoptics speak of Jesus' paschal death and Resurrection as the source of eternal life. John draws out more explicitly how believers become the "children" Jesus said they must become. His insight into the "heavenly origins" of Jesus makes him look more deeply into the mystery of the Cross where he finds the supreme meaning of that event to be God's great love for the world. The data is the same, it would seem. The expression of the data is the most creative and profound of all. And John would remind his readers that most of the credit should go to the Spirit for he is the one who guides him in the transposition and interpretation of the data.

FURTHER PARTICULAR COMMENTS:

As noted, chapter 3 presents some "literary" problems. The chapter begins with a dialogue which soon turns into a monologue addressed to "you people." Vv. 13-21 and vv. 31-36 speak of Jesus in the third person and vv. 31-36 seem repetitious of vv. 13-21. And as stated, vv. 22-30, the JB insertion, seem to break up the discourse. Various theories seek to explain these difficulties. If we accept John as transposing Jesus data into discourses more his own style and if we think an insertion of his own understanding of Jesus into the discourses is a legitimate use of the data, the problem is less vexing than some make it. Vv. 13-21 and vv. 31-36 (the more impersonal sections) indicate John (or his editors) reworked an earlier version of the discourse, expanding it more fully to explain the correct meaning of the *son of man*, the deeper meaning of this *man's* death, and the "judgment" this *man* effects on people's lives. Discourses are not tape-recordings of Jesus; they are Jesus speaking to this community with its distinct spiritual and theological problems.

Vv. 3, 5, 11 . . . Again Jesus uses the "divine" mode of speech, the double Amens, to start his statements, indicative perhaps of his "higher origins."

Vv. 3, 5 . . . John's only use of the common Synoptic term, Kingdom of God. He now knows the essential meaning of this mystery: generation into the life of the glorified Jesus.

V. 3 . . . *"born from above"* can also be translated "born again." Nicodemus, the earth-bound rabbi, takes an "earthly" understanding of the words.

V. 10 . . . a *"teacher of Israel"* *should* understand about a "begetting by the Spirit," a "divine breakthrough" expected at the coming of the New Age (cf. Is 44:3; Jr 31:31-34; Ezk 36:26-27; Jl 3:1; Ps 2:7). Also it should be noted a bit of the "divine-breakthrough" was *"seen"* at Cana.

V. 14 . . . note the Wisdom literature, of which John seems to be a student, has this "image" too (Ws 16:5-7).

Vv. 16, 17, 19 . . . John uses the term "world" in two ways. It is where God's people dwell (vv. 16, 17). It is also a place where sin and sinners oppose the light and this seems to be its meaning in v. 19.

V. 30 . . . the Christian feast of JB was fixed at June 24, the time of summer solstice, when the light begins to grow shorter; Jesus' feast was fixed at Dec. 25, the time of winter solstice, when the light begins to grow longer. This verse played a significant role in that determination. With this verse JB's limited role in salvation history is concluded.

Vv. 1-30 . . . not a few scholars see these verses as an "instruction" for John's Church on the meaning of Baptism.

V. 36 . . . *"God's wrath."* Demythologized this translates to "option # 2" ("option # 1" being the ability to give faith and to live righteously). Jesus does not condemn (v. 17); and yet "condemnation" is in the scheme of things. Ancients (because of an inability to be philosophically precise) often put God more actively in the "wrath" situation than he should be. Now modern believers would say because they choose to follow "option # 2" *they* are the main cause of "wrath" in their lives.

In ch. 4 Jesus meets non-Jews

Chapter 4

GENERAL COMMENTS (and reflections):

Thus far Jesus has revealed himself only to Jews and with mixed success. Some find him the Messiah they searched for (with elements of a "glory" from above) and have become his disciples. Others fail to find in him Messianic or other worthy attributes and remain uncommitted (soon to become hostile). Some find his works impressive and follow him as a wonder-worker, but without recognizing the person his works reveal him to be. With this chapter Jesus turns to people outside Judaism, people whom Jews consider paganized heretics (a Samaritan woman and other Samaritans) and one who is probably a Gentile (the royal official). Unlike Jews, these two people and their confreres are not properly *born* (of Israel). Lacking access to the complete Scriptures or having access to none, their *knowledge of God* is false or incomplete. They are also people who do not *worship* God in approved ways. Nicodemus as a Jew could boast of proper birth (he is a son of Abraham), proper knowledge (he believes in all the books of the OT where God reveals himself), proper worship (he worships in God's approved Temple in Jerusalem). But with all these advantages he does not *see* the fuller advantage to be found in Jesus; he does not accept him or what he offers. The Samaritan woman and the royal official, lacking all the proper advantages, come to Jesus with open, honest and searching hearts and find in him not only their "missing advantages" but infinitely more besides. With Jesus it is not so much a question of "where you've been" as "where you are now."

Chapter 3 has already established the point: Jesus can make available to believers the only *birth* that matters. When his "hour" arrives he can send his Spirit who will *generate* them into a living interpersonal "new birth" relationship with God. And since Jesus is God's Word and Wisdom incarnate, his presence gives believers immediate, humanly perceivable *knowledge of God*. And chapter 2 taught them in Jesus they have God's new Temple, the place where God seeks to be encountered. This Temple is theirs to enter when Jesus completes his "hour." It is true Jews had access to the "waters" of God's revelations in the OT, but these were not the final waters God wanted for them. The OT and its waters have served their purpose . . . they flow towards Jesus . . . and Jesus is God's "definitive waters." Nicodemus, relying too much on the "waters" he now has, hesitates to take the plunge into the new "waters" Jesus offers. The Samaritan woman and the official, with few advantages to boast of, because of their open hearts and exercised faith make the jump and find in Jesus the fullness Nicodemus and many Jews doubt is there. But having been to the Wedding Feast at Cana, all readers of this gospel should know that in opting for Jesus they will not lose anything in choosing his "waters"; he has the power to perfect and change the OT and its waters to something far better (readers should be reminded again of the "Johannine presumption"—they must bring to each new scene, the lessons and insights learned from previous episodes).

Not only does the Samaritan woman lack Nicodemus' advantages, she seems weighed down with disadvantages. Her Jewish blood is mixed with pagan blood (Samaritans intermarried with the Assyrian conquerors of Israel and let pagan ideas and practices corrupt their ancient faith). As such, Jews would consider her outcaste and impure, a deserving object of Israel's hatred (more hatred even than is shown Gentiles). Half pagan-half Jew, the Samaritans still continued to embrace the Torah (the five books of Moses). They, however, rejected the "prophets" and thus to Jews would lack the deeper knowledge of God these books provide. Their worship was not only false in God's sight but was celebrated on a mountain unapproved by God. Despite these disadvantages, she will be open and receptive to Jesus' words. What he reveals, she will respond to; what he offers, she seeks to have; what she finds in and receives from him, she shares with others.

The other tradition is silent about a "Samaritan ministry." Luke's gospel, however, includes the parable of the "good Samaritan" (Lk 10:29-37) and mentions a grateful Samaritan cured of leprosy (Lk 17:11-19). The book of Acts (attributed to Luke) indicates Samaria embraced Christianity with enthusiasm after the death of Stephen at Jersualem. This could mean there was a predisposition to do so because of some prior knowledge of Jesus. It is not unlikely that John (with Samaritan Christians in his Church) knows of such a (hidden) ministry. In any event, the Jesus of this gospel because of his divine origins would not be subject to the usual Jewish biases against Samaritans. Jesus is discoverable in the Torah as well as in the Prophets and there is little reason for him not to reach out to people of the Torah wherever or whoever they are.

This episode reveals a Jesus who is quite *human*. Hot and tired, thirsty and talkative, John's Jesus hardly qualifies as a "gnostic" (fleshless) redeemer. Though definitely God's Word come from above, he is truly encased in human flesh. It is in the human after all that the divine is *seen*. Jesus initiates the conversation with the woman and since the hour is about noon (v. 6), a time of light, the reader suspects something "good" is to happen. John sees the dialogue beginning with an ironic paradox (as pointed out earlier, he has a passion for the ironic). Jesus is thirsty and *needs* some of *her water*. Actually it is the woman who is *thirsty* for God and human meaning and the water that will quench her thirst is Jesus. This conversation is most unusual . . . a Jew talking to a Samaritan (and a woman at that) and drinking from her cup (this is unlawful and incurs legal impurities). She calls his attention to the unusualness of the situation (v. 9). But this Jesus worries little about legal taboos, and is no respecter of persons. He and his gifts are meant for all. When one comes to Jesus with honest questions, he replies. He reveals to her through the earthly *water* she gives him, that he can give her an even better gift, and even *better water*—indeed he has *Living Water* to give (v. 10). Jesus (and John's listening/reading community knows this well) is referring to *himself* under the terms, *gift* and *living water*. When God *revealed himself* in the OT this self-revelation was often called *God's gift* to Israel (Is 12:3; 55:1; Ezk 47:1); this gift of self-revelation was also called at times *water* or *living water* (Si 24:19-27; 30-33; Pr 14:27; Jr 2:13; Is 55:1; Pr 13:14). So Jesus is informing the woman *he* is a *revelation* from God (indeed the fullest one this world is to receive). If she would listen intently and look deeply into him she would find God.

Moreover, the use of the word *water* makes John's people hearken back to the previous chapter where Jesus equivalently offered Nicodemus a new birth in water and the Spirit, meaning that Jesus because of the giving of himself through "lifting up" can make available to believers in the *waters* of Baptism, the generating *Spirit of God*. Jesus as *gift* and *living water* makes available to them God's definitive revelation of himself . . . and gives them access to the *Spirit* who generates them into a psychic interpersonal "new birth" relationship with God. But the woman has not reached this mature a faith so soon, and so she "misunderstands." She is listening to Jesus on the wrong level. Like Nicodemus she at first comprehends only the surface meaning of his words. Just as well, this gives Jesus the opportunity to explain the *water* he is really talking about. She wonders, does Jesus know about a source of fresh, running, earthly water better than Jacob's? And again we pick up the irony of her question: " . . . you don't mean to say you are *greater* than our ancestor Jacob do you?" (v. 12). Without knowing it, she has stated a truth about Jesus (and John's readers must be smiling; they are all graduates in his school of irony). A flashback to 1:51, shows that Jesus earlier claimed to be *greater* than Jacob's ladder; and the gospel *in toto* will show how much "greater" his *waters* are than Jacob's. And so Jesus clarifies what he offers. His *water* need only be tasted *once*, for it has an eternal, "from above" character about it. What this woman really thirsts for is a meaningful knowledge of and relationship with God and she can find this in Jesus who sits before her; Jesus has come from God and is present to her in human form. But this again is a truth too deep for her present faith-comprehension, and so once more she "misunderstands." But even so, she *asks* Jesus for such water, showing her desire to understand his words and his offer (v. 15).

The whole scene shows readers how to believe in Jesus. They must come to him with no preconditions for faith; they must come open, searching, and listen to him receptively. If they do not fully understand, they must stay and continue to search, to listen, to ask. Jesus will reveal who he is in proportion to the openness of their coming and the honesty of their looking (seeing). And since the woman has been open, honest and receptive to a sufficient degree he now reveals to her something of his "from above" identity. He asks her to call her husband (v. 16), whom she is reluctant to identify since he is not legally her spouse (she has been "married" five times and we recall Moses permitted only three marriages and Samaritans probably concurred in this). As she evades Jesus, saying she has no husband, he informs her of her past "marriages." Again without knowing it (v. 18) she speaks the truth (her present companion is not legally her husband). Still, she is there listening, and so

Jesus reveals who he is. He is the one who knows the personal histories of people. Who could this be except God or one who comes from God? And with her "limited" Samaritan comprehension of God this could mean that Jesus is the "*prophet.*" This is by no means all that Jesus is, but as long as she believes he is her prophet, Jesus can build on that belief to further reveal himself.

As we found out in chapter 1 with the first disciples, Jesus reveals himself progressively as their openness continues and their faith-seeing matures. When they come to Jesus with openness, he reveals himself. As they absorb his revelations, more revelations ensue, until they see more fully who he is and then can more fully believe in him. (In the coming sequence Jesus will speak next as the Samaritan *prophet* she takes him for, and he will clarify the question of how God is to be more perfectly worshipped in the time of the New Age, now arrived. Next he will reveal himself to be the Messiah. After that he seems to identify himself as the revelation of "*ego eimi*" present on earth. And finally he will reveal that he is the Savior of all the world.) If one believes the revelations as they come, remaining receptive and open, more will come until finally the fullest meaning of Jesus will be made known.

The next verses (20-24) where Jesus speaks about the place and manner of worship seem like a digression, but they fit in under the term, *prophet.* The Samaritans, although they did not accept the post-Moses prophets, did accept Moses and believed in the prophet he foretold would come (Deut 18:15-18). This prophet was to "tell . . . the things that are to come" (v. 25). He would settle the dispute over the most fitting place for worship, Jerusalem or Gerizim, and the expectation was that Gerizim would be the place. He would also inform them how the "world" was to be *saved.* And these verses show that Jesus is the bringer of these expected revelations. Again, *he* is God's answer to the question where and how God is properly to be worshipped (v. 24) and how the world is to be saved (v. 42). Jesus once more speaks of his "hour" (v. 23). Through that "hour" he will be able to send his generating Spirit who will catch up believers in a psychic interpersonal "new birth" relationship with God. They will be able to confront God as his very own children. Through the Spirit they will be able to enter into the pure and indestructible Temple of Jesus (cf., 2:19-22) and there encounter God, for he is truly present in Jesus as Jesus is truly present in the Spirit. And it seems this more perfect worship is realizable any place where the "born from above" gather. Jesus comes to all peoples, but through Judaism (v. 22) and so salvation happens in and though Jesus who is a Jew, but as bringer and giver of life from above, he also *transcends* Judaism. All peoples, be they Jews or non-Jews, can receive from him the Spirit through faith and know this new birth. New-born, they come to God no longer as servile creatures; they come as sons and daughters, having been generated into his family through the Spirit. This is worship in "Spirit and truth" (vv. 23-24). God stands before any and all believers as *real* Father; they stand before him as his loved and loving *real* family.

Already accepted as prophet, Jesus will reveal more of his identity if the woman seeks to know. And she does. She wants to know if *prophet* also implies *Messiah* (v. 25). This might be just a synonym Samaritans use for their expected prophet, but to John's people, Jesus is the Messiah foretold in the post-Moses Prophets as well, and so Jesus identifies himself as this expected figure. And this truth is most strikingly revealed (v. 26). This seems to be the first use of the frequently found phrase— "*ego eimi*,"—that Jesus will often use to identify himself (although scholars are not in full agreement that this is Jesus' first use of the phrase). This was the name of God revealed to Moses—"I am who I am" (Ex 3:14). The titles, prophet-to-come and Messiah, have so many different meanings depending on different Jewish theologies and expectations, that Jesus seems here to hint at the true and *ultimate meaning* of these terms. This prophet-Messiah is in truth the incarnate Son of Moses' God who comes to the world to reveal the mystery of God in human terms. The heavenly "*ego eimi*" is made known in the incarnate, humanly perceivable "*ego eimi*," Jesus. As Jesus will say in c. 14:9, ". . . Philip, he who *sees me sees the Father.*"

The Disciples Return: 4:27-38

As Jews the disciples are naturally shocked that Jesus talks to Samaritans. Jesus, however, transcends Judaism and can talk to all peoples. It seems the woman has forgotten all about the "earthly" water she came to fetch (v. 28). She goes to tell others of the "new water" she discovered. As she came and saw, so she invites others to "come and see" (v. 29) and they are eager to do so. And there is no talk of coming to see signs and wonders; they want to see and listen to Jesus. His word convinces the woman; her word about him brings others to see. Jesus will not disappoint. He is by John's definition, the Word, the Revealer of divine truth.

The dialogue Jesus carries on with the returned disciples (vv. 31-38) sounds like John has set off on something of a detour. However, when the chapter is seen not only as a revelation of Jesus' identity and his ability to make available to believers his Spirit, but as also an instruction in the dynamics of faith, one sees that this section fits in quite logically. After Jesus' initiative to draw faith from the woman, she comes to believe in him and seeks to bring others to faith through her word. It is Jesus' work to draw people to faith through his words and works. It is the work of the *disciples* to draw others to him through their words about him. Jesus makes this point through the symbol of "food." They try to make him eat the bread they brought from town. He says another food sustains him . . . his food is to do the work of his Father (v. 34). Actually the Father's work will not be fully done until Jesus goes through his "hour"; then he will be able to say . . . "it is finished" (19:30). Jesus can speak of his work (his life, death, and Resurrection) and draw believers to himself while historically on earth. But who does this work after his Ascension? As he lived the mystery and drew people to a belief in it while on earth, so disciples must continue to sow (preach) the mystery and reap (draw to faith) others to believe in the mystery after he returns to the Father bodily. John believes, through the use of what seem to be two proverbs (vv. 35-37), the disposition of many people near his community (doubtless refugees from Samaria) is such that they are ripe for conversion to Christ. In this chapter Jesus is depicted as going to Samaria, and the Book of Acts recounts deacons went there early to preach the word (ca. 36 AD); so seeds have been sown in this country. It is the task of John's people to reap those sown seeds for Christ. The OT spoke of an abundant overlapping of sowing and harvesting (Ps 125:5-6; Lv 26:5; Am 9:13) in the time of the New Age; with Christ this Age has come and there is an urgency that the disciples reap an already sown Samaritan harvest for God. Samaritans surely are the intended harvest but in John's preaching they probably symbolized the whole non-Jewish world that surrounds this Christian community. All peoples beyond Judaism are ripe for harvesting.

Brought to Christ by the believing word of the woman, the townspeople too become believers. Jesus *is discoverable* in the lives and words of *believers*. When new believers find Jesus in existing believers, he then comes to reveal himself further to the new believers (v. 41). The peak of the progressive revelation of Jesus is reached when they discover him to be the "Savior of the world" (v. 42). The title is ascribed to God in the OT (Ps 24:5; Is 12:2) and thus it seems the Samaritans have penetrated to the "divine dimension" of Jesus. Hellenistic religions too had many savior-gods; ancient peoples looked to their kings, heroes and emperors as savior figures. It seems through this title John seeks to show Jesus is the fulfillment of the desires of all peoples for a spiritual savior. As *"ego-eimi-with-us"* and "Savior of the world" Jews and non-Jews alike can know that Jesus is the Savior they yearn for.

As the episode ends we feel a warm affection for this Samaritan woman and her fellow townspeople. Many scholars believe John's Church contained a fair number of Samaritan converts, perhaps indicating further that this Church deriving from a non-mainstream form of Judaism itself, wants other non-mainstreamers to feel at home in its midst. Still, if Jews of a more orthodox bent are in the Church (and this seems to be the case also) latent antipathies could spark old antagonisms and this could make the lot of Samaritan converts difficult. This episode shows such imbedded biases are no longer to be tolerated, for Jesus "stayed on there" in Samaria (v. 40) and revealed his identity and shared with Samaritans his "living waters." The missionary thrust of the episode (vv. 32-38) seems to indicate other Samaritans are nearby and "ripe for harvesting" and John's people are charged by Jesus to bring the word to them.

Did John intend this episode to have a baptismal meaning? The main meaning of these scenes as we saw was to identify Jesus as God's definitive revelation of himself (Jesus is God's *gift* and *living waters*). His hour brings believers the *Spirit* who regenerates them to new life, to a new relationship with God rendering them capable of worshipping him truly in interpersonal familial intimacy. And they explain how disciples are to relate to Jesus through faith. But the early writings of the Church indicate this chapter was also used by catechists to instruct catechumens in the meaning of Baptism (and we note the catacombs have a painting near a baptismal font depicting a deer *drinking* water ["whoever *drinks the water* I will give . . .'' v. 14]). So a baptismal meaning could be here also, at least on a secondary level. Surely for Johannine Christians the term *water* has two obvious associations. It signifies the revelation and Spirit Jesus gives them . . . *and* . . . it signifies the communal symbol in which they ritually find the Spirit encased, namely, Baptism.

Cure of the Official's Son: 4:46-54

Vv. 43-45, provide a transition to get Jesus from Samaria to Galilee where he is to work his second sign. Here he will be ''honored'' by Galileans but for the wrong reasons. They welcome him for what ''he does'' (v. 45) but fail to *see* the revealing significance of what he does. They see the works but do not listen to Jesus' revealing words as he performs them and fail to discover God's ''glory'' in his signs.

Jesus arrives at Cana again and continues his initiative to non-Jews. The word ''royal'' probably indicates this man works in the household of Herod (Antipas), tetrarch-king of Galilee, and that he is a Gentile. He approaches Jesus to cure his son who is near death. Jesus appears to rebuke the man, but actually he is speaking to a plural ''you'' (v. 48), indicating his rebuke is intended for the crowds and the ''Galilean attitude'' toward signs spoken of in vv. 43-45. This man approaches Jesus seeking continued *life* for his boy; it must be that to some point at least he believes Jesus has power over *life*. He is not put off by Jesus' words to the crowd; he asks a second time, indicating again he believes Jesus has power to give *life*. Jesus is impressed with those who seek life from him and he assures the man his boy *will live*. The man does not insist Jesus come personally to ''perform'' some dramatic healing act. The man accepts Jesus' word that his boy will live and returns home, discovering his boy is indeed alive (vv. 50-53). Miracles illustrate the mystery that life is within Jesus to be given; they do not make one believe that this is so. The Galileans (and not a few Christians) think it works the other way around, viz., one believes in Jesus only because he works miracles. John is the theologian who teaches this is the wrong way to look at miracles. The Jesus who speaks to the world in John is the divine Word who comes from heaven with God's life and glory and who is eager to share himself and his gifts with the world. His signs reveal that this is so. Jesus gave a new ''life'' to the waters at Cana; now he gives renewed ''life'' to the official's son. This is Jesus' *nature*, his divine function . . . to give "life."

The family of the official comes to believe through his faith. Their only access to Jesus in fact was the word given to them by the official. As the first two signs of Jesus resulted in a very positive reaction: deeper faith in Jesus on the part of the disciples and the conversion of the official's family, the coming signs will receive more hostile, negative reactions. John will thus show that with Jesus, his signs and his words, one can react in two different ways. Free creatures have two options vis-à-vis Jesus—rejection or acceptance.

Two of Jesus' signs take place at Cana. This could be the order John finds in his "signs source" or it could be his way of alerting readers to what the remaining signs after the Wedding mean . . . they further reveal what happened there. As he inaugurated the New Covenant first at Cana, his further signs reveal the fuller and deeper meaning of that Covenant. It is the Covenant of New Life.

FURTHER PARTICULAR COMMENTS:

Vv. 1-3 . . . In these transitional verses, John mentions that both JB and the disciples of Jesus are baptizing. This could mean the author is telling the reader there is a baptismal motif contained in both these chapters. For those who seek to know how they receive the Spirit and the New Birth, they can know this mystery comes to them encased in the symbolic waters of Baptism. Since the Spirit is stressed in both chapters, this highlights the essential difference between the two baptisms (Jesus' contains the Spirit). The stress that Jesus did not himself baptize shows that he is not some breakaway disciple of JB who *imitates* JB's role as baptizer.

V. 6, *Jacob's well.* Not clearly mentioned in the OT (Gn 29:1-21?); rabbinic tradition, however, seems to locate the well where John places it.

V. 14 . . . The verb "*drinks*" is in the aorist, indicating Jesus' waters need be taken only once; perhaps an implied reference to Christian Baptism.

V. 20, *Mount Gerizim.* Samaritans regard it as God's approved place of worship. The "prophet-to-come" foretold by Moses was expected to validate this view.

Vv. 22-24 . . . Terms in these verses are unique to John in the NT, but they do reflect similar expressions found in the writings of the community at Qumran (a non-mainstream form of Judaism). This group understood itself to be God's eschatological community whose worship was celebrated in "Spirit and in truth." If, as some say, John and his early disciples were also of a non-mainstream mindset whose faith-expressions were in part similar to sects like Qumran, then, once converted to Jesus, they would also see themselves as God's eschatological community, worshipping in "Spirit and in truth." This latter expression, however, is not seen by many scholars as a repudiation of external worship. The expression in John has to do with the Christian's relationship to God in the acts of worship. Surely a gospel written for a "community" that discovers the "divine" in the "human" would seek to encounter the divine in and through the meaningful human symbols of its community.

V. 23 . . . Both Christian eschatologies are here, *final* and *realized*, giving evidence that John's community underwent an evolution in its understanding of the mystery of the "end-time."

Vv. 35-38 . . . Echoes of these ideas are heard in Mt 9:37-38 and Lk 10:2.

Vv. 46-54 . . . The Synoptics seem to have counterparts of this miracle: cf. Mt 8:5-13; Lk 7:1-10.

Chapter 5

GENERAL COMMENTS (and reflections):

All who have followed John's story of Jesus this far (who have seen the witness of JB, the call of the disciples, the Wedding Feast, the cleansing of the Temple, the dialogues with Nicodemus and the Samaritans), and have observed Jesus' actions and words without bias or preconditions would conclude (John thinks) that he is God's Messiah. As such he is a "fulfillment" figure. While securing the present relationship with God and the gifts the covenant brings to Israel, he should improve this relationship and perfect the gifts that come with it. Fulfillment (and the Messiah who brings it) means Israel is to lose nothing of her spiritual goods and values, but is to receive blessings and promises far greater. Does the story show this kind of fulfillment is happening? The heavenly origins of Jesus and the glory he brings and gives indicate he is improving the covenant and enhancing its gifts. His own relationship with God, his sharing presence with believers show the covenant is entering into a more perfect state of union with God. If Jesus is God's Word and shares with believers his life and glory, he brings fulfillment far greater than they could have hoped for. But how is Jesus to convince the yet unconvinced that he is the "fulfillment" of God's promises? He can *tell* them as he did with Nicodemus and the Samaritans and as he will do so again here in chapter 5, vv. 16-47, and continue to do so in upcoming chapters. But more than *tell*, he must *show* that he is "fulfillment" (many Jews after all are in a sense "from Missouri").

And so in this and coming chapters Jesus will involve himself with the specific institutions, goods and values of Judaism (in this chapter, the Sabbath; in coming chapters 6-10, significant feasts of Israel, all symbols of present Jewish blessings received from God) and he will absorb them into himself. In a sense he will "take them over," improve on them, transcend them, showing he possesses within himself everything of value Jews and Judaism already have, and that he contains in himself infinitely more. Indeed if Jesus is not shown to be "fuller" and "greater" than what the Jews presently have from God, why should they come to him?

Jesus, then, works his third sign, the cure of the cripple. Like his two previous works Jesus here gives "new life" as a *sign* of the "heavenly life" and the glory he is able to give (in a sense he gave *life* to the waters of Cana by changing them to wine; he renewed the *life* of the boy near death, and now he will give *life* to human legs thirty-eight years *dead*). It is true, Messiahs were expected to do such things, to work wonders. But Jesus is less concerned with wonders and more concerned with giving *life*. It is his function as "high" Messiah to give life and this is the "fullness" he brings to Israel. And we notice when Jesus gives life this third time he does so on the *Sabbath* (v. 9). This says something about who Jesus is, his origins, and the particular fullness he offers Judaism. He is one who like God possesses life in himself and can give it as God gives it, even on the Sabbath. It is true, the Synoptics show Jesus working miracles on the Sabbath (e.g. Mk 3:1-6). But in the earlier tradition these works were manifestations of Jesus' compassion and kindness toward the sick. They also revealed that his authority was approved by God. In John, Sabbath cures identify who Jesus is and point to the fullness he brings. As Jesus will say in v. 17, the reason he does this work on the Sabbath is "... *because* his Father works on that day and so he *must* also." Jesus in other words works on this day—a legitimate workday only for God—because he and the Father work as one.

Though Gn 2:2-4 spoke of God resting on the Sabbath, most rabbis "knew" this was not the case, for God cannot rest on any day. He is a God of life and judgment and often gives life and pronounces judgment (takes away life) on the Sabbath. Indeed if anyone *must* continue to work on this day, it is God, and so Jesus now insists he too *must* work on this day. As God gives life so Jesus can legitimately give life and does so to the cripple's legs. To claim power over life is of course blasphemy if Jesus is *not* one with the Father, working in tandem with him. To encourage the man to carry his mat seems a clear case of breaking the law. But note, the miracle happened. The cripple stands and walks. God has not contradicted Jesus' action or claim. A work of life has been done . . . it is therefore revelatory of Jesus' oneness in life with the Father, natural

NB

Lord of the Sabbath! The "Jews," however, have not been observing Jesus honestly or fairly and cannot see this. This is obvious because the beauty of the happening is lost on them entirely. Rather than rejoice at a lifelong cripple walking, they notice only that an unnecessary "work" has been done on the Sabbath. And when Jesus informs them that the work was equivalently done in tandem with the Father (and thus not a breaking of the law)—oblivious to his "divine connection," they accuse him of blasphemy. The cure should have shown Jesus' union with the Father but the "Jews" are unconvinced. And so Jesus must *explain* why he can cure a cripple on Yahweh's day. It is true the ears of the "Jews" will be as closed as their eyes, and his explanatory discourse will not convince them. But the sign (vv. 1-15) and the discourse (vv. 16-47) are meant for Johannine Christians. In seeing it and hearing Jesus' defensive explanation of it they will know how to defend him and themselves against the persecution and threats they are now experiencing (ca. 90-95 AD).

Jesus, then, as the one who fulfills and transcends Judaism, comes to Jerusalem to celebrate an unnamed Jewish "feast." In coming chapters he will fulfill and surpass the feasts of Passover, Tabernacles, Dedication and a final Passover. Here he fulfills and transcends the "weekly feast" of the Sabbath. Jesus takes the initiative and comes to a pool associated with natural cures (perhaps the pool contained some sort of healing properties that attracted the sick and disabled) (vv. 1-7). But as John tells the story he seems to say the pool (since he identifies its Hebrew name, Bethesda) is a symbol of the OT (the OT possessed God's waters too, but they are not as filled with "life" as the "living waters" of Jesus who stands before them.) Certainly this OT pool was not able to give life to the cripple's legs (vv. 5-7). Jesus has claimed access to waters containing eternal life (c. 4); now he *shows* the truth of this claim. The man's legs have no life in them. Jesus speaks and life comes into them. In a human, visible action of giving physical life where there was none, Jesus shows he can give heavenly life where there is none. Miracles are revelations in human terms of the "life from above" that Jesus can give. Human persons cannot see heavenly life directly; they see it indirectly in the human life-giving action. Moreover, ancients associated moral evil with physical affliction, and so the sign seems to say that as Jesus takes physical evil from the cripple this signifies his ability to take moral evil, sin, away from him too. Jesus like God speaks . . . and his words bring forgiveness and new life. The sign *shows* this . . . it visibilizes the beautiful "fullness" that Jesus brings to Israel (v. 9).

Earlier we stressed that Jesus gives his gifts especially to those who are open and receptive (his mother, the Samaritan woman, the official). The cripple seems not nearly as receptive and at first will not even know who Jesus is. Still, he listens and obeys; he does not question the key command . . . "stand up" (v. 8). Jesus may not be able to save the disbelieving, but he can certainly save slow learners. This sign, perhaps more than all the rest, shows that salvation happens mainly because of Jesus' initiative. Grace is grace and is available to all because of the graciousness of God's love and not because some deserve it, some do not.

The beauty of what has happened would overwhelm most people and prompt them to ask who has done this wonderful act. Certainly Johannine Christians who know what Jesus has said and done, who know what Jesus *will* say and do, are rejoicing because they see in the sign the revelation of his "from above" powers. Not so, "official Judaism." Rather than see God revealing himself in this act, they see only that a man has broken the Sabbath. This negative reaction symbolizes the problem Jesus confronts so often. Israel's present value-system, symbolized by super-devotion to Moses' law, is more important to some people than the *new* gifts Jesus brings to Israel. Doubtless the regulations surrounding the Ten Commandments served important preparative functions in getting Israel ready for the New Covenant . . . but can't these people see that new life in legs thirty-eight years dead has more value and significance than "not lifting a heavy object" on the Lord's day (v. 10)? Surely, as people of the law, they should know that "life" is not the work of charlatans, for only God can give it. Can't they see God is present in Jesus and if so no law is being broken at all, for God's work is to give life (even on the Sabbath)? They do not see this and so for them Jesus has broken the law. That's it! He can't be the Messiah! Nor can he be anything "higher" than the Messiah!

The reaction of disbelief, so incredible to the Christian reader, indicates the truth of the original Hymn (as John's dualism expressed it) . . . when Jesus' *light* came it was met with willful, uncomprehending *darkness*. But this document is written for believers who are encountering the same kind of darkness; they too are being persecuted (v. 16) and threatened with death (v. 18) for their faith in Jesus as the Messiah who comes and brings life from above (synagogues are expelling many of them; some it seems have been executed as heretics). Thus Jesus must answer this uncomprehending response to him and his work in strong terms, so that his disciples (ca. 90-95 AD) undergoing persecution may vigorously defend him and themselves against the ongoing darkness that surrounds them (vv. 19-47). The accusation of the years ca. 27-30 AD seems pretty much the same as the accusation of the years ca. 90-95 AD. Jesus is a lawbreaker; he commits the Adamic sin (Gen 3:5-6) and makes himself equal to God. He therefore cannot be God's Messiah in any expected or unexpected way. How does Jesus (and John's Church) answer this?

Again, John expects the reader to call to mind the full evidence of the gospel, both the chapters seen and the chapters to come. One should recall Jesus' signs, his words, and conclude that Jesus in everything he says and does is never alone . . . the Father is with him and he is with the Father . . . and this is why it is his function to work and give life on the Sabbath (v. 17). This is essential to Jesus' defense; unlike Adam he does not work in opposition to the Father or fail in his efforts to be equal to God. He works in union and cooperation with the Father but in subordination to him. All Jesus' works flow from the Father's instructions, are done in union with his will and love (vv. 19-20). The works, the discourses are not solo accomplishments: they are tandem works of both. If Jesus gives life and acts as a judgment on the world, it is because the God who gives life and pronounces judgment (the God of the New Age especially) has given that work over to him (vv. 20-22). V. 21, seems to draw the reader's eyes and ears forward to chapters 9 and 11 where further tandem life-giving works are to be done, the cure of the blind man and the raising of Lazarus. Jesus does these actions not alone but with the Father.

And the sign just worked by Jesus has not only been a source of life (physical *and* spiritual) for the cripple, but the refusal of people to see a "divine breakthrough" in it results in these people being deprived of the "given life" of Jesus—this is judgment. By refusing to see life in Jesus, they condemn themselves to live without his life. The Father, v. 23, is not aloof or indifferent to what Jesus does or how people react to him. The Father has in fact put the whole case for his own power, judgment and

believability on Jesus. Belief in Jesus *is* belief in the Father; honor given
Jesus *is* honor given him (v. 23). The works of Jesus from chapters 2
through 20 are as much the Father's as his own. Reject Jesus, God's
Agent and Son, and we reject the Father. The claim of Judaism is that it
has access to the Father and does not need Jesus. The belief of John and
his Church is that repudiation of Jesus is tantamount to repudiation of the
Father. It is most important to see Jesus in this light if Johannine
Christians are to remain faithful to Jesus who is now receiving such
intense hatred and rejection from the Synagogue.

Vv. 21-30, scholars note, give side-by-side examples of two Christian theologies of the *end-time*. Vv. 21-25, illustrate *realized* eschatology; vv. 26-30, *final* or *future* eschatology. The verses reveal what
believers receive in their faith-acceptance of Jesus; they speak also of the
time when the gifts of faith are to be experienced. The earlier verses
(illustrative of John's later, more predominant view) show believers
possess "life" in their present lives (v. 24). Again, the "Johannine
presumption" seems to want the reader to flash back to the boy and the
cripple and forward to the blind man and Lazarus (v. 25) where Jesus'
gifts of "life" were and will be received in the present lives of the people
involved, indicating that eternal life symbolized in these signs is experienced *now*. The later verses, 26-30, probably illustrative of an earlier
understanding of John's Church, indicate these gifts come after death.
The points stressed are the same—faith gives life; non-faith brings
judgment—but the "timing," the "eschatology" of reception, is different. Why they are put side-by-side in the same discourse is a matter of
debate among scholars (some speculations can be seen in the "particular
comments" at the end of the chapter). But certainly, John, as the
pre-eminent NT theologian of *realized* eschatology, has in his end-time
theology made Christianity all the more relevant to believers in stressing
the *now* aspect of living with Christ. His people find Jesus to be Messiah
and Savior in every minute of their human histories as they work their
way toward eternity. To know that believers are now with Christ as well
as to be, and that Jesus is with them in grace through all of life makes
every aspect of human life extremely important and valuable. And it is
good to have Jesus pictured not as the blood and thunder condemner of
evil (preached by some as Christianity's main message), but to have him
presented as the offerer of life, light and love from above. Judgment is not

his condemnation of a person; it is one's rejection of him. If one rejects Jesus' life and love, such a one must live with that decision, that void. Jesus is always Savior, always life-giver.

As noted earlier, scholars find John's gospel to be generally (and at times particularly) constructed along the lines of a Jewish trial. Jesus' action and words are considered *unlawful* to some and he must *defend* them. The recent verses, 16-30, had Jesus *defending* himself before authorities who *accused* him of breaking the law and committing the capital *offense*, blasphemy (v. 18). Earlier JB was put forth as a *witness* in Jesus' *defense*. The Temple cleansing had to be *defensively* explained. Nicodemus, the disciples (and from here on out, the Pharisees) put prosecutorial *questions* to Jesus (and other "court-room" terms appear: *judge, judgment, paraclete,* etc.) . . . and now with vv. 31-47, the remaining discourse of Jesus takes on more formal aspects of a trial. The earlier verses along with these indicate the main objections the "Jews" (both in the Synoptics and in John) have against Jesus—his approach to the office of Messiah suggests a blasphemous intimacy with Yahweh. Surely Jesus' actual trial before the "Jews" would have taken place later than John has it here. John seems to be moving and transposing that trial into a stylized, creative discourse and placing it here for theological reasons. Through the cure of the cripple he wants everyone to know . . . the "Jews" in their accusation, without realizing it, have hit upon a profound truth. Jesus by curing this man on the Sabbath is showing himself to be equal to God, and if so . . . the trial against him on that "count" should begin now. And Jesus should defend himself. John is a theologian-interpreter and little bothered about the exigencies of exact chronology. In this gospel Jesus *is* equal to God and must reveal and defend his equality.

As one accused of a capital crime, Jesus has the right to present a trustworthy witness in his defense (and more if he has them). He is not, however, by rabbinical law allowed to witness on his own behalf. Johannine Christians know Jesus has the most trustworthy witness anyone could call, viz., the Father (v. 32). And alone he would be more than enough to exonerate Jesus from his accused crimes. What Jew could question the testimony of God? But John is an evangelist and knows the Father has been witnessing to Jesus in many ways all along, and so he presents along with the Father, three other "witnesses," thus giving

Jesus a formidable array of *four* trustworthy defenders: JB, Jesus' deeds, the Father himself, and finally the Scriptures. It is John's way of getting his readers to *recall* the full gospel evidence in Jesus' favor.

First, the Baptist (vv. 33-35). He was viewed by many as a true prophet called by God to bring Israel to penitence. He was a man of great integrity who stood up to the lascivious Herod and died a martyr to the faith. Flash-backs to chapters 1 and 3 would recall the good things JB said about Jesus: that he was the Messiah, the Prophet, the Elijah-figure, the Lamb of God, more worthy than JB, who baptized with the Spirit, whose light was to increase as his decreased. A most valuable witness!

Secondly, Jesus' deeds (v. 36). Even Nicodemus and the Galileans were impressed with these actions, seeing them as an indication Jesus was " . . . from God" (3:2). The three signs seen, the four to be seen—all life-giving in character—reveal that Jesus is united with God, the giver of life. As the gospel proceeds it becomes more obvious to the attentive reader that all Jesus' works are tandem signs done not only *by* Jesus but *with* the Father.

Next, the Father witnesses for Jesus (vv. 37-38). The Father is invisible to the "Jewish court" but not to Jesus nor to those who look at Jesus with honesty and openness. Jesus always hears his voice, sees his face; as one *sent* by God to be his Agent he projects the Father's presence to others. Again, the obvious life-giving character of Jesus' signs indicates he is in union with the life-giving Father.

Finally, the Scriptures (vv. 39-40). John need not specifically quote the Scriptures that reveal Jesus fulfills God's promises to Israel. His people know most of the gospel by heart and see it filled with biblical motifs (the Creation Story, allusions to the Wisdom literature, Moses motifs, to recall but a few) and allusions and quotations from many parts of the Bible (the gospel contains references to Genesis, Exodus, Numbers, Deuteronomy, 1 & 2 Kings (Elijah) Ezekiel, Isaiah, Amos, Daniel and many more). By the end of the gospel the biblical evidence for the fulfilling nature of Jesus' work will be exceedingly rich and varied. But unfortunately Jesus' accusers will be as blind to Scripture as they are to Jesus. They will misread both.

Still, listening to such witnesses, any honest, open, receptive "jury" would surely acquit Jesus of the crimes he has been accused of. This jury does not and Jesus tells why. They listen more to the vision of

God they have constructed themselves than to the vision of God revealed in Jesus (v. 42). They listen to those who tell them what they want to hear (false Messiahs); they do not listen to what God says through Jesus (they think they "know" what a Messiah is better than God or his Agent-Son) (v. 43). If they really looked and listened in openness they would discover the heavenly worth of Jesus. This they refuse to do, since they fancy themselves the only true discerners of God (v. 44). The Johannine dualism becomes very strong in this defensive discourse, but John must make it clear to his own people (who are the present ones being "tried" by the Jewish authorities) who is right in this dispute over Jesus and who is wrong. Their accusers are *not* on God's side. With Jesus and his witnesses, *they* are on the right side and are innocent and even though they die will share with Jesus the vindication of his Resurrection. All human beings possess two options, but many members of the Synagogue are opting wrongly. They deliberately choose to walk in darkness rather than embrace the light incoming.

In this creative "trial" Jesus presented four very persuasive and trustworthy witnesses. The prosecution really has only *one* witness to give testimony against Jesus, viz., Moses (with the commandments upholding the Sabbath and inveighing against blasphemy). In a Johannine *tour de force* Jesus "pre-empts" *their* witness for his own defense (vv. 45-47). Moses, the expected defender of Israel on the Last Day, steps forward to defend Jesus instead. It was Moses who foretold there was to come a prophet that Israel must listen to (Dt 18:15-18). The reader can almost see Moses pointing to Jesus as the prophet he referred to. But blind to other prophecies that point to Jesus, they are blind to the prophecy of their own witness, Moses.

* * * * * * * * * *

It is time to explain the frequent and quite harsh use of the term "Jews" that appears in John (a term that seems a synonym for all those who blindly and unfairly oppose Jesus). The term is not meant to indicate that Jesus condemns a religion or a people (Christianity of a later era unfortunately took parts of John to mean this). But this cannot be so. Jesus and John are themselves Jews as are many members of his community. The term is used by John to *symbolize* "certain Jews" (the attitudes of certain Jews) of Jesus' time and of his own (Pharisees especially) who refuse in his view to look at Jesus (and the evidence for Jesus) with open minds and hearts and who moreover have persuaded others not to "come and see" what is to be found in Jesus. Such people in John's dualistic view of things are committing the darkest of all sins, preventing themselves and others from coming to Christ. He has locked this type into the term— "Jews." As Jesus debated with this "type" for some years, so John and his Church have debated many years with a like group and find them still adamantly opposed to Jesus; as darkness resists light, they continue violently to resist Jesus. Furthermore it seems some of them are even confusing pagan converts about the saving value of Jesus. John, the strong dualist, needs a strong term, a dramatic category to put such a diabolical attitude into focus, so that his people can locate the enemy, answer that enemy, (or avoid that enemy). He picked the term, *"Jews"* (not knowing what history would do with the term). Now with a more sophisticated and less dualistic mindset, modern Christians have no further need of that term; they know that John was talking about a "sin" and not a people. Being born into God through his "Jewish" Son, Christians have no cause to be anti-semitic in any sense of the word whatsoever.

FURTHER PARTICULAR COMMENTS:

The reader's attention should be called to a dispute about the present ordering of cc's. 4-6. The material in these cc's. seems out of proper "location." Scholars feel the gospel would flow more smoothly in a geographic, theological and chronological sense if the chapters were arranged in this sequence: 4, 6, 5, 7f. But again the reader is reminded that John seems to want his readers not to take each section in isolation from the sections immediately "nearby." What has happened and what is to happen, with its events and insights, should be kept in mind as we read each section (we have called this the "Johannine presumption"). If we do this, the "dislocation" problem becomes less bothersome. The oldest MSS. follow the present order.

Vv. 1-9 . . . The episode seems quite similar to Synoptic cures of paralytics, cf. Lk 13:10-17; Mk 2:1-12. But John gives the deepest reason why Jesus works these cures on the Sabbath. It is "of his nature," as one united with God the life-giver, to do this.

V. 2 . . . This pool has been unearthed by archeologists; as John describes it, it has five porticoes.

V. 4 . . . This verse is not found in the early MSS. of the gospel and is considered to be a gloss. But perhaps the gloss reflects a tradition associated with the pool. Since v. 7 describes it as bubbling and spring-like, it could have been considered to contain healing properties and would thus attract the sick and disabled.

V. 17 . . . Some commentators see this verse as meaning Jesus hereby dissolves the Sabbath obligation. Although Christians in early years kept both days holy, in a short time the first day of the week became the exclusive holy day for Christians.

Vv. 19-30 . . . These verses which speak of Jesus' unitive relationship with the Father and later verses which speak more of this relationship and also his relationship with the Spirit (cc's. 14-17, 20) provide much of the basis for the Church's later understanding of God as trinity. It is in the words and actions of Jesus that Christians came to see that monotheism was not violated in this remarkable triad.

Vv. 21-30 . . . As noted, these verses contain examples of two under-standings of the "end-time." These duplicate versions (21-25; 26-30) placed side-by-side are thought by some to be the work of editors. The *final* eschatology verses, 26-30, would be an earlier expression of Christian belief; the *realized* verses, 21-25, reflect a later understanding. An editor includes them both since the Church expressed its belief in both ways at various times. Others explain the duplication as evidence the Church does not see these two eschatologies as mutually exclusive. The eschatology of *now* does not rule out a more intensely experienced "coming" *in the future*. The duplication could indicate there is an ongoing debate about this.

Vv. 31-47 . . . Contrast this stylized "trial" with the actual trial of Jesus before the Jews found in Mk 14:15 f. Jesus is much less talkative there. The Synoptics in general seem to want to underscore the *suffering servant* character of Jesus (silent and humiliated before his captors). John's Jesus is always the *revealer* and can leave no doubts in anyone's mind that as Word he is not a breaker of the law or blasphemer. But in both versions the accusation against Jesus comes down to the crime of blasphemy. The accusation of the "Jews" in this chapter will again be stated in the major formal "trial" narrated by John, Jesus' trial before Pilate, cc's. 18-19.

Chapter 6

GENERAL COMMENTS (and reflections):

The OT has often been called Salvation History. The God of Israel is one who *saves* and *liberates* his people from their enemies and calls them to share in his life through loving faith and obedience to his will (revealed especially in his Law). As they continue to believe and obey in love, he continues to *save* them with his providence and care. Their history began with Abraham, but it came into sharpest focus with Moses and the events of Exodus. The Moses-Exodus-Passover mystery is the centerpiece of the OT, for it shows conclusively that the Lord of Israel is a *saving* God. Through his prophet Moses he saved his people from bondage in Egypt and led them to freedom and deeper covenant by giving them his Law at Sinai-Horeb.

Little wonder, then, that Jesus (if he is to convince Israel that he, and not Moses, is God's intended centerpiece in the history of Salvation) must fulfill, indeed transcend Moses and all the saving events of Exodus-Passover (which, with his coming, will be seen as a *prophecy* of his own Paschal Mystery). And so in chapter 6 near Passover (the second one in the gospel)—the feast that recalls the glories of Moses and the saving events of the original Passover—Jesus will show that he is the fulfillment of this OT mystery. The chapter is filled with motifs showing that Jesus is a new, better, more saving instrument for God than Moses. In the first four verses Jesus parallels the actions of Moses at Exodus: like Moses he "crosses the sea"—with "large crowds following him"—"attracted by his signs"—Jesus like Moses ascends "the mountain." In the verses that follow, as Moses fed the Israelites with *manna* in the desert, Jesus provides barley *bread* to feed thousands (his fourth sign, vv. 5-13). As Moses spoke of a *prophet* to come (Deut 18:18), Jesus will be acknowledged by the crowd as that prophet actually come (v. 14). As

Moses and his God saw the Israelites safely through the rough seas of
Exodus, so Jesus walks on the waters (his fifth sign) and brings his
disciples safely across the sea of Tiberias (vv. 16-21), hinting as he does,
that he is very closely linked to Moses' God, *Ego eimi* (v. 20). Even Jesus
meets with the "murmuring" Moses experienced in the desert (vv.
41-42; 60-61).

The feast of Passover summoned up expectations of another liberating and saving prophet-to-come, a new Moses as it were for the New and
Final Age. He was expected to free the Israelites from their present
enemies and give them a more lasting *manna* to sustain them. Jesus in this
chapter will speak with greater authority than Moses or any prophet and
will announce that he not only can give the expected new *manna*, but that
he himself *is* that *manna*, bread come from heaven, which if eaten gives
eternal life. No doubt about it, as Jesus earlier in the gospel absorbed into
himself the purifyng waters of the OT (c. 2); as he cleansed and replaced
the Temple (c. 2); as he made it possible for those born of Abraham and
Adam to be born of the Spirit (cc's. 3, 4); as he took over with the Father's
approval the life-giving works of the Sabbath (c. 5); so here in chapter 6,
Jesus begins to take over (since he has one more Passover to go) the
Moses-Exodus-Passover event, replacing it with a new, better, eternal
bread-from-heaven and giving Israel a New Moses whose Exodus and
Passover is to lead to the literal life and land of the Father.

Multiplication of the Loaves: 6:5-13

Jesus' fourth sign, the multiplication of the loaves, appears in all
four gospels (twice in Matthew and Mark; the second miracles, however,
seem variants of the one multiplication event). This commonly narrated
miracle must have had special significance for early Christians. Many
scholars think Christians saw it as a prophetic anticipation, of the
Eucharist which from the beginning was the distinctive liturgical act of
Christians (cf. Ac 2:42-46). Catacomb paintings bear out an early Christian linking of the two. The miracle seems in fact to be narrated by all
evangelists in quasi-liturgical style: Jesus "looks up"—"blesses the
loaves"—"breaks them"—"distributes them"—"gathers the frag-
ments left over" (all eucharistic rubrical actions). And John retains
(some say heightens) these liturgical aspects as he tells the story. He

alone mentions that the miracle takes place near Passover, seeming to infer that the Eucharist which became the Christian Passover Meal is prophesied in this sign. But it would only be later (with post-Easter reflection) that Christians would pick up the eucharistic symbolism of the miracle. The immediate viewers are impressed mainly with the *wonder* of it. They look at the surface meaning of the sign: Jesus providing abundant earthly bread for earthly hunger. They do not see in his words and actions that he comes from God and is sent to give bread that will satisfy a deeper, interior hunger for God. Jesus' signs are always and mainly that, revelations of who he is and what he can do for the world; the visible symbol encases his spiritual identity and functions. But most of the crowd see only the earthly effect and since their views of messiahs and prophets-to-come are very earthly, they see Jesus as a provider of material food only. And Jews expected the "prophet" to be more than a good provider; they envisioned him as a political deliverer (Passover seemed to intensify hopes of political liberation from Rome) and so the upshot of Jesus' remarkable sign is that they want to make him their prophet-king in a nationalistic sense (vv. 14-15). Jesus, however, is not their desired prophet-king. He is a prophet in God's sense—one who reveals God and his will. He is a King who will liberate and rule the world spiritually through the giving of his flesh and blood.

Jesus Walks on the Waters: 6:16-21

The evening of the day Jesus multiplied the bread (this sequence is also found in Mark and Matthew) he works his fifth sign. Jesus normally explains the deeper meaning of his signs, and we might wonder why he walks on the waters before explaining the meaning of the bread-sign. But in John's thinking the explanation of Jesus as the "bread from heaven" (which will be revealed in vv. 35-58) can only be understood if one accepts him as the Word come from heaven. Jesus can bring better bread than Moses because he is *greater* than Moses in a remarkable way. He is the *incarnation* of the Son of Moses' God (who since the time of Exodus has also been known as *Ego eimi*). *Ego eimi* was with Moses and the Israelites during that first Exodus, getting them safely through the seas from Egypt to Sinai. Jesus must show (at least to those in the crowd who are receptive to his words, the believing disciples) that in him believers can find and hear the mystery of *Ego eimi* also. The Moses-Exodus-Passover motif continues: it is night—it is dark—the seas are rough (vv. 16-18) and as *Ego eimi* came to the ancient Israelites, so Jesus sent by God to be *Ego-eimi-with-us* comes to the new Israelites, the disciples, and gets them safely across the sea (cf. Ex 14; Ps 77:19; 78:13). Knowing the "divine origins and power" of Jesus, the disciples will be able to accept the divine claims that will be made in the Bread of Life Discourse.

Verses 22-24, make up a transitional passage to get the witnesses of the multiplication miracle and others to Capernaum where Jesus is to "deliver" his Bread of Life Discourse. Scholars see the verses as awkwardly put together and think John is telescoping two or more events into a sequential story. To understand the discourse the reader should see it in the context of these *two signs* and so John in chapter 6 brings the audience of the former into the synagogue where the discourse is to be given. The signs and the discourse are theologically connected and so must be witnessed by the "same people" (although John's discourse data indicates new people are present also).

Verses 25-34, a rabbinical debate carried on between Jesus and the crowds, provide a lead-in to the Bread of Life Discourse. The crowds wonder how Jesus arrived at Capernaum without a boat (believers and all who look at his signs with open, seeing eyes know how Jesus is able to accomplish this). But Jesus informs them they look only at the surface of what he does and so they see only that he has power to provide earthly food (v. 26). Such food lasts only a short while. Human life in fact lasts only so long. Jesus transcends earthly food and human life. He can give eternal life and sustain it; his bread is of a different, transcendental category, and yet they seek him only for perishable food to sustain their perishable lives. Verse 27 reminds them—though admittedly the claim to have access to eternal life and heavenly bread is a startling claim—that the Father backs up Jesus' claim. The two signs of the chapter joined with the others of the gospel indicate the Father works in tandem with Jesus. The trouble is, the crowds are not doing the *work* (vv. 27, 28, 29) that would help them see Jesus has access to bread from above. They must open their eyes and hearts to his actions and words. The essential *work* they must do to penetrate Jesus' identity and power is this: they must look at and listen to him with total openness, and with no preconditions. People should not tell Jesus what he can do and who he should be. They should let *him* do his thing . . . and say his piece. They should listen to him as he tells them who he is. He (and the gospel generally) told them he is one sent by God and that he is not the provider of earthly food only. He has told them he was sent by God to give new life. If they believed *that*, then the signs will show what he says is true.

But the crowds are nowhere near that openness or faith, and so again they seek only earthly groceries from Jesus. They quote Scripture as a "come on" for a do-it-again multiplication miracle. They recall that their ancestors were given *manna* in the desert to eat . . . but "God gave them bread from heaven to eat" (Ex 16: 4, 15; Ps 78:23; Ws 16:26). So the ancient *manna*, though earthly, is actually "bread from heaven" they argue. God through *Moses gave* it to them . . . and . . . Jesus, if he is really Moses' prophet, should give it to them *again*. That is their rabbinical interpretation of the OT text quoted in v. 31. Jesus (a good Rabbi too) counters with his own interpretation of that text. The Bread from heaven that God was talking about is none other than Jesus himself; *their* text was a prophecy of *him*. It explains who Jesus is and why he comes. The gospel from the beginning has described Jesus as the Word of God. God's Word in the OT was often described as food or bread (cf. Am 8:11-13; Pr 9:4-6; Si 15:3; 24:21). *Jesus* then is God's food, *God's bread* sent from heaven and such a bread or word is always life-giving, more so than any earthly bread (cf. Dt 8:2-3; Ws 16:26). A Johannine "flash back" and immediate "flash forward" will confirm that Jesus' signs all show the life-giving character of his works; taken in conjunction with his discourses Jesus always indicates that the *life* in his signs is symbolic of the *life* he brings from above. Thinking in terms of earthly perishable bread and hearing Jesus speak of imperishable bread, they (like the Samaritan woman when she heard of Jesus' new waters) ask to have this bread (v. 34). [*The irony is that Jesus gives his life to all who seek it honestly; they ask, but really do not seek his heavenly bread, so Jesus speaks here mostly to Johannine readers.*] Jesus nonetheless informs all listeners (along with John's people) in clear terms that *he* is God's imperishable *bread* given for the life of the world, and this bread is theirs to have if they would believe.

Bread of Life Discourse: 6:35-58(59)

We recall that the crowds in verse 31 gave Jesus his discourse text ("He gave them *bread* from heaven to eat"). Jesus has already explained the *he* in the text is his Father and *not* Moses. Since Jesus has been described often as the "one sent from God" the implication is that Jesus *is* the bread from heaven. But this must be stated clearly. Jesus begins his revealing statement with the dramatic *Ego eimi*, indicating what he is about to say is not just good rabbinic interpretation—it is God's interpretation of the text. He clearly identifies *himself* as being the heavenly bread of life (v. 35).

Since the coming verses of the discourse (51b-58, 59) are so obviously eucharistic in meaning, it has often been thought that the *bread* Jesus speaks about in verses 35-51a is also intended to be eucharistic in meaning. Most scholars, however, now agree that these initial verses refer to Jesus mainly as *bread* in a *Wisdom* sense (again, cf., Pr 9:4-6; Si 15:3; 24:21; Ws 16:26). Jesus is describing himself as the OT described Wisdom and indeed all of God's revelations in the OT, including the Law, were spoken of as God's food or bread sent from heaven. Jesus, then, in these verses is describing himself as the bringer of God's Word, his message of Love, his plan for the world. If one accepts him as sent by God and embraces his message one will "know" the life that is in God. Jesus is God's Word. In the OT God's Word was always life-giving. And so it is with Jesus; his words are not just information about God . . . they contain the mystery of God and the life within God. When one listens openly and accepts his words sincerely . . . one experiences in a way his presence and life. Jesus in these early verses seeks the key response all people must give to God's Word (God's self-revealing Wisdom) . . . *faith*, openness, readiness to believe what God says. If Jesus receives this he can satisfy people's hunger and thirst for a sharing in God's life (v. 35) . . . those who listen to and accept him will never be forsaken (v. 37) . . . they will have eternal life (v. 40) . . . they will be raised up on the last day vv. 39, 40).

The Father is the key to Jesus' self-identification (vv. 35-40) . . . for Jesus is *his* Word. Jesus does not speak only his own thoughts and plans for the world . . . his are identical with the Father's. Some of those present in the original audience at the synagogue *and* some in and near John's Church (ca. 90-95 AD) doubt that Jesus' words are also the Father's. John must make it clear that Jesus *and* the Father both identify Jesus as the bread from heaven. No one can say they have the Father's bread and do not need Jesus. Jesus *is* the bread the Father gives to the world (v. 33).

But this is so hard for "surface observers" of Jesus to see. How can he be the Father's bread sent from heaven when earthly evidence identifies his origins as not from heaven but from Nazareth, from Joseph (vv. 41-42)? If they had taken Jesus' words as truly spoken, if they had looked deeply at his signs and opened their hearts fully to his words, they would discover Jesus' "higher origins." But again these verses indicate they cannot take Jesus at his word; what he says and does originates only from a human source, and so as the Israelites reacted with incredulity to Moses (Ex 16:2, 7-8), the crowds "murmur" against Jesus' self-identification as the bread the Father sends from heaven (vv. 41-42).

Being himself so convinced of Jesus' divine origins, John must have wondered why so many people refused then and during his own time to see what he so clearly sees. John, as Jewish dualist, knows free human persons are two-option beings, and this to some degree answers the riddle of rejection. But the option for Jesus is so attractive, so compelling, he still is hard put to know why so many do not choose Jesus. Verses 44-50, give him part of the mysterious answer he seeks. He finds it in Isaiah 54:13. These people are not listening as deeply as they should to the Father of Jesus; he is discoverable in the Scriptures; they prepare Israel for Jesus (v. 45). But to accept Jesus one not only needs openness; one also needs some help, some "grace" from the Father (as Christians will later put it) to discover that Jesus is his bread from heaven. The Father is not standing silently by hoping the world will accept his Son; he is drawing the world to him through the Scriptures and through his attracting grace. It can only be that many do not look honestly and deeply into the Scriptures *and* many reject his attracting graces. To John, the strong dualist, it must be that many are blinding themselves to the Father's "evidence" for Jesus (chapter 9 upcoming will explicitly show this to be the case).

Many rejected Jesus (despite his miracles) because, in comparison to Moses, he did not quite measure up to the glories and glamor of Moses and Exodus. Since God in their view seems more obviously with Moses, they opt to stay with him (some of John's people actually seem to be leaving Christ and returning to "Moses," i.e. going back to the synagogues). Jesus (and John) answer those taking the "Moses option" by saying . . . "that one [viz., Moses] has not *seen* the Father." It is dangerous to choose Moses over Jesus, for Jesus . . . "is from God and has *seen* the Father'' (v. 46). In retrospect Christians know that Moses' *manna* is only earthly bread, and his revelations were not end-of-the-line revelations, but anticipations of Jesus. To return to him would be to settle for a half-told, half-fulfilled story.

Johannine realized eschatology, so strong in vv. 35-40, emerges again in strong terms as Jesus concludes the ''Wisdom'' portion of his discourse. If one at all doubts that faith in Jesus has value for the present (as over against the OT and the earthly *manna* it offers) Jesus assures those who believe in him and his message (the bread he brings)—they *now* are in possession of eternal life (v. 47). Unlike those who hope for another earthly *manna* that cannot keep them alive for long, believers, *now* possessing the bread-life of Jesus' Word, are never to die (vv. 49-50).

The Sapiential character of verses 35-51a (even though Jesus speaks of his Wisdom as *bread*) is evident to many commentators from the response Jesus seeks. ''Eating'' does not specifically come into the discourse until v. 50 and from then on until v. 58 ''eating verbs'' will predominate. Here (vv. 35-51a) Jesus seeks the *response of faith* to his words; note the *verbs*, they are all synonyms for faith: e.g., Jesus wants us to *come to* him (used 5 times), to believe in him (used 4 times), to look upon, to be drawn to, to hear, to learn, to be taught by the Father. It seems, then, in the earliest form of chapter 6 the discourse was primarily intended to identify Jesus as life-giving *sapiential* bread.

With verses 51b through to v. 58 (59) Jesus speaks of himself in another way than as Word. The meaning of *bread* in these verses seems obviously to be eucharistic. These verses would be artificial in a discourse given this early in Jesus' ministry. Their meaning could only be understood in the context of the Last Supper. So what John has apparently done in these verses is artificially to move the ''data'' of the Last Supper to chapter 6 (John by the way will not include the institution of the Eucharist in his Last Supper account, cc's. 13-17). Jesus' discourse here is meant especially for the Church of John and those with whom his Church is engaged in debate about the meaning and value of Jesus. Jesus is *now* (ca. 90-95 AD) understood to be the ''bread from heaven'' in two ways. He is God's Wisdom bread still teaching believers God's life-giving message through the Spirit. *And* he is with them in the eucharistic bread received in the Supper each first day of the week. If Jesus is understood to be these *two breads*, then he should speak of himself as such in the *same* discourse (this seems to be John's rationale for moving the material here). Thus in a later version of the Sapiential-bread discourse, John (and/or his editors) *inserted* these verses (51b-58, 59) to show Jesus is *also* with believers in the eucharistic bread (v. 56).

John's people need and must accept Jesus as *both breads*; the opponents of Jesus (ca. 90-95 AD) deny he was ever Wisdom-from-heaven and that he is in the eucharistic bread where supposedly (God forbid) his "body and blood are eaten." It must be established for believers and non-believers alike that Jesus himself taught this, so that Johannine believers can firmly believe this truth and defend it vigorously before those who deny it. Wisdom never spoke of herself as "flesh to be eaten" (bread, yes; flesh, no); it is Jesus at the Last Supper who said this. Flesh-or-blood will be used ten times in this section; eating-drinking-feeding on will be used ten times also. When can Jesus have said this except at the Last Supper? To eat the bread of Wisdom means "to accept and believe her words"; to eat and drink the flesh and blood of Jesus can only mean to accept his personal love present in the symbols which Jews can legitimately eat and drink, namely the eucharistic symbols of bread and wine. Jesus speaks here on a deep spiritual level. His hearers understand him on a very surface, earthly level. In surface meaning, to eat flesh and blood is incomprehensible to Jews and in fact unlawful (cf. Lv 17:11-14) . . . but on the spiritual level of meaning Jesus can very definitely invite believers to "eat" of the deeper meaning of "his flesh and blood" for the words idiomatically mean his "offered life and love." Jesus is not making cannibals of believers (v. 53). He is making them symbol-partakers of his loving transcendental presence by inviting them to share in the meaningful meal-symbols of bread and wine. These were the symbols he chose at the Last Supper to be the encasement of his given life and love. Jesus has not only given believers his words to live by; he has given them himself, his life, his body crushed, his blood poured out—in other words the loving act of his death—to live by and has made it available to them in the eucharistic symbol of bread (v. 56). They must *hear* and *listen* to Jesus (the Sapiential bread); but just as importantly, they must know that they *have* Jesus with them in the eucharistic bread. Lovers must speak to one another surely; but lovers must have each other, must "touch" one another. This is necessary *bread* too (v. 55). Human persons are symbolic-psychic beings and can only communicate love to each other in the symbols of *word* and *touch* and so Jesus has given himself in both symbols, both forms—the word *and* the touch. It is a tragedy of Christian history that Christians thought they could get along with one ignoring the other. Perhaps John teaches modern believers as much as he taught his own people . . . Christians to be fully nourished need both the bread of the Word and the bread of the Sacrament . . . they cannot survive on less. Jesus must speak to them and they to him . . . but each must also touch the other . . . how else are they really to know and feel how close Jesus wants to be to them; how else know what this lofty term "eternal life" is all about? And since the Word was heard and the Eucharist eaten weekly in a community setting, the reader knows that John understands Word and Sacrament to be Jesus' principal bread-gifts to his Church enabling her to stand up and witness him before the world. Believers listen to and share him publicly knowing the world needs *these breads* as badly as they do, and it should know about them too.

And when Jesus says the eucharistic bread contains his "blood," one knows that Jesus as a Jew understands it to mean the bread encases the mystery of his "life" (life is in the blood). To be forgiven of sin, Jews had to symbolically give their life in penitence to God; this they did by giving their "blood" symbolically in the blood of an offered animal. Now sinners know that the "blood" Jesus gives in the Eucharist contains his life and it is in his giving of self that they know forgiveness of sins. Thus the Eucharist is not only experiencing the "touch" of Christ; it is feeling the "*forgiving* touch" of Christ. (*Is this what Jesus meant in c. 4:21-24 when he said the day is now here when the world will "worship God in Spirit and in truth"? What better worship could anyone devise than this—to hear Jesus actually speak . . . to experience the forgiving touch of Christ in the presence of his Father and Spirit?*) Jesus repeats what he said of himself as Wisdom (v. 50), that those who eat of his eucharistic bread, will never know death (v. 58). Jesus is exceptionally categorical about the "eating of his body" (said 8 times). This obviously reflects a dispute his Church is having (with itself and others) over the presence of Jesus in the bread-symbol. Difficult for non-Jesus people to believe; difficult for Jesus people to believe . . . *still* fully believable because the Jesus who says it is indeed from heaven. Surely if human beings can encase their love in human symbols, all the more can God's

Word do so. In fact Jesus is much better at it than they will ever be, since they often claim to be in the symbols of their love—the kiss, the squeeze, the hug, etc.—when often they are not. Jesus, the truly authentic one from heaven, can never be absent from the symbols he chooses to encase his love in. If he, *Ego-eimi-with-us*, says his love, his body given, his blood shed, is in the bread, then most certainly believers know that it is there.

With verse 60, the chapter takes up again where an earlier form of the discourse left off in v. 51a, where Jesus first mainly spoke of himself as the Sapiential bread from heaven. This of course scandalizes those who regard Jesus on the level of the human only and who see no "divine connection" in him at all (a connection revealed in the two signs of the chapter). He (some have said) is *only* the son of Joseph, only human, and as such must be (ca. 90-95 AD) dead. But Jesus must remind them that his history did not cease with his death. The Jesus of this gospel, besides being God's Word who descended, is also the incarnate Word who ascended and whose Spirit has been sent to believers (vv. 62-64). Jesus is not just the human son of Joseph; as such he could not feed them with eternal life . . . "the flesh is useless" (v. 63) . . . he is the ascended one and therefore can make good and has made good on his boast to give believers the life of one ascended to God.

Sadly John recounts that some disciples (of superficial faith) broke away from Christ, apparently having chosen to return to "Moses" and the synagogues. This undoubtedly is happening to John's Church (it seems mainly because of John's "high" Christology . . . Christ is professed as true bread-from-heaven . . . and also the "high sacramentology" of the Church which places Jesus *really* in the bread and wine of the Eucharist). Knowing the "facts" of his gospel, John is in a quandary why people cannot accept this. His refuge again is in the mystery of "belief." Even though the option of belief is open to all, it is not easy to believe. The Judas-enigma must have repeated itself many times in John's Church (vv. 64, 70-71). All need the help of the Father (v. 65). To follow Christ is *grace* as well as *option*. It seems to be John's conclusion that some willfully reject that help and are not listening to Jesus' key Witness, the Father (c. 5). Having lost some followers, Jesus now turns to Peter to learn of his reaction to the identification of himself as the bread-from-heaven; does he believe this to be true? Speaking for the Johannine

Church (and doubtless reflecting a more mature, post-Resurrection faith of that Church), Peter (who witnessed both of the chapter's signs and saw in them "epiphanies" of a true bread-from-heaven) acknowledges his belief in and acceptance of the revelation (vv. 68-69) . . . "Lord, to whom can we turn? You are the one with words of eternal life."

FURTHER PARTICULAR COMMENTS:

Verses 1-13 . . . cf. Synoptic counterparts: Mk 6:30-52; 8:1-19; Mt 14:13-21; 15:32-39; Lk 9:12-17. Scholars find John's account quite close to Mark's, indicating he seems to have had access to the data of Mark, if not to the gospel itself.

V. 4 . . . *Passover,* the holiest and most significant feast for the Jewish family, would be an especially anxious time for Christian Jews separated from their families by synagogue "excommunication" (ca. 90-95 AD). The chapter helps to convince Christians that they have in Jesus a new and better Moses, and in the Christian community a new family with whom to celebrate the Passover of Christ.

V. 15, *the prophet* . . . In the popular beliefs of many this prophet was expected to provide better *manna* and *water* for Israel; he was also to come on a *donkey*. Remarkably Jesus fulfills all three of these expectations in John. A Davidic king in a "nationalistic" sense was expected by some. Jesus is not such, so he refuses the offer to be this kind of king.

Verses 35-51a . . . Though these verses seem primarily to identify Jesus as Wisdom-bread from heaven, some commentators think that to the Johannine community the term *bread* would evoke in a subordinate sense thoughts of the Eucharist as well, especially since the eucharistic "miracle" of multiplication has just taken place.

Verses 44-45 . . . *the Father draws him* . . . *everyone who hears the Father* . . . These verses seem also to recall c. 5:32-39 where the Father draws people to Jesus through the words of JB and Jesus' signs.

Verses 51b-58 (59) . . . Since the earlier verses of the discourse are mainly Sapiential, some have wondered, could not these verses be just a graphic or dramatic metaphor for accepting Jesus as Wisdom (and thus not a reference to the Eucharist at all)? Contemporary (1st century AD) metaphorical speech involving eating someone's body and blood all ends up with negative, hostile meanings. Jesus could not be inviting us to think of him in hostile ways. The words here take on meaning in light of the Last Supper words of Jesus found in the earlier tradition. John is a theologian and moves his material where it has the best theological effect for his people. Even Rudolph Bultmann concedes the obvious sacramental character of these verses. He finds them, however, not to be here by John's intent, but as the work of a "sacramental redactor" who seeks to make the gospel (in Bultmann's view a Christianized gnostic document) safe for more conservative Christian consumption.

V. 63, *"the flesh is useless."* . . . Zwingli and others at the time of the Reformation understood this verse as referring as well to vv. 51b-58, and concluded that Jesus was not *really* in the sacrament of the Eucharist. He thought emphasizing personal faith over a supposed objective real presence could correct superstitious practices that surrounded eucharistic celebrations of his time. As is evident, if Jesus is not in his symbols, the symbols become less important and in time eucharistic practice all but disappeared from churches in the Zwingli mold. As noted in the general commentary, v. 63 more properly applies to the content of vv. 35-51a. If Jesus were *only* of the *flesh* of *Joseph*, then he would not be bread from heaven nor be able to give the Spirit. It is as the Word and as the ascended Christ that he gives believers the Spirit, in whom they find Christ's presence.

Verses 67, 71 . . . A rare appearance of the term *"twelve"* in this gospel, again indicating why some scholars think John is from another (less mainstream) tradition than the *"twelve,"* i.e. the tradition of the *Apostles* (another mainstream term missing from John).

Chapter 7

GENERAL COMMENTS (and reflections):

By this time (having worked five revealing signs and given clarifying discourses about himself to Nicodemus and the Samaritans, having presented worthy witnesses to speak on his behalf, and having spoken to the crowds and the disciples at Capernaum), Jesus' identity and saving functions as "high" Christ are fairly well established. His works (especially after c. 5) are understood to be tandem actions done by him *and* his Father. Jesus has said and implied often that his origins go far beyond Joseph or Nazareth.

The prologue stated that Jesus is a light which comes to the world from heaven (1:4, 9). But it also said that not everyone accepts this light (1:10-11). The gospel makes clear that the world can react in two ways; all human beings have two options. They can embrace this light, or they can reject it and remain in darkness.

The theme of "darkness" opposing light has been present in the gospel since the cleansing of the Temple; the theme became more noticeable in chapters 5 and 6. From chapter 7 to the death of Jesus, the struggle between light and "darkness" will grow in intensity.[1] Some reject Jesus' light outright. He is not a Messiah they seek (the deliverance he offers is not politically or economically sufficient or suitably law-oriented, etc). He offers *too little*. For others, as Messiah he blasphemously offers *too much* . . . new birth, living waters, bread from heaven, eternal life as though it were his own to give.

John, the Jewish dualist, has meditated many years on the meaning of Jesus' life on earth and sees it this way: God's light came into the world to share itself with human creation, but much of creation refused his light

[1] The theme will be toned down a bit during the Last Supper Discourse, but even there it will be talked about.

and in fact struggled to extinguish it. The opposition Jesus met and the death he suffered were no accident; they were willed and accomplished by the efforts of people who loved darkness more than light. There cannot for long be neutrals in John's world; there are only two options open to all and the options are soon made and the struggle between them soon undertaken.

The war of "darkness" against the light is to become so intense that it will seem to shallow observers that "darkness" comes off victorious in the end; the light is seemingly extinguished in chapter 19. But John knows that Jesus is not a light that can be put out by human effort. As much as the world of "darkness" tries to extinguish his light, it can never do so. Rather, the light "gives itself up" for the world. It is by laying down his light that Jesus makes it eternally available to all who open themselves to it. In a sense his death is the "work of darkness" because its children want it to happen and try their best to bring it off. But in John's theology the death of Jesus is mainly his and the Father's work . . . "a work of light" . . . the selfless surrendering of his light for others. And to understand the upcoming chapters, this must be kept in mind. What superficially looks like a series of disjointed, repetitious complaints about Jesus and his repetitious *ad hoc* answers to these complaints, is really John showing how steadily the powers of "darkness" work to bring down Jesus' light and yet how powerless they are to do so. This "darkness" often took the form of sheer stubborn unwillingness to see anything good in Jesus; certainly darkness can find no "heavenly" dimension in him. He is earth-born and not from above. His works are not revelations of the divine but of the demons who possess him. For him to claim "heavenly connections" is blasphemy. But is this a truthful and proper judgment of Jesus? *Or* is it a judgment made by the powers of darkness in the presence of inextinguishable light? The gospel makes the point over and over again: as much as "darkness" tries to prove (through opposition, ridicule, plots to eliminate him, etc.) that Jesus is not who his words and discourses reveal him to be, it can never prove him false in his claims; it can never extinguish his light. Jesus is always in control of his own destiny. And when he finally is arrested it will be because *he permits it*. Even then the trial of Jesus against the world goes on and the gospel will clearly show that light is the winner. The final verdict favors Jesus who at the end is more than ever the light invincible.

Most of the complaints against Jesus found in cc's. 7-9 will in some degree or other still be current in the Johannine Church-Synagogue debates occuring ca. 90-95 AD. The battle still goes on sixty years after the verdict of innocence and triumph has come in, so the gospel must show once more that darkness (now the Synagogue complaints against the high Messianism of Jesus as well as the troubles they and others have with Jesus even as "low" Messiah) cannot win out over light. If the descriptions of "darkness" (confusion, befuddlement, wild and false accusations, legalistic stuffiness, missing the point, misunderstanding, general nastiness) are painted perhaps too darkly for modern taste, keep in mind John's dualistic mindset and his theme: to keep his people firmly loyal to Jesus, he *must* paint him with lustrous and brilliant light while at the same time painting the opposing option of uncomprehending and obstructive evil in the darkest possible colors. Against a "backdrop" of stubborn unseeing darkness, the light of Jesus like a pearl of great value will shine all the more brilliantly and to its best advantage. So remember, a talented and dramatic dualist is at work here.

The Feast of Tabernacles

Chapters 7 and 8 are set in the context of the feast of Tabernacles (c. 9 happens in its after-glow). So the feast with its theological meaning and liturgical ambience provides a good forum for the further self-identification of Jesus. By what he says and does during this time, Jesus will further reveal who he is in himself and who he is "for believers." It is the fall harvest feast for Israelites, a time of thanksgiving to God for the products that provide for "life" and sustenance. In time Christians will see Jesus (who gives them *harvest-life* infinitely better) as the subject of their supreme *thanksgiving*. The feast made dramatic and prayerful use of *water* and *light* (symbols of the gifts of *rain* and *sun* that made the crops bountiful). Water was carried in procession from the nearby pool of Siloam to the Temple and there poured out over the altar as a "prayer" of thanks and need to God for his waters (without this precious gift there would be no past or future harvests). Also the Temple area at night was beautifully illumined with massive candles, so that for all twenty-four hours it was aglow with light; the feast, day and night, was remembered as a festival of light. The feast, then, was a thanksgiving to God for his generous bestowal of *water* and *light*, and so it will be an opportune time for Jesus dramatically to reveal again that he can give even better gifts than earthly water or created light.

The feast was one of the three pilgrimage journeys devout Jews made to Jerusalem each year. As they lived in temporary "huts" or "booths" during the harvest feast, they hearkened back to the early days when as nomads they lived in tents in the desert. The feast recalled their ancient desert pact with God and it became a time of spiritual thanksgiving for and renewal of the Mosaic Covenant. The Synogague readings referred to Exodus and the time God gave their ancestors abundant water for their desert sojourn (Ex 17:1 f; Ps 78:15-16). Jesus by being here will infer that ancient covenants can be made better—their "earthly waters" replaced with even better water (vv. 37-39).

At Tabernacles the expectancy of the Messiah ran high. Many thought this Agent of God would come during the feast and usher in the New Age (Zc 14:16-21). The Synagogue readings for the feast (Ezekiel's vision, c. 47, and Zechariah's prophecy, cc's. 9-14) spoke of the Messianic Age as a time when abundant waters would stream forth from the side of the Temple and living waters would issue from Jerusalem and flow endlessly. What better time, then, for Jesus to indicate that the expected person . . . the expected Age . . . the expected waters are *now* here (v. 37)? Messiahs are "sent" by God to teach and to display God's power. Jesus during Tabernacles will be called "Rabbi-*Teacher*" and "*Messiah*" . . . he will call himself the "sent One" . . . he will display that he is God's water and light from heaven as he cures the lightless blind man in the pool waters of Siloam which bears his own name, the "sent one." Moreover, the feast which bathed the Temple so beautifully in twenty-four hour light was a time of thanksgiving for God's gift of the Temple (Israel's first Temple was dedicated on this feast). Jesus spends most of his time during the feast in the Temple precincts, inferring it seems that *he* is the Temple from whom the expected abundant flow of living waters is to emerge (cf. Ezk 47). In sum, then, the feast with its several meanings and high Messianic expectancies is a *natural* for Jesus to be present at; there he can identify himself once more as the "high" Messiah (sent by the Father) who can offer living waters (c. 7) and eternal "light from above" (c. 8).

As chapter 7 begins, the opposing darkness to Jesus' light is identified as present: the "Jews" are seeking to *kill* him (v. 1). His "brothers" also illustrate the elements of "darkness" present opposing Jesus. They view him only as a sign-performer (fast losing supporters, and thus losing any "public" or "political" value he could have for the "family"). By urging Jesus to continue his works of power in Jerusalem they show they do not understand that he is light from above (vv. 2-5). Jesus in verses 6-7, equivalently identifies himself as the light the world hates. The attitude and request of his brothers show that they are part of the world of darkness, and Jesus refuses to go to Jerusalem with them. He will, however, go for his own reasons. He will go to reveal that with his "time" and "hour" fast approaching, he is soon to go to the Father whence he will be able to give to believers his Spirit in whom they will find his eternal water and light. His refusal to go and then going, v. 9, is John's way of indicating Jesus reveals himself only on his own terms (cf. other examples of this: cc's. 2, 4, 11).

With verse 12, Jesus is equivalently accused of being a deceiver, a false prophet (i.e., he lies about his origins, the source of his authority, etc). To the "Jews" of ca. 27-30 AD and to the Synagogue opponents of Jesus in John's time a "high" Christ can only be a deceiver; and such a deceiver can justly be condemned to death. No one says that Israel is not within her rights in testing Jesus as a valid prophet. The "darkness" of his opponents shows itself in their refusal to see him as a true prophet who has produced good witnesses to vouch for the truth of his prophetic identity. They refuse to see the "divine dimension" in him, his words, or his signs (wherein the Father is discernibly present).

At a time when people are wondering: if this is the year of the Messiah's actual coming, Jesus arrives to say and do things that strongly infer he is the expected Messiah. But Jesus (despite his words and actions) *cannot* be Messiah as non-believing "darkness" views the situation. He teaches without ever having had a reputable and respected teacher to train him in the meaning of the Scriptures and in the proper functions of messiahs. John's people pick up the irony of this complaint, for they know Jesus was taught by the "best." Jesus when he teaches is not only giving his own opinions. His doctrine is the *same* as that of his *instructor* (the Father) (v. 16). Jesus seems again to infer that his Father (whom darkness has not been listening to very closely) reveals his approval of Jesus by making his works *fruitful* (v. 18); five signs to date, two more within the reader's "flash-forward" view would seem to show that Jesus must be speaking the truth about his rabbinical training and his heavenly instructor. His works are not solo but tandem works, after all.

The Father (5:37-38) and the Father's Scriptures (5:39-40) have in a sense already "testified" for Jesus at his "trial." He did not arrive at Tabernacles a stranger off the streets. He came announced by the Scriptures; he came "sent" by the Father. What better Messianic preparations could there be than this? The Law of Moses might justify putting to death a "false prophet," but a *true* prophet, proven true by the Father and his Scriptures? That is a clear breaking of the Law (viz., murder), and so Jesus reminds the law-bound leaders of Israel (and the law-bound leaders of the Synagogue, ca. 90-95) that by wishing Jesus (or his later disciples) dead, they are breaking their own law (vv. 19-20). Again, the evidence is clear; "darkness" (as it did in Jesus' time) is still opposing the light. Its followers feign innocence; but the truth is out—they *do* want Jesus *dead* and are plotting his death (5:18; 7:25), and so rather than Jesus being found guilty of deception and lies, it is the authorities who deceive and lie (as "darkness" always does).

Jesus (say the opponents of his light) cannot be Messiah because he breaks the Law. This chapter assumes the miracle of the cure of the cripple worked on the Sabbath in chapter 5. Can "darkness" be shocked into seeing that such a work was not a breaking of the Law? God's law is difficult to follow but it is not designed to crush the human spirit; it is God's effort to make human persons truly whole and authentic. If "good works" can legitimately be done on the Sabbath, as for example the circumcising of a male child when the eighth day after birth falls on the Sabbath, cannot Jesus give *life to crippled legs*? The *spirit* of the Law after all is to make people fully whole. In chapter 6 some of Jesus' followers went back to the sterile milieu of the law-bound Synagogue (the place where Moses prevails, vv. 19, 23). Verses 21-24, seem to recall again the words of the prologue (1:17), reminding the reader that if one opts for Moses one ends up *only* with the Law (and often without its spirit); with Jesus believers have God's "enduring love" given to restore humanity's crippled condition. To think the former is more important than the latter is indeed to opt for "darkness" over light. The irony of the situation is not lost on John's readers: Jesus seeks only to bring life where there is none; the officials of Judaism seek to bring death to one who only wants to give life to those who are humanly crippled (v. 25). To want to do this is surely not breaking the Sabbath.

Jews of an apocalyptic bent thought the Messiah would appear suddenly without anyone knowing his exact origins (v. 27). This, then, would rule out Jesus, for "everyone" knows where *he* comes from (6:42). The irony of this complaint is obvious, too. As things are turning out, Jesus, to the complaining children of "darkness" *is* actually the *hidden* Messiah, for they do not really know where he comes from (ironically what they demand of the Messiah is true in Jesus' case). So Jesus reveals again the "hidden identity" he has made no effort to "hide": he comes from the Father, has been sent by the Father (vv. 28-29), and the reason this is not obvious to them is that they never look honestly and openly at Jesus, who reveals the Father ("darkness" never wants to look directly into the light).

Darkness—symbolized in the reaction of priests and Pharisees to Jesus' identification as "high" Christ—attempts to arrest him (v. 30). But again, "darkness" has no power to extinguish the light of the "high" Christ (v. 30). At his "hour" he will submit to it, but not as to a victor; "darkness" will make possible Jesus' death but his death is not a finale—it is a preface wherein Jesus' light takes on eternal, glorified proportions redounding to the good of all creation. What looks superficially like a victory for "darkness" (John uses here and later the terms "*a little while longer*"—cf., also 12:35; 13:33; 14:19; 16:16-22—to signify his *death*) is not a victory for "darkness" at all but his "*going to the Father*." As his light goes through the mystery of death to the Father, so those who believe in his light will be able to "go there too" and find it. Not so, the supposed victor, "darkness"; wanting the light extinguished, darkness ends up with no eternal light whatsoever (v. 34).

Since "darkness" makes no effort to comprehend Jesus (especially his "high" nature), it again "misunderstands" his statement about "going away" where he cannot be found. This departure is interpreted to mean he is going off to teach the Greeks (apparently Jews think Greeks will swallow anything). Ironically in "going to the Father" (and returning through the Spirit) Jesus has indeed (ca. 60-95 AD) "gone to the Greeks" (many Gentiles have accepted Jesus when the gospel was written; in fact, the Church world-wide, ca. 90 AD, is mostly "Greek") (vv. 35-36).

With verses 37-39, John reaches the climax of chapter 7, where on the last and greatest day of the feast Jesus cries out in the Temple that all who thirst should come to him and drink ... all who believe in him shall have living waters flowing within them. The first two of these verses are frustratingly ambiguous to many scholars. Who is the source of living water—Jesus or the believer? It could be they view the words too much in isolation. Jesus has already claimed in this gospel to be a source of *living water* (4:10) and *water ... leaping up to eternal life* (4:14). The Synagogue readings of the feast (a presumed motif for the chapter) speak of God as the provider of life-giving water for his people wandering in the desert (Ex 17; Ps 78). Other readings refer in vision and prophecy to the coming Messianic Age (the feast is a time of high Messianic expectancy as we saw) which is envisioned as a time when God would gift Israel with abundant waters flowing from the side of the Temple (Ezk 47) and from Jerusalem (Zc 14:8). The gospel has established the Messianic identity of Jesus. This chapter has reaffirmed it ... *as much as to say the expected Messiah ... the expected Age ... the expected abundant waters ... are here!* It would seem, then, that Jesus is the primary source of the living water, especially if we "flash forward" to 19:34 (every passage in John should be read against the background of the whole gospel) and see there the "waters" flowing from the opened side of Jesus (again, cf. Ezk 47), from Jesus who has been established (since cc's. 2 and 4) as the true Temple of God.

The Jesus of chapter 7 (viewed also as the Jesus of the gospel *in toto*) seems to invite believers to come to *him* (especially at his "*hour*") so that they can receive the Messianic waters of God flowing from his side, as the Temple of the New Age. As for believers, the waters of Jesus do not cease to be living or flowing as they reach the person of faith. The source of Jesus' life is the Father; the source of the disciples' life is Jesus who remains in them through the Spirit he sends. Jesus dwells within them and from them flows outward to others. As Jesus will pray at the Last Supper: "Father . . . may the love with which you love me dwell in them as I dwell in them myself" (17:26). Only a "high" Messiah could offer so much. And to get the impact of vv. 37-38, one must take them in their context: the theological, biblical, liturgical and Messianic ambience of the feast of Tabernacles (remembering especially that on the last day of the feast the dramatic rite of carrying the waters from Siloam to the altar of Yahweh is taking place most solemnly).

On the following page is a diagram that in a limited way indicates the dramatic effect John seems to be working for. If one takes Jesus' words in the context of the feast, while setting the feast in the context of the whole gospel, one ends up with words of great impact. Such placing of scenes has been going on all along (the "Johannine presumption" as spoken about earlier); it is illustrated here in rough outline and in the following chapter to show there is a "Johannine presumption." Hearing these words from Jesus at Tabernacles (and knowing at the same time that Jesus can and did give believers Spirit-filled waters), who in John's community would settle for water less than this (e.g., waters of the Synagogue, waters of the OT Law)? Surely John's people see Jesus as truly the "high" Christ whose death gives them the Spirit in the living waters that flowed from his side, the side of God's glorified Temple (Ezk 47). Jesus not only eloquently identifies himself once more, but does so at the most meaningful of times and in the most appropriate of settings.

Verses 40-41, seem to echo the conclusions that hearers of Jesus should make. In light of what they have seen and heard in chapter 7, what they will see and hear in chapters 8-20, Jesus *is* the prophet (Dt 18:18), and he *is* the Messiah (Zechariah was right! The Messiah did come at Tabernacles. Zc 14:16-21). But the reader must remember the immediate chapters are also attempting to show that "darkness" is trying to extinguish the light, and so it continues its opposition to Jesus. He cannot be the Messiah, say some; he is from Galilee (nobody ever made it to the big leagues from there). Many Jews of course expected a Davidic Messiah, Mi 5:1-3 (especially those who viewed the Messiah's role as kingly in a nationalistic sense). David was from Bethlehem. Jesus is from Galilee. This could be ironical for two reasons. Surely if a Messiah comes from heaven, this would render the Davidic expectation totally irrelevant; if given a choice between Bethlehem or heaven, heaven should win out, no? *And* if John is aware of the nativity tradition of Matthew and Luke (and ca 90-95 AD, why wouldn't he?) he must know that Jesus through Joseph was of David's line and was born in Bethlehem. "Darkness" which variously looks for a "hidden Messiah" *and* a "Davidic Messiah" can find *both* in Jesus, but finds neither (it is difficult to see in the dark, wouldn't you say?).

As the soldiers return without an arrest (expected since Jesus determines his own fate), verses 45-52, seem to sum up the recent objec-

A diagram to show John seems to want his readers in a general way, and on dramatic occasions, in deliberate ways, to attempt FLASH-BACKS and FLASH-FORWARDS. His episodes set against a background of the whole gospel become more comprehensible and richer in meaning.

FLASH-BACKS

c. 1 . . The Hymn describes Jesus as coming from heaven; surely such a one could deliver on the c. 7 promise to give us the Spirit and living waters.

c. 2 . . Jesus can change WATER into wine (he gives us better than OT Waters to drink).

c. 3...Jesus tells Nicodemus that "he must be born again of WATER and the Spirit" (water in John is often symbolically associated with the Spirit).

c. 4 . . Jesus says to the Samaritan Woman: "who drinks of the WATER I shall give, will never THIRST again . . ."

c. 5 . . Jesus and the Cripple. . what the OT waters (pool of Bethesda) could not bring the Cripple, Jesus can bring (does he have better water than the OT?).

c. 6 . . Jesus dramatically walks on the WAT-ERS (like "Ego Eimi" of Exodus he too can calm and walk over the Waters.)

FEAST OF
TABERNACLES,
c. 7

"Jesus cried out: if anyone thirsts, let him come to me; let him who believes in me come and drink! As Scripture says: from him shall flow fountains of living water." 7:37-38

The context, ambience of the Feast:
Water ceremonies: during the Feast "abundant waters" (past and future) are on the minds of the people.

Readings heard in Synagogues during the week of the Feast:

Exodus 17:1!
Ezekiel c. 47
Psalm 78:15-16
Zechariah cc's. 9-14

Here we find readings that recall Israelite rescue from thirst at Exodus and readings that anticipate the Messianic Age when there is to be given "abundant waters."

Here if WATER is on the minds of the people as a past and future good. Jesus can use the term and image to describe the good he now brings from heaven.

FLASH-FORWARDS

c. 9 . . Jesus heals the Blind Man with WATERS that have a name like his — "the one sent."

c. 18 . . Jesus on the Cross about to return to his Father says: "I am Thirsty."

c. 19 . . . Jesus' side is pierced and WATER flows forth (a symbol encasing his Spirit?).

c. 20 . . Jesus gives the Spirit to his disciples (John's people would likely associate water as the post-Resurrection symbolic encasement of JC's Spirit).

c. 21 . . . Jesus meets disciples by the WATER and directs them to find a good catch from those waters.

etc. etc.

tions of "darkness" against Jesus' light (objections of both ca. 27-30 AD and ca. 90-95 AD). Impressed with Jesus' charismas preacher, the soldiers hesitate to arrest him. Jesus has great speaking ability and uses it to deceive (he is still the false prophet, the liar) (v. 47). Only those ignorant of Scripture (and Pharisaic interpretation of the OT) could accept Jesus (v. 49). Pharisees have their own peculiar Messianic expectations, their own way of reading Scripture . . . and nowhere do they find or expect a Messiah "high" or "low" like Jesus; it is only the uninformed "mob" that could fall for his line. But is the reaction of the Pharisees to Christ a true one or is it again an example of "darkness"? One of their own shows them that their conduct illustrates "darkness" more than truth . . . they desire to condemn a man without fully knowing the facts about him or giving him a fair hearing (v. 51). How can people of the Law be so free and easy with it? Nicodemus makes a good point but since it is a pro-Jesus, pro-light point, those who symbolize "darkness" must try to put it out (by putting the critic down). Nicodemus, they say, must be a *Galilean* (this term along with the name "Nazarenes" seems to have been a common demeaning "put-down" used against Christians generally). The reader seems to catch echoes of Nathanael's ironical question: can anything good come from Nazareth? Stay tuned.

FURTHER PARTICULAR COMMENTS:

V. 3, *his brothers* . . . The Synoptic tradition also infers Jesus' relatives did not understand or appreciate his ministry; cf., e.g. Mk 3:21, 31 f; 6:4. *Brothers*: a general term for male relatives (brothers, half-brothers, cousins, etc).

V. 4, *display yourself to the world* . . . The three temptations of Jesus found in the Synoptic tradition (e.g., Mt 4:1-11; Lk 4:1-13) on first inspection seem to be missing from John. This verse perhaps picks up echoes of the last temptation: Satan invites Jesus to "*display himself*" by jumping from the pinnacle of the Temple. In a "flash-back" to chapter 6, one may possibly discover the other two temptations: 6:15 . . . the people (like Satan) want to make Jesus *king*, and 6:31 . . . the people (like Satan inviting Jesus to turn stones into bread) invite Jesus to produce *miraculous bread*. The temptations, then, seem to be in John but in less heightened stylized form. To John "darkness" is not confined to the dramatic personified singular (Satan). "Darkness" is potential to the two-option nature of human beings, many of whom choose to follow the prince of darkness.

Verses 15, 46 . . . The impressive charismatic character of Jesus' teaching is found in the Synoptic tradition also; cf. Mk 1:22; 6:2. Jesus is a unique Rabbi. He taught with no formal education and yet with great authority and knowledge of Scripture.

V. 20, *demented* . . . A charge found also in Mk 3:22. Jesus' signs could be dismissed, then, as not being revelations of God, but works of the devil (the demons)—a charge that is still current ca. 90-95 AD apparently.

V. 21, *circumcision originates with the Patriarchs* . . . Possibly this indicates John's Church was ridiculed because it gave little value or importance to circumcision. John's defense for this was to minimize the value of circumcision, ascribing it more to ancient custom than to divine law.

Verses 23-24, a cure *on the Sabbath* . . . This was a point of contention in the Synoptics too; cf. Mk 2:23-28; 3:1-6. In his Sabbath works, however, Jesus always insists he is keeping the *spirit* of the Sabbath and the Law.

V. 27, *no one is to know where he is from* . . . An apocalyptic strain within Judaism seems to have held that the Messiah would only be known when Elijah returned to identify and anoint him. Remarkably JB who implies Jesus is Elijah-returned (1:21), also "identifies" him as the Messiah (1:29). Thus the Messiah of apocalyptic expectation can also be found in Jesus.

Verses 28, 37 (cf. also 12:44) *he cried out* . . . This seems to be a Wisdom motif (Pr 1:20-21; 8:1-4). Wisdom occasionally speaks in this manner.

V. 34, *look . . . and not find* . . . Again possibly a Wisdom motif (Pr 1:28), for Wisdom when ignored, was also difficult to find.

Verses 37-39 . . . St. Paul (1 Cor 10:4) sees in the "Rock" of Exodus (Ex 17) a foretelling of Christ, indicating that Jesus in the Pauline tradition at least was seen as fulfillment water to that of Exodus. Since this text was also read at Tabernacles this could be another indication that John sees Jesus as the primary source of living water for Christians.

V. 52, *a prophet arising in Galilee* . . . True, there is no OT passage that says a prophet is *to arise* from Galilee. But John could well know that a prophet *had come* from Galilee (Jonah from Gathhepher, a town near

Nazareth), whose life (three days in the belly of the fish) was a *prophecy* of Jesus' "hour." Perhaps some Johannine irony is at work here.

To the question: does chapter 7 contain a baptismal motif, the answer seems to be . . . quite possibly yes, at least in a secondary sense. The early Church picked up on Jesus' self-descriptive words in chapter 7 (linking them with 4:10-14 and 19:34) and found the chapter evocative of Baptism. The term *water* has rich biblical associations (identifying God's Spirit with water, his word and Law with water, his providential gifts with water, his Coming Age with abundant waters), but it must have had (ca. 90-95 AD) liturgical associations as well, especially in a Church fast becoming Gentile, whose understanding of the term would be more liturgical than biblical.

Chapter 8[1]

GENERAL COMMENTS (and reflections):

Continuing in the context of the feast of Tabernacles with its several theological meanings (discussed in c. 7), but particularly in the knowledge that it is a time of thanksgiving for God's *light* (the Temple, e.g., is beautifully ornamented at night with lighted candles and vats of oil set afire), Jesus in v. 12, dramatically identifies himself as the "light of the world." When the people are thanking God for his created light (the sun, the gift that allows them to see and their crops to grow), when they are thanking him for the pillar of light (Ex 13:21-22) that saw their fathers through the darkness of Exodus, when they are enjoying the beauty of the Temple bathed in light, when many are expecting the Messiah to usher in a New Age of "perpetual light" (Zc 14:6-7), Jesus claims to be the bringer of heavenly light to the world. He wishes to share his light with believers so that they will never walk in darkness again.

To Jews God was light and the author of light (Gn 1:3-5; Ps 27:1; Ps 36:9; Ps 56:13; Jb 33:30; Ba 5:9, etc.); his revelations in the Torah and the Prophets were "light" revealing his nature, goodness and power, his will that gave direction to life. Not to know God and his will was darkness; to know him and his Law was to have *light* and *truth*. Wisdom (cf. Ws 5:5-6; 6:12-13; 7:29-30) was described as the mystery that brought God's light and truth to Israel; with her teaching and revelations God further illumined the minds of the Israelites to his goodness, mercy and love.

And so as Jesus identifies himself as the "light of the world" he seems to say that God, who has already revealed much of himself in the OT through his Prophets and Wisdom, is now through him revealing the fullest word about himself and about human life. In seeing him the world

[1] For comment on c. 7:53-8:11, see the "particular comments" at the end of this chapter.

is seeing a revelation of God ("to see him is to see the Father," 14:9 . . .
"to know him is to know the Father," 8:19). To hear his words is to
receive God's ultimate teaching about the meaning and purpose of human
life, that God not only shows himself, but in Christ offers himself to be
shared. Human persons are to walk in Jesus' light . . . to possess the light
of life, to be interpersonally related to God-revealed-in-Jesus "forever"
(v. 12). But John knows God's light is an *offered* gift, not one forced on
anyone (as indeed love to be fully *known* must always be a mutuality of
freely shared lives). Human persons to John are two-option beings who
must opt for the light or oppose it. The theme of darkness-against-light
continues strong in c. 8; Jesus is a light inextinguishable here, as in c. 7.

But to claim to be such a light (fully revealing God and the purpose
of human life) is again a claim that only a divine messenger could make,
and many do not accept Jesus as "high" Christ. And so with v. 13,
"darkness" once more objects that Jesus' claim to be such a light is
without foundation for he (only human after all) has no witnesses other
than himself to back up his claim. John's readers (and indeed the
Pharisees of 90-95 AD, who have heard John's defense of Jesus many
times) know that Jesus has *already* presented his witnesses to speak for
his claims, one of whom was a "favorite" of Jesus' objectors, viz.,
Moses (cf., c. 5:30-47). Only "darkness" would refuse to see and listen
to such witnesses. Still, if Jesus were *only* human, it is true, his solitary
witness would not be sufficient to convince others that he speaks the truth
when he says he is the "light of the world." But Jesus by this time (to
John's people especially) is known to be the "high" Christ and such a
person is not bound by rules for human speakers or prophets. If one
descends from heaven and, after incarnation, *ascends* to heaven (and
when the gospel is written it is always the *Risen* Jesus as well as the
"high" Christ who speaks Jesus' words), then such a one can solitarily
witness to the truth of his statements, since no one should question the
words of one sent by or ascended to God (v. 14). The trouble with the
Pharisees is that they judge Jesus only by "human standards" and thus
seek other witnesses (v. 15). But since darkness prevents the Pharisees
from recognizing Jesus as "high" Christ, he again must remind them
(and their mentality) that he has the witness of the Father always testify-
ing to the truth of his statements. To see the Father present takes an
openness "darkness" does not have, but the believing readers have seen

the Father present in all of Jesus' works and discourses. There is no explanation for Jesus' signs (or his coming Resurrection) other than the Father being at his side (vv. 16-18). Jesus is not a solo speaker or performer; he always works in consort with the Father.

The situation behind c. 8 again seems to be the dispute between John's Church and the Synagogue which has excluded Christian Jews. The latter claims to have the *light* of the Torah and therein to have exclusive access to the Father. At Tabernacles John assures his own people this is not the case. In Jesus they have God's total light, his fullest revelation, the New Torah as it were to help make sense of their lives and to guide them to God. In Jesus they *have the Father* ever standing by his side (v. 16). Rather than feeling deprived of the Father when they opt for Jesus, they must know, with Jesus they *have* the light of the world *and* the Father. A "flash-back-and-forward" shows the Father working with Jesus from the beginning of the gospel to the end. This is the sticking point of the adversaries of Jesus—he always talks and acts as though he were working in tandem *with the Father* (cf. c. 5)—when actually *we Pharisees* "know" this is not the case! In v. 19, Jesus says the invisible Father is visibly seen in him . . . but the "visible" and the "invisible" are *two* divine mysteries always standing side-by-side. But the opponents of light are not looking for God to reveal himself in Jesus. Apparently they seek from "their" prophets and messiahs only confirmation of their own views about God and nothing *new*. And so they do not recognize or *see* the "invisible" Father standing by Jesus' side (v. 19).

Jesus as light seeks to reveal God to people and to draw them to an acceptance of the God he reveals, but if this is not seen and the invitation to believe not followed, then the disbeliever refusing to see commits the worst possible sin. Denying the revealing light of God in Jesus, such a one cannot find God (v. 21). He dooms himself to walk in darkness. Light is not forced on anyone: human persons have two options, to embrace or reject it. If they reject it, they cannot follow Jesus to the Father whence he came and where he goes. There is only one God, the one humanly reflected in his Son. Reject the Son, and one loses the Father.

The reaction of the Jews to Jesus' warning that they cannot follow him is crudely misunderstood to mean Jesus is about to commit suicide (few Jews would think God would reward with eternal life one who shows so little regard for human life). This wild missing of the point is meant to illustrate how dark "darkness" can be at times. It could also reflect current gross misinterpretations of Jesus' crucifixion (if Jesus so willingly submitted to an unnecessary death . . . even sought it, this could be interpreted by some as suicide perhaps and thus Jesus could be dismissed as an unworthy and condemned messiah). ✗

The crucifixion (whose horror and cruelty seem to many "Jews" God's judgment on Jesus as false messiah) cannot be rightly understood unless one accepts Jesus' premise that he *is* the "high" Christ. Judge his death in a "worldly way" (v. 23) and it can be misread. But if Jesus came to *reveal ego eimi* to the world and death is a part of that revelation, then it is not suicide; it is the last and fullest revelation of who *ego eimi* is in himself and who he is for the world. If the life *and* death of Jesus is a revelation about God and his love and will for the world, not seeing this, not believing or accepting this, will mean (in John's two-option view of things) that disbelievers opt not to know the revelation nor to share in it. This to John is the supreme and only sin that defines all sin: to reject the light which displays God's love and to die without it, to will not to have it, to choose rather to walk in "darkness" (v. 24). This chapter will contain three examples of the "absolute use" of *ego eimi* (vv. 24, 28, 58).[2] Since this is an OT *name* for Yahweh, Jesus seems clearly to be saying just that: he and his death are in human terms a revelation of *God*. This is why Jesus is the light of the world . . . he reveals in a human way God and his love and will for the world. To be offered this revelation and to reject it would be the only real human tragedy. Such people would deny themselves access to God. And of course if one does not see the death of Jesus in a faith-context as the offered, surrendering love of God for the forgiveness of sin and for the light and life of the world, then one deprives himself access to God's forgiveness, life and light and will surely "die in his sins" (v. 24).

Jesus' opponents do not at first penetrate the implications of his *ego eimi* identification and are expecting him to finish the sentence . . . "who are you, then?" (v. 25). So Jesus must draw attention back to what has been revealed since the gospel began: everything he said and did indicated that he was revealing God; as God cannot lie in his self-revelations, neither can Jesus who has been sent by him (v. 26). It was so often the

---

[2] An explanation of John's use of the phrase, *ego eimi*, precedes the "particular comments" at the close of this chapter.

strategy of Jesus' enemies to separate him from the Father. John never lets Jesus' opponents do this. Take Jesus and you get the Father; reject him and you lose the Father . . . this is his methodology. Jesus has no identity apart from the Father (he is God's Word, he is sent by God, he seeks only the glory of the Father, to do his Father's will, etc). That is the only judgment (v. 16) Jesus makes on the world . . . "do you believe that I am a human revelation of *ego eimi* or don't you? If not, then you opt not to share in the life of *ego eimi* in an interpersonal way." This is supreme, willed "darkness" . . . this is sin . . . this is judgment.

Verse 27, seems to echo the key complaint of "darkness" . . . the Father we love, but Jesus, the crucified one, we have no use for (as mentioned, his ignominious death seems to many a divine judgment on his mission). John goes right to the heart of this accusation. Jesus' death (John's term for this here is "lifting up") is not "proof" that he is a false prophet; it is "proof" that he is the true revealing light of God. Because it was from the Cross that he returned in light-filled Resurrection to the Father. Surely if Jesus' seven signs do not reveal the inner mystery of his oneness with the Father, the Resurrection should. If Jesus was a solo false prophet, if his claim to be light was human bravado and conceit, he would have been extinguished forever; his death would have been the end of him, his damnation. But if he is, as he has said and implied many times, a tandem prophet, then his death is not the end of him. Since the Father, who was with him throughout his human history, is always with him, he was with him in death, and shows his being with him by taking him to himself in Resurrection (vv. 27-29). The teacher who trained him welcomes him home. Indeed Jesus in surrendering his life and light mirrors the very love the Father has for all human persons. It will be by *transcending death*, by being "lifted up" to the Father that Jesus will conclusively show that he was indeed *ego-eimi-with-us* (the author of all life and light).

8:31-59

When disciples of Jesus are excluded from the Synagogue and in the process seemingly fenced off from almost 1800 years of God's revelations to them, is not some of his truth and light lost as they leave the Synagogue? Jesus informs these excluded disciples that in him as "high"

Christ they know *all* the truth God has given Israel and infinitely more besides (vv. 31-32). The total revealing truth they have in Jesus can set them "free" from the Synagogue with no fear of loss whatsoever (v. 32). In Jesus' word and those who abide in it is total truth, total light, freedom unlimited. The prologue (1:17) told the reader that in Moses (a symbol for the Synagogue) one finds *only* the Law, but in Jesus one receives God's enduring love. It is God's love freely given, his love freely and faithfully accepted by the disciple, that brings the full "knowing of God's truth" (v. 32). It is not Moses, nor the Synagogue, nor the Law, nor Judaism in and of itself, that saves, but *only* Jesus who is Judaism's fullness. In him is found *freedom from* Law and its Synagogue, *freedom from sin, freedom for grace*.

This is the sticking point. Is it all there in Jesus? Is total light, freedom, forgiveness all really there? Is it not safer to stay with the religious system, the Synagogue, the Law, with Abraham as physical father? Salvation is in and of the Jews after all. Jesus is too risky to follow *alone, separate* from the OT with its traditions, laws, and structures. By promising this "freedom" in him Jesus has implied that the OT *without him* is slavery: it is to settle for half-light at best and non-freedom (v. 33). As Paul pointed out years earlier to the Judaizers of Galatia and Rome (Rm 4; Gal 3), the Law and its structures have no power to forgive sin; only God can forgive and only in his forgiveness will one know true human freedom. Presently the OT authorities that persecute members of John's Church are locked into the "sin" of disbelief (as well as the sin of presumption that equates salvation with physical descendancy from Abraham) and thus they are spiritual *slaves* to sin and can find a light out of the "darkness" only through the forgiving power of Jesus. Jesus after all is the coming to the world of the *Son* of the *forgiving Father*. As an earthly son of the Graeco-Roman world newly come into his inheritance sometimes freed his domestic slaves (vv. 35-36), so the divine Son frees all from the slavery of sin at the time he comes into his inheritance, i.e., in the moment of his being "lifted up" to the Father (his "suicide" as "darkness" crudely puts it). It is not the disciples of Jesus who need Abraham or the Synagogue; it is the descendants of Abraham and the Synagogue who need Christ for the forgiveness of their sins. And not only will sin be taken from them through Jesus, but as *Son* he can give them the freedom of grace that relates them properly to God in an interpersonal relationship of sons and daughters psychically loving their true Father, God.

Descendants from Abraham

To show again that it is not risky to put total faith in him, Jesus, who earlier had shown he transcends Jacob and Moses, now begins the process of showing he transcends Abraham (not in the sense of turning his back on close to 1800 years of salvation-revelation history, but by containing in himself all the values, blessings and realized promises of that history and infinitely more besides). Jesus' adversaries who refuse to accept him as the "light of the world" do not even act like proper sons and daughters of Abraham . . . they personally seek to kill Jesus and to destroy his revealing words about God (v. 37). Abraham was a true believer in God's word; he accepted the "light" given to him; he received in joy the promises made to him. Not so, his "literal children"; they seek to kill God's Word (v. 38). Their sin is all the worse because the one who reveals God's word is more than angel or human prophet . . . he is the Son who sees the Father face-to-face (vv. 38-40). Again we seem to catch variations of Paul (Romans, Galatians) where he extolled Abraham for his faith as against the Judaizers who saw Abraham as a man rewarded for his works. The "literal descendants of Abraham" are lacking the *key Abraham virtue* . . . faith, willingness to open themselves to God's revealing word, and thus their conduct is not much like their claimed father. Since they, like the devil, seek always to oppose and destroy God's word, the implication is that Jesus' opponents act more like children of the devil (vv. 40-41).

The dualism of John is very strong is this chapter, but allowing for his mindset and dualistic background, how else can he put it? The situation comes down to this: the "Jews" have settled on the Father to the exclusion of Jesus (they believe the disciples with their "high" Christ are reductively anti-Father people). This cannot be. Jesus and the Father are inseparable; to be anti-Jesus for John is *ipso facto* to be anti-Father. Jesus again states the "high" Christ premise: he comes from the Father, is sent to the world by the Father. He is the human *locus* of the Father's love inviting the world's love in return (v. 42). If this claim were made off the top of his head, it would be conceit in the extreme. But these words and dialogue of light with "darkness" are set against the backdrop of the whole gospel (indeed against the backdrop of sixty years of history where John's group has been making the gospel "case" for Jesus and the Father with the same result; "darkness" refuses to see any "light" in Jesus whatsoever). Jesus is not mouthing macho-bravado claims. His oneness with the Father and the Father's light has been and will be manifested many times. Again, the diagram on the opposite page will show that there are grounds for John's heavy dualism. And so it seems in John's mindset that "darkness" has rendered itself almost "incapable of hearing Jesus' words" (v. 43) (not, however, in a deterministic way, since Jesus still "dialogues" with them). Their opposition to light makes them look more like children of the devil than of Abraham. Since the devil from the beginning was a murderer (cf., Cain: Gn 4:8; 1 Jn 3:12-15) and a liar (cf., Adam-Eve: Gn 3:4-5) and the key sins of the disciples of darkness are their desire to destroy Jesus and his words, to tell lies about him, it would seem they are true sons and daughters of *that father* (who else could spawn children who love to murder and lie so much?)

Certainly to the modern reader John's dualism is almost *too heavy*. But remember, John is busy making a statement to his people about who Jesus is and how absolutely necessary he is for their salvation. This is a gospel and not an historical documentary exactly recording first-century Christian Jewish debates and the motivation behind them. There are not several paths human persons can follow to reach God; there is only one, and historically in his world Jesus as the one true path is being rejected and his disciples persecuted. John cannot leave any confusion or doubt in the minds of his people that this is objectively wrong (as a first-century Jew he knows precious little about the limitations and vagaries of human psychology—that people can be wrong for the best of subjective reasons, etc.) He knows what the choices are: they are two . . . Jesus is obviously the right one and yet so many do not opt for his light. The stakes are too high to let this be reduced to an "unfortunate situation," ecumenically to be pussy-footed around. No, the rejection of Jesus must be seen as wilful choosing not to "belong to God" (v. 47). Subjectively John may have been totally wrong about the Pharisees; but objectively, he was completely right. To reject God's light and Son sent into the world . . . this is not what the Father expects or wants of his creatures. This is a work of "darkness."

Diagram #2 on the Flash-Back, Flash-Forward phenomenon.

FEAST OF TABERNACLES, c. 8, c. 9

"Jesus . . . said: '*I am the Light* of the world, anyone who follows me will not walk in darkness; he will have the *light* of life!'"

8:12

"As long as *I am* in the world, I am the *Light* of the world."

9:5

FLASH-BACKS

c. 1 . . . The Hymn where Jesus as Word is described as the "*light*" of men that "*darkness*" cannot overcome.

c. 3 . . . Nicodemus who comes to the *light* but in some "*darkness*" (for it is *night*) is told: "the man who lives by truth comes out into the *light*."

c. 4 . . . Samaritan Woman comes "open" to Jesus at "*noon*" and finds out who Jesus is.

c. 4 . . . So also the Official whose son is cured at the hour of greatest *light*.

c. 6 . . . Though *night*, Jesus' disciples are able to *see* him walking on the waters.

cc's. 5-8 . . . The many dialogues Jesus has with unbelieving "Jews," illustrating they are in "*darkness*" and even though they attempt to overcome Jesus' *light*, their efforts do not succeed. Heightened *dualism* in these cc's. shows that Jesus is the *light invincible*.

FLASH-FORWARDS

c. 9 . . . The Blind Man who has no *light* in his eyes, receives light from Jesus (physically and spiritually).

c. 11 . . . Lazarus has no "*lights*" at all; he receives the light of life from Jesus.

c. 13 . . . Judas leaves to betray Jesus "*at night*."

c. 18 . . . Jesus' enemies need "*false light*" to find him.

Peter leaves Jesus for a "*false light*" and there denies him.

cc's. 18-19 . . . dialogues of "*darkness*" *vs. light* continue: Pharisees, Pilate, (c. 20) disciples, Thomas; still darkness is not able to overcome Jesus.

c. 20 . . . Jesus lays down his *light* to take it up again at the Resurrection.

etc.   etc.

The *context, ambience* of the Feast:

The *Light ornamentation* of the Temple during the week of the Feast.

Readings heard in Synagogues during the week of the Feast:

Exodus 13:21-22 . . . recalling how God's PILLAR OF FIRE (*Light*) got the Israelites through the nights of Exodus on their way to freedom.

Zechariah 14:6-7 . . . where the Messianic Age is described as a time of perpetual *DAY* (*Light*).

Here we find readings that recall the light-gift of Exodus and which anticipate the Messianic Age where there is to be an abundance of "light" . . . thus if LIGHT is on the minds of the people as a past and future *good*, Jesus can use the term and image to describe the *good* he now brings from heaven.

Again, with v. 48, the "Jews" seek to isolate Jesus from the Father, this time by ridicule: he is a man possessed by demons, they say, or a Samaritan who with the power of demons works magical signs (Samaritans were ridiculed by Jews as lovers of magic). A review of all twenty chapters of the gospel hardly indicates Jesus is demented, and c. 4:9 indicates he is certainly not a Samaritan (so who are the liars here?). Jesus again in answer is the "high" Christ, whose whole life has been dedicated to revealing and honoring the glory of his Father. As "high" Christ he will go through death to eternal life and thus be vindicated as "high" Christ by God. And those who keep his words will pass through death to eternal life also (v. 51). The Johannine reader it seems would link this claim of Jesus to be able to give life with at least three disciples who kept Jesus' word in some degree: the cripple of c. 5, the blind man of c. 9, and Lazarus of c. 11. The cripple's legs and blind man's eyes were *dead* and yet in faith they saw new *life*; Lazarus went to human *death* as a believer, a keeper of Jesus' word ("see how much he loved him"-11:36), and came to know *life* again. The claim is not only mouthed; it has been and will be revealed in symbolic life-giving actions.

But the opponents of light are obviously not "flashing backwards or forwards" to these episodes and seek again to destroy Jesus, denying that he is the "high" Christ of the Father. He is merely a human being (obviously crazy to make such outrageous claims). How can a human being insure against death? The greatest human members of Israel's past all experienced death and so will Jesus and his disciples (these again are statements made in "darkness," since these people know in the preaching of John's community about the cripple, the blind man, and about Lazarus—*and* about the Resurrection—and yet they still insist what is human dies and no human being has power over life or death). Who does Jesus *pretend* to be (was there *pretended life* in the cripple's legs, the blind man's eyes, in Lazarus' body?) (v. 54).

Jesus again can only counter the ridicule of "darkness" with a re-statement that he is the "high" Christ. He is not like the demented Samaritans, a solo worker of magic or wonders. He "knows" the Father (v. 55)—this biblically means Jesus is interpersonally united in the love of his Father, and his whole mission on earth has been to reveal and bring his Father's word to the world. To be what you are, to tell what you have been told by the Father to tell, is not to lie (in this gospel Jesus tells no lies;

"darkness" does all the lying). And since the Synagogue always opposes the privilege of 1800 years of historical covenants with God against some supposed "fullness" to be had in Jesus . . . Jesus must take the symbol of that 1800 years of history away from his Synagogue opponents and claim it for himself. *Their Abraham* rejoiced over *him* (v. 56). The OT was prophecy of Jesus. Judaism can only find its fullness in Jesus. The rabbis saw in Abraham's rejoicing over the announcement that he was to have a son (Gn 17:17; 21:6) that he somehow could see down the years of history to his progeny of "many nations." The *Christian rabbis* theologically see Abraham rejoicing over Jesus, for Jesus is the one who "descends from Isaac" surely, but who also "descends from God" and thus brings to the sons and daughters of Abraham the ultimate promise of salvation God wants for them.

But how could Abraham (dead 1800 years) see Jesus, and Jesus (less than fifty human years old) see Abraham? Jesus' answer is the fullest statement by him in this gospel that he is indeed the pre-existent, divine "high" Christ . . . "before Abraham came to be, *I AM*" (v. 58). Only one mystery could pre-exist Abraham . . . and still be present speaking to people on earth, and that mystery is God. And it is obvious to the Jews who hear these words, that the words not only mean pre-existence of some sort; the words since Moses' time were a biblical name for God (Ex 3:14), and so Jesus is clearly assuming the *name* of God. The Synagogue has their Jacob and Moses, and Jesus proved "greater" than both (4:12-13; 5:46; c. 6). The Synagogue has Abraham and all the promise and privilege that term implies, and now Jesus proves "greater" than Abraham (v. 58). What disciple of Jesus could ever doubt that his word, his light, his truth is insufficient in some way? Is not God's Son, with or without the OT, with or without the Synagogue, enough for them? But if Jesus is not what this name implies, then he has committed a blatant sin of blasphemy and should be stoned (Lv 24:16). Did Jesus speak the truth? Is he able to give the eternal life and light he promises? John would want the reader to review again the whole gospel for the answer. And note also that the symbols of "darkness" in the immediate chapter have tried twice to extinguish his light and were not able to do so (vv. 20, 59).

* * * * * * * * * * * * * * *

EGO EIMI, I AM

Although this expression appears a few times in the Synoptics, it is almost a trademark of John. He uses forms of it many times. John believes Jesus is a pre-existent, divine being sent by the Father (the "high" Christ as we often call him). He believes that his words and works supremely reveal the nature and goodness of God and his will. He is not merely an inspired spokesman for God; he is God speaking to the world in human flesh. John seeks a way to convey this insight without seeming in any way to deny the monotheism of Judaism.

The Jewish and Hellenist world of his time provides him with the expression, *ego eimi*, which helps him convey his insight into Jesus' divine person, his saving words and functions. The gods and goddesses of contemporary pagan religions often used the phrase to introduce themselves to their flocks, to indicate their origins, to spell out the gifts they offered, the demands they made on believers, etc.; e.g., "*I am* Isis . . . taught by Hermes . . . *I am* the wife of Osiris . . . *I am* the one who gives laws that must be obeyed and not changed, etc." (*Later gnostic sects make great use of the phrase, "I AM," to introduce the revelations of their heavenly revealers*). Thus, the expression in pagan and early gnostic circles connotes a deity and revelations of or from a deity.

The OT also contains the expression. When Moses asked God to reveal his name in Ex 3:14, God told him . . . "*I am*: that is who *I am*." In a sense the phrase could be understood as God's translation of his name, Yahweh. Later when the Hebrew Scriptures were translated into Greek, the phrase, *I, Yahweh* (say or do such and so) came out very often as *Ego Eimi—I AM* (say or do such and so: e.g., Is 41:4; 48:18; Ho 13:4; Jl 2:27). The Greek translation of Deutero-Isaiah (cc's. 40-55) frequently uses the phrase as a name for Yahweh (and John's Jesus sounds quite a bit like Isaiah's God). Generally in the Greek OT the phrase is used to speak of the existence of Yahweh against those who question it, his consoling presence with Israel, his uniqueness as a one-only God. Again, the expression intends to name the Jewish deity and to introduce revelations from or about him. Late Judaism often understood the expression as a *name* for God (as such the words "*I AM*" in any context were piously avoided out of reverence for God's name; Jesus will not piously refrain from using them at all).

Scholars note that in John Jesus uses the expression three ways (two pretty much as name-identifications for himself, and the third to identify but also to spell out in concrete ways his relationship to believers): 1) the phrase is used by itself in an absolute sense as a name: 8:24, 28, 58; 13:19; then, 2) the phrase is used by itself, as a name, but with a predicate understood: 6:20; 18:6; and possibly 4:26 (the first two cited examples seem almost to be quasi-divine "epiphanies"); and, 3) the phrase used with predicates: e.g. 6:35, 51 . . . "*I am* the *bread* of life"; 8:12 . . . "*I am* the *light* of the world"; 10:7, 9 . . . "*I am* the *sheep gate*"; 10:11-14 . . . "*I am* the *Good Shepherd*"; 11:25 . . . "*I am* the *Resurrection* and the *life*"; 14:6 . . . "*I am* the *way*, the *truth*, and the *life*"; 15:1 . . . "*I am* the *Vine*" (these too seem closely related to absolute usage, indicating the functions of a divine Jesus vis-à-vis the believer). The predicates used in the above instances often appear in the OT used of Yahweh, or of Israel as a community. Contemporary pagan cults use the phrase with understood predicates or with predicates but never absolutely as a name . . . only the OT and Jesus do this.

It is interesting to note that John also uses the term, *Name*, to identify Jesus and the Father (cf. 3:18; 5:43; 10:25; 12:23, 28; 14:13; 15:16; 16:23, etc.). For John, Jesus can use the two ways of speaking God's name—"*ego eimi*" and the "*name*"—because he *is ego-eimi-with-us* . . . and . . . the *name-with-us*.

The phrase, then, helps John identify Jesus as more than human, as truly a divine "from heaven" mystery. Jesus is *from* God, he *is* God and he speaks as God-with-us, God-for-us. Since both pagans and Jews understand the phrase to mean God and God speaking, John uses it to indicate that Jesus is divine and his revelations are not just inspired utterances, but the speech of God. And indeed Jesus by using the phrase is understood to be the only one who legitimately and truthfully can speak in this manner (all pagan gods and pagan revelations must give way to him and his revelations; all the attributes given to these gods, as e.g., light, life, food, vine, etc. must now be exclusively given to Jesus). Most importantly Jesus can boldly use the phrase because it properly belongs to him as one "who comes from God." He is the "high" Christ. As the name of his Father, it is also rightfully his name too.

FURTHER PARTICULAR COMMENTS:

C. 7:53-8:11 . . . This story of the woman caught in adultery is not found in the earliest texts of John. It appears in western manuscripts for the first time in the fifth century. Scholars find the episode in style and vocabulary more like Luke than John. It is quite similar to situations where Jesus is asked to make two choices meant to trap him into some sort of compromise and he answers with a third alternative (cf., e.g. Lk 20:20-26, 27-40). St. Jerome included it in the Vulgate version of the NT as part of John's gospel, and Catholic Christians have considered it a part of the inspired Scriptures ever since. In time it came to be regarded as inspired by most Christians. Why it was so late to appear and find acceptance is a matter of speculation. Those guilty of this sin in the Church's early history had to submit to a very harsh discipline for its forgiveness. Perhaps Jesus' less harsh approach to the sin seemed difficult to reconcile with the Church's early attitude and practice, and so the text was for a time suspect. When the discipline for the forgiveness of this sin relaxed, then the passage became less suspicious. How it found its way into John's gospel again is not clear. The passage immediately following (8:15) does speak of Jesus not passing judgment on anyone (at least in a condemnatory way). The Pharisees by contrast judge the woman guilty even though as sinners they should not be so harsh to judge others. They also have judged Jesus a sinner and have determined he should die. Moreover, the episode illustrates John's darkness-opposed-to-light theme (very strong in cc's. 7 and 8). The Pharisees, symbols of "darkness," attempt to overcome Jesus' light by entrapping him with an insoluble dilemma (whichever way he goes, he will be in trouble, either with Rome or the Law, Lv 20:10) and yet "darkness" is not able to trap him.

Verse 12, *light-darkness* . . . Normally in the OT, light and darkness are not pictured as opposing principles, good versus evil, as they are in John. This phenomenon does, however, appear in forms of non-mainstream Judaism, as, for example, the Essenes of Qumran (with their prince and sons of light; their prince and sons of darkness). Thus, again, John's theme of "darkness" opposing light seems to indicate that his background is quite probably from a non-mainstream variety of Judaism, not necessarily from Qumran, but from some sort of Judaism (perhaps a hellenist oriented form) that employs heightened dualism in its expressions of faith. In passing, it is good to note, that moderns, in comparison to the ancients have little appreciation for the "gift of light" (a simple flick of the switch supplies light when needed). In the era of the gospel most activity, for the poor at least, virtually ceased with sunset. To have the promise of "light always" was a blessing devoutly to be wished for.

Verse 13, *your own witness* . . . (cf. Dt 17:6; 19:15; Nb 35:30) . . . Though these texts refer to the need of more than one witness in the condemnation of capital offenders of the Law, the positive principle of a need for independent witnesses to establish the truth of a statement seems to derive from these verses of the Torah.

Verse 28, *lift up the Son of Man* . . . Like the Synoptics (cf., e.g., Mk 8:31; 9:31; 10:33-34) John also has Jesus predict his Passion three times: here and in 3:14 and 12:32. The early Christians sought to explain as best they could the enigmatic character of a "crucified Messiah" by showing that both the Messiah and the God who sent him *somehow* "knew" of this mystery before it happened (it could not therefore be summarily dismissed as proof that Jesus was a false messiah, etc.).

Verse 32, *set you free* . . . As Paul graphically puts it in Gal 3:13, Jesus *sets us free* from the "curse" of the law.

Verse 39-40, *works worthy of Abraham* . . . *Abraham did not do that* . . . Some commentators see Abraham's *work* as welcoming the messengers God sent to him (Gn 18:1-8). The "Jews," however, do just the opposite; they always darkly resist Jesus, God's messenger.

Chapter 9

GENERAL COMMENTS (and reflections):

In chapter 9 Jesus will work his sixth sign, the cure of the blind man. The sign will illustrate in a symbolic action the truth of Jesus' remarkable claim made during the feast of Tabernacles and repeated here, that he is the "light of the world" (8:12; 9:5)—that is, he is the one who reveals in human terms *ego eimi* to the world—he is the one who frees human persons from their sins as well as the spiritual "darkness" emanating from the Synagogue (ca. 90-95 AD)—he is the one who frees them *for* a new grace-relationship with the Father. In a sense the *discourse* that explains the deeper meaning of this sign has already been given at the feast of Tabernacles in chapter 8. All Jesus need do is to give light to a man receptive to his words. How this action affects the lives of the blind man and others will show that Jesus is what he said he was—the "light of the world."

Something beautiful happens to the man's physical eyes; something *more* beautiful happens to his inner, spiritual eyes. As the story progresses he sees more and more deeply into the meaning of Jesus as God's light sent to him. The story in a sense is a "dramatic discourse," a "story explanation" that Jesus is God's light in and for the world, a light some accept, some reject. It further shows that those who receive this light must never deny or hide it; they should "witness" it openly before the world, no matter what the consequences. Thus the situation behind chapter 8, namely the dispute over who more fully possesses God's light—the Synagogue or Christian Jews excluded from it—continues in this chapter. The former blind man will be excluded from the Synagogue because he is a disciple of Jesus and yet will come to know that Jesus is the Son of Man, while the Synagogue will know further "darkness" and be judged to be spiritually blind.

To the ancient Jewish mind the blind man or his family because of this affliction would be understood to be sinners in some way. Jesus seems to repudiate theories that too simply see sin as the cause of human sickness or disability. Rather, the event will be a "work of God" (v. 3), revealing that Jesus is the "light of the world." As this is being revealed, it will at the same time become clear which sin draws from God loathing and judgment. That sin will be the willing refusal to see that light has come into the world in Jesus (the sin of spiritual blindness that prefers "darkness" to light) (3:19). Jesus will perform a work of light confirming his claim to be God's light and the Pharisees will see no light in it at all. Jesus wants and seeks to give his light; he refuses it to no one who listens to or obeys his words. But again the world is a place of two options. This story shows the two options in operation . . . the acceptance-belief option: it brings the insight that Jesus is indeed God's Son come to share the light of his presence and love with the world . . . and the rejection-disbelief option: that seeks no new light and which results in one becoming even more spiritually blind to God. The blind man, of all God's creatures, seems the most disadvantaged (he is a sightless, "sinful" beggar, ignorant of the revelations of God and the Law of Moses) and yet he has the one necessary thing it takes to bring God's light into his life . . . faith, openness to God's Word. And the Pharisees: they have all the supposed advantages (they are the learned leaders of the Synagogue, devout descendants of Abraham, knowledgeable in the Scriptures, "righteous" in their knowledge and fidelity to Moses and the Law) and yet they are lacking the key virtue of faith and openness. It is not one's genetic, religious, educational credits or purity that bring light, only faith and openness.

The theme, then, of darkness-opposed-to-light continues very strong in chapter 9. And as much as "darkness" seeks to overcome Jesus' "work of light," it cannot do so. The miracle is too eloquent to show Jesus is and has light to give. In its several repetitions it more and more reveals this fact. And in the negative reaction to the telling of the sign, the forces of "darkness" are more and more revealed to be *blind* and unable to put out Jesus' light. Nor can they put out the light (physical and spiritual) that Jesus gives the believing blind man; he stands firm in his new light and receives still further light about Jesus as the story progresses.

The Sign

As Jesus walks in light (v. 1) he sees a man in physical darkness (like all human persons without God's light, the man lives in spiritual darkness also) and Jesus seeks to give him light. Jesus has mainly "spiritual light" to give, but such light is invisible and so Jesus encases his heavenly light in the physical light he gives to the man, whom he finds obediently receptive to his words. But the disciples, like most Jews of this time, are distracted by the physical affliction of blindness, seeing it as somehow a punishment for sin (the bio-genetically naive OT seems ambiguously to agree with this view: cf., Ex 20:5-6; Dt 5:9, and sometimes to question it, cf. Jb). Be that as it may, Jesus informs them that no immediate sin (of the blind man *or* his parents) was involved in the darkness this man suffers. If they seek to know the sin that produces real affliction, the episode will reveal it (it will be the refusal of some to find light in Jesus; this is the sin that brings God's judgment on the world, v. 39). Rather, they are to see in the coming cure a "work of God" (vv. 3-4). All of Jesus' signs are revelations of who he is and this one is to show and reveal that Jesus is the "light of the world." By bringing human light to the blind man's eyes Jesus shows he can bring transcendental light to his spirit. Jesus' work is not mainly to cure people of their physical ills (vv. 4-5); it is to reveal God's love and to share it with those who open themselves to it as the blind man will do, and so he is anxious to reveal that he can do *this work* (vv. 4-5), anxious because his work of final revelation, his "lifting up," is fast approaching (v. 4 . . . "the night comes").

Jesus is no secret giver of light; he has actively sought out the blind man and now actively sets out to cure his darkness. He takes the *soil* of Israel and with his saliva makes a muddy ointment and applies it to the blind man's eyes (the reader seems to catch echoes of the first creation, Gn 2:7, where God fashioned Adam from *dust* and breathed life into his nostrils; here Jesus through his anointing symbol is to give more beautiful life and light than was given Adam). Also, the Pharisees will later try to convince the man, Jesus had no active part in his cure. The blind man *feeling* Jesus' anointing *touch* will never doubt *who* cured him. Jesus is God's light surely, but he is also *God's-light-with-us* in such a way that it can be "felt" and "touched," and so Jesus in a sense with his anointing hands "touches" his transcendental light into this man's eyes (and soul)

(v. 6). Jesus then tells the man to wash in the pool of Siloam (v. 7). For reasons that escape most scholars, John finds that the name Siloam in its Hebrew form sounds like the word "sent" and he gives the pool the name given to Jesus in the gospel, the "sent one" (cf., e.g. 3:17, 34; 8:16, 29, 42, etc.). By doing this it seems John wishes to indicate that the water encases or symbolizes the mystery of Jesus and the light he brings from the Father. Jesus' light comes humanly encased in the sensually felt anointing and sensibly experienced submersion in water, v. 8 (the episode has many baptismal motifs which will be noted at the end of the chapter).

The earlier tradition has Jesus working similar cures of blind men (cf., e.g., Mk 8:22-26; 10:46-52; Lk 18:35-43; Mt 20:29-34, and so John seems to be working here with traditional Jesus data), but in his account with telling drama and artistry he reinterprets the data and reveals the deeper meaning of these cures. The cure encases the transcendental revelation of God found in him; as Jesus "gives" human light the reader knows that he is more profoundly "giving" himself—God's light. But the drama that ensues also indicates that his desire to give light is often opposed by "darkness." As beautiful as his light is, there are many who lock themselves into their personal world of "darkness" and who seek no part in it; they love "darkness" more than light (c. 3:19). Jesus' light is beautiful but comes through a "death to self" and many are unwilling to give up the "darkness" in their lives to receive it. As earlier, "darkness" opposed Jesus without much success, so "'darkness" will oppose one sharing Jesus' light, but without much success. It cannot snatch his new light from him; by remaining faithful and open to Jesus, the former blind man in fact receives more and more of Jesus' light.

With masterful irony John shows that disbelieving "darkness" is little interested or impressed with Jesus' light. First, the man is personally overwhelmed with what has happened to him (as other honest and open observers should be), and yet his "neighbors" debate about the beggar's identity (vv. 8-9) . . . is this the blind fellow or isn't it? . . . he looks so different (is this so strange? . . . he has just experienced light after a life-time of darkness) . . . well, what happened? . . . tell us again, what happened? . . . Jesus, you say, did this . . . well, where is he (v. 11)? One would expect and hope for a *different* reaction: . . . something like . . . how beautiful, how wonderful! Whoever did this *must surely be from*

God. Didn't Jesus say just recently at Tabernacles (c. 8) that he was the "light of the world?" . . . could this possibly be a "sign" to reveal the truth of his claim there? But since none of the man's "neighbors" is flashing-back or making expected connections between the sign and Jesus' words in chapter 8, the point seems to be clearly made: "darkness" does not easily recognize light, even when overwhelmingly confronted with its beauty.

The blind man has received light and can receive more if he remains faithful to Jesus as the source of his light. Presently Jesus is seen only as the good "man" who restored his sight (v. 11). Pressures will mount to dissuade him from believing that Jesus gave him new light, but the man will never back away from this conviction. He is next taken to the Pharisees who far from finding the cure a "work of God" (vv. 3-4), find the one who did it to be a violator of the Sabbath Law (kneading material for ointments and unnecessarily initiating cures for people not in life-threatening situations on the Sabbath are not allowed according to their "reading" of the Law). Johannine "readers," however, know that as a work of *ego-eimi-with-us*, the giving of life to blind eyes is not a breaking of the Sabbath. It is a "work of God." If Jesus is in union with the Father and works in tandem with him, then he is allowed to give life on the Sabbath as God does.

But "darkness" is not about to surrender to Jesus as *ego-eimi-with-us*, or as the *giver-of-light-from-above*, so it seeks another telling of the cure in hopes of discovering some other source for the light this man has received. The former blind man consistently attributes his new light to Jesus (v. 15). Since he remains faithful to the source of his light, that source will further identify himself. While "darkness" finds Jesus not to be from God because he breaks the Sabbath, the former blind man finds Jesus to be certainly a "prophet" (a common Jewish expression for "one who comes with a mission and message from God") (v. 17). No need for Jesus to tell readers again the Pharisees love "darkness" more than light. The story itself shows they are blind to the light-giving works of God, and Christians who are "fearful" of them should "fear" them no more; they are blind leaders and not conveyors of God's truth. As the former blind man illustrates the proper attitude and option readers should take toward the light, the Pharisees illustrate the wrong attitude and option. This man is obviously a *model* for the Church of John (some of whom are vacillating in their Christian faith); he remains faithful to Jesus' light, no matter what the pressures are to deny Jesus as the source of light.

The miracle, which, after its first telling, has now been retold three times, is still not believed to be a true giving-of-light to a blind man (v. 18). "Darkness" faced with an obvious giving-of-light sign can only save face by saying it never happened. The man must be a liar; he was not really blind to begin with. So his parents are summoned. Admitting they are the man's parents and that he was truly born blind, they refuse to speak about the "light" now in their sons's eyes. This part of the chapter especially shows that John is adjusting the miracle data to the problems of his own Church in its disputes with the Synagogue (see the "particular comments" at the end of the chapter for some historical notes behind these disputes). The parents are "fearful" of being excluded from the Synagogue if they acknowledge Jesus as a light-giving Messiah (this is more a problem of ca. 85-90 AD than ca. 27-30 AD) and so they do not take a stand for Jesus. As the former blind man is a model of the "good disciple" by his unshakable profession of faith, so his parents are examples of "crypto-Christians" with shallow faith who hope to remain *secret* believers while remaining in the Synagogue. This to John is reprehensible; no one can believe Jesus is the light of the world and not profess him openly (vv. 18-23).

With verses 24-33, the former blind man is summoned a second time before the Pharisees. His words to them will give John's people a short, eloquent, apologetical way of defending Jesus as the "light of the world." The Pharisee-Synagogue argument against Jesus is that he blasphemes, breaks the law, and as a man crucified (remember, all gospels are post-Resurrection "look back—read back" documents) is obviously not the Messiah but a "sinner." And those who believe in him are sinners, too; they tell lies like *their Jesus*. Confess . . . you were *not* blind (no light ever came to you). Repent your lies . . . "give glory to God" (v. 24). Nice try. But the blind man is not about to deny Jesus or what he did for him. He speaks with abrupt and telling eloquence. The facts of the matter are these: I was blind . . . Jesus came to me . . . and now I see (v. 25). You people obviously pay little attention to what Jesus does or to what *we* (i.e. the Church of John; the use of *we* in vv. 27 and 31 shows the episode is refashioned in light of the on-going Church-Synagogue disputes) say about him. How many signs must he work . . .

how many times must *"we" repeat* what he said and did . . . to convince you that neither Jesus nor *"we"* sin by giving and receiving light? It is not some work of magic; it was God's light sent to us in Jesus that we received.

The former blind man ironically turns the pressures exerted on him back on his adversaries. Is the reason they want so many "repeat explanations" of this work of light because they find it so beautiful that they too wish to become disciples of the man who did it? (v. 27) Obviously they have no such intent. The tragic irony is that the Synagogue opposes and prefers Moses to Jesus; masters in the laws and methods of Moses, they are blind to *new* revelations coming from Moses' God. Moses, in fact, had foretold another prophet would come to Israel with *new* revelations (Dt 18:18). Strange, Moses' *origins* are clear to them, but not Jesus' (v. 29); although Jesus has never been bashful in speaking about his origins. Strange, Moses' *signs* revealed that God was on his side, but Jesus' *signs* (and there are now six) reveal nothing to the Pharisees about whose side Jesus is on.

Could it be that they never really look or try to *see through the signs* to Jesus' *origins*? No one can give what he does not have. If Jesus gave light, it must be that he possesses it. Before he worked it, he notified all that what he was about to do was a "work of God." If physical light (a good thing, a blessing) was given to eyes in darkness (an evil condition) it must be that in doing good and destroying evil he was doing a "work of God." Only God can give light. Jesus at the feast (c. 8) claimed to be the "light of the world." It must be that the light in the blind man's eyes is a revelation in human terms of the light Jesus brings from above. No sinner could give (and according to the OT, no one had ever given) sight to a person *born* blind. Since the light came from Jesus, he cannot be a sinner (vv. 30-33).

This man now sees deeply into who Jesus is and thus the reader knows he is the recipient of Jesus' transcendental light (the "from God" character of Jesus) as well as physical sight. Here is a simple beggar, a "sinner," ignorant of Moses and the Law and yet he has completely unmasked the shallow complaints and arguments of the feared authority-figures of Judaism. These people do not seek God's light or truth, for the truth of God and Jesus is present to them in the *true* eyes and *true* words (his "lecture" as they sarcastically put it, v. 34) of the blind man and they refuse to see or hear it. They have no way to answer this man's theological defense of Jesus as "light of the world" except to ridicule him. They say he is steeped in sin; his blindness shows that. *And yet he is no longer blind!* "Darkness" has its own strange and senseless logic. It is the Pharisees who are steeped in sin, for they refuse to see light not only in Jesus but in those who obviously share it.

And so he is expelled (v. 34). Again, this man, besides being a recipient of Jesus' light, is one who represents those in John's Church who have been expelled from the Synagogue. The man obviously serves the role of *model* for these members. His faith in Jesus as light has been tested, pressured, insulted, persecuted, and finally punished by exclusion from the Synagogue, and yet he refuses to deny Jesus as the source of his light. His explanation of the sign and Jesus' part in it is simple, direct, totally convincing. John's people need but repeat the sign over and over again along with the man's simple defense of Jesus to present convincing proof that Jesus, true to his words at Tabernacles, is indeed the "light of the world."

Still, to be excluded from the familiar *locus* of one's religious and cultural heritage is not easy to accept, and so Jesus goes directly to the man expelled (6:37; 10:28) to assure him that in *losing* the Synagogue he has actually *found* the Son of Man, the Savior and Judge of the world. Not only has the man found light for his eyes, he discovers the deepest meaning of Jesus. The title, Son of Man, was used in chapter 8 where Jesus predicted his Passion, his "lifting up (8:28). It was earlier used to foretell this "hour" in 3:14, and will be used again, in 12:32-34, for the same purpose. It will be in Jesus' *death* (and Resurrection) that he will be fully revealed as *ego-eimi-with-us* giving his life and light for the world. The Son of man is the one God sends from heaven to reveal himself and his love. It is especially in the *death* of the sent-one as *man* that he will reveal *in human terms* the giving nature of *God's* love. This giving of the Son of Man is also God's judgment on the world, for the Son can be believed in or rejected; belief brings to believers the given life and light that Jesus offers in his "lifting up" . . . rejection denies one access to the life and love offered there. It brings only "darkness." The man who began the chapter walking in darkness walks in it no longer; he not only has his human vision, he has full spiritual vision into the transcendental mystery of who Jesus is—the eternal, saving, judging Son of Man (a mystery to be worshipped). In a sense, excluded from rightfully participating in his own *Jewish* history, he ends up possessing the light of the incarnate Lord of *all* history.

It is a tragedy that many "Jews" rejected the fuller light that came in Jesus, revealed by *word* in chapter 8, revealed in a *sign* in chapter 9. Jesus does not seek to reject or undo Jewish history, only to fulfill it. If they were open and sought more light than they had, they would have found new and fuller light in him. But they refused to see. Jesus' light in its fullest meaning is an *offering* . . . it only becomes *judgment* when it is refused. The sin of the Pharisees is thinking that they have full light when full light is found only in Jesus (v. 40-41).

Here again, John's dualism may appear too heavy for modern taste (allowing for few if any subtleties to explain the conflict between Christ-ian and non-Christian Jews), but his background is strongly dualistic to begin with, and the situation confronting his Church calls for a clear statement on his part of the options, good and bad, his people face. Ideally Jewish members of his Church should be able to be Jews and Christians at the same time. The situation ca. 85-95 AD, however, no longer permits this; a choice must be made. In leaving the Synagogue, will Christians lose their advantage before God, suffer some irreplace-able loss? The episode shows them they lose nothing of eternal value; they rather gain the Son of Man, the light of the world, God's Savior and Judge. It is the Synagogue that suffers loss; they choose to exclude from their lives the light and life of God present in Jesus.

Although the episode is primarily the revelation that Jesus is the light sent by God to the world, there seems clearly to be present in the chapter a baptismal motif. Early Christian history often associated this chapter with the Sacrament. Several paintings in the catacombs illustrate that the episode had a baptismal meaning for early Christians. The chapter was seen as teaching the theology of Baptism in a story and was used in the instructional preparation of catechumens for their Baptisms. Often it was read as a preface for the actual celebration of Baptism. The chapter seems to contain ritual actions close to those used in early forms of Baptism, e.g., the blind man is "anointed" (Jesus uses spittle in his anointing and so did early Christian ministers of the Sacrament; they used spittle *and* oil). The blind man is asked to *go into* the pool (much as the candidates for Baptism *went into* baptismal pools). The pool is given the name, "Christ." Paul, for one, taught Christians (Rm 6:3-4) that the pool they plunged into at Baptism was *Christ's death*. Near parallels to ancient baptismal scrutinies seem present in the chapter, e.g., the man is asked about Jesus . . . "who do you say he is" (a question asked of baptismal candidates). The man replies . . . "he is a prophet," v. 17 (close to what the candidates for Baptism were expected to respond . . . "he is the Christ"). The man is asked if he "believes in the Son of Man?" (as the candidates later were asked if they believed . . . "Jesus was the Son of God," v. 35). Verse 38, "I do believe," is viewed by some scholars as an editorial insert from the actual profession of faith asked of the baptismal candidates in John's Church. Finally, Baptism was spoken of as a mystery of "light" or "enlightenment" even in some books of the NT (e.g., Ac 9:17 f; Heb 6:4; 10:32; I P 2:9) and in the writings of the early Fathers (e.g., Justin, *First Apology* 61:13, PG 6:421). Certainly a gospel that shows the Word of God came encased in the symbol of human flesh, is not adverse to showing that the Word is still met in the faith-encounters of his Church under the symbols of bread (c. 6) and water (c. 9).

FURTHER PARTICULAR COMMENTS:

Verse 22, anybody who confessed Jesus as Messiah *would be put out of the Synagogue* . . . As noted, much of the gospel since c. 5, has been set against the backdrop of disputes that took place between Christian and non-Christian Jews in the Synagogue (scholars think these disputes took place through the decade of the eighties AD). Much of these disputes centered around faith in Jesus as Messiah, especially it seems around faith in Jesus as "high" Messiah. Some time before the gospel was written, many Christian Jews because of their faith in Jesus were permanently expelled from the Synagogue (9:22; 15:20; some possibly executed as heretics, 16:2). As the gospel is being written the expulsions could still be taking place; certainly many are feeling the pain of ostracism and are experiencing various forms of persecution from the Synagogue.

How this came about is pretty much an accident of history, since Judaism had been sufficiently pluralistic to be able to tolerate widely differing forms of faith-expression. But after the Jewish-Roman wars and the chaos that followed the destruction of the Temple, with the exile of many Jews from Jerusalem, a pluralistic approach to "being a Jew" proved very difficult to sustain. Jamnia, already a religious center for Judaism, with the destruction of Jerusalem became the leading center for the teaching of the Jewish faith. As it happened, Jamnia was dominated by the Pharisees, and their form of Jewish faith "won out" over other formerly tolerated expressions. Pharisee-rabbis became the leaders of the Judaism that survived the Jewish rebellion. To keep exiled Jews loyal to their religion, the Pharisees put great stress on the strict observance of the Mosaic Law, as interpreted by them. Messianism continued as a tenet of faith, but "true messianism" was seen as that which conformed to the expectations Pharisees had for the Messiah. Most Pharisees, controlling the Synagogues, were ill-disposed to accept the "high" messianism and the allegded anti-Temple, anti-Moses, anti-Law attitudes of the Christians. And so to weed out this very vocal and disruptive group, the rabbis reintroduced ancient Synagogue prayers (the Eighteen Benedictions so called) and reworked the Twelfth Benediction so that it became a prayer to God to reveal and expose (even "curse") all who "deviated" from the true faith of Israel (the Christians would surely qualify as deviators, or heretics). These prayers were required to be recited each Sabbath. This made public decision for or against Jesus critical and imperative. Christians had to make public profession of their faith; or at the very least they had to refuse to say the "curse against the deviators "prayer," but in so doing they were exposed as minim, heretics, and expelled. Some (like the parents in this episode) attempted to *hide* their faith in Jesus so that they could remain in the Synagogue (John shows little patience with these people, known as the "crypto-Christians" cf., also 12:42-43). It is understandable why some would attempt to keep their faith *secret*. It took an immense act of sacrifice for Christian Jews to leave the Synagogue; it was their religious, socio-economic and cultural matrix. To leave it was to leave the "family" and all the advantages that implied. It seemed as though they were again being sent into exile; this time by their own family (1:11).

So the "Jews" in John's gospel are for the most part those who expelled Christian Jews from the Synagogue (ca. 80-95 AD). These "Jews" had written Jesus off as a false Messiah; they considered his disciples, minim, heretics, who were leading the children of Abraham astray from the true faith (as interpreted by the Pharisees; note, few other anti-Jesus Jewish groups are even mentioned in the gospel). This dispute and expulsion and its continuing effects would naturally compound John's natively strong dualistic manner of speaking.

The blind man, however, gives Christians who were expelled a very eloquent and forceful means of countering the arguments of those who expelled them. The position of the Pharisees is revealed to be ominously "dark" in comparison to that of Jesus which is filled with light. And besides, the brilliance of a beautiful pearl is best displayed against a dark background.

Chapter 10

GENERAL COMMENTS (and reflections):

The Pharisees, religious shepherds of Israel, have expelled the former blind man from the Synagogue, because he accepts and defends Jesus as the source of his new light. Jesus has given him light for his eyes and also the light of faith to penetrate his "from heaven" identity. Chapter 9 has shown that the shepherds who expelled him suffer a far worse blindness than he formerly knew; they are blind to God's love and light present in Jesus. Those who are "excommunicated" by such blind and uncaring shepherds need have no fear of them or regret. They will find in Jesus not only light from God but a Good Shepherd who will keep them safe in his light and provide them access to God's life.

As this chapter begins, the theological and liturgical ambience of the feast of Tabernacles lingers on; it was at this "feast of light" that Jesus identified himself as God's "light" (the blind man is spoken of again in v. 21). The coming feast of Dedication, at which Jesus will arrive in v. 22, is also a "feast of light" and Jesus, by being there, will reinforce the theme that he is the light of the world who reveals and shares God's light with believers. It will also provide the material for Jesus' words in the early verses of the chapter. This relatively new feast (est. ca. 165 BC), due to its historical origins and a biblical prophecy associated with it, Ezekiel c. 34 (possibly a Synagogue reading for the feast) invokes thoughts in the minds of devout Jews of the "good and bad shepherds" Israel had known in her history (since so many of her great leaders had been shepherds, e.g., the Patriarchs, Moses, David, etc., the term became a synonym for Israel's leaders, both spiritual and national). Ezekiel's prophecy was made during the Jewish exile in Babylon (ca. 587-537 BC). The prophet attributed the "disastrous day" (the destruction of Jerusalem and foreign exile) in part to the corrupt shepherding Israelites experienced before the exile, which still continued during the exile. He spoke particularly of Yahweh's displeasure at the selfish and uncaring attitudes of Israel's shepherd-leaders and spoke of a day when God (always considered the principal, transcendental Shepherd of Israel: cf., e.g., Ps 23; 78:52; Is 40:11; Jr 31:10, etc.) would take a more immediate and personal hand in the shepherding of his people. It was assumed by many that this would happen at the coming of the New Age. Since chapter 34 of Ezekiel will help the reader understand Jesus' words in vv. 1-18, we note here pertinent parts of it:

> . . . prophesy against the shepherds of Israel . . . who feed themselves and yet fail to feed their flocks . . . who sacrifice the sheep . . . who fail to make the weak strong . . . to bring back strays or look for the lost . . . who rule cruelly and violently . . . for want of a shepherd my sheep are scattered . . . I will call these shepherds to account . . . I will not allow them to feed my flock . . . I am going to look after them myself . . . I shall bring them back . . . feed them in good pastures . . . I myself will be their pastor . . . it is the Lord Yahweh who speaks . . . I shall be a GOOD SHEPHERD to them (Ezk 34:2-16).

Four centuries after the Babylonian exile, the Israelites once more fell under foreign and pagan influence. Israel's shepherd-leaders again seemed more interested in "feeding themselves than the flock" and created situations that contributed to the profanation and desecration of the Temple by the Syrians. Even a statue to Baal (oriental Zeus) was erected on the altar of holocausts (1 Mc 1 f). Ezekiel's words of warning seemed as appropriate during the Syrian domination as during the exile in Babylon. Through the Maccabees (2 Mc 4:1-29) these pagan invaders were driven from the land. The Temple was reclaimed and purified and a new Altar of holocausts was built and consecrated. The feast was established to celebrate the purifying of the Temple and the *dedication* of a new Altar to Yahweh. In their prayers devout Jews thanked God for the "zealous shepherds" he had given them to effect this liberation. As the years went by and "shepherds" became less zealous in keeping Israel free from political and religious persecution, the annual celebration of the feast revived hopes that Ezekiel's prophecy would come true and find Yahweh taking a more personal hand in the shepherding of Israel.

John views Jesus' day and his own as a time when Ezekiel's warnings seemed still as appropriate as ever. Israel's shepherds (in John's time, the Pharisees almost exclusively) in their "blindness" and darkness were robbing God's people of the light God had sent them. Rather than feed the flock with the food God was providing them, they deprived the people of the "bread from heaven" and the "living waters" of Jesus. But John knows that in Jesus God has fulfilled in fullest measure the prophecy of Ezekiel. His Jesus is *Yahweh's-Son-come-to-Israel* who personally provides for her spiritual Shepherding. Jesus in chapter 10 will again speak as the "high" Christ, but now under the image of the GOOD or MODEL SHEPHERD. The former blind man (and other Jewish members of his Church) may be physically separated from the Synagogue, from their former shepherds, but they are not spiritually separated from Israel or God's promised Shepherd. They have for Shepherd, Jesus the "sent one," Yahweh's Son, the light of the world. What they are separated from is the uncaring, blind shepherds of "darkness," indicted by the God of Ezekiel.

Jesus, the Gate and the Shepherd

It has been noted that parables, so commonly used in the Synoptic gospels (and doubtless reflective of Jesus' own teaching style), are not used by John to summarize Jesus' message. He prefers the "unified discourse" instead. Chapter 10, however, indicates that John seems to have had access to some of Jesus' parables, for here we have a discourse based on two of them: one about a gate, the other about a shepherd. Since both parables involve *sheep* (a Jesus data word for repentant believers; cf., e.g. Lk 15:4-7; Mt 18:12-14), John by merging them in a discourse can show how Jesus generously provides his sheep with the knowledge of God and a sharing in his life. Jesus does not tell a story so much as use the terms of two stories to further identify himself (in the process, he seems to mix a metaphor). Some of John's people have just been cut loose from their Jewish moorings by their Pharisee shepherds. These Pharisees, like earlier leaders (at the time of the Babylonian and Syrian "captivities") do not provide the people with full gate-access to God, nor do they shepherd

Israel selflessly and caringly, and so they will be contrasted with Jesus who is God's approved access-gate for Israel's sheep, as well as the Model or Good Shepherd who cares for and feeds them.

The new descriptive terms for Jesus' self-identification become clearer as we recall the shepherding practices of ancient Palestine. At night several flocks of sheep would be kept in a common fenced corral behind a sturdy gate, with a trusted sentry assigned to guard the gate and watch out for the sheep. When morning came, individual shepherds returned to the corral, were recognized by the gate-keeper, and let in to "call" their particular sheep by name. Sheep only came when they recognized the voice of their shepherd. In a sense sheep were like personal pets, each had its own name, knew it, and at the voice-call of the shepherd came running to follow him. The shepherd then led them out to pasture. The gate kept them safe at night from their enemies, predatory animals and thieves who could steal and kill them; it allowed them access to their shepherd in the morning. The shepherd looked out for their feeding and protection during the day. The terms are now sorted out: a gate, a shepherd, sheep in a sheepfold. And the elements of Johannine "darkness" are here too: thieves, bandits, strangers. In the coming verses Jesus will explain that he is the gate *and* the shepherd . . . the present leaders of Israel are thieves, bandits, and strangers, with no true interest in the sheep; they are more concerned about themselves and their narrow views of religion than the good of the sheep (vv. 1-13). The prophecy of Ezekiel (c. 34) seems to foretell their selfish, careless shepherding, while at the same time pointing to the coming of Jesus as the selfless, caring Shepherd.

The "Jews" (and these seem to be the Pharisees, since no other Jews have entered the gospel since c. 9) fail to detect whom the terms correspond to, so Jesus clarifies the key terms for them. He tells them *he is the Gate* (v. 7). And since Jesus introduces this self-identification with an "*ego eimi*," the implication is that he speaks as the "high" Christ, the one sent by God to reveal himself to the world. Scholars see Ps 118:20 as Jesus' biblical source for this term . . . "this is the *gate of Yahweh* . . . the good man enters *through* it." God is found as one goes *through the gate*. Jesus will seem to claim again in 14:6 that he provides a similar gate-access to God when he tells his disciples at the Last Supper: " . . . *I am* the *Way* . . . no one comes to the Father except *through me*." As the one who reveals the Father, he thus provides visible human gate-access to God (who sees him, sees the Father; who comes to him, finds the Father). The access to the that Father Jesus provides is a sharing access, for through him one can find pasture and fullness of life (vv. 9-10). Jesus invites all to share in his heavenly bread (6:35 f), his living waters (4:14; 7:38), his light from above (8:12; 9:5). Now the *ego eimis* heard here seem to imply that the bread, water and light of Jesus are *tandem food* and *light*. In Jesus one finds not only his own food but the Father's (*ego eimi's*) as well . . . it is food *"to the full"* (v. 10). And God's full life comes through "entering the gate" (v. 9) . . . one must come to Jesus, go *through Jesus* . . . and this is *faith* . . . the necessary "ticket" that gets one to and through the gate.

"All who came before me" (v. 8) could include the whole gamut of opposing shepherds that frustrated people from recognizing or coming to Jesus as "gate"; surely in John's time, this would include the Pharisees. In John's strong dualistic mindset he sees them as people of "darkness" who "steal" and "kill" the sheep (vv. 8, 10), at least in the sense that they prevent God's sheep access to the full life and pastures he wants for them. The Pharisees have committed the fatal sin: they themselves reject the light God sends and deprive others from coming to that full light. Ezekiel's warnings seem particularly aimed at them: they feed themselves, but not the flock (whom they deprive of Jesus' heavenly bread, living water, and light) . . . they sacrifice the sheep . . . they rule them cruelly; whereas in Jesus the sheep can find a good Shepherd and rich pastures (Ezk 34:2-16).

As the prophet spoke of Yahweh, the heavenly Shepherd of Israel, assuming more direct care of his flock (Ezk 34:15-16), so Jesus by using his Father's name, *ego eimi*, seems to identify himself as the expected Shepherd of Ezekiel (v. 11) And uniquely so! Present shepherds, as Ezekiel had warned, let God's sheep be snatched, scattered and sacrificed; they work only for hire and their own selfish interest. But Jesus as Shepherd works solely for God and the flock and he is to sacrifice his life selflessly for the sheep. As the Father loves them by sending his Son (3:16-17), Jesus will show that love by giving his life in death for them. His willingness to die indicates the depth of his love. One sees here John's positive interpretation of Jesus' death. It is not a negative work done by "darkness." It is a work of sacrificial love accomplished by Jesus and the Father for the love of the flock (vv. 11-13). It will provide them with the fullest possible pasture and life (vv. 9-10).

Verses 14-15, further point up the fact that the relationship which exists between Jesus as Shepherd and believers as his flock is one of interpersonal love. He "knows" them and they "know" him. In the biblical use of the word, when persons "know" each other this implies that there is deep, intimate understanding and shared love between them. The fact that Jesus is to die for his sheep again underscores this meaning (as he will explicitly say in 15:13 . . . his dying manifests his great personal love for his disciples). Jesus thus informs believers that the "knowing love" which exists between him and the Father is to be shared with them. Not only is there something beautiful going on between him and the Father, but now believers are in on that beautiful "knowing."

Unlike the Pharisees, who seek to limit their flock to those who reflect their own narrow views of God and salvation, Jesus seeks to bring all sheep into his fold (v. 16). Certainly this indicates that Jesus has a special interest in bringing yet unconverted Jews and Gentiles into his flock (although many are there already). Perhaps John is thinking too of other nearby Christian Churches who do not yet share the depth of his understanding of Jesus as the "high" Christ. Jesus the Shepherd thus calls all Christians to an even deeper faith in him and to a union that will merge the "several Christian flocks" into "one fold." Jesus like the Yahweh-Shepherd of Ezekiel's prophecy is one who gathers and unites; he is not a scatterer like the Pharisees (Ezk 34:2-16).

Jesus has shown he is a deeply loving and caring Shepherd because he dies for his sheep. But in light of the horrible form his death took, Jesus, in vv. 17-18, must reveal again as he did in 3:16-17, the Johannine understanding of this death. As mentioned before, many Jews saw the crucifixion as a "stumbling block," a sign of God's disapproval, that Jesus was in fact a condemned sinner. John has penetrated the deeper meaning of this death and sees it as a "positive work of love." The Father did not tell Jesus to get himself killed. He told him to show his people how much he loves them. One shows love by giving of oneself and Jesus gave himself fully in death. It is little matter that "darkness" conspires to destroy him. While it plots and schemes, a more profound plot is being acted out: God's eternal love incarnated in his Son is being "given up" so that the world might share in it. And the remarkable beauty of Jesus' death is not only that through it believers are able to share in the love of

Jesus and the Father, but in it and the Resurrection they see that their "dying Shepherd" ultimately transcends death, survives to be an *eternal Shepherd*. His death proves the depth of his love and his death-unto-Resurrection shows that this love is to be shared with believers *forever*. The Shepherd of Christians is indeed what Ezekiel implied, *ego eimi* Shepherding them *forever* (vv. 17—18).

As attractive as a totally loving and eternal Shepherd is to believers, it is not so appealing to those who close their minds and hearts to Jesus' words and works. Some regard a "descending-ascending" Messiah difficult to accept, summarily dismiss him, and (true to the polemics of the time) call him possessed and insane. John again shows that Jesus does not force his Shepherding or profound love on anyone; he is a Shepherd of light and life who can be opted for or against. If one opens one's spirit to Jesus as the blind man did, then such a one receives light. If one judges Jesus by human standards and expectations and seeks no new word about God from him, then Jesus sounds very much the blasphemer and possessed. But in doing so one chooses to live without the Good Shepherd. This is the option of "darkness" (vv. 19-21).

The Feast of Dedication

With the reference to the blind man in v. 21, John wants the reader to know that his theme of Jesus as the light of the world still continues. And as "darkness" opposed Jesus' "light" at Tabernacles, so it will continue to oppose him at the feast of Dedication. Set in the middle of December (a time of natural darkness), the week-long feast is also a "feast of lights" (Hanukkah). The Temple, whose reclaiming and restoration is being celebrated, is illuminated brightly, as are the streets and homes of Jerusalem. As the Jews thank God for the present Temple and Altar (in the ambience of beautiful lights everywhere), Jesus by his presence and solemn declaration that he is the "high" Christ, shows again that he is the New Temple and God's consecrated Altar (this is part of the *light* that God reveals to the world through him.) But, as the reader knows, when Jesus reveals himself as *light* from above, "darkness" is always present to oppose him. "Darkness" does not accept him as the divine Shepherd Yahweh sends; still, it knows that Jesus called himself a *Shepherd*. To many, the term *shepherd* connoted the coming of a new Davidic Messiah (cf., again, Ezk 34:23f; these verses show that Yahweh's "Shepherd coming" was to be accompanied by the arrival of a new David also) who, it was assumed, would overcome Israel's political enemies (the feast, it seems, had political overtones and nurtured dreams of political freedom through the efforts of a new military-type "David"). "Darkness" *demands* to know if Jesus is claiming to be *this kind* of (Davidic) Messiah (v. 24). The *insistence* of some to know this recalls the trial of Jesus before the Jews in the Synoptics; there was this same kind of insistence there (cf., e.g., Lk 22:67; Mk 14:53-65). And so it seems that John moves and transposes some of the trial material here for the remainder of chapter 10, so that Jesus can unequivocally reveal that he *is* indeed the Messiah, but one (as the reader has seen time and again) far beyond the limited, earthbound expectations of many Jews. He *is* the "high" Messiah (vv. 25-30).

Jesus informs them of what the gospel has been at pains to show since the beginning—that he has been sent by the Father and his *works* reveal this fact. If he is from God and works in tandem with the Father, giving light and life to believers, who else could he be but the Messiah? A "high" Messiah *a fortiori* contains all possible authentic *lower* expectations Israel associates with the person and title. The reason many do not see this is because they refuse to have him as their Shepherd, to be his disciple-sheep, listening openly to his words, viewing his works as further revelations that his words are true (vv. 26-27). They look and listen but really do not see or hear. What Jesus has been saying by strong implication for some time, he now says clearly and explicitly, that as Messiah he is the visible encasement of God's invisible presence . . . that all his words and deeds are tandem revelations made in union with the Father . . . "the Father and I are one" (v. 30).

Jesus never speaks or works alone. He has never set himself up as a blaspheming solo competitor to God. He is the sent-Agent of God, the one who works in his name, whose power derives from God. Jesus would not nor could not speak or act as he does if this were not so. His life and light-giving signs have revealed the life and light-giving Father with whom he is united. John's readers would instinctively be "recalling" the nearby "noble works" (v. 32) of the blind man's cure and the raising of Lazarus as well as Jesus' own Resurrection. But in the thinking of some "Jews," Jesus cannot claim a tandem union with God. He is, after all, only a man. This, of course, shows how little they pay attention. The gospel is not about a man claiming to be blasphemously close to God. It is about the Word of God becoming man and coming wonderfully close to his own people. But this is "too hard" for some to believe, and so, not believing Jesus, the man, he becomes for them the blasphemer (vv. 31-33). The fitting penalty for such arrogance is, of course, stoning (Lv 24:16).

Since the Pharisees do not listen to Jesus (he tells lies), perhaps they will listen to their Scriptures (which cannot lie; vv. 34-36). Jesus (not unlike the clever rabbis of his time) quotes from Ps 82:6. There the Judges who followed Moses as leader-shepherds of Israel (some corrupt and dishonest, by the way) were spoken of as "equals to God" because they were his appointed instruments to rule Israel and to *reveal his words* and will to the people. They were to make fair *judgments* in the earthly affairs of God's flock. The psalm said of these people: "You are *gods . . . sons of the Most High.*" If such titles can be given to corrupt and mortal judges, Jesus has even more right to use them, for *he is God's Word; he is the sent Son of God; he is God's judgment* on the world. And unlike the "works" of many of the unjust shepherds and judges of Israel, Jesus' "works" have always revealed the Father's love and will for Israel. In him Israel has at last found its authentically true Shepherd and just Judge (Ezk 34:22-23).

Jesus, moreover, reminds them during the feast that he is not a usurper of God's titles or functions. He comes as one "consecrated" and "sent" (v. 36). The feast, a thanksgiving for the Temple and Altar restored to purity after their desecration by pagans, gives Jesus again an opportunity to identify himself as God's perfect Temple and Altar on earth. Not only is Jesus a Shepherd and Judge who speaks about God . . . he is the *locus* where one encounters God. To defile God's Temple and Altar is to defile God; to deny that Jesus' works are also the Father's, is to deny the Father. In Jewish law the works of one *sent* in a "consecrated," official and approved way, were to be understood as the *very works* of the "consecrating" sender. The officially-*sent-one* could speak with the full authority of the *sender*. Jesus has never taken advantage of the role of the "sent one"; his "works" have always reflected the Father and his will for the world. All of them show God anxious to share with his people life, light and love (again, the nearby "signs" of the blind man, Lazarus and the Resurrection eloquently reveal this). If one looked at Jesus' signs openly, the "Father's presence" in them would be seen. God is not asking people to believe in an *unknown*; he *makes* himself and his will *known* in Jesus' words and *signs* (v. 37). The chapter ends with Jesus restating in an explicit way that he is the "high" Christ. Jesus' flesh not only encases his own spirit; in a human way it encases the spiritual being and presence of the Father as well (v. 38). "Darkness" again attempts to extinguish the light but in this gospel, this cannot be done. Jesus' light will be surrendered for the world. It will not be taken from him (v. 39).

As JB is again referred to (vv. 40-42), scholars believe the public ministry of Jesus in an earlier form of the gospel concluded with this chapter (thus cc's. 11-12 are seen as later supplementary additions to the Book of Signs). The public ministry began with JB's witness of Jesus in chapter 1. As Jesus was identified as the Messiah then, in the subsequent nine chapters, having listened to and seen Jesus' words and works, the reader has come to see that he is indeed the Messiah, but an even *greater* Messiah than JB recognized.

Chapter 11

GENERAL COMMENTS (and reflections):

In chapter 10 Jesus identified himself as the "dying and rising" Shepherd (10:17-18). His sheep love him and know his voice; he loves them and knows them by name (10:3). They come when he calls (10:4); he leads them to eternal, never-ending life. None of them will perish or be snatched from him or his Father (10:27-29). This is saying quite a bit, especially when the one who says it is about to die (two arrests and two stonings have already been attempted; three times the word has gone out that "he must die"; a firm decision on his execution will be reached at the close of this chapter). And now a beloved disciple, Lazarus, is about to die. Both the Shepherd and one of his sheep, in light of their imminent deaths, seem "snatchable" from the Father. Is the Jesus of chapter 10 to be believed?

Most disciples, after hearing Jesus' words and witnessing his six signs, would be convinced that Jesus speaks the truth when he says he is the Shepherd of eternal life. Certainly the new life in the cripple's legs and the light in the blind man's eyes would symbolize for them the eternality of the life and light Jesus possesses and offers. And yet a crucial element of Jesus' claims has not yet been fully "displayed." What about death? Can the Shepherd and the sheep *really* survive that and actually live on with the Father forever? The cures would seem strongly to infer that they can. But up to the blind man, the reader has "only" *seen* Jesus as healer, one who has effected wonderful cures with the living. The critical question is, is Jesus what he equivalently claimed to be in chapter 10 . . . the Shepherd of life beyond the grave . . . the Shepherd of Resurrection-Life? To be eternal light and to be seen as one who can share that light with believers forever, Jesus must give a "revelation display" that shows his "light" survives the one thing that *seems* to overcome it, namely, death.

Thus John has saved Jesus' most dramatic and convincing display that he is the Shepherd of eternal life until the end. The "glory" he contains and the glory he promises is glory-unto-eternal-life and nothing less. In this chapter the "deep love" that exists between Jesus and Lazarus is stressed; he is a believing and loving disciple, deeply loved by Jesus. There is no doubt about this (cf. vv. 3, 5, 11, 36). It could be said that Lazarus is put forth as a model believer; and more particularly he is a believer who suffers the seemingly light-and-life-ending enigma of human death. Is Jesus still *his* Shepherd, providing *him* with eternal life? In a sense, *if* there is an "eternal there" beyond death, Lazarus, in a few verses after the chapter opens, is "there." There is no doubt in Jesus' mind about the "eternal there"; he will say in v. 26, "he who believes in me *shall never die* at all." What can symbolically reveal this? A "cure" will not fully do it; and besides, Lazarus after four days is surely dead and beyond a cure. The sign that will display that Jesus' Shepherding role extends beyond death is to "bring back" one of his sheep who has passed beyond death. Only the Shepherd of eternal life . . . only a Shepherd of the Resurrection could bring back one of the sheep from "there." And the sign will be a dramatic prophecy of and preparation for what is to happen to Jesus the Shepherd in his own fast-approaching death. This sign will show that Jesus' death will be like Lazarus', a "door" to Resurrection, to eternal life and glory. "Darkness" thinks it has "snatched a sheep" from Jesus in the death of Lazarus; it plots and plans to "snatch" his own life away. The irony of such a plan is that rather than "snatch" anything from anybody, Jesus' death will insure eternal life for him and all his sheep. The most powerful weapon "darkness" seems to have against light is *human death*, and yet as things turn out it will be the "weapon" that Jesus uses to overcome "darkness" forever.

The Death and Raising of Lazarus

As the chapter begins, Jesus' close friend Lazarus is near death and his sisters inform Jesus. They seem to want him to hasten to Bethany to *cure* their brother (v. 3). Jesus refuses to come immediately, saying Lazarus' sickness is *not to end in death* (v. 4). Jesus could show his "power" by a cure; he seeks to show something more beautiful . . . to reveal that the "glory" he possesses from God is *eternally* communicable to believers. The refusal to come, looked at superficially, shows a lack of love and concern on his part. By the end of the episode the reader will see Jesus has given Lazarus a more profound gift of love than a few years of transitory earthly life. By delaying his departure for Bethany some days and letting Lazarus pass through the enigmatic "gate" of death, he will show he can even penetrate that enigma and reveal the eternal life and love that exist for his sheep who have passed through it. This is Jesus' work—to give *eternal* life, light and love; he must not let others reduce his work to that of "temporary healer," the here and now "lover" only. Jesus is the Shepherd of eternal life, eternal light and love and must reveal that clearly before he passes through the enigma of death himself.

And the shadow of the Cross pervades the chapter. Jesus' disciples fear that he is returning to Judea too soon. They fear that some form of death awaits him there if he goes back; the powers of "darkness" in their plots against him seem in the ascendancy (vv. 7-8). Jesus, however, is not fearful in the least. As the Shepherd of light he is not about to stumble now; he is eager to walk steadfastly toward his hour (vv. 9-10). And the sign he is about to work will show the deeper significance of his approaching hour. The raising of Lazarus will be a prophecy of his own death and Resurrection, which will be the last saving work his Father has given him to do; to defeat "darkness" radically by making his light eternally available to all.

Jesus informs his disciples that Lazarus has died. But dying as a "believer" is different than simply dying. Jesus attempts to see if his disciples now realize this. He says Lazarus has "fallen asleep"; he must be awakened (v. 11). The disciples' faith is not yet where Jesus wants it to be, and so they "misunderstand" him. Lazarus is not just physically asleep as they mistakenly interpret Jesus' words; he is dead and has passed beyond earthly life. But Lazarus is one of Jesus' sheep; he really "never dies." The miracle will show that what appears to be permanent death, in the case of believers, is not permanent at all. He hopes the sign will elicit the faith he seeks from them: that all who experience human death merely pass through the "gate" of Jesus to eternal life, having already possessed the life of their eternal Shepherd when they died (v. 15;

cf. also, 10:1-3, 7-10). Lazarus in death does not cease to be a sheep of the eternal Shepherd; Jesus feeds him with life forever. The "waking up" will show this (no one could be awakened, brought back, if he were not "there" to be brought back).

Thomas bravely decides to go to Judea and if need be to "die with Jesus" (v. 16). Immediate history shows this to be empty bravado, but nevertheless Thomas utters a prophecy. Unless Jesus "dies" there will be no "eternal awakening" for anyone; and unless Thomas dies to self and enters into Jesus' "death-Resurrection" he personally will never know that "awakening" (v. 16). Thomas ultimately came to Resurrection-faith (and it is assumed after years of arduous ministry) and did "die with him" (c. 20:28).

Since scholars think chapter 11 is an added clarifying chapter to the Book of Signs, which in an earlier version of the gospel ended with chapter 10, the "Jews" at Bethany seem less hostile to Jesus. Rather than serve the role of "darkness" (as they did in cc's. 5-10), they seem more receptive to Jesus. Some, witnessing the sign, will end up believers; others will be hesitant to forsake the influence of the Pharisees (v. 19). It is established in v. 17 that Lazarus is fully dead in the earthly sense; the "four days" since his death in rabbinic belief would signify that his body can no longer encase a human spirit. Jesus is not to work a *cure* then. The sign is not a revival of life but a symbol of Resurrection (Lazarus, as a believer, though seeming to be dead, is *not* "eternally" dead).

As Jesus arrives at Bethany days after Lazarus' death, Martha greets him with affection and yet with a "faith" that sees him more as "healer" than the "eternal Shepherd" who loves Lazarus actively beyond the grave. Rather than thank Jesus for providing eternal life for Lazarus, she seeks again something like a "cure" (v. 22). She treasures the human earthly company of Lazarus more than the eternal life her brother now knows. So Jesus must solicit from her a deeper faith and a more "Christian" view of death. He informs her: "your brother will rise again" (v. 23). While Jesus thinks in terms of that life coming in full measure to Lazarus as Jesus passes through his own death (he must be experiencing a limited, anticipative form of it now; he can't just be on "hold"), she thinks in terms of OT Jewish resurrection (cf., e.g. Dn 12:1-3; Ps 16:10-11; 2 M 7:13-14, 29) which many Jews for a hundred or more years believed in, which saw the good and bad rising at the end of the world: the righteous to receive their reward, the evil to be punished (v. 24).

Jesus as the sent "high Shepherd" of Yahweh (the *ego eimi* of v. 25 should indicate the "from heaven" aspect of Jesus' Shepherding powers) transcends and surpasses this earlier notion and belief. Jesus possesses eternal life and makes it available to all in the moment of his "lifting up": all one need do to receive it is to accept him as Shepherd (Lazarus has obviously done this). Jesus must inform Martha that there is an even more beautiful understanding of Resurrection than her partial view, and the source of it is standing there before her. Jesus for believers *is* the Resurrection . . . he *is* eternal life . . . all who live and die in faith live in his life forever. In a sense Martha's eschatology is a primitive form of "future eschatology." Jesus is not denying a fuller resurrection for Lazarus after his own Resurrection comes to pass. But John understands Jesus to grant his life *now* through *belief*, and so Jesus solicits from Martha belief in him as the source of realized-Resurrectional-life *now*. Since her brother Lazarus was obviously a loving disciple of Jesus, he knows that "resurrection" *now*, in some measure at least.

Jesus in verses 26-27, asks for this belief and Martha at least "technically" in the titles she gives him (Messiah, Son of God, the One who is to come into the world) seems to accept him as the "Resurrection and eternal life." In the immediate context of the episode she has not arrived this far yet (v. 39 shows that). But as a symbol of the post-Resurrection Church which hears vv. 25-26 in the light of Lazarus' and Jesus' Resurrection, she speaks for Christians who *then* see Jesus as "Resurrection and life."

Now "believing Martha" (and the Martha of v. 28 is in a sense post-Resurrection Martha), in true Johannine fashion, must go and tell others (her sister) of her faith. The "Mary" story seems pretty much a repeat of the "Martha" story (but her identity must be established, for she features in an episode in c. 12). What is Jesus' reaction to Mary's faith which sees him more as the "healer" than the "Shepherd of eternal life"? He shudders with the deepest emotion; he even cries (vv. 33, 35, 38). This is interpreted by the onlookers as Jesus' "great love" for Lazarus (v. 36). On this score there should be no doubt (cf. v. 11); but Jesus shows the depth of his love in the eternal life he grants Lazarus, not the earthly. Mary and the accompanying crowd obviously have inadequate faith. She seeks a "cure"; they seek some "wonderful healing" like that of the blind man (v. 37). If Jesus did work "cures," they were *signs* of something far more transcendental than the granting of human life. They were all signs that Jesus is the eternal Shepherd who provides death-transcending life for believers. For many he is still "Mr. Fixit" . . . the one who prevents death, not transcends it . . . for many he is still *not* the "Shepherd of Resurrection." To a degree "darkness" has overtaken believers. It is "darkness" that sees Lazarus' death and Jesus' own coming death as somehow a defeat. Jesus, then, as he approaches his own death, enters into the most crucial phase of his struggle with "darkness." Before he dies he must be believed in as the source of eternal life and Resurrection; otherwise with his death, "darkness" will seem to be the winner in this struggle. This must not happen. Death is not the enemy. Lack of belief in Jesus' power over death is the enemy! Jesus' greatest love for Lazarus will be seen in his death: disciples should know this (cf., e.g., 3:16-17; 8:28; 10:11; 15:13). Mary and the crowds preoccupied with a "temporary cure" show their inadequate faith and thus Jesus is moved to deep emotion and tears (cf., also a similar weeping of Jesus in Lk 19:41-44).

Martha now reverts to "pre-Resurrection" Martha and worries that obeying the Shepherd of life and rolling back the stone before the tomb will release unpleasant odors; she is not thinking that the action could reveal Jesus' lordship over life . . . his "glory" . . . that Lazarus is even *now* in union with the Resurrection and the life (v. 39). By this time, having spent "eleven chapters" with Jesus, she should know that he is not just the "healer" but as *ego-eimi-with-us* he is the depository and communicator of God's glory and light to the world.

Jesus, who so often has been accused of blasphemously making himself God's equal, when in truth he was working in tandem with the Father in everything he said and did, now makes sure that all witnesses of this sign realize it is not some work of a demon-possessed magician (who by the way would never solicit the Father's power); it is a work done in tandem with his Father. And so Jesus in vv. 41-42, audibly addresses the Father and reminds the bystanders that he performs this work as one "sent." This means the work must be considered the Father's as much as his own. Jesus as the "high" Christ who bears the same name as his Father can convey Resurrectional-eternal life to those who, like Lazarus, choose him for their Shepherd. "Darkness" thought it had put an end to a believer. Jesus will show that nothing puts an end to those who open themselves to his life and light. All believers are in the "Resurrection life" of their risen Shepherd. This must be demonstrated. Jesus transcends death, his own and the death of all believers. What symbolizes Jesus' possible inability to give transcendent Resurrectional life—the corrupting corpse of one of his sheep—must be "overcome." The miracle is a revealing demonstration that Jesus spoke the truth in v. 25 when he told Martha: "I am the Resurrection and the life." The "dead" Lazarus coming forth from the tomb is "*shown*" to be "*eternally* risen" by his "*earthly* raising." The Father and Jesus do not want us to believe in a completely *unknown* and *unknowable* mystery; the sign will and does *to a degree* make the mystery of Resurrection *knowable* to us in human terms.

As the sign happens, Jesus' words of chapter 10 come clearly to mind. Jesus, the Good Shepherd, calls one of his sheep by name to come and follow him (10:3-4) . . . ("Lazarus, come out!") . . . this sheep recognizing his voice follows his Shepherd (10:27) . . . ("the dead man came out") . . . now we know that, true to Jesus' promise in chapter 10, believers like Lazarus . . . have eternal life . . . they do not perish . . . they cannot be snatched away from him or the Father by "darkness" (10:28-29). Moreover the prophecy of Jesus spoken in 5:25-29, against those who denied his tandem union with the Father, seems fulfilled here also, showing again the tandem nature of this seventh sign . . .

> . . . the dead will hear the voice of God's Son . . . the Father who is a source of life has made the Son the source of life also . . . do not be surprised at this, for the hour is coming when the dead will leave their graves . . . [they] will rise to life . . .

Can there be a more eloquent "display" of the truth that Jesus is for believers the "Resurrection and the life?" Only one . . . the Resurrection of Jesus himself, which has now been immediately prepared for by this, the last of Jesus' signs.

Jesus Condemned to Die

Throughout the gospel there have been two reactions to Jesus' words and signs: belief and rejection. And so with the performance of his last and most striking sign this twofold reaction takes place. Some came to believe and will even salute him as their Messiah-King in the coming chapter; others, specifically the Jewish Sanhedrin, convene to decide once and for all that he must die. That decision is made in vv. 47-53, although Jesus is absent. In the immediate afterglow of Jesus' most *life*-giving sign, his enemies with paradoxical irony decide he must be put to *death*. The Synoptics put the counterpart of this trial at the very end of Jesus' life. John has shown Jesus equivalently on trial before the "Jews" since chapter 5 (charges have been made, answers to charges demanded and given, witnesses asked for and given, attempts at execution undertaken, etc.), and it continues here. Of course John could not let the opportunity go by to insert elements of the *actual* "trial" here, for he sees Jesus' life as a struggle between light and "darkness." When Jesus' work of giving life and light reaches its highest point, it is then that the most damaging decision of "darkness" should take place also. As we have mentioned before, gospels are theological interpretations of Jesus which seek to show the deepest *meaning* of his life and death. They are not biographical documentaries concerned with exact chronology.

As Jesus is "tried" *in absentia*, John notes a profound irony in the two main complaints that the Sanhedrin and the Pharisees lodge against Jesus. First, with his "signs" he is becoming *too popular* and is drawing great crowds to himself (and obviously away from the present religious leaders). Secondly, his success with the crowds causes Rome some concern. Because of the religious ferment over Jesus, the Romans could *destroy the Temple and the nation* (vv. 47-48). When the gospel is written (ca. 90-95 AD) its readers know, that although these leaders put Jesus to death, his *popularity* and drawing power with the people did not decrease; it increased immensely. And Rome, despite the death of Jesus, came and *destroyed the Temple and the nation*. What the Jews feared would happen if Jesus were *not* killed, actually happened. This, if nothing else, shows that the blame for the destruction of the Temple and the nation cannot be ascribed to Jesus; these happenings were rather brought about by the actions of those who lived to that time who are now sitting in judgment against Jesus.

What the Sanhedrin implies must be done—the execution of Jesus—Caiaphas the high priest (again continuing the ironical verdict of this "trial") urges be done, namely . . . "it is better that one man die to save the whole nation from destruction" (v. 50). The high priest (some rabbis thought the gift of prophecy went with his office) in John's opinion prophesied more profoundly than he realized. Jesus' death brought about not only the "spiritual" salvation of the nation; it accomplished the salvation of the world (vv. 50-51). When Jesus, the Shepherd, was struck down, there was a momentary "dispersion" of the flock; but the mystery of his "death-Resurrection" worked to gather them back into the flock. These gathered disciples in turn went off to the radically "dispersed" people of the world, the Gentiles, who are now being led into the one true fold. As Ezekiel (c. 34) had foretold, Yahweh's Shepherd unites the sheep others scatter; his death so devoutly desired and determined on by Jesus' enemies turned out to be the ultimate cause of the union of the "dispersed" people of the world. The *end* of Jesus ironically was actually the real *beginning* of the *world's* salvation.

FURTHER PARTICULAR COMMENTS:

A word about "constructs." Commentators note that the Lazarus miracle is not in the Synoptic accounts; in fact no dramatic raising of a dead man is narrated in Jesus' life just before his arrest and trial. John seems to solidify all of the opposition against Jesus around this dramatic sign; he is arrested as a consequence of Lazarus' resurrection. Jesus' opponents in the Synoptics unite against him because they are incensed at his cleansing of the Temple (in John this happens in c. 2); his predictions that he can destroy and raise the "Temple" in three days, and the way he claims to be Messiah amount to arrogant blasphemy according to the authorities. These are the "offenses" that trigger his arrest and condemnation in the Synoptics. With some commentators, then, the question arises: since there are differing accounts of what led to Jesus' immediate arrest and condemnation, could not John (the odd man out) in the Lazarus sign be "constructing" a fictional miracle from data available to him? If so, then chapter 11 contains a "theological story" about Jesus rather than an historical event of his life. If John, for example, knew of Luke's gospel or at least Luke's sources, he would have the material for his "constructed" story. In Luke one finds the following material: in c. 7:11-16, Jesus raises a widow's dead son to life; in c. 19:29, Jesus arrives at Bethany to stay there just before he goes on to Jerusalem to his death; in c. 10:38-42, Luke narrates a visit of Jesus with Martha and Mary, both described similarly to John's description; and in c. 16: 19-31, Luke recounts a parable of Jesus about a poor man who dies and was carried to Abraham's bosom. Abraham is asked by a sinful rich man now suffering in hades to send the man back from the dead to warn his brothers so that they will not be selfish like him and end up in hades. The parable says that even if the man "returns from the dead" his brothers will not listen to him and mend their ways. The beggar's name is Lazarus.

If John did "construct" an episode from the Lucan data, would he, by the standards of NT evangelists, be doing something dishonest, narrating the unhistorical as though it were historical? Not according to the purpose of NT biblical "constructs." Such constructs work with Jesus data and do so selectively and creatively. The aim of these constructs is to synthesize dramatically and heighten material in a memorable and memorizable way (since most ancients cannot read) so that reader-listeners will be able to catch the theological meaning of the data . . . the true understanding of Jesus' miracles . . . why he works them . . . what they say to the spiritual needs of the evangelist's Church, etc. Gospels are not strict biographies; they are theological interpretations of Jesus. As John sees Jesus, he is God's light and life who has come to the world to share his divine gifts with believers. "Darkness" is opposed to Jesus mainly because he *is* light and life, and it refuses to surrender its "darkness" to his light. Thus the "element" that brings Jesus in climactic conflict with his enemies is his granting of "resurrection" life. John in his Lazarus episode is not giving the reader the exact historical happening that brought about Jesus' arrest and death; he is synthesizing the data and giving the "theological happening" that *radically* brought about his arrest and condemnation. Jesus gives life and light; "darkness" must either yield to this light or seek to overcome it. Arrest and condemnation shows that "darkness" decides to overcome the light.

Now having said this, it is good to note that many scholars, realizing that John is giving the deepest theological reason for Jesus' arrest and death, believe also that the "sign" is basically historical (some "constructed" elements could well be introduced into the episode as they would be in most gospel narratives, since evangelists always do some synthesizing, some adjusting of their material for polemical, pastoral, liturgical and other reasons), but the basic sign historically happened. Jesus did raise his friend Lazarus from the dead. In brief, they note:

John's sources are in part independent from the Synoptics. The miracle happens in Judea and this is the area in which John's narrative always comes into sharpest focus. There is in this episode great personal and emotional detail, a real "ring of truth." This type of miracle is in all the gospels (John the dramatist-theologian has no qualms about placing his data where it will do the greatest theological good). Such a miracle happening somewhat near the end of Jesus' public ministry would make the great welcome Jesus receives on Palm Sunday more understandable (the Synoptics give the "welcome" with little of the motivation behind it). And incidentally scholars note that unlike most of Jesus' parables, the hero of Luke's parable is *named*. It could well be that Luke has added some lines to the original parable he found in his data (for theological reasons of his own) and that he (not Jesus) gave the name Lazarus to the beggar-hero, since there are some parallels between the hero of the parable and the "historical" Lazarus (whom Luke could have learned about later). Also, they note, John has been very selective with the signs he narrates, giving only seven. Just a few verses before the raising of Lazarus, Jesus said in 10:37-38 . . . "if I do not perform my Father's *works* put no faith in me. But if *I do* perform *them*, even though you still put no faith in me, *PUT YOUR FAITH IN THESE WORKS*." It would seem Jesus has very specific historical "noble works" (10:32) he wants his audience to recall for the true identification of who he is (not some general feeling that he here and there performed life-giving activity).

Verse 2, *Mary . . . who anointed the Lord . . .* This scene does not happen until c. 12. This unconscious "reminder" of a scene that has not happened yet, could indicate that John (or possibly his final editors) wants the reader to view his episodes not only in light of what has already transpired, but in light of what is to transpire (it is probable that many Johannine Christians knew most of this gospel by heart). The Mary who "fears" death in c. 11, shows no fear of Jesus' death in c. 12. The "sign," it seems, has brought her to something close to Resurrection-faith.

Verse 43, *shouted with a loud voice . . .* Commentators notice an ironic comparison between this verse and what happens in cc's. 18-19. As Jesus "shouts" to give *life*, so the "Jews" there will "shout" to bring about his *death*.

Verse 44, *bound in linen strips . . .* Some scholars note a cross-reference here to c. 20:5-8. Lazarus must yet endure another physical death and will need his funeral clothes once more. Jesus comes forth from the tomb leaving them behind; he is never to die again.

Chapter 12

GENERAL COMMENTS (and reflections):

The raising of Lazarus, Jesus' most dramatic life-giving sign, has united the powers of "darkness" against him. They have decided he must die (11:53). The sign has drawn some to faith, others like the sisters of Lazarus to deeper faith. They are beginning to see that Jesus is more than "healer"; he is the source of Resurrection-life. But with the sign, believers sense that Jesus is close to death himself. The pieces are beginning to come together and they indicate his "hour," his death, is very near. JB earlier identified Jesus as the Lamb of God (1:29, 36). As Jesus comes to celebrate the feast of Passover, with so much opposition mounting against him, the feeling is that he, like the Paschal Lamb, is about to be "sacrificed" (v. 1). Jesus has already spoken twice of his "lifting up"—the Johannine term for crucifixion (3:14; 8:28); he will refer to it again at the close of this chapter (v. 32).

But the recent life-giving sign helps believers recall that Jesus also spoke of his death as a source of life for believers (3:14-17; 10:17, 27-28). And although a sense of Jesus' death is in the air, the feeling is that it will not result in his total destruction as "darkness" intends. Jesus' death is to have cosmic saving effects; it is to be his and the Father's greatest act of love for the world (3:14-17; 15:13; 12:32). And Mary, after seeing her brother recalled from "death" by the Good Shepherd (remembered to have described himself as a dying-rising Shepherd, c. 10:17-18), seeks to show her love for Jesus who now is about to lay down his life for all the sheep. She *knows* that Jesus will overcome his death as he overcame her brother's (2:19; 10:17-18), but she *knows* the act is a deep expression of his love for her and all believers, and she wishes to show her deep love for his great love. (*We say Mary "knows" because the episode, though happening before the Resurrection, contains ele-*

ments of post-Resurrection insight read back into it. Also, as a "Johannine Christian" she can "see" what lies ahead as well as what has transpired.)

Jesus' Anointing

How will Mary show her love? Scholars believe John has reworked material he finds in his sources (these sources are thought to contain episodes similar to those found in the Synoptic tradition). There Jesus is twice anointed by unnamed women (cf., Mt 26:6-13; Mk 14:3-9; Lk 7:36-50). The episodes are symbolic gestures of the deep love these women have for Jesus. In the episodes of Matthew and Mark, the perfumed anointings are said to be for Jesus' "burial." The women, however, anoint his head. In John, Mary anoints his feet. The episode in Luke has the woman, a sinner, crying over Jesus' feet; she dries them with her hair, and anoints his feet with perfume. Mary anoints Jesus' feet with perfume and then wipes them with her hair. In all cases, although complaints are made against the women, Jesus defends their actions as done "out of love" for him. Either John does a little "constructing" here or the data comes to him a bit confused. In either case he lets Mary anoint Jesus' feet, since it will be a loving as well as a prophetic gesture. It indicates her great love for Jesus and it shows that her love is directed at his greatest act of love for her and all believers, namely, his death. Anointings meant to honor the living were usually applied to the head; honor and love for the *dead* were shown by an anointing of the whole body, including the feet. If Mary was not actually the woman in his sources, John's thinking would be that this kind of "love" for Jesus is in her heart. The reworked episode says what Mary feels for Jesus because of what he has done for her brother and for her faith and what he will do for all believers (v. 3).

In the data for the "burial" anointing of Jesus (Mt and Mk), complaints were made of the "waste" of so much expensive perfume. John names the key complainer as Judas, who seems to "worry" about the money-value of the perfume. He is thinking of the poor (oh?). John informs the reader that Judas was a thief and it is unlikely that any money realized from the sale of the perfume would have gone to the poor. Mary and all genuine Israelites would think it a matter of justice that the poor be provided for (Dt 15:11); the gesture will not deprive them of their needs or dispense her from her obligations toward them. The gesture symbolizes the extravagance of her love for Jesus in giving up his life for her. That is to happen only once and believers can never thank Jesus "too much" for that act, for it makes available to them his eternal life, light and love (and besides, the rabbis always taught there was "no waste" to an act of merciful love, done to the living or the dead). Judas, as "thief," shows love neither for the poor (he *robs* from the treasury the alms due them), nor for Jesus whom he is about to betray (he seeks to *rob* him of life) (v. 4). There is no more striking example in the NT of the two options open to people confronted by Jesus. As a disciple, he must have had a modicum of faith and love for Jesus; now it is apparent that he has withdrawn that love and faith and has followed the other option, the option of self-love and "darkness" (in c. 10, those who opposed the Good Shepherd were called "thieves," vv. 1, 8, 10).

Though scholars are in disagreement about whether a "kingly theme" is beginning to emerge here at Bethany, some do see it. The kingly aspect of Jesus' mission is not stressed in John's gospel until Jesus draws close to his death. The Messianic King was so often given nationalistic and political meanings, that John wants to guard against this. Jesus can only *safely* be identified as "King" in the context of death. He will be saluted as "King" in a few verses and he will not discourage the salutation completely. Through the trial, crucifixion and actual burial of Jesus the kingly theme will intensify. Here some see Mary's extravagant burial anointing (worth about 300 days' wages) as more fitting for the burial of a king than for a humble "son of Joseph" (6:42). But Jesus *is* a King. It is in death that he will "rule" over the hearts and minds of his subjects; it is through the Cross that he provides eternal "welfare" for his people.

Jesus' Entry into Jerusalem: 12:9-19

The next scene still involves Lazarus. For John, his raising is the particular sign that prompts Jesus' "kingly" welcome to Jerusalem. The crowds, however, seem to be captivated by the wonder of the miracle, rather than its symbolic meaning: that Jesus is and can be the source for others of "Resurrection and Eternal Life" (v. 9). As "darkness" intensifies its hatred against Jesus, so this redounds to those who derive life from him. Lazarus' life is also in jeopardy (v. 10). It seems John has a lesson here for his own people (ca. 90-95 AD). They, like Lazarus, can expect (and are getting) the persecution and rejection Jesus experienced.

This scene is in all the gospels (Mt 21:1-11; Mk 11:1-11; Lk 19:28-40). So John is working with common data. Scholars naturally detect Johannine nuances in the use of the material. He sees the welcome due in large part to the "Lazarus sign" where life was given to a "dead" man. John sees this as theologically correct; this is why Jesus should be welcomed as King. He offers life to those who come to him when he calls. But in John's telling of the event, the crowd is thinking of a different kind of king, a military-type liberator, a nationalistic leader. There are clues that indicate this: the crowd waves palms and shouts a "royal psalm" at Jesus (Ps 118:26). This gesture and the recitation of the psalm have political connotations; Israelites did this when they welcomed kings back from military victories as they approached the Temple (cf. 1 M 13:51; 2 M 10:7). The crowd "comes out to meet Jesus" (an action done when kings came to the city). They add an extra line to the psalm—"blessed is the King of Israel" (a Messianic title, but often popularly understood in a military and political sense). It is obvious from these clues that the crowd would like Jesus to be their earthly liberator-king (vv. 12-14).

Jesus has already discouraged an attempt to make him this kind of king (6:15). This time he does not reject their salutes, for he is about to become their King in actual fact, but in a profoundly more spiritual sense than they suspect, and so he seeks to reveal this to them. He is not to rule them and the nation as earthly kings do; he is, as was noted earlier, to rule over their minds and hearts and provide for their (and the entire world's) spiritual welfare. How tell them this? Jesus performs a prophetic action, a symbolic act that contradicts the nationalistic hopes and expectations of the crowd, which will also prophetically reveal the spiritual nature of his kingly office. Jesus finds a donkey and sits on it. The act recalls, or should recall, the prophecy of Zechariah (Zc 9:9) where the Messiah was described as "coming seated humbly on a donkey." This Messiah in the very next verse of the prophecy is further described as one who comes "to proclaim *peace to all nations*"; his reign is not to be nationalistic, it is to be universal (the crowd is thinking of a new king just for the "nation").

John leaves out the word "humble"; still the act is most unlike the acts expected of nationalistic kings (most of whom suffer from the "Cadillac" syndrome).

Moreover, some see John in his recording of Zechariah (Zc 9:9) to be inserting an allusion to Zephaniah (Zp 3:14 f) which describes Yahweh as one who comes to his people with justifiable anger at their sins and lack of faith, and yet who comes to overcome the misfortunes of the lame and the outcasts and who is to gather strays and draw them all into his love (much as Jesus overcame the "misfortune" of the "cripple" in c. 5; came to the "outcast" blind man in c. 9; and as Good Shepherd, came to gather "strays" into his fold in c. 10; and whose death is seen as drawing the world to his love in c. 12:32). The "universal" character of Jesus' kingly office spoken of in Zechariah (Zc 9:10) has just been hinted at in 11:52 (Jesus there was to gather together all the "dispersed children of God"), and it is hinted at again in the coming near verses, 12:19, 20. These verses show that Jesus is a King interested in all the nations (they are seen in the words, "the *world* runs after him," v. 19, and in the term, "the *Greeks*," v. 20).

The donkey and Zechariah-Zephaniah may be a little subtle for modern readers, but to John and his people they are enough to set them on the "research trail." In Zechariah and Zephaniah they will see that Jesus is a different king than this crowd immediately asks for or wants. And certainly the "lowly transportation" hints at the "different" King Jesus is to be. As the gospel advances, the "different King" will be dramatically displayed in the events that surround his last hour; e.g., his crown will be made of thorns; his purple robe is put on him in mockery; his throne will be a Cross; his coat of arms an intended insult, etc. (vv. 12-14).

But if the crowd really wants to see what kind of King they are getting in Jesus, they should look to Lazarus (vv. 17-18). What happened to him is a symbol of the "gifts" this King offers his "subjects." He is not offering them political liberation and peace or national, earthly welfare; he offers them freedom from "darkness" and eternal peace and life . . . and not only is he offering it *to them*, but as Jesus will tell them in v. 32, he offers his gifts *to all the world*. And most remarkably this liberation, peace and life will not come through great and mighty acts or military victories, but by the selfless act of "entering into his hour"— which he is about to explain.

The size of the crowd that comes to see Jesus because of his raising of Lazarus (v. 19), prompts the Pharisees to exaggerate that the "world" is running after him (making it all the more imperative that he be stopped if the nation is to be saved). Ironically the action they design to stop his popularity will be his most kingly, (and in the long run) his most popular act, and the act will redound to the salvation not only of this Jewish "crowd" (if they accept him) but of the "world" (who in John's time, ca. 90-95 AD, continues to "run after him" in ever-increasing numbers).

The "Greeks" and Jesus' *Hour* 12:20-36

If Jesus is the "world" spiritual King, as well as Israel's, then the world should "come to see Jesus" (v. 21). And so the "Greeks" arrive asking to *see* Jesus (v. 20). In Jesus' time these would probably have been Gentile proselytes who came to Jerusalem to prepare for their conversion to Judaism. John sees them as prophetic symbols of the "Gentiles" who were to come and submit to Jesus' reign of eternal peace and life after his death and Resurrection. How these Gentiles are to "see" their King and enter into his "Kingdom" is now explained to them. It is in the mystery of his "hour," his "lifting up" (v. 32) that they will "see" Jesus (a Johannine word for "believe in"). On the surface, this sounds preposterous: in the cruel crucifixion of a Jew the Gentiles are to find their kingly Savior! But it *is* true, and Jesus must explain why it is true (again, it seems, using images from a harvest parable or proverb, as he did in c. 4:36, when speaking about other non-Jews he sought to harvest).

When Jesus dies, his kingly power to save, to give life, light and love to believers, will go fully out from him, be fully given "for others." What he came to share will be totally "shared" in his death, but quite remarkably its total "givenness" in death does not render its acquisition difficult to realize; no, Jesus' "given life and love" enters into a new *Mode of reachability* (from here on out we will refer to the Jesus of the "hour" and beyond as the Jesus of Mode #2; the Jesus of Mode #1 is the Jesus who lived with and spoke to the "Jews" publicly ca. 27-30 AD; and here we are, God help us, "theologizing" a bit on Jesus' explanation. We now confess, God forgive us, to have been doing this on occasion). The blind man and Lazarus could find life in the Jesus of Mode #1; they encountered their "King" when he existed in that Mode. But the "Greeks" (and indeed all future believers), how will they (and such believers) after the "hour" removes Jesus from history, contact him and submit to him and find his life? It is through the hour that they (and future believers) are able to do this. Jesus then like the seed (v. 24) goes into the ground and "dies," i.e., he passes beyond the limitations of space and time, beyond the limitations of his short personal human history to become the transcendental, trans-historical, universally reachable Jesus who can be "seen" through faith in any time, in any age. If Jesus had not died, would coming believers see that his life and love have been "fully given" for them? If Jesus had not died, would he be a Jesus fully reachable to the "Greeks" throughout history? It is in death, that Jesus "displays" his totally given, totally reachable love and life. It is in his death and Resurrection that believers know that the historical King of Lazarus and Palm Sunday is now the trans-historical King who can be "seen" forever as long as one comes and submits to him in faith (vv. 23-24). The Jesus of Mode #2 is the Jesus who through death and Resurrection can potentially embrace *all the "world," all of creation.* "Unless the seed dies, it bears no fruit; if it dies, it bears *much fruit*" (v. 24).

And when Jesus has died and entered into his trans-historical Mode #2, how do the "Greeks" come, how do they submit to and find Jesus and his life? By doing in their portion what Jesus did in his "hour." As Jesus, in his human Mode, at the time of his death, found his Father's glory pouring into him as his own glory in death was pouring into the Father and into an infinite reservoir of glory for the "Greeks" . . . so the one who seeks to share in Jesus' glory must also "give up his own human glory," i.e., "die to self" (v. 25). Paul used the word "emptying" when describing the mystery of the "hour" (Ph 2:5 f), seeing Jesus' death as the total surrender of himself for others; but in rendering himself totally empty of self, he rendered himself totally able to receive God's fullness. Paul's Christians were to imitate this "emptying process" to receive of Jesus' fullness. In John, when Jesus "dies" he enters into a new Mode reachable to all through faith. So the believer in "dying" will find the "given love" of Jesus ready to fill him or her with life. This is really the mystery of how human-divine love works. If one only loves oneself, no love can get out or come in. It is in "hating one's life" (a hyperbolic semitic expression calling for one to be more selfless, to get out of self, to

live for somebody other than oneself) that Jesus' love "out there in Mode
#2" can get in (v. 25). It is in serving and loving another that one "dies"
to self; this is how one renders oneself open to another's love which is the
love that truly completes and fulfills. "Death" is the key; it makes love
communicable and receivable. The "Greeks" in their serving and loving
faith will find Jesus' kingly life and love always "there" . . . *findable*
because through his dying and Resurrection Jesus has entered into a
trans-historical Mode in which the nations and the ages of any time can
"*find*" him through faith and service. And when one finds Jesus, one
also finds the Father. The Jesus of Mode #2 is *in* the eternal Father; if
Jesus is reachable, so is the Father (v. 26). There are many levels of
meaning to the mystery of Jesus' "hour." John has penetrated to a very
deep level indeed.

In verses 27-28, we find John's reinterpretation of Jesus' prayer in
the garden just before he entered into his "hour" (cf., Mt 26:39; Mk
14:35-36; Lk 22:42-44). In the Synoptics, facing the dreaded moment of
death, Jesus prays that he be spared from the "cup." In John, Jesus
speaks to the Father, but seeks no escape from his "hour." He rather
speaks aloud to inform bystanders that his "hour" is the climax of his
earthly mission. And he wants them to know that the Father is a tandem
partner with him in his "hour." What is "visibly" to happen to him
there, mirrors what is happening for them in the Father's heart. "Father,
glorify your *name*" (v. 28), i.e., *reveal that your love is in this act too!*
As the Father's glory was seen in all of Jesus' words and deeds up to now
(v. 28a), so it will be seen in the "deed" that is to happen (v. 28b). If
Jesus' soul is "troubled," it is not from dread or fear of the "hour"; it is
only because so many refuse to see the "hour" as the moment of his and
the Father's supreme glory, that is, the moment in which they both
manifest and communicate the depth of their love for the world (3:16).
(*Jesus, we recall, was also "troubled" at this blindness to his Resurrection power in c. 11:33, 38. And Jesus is further "troubled" because
people, ca. 90-95 AD, refuse to see glory in the "hour"; they see only its
"scandal."*)

The "voice" of the Father in v. 28, is in a sense "audibly" heard:
some hear "thunder" (an ancient symbol of God's voice); others hear the
words of an "angel" (an OT speaking instrument for God). The equivalent "voice" appears in the Synoptics at Jesus' baptism (Mt 3:17; Mk

1:11; Lk 3:22). There the Father showed his approval of the mission that Jesus was about to undertake. In John, the greatest work Jesus undertakes is his death, and so the "voice" must indicate that he is invisibly with Jesus in that work which is about to happen. The "voice" (whose words are mostly heard by the readers of the gospel and not by the episode's audience) seems to be John's way of reminding his readers to "remember" the many times Jesus informed them that his words and works were tandem mysteries performed in union with the Father (*"I have glorified* my name", i.e., in the whole Book of Signs, cc's. 1-12: *"I will glorify* my name", i.e., in the coming Book of Glory, cc's. 13-20, 21).

With verses 31-32, the "Greeks" must be told that the enigma of the Cross is not the scandal or stumbling block many find it to be. "Darkness" believes the Cross conquers Jesus by destroying the Shepherd and extinguishing his light. But as foretold, this Shepherd and his light are radically inextinguishable (c. 10:17-18), and so beholding the Cross, the "Greeks" should know that the Jesus who hangs there is to rise and thus they are to realize that "darkness" when it seems to be winning is actually losing the light-darkness struggle (v. 31). And rather than separate any sheep from him (Jewish or non-Jewish), the Cross will "draw *all* people to him" (v. 32). John must see the outstretched arms of Jesus in death as a symbol of his all-embracing desire to draw believers to his life, light and love, which are now through the mystery of the Cross becoming transcendentally, trans-historically, indestructibly reachable for all. Jesus is the winner over evil through this enigmatic act; he is the winner for all believers who follow by years or centuries this act, whose effects are reachable through faith. In a world of so much personal and structured evil, believers sometimes wonder if anyone can destroy the evil within and outside of them? They know how difficult it is to bring the world's structured evil to the Cross. But it is profoundly consoling to know that with Jesus' Cross now being transformed into an eternally reachable Mode they can bring their personal sins and stupidities to Jesus to have them "driven out" (v. 31).

With verse 34, we realize again how difficult it is for people who look at and listen to Jesus superficially, to see "good" coming from the cruel form of his final "hour." Though its mystery has to some degree been explained, recurring "darkness" concentrates only on the "death" aspect of it. And a Messiah, indeed a Messiah-King, who is so soon and so cruelly to die is not a king "darkness" expects or wants. And so the worn-out complaint, the literalist expectation, is heard again . . . "the Messiah is to remain *forever*" (cf., e.g., Ps 45:7; 89:5; Is 9:6-7; Dn 7:14). How little they pay attention. The Jesus of John is a "from *forever*" and a "for *forever*" Messiah: he is the indestructible Temple . . . the Bread from heaven and the living waters . . . the light come into the world . . . the Shepherd of Resurrection . . . the fruit-bearing seed . . . in sum the Messiah of eternal life and Resurrection. But all of this is not enough "*forever*" for some.

Jesus is Messiah in a different way than expected. He is the "Son of Man." The title, as noted in chapter 1 (in the images of the Book of Daniel and apocalyptic literature) describes the Messiah as one who "comes from heaven," who brings "hidden treasures," who establishes a "new order," and who "comes to bring God's judgment on the world." And yet he is called *Man*. As such he could be subject to the mystery of being "lifted up" (all three predictions of the "lifting up," 3:14; 8:28; 12:32, call the *lifted one* "Son of Man"). Superficially looked at, all the expected attributes of this Messiah are acceptable to most Jews, *except* the "unacceptable" last possibility. Jesus (or John) could very likely have preferred the expression "lifted up" precisely because this indicates that his death as *Man* is not the "scandal" many choose to call it . . . it is rather his transforming "return to heaven," the act that creates his new Mode of existence that makes his presence there reachable to all who open themselves to him in faith. These people, now obviously symbols of "darkness," refuse to give faith and thus the light of Jesus made fruitfully reachable by his death on the Cross will be wanting to them because they do not have faith to see that light shines even there (vv. 35-36). To see Jesus as the descending "Son of Man" and as the "Son of Man" *who will ascend* through "lifting up" requires an openness of mind and heart. These people refuse to give Jesus such openness. The blind man in chapter 9 was asked if he believed in the Son of Man and said: "Who is he, that I may believe in him?" This crowd asks the same question (v. 34), not really caring to hear the answer from one about to die. But Jesus identified himself then and now as the "Son of Man": he showed the blind man he was that Son by giving him light symbolic of the light he brought from heaven. He will show it to these people and to all the world, when after death, he is truly "lifted up" to eternal light (vv. 35-36).

As John had closed the earlier and shorter version of the Book of Signs (10:40-42); so he now closes the expanded book. John has made a very good "case" for Jesus as the Messiah who fulfilled authentic Jewish expectations; he has also adequately established that Jesus is a Messiah far beyond expectations, namely, the "high" Christ. And yet so many of his own refused to accept him (1:11). Early believers found this rejection difficult to understand and just as difficult to explain. To the modern Christian mind the answer seems a little easier to articulate. Christians now realize that God leaves them free to choose good and evil. They see that God had to leave them free to choose his life, light and love. Love cannot be forced on anyone; it has to be given and received *freely* to be meaningful and fulfilling. The ancients could not so easily put most of the mystery of rejection on a human being's choosing causality alone (secondary causality as we say). God for them was not only the principal cause of all created activity (God's all-embracing primary causality is everywhere in the OT); he was there imprecisely involved in the secondary causality of human choosing (which now Christians see is quite autonomous).

Early Christians, philosophically less sophisticated than their modern counterparts, saw in Isaiah (Is 53:1; 6:16) part of the answer to their question: why do some reject Christ? (vv. 38-40) God warned the prophets that they would be rejected. If Isaiah can know rejection, surely Jesus also. The blinding of eyes, the numbing of hearts, the not-perceiving, the not-converting, etc., happens because God sees it in the *plan* and to a degree "causes" it; he is the author of the plan (v. 40). This did not mean the ancients saw God determining it to happen, but that it was "bound to happen." If they were as philosophically sophisticated as moderns, they would say God *allows it to happen* in light of the necessity of the love he seeks to give and receive. But at least the point is made. It is part of the "plan." God knows it will happen. Those who easily dismiss Jesus as a "false Christ" because he is rejected should recall God's words to Isaiah. God "knows" that people will reject his true prophets; if the last one was his only Son, the inference is that he too can be and was rejected as true Messiah. This helps them understand the mystery some what; it also lets Isaiah warn present Christians who may be having second thoughts about Jesus. They have no excuse for rejection themselves after having witnessed the Book of Signs (God's book of true revelations about Jesus). The Father who forewarned the prophets, is also the Father of Jesus and his approval remains ever with the prophets and Jesus as against the rejecters (whom God knows about).

The forewarned prophet "saw" the glory of Christ (v. 41). At least from Is 6:1-6, Isaiah in describing his own call to be a prophet, says he saw the "glory" of God filling the earth. This is assumed to be some sort of visible reflected manifestation of God's presence. John knows that God's reflected glory is now fully encased and localized in Jesus, and so if Isaiah "saw" God's glory, that would have to be Jesus.

Verses 42-43, reflect a situation that existed in John's time that he vehemently disapproves of. Jews claiming to believe in Jesus, are not owning up to it in the Synagogue. Thus they avoid exclusion and persecution. It would seem that John's dualistic mindset has a hard time justifying "secret faith" for any reason: especially in synagogues which demanded members to curse "the heretics" (i.e. the Christian deviators) and who officially label Jesus as a demented "false prophet." The term "crypto (secret)-Christian" for John is a contradiction in terms.

The discourse in verses 44-50 is obviously "unattached"; it has no known audience or recognizable setting, although it sounds like a variation in part of c. 3:16-19. Since it "duplicates" previous discourse material, this indicates that probably not John but a post-John "editor is at work." He apparently concluded that this left-over discourse would be a nice summary of Jesus' message: that his words and signs have shown him to be the "high" Christ, sent by the Father and ever in union with him. The mentality of the Synagogue, ca. 90-95 AD, seems to have been: "we have the Father . . . you people can have Jesus." This summary discourse shows the falseness and danger of that premise, for again Jesus draws out the tandem union between him and the Father: Jesus is the *sent-Agent* of the Father; who sees him, sees the Father; who hears him, hears the Father. To exclude Jesus is to exclude the Father's light sent to the world; it brings judgment on those who do it. The Father is "over here" in John's community (vv. 44-50).

FURTHER PARTICULAR COMMENTS:

Verse 8, *the poor you have*, etc. . . . . This verse is missing from many MSS. It is a direct quotation from Mt. 26:11, and is considered by many to be added by a scribe.

Verses 24-26 . . . Synoptic counterparts to this idea that sees the need for Christians to die in order to have life are found in Mt 10:38-39; Mk 8:35; Lk 9:23-25, 17:33. Implicit in this concept that Jesus is the seed who "dies," could be another important truth for the "Greeks." It is Paul's insight that when Jesus died, the Law died also and with it its cultural-religious structures. Thus the Gentiles are no longer bound by the external forms of the Law, but can find Jesus through the simple path of faith and Baptism (cf., Gal 2:19-21; 3:13, etc.).

Verse 31, *prince of this world* . . . A term for Satan that is distinctive of John. It is, however, close to Qumran's angel of darkness who opposes the "prince of light." Again, a possible indication that John's background seems to be from a different, more heavily dualistic form of Judaism than the background which produced the Synoptics (though John need not have come particularly from the Qumran people, a known minority-stream group).

Verses 35-36, *the light among you . . . a little while longer* . . . Some scholars see John's term "lifted up" deriving not only from Numbers 21:4-9, but also from Isaiah's Suffering Servant (Is 52:13). The Songs of the Servant (Is cc's. 42-55) speak of the Servant not only as one who will be "lifted up" (52:13) but as one "who will provide light to the nations" (Is 49:6). Thus for John the title "Son of Man" could be a synonym for the "Suffering Servant," who once "lifted up," provides eternal light for the "world"—the "Greeks" of this chapter (vv. 32, 35-36).

Chapter 13

The Book of Glory Begins

GENERAL COMMENTS (and reflections):

With the close of the Book of Signs (cc's. 1-12), Jesus has clearly identified himself to the world. His works and discourses have revealed that he was sent by the Father to reveal that God wishes to share with human creation his life, light, and love——in sum, his "glory." Jesus was the human manifestation of God and his glory. Some accept him. Others reject him. Some in fact seek his death. If the Book of Signs could not convince these people he spoke the truth, Jesus, nevertheless, leaves them with this Book. It is an adequate "brief" for his true identity and purpose. He must move on. His "hour" has come. Perhaps when it happens and is witnessed by believers it will bring non-believers to an understanding of that first Book.

But the time has come for Jesus to complete his work on earth. He must radically and fully reveal God and his love for the world. He must show that God's love has been fully given and is forever reachable through faith. Through his "hour" he will not only return to the Father; he will also enter into a new Mode of glorification as Son of Man that will render his and the Father's "glory" reachable to believers for all time (it is when the seed *dies* that it becomes fruitful, 12:24). That this is to be accomplished through death (through a cruel and hateful death), is not easy for human minds to comprehend, and so Jesus will take believers *aside* and explain to them the "mystery of his hour": why it must happen, what it reveals, especially the repercussions it is to have for believers.

This is the Book (cc's. 13-20, 21) specifically designed for believers. They alone can profit from the "hour" because they alone open themselves to Jesus. They have accepted him as one sent from God. In

him they have seen "God's glory" (it was visibilized in the signs he
worked in his earthly Mode of existence, Mode #1 as we call it). But now
Jesus (and the "glory" he possesses) is about to leave the world in that
Mode. He is to die. On the surface this seems like the "glory" believers
saw will no longer be seen. Jesus must explain that this is not to be the
case. The glory he revealed will be fully seen; it will be made fully
reachable through his death and Resurrection. These next chapters (cc's.
13-20, 21) are rightly called the Book of Glory. Not that the First Book
was not a Book of Glory. But this part of John's gospel will show the
eternality of Jesus' glory (that it is truly eternal and indestructible); it will
show that the "glorification" of Jesus makes his "glory" eternally
reachable . . . as the glorified Son of *Man* in the unlimited Mode of
Resurrection he can reach out to all believers and include them in his
glory.

The Last Supper

As in the Synoptics, Jesus eats a farewell Supper with his disciples
before his arrest and trial. John's telling of the event, like the earlier
tradition, will have about it a feeling of apprehension and concern over
Jesus' impending departure, but the meal (once Judas departs) is one of
shared affection and intimate love between the Master and his disciples.
John, of course, must recount things his own way. We note at the start
that the timing of the meal is different. For the Synoptics, the Supper is a
Passover Meal and Jesus will be condemned and die on the feast of
Passover. For John, the meal comes earlier. Jesus will be in the tomb
before Passover begins. The Synoptics stress the institution of the
Eucharist as a main feature of the meal. John does not mention the
Eucharist taking place at the Supper. He stresses Jesus' washing of his
disciples' feet. Also Jesus will give a lengthy farewell discourse. These
differences seem major to the "modern mind." But one must realize that
gospels are religious documents, theological interpretations of Jesus and
the events of his life and death.

The two "Supper traditions" are making theological statements
about Jesus' death, and it seems both are drawing out the Paschal nature
of his final "hour." The Synoptics want to show that Jesus replaces and
fulfills the mystery of Passover. The mystery of Jesus' death and Resur-

rection accomplishes his and the believers' Passover to God; it is the New Exodus from sin to life and Jesus leaves believers the Eucharist as the meal that symbolically encases his Passover. It enables true Israelites to celebrate Jesus' Passover with him; it helps them realize that they too are part of this mystery. As for John, many commentators believe he has already shown in chapter 6 (vv. 51b-58), that Jesus leaves believers his Paschal "body and blood" under the symbol of bread. Moreover, many of these same commentators detect a "eucharistic setting" for the long homily discourse Jesus gives at the Supper. Jesus' discourse will put heavy emphasis on the fraternal love and unity he expects of his disciples. Christians early on came to understand the Eucharist as their great Sacrament of fraternal love and unity (cf., e.g. Paul, I Cor 10:14-17; 11:17-34). So in a sense the Eucharist is the "setting" for Jesus' discourse in John.

But the Jesus of John and of this Supper is also the Passover Lamb (Johannine hints here and nearby show this). Three times he reminds his readers the Passover feast is near (11:55; 12:1; 13:1). The meal has about it a Passover ambience (there are Passover ritual gestures; Father-children dialogues; a solemn concluding prayer, etc.). Jesus shortly after the meal is sentenced to be slain as the Paschal lambs are being slain. On the Cross, Passover images are referred to (the hyssop reed, his bones left unbroken). Jesus for John is dying as the Good Shepherd, but a Shepherd who is like the Lamb who gave his blood that others might live. He dies as both the Shepherd *and* the Paschal Lamb of God. The timing of the Supper is not that important; the theological statement that Jesus' death is "Paschal" is more important (some scholars in fact view John's more drawn-out version of Jesus' last "hour" as probably closer to the actual facts; they see the Synoptic accounts, with so much happening so quickly on the very holy day of Passover, as quite unlikely). Both traditions, then, see Jesus' "hour" as fulfilling and surpassing the religious meaning of Passover. As John will say: "the hour had come for him to PASS FROM THIS WORLD to the Father" (v. 1). In his death he frees the world from more than human bondage. Through Jesus' Passover he frees it *from* eternal darkness; he frees it *for* eternal light and love. The major difference between John's Last Supper and the Synoptics is the footwashing and the extensive discourse that Jesus gives. We turn to them now.

The Footwashing

The gospel has been describing the gifts Jesus offers from the Father as God's life, light, and love (the summary word for all three would be "glory"). In the Book of Signs Jesus spoke of this glory most often under the terms *life* and *light*. The Book of Glory uses very frequently the term *love*. The "hour" he is about to endure is not some enigmatic exercise the Father requires of him—the suffering of a cruel and unjust death. No, it is Jesus "showing his love to the full" (v. 1b). Judas is mentioned here, it seems, because John sees him as a symbol of "darkness." He specifically rejects Jesus' *love*. He was a disciple; he must have had love for Jesus at one time, but this love has now been withdrawn. To leave Jesus, to betray his love is to reject God's love incarnated in him. How could this happen? John says the "devil" induced Judas to betray Jesus (v. 2). To many first-century minds the simple "freedom" of Judas is not sufficient to explain the awful choice and decision he makes. The choice is "so diabolical," that a diabolical force must be in the picture too (and, of course, in some heavily dualistic forms of Judaism, the "prince of the world" had powerful influence over those who chose to live out their lives as children of "his darkness"). But the rejection of his love cannot dissuade Jesus from "showing it to the full" (v. 1b). The full showing of it not only represents the depth of Jesus' own love for the world; it displays the Father's love also. Jesus' "hour" is above all an hour of his *and* the Father's love (v. 3).

The action that follows is found only in John. But John, as we saw, seems to have had access to data independent of Synoptic source material. The action could likely recall a demonstration Jesus undertook toward the end of his life to teach the "serving attitude" he expected his followers to adopt in imitation of him. And since he has already revealed the mystery of the Eucharist in chapter 6 (vv. 51b-58), he need not mention it here as the Synoptics do. He will instead have Jesus act out his ultimate love in the symbol of footwashing. In John's thinking both symbols "say" the same thing: "Jesus shows his 'love to the full' through his death and Resurrection" and he leaves the disciples the mystery of his total love in a washing-symbol (as in the earlier tradition he left the mystery in a bread-meal-symbol). The two primary Sacraments that symbolically encase Jesus' "ultimate love" are the Eucharist and

Baptism and many scholars see the footwashing as an allusion to
Baptism. John, by choosing to recount only the footwashing can, teach
his people two important meanings of Jesus' final "hour." First, that his
hour is his "full love" given *for* and *to* them (Jesus "washes" them into
his love); and secondly, being in his love, they must then live out their
lives in the service of one another.

Looked at on the surface, Jesus' action seems to be an extraordinary
act of humility. Guests coming to a supper with tired and dusty feet would
(as an act of hospitality) be offered the opportunity to wash their feet; in
this act they were often assisted by wives, children, or a lowly slave . . .
but never by the father-host of the family. That Jesus as the Master-
Teacher would "stoop" to this act shows his extraordinary love for his
disciple-friends. But Jesus' *humility* and *love for his friends* is more
profound than this. John again gives clues to the deeper symbolism of this
action. He recalls that Jesus "*takes off* his robe" (v. 4). He uses the same
verb found in c. 10:17-18 to describe the "Shepherd *laying down* his
life" (*tithenai*). When Jesus finishes the washing, he "*puts on* his robe"
(v. 12). Again the verb used is the same as that which described the
Shepherd's power "*to take up* his life," (10:17-18) (*lambanein*). Jesus is
thus "acting out" symbolically the ultimate and full love of his
"hour"—Jesus is to *take off*, i.e., he is to *lay down* his life: and he is *to
put on*, i.e., he is *to take up* his life again "for love of the disciples" . . .
and he is to bring this love to them in the symbol of "bathing." Jesus
loves them "unto death" and he washes them into his loving death and
Resurrection. Later the action will be seen as a model of Christian love
for the brothers and sisters, but first Jesus shows the disciples the extent
of his love and shows them he wishes to give them his love. His given
love is the mystery they must be rooted in if they are to love each other as
Jesus loves them. This action will only be understood after the "hour"
has historically happened, and after the faith-symbol-community life of
the disciples begins and develops; but Jesus "acts it out" before the
"hour" takes place (vv. 4-12).

That Jesus is symbolically displaying his Paschal love and humility
and offering it to the disciples is seen in the reaction of Peter. Peter
refuses this extraordinary and "improper" work of his Master-Teacher.
Peter thinks he should be doing this humble act rather than Jesus (disciples often washed their Rabbi-Teacher's feet to show their respect and

devotion). But Jesus insists. Peter must let him do this, otherwise he can have no part in the inheritance Jesus is to gain and share with his disciples when he returns to the Father (v. 6-9). Peter's attitude of refusal is very close to the reaction he showed in Mt 16:21 f, when he "lectured" Jesus that he would not die as he had just revealed he was about to. Without realizing it, Peter has refused to accept the symbol that encases Jesus' death. Jesus both here and in Matthew tells Peter he will be lost if he does not accept this act. This is a problem then, not only for the disbeliever, but for the believer. The crucifixion-death of Jesus is not an evil to be rejected, a scandal that proves the unworthiness of the one who dies that way. It is God's fullest act of love, and unless Peter and all believers embrace it and let it embrace them, there will be no sharing in Jesus' inheritance. Peter and other believers forget too soon the words of Jesus in 3:14-16:

> Just as Moses lifted up the serpent in the desert, so the Son of Man *must* be lifted up, that all who believe in him may have eternal life. *So great is God's love for the world that he gave his only-born Son*: everyone who believes in him is not to perish, but is to have eternal life.

Peter, even though he does not grasp Jesus' meaning (the "hour" must take place before deeper understanding dawns), does not want to be separated from him or his gifts. He then asks that Jesus wash more than his feet. The commentators give no clear answer to the meaning of Jesus' response to Peter. It refers to the situation of a guest coming to a supper with dusty feet; in such cases the guest only need wash his feet to feel clean and at home. Judas is referred to in Jesus' reply. Since it seems that the feet of both Peter and Judas were washed by Jesus, why could one of them be called clean and the other not? It could be John's way of saying that Peter brings to Jesus' "hour" (or will ultimately bring) what Judas does not bring, namely, faith and love. Without it, Judas or anyone, even *with* the "hour," is "unclean" because he refuses to let the cleansing power of Jesus' love come through to him. "The person who is washed [i.e., who believes in me and loves me] has need only that his feet be washed once [i.e., needs me to bring my "hour," my love to him in a bathing symbol only once]" (vv. 9-11). We admit many scholars do not

see a baptismal motif in the footwashing episode; most, however, see the
"dying-rising" symbolism of the action. Still, Jesus speaks of his action
as needed "*only once*" (as Baptism is needed only once). The verb used
is the common baptismal verb, *bathing*. Baptism was always viewed as
done *by Jesus* (no matter who the earthly minister was). Paul in Romans,
c. 6, speaks of Baptism as a "plunging into Jesus' death." An immediate
"flash-back" to chapter 12 shows Jesus' "feet" in a sense bathed in love
by a believer . . . and close upon that scene we have this one showing
Jesus "bathing" the "feet" of believers (both "bathings" have to do
with "his burial"). Could the Jesus of Mode #1 be showing the disciples
how they appropriate the love of the Jesus of Mode #2 . . . namely,
through the symbolic act of Baptism? At least some scholars think so;
they discover in the scene a baptismal motif, although on a secondary
level.

With verses 13 f, Jesus speaks of another meaning of his action,
closely related to its deeper meaning. Once "incorporated" into the
mystery of Jesus' death and Resurrection—Christians come to the
mystery through faith; Jesus brings the mystery of his love encased in
symbol—how do believers live out their lives united in the mystery of his
"hour"? If Jesus is a Master who "serves" the disciples "unto death,"
then his disciples now living within their "serving" Master, must try to
do as he did (v. 15). As Jesus renders his glory communicable by the
"giving" of himself, so his disciples must give themselves to the service
of the brothers and sisters. In verses 16 and 20, the disciples are now
identified as "sent" by Jesus. The term is very familiar; Jesus has been
the one "sent" by the Father. As the Agent of the Father he audibilized
and visibilized the Father's words and love. Now Jesus is to ascend to the
Father in death and thereafter will not be directly perceivable as he was in
Mode #1. When he becomes invisible and transcendent, where will his
love and service be *seen*, be made visible? It will be seen *in those he
sends*. His love residing in them spiritually will go outward in service to
the brothers and sisters. What makes the Jesus of Mode #2 visible, is the
visibility of his disciples; Jesus, his death and Resurrection lives in them
spiritually.

Judas again is referred to in vv. 18-19. Not only did the "Jews"
reject Jesus, whose blasphemies they believe brought him deservedly to
the Cross; but *one of his disciples* rejected him and betrayed him to his

enemies. The *Cross* and *Judas* are both "scandals" that continue to be used against Christ and the disciples even in John's time, ca. 90-95 AD.

For John (like many NT documents) part of the answer to these "scandals" is to be found in the OT. Scriptures indicate that God knew about the *lifting up* and about *the one who eats bread and yet raises his heel against him* (Ps 41:9; cf., also 2 S 15:31; 16:23; 17:1-4, 23: Ahithophel's betrayal of David and subsequent hanging were seen as a prophecy of Judas' action and fate). God's plan will know acceptance *and* rejection and he is aware of this. Furthermore, Jesus as *ego-eimi- with-us*, the "high" Christ, can read men's hearts and he knows that many choose to do evil (v. 19). The great drawback to this explanation is that it often leaves the mystery of "rejection" sounding like it *had* to happen in a deterministic way. The full OT and NT revelations teach otherwise; they show that all human persons are basically free in their choices. One suspects with the frequent reference to Judas, that he was not only a "current argument" used against the true and valid Messianism of Jesus (i.e., a "high" Christ would never have chosen such a disciple), but that he was also cited as a "type" of on-going defections happening in the Church (cf., the Johannine Epistles). These Judas references could indicate that the Church saw more than one Judas being foretold in Ps 41. To reject and leave a community "sent" by Jesus would be a "Judas-act" too. Latter day Judases by leaving the community not only reject Jesus; they reject the Father who sent him (v. 20).

Jesus Predicts His Betrayal 13:21-30

Jesus earlier was "troubled": once because he was confronted with "darkness" that refused to see him as a source of Resurrection-life (11:33); the other time because people refused to recognize that life could flow from his death (12:27). Here again Jesus is "troubled" (v. 21). It is not fear of death that elicits this anxiety; he is disturbed at the "darkness" of Judas' heart. The former disciple has stopped loving; he does not recognize the love Jesus offers him in the symbolic action of the footwashing. Again, an inexplicable enigma! But Jesus is the "high" Christ and he knows the thoughts of the human heart. And even though he is rejected by a disciple, he will not reject the disciple. He offers Judas bread (an ancient gesture of love and affection for a special friend or guest). But Judas seems beyond reconciliation. He eats the bread, but without love (fulfilling again Ps 41:9). He opts for betrayal, an act that seems more diabolic than mere human choosing of evil, and so as a Jew of strong dualistic mindset, John sees "Satan entering into him" (vv. 26-27). Even then, Jesus gives the challenge: "do what you must do" (v. 27). That Judas remained solid in his decision to reject Jesus is dramatically expressed. After hearing Jesus speak words of love for his disciples, and after being offered two symbols of love (the washing and the morsel of bread), he chooses to follow "darkness" instead of the "light" . . . "he went out and . . . *it was night*" (v. 30).

John mentions for the first time the "disciple whom Jesus loved" (v. 23). Since his love for Jesus will be shown many times (18:15; 19:26, 35; 20:8; 21:7), we know that, unlike Judas, his love is constant and reciprocal. He will represent those who accept Jesus and listen to his words with openness. The discourse about to be given on the deepest meaning of Jesus' hour is meant for him and like believers. With Judas' departure, the scene is set for the discourse. * * * *Many scholars believe this disciple is identified now and will continue to be mentioned as remaining with Jesus through his "hour" because he is the eyewitness authority behind the gospel. His deep love for Jesus in the beginning and his long years of faithful love after the Resurrection show that the tradition behind the gospel derives from a trusted early source, one loved by Jesus and one who reciprocated that love. He personally witnessed and experienced Jesus' love for the world and is (with the help of others) recording it in this book.*

The Last Discourse

Jesus has given many discourses; they have helped draw out more fully his true identity and have opened up the symbolism of his signs: e.g., in c. 5 his discourse explained that he worked in tandem with the Father and could give life on the Sabbath. In c. 6, he explained he could offer better bread than Moses' manna and the barley loaves he himself multiplied. In cc's. 7-9, he explained the revealing light he was bringing from heaven. Now Jesus is to work his greatest sign and on the surface it seems sadly tragic . . . Jesus is to leave the world rejected and in suffering. Disciples facing Jesus' imminent death, obviously do not want it to happen . . . they do not understand why it must happen. And so Jesus must spend time with them and explain why it has to happen and what the effects of its happening will be for them. If any sign of Jesus needs a discourse to draw out its meaning, it is the one that is about to happen.

And the Jesus who gives the discourse is most remarkable: he is the Jesus about to go through his "hour," but *also* the Jesus who has gone through the "hour" and returned in a transcendental, trans-historical Mode to tell the disciples about it. He is mostly the Risen Jesus who has gone to the Father and who has returned to live with the community of John through the coming of the Spirit for fifty or more years. Thus the audience for the discourse is also (and mainly) the community of John (they, like the original disciples, must learn from Jesus the meaning of this "hour"). The discourse is an explanation of the "hour," but it is also a commission to tell others about it. The Spirit therefore has many other people in mind besides John's Church when he inspired him to "record" this discourse. Historically, it has proved to be for countless Christians the most beautiful, meaningful, and challenging explanation of Jesus' "hour" that Christians possess, a much treasured masterpiece.

As one looks at the length of the discourse one wonders: did Jesus actually say all this (or something like this) at the Last Supper? Scholars see it as unlikely that the discourse in its present length was given in one sitting. In fact the discourse actually "ends" in c. 14:31, and then continues on for *three more chapters* (a clue that there may be a "collection" of discourses here). On close inspection scholars further detect that the Jesus who gives the discourse is understood with different levels of insight (thus a "collection" of data from different periods in Jesus' ministry is indicated.) Also, some of the data seems more suitable to other settings than a Last Supper (e.g., words about the Vine and the Branches would more likely be given when Jesus was in or near a vineyard). So the discourse seems to be a collection of many sayings of Jesus that speak of his "going away" and the repercussions his "going away" will have for the disciples; also sayings that speak of the manner in which he is to return to them after his Resurrection. What John seems to have done, then, is to have gathered material from which he can construct Jesus' LAST WILL AND TESTAMENT for believers as he approaches his "hour."

If the discourse is a collection and therefore a "constructed discourse,'' is the idea of gathering data under the general theme of a Last Will and Testament original to John? One who is familiar with the OT knows that the "Last Discourse" is in fact a literary form found there quite often. The OT contains these artificial discourses for such great religious figures as the Patriarch Jacob (cf., Gn, cc's. 47-49); Moses (cf., Dt, cc's 31-34 especially); Joshua (cf., Jos, cc's 22-24); David (cf., I Ch: cc's. 28-29), and others. Even the NT uses this form; cf. Ac. c. 20 and 2 Tim, for ''last discourses'' of Paul; 2 Peter for Peter's ''last discourse.''

John, then, seems to be constructing a discourse along the lines of these Scriptural precedents, for his discourse contains most of the common elements found in them. These discourses are given as though the "Great Religious Figure" were about to die. First, he assembles the family or the nation and announces his imminent death (Jesus will do this). Next, there are reactions of concern and anxiety on the part of the family or the nation left behind (this is discernible in Jesus' discourse). The "Great Man" then reassures his family and his people that they will survive his passing. He gives instructions that will see them through the crisis and he gives them rules that will help them live as he and God would want them to live as he leaves them. He exhorts them to remain united with and loving of each other. He warns them of the difficulties ahead, but he leaves them the commandments as protection against their enemies and problems. He promises them God's help in their lives and concludes with a prayer invoking God's help for their survival and safety. The device is intended to give a summary picture of the "Great Man" and the meaning and purpose of his life for the people.

Jesus in the Last Discourse will be doing much reassuring, much explaining of the consequences of his "going away." He will leave his disciples a special commandment. He will stress the need for unity and love. His promises will differ greatly from those of the Great Men who preceded him. He will promise *to return* and *to be with them forever* through the mystery of the Spirit. God's promised protection will dwell within them. The discourse paints a most beautiful, spiritual picture of Jesus—who he is, what he does for believers, what he expects of them. The discourse ends with Jesus' prayer to the Father for his disciples. This "Great Man," of course, is also God's Son, who dies for the world and returns to it. The thoughts originate from the data of Jesus Mode #1, but they have been transposed by John and are mainly spoken by the Jesus of

Mode #2 who dwells within this community through the Spirit. A truly remarkable discourse. When we ask again, did Jesus really give this discourse, John would undoubtedly say, "yes." "His Spirit helped me gather this material together. His Spirit helped me set down these words as Jesus' *intended* Last Will and Testament for believers."

13:31-38

Judas no longer listens or believes; he has chosen darkness and cannot follow Jesus where he is about to go. The disciples believe in Jesus and listen to his voice; in time they will be able to follow him (v. 36), and so he will explain his "going away" and what it means for them. The disciples naturally think of "going away" in terms of stoning or crucifixion. Jesus must take them immediately to the deeper meaning of his death. With chapter 12 so close they should be thinking of his death as a full dying of himself into the Father's love, which death will produce a reservoir of reachable glory for them. In Jesus they have been seeing the reflected glory of God (his words and signs have been revealing God to them). In his death and "going away," since Jesus is incarnated in human flesh, they will *see* it in full measure. If Jesus gives himself fully to the Father and for the children of the Father, it means that the Father he gives himself to will give himself fully to Jesus (for Jesus and for the disciples of Jesus). The full giving of Jesus to the Father will be seen in his death; the full giving of the Father to Jesus (his glorification) will be *seen* when Jesus rises (vv. 31-32). Thus Jesus' "dying bears much fruit," for his glorification is, as we said, a "new Mode for Jesus," in which disciples can reach him and share in his realized glory.

Jesus had told the powers of "darkness" they could not follow him; the reason for this was that their "non-believing" closes them to his life of glory. The disciples cannot follow Jesus only because Jesus has not been glorified, i.e., he has not entered into the new Mode of existence that will make this possible (v. 33). Jesus once glorified, then can come to them and lead them to this glory. As the "Great Man" about to die, Jesus announces his departure (v. 33). He addresses the disciples as "his children." He leaves them the "commandment" that insures they will survive to share in his glory. The commandment he leaves is "love one another" and he calls it *new*. Since such "fraternal love" was expected of Israelites (Lv 19:18, 34), scholars debate why Jesus calls his commandment *new*.

It would seem that it is new because the model of love God has in mind for his people is now made known. It is the model of Jesus' way of loving . . . selfless, totally serving of others, sacrificial, "dying." As Jesus and the Father's love were always directed selflessly at others, so the love of the disciples must be directed at others. They are loved by Jesus and the Father; they must give that "given love" to others. And rather than lose it in the mystery of giving, they find more of that love returning to them because of their selflessness. They find it in the "brothers and the sisters" who are the possessors of Jesus and the Father's love also. Jesus and his Father are not loved and served "up there somewhere"; they are loved and served and discovered in the disciples. Unless the disciples learn how to love selflessly, they can never "follow Jesus," who arrived at his "fruit-bearing" glory by loving selflessly. And as Jesus' selfless love draws people to him; so the selfless love of Christians for each other will identify them before the world and draw the world to them and thus to Jesus. Members of the Synagogue are known for their "busyness" with the Law. Christians are known and identified by living not for themselves, but for each other. This love is so selflessly "different," that it identifies them before the world. Jeremiah spoke of a time when there would be a "new law," a Coming Age when the covenant would be interiorized in people's hearts (Jr 31:31-34). Now the disciples know what that means and why the commandment of Jesus is called *new*. Of course the ability to love this selflessly is beyond their capacities, and the disciples will be "troubled" about it (14:1). Jesus will shortly reveal that in the new Mode realized by his "going away" he, his Father and Spirit will be with them and will help them keep this *new* commandment.

Verses 36-38, contain John's version of the common datum which spoke of Peter's boast that if Jesus were to die, he was ready to die with him. All the gospels attest to Jesus' foretelling of the immediate emptiness of this boast, (cf., Mt 26:30-35; Mk 14:26-31; Lk 22:31-34). The insertion of this datum is not meant to embarrass Peter; it is put here to help John show the disciples that by themselves they cannot keep the commandment of "selfless love." Peter cannot "follow Jesus" (v. 36) until he enters into the "selfless love" of Jesus in his new Mode and there learns how to love selflessly (it was the Jesus of Mode #1 that Peter denies; it will be the reachable Jesus of Mode #2 that Peter returns to in repentance and love—this Jesus "drives out" all sin, 12:31). The readers of the gospel, ca. 90-95 AD, know that ironically Peter did "follow Jesus later" in death after some thirty years of selfless serving (tradition tells us by martyrdom also, about which there seems to be a referencein 21:18-19). John would see Peter's boast and Jesus' reply as again an indication that Jesus knows all things. The discourse is not the Church's "rationalization" about the death of Jesus; it is the explanation of the death by the "high" Christ who endured it to express visibly how total and selfless his love was.

FURTHER PARTICULAR COMMENTS:

V. 13 ff . . . The Synoptic gospels also speak of "service to one another" as the moral imperative Christ asks of his disciples (cf. Mt 20:28 f; Mk 10:44-45; Lk 22:26 f).

Verses 23-24, *the disciple whom Jesus loved . . . Peter signaled him . . .* Some commentators note that the beloved disciple (also the "other disciple") is frequently mentioned juxtaposed to Peter (cf., also. 18:15-16; 20:2-9; 21:7,20,23). Could this be an indication that the two traditions (Petrine and Johannine) are both seen as flowing from authentic discipleship, although the traditions developed for the most part independent of each other . . . that they are now, ca. 90-95 AD, seeking closer association because of the original closeness of their two traditions to Jesus?

Verses 31 f . . . the "Discourse." Scholars, admitting the uniqueness of John's discourse, find a corresponding "Last Discourse" in the Synoptics; not at the Supper but in statements Jesus makes just before the Supper, the so-called "Eschatological Discourse" (cf., Mk 13; Mt: 24-25; Lk 21). There in rather apocalyptic style Jesus describes what will happen when he "goes away." The Temple is to be destroyed. There will be perils, persecutions and wars. The gospel must be preached but under great difficulty. Jesus will return in apocalyptic glory in the final days as the Son of Man to judge the world, to draw the good to eternal life and the evil to eternal judgment. Before that time, believers are to remain alert and faithful. Since "mature John" believes that Jesus has returned in the

Spirit (the "second coming" is *now*), these scholars see John transposing the Synoptic eschatological discourse from its " future eschatological" form (quite apocalyptic) into a "realized eschatological" *now* form. And since Jesus has returned, he must speak at the Supper as one who is soon to return. He will address not apocalyptic problems but the specific problems his fellow Christians confront in the life of this Church, ca. 90-95 AD. In his review of the data he has found very appropriate "going away" material for a community that believes eschatology is "realized." V. 32a . . . This verse is missing from important MSS.

Chapter 14

GENERAL COMMENTS (and reflections):

The disciples, aware of the forces that oppose Jesus, are fearful for his life. Now he speaks of his imminent betrayal. He says that his final "hour" is at hand and that he is to leave the world. As awesome as the description of his death is—*glorification*—the disciples are still "troubled" (v. 1). How can they survive his death? Alone, how can they keep his "commandment of love" (even Peter has been forewarned that he will deny Jesus)?

Jesus informs them his departure is part of God's plan. Since God never forsakes his people or plans, their faith should not be shaken when he departs. They should understand his death as God carrying out his plans for them (v. 1). The sum of what Jesus has been saying in chapters 1-13, is that he has come from heaven to reveal the Father and his love for the world, that the Father wishes to share his life, light and love with all who open themselves to Jesus in faith. All of what he is and brings from the Father can be shared with believers when he is "lifted up," i.e., when he returns to the Father through death. The reason he came was to reveal and demonstrate the Father's love; the reason he goes is fully to reveal and finally to make that love available to them. As Jesus puts it, he goes "to prepare a place for them" (v. 2).

The language of "going and preparing a place" recalls the eschatology of early Christianity—"many *dwelling* places." At first, "heaven" was understood as what awaited Christians after a life of faith, hope and love. Jesus would take believers there after his final coming. John to a great degree demythologizes this view and shows that the "dwelling places of heaven" are here *now*. The process of "dwelling with God" begins long before the final coming.

Jesus described his "going away" as his glorification (13:31-32).

The term (unlike the actual form of his departure) sounds "great." The disciples, however, do not clearly see that Jesus' glorification is great *for them*. So he tells them. He must go so that they can dwell in his "Father's house." Not only God dwells there, but there are places for many to dwell there. "Going away" is the mystery of the seed dying, so that it can bear fruit (12:24). Unless Jesus fully gives himself in love to the Father and for the world, he cannot receive the communicable "glory" of the Father for the world. Love must fully *go out* before the loved one's love can fully *come in*. And when it comes in through death, Jesus, then, enters into that "glorified Mode" which renders him capable of giving his and the Father's glory to believers of any time or age (v. 3).

Jesus must review for his disciples why his departure is a "going to the Father" for them (v. 2). They should be well aware that Jesus knows the "way" to the Father; after all, he came from "there." Jesus plays on the word "way" to see if they remember why he will surely find the Father when he goes through death . . . "you know the way to where I go" (v. 4). Thomas *misunderstands*, showing that he has not seen in Jesus what is there to be seen. In other words he has not sufficiently understood that the visible and audible deeds and words of Jesus were revealing also the deeds and words of the Father (he has not seen the deeper meaning of the Book of Signs); *and* it could be that he thinks Jesus is about to reveal some *new* way to the Father. Jesus gets him and all believers to do some *recalling* (i.e., flashbacks to what was going on in chapters 1 through 12). In those chapters Jesus showed that *he was* the "Way, the Truth, and the Life" (v. 6). The gospel has revealed that Jesus was the sent Agent of the Father whose words and functions derive from and reveal the Father. Hear him and one hears the Father; see him and one sees the Father. Earlier he had equivalently called himself the "way" to the Father when he spoke of himself as the "*Gate*" believers were to enter and go through if they were to have access to "full life" (10:9-10). Human persons cannot see the Father, but they can see Jesus, and so for them Jesus' actions in the Book of Signs were the seeable revelations of the Father. To say that Jesus is the Way and that he is the Truth means his words and deeds *truly reveal the Father.*

Jesus has also been sharing with believers that which he reveals: *life* was given; *light* was given; soon *love* will be given. This indicates that Jesus is *sharer* as well as *revealer*; he is thus the *Way to Life* as well as the

Way to Truth. Thomas and all the disciples have been challenged to review what they have seen and heard; on reflection they should conclude that in Jesus they have *seen* the Father. The question of v. 5, therefore, shows lack of proper faith. From the Book of Signs they already know the *way to the Father.* The question should not be "where is the way?" The question is, how remain with the Way when Jesus is "going away"? (v. 5) As the discourse develops, Jesus will show that in death he enters into a Mode that transcends all "going away"; his death will make possible his always being present to believers as the "Way" (vv. 5-7). And of course when his death and Resurrection happen, the disciples will *see* even more clearly that Jesus is *in and with the Father.* His "lifting up" takes him there, and so the Risen Jesus (whom the disciples are to witness) is even more so seen to be the *way to the Father.*

But the post-Resurrection, transcendental Jesus is not visible except through faith, and it seems the world will not believe what it cannot see. Philip's question seems to echo a current problem, ca. 90-95 AD, against John's Church which preaches that Jesus is the "only way to the Father" (v. 6). If he is the "high" Christ, and if he truly passes through death to the Father, why doesn't he show his "being with the Father" by some dramatic display, perhaps as God displayed himself to Moses? (Ex 33:18-23) (*Readers should again be reminded the Last Discourse is in two time zones at least; Jesus is to die, but he has already died and Risen. John intermingles these zones.*) Again, the Philip-question seems to be Jesus' (or John's) device to get believers to remember where they have been, what they have already seen and heard. Sufficient "showing," sufficient displays have already been made to reveal that the Father is with Jesus (cf., cc's 1-13); one last "display" is shortly to be given (cf., cc's 20-21). In sum, Jesus' words (e.g., his frequent appropriation of Yahweh's name, *ego eimi*; the application of so many Yahweh images to himself: light, life, love, bread, shepherd, etc.), his deeds, his Resurrection—these are the *displays* that show Jesus is in tandem unity with the Father, that he is the human visibilization of the Father's presence, will and love. This Agent-messenger of the Father was lifted up and brought home, "glorified" and has "since" *spiritually* returned. Does the world need more "displays" than this?

Now Jesus states this mystery unequivocally. "I do not speak *on my own,* nor do I perform works *on my own*; it is the Father who resides within me who does these things . . . I am in the Father; the Father is in me" (vv. 10-11). No stronger statement on the mutual tandem indwelling of Jesus and the Father can be found anywhere in the NT (vv. 9-11). This for Christians is the primary truth that must be believed (v. 11). And the gospel has shown the existence of this relationship from the beginning. Believing in this truth, then the disciples can not only survive Jesus' "going away"; their faith in the Jesus-Father indwelling brings them into that mystery themselves (v. 12). *Faith* is the *key* (v. 12a)—it makes their human spirits capable of participating in the mystery of the Risen Jesus. *Jesus' departure* is the *key* (v. 12b)—it renders the Jesus of the Resurrection reachable (as will soon be seen). They can now through faith enter into the mystery of Jesus' and the Father's mutual indwelling.

And there they will be able to do the "same works" Jesus did. In fact, they will be able to do even "greater works" than he did (v. 12a). Some have thought that the "greater works" referred to the miraculous activity of the early Church. John probably sees the words as referring to the mystery we have been speaking about, the mystery of Jesus, Mode #2. This Jesus can bring life, light and love to believers, and through them, communicate his love for the world to the end of time. The "works" Jesus will do in union with believers, the "works" of the Jesus of Mode #2, are "greater" than the works that Jesus does alone (the Jesus of Mode #1, the Jesus before the mystery of his "going away").

But to be charged with doing the "same and greater" works, to be charged with the "commandment of selfless love" (13:34-35), seems to believers "beyond doing." How can they do this? They can do it through prayer. "Whatever you ask in my name I will do" (v. 13). The prayer they say is not the prayer for selfish or petty needs; it is the prayer believers say to the indwelling Jesus to help them do the "greater works," the works of selfless love. Jesus continues saving the world through the works of the believing brothers and sisters. The Father continues to give his glory to this community and, through them, to the world. To carry it off, believers need always say the *prayer of union with Jesus and the Father*; otherwise the human part of the "indwelling equation" cannot properly "perform the works" of Jesus. He was and is always selflessly united with the Father. The disciples are not yet so selflessly united, so they need to overcome the selfish options they confront if they are to do saving works. Jesus assures them he is committed to helping them do the works of selflessness, the works of love. That they are there within the mystery of the Jesus-Father indwelling and can pray *from within*, is next to be revealed.

14:15-24

Jesus, while telling the disciples he is to depart, makes great demands on them: they are to believe, to keep the "commandment," to do "greater works," to pray to him for help. Even if they know Jesus is "going to the Father," his "absence" in the Mode they are familiar with makes Jesus' demands difficult to meet. Thus, he must further explain the nature of his "going away"; how, in fact it makes possible his spiritual return. The demands he makes will not be met apart from him. No, the believing, loving, working, praying, are to be done in union with him in a new Mode. His departure makes Jesus able to send back to them the Paraclete, John's Last Discourse term for the Holy Spirit (this is the first of five LD references to the Spirit). The term "Paraclete" seems to be a borrowed first century legal term. Paracletes were counselors, people who *stood by one's side* in court to help defend and justify a person. Though the word must have had several meanings in John's milieu, he apparently likes the "standing with us" meaning of the term to describe the special role of the Spirit. Thus as Jesus was never alone, so also believers are never alone, even though Jesus will be physically absent. Since the Spirit is called "*another* Paraclete," Jesus is seen to have been their first one, and the Spirit's task will be to continue with believers the work of the first Paraclete, Jesus. Like Jesus, he too is a revealer of God, for he is said to be the *Spirit of Truth* (v. 17). His revelations, however, will not be different or additional to those received from Jesus, for as will soon become evident, one of his functions will be to continue to teach and make more understandable the revelations of Jesus (v. 26). Like Jesus, he is a "sent gift" of the Father (v. 16). In a sense, as Jesus was God-with-us in visible form, the Spirit will be Jesus-with-us in spiritual form. He will be a "forever gift" in a "forever reachable" Mode.

Since the possession of the Spirit is not visible as the presence of Jesus in his earthly Mode was, non-believers will not be able to *see* him. The time of the *visible seeing* of Jesus, the time of Mode #1, is (will soon be) over. The post-Resurrection *seeing* of Jesus in the Spirit is through inward vision possessed only by those who believe and love as Jesus demands. The Spirit makes believers aware that Jesus is alive in union with them; his meaning and love are communicated to them. This post-Resurrection awareness of Jesus in the hearts of believers shows them that the Spirit is within them revealing the Risen Jesus to them (vv. 17, 19). The world neither believes nor loves Jesus; thus it cannot *see* him or the Spirit.

Jesus has been the Rabbi-Teacher of the disciples, but unlike the rabbis of old his death will not leave his students "orphans" (v. 18). Jesus too, in his post-Resurrection Mode will be able to come back to them. This "coming back" is more than the Resurrection appearances, for Jesus speaks of himself as he did of the Spirit. He will come in an indwelling, permanent Mode. Having died and gone fully into the Father's glory, he lives in glory and can communicate that glory and life to believers. This "coming back" is of course the realized eschatology of John. If Jesus were to come back at the "literal end" of the world, even non-believers would be able to *see that* coming, for it would be their final judgment. The Jesus of John returns unseeable to the world (v. 19), but seeable to the believer through the inner eye of faith and love. The life of the "end time"—the "parousia"—"that day"—is with believers *now* (v. 24).

It would seem, then, that the gift of the Spirit not only illumines believers to Jesus' meaning—the "gift" brings them the indwelling presence of Jesus in his post-Resurrection Mode (vv. 18-19). And the Christ who dwells within them is the Christ who dwells with the Father (v. 20). The "departure" of Jesus which looked so "troublesome" and separating in verse 1, is looking less troublesome, less separating, more unitive all the time.

Especially now, the "commandment of love" is seen as the way believers grow in their love of the post-Resurrection Jesus. Now they know that Jesus lives in the brothers and the sisters; in serving and loving the brotherhood they serve and love him. It is from "there" that he communicates his and the Father's love. If Paul came across something like this passage, he would doubtless see it as an alternate reading of his own insight (cf., e.g., I Cor 6:13-17; Gal 3:28; Ep 2:13-16; 4:1-16, 25, etc.). The transcendental Risen Jesus (in Mode #2) has now a new post-Resurrection body as his dwelling place, a new *locus* to live in, to love and be loved. Believers are the *body* of Christ, in whom he lives (dwells), and loves. As they love the seeable body of Christ (the community of faith), so they are at the same time loving the unseeable (but indwelling) *head* of Christ. John's Jesus equivalently says: "Love the brothers and sisters and you love me." "Love me and you love the Father." "Love the brothers and sisters and we will love you and dwell within you" (vv. 21, 23). The mystery of Jesus' "going away" has put us all together (Father, Spirit, Jesus, the brothers, the sisters) in one new Mode of interpersonal love and service. It is in dying that the seed has become so fruitful; his life in death expands to go out fully to embrace all who love and believe in him. The Pauline and Johannine expressions of Christian morality are one and the same. It is in the brothers and sisters that Christians find Christ. It is in the brothers and sisters that they love Christ and the Father. If Christians ever really believed and lived the mystery of the "indwelling," the world would *see* a moral revolution indeed!

The "other" Judas continues to ask the question that challenges the truth of John's teaching about Jesus. If he is what John says he is, if he has actually returned to the world, why did Jesus not show himself in his Risen Mode to his enemies? (v. 22) John, not at all denying that Jesus will come at the literal end of history for a final "show" before the judgment of the world, knows that Jesus *has returned* through the "indwelling" which his death and Resurrection make possible. The reason why some are *aware* of this coming and some are not, is that the indwelling is a mystery reachable and seeable only through faith and love. As lovers know, the mystery of interpersonal psychic (indwelling) love only *happens* when people are *truly* open to each other, and when they *live for each other*. Since the disciples "believe and love" Jesus in this way now, the "dwelling with God" (v. 2) does not have to wait in heaven for them (future eschatology); the "dwelling" (v. 23) is happening *now* (realized eschatology). The "world" is not open to Jesus; certainly it lives and acts selfishly and rejects Jesus and so cannot *see* the "coming" or experience the "indwelling."

14:25-31

These final verses of the "first edition" of the Last Discourse seem especially directed at later generations of Christians who think that the Jesus of Mode #1 is *more real* than the Jesus they have encountered spiritually in the community through faith and love, the Jesus of Mode #2. Some regard the disciples who knew the pre-Resurrection Jesus as having some "advantage" over later believers. The "pre-Resurrection Jesus" here answers the shallowness of such a position. The Paraclete (now identified as the Holy Spirit) comes to "*teach you everything*"; he will "recall to you *all* I have told you" (v. 26). The later additions to the discourse (cc's. 15-16) make clear that the original disciples did not at times know as much as later believers. It is actually the Spirit who brings insight and meaning about Jesus. With the Spirit, later believers not only have the "essential Jesus"; they have Jesus *and* insight into the meaning of Jesus.

That the post-Resurrection Jesus is just as real, if not more real, than the Jesus of Mode #1, is now said in another way. As Jesus leaves the world he leaves believers his Peace. The age-old greeting and farewell blessing that Jews wished each other, Peace or *Shalom*, was a wish of earthly peace, harmony and well-being. The wish came in time to mean the deeper spiritual Peace that God would grant them in the Last Age. In a sense, Peace was seen by many as God's supreme "Messianic Gift," the full salvation-happiness he would give his people "at the end" which was to last forever. Jesus' Peace will be the fulfillment of this expected "*eternal* gift" (cf., e.g., Ps 29:11; Is 57:19; 9:6; Zc 9:10; Ezk 37:26).

By this time the disciples should be well aware that Jesus is the Messiah-Agent sent by the Father who brings the expected "eternal gift," the "forever covenant" of the Last Age (a theme that John has been developing all along—faith brings "*eternal* life"). Jesus as the departing "high" Christ has informed them that his departure brings the indwelling of the Spirit, the Son and the Father. As Jesus so often said, he comes to give life, light and love . . . the shared life of God. He does not promise believers an escape from the normal tensions and anxieties of human life, nor that they will be uniformly equal in talent, health or opportunity (v. 27). He offers Peace. He offers salvation. Now we know he offers them the "indwelling." This is the "setting" they can now presume as the reachable "setting" for any man or woman's history. If one accepts with thanks and tries to live the mystery of the indwelling, then one's life will not be "troubled" or "fearful"; it will have the deepest meaning and know the truest Peace. If all believers have Peace, how can there be any time-space advantage of one believer over another?

And since the Peace of "indwelling" can come only through Jesus' death, through his "going away," the disciples should rejoice that it is about to happen (vv. 27-28). Jesus in death goes to the Father, who he says is "greater than I" (v. 28). John is not trying to "explain" the Trinity here, that the human Jesus plays a subordinate role to the Father in that mystery (neither he nor the early Church yet think in these categories). He is trying to explain the *beauty* of his *not-so-beautiful* "going away." Jesus cannot, in his limited earthly Mode #1, give the Peace he promises. He can only do this when he arrives at the "greater" mystery, the mystery of the coming Resurrection, the mystery of the Mode of post-Resurrection existence. Death will bring him as Son of *Man* fully into the life and love of the Father; as he surrenders his love, the Father surrenders his love to Jesus and Jesus enters into the Mode that can render both his and the Father's love communicable to believers. The disciples would like the Jesus of Mode #1 to stay on. He informs them that the Jesus who goes to the Father is for them a "greater," more salvationally efficacious Jesus. The Father who loves them through the "lifted up" Jesus is for them a "greater" Father (v. 28).

Verse 29, again shows that the Cross, the "going away," is not the *scandal* some people judge it to be. Jesus admits that his death involves the devil. Satan is the force behind the "darkness" that opposes him, its personification as it were . . . "the prince of the world comes" (v. 30). The Cross is the final attempt of "darkness" to extinguish his light. Superficially viewed, it seems that could be what happened; it appears that Jesus dies a sinner rejected by God. The Last Discourse has shown that such will not be the case. What "darkness" views as victory, ironically is actually its own defeat and Jesus' victory (v. 30). For Jesus in dying keeps the commandment he gives believers and receives the fruit of that commandment. His death is not punishment; it is revelation. It is his total loving surrender to the Father for the world. Jesus was not told to go and get himself killed. He was told to go and *show* the Father's (and obviously his own) full love for the world. The rejection of his "coming" took the final enigmatic form of crucifixion (willed by "darkness"), but even in this awful form of rejection, Jesus triumphs over "darkness" and demonstrates his love for the Father and the world . . . he shows the

Father's full love for the world. Through this enigmatic act, Jesus surrenders his love and renders that love reachable to all people for all time(v. 31). The "high" Christ knows about this act and informs the disciples about it before it takes place. When the Resurrection happens, then they will know the Cross was his means of getting to the mystery of the "greater"; it was not some victory for "darkness." Hopefully, then, they "may believe" (v. 29).

With verses 30-31, we apparently come to the conclusion of an earlier form of the Last Discourse. What follows (cc's 15-17) is a collection of additional "going away words" of Jesus that either John or his final editors find suitable as an appendix to the original discourse; the "words" are found to be appropriate material for Jesus' *Last Will and Testament*.

FURTHER PARTICULAR COMMENTS:

Verse 6, *I am the Way . . .* The word "way" is a new term that Jesus uses to identify himself. Scholars debate about John's source(s) for this term. Some, noting use of the term in later gnostic literature (Hermetic and Mandean writings especially), speculate that John (a Christianized gnostic) may see Jesus as something of a "gnostic redeemer" who knows a "secret path to God." Others see OT parallels to the term: Israelites who attempted to live lives in full conformity with the Law were seen as following the "*way* that leads to truth" (cf., Ps 119:30; Tb 1:3; Ws 5:6). Others note that some sectarian Jews (the Qumran group, for example) designated their own community as the "*Way*" (by their study and exact observance of the Law in the desert, they saw themselves as "preparing a *way* for the Lord") (cf. Is 40:3). It could be that the Synagogue opposing John's Church, ca. 90-95 AD, with their ever stricter adherence to the "observances of Moses" have become "sectarian" to a degree and style themselves as the "only *way* to God," and thus John must insist on the contrary: his Jesus is the "only *way*" (v. 6). In the Book of Acts, the early Christian community called itself the *Way* (cf., Ac 9:2; 19:9; 22:4; 24:12, 22). John seems to like to take "community" terms (terms that are used to describe Israel or the Christian community) and apply them personally to Jesus. For example, if the community is the "temple" (as in Paul), for John Jesus becomes the "Temple." If the Kingdom of God (in the

Synoptics) is like such and so, then in John this becomes "*ego-eimi*," "I, Jesus am such and so"; e.g., the "Kingdom of God is like a man with a vineyard" (Mt 20:1-16) becomes "*I am* the Vine." Most scholars, it seems, find John working more with the OT, Jewish sectarian, Christian usage of the term, than "gnostic" parallels, transforming the term to conform to his own unique understanding of Jesus. Jesus has surpassed the way to truth, viz. the Law, and so *he is* the Way *to ultimate Truth*. *He is* the source of eternal life, and therefore he is the *Way to Life*.

Some see the term as meaning mostly that Jesus is the Moral Model of how Christians are to live their lives. No one can deny that Jesus is a good Moral Model, but to reduce him only to this is greatly to minimize the existential mystery of the Jesus John is describing.

Verses 9-11 . . . Some commentators see these verses as possibly directed at other Christian communities who accept Jesus as the Messianic instrument of salvation but do not yet see his full divine dimension. Thus the stress that Jesus is "in the Father and the Father is in him."

Verses 30-31 . . . John does not include the traditional "agony in Gethsemane" scene in his gospel. Still, his book seems to contain snatches of that episode (cf., e.g. 12:27, where some scholars catch echoes of Mk 14:34-36). Again, elements of the "scene" seem present in these verses; they sound close to the expressions narrated in Lk 22:42, 53 and Mk 14:42.

Chapter 15

GENERAL COMMENTS (and reflections):

The Last Discourse which seems to have ended at the close of chapter 14, will continue on to the end of chapter 17. There are many opinions on who composed these "appendix" discourses, and how they were formed and became part of the final edition of the gospel. Most scholars accept their content as Johannine and see the material coming either from John or an editor-disciple(s) familiar with his Christology (this part of the gospel, for instance, has been seen to have close affinities to the First Epistle of John and some scholars conclude that the author of the Epistle had a hand in the addition of these chapters). The content of this section, though transposed into homiletic form, would be based on Jesus data adjusted to the spiritual-pastoral-apologetical needs of John's community. The material has been judged as appropriate to the general literary form of a "Last Discourse." Chapter 15 especially contains "going away" thoughts that complement and develop what Jesus (the departing "religious figure") has already said about the *commandment* of love he leaves his disciples (the "survivors"). The mystery of the "indwelling" which results from his "going away" (his "survival revelation") is further developed.

The descriptive images of Jesus as *Vine* and the disciples as *Branches* are new for John, and scholars debate about his source for the imagery. The figure of the divine tree (vine) producing life is a myth found in contemporary pagan religions. Post-Christian gnostic sects (which doubtless had first-century antecedents) develop elaborate mythologies of a heavenly *vine* (cf., e.g., the Mandean literature). But again the *vine* and the *vineyard* are not uncommon OT images for *Israel* (cf., e.g. Israel as *vine*: Ezk 15:1-6; 17:5-10; 19:10-14; Jr 2:21; 8:13; Ps 80:8-18; cf., e.g., Israel as *vineyard*: Is 5:1-7; 27:2-6). In the OT, God made great efforts to care for and cultivate the vine/vineyard of Israel, but with minimal success. Israel as vine failed God's expectations and produced either no fruit or inedible fruit; God was displeased and threatened radical reform. Even the earlier gospels pick up on this imagery as Jesus gives three parables involving vineyards (Mt 20:1-16; Mk 12:1-11; Lk 13:6-9). Jesus could have seen himself as the true and fruitful Vine of Israel (in contrast to the nation as a whole). Certainly in John's view Jesus fulfills and surpasses Israel; perhaps his data specifically shows that Jesus revealed this truth in a parable or a viticultural metaphor about a "vine and branches." In any case, John tends to transfer "community images" (either of Israel or the Christian Church) to Jesus personally; thus the Scriptural usage of the vine/vineyard imagery for Israel could well be the main source for John's usage here.

In this connection, the OT may have contributed to John's insight that Jesus is God's real Vine. Some scholars note that John could likely have seen a prophecy of Jesus as the true Vine of Israel in Ps 80:14-18. There the psalmist asks God to restore the ravaged Vine of Israel; at the same time he appeals to God to strengthen the "son of man whom he has approved" (apparently meaning Israel's present leader). Also, in cc's. 15 and 17 of Ezekiel, God expresses his displeasure at the Vine of Israel to the prophet, whom he calls the "son of man." Scholars wonder if John may have seen Jesus prophetically revealed in these two side-by-side images: vine and son of man. Further, John (an evangelist who makes frequent use of Wisdom motifs) would quite likely be familiar with Si 24:17-21, where Wisdom is described as "a Vine producing rich and graceful blossoms." Those who followed her were to be filled with fruits; those who drank of her were to thirst for more. And so, if Wisdom is God's Vine, Jesus, who seems to be for John the incarnation of Wisdom, would be regarded by him as God's Vine also.

It is evident that John is very knowledgeable in the OT. The Vine/Vineyard imagery is there. It is also in contemporary religion. The Vine/Branches phenomenon naturally corresponds to the spiritual relationship that exists between Jesus and his disciples (the life of the vine naturally flows into and feeds the branches, as Jesus' spiritual presence flows into and nourishes his disciples). And so he finds the image aptly universal, easy to comprehend, easy to adapt and reform so that it appropriately and dynamically describes Jesus' true identity, especially as that identity relates to believers after his "going away." Jesus is the New Israel who produces the fruit Yahweh desires; he remains transcendentally in an intimate life-love relationship with believers. The *realism* of the imagery helps to show that the Jesus of Mode #2, though present spiritually and invisibly, is *really* present, for the Branches "alive" and "visible" could not be such if they were not *united* to a *real Vine* (even though that Vine is not physically visible).

If the image derives from a parable of Jesus (or viticultural metaphor), it probably would have been given in an earlier and different setting than the Last Supper (in a vineyard perhaps). Still, John would reserve Jesus' reflections on the image for the Last Discourse. Up to the Supper, Jesus has been the Vine, doing all the works of his Father. Little was expected of the disciples while he was on earth revealing himself in Mode #1 (no need to talk of the Vine *and Branches* then). But now that Jesus is about to depart, the time has come to speak of the mystery of indwelling in the "tandem metaphor" of the Vine *and* the Branches. If Christians see the Incarnation as the high point in human history (one can picture it as God planting his truly fruit-bearing Vine on earth), they must know that *that story* is by no means over with his "going away." The Incarnation is to live on in the disciples, in the Branches of God's true Vine.

So much of the Book of Signs showed the reader that the Father was living on in Jesus spiritually. "Tandem mysteries" like that *can* happen—the invisible living in and with the visible. Now Jesus will become invisible to the disciples in the flesh, but as the Father lived in him, they are ready to *believe* he can transcendentally, invisibly live on in them, and thus the work of the Father, the work of Jesus continues on visibly through history in the brothers and sisters. Jesus in death will no more be separate from Christians than the Father was separate from him; the only thing that will be different will be the Mode (and as we saw, the Jesus of Mode #2 is even a better Jesus, if you will, than Mode #1, for this simple [and beautiful] reason: the Jesus of Mode #2 has *Branches*).

If there is a theology of the Church in John, it would surely be here in chapter 15. Jesus will be living in his Branches and he will expect of them "works" that the Father expected of him. As Jesus did the Father's works because of his union with the Father, so believers do Jesus' works because they are united to him. Many commentators see close parallels between the theology of chapter 15 and Paul's teaching about the Church as the Body of Christ. If Paul's metaphor lasted longer than John's, John's is no less informative of the ecclesial mystery. Some would see his imagery as even more revealing and beautiful, since it shows that the life that flows between Vine and Branches is actually a unity of love. (*Further ecclesial motifs are found in cc's. 17, 20-21*).

This revelation at the Last Supper would have special meaning for John's community, ca. 90-95 AD. Separate from the Jesus of Mode #1 by many years, some might wonder about the *realism* of the Jesus they "live with" (Mode #2 Jesus). The chapter should help dispel doubts about the realism of the relationship. Some, viewing John's theology of the "high" Christ as a compromise of monotheism, might be contemplating a return to the Judaism of the Synagogue. Or Crypto-Christians might rationalize that it is possible to be a secret Christian in the familiar but unbelieving setting of the Synagogue. John must inform these people that they are opting for an Israel that is not fruit-bearing like the Vine of Jesus; their vine is not approved by the Father. Also, his community and Christian Churches generally have seen and experienced persecution both from the Synagogue and Rome. They must be given the *theology* behind such suffering. The present discourse gives a very profound theology on that subject. They are in union with the loving Christ and so must continue to love as he does. They are in union with the suffering Christ and so will know the sufferings he knew. If their lives are not seen to be loving or to be opposed by "darkness," then they can truly wonder whether they are in the loving, suffering Vine of Jesus.

15:1-17

Jesus here speaks as the "high" Christ (*I Am, ego eimi*) and so can describe himself as the *real* Vine (v. 1). The Father fulfills his will to have a truly fruitful Vine on earth by sending his own Son from heaven. Jesus, we recall, was earlier the "*real* bread from heaven" (6:32); so here as Vine he is truly from heaven and speaks as God's approved Agent. The nearby vine of the Synagogue cannot claim this "sent from heaven" authority. John's dualism would see the Vine/Branches metaphor as helpful in explaining two "enigmas" that his Church is experiencing: the loss of disciples (Judas, and those who followed Judas in a like rejection of Jesus, cf., e.g., the Johannine Epistles), and the present "suffering" of the disciples. Branches, once alive, can become dead, and if such a thing happens, for the good of the remaining Branches, they are to be cut off. John in his dualistic mindset can see only two categories of people in the world: those who choose life and those who choose selfishness and death, and Branches who choose death are not to be left on the Vine. Such bold "cast off" imagery (v. 2) would also be a "scare" warning for crypto-Christians. By not professing Jesus, they are not secretly living in him as they suppose; they could be cut off by the Father's pruning ax. Secondly, Branches are naturally *trimmed* to make them more fruitful. The mystery of suffering is the "pruning action" of the Father aimed at producing more fruitful Branches (n.b., he did this in the OT too, cf., e.g. Jr 5:10; Ezk 17:7). This pruning has an inward effect in that it draws believers into deeper love of him and his Son, and the pruning of suffering has an outward effect in that it draws others to become a part of the Vine.

The disciples are said to be "clean" already (v. 3). This seems to recall 13:10, where Jesus referred to his disciples after the *footwashing* as "clean." The disciples (with the exception of Judas) believe in Jesus' words and bring faith to his "hour" given to them symbolically encased in that action (v. 3). As disciples they believe in Jesus and so are Branches of the Vine, but more will be required of them than being clean. As Branches they must now "bear fruit"; *doing* must follow *being*. It is possible that by not doing, not bearing fruit, they could end up without being. They could end up dead Branches. Of course it is always more difficult to live, to act as a believer than simply to believe, so Jesus must explain why the doing, the fruit-bearing, is ever possible for believers.

Jesus then in vv. 4-5, makes clear to the disciples that their belief puts Jesus in their lives. He is *within* them. The indwelling is *for real*. The tandem mystery that made him able to work and bear fruit, viz., his being spiritually one with the Father, is now moving into a new Mode to the point where it now includes them. As the Father "remained in" Jesus, so now he, Jesus, "remains in them" (but in his post-Resurrection Mode). The disciples are now told they are to be tandem agents of Jesus. This is not pious supposing, for Jesus in v. 5, when he identifies the disciples as his "Branches" speaks as *ego eimi*. No one (again, John's categorical-dualist mindset is in operation here) can do the works of God unless he/she is joined to Jesus; the life, light and love of God is

channeled to the world *only* through him—an obvious warning to defectors and crypto-Christians. Unite with the Synagogue and you disunite
with the fruit-producing Jesus. Defections produce death; unity with
Christ produces life and fruit.

Verse 6, seems to reflect final eschatology (and this would not
normally be expected in a Johannine Last Discourse). John, however,
could find the OT eschatology "cast off and burn" imagery (cf., again
the OT Vine/Vineyard references above) better left *as is*, than transposed
to realized eschatology, for in this case final eschatology makes good
polemic against the defectors and crypto-Christians. His dualistic mindset sees choosing not to be united with Jesus as a choice that inevitably
leads "to fire."

Scholars see vv. 7-17, as a collection of Jesus sayings that speak of
the consequences of the indwelling he promises his disciples at his
"going away." John (or his editors) has molded them together in something of a mini-discourse within a discourse; the background of the
Vine/Branches mystery will reveal new depth to these sayings. In the
earlier discourse (c. 14) Jesus spoke of the "greater works" his disciples
were to do after his departure. Again Jesus stresses that these works must
be understood to be "tandem works" (v. 7). The "fruit-bearing" prayer
of the disciples is said in the certain knowledge that they do these works
with Jesus, never "apart from him" (v. 5). They pray to Jesus as
Branches, not as unattached "do-gooders." As the Father *radically*
"works" the salvation of the world through Jesus, he *practically* "works
out that salvation" in the Jesus of Mode #2 (the glorified Vine united
invisibly to the visible Branches of believers through all of history). As
the Father up to the Paschal Mystery of Jesus was *glorified* in Jesus and
his ministry (cf., e.g. 12:28; 13:31-32; 14:13), so now he receives *glory*
in the mystery of Jesus, Mode #2, Jesus living transcendentally in the
brotherhood (v. 8). If the brothers and sisters are not reflecting the
Father's love as Jesus did, John would wonder whether they are really
"disciples" (v. 8).

As noted, John has stressed in the earlier chapters of the gospel that
Jesus shares his life and light with disciples; now the emphasis is put on
his *love*. These earlier terms seem to be saying this too, but nothing says it
better than the term itself. Jesus will explain the deeper meaning of love,
since so often the term can be reduced to a sort of shallow "emotional

attachment'' one has for another person, a now-and-then sort of thing. The love Jesus gives is more constant and profound than that. In v. 9, he recalls the great love the Father had for him (both the pre-and post-Resurrection Jesus seems to be speaking here). The Father's love was the giving of total love to Jesus who gave himself totally to the Father for love of the brethren . . . two sharing totally surrendered love . . . this is the love that Jesus' death will display, the love he can give to disciples once he is Risen (v. 9).

And if Jesus gives disciples such a total love, the response he expects is "totally surrendered love" also. Unless this happens, the most profound meaning of love never happens. How human beings, weak, selfish and living in a world of "darkness," can love like this, was told them in the Vine/Branches mystery. They can love this way because they are in tandem unity with Jesus, the selfless, sacrificially loving Vine. Where and how they surrender such love to Jesus and the Father (and this is the kicker) is again revealed to them. They love Jesus and the Father when they keep his commandment, when they love and serve the brothers and sisters selflessly. To the question, "Won't they come up short if they surrender too much of themselves to the service of the brotherhood?" Jesus seems to answer . . . "did I?" If Jesus ends up *remaining in* the love of the Father (v. 10) after his total giving, then so will they end up with Jesus and the Father in their total giving. Jesus is not only "inside" helping them to go out to others; he is "outside" in the brothers and sisters trying to come in (v. 10). It is in "keeping the commandment" that the mystery of indwelling really takes off.

Jesus reminds them that what they most desire . . . the fullness, the ultimates of Peace, Life, Love and Joy (all eschatological descriptions of ultimate salvation; for Joy, cf., e.g., Is 25:9; 61:10; Zc 9:9 f) are to be found in a life of *faith* (being with Christ) and in *love* (keeping the commandment) (v. 11). Verses 12-14 repeat again the enigmatic truth which seems to contradict popular attitudes and conceptions about love. It is in *sacrificial love* that one gives and experiences God's love. Jesus is the primary model and convincing proof that sacrificial love is the most beautiful and rewarding. His sacrifice led to his glory and to the disciples' sharing in his glory; can anyone do better than that? Paradoxically, to borrow a word from Paul, it is the "empty" who end up with "fullness"; selfish lovers end up with little or no fulfilling love at all.

Verses 15-16, further define the love Jesus has for his disciples. It is the communication, the sharing, the giving up of one's innermost secrets and knowledge. Jesus does not only take care of and look after them as a Master would a faithful servant. His whole psychic life is to be shared interpersonally with believers. And since Jesus' psychic life is lived in union with the Father, the believer is to be caught up in the interpersonal psychic love of Father and Son. *Servants* have partial, limited knowledge of their *Masters*; no such limitations are to exist between Jesus and the disciples (v. 15). Nor are they loved because they in any sense "earn" or "merit" Jesus' love. No, disciples are such *by choice* . . . again, the language of selfless, outward-going love (v. 16). Jesus especially loves and chooses disciples, for he sees them capable of bearing his love to others. His indwelling capacitates them for this. It moves them to do this. If disciples have Jesus' love with them, it is there to be "passed on" to others. No one says that it is easy to "pass it on," but Jesus reminds them that they are *in a union* (which prayer makes explicit and manifest) which enables them to do this (v. 16). Jesus does not say "do this if you can"; he says "*do* this" ("this I command you"). It is only in doing the commandment that they will ever really know and experience the happiness of the love-indwelling that is theirs because of his "going away" (v. 17).

Is there a Eucharistic Motif in 15:1-17?

Would John's people, reading or hearing these verses, associate Jesus the Vine with the Eucharist, especially under the symbol of wine (a natural fruit of the *vine*)? Though the primary motif of this passage is the revelation of Jesus' indwelling love in the disciples and the demands this mystery makes on them, a number of scholars see a secondary eucharistic motif here. John's people, ca. 90-95 AD, would be aware of the eucharistic words of Jesus. The tradition, for example, behind Mark 14:25, could be known to them. There Jesus speaks of the "cup" of his covenant blood as being the "fruit of the *vine*." Christians would see the Eucharist as a Sacrament-symbol of Jesus' death, and the motif of death—Jesus' "going away"—is very strong in this passage (cf., v. 13, especially; and the implication of this verse is that when Jesus lays down his life, he does so as the *Vine*). A very ancient Christian document (Didache, 9:2), refers to the Eucharist in this way: "We *thank* you [Greek word from which the term *Eucharist* derives], O Father, for the *Vine* of David.'' In what many consider John's ''eucharistic text''—6:51-58— the bread which is also Jesus' ''body'' is spoken of as his ''flesh for the life of the world,'' connoting that his *body was given in death* for all humanity (6:51). The language of ''remaining in,'' so strong in this passage, is also found in John's ''eucharistic text.'' When one eats of Jesus' body, it says in chapter 6, one ''remains in him'' (6:56). Some indeed think that the Johannine equivalent of ''This is my Body'' would be ''*I am* the Bread from heaven'' and the equivalent of ''This is my Blood'' would be ''*I am* the Vine.'' On reflection, since Christians have a symbol that shows they are truly sharing in Jesus who is the ''*Real Bread* from heaven,'' viz., the eucharistic bread, would it not be instinctive for them to regard the eucharistic wine as the symbol that shows they are in union with the *Real Vine* from heaven, the Vine which shed its life-blood for them?

15:18-16:4a

Jesus, about to depart, has informed the disciples that he is to remain with them in a spiritually indwelling Mode; this capacitates them and charges them to love as he loved. This is how his love is communicated through time and history. But as the OT ''Last Discourse'' form warns ''survivors'' of the ''difficulties'' that lay in store for them, so Jesus alerts his disciples to the problems they are to face. Jesus brought the Father's love to the world and was hated and rejected by ''darkness.'' If the believers are indwelt by this same Jesus, they can expect no better. ''Darkness'' is still ''out there'' and will oppose believers as long as there are believers. One can almost feel the rejection and opposition, the forewarned hatred and persecution happening to John's community. Part of the Church has been excommunicated from the Synagogue (possibly this is still going on); opposition of one sort or another is coming from that quarter. Christians have also known persecutions on the part of the Romans (cf. Domitian's persecution in the last decades of the first century). The indwelling means being and growing in Jesus' love, but it *also* means rejection and suffering, and so Jesus informs them of this (v. 18).

The *world* is used here in a technical Johannine sense as those ''who choose to remain in 'darkness' and who oppose those who share Jesus' light and love.'' To the modern mind (which is aware of the vagaries of human psychology, the ambiguities that religious and cultural condition- ing can work on one's moral choices, etc.), the categorical division of human beings into two groups is terribly simplistic. John, however, is born and brought up in a heavily dualistic mindset. He knows that Jesus is truly the ''high'' Christ, that he has been rejected by many—and he only has two categories to put people into. He makes the Jesus category as attractive as he can. He makes the non-Jesus category as unattractive and negative as possible. And indeed the history of his time worked to solidify him in his categorical mindset (no ''live and let live'' in those days). Thus John makes opposers sometimes look as though they were locked into the ''opposing darkness'' (the ''over-all'' John, however, knows this is not the case; Jesus is trying to win everybody's faith, and so everybody is winnable). Still, the *sound* of determinism suits his polemi- cal purpose. He wants to keep the right-choice people where they are. He wants to paint the wrong-choice people as ''far-out'' as possible, so that they will be *shocked* into some awareness that they are *wrong-choice* people. Either that, or he wants truthfully to label these people as ones who have taken a stand against the true light of the world. From such people, believers can only expect persecution and opposition (v. 19).

In 13:16, Jesus warned that the disciples as his servants would fare the same as he (ca. 90-95 AD as well as 27-30 AD). Here he specifies that this means persecution and people contradicting their words (v. 20). Scholars find in v. 20, echoes of Jesus' missionary warnings to his disciples in an eschatological passage in Matthew (Mt 10:14-25). The Jesus of that gospel warns, as does John's Jesus here, of persecutions and rejection that his disciples will experience. Matthew's Jesus, like John's, promises the Spirit who will give them strength to witness despite opposition (Jn 15:26-27). Thus John seems to be reworking traditional material (in Matthew the ''going away'' and its effects are more apocalyptically described; in John the ''going away'' and the problems are spoken of in actual and more realized terms).

Persecutors are especially upset at the *names* the disciples give Jesus. It is disturbing to Jews that Jesus can be so ''high'' a Messiah that he often pre-empts the titles *ego eimi, the name*, etc. The common Christian title, *Lord*, would be upsetting both to Jews (it became a Greek word for Yahweh) and to Romans (who know it as a title of the emperor). Believers, then, are persecuted because of Jesus' *name*. But Jesus informs them that as "sent," as the approved Agent of Yahweh, he can certainly use the *name* of his sender (v. 21). To tell Jesus (or Christians speaking for Jesus) that he cannot use these names, is to tell the Father that he does not much know what his Agent is up to. Christians should not hesitate to continue using Jesus' name. The Father is always with his Agent, Jesus. He is with the agents of Jesus, the disciples. He is not with those who deny Jesus or persecute his disciples.

The dualism of John, so strong in this *warning section* of the discourse, is not, however, so heavy as to be deterministic, for in vv. 22-24, Jesus speaks of the *guilt* of those who oppose him and the disciples. Guilt follows upon hearing and seeing Jesus' words and works. He comes to those who will ultimately reject him just as he comes to the disciples. Sin and guilt happen in and after the coming. It turns out that those who reject Jesus never gave him a fair hearing or an honest look (they even denied that the blind man had been cured); the disciples on the contrary were open to Jesus' words and deeds. The Father was recognizable in what Jesus said and did. That some failed to recognize him shows that their attitudes were *sinful*, that they chose *sinfully* to close themselves to God present revealing himself in Jesus.

Still, being the recipients of such deep hatred would make some early believers wonder. Can something so good, be so hated, especially by those who with their Scriptures, prophets and Law were supposed to be prepared for Jesus? Christians should have said: yes, all people are capable of this deep hatred. For love between God and human persons to work, everybody's will must be left autonomously free. But Christians were not this psychologically sophisticated, and so they answered the "mystery of rejection" by referring to the Scriptures (we saw this earlier, in 12:38-40). God knew about the "rejection" and the "hatred" and that it would be without cause (Ps 35:19; Ps 69:4). He sent Jesus to the world despite foreknown rejection.

When Jesus in the Eschatological Discourse of the Synoptics (cf., esp. Mt 10: 16-20; Mk 13:11) foretold that persecution and hatred would be the lot of his disciples after his "going away," he also promised the Spirit to help them bear witness to him in the sufferings of that time. So Jesus in John (reworking the "eschatology" of this discourse to conform

with the "realized" problems of his own community) promises the
Paraclete. This "invisible" Witness will reside within believers and help
them to witness Jesus "visibly." The "tandem Jesus-Father mystery"
was opened up to believers; their faith and love have brought them into
the indwelling (cf., cc's. 14-15, 17). The Paraclete is now seen to be part
of that mystery. As Jesus received the Spirit to bring God's message of
salvation to the world (1:32-33), so believers will be indwelt by the Spirit
to speak that message of salvation throughout history.

16:1-4a

As stated above, some members of the community of John have
been excommunicated from the Synagogue; some perhaps have been
executed either by Jews or Romans (even Paul before his conversion
acquiesced in the *death* of Christians; cf. Ac8:1; 26:9-11) (vv. 1-2). This
is the "scandal" John's confreres have experienced, ca. 90-95 AD. It is
part of the mystery of indwelling. If Jesus suffered his "hour" before he
knew his full glory, believers must also share in the suffering aspects of
the "hour" (v. 2). The Spirit sent by the Father and Jesus "reminds"
believers of the inevitability of such suffering when one lives in a world
of non-belief. But the "reminding Spirit" is also understood as the
source of strength that helps believers witness Christ even in suffering (v.
4a).

FURTHER PARTICULAR COMMENTS:

Verse 1, *I am the Vine* . . . If John sees in Jesus the fullest meaning of
Israel (i.e., the full meaning of what God wants Israel to be), if he and not
historical Israel is God's *true, real* Vine, through which he transmits to
the world his life, light and love, then John does not seem very distant
from Paul, who views Jesus in a similar light. For Paul, Jesus is the one
faithful, legitimate heir of Abraham who inherits the Promise; when
people believe in Jesus they become coheirs with him of that Promise;
(cf., e.g., Gal 3:28-29; 4:7; Rm 11:16-24).
Verses 1-7 . . . In passing, it might be noted that Catholic Christians find
in these verses a theological base for their devotion to the saints. In these
model Christians they have found Jesus "truly remaining" within. The

saints are not "prayed to" in isolation from Jesus; it is their witness to the indwelling Christ that draws others more deeply to believe in the Vine/ Branches mystery. Saints are "prayed to" as Branches of the indwelling Vine; in a sense they are *proof* of the truth of the mystery.

Verse 20 . . . the close of the verse seems to be John's way of saying that the "world" will give ear to Christians about the same way they gave ear to Jesus (often a "deaf" ear).

Chapter 16

GENERAL COMMENTS (and reflections):

Scholars see the present Chapter as a variation of the original Last Discourse of 13:31-14:31 (the themes of impending departure, sadness-reassurance, the coming of the Paraclete, the gift of Peace, need for prayer, are here). They see it, however, as less theologically developed (especially about the "indwelling" and the "commandment of love") and so suggest that it is an earlier form of the discourse in cc's. 13 through 14. Be that as it may, the Chapter ended up as an integral part of the gospel where it now stands. Why would John or his final editor(s) include material which seems to repeat what has already been said? Apparently because he or they judged the material appropriate for some of the community's current problems, ca. 90-95 AD. It could be that some do not fully appreciate the presence and functions of the Spirit in their lives. Chapter 16 will remind them of important roles that the Spirit fills. For one thing, he proves to Christians that the world now persecuting them is totally wrong in its judgments about Jesus and indeed stands condemned by God for such judgments. Moreover, the Risen Jesus whom disciples should believe is transcendentally "remaining with them" (cf., cc's. 14-15) is being interpretatively disclosed to them in their day by the Spirit. Still, some may be "wondering" about the reality of a Jesus remaining with them whom they cannot "see." Most never saw the historical earthly Jesus or experienced an appearance from him. Do they feel that those who experienced this have an advantage? Did early Christians "see" Jesus *more* than they "see" him? In the second half of the Chapter, Jesus will remind them that their present "seeing" is the seeing that counts, and that they should cease all "wondering" about who best "sees" him.

16:4b-15

Jesus, as long as he was in his earthly historical Mode, did not have to explain to the disciples the deeper meaning of his "going away" or the different Mode in which he would "return." He was there to reveal God and his love for the world. He was with them visibly to answer all their questions. But the time to speak of the consequences of his "going away" and "return" has arrived; both are now close at hand. His present form of "being with them" is about to change and they must know about it. But to lose Jesus in his familiar earthly Mode naturally creates sadness; visible human presence always seems more real. Jesus must now reveal why any kind of lasting sadness should not be their proper reaction to his "going away" (vv. 4b-6). (*The question Jesus asks in v. 5, shows that this "discourse" is probably antecedent in composition to 13:31-14:31. Peter did ask Jesus about his going away in 13:36, as did Thomas in 14:5.*)

Jesus informs the disciples it is for their deepest good that he departs. If he does not go, they will never receive the Spirit whose role (it is now becoming apparent from earlier revelations: 1:33, 3:3-8) is not only to teach believers the full meaning of Jesus, but to beget them into the mystery of God wherein Jesus will return to them in his post-Resurrection Mode. Unless Jesus goes fully, totally, selflessly through death into his "glory for others," he can never catch believers up in that glory through the Spirit. In death and Resurrection he reaches that glory and sends the Spirit who brings them into that arrived-at mystery. The seed must *die* if it is to become fruitful, 12:24 (v. 7).

With v. 7, John's community is solemnly reminded by the Jesus of the Last Supper that he *did* go to the Father. He *did* send the Spirit. They are now, through the Spirit, living with him in his transcendental Mode. If the opposing, persecuting world has caused some to doubt the Spirit's and Jesus' presence, Jesus reminds them again in this Chapter. Moreover, the Spirit as witness for Jesus, now in vv. 8-11, is shown to be the witness against the world that opposes both Jesus and Christians in their time. The trial motif used so frequently in the gospel emerges again strongly in these verses. The Spirit in this passage is not so much the attorney who defends Jesus; he is the one Jesus sends to "prosecute" the false judgments of the world (earlier we recall that Moses, a supposed witness *for* the "Jews" against Jesus, became the "prosecutor" *against* them, 5:45-47). The "prosecution" speaks here especially to persecuted Christians (since in John's view the world does not much listen to Jesus or the Spirit). Christians must know that the world has "no case" against Jesus, and the Spirit will show them this is so. Verses 8-11, are quite condensed, and while the "case" was clear enough for John's community, it is more difficult for modern readers to follow the lines of the Spirit's argument against the world. But the main thrust of the argument seems to be as follows.

The Spirit shows that the world was wrong about Jesus on three counts: sin, justice (righteousness), and judgment (v. 8). The world (especially the "Jewish" segment of the term) regarded Jesus as a *sinner* (he told lies about his origins, he broke the Law, he blasphemed; none of which as "high" Christ he actually did). So as it turns out, it was not Jesus who *sinned*, but the "Jews." They refused to believe God's Agent sent from heaven to reveal his will for the world. And Jesus was shown to be God's Agent by his "going away"—his "lifting up"—his "return" in the Spirit. No other *sin* could compare with refusing faith in one so obviously sent from God. Nor was it an honest mistake on the part of the world. As John sees it, the refusal to believe was wilful (cf., e.g. 3:19; 9:41; 12:37; 15:22-24) (v. 9). So it is the world who sins, not Jesus!

Secondly, Jesus was thought not be be a *just* and righteous man (again apparently because he lies, breaks the Law, and blasphemes). The Spirit shows the blatant falseness of this accusation by reminding believers that Jesus actually went "to the Father" (v. 10). The Father can only take the righteous to himself. The unrighteous could not send God's Spirit to them. That believers are now experiencing Jesus' return through the Spirit, shows how blasphemous and unfounded the charge is that Jesus was unjust. And those people who accuse Jesus of being unrighteous "can see him no longer." They saw to this, having conspired in his death. The only place they can "see" him now would be in the brotherhood (the Jesus of Mode #2), and they refuse to listen to the brotherhood, in fact persecute them. So who is "*unjust*"?

Finally, Jesus was ridiculed as one "condemned," one "*judged*" guilty of crimes that called for his execution (he blasphemes, say the Jews; he is pretender-king, say the Romans; and is thus *judged* deserving of death. Who would take such a one for Lord and Savior?) The world which judged Jesus worthy of death was acting under the leadership of the "Prince of the world" (since it was the darkest act of all history). Was the judgment of the devil and his cohorts right? No, the Prince of the world and his followers were condemned by their own executed *judgment*. Jesus' death brought him to the Father, not to ignominy or oblivion. The death and Resurrection are God's definitive *judgment* on the devil and the world. As God sees it, Jesus is *judged* worthy of only one thing: total, eternal life, light and love in a form communicable to all who open themselves to him. That he is fully in that "glorious state" is amply shown by the experienced Spirit, the experienced Risen Jesus living with the Church. In fact, the Spirit's being with Christians "proves" that Jesus is sinless, righteous, and judged by God as the one deserving to share his full glory. How could the Spirit be here, if Jesus, the just one, did not send him? (v. 11)

Of course John's community, beset with trials and persecutions, might "wonder" whether the devil has been fully "condemned and conquered." But John knows the defeat is radical, and Christians to remain faithful and loving in such circumstances need only remain within Jesus to "defeat" the devil every time he opposes them (John's realized eschatology means not only that "life with and in Jesus" is *now*; it means that "defeat for the devil" is *now*). He can no more destroy Christians than he could destroy Jesus. Suffering they may know; defeat because of suffering and persecution they need never know.

Verse 12, seems to be the pre-Resurrection Jesus informing Christians that it will not be more pre-Resurrection words that will answer their questions about suffering. What they need is the post-Resurrection Jesus who can send them the Spirit of Truth who will give them all the support they need to endure the sufferings of their time, a Spirit who will teach them the full meaning of God's love that comes to them in the person of Jesus. The Spirit can "defend" Jesus against any and every enemy that opposes him. He can interpret Jesus for each new generation ("he can declare the things which are to come"). But first, Jesus must go into his "totally surrendering death" so that he can send the Spirit to do these things (v. 13).

His telling of the story of Jesus was so novel that John must have been accused of radically altering the story, to the point of telling it wrong (his "high" Christ, etc). His answer must have always been: "it is the

Paraclete who repeats and explains the story to me; It is he who unfolds the full meaning of Jesus as the situations of Christians require.'' The Spirit is not some new or other revealer improving on Jesus; he is the ''declarer'' of the true meaning of Jesus (vv. 13-14). Christians have no need of another word or revelation, since Jesus was the definitive Word, the ultimate revelation about God. What they need is a good teacher to review and interpret what was definitively taught by God's Word. And they have this in the Spirit.

And as they saw Jesus' ''glory'' in his life and works, so now they can continue to see his invisible glory in the good works of the visible brotherhood, works made possible by the presence of the Spirit within them. As the ''sent one'' the Spirit also brings them the transcendental presence of the glorified Jesus: the *sender* is in tandem union with the *sent* (v. 14). How is Jesus *seen*; how does he draw people to his love in John's day? Largely through the Spirit-filled, Jesus-indwelt lives of believers. And at this stage of the Last Discourse, believers should know that when they have the Spirit of Christ, they also have the Spirit of the Father. They may be momentarily saddened by Jesus' death. They may be plagued with suffering and persecution as they live out their lives. But Christians, because of this mystery, can know that they presently live in union with Jesus and his Spirit-vindicated love and goodness. They live in union with the Father who has given his full love to Jesus for love of him and them. Can the *world*, can the Synagogue (both disturbing John's community in some way, ca. 90-95 AD) do any better for them than this? (v. 15)

16:16-33

It seems that these verses have something to do with how a believer *sees* Jesus after his death. Jesus says the disciples will see him in a ''little while'' (v. 16). He is to return and be ''seen'' in his Resurrection Appearances (cc's 20-21). This will be a ''little while.'' In the common tradition of the early Church, it was thought that Jesus would return at the parousia and be ''seen'' by all. But in John's time, the ultimate parousia had not taken place and so the intervening sixty years or so would not be considered a ''little while.'' Could the ''little while'' refer to a less selective and more general post-Ascension but pre-parousia *seeing*? It

would seem so. Chapter 16, after all, is set in the gospel immediately
after cc's. 13:31-15:27. There, Jesus spoke of his return to "remain with
you." The "indwelling" happens in a "little while" after Jesus' Resurrection and this is *seeing* of a real and profound order. For the glorified
Jesus to be with them in the Spirit, this is "to see" Jesus. He says to the
disciples: "you will *see* me . . . because I am going to the Father" (v. 17).
Jesus' death ends the time when anyone thereafter can see him in Mode
#1. His death and Resurrection (his "*going to the Father*") have brought
him to the mystery of his glory, his "glory for others," to the Mode
which makes him seeable to believers. This is the Jesus who has reached
full glory in the full surrendering of self, the Jesus who is reachable and
seeable to all who give faith to him after his Resurrection. But is this
spiritual seeing really seeing? It seems that some of John's people
"wonder" about this. And so Jesus must put an end to all such "wondering" (vv. 16-19). It *is seeing* and it *is* "seeing in a little while." From
Jesus' already given words of the "discourse" they should know this.

The new Mode of "faith-seeing" was brought about through the
tragic and cruel event of crucifixion, through suffering and physical
death. Naturally believers are "sad" about this kind of "going away" (v.
20). For one to surrender his earthly life as Jesus did is a very painful act,
much like the mother giving birth to a child (an image, by the way, the OT
and NT use to describe the sufferings that are to happen before the joys of
messianic fulfillment will be experienced; cf. e.g., Is 26:17-18; 66:7-13;
Mk 13:17-19; Mt 24:19; Lk 21:23). But the death of Jesus, like the
suffering of a mother, is the prelude to a most joyful event: the coming of
Jesus to his glory; the mother to the joyous birth of her child (vv. 21-22).
Again, a mystery is being revealed here (n.b., v. 21 begins with an
"Amen, Amen," and so Jesus speaks with divine revealing authority),
and the mystery is that eschatological joy follows upon human surrender,
human giving; the "seed must die" before it can know joy and bear joyful
fruit for others.

And Jesus reminds his disciples (the pre- and post-Resurrection time
zones seem combined here) of a beautiful fact. As he will return to them
in the "Resurrection Appearances" all the sadness they feel at his death
will turn to joy, but it will be rather remarkable joy in that it never leaves
them, even when the "appearing Jesus" leaves them. The joy Jesus will
give them at that time "no one can take from them" (v. 22). The felt joy,

then, is "seeing" Jesus *forever;* it is "faith-seeing" and it will happen in a "little while." Suffering continues (since believers remain on in the human Mode. John's people know this well; his Church is experiencing spiritual and physical suffering) but such human suffering after Jesus' post-Resurrection return can never destroy their "seeing." Jesus and his given joy will always be in believing hearts because of his new Mode of "being there" made possible by his "dying." The *joy* no one can take from the disciples is the *indwelling*.

For John, if the seeing, the eternal joy, will come to disciples in a "little while," then the parousia . . . "that day" . . . is with the disciples *now* (even though human sorrow continues). With this "seeing," Christians should not "wonder" anymore . . . they should not have to "ask questions" anymore about the "little while." Eternity is *now* . . . the Jesus of the eternal Mode #2 is with them . . . the "seeing" is now and forever (v. 23).

When Jesus goes away and returns to remain with the disciples through the indwelling, all they need to ask for is that God keep them firm and constant within that "seeing." Being within the mystery of the "returned Jesus" in his new Mode, they know that they are in the mystery of the Father also, the Father who is totally united with Jesus, and so whatever believers ask of the Father in the matter of constancy to the mystery will be granted them (v. 23). Before his death the Jesus of Mode #1 was the mediator before the Father for the needs of the disciples. Now in death and Resurrection Jesus is "there" with believers in the mystery of the Father . . . their tandem unity is shared with believers . . . Jesus' agency includes the agency of the disciples. Now believers speak their "mystery needs" to Jesus in Mode #2, in whom they dwell with the Spirit. They pray for the grace to be faithful to the mystery; they pray for the grace to be capable of the love the mystery demands; and they pray *from within the mystery* and are assured of that grace (v. 24). Disciples should never forget they are branches within Christ (v. 15). The Father will prune these branches to make the joy Jesus gives them fuller and more fruitful. Thus prayer is necessary to help them grow spiritually "within the mystery." The Father seeks this growth.

Before Jesus went into his death and arrived at the Mode of eternal reachability, he could speak of the mystery of the "little while" only in figures. Once arrived at the mystery which renders indwelling possible, once he communicates the indwelling to believers, then he can speak of his and believers' "being there" in *plain words* (v. 25). The coming of the "hour" has made the indwelling a reality (*plain*, understandable, realizable) not just a promise (*figures* that foretell and demonstrate the mystery symbolically). Further, the "asking prayers" still necessary for believers (for as free participants in the mystery before their own final surrender in death, believers can opt out; they can be unfaithful and unloving), are said (Jesus reminds them again) within the mystery of indwelling, not from outside. These prayers then are *within the Father's love*. The Father is committed to keeping believers faithful and loving . . . "ask the Father *anything* and he will give it to you" (v. 23). The Father knows that in believing and loving his Son, they gave faith and love to him as the Father; Jesus, after all, was revealing *him*. They are truly brothers and sisters of Jesus and the Father's own children begotten by his Spirit. How can the Father not desire that his *own family* stay united in his love? He will provide all the strength they need to stay where they now are. If Christians are within the post-Resurrection mystery of Jesus sharing in the Father's love, why should there be any "wondering" about the "little while"? . . . about when they are going to see Jesus? . . . about whether the Father listens to their prayers? (vv. 16-19) Giving faith to Jesus, loving his brothers and sisters, praying within the Father's love: this is *seeing* Jesus. Much of this whole chapter seems to be derived from a homily of John to his own community about the inappropriateness of his people "wondering" about how and when they "see" Jesus. If they believe, love and pray they are dwelling within the mystery of God's love and are "seeing" Jesus. Jesus' first coming was the revealing of this mystery; his return after death in a Mode reachable through faith is the giving of this mystery (v. 28).

Verses 29-30, seem to be John's way of again showing his own people that they are not disadvantaged in not having seen the Jesus of Mode #1, nor in having a *personal* post-Resurrection appearance of Jesus. The episode depicts the disciples who had that "advantage" as not really understanding what Jesus said to them (they seem to say they believe fully that Jesus is the "high" Christ, e.g., he knows questions before they are asked, etc., but they do not really understand). Historically no one can comprehend the deeper meaning of Jesus until after he has gone through the mystery of his death. Jesus' words only become *plain*, understandable, *after the "hour,"* and John's people are just as much "after the hour" people as the first disciples, and thus are at no disadvantage. A Christian is a Christian is a Christian!

Jesus continues to rub off the glamor some of his own people attach to the "first disciples." He notes that at his "hour" they all scattered (John's sources parallel Synoptic accounts: Mk 14:27; Mt 26:31, who see the defections fulfilling Zc 13:7) leaving him alone (not much brave "we know you know everything" conviction there) (vv. 31-32). It is not beholders of his Mode #1 existence that Jesus wants; it is believers of him in his Resurrection Mode that he seeks.

On the Cross he seemed most alone and abandoned, but this was not actually the case, because the Father was with him there. And as John's people still know suffering (they are not yet possessors of full joy and glory. As long as they are this side of death and full surrender, they will know persecution; they will be faced with temptations against faith and love), they must realize they are never alone but possess the Peace of Jesus (like Joy, a synonym for the "indwelling"). With such Peace they can overcome all the sufferings that afflict them on the way to full glory (v. 33).

Chapter 17

GENERAL COMMENTS (and reflections):

John (and others involved in the final edition of the gospel) for more than three chapters has been assembling material that properly fits into the form known as a "Last Testament Discourse." This literary device gives biblical writers an opportunity to select material from their sources which best "sums up" the meaning of the departing leader and which suitably prepares those who are to survive him for the life and tasks they will confront once he dies. The form often ends with the leader's *prayer* for the people (cf., e.g., Moses, in Dt 32, 33; Samuel, in I S 12; Paul, in Ac 20:17-38). And so John, after Jesus concludes his last remarks to the disciples (16:33), sets down Jesus' special "going away" prayer for them. Scholars have heard in the prayer echoes of other NT prayers of Jesus: the Lord's Prayer, his prayer in Gethsemane—some even detect a eucharistic tone to its mid and final verses. Doubtless John has gathered, reworked and transposed elements of these prayers into his own composition. But it seems the *prayer* is mainly the majestic and original creation of John himself, based on his understanding of many of the deepest wishes and thoughts that Jesus had for his disciples as he confronted his death; parts of the prayer are based on the words he spoke to his disciples about the mission he was entrusting to them at his death. Both pre— and post-Resurrection time zones are here; but mostly it is Jesus Risen and Transcendent who prays.

The prayer is said to the Father, but is intended for the ears of disciples, both present and to come. Jesus will be consoling them, interceding for them before his Father (thus the prayer has been called from an early date, his "Priestly"-Intercessory prayer), but again Jesus in the prayer will be doing what he has been doing all along, namely, *revealing* his identity and his relationship with the Father and believers and so the prayer is "revelatory" as well. What he has been saying about himself, the Father, and believers will be said again, this time even more majestically and memorably. The Jesus who is about to leave and return to heaven was ever in tandem unity with the Father, and the prayer eloquently confirms and illustrates this unity. No true understanding of Jesus can be had unless this premise is accepted. And since Jesus (after a few "appearances") is to leave the world visibly, he must reveal as resolutely and clearly as he can that the disciples at his death now become a part of the mystery of his tandem unity with the Father. The prayer is really the prayer of the Jesus who has reached his glorified Mode, said for the visible brotherhood who are is now part of that mystery (both ca. 30 AD and ca. 90-95 AD).

17:1-8

As Moses did in his final discourse (Dt 32), Jesus *looks to the heavens* to address a prayer to his Father; like Moses (Dt 33), Jesus prays *to be heard by his disciples*. He reveals again that his "hour" is bound up in the mystery of his and the Father's glory. God's glory is the life and love he wishes to share with human creation. He has sent it into the world humanly encased in Jesus. It has been seen to a degree in the Signs he has worked. It is to be seen in the fullest measure in his final "hour"—his death and Resurrection. Jesus then prays: Father, as I show how great my love for you and the world is, show also your great love for me and the world (v.1). God and Jesus not only have *love to give*; the "hour" shows that their love is eternally, forever, fully *given*. It is eternally *there* available to be shared in by anyone who comes in faith to the Jesus who endured this "hour." The Father's given love is there in the given love of Jesus. And so if the Father is to share *his* love with believers, *he* must take them and give them to Jesus (v. 2).

Disciples are not first Jesus-people who win their way into the affections of the Father. Disciples are Father-people whom he "gives to Jesus" so that Jesus through his "hour" can make the love the Father wishes for them available to them. The Father wills the salvation of all, but his salvation has been enshrined in Jesus by means of his "hour" (so often opponents of John's community claimed to be Father-Moses-people with no taste or need for Jesus. For John, the Father brings *all* people who seek salvation from him to Jesus; if they seek his love and glory, they will find it there and only there). The "hour" is the mystery that makes God's love sharable. In Hebrew thought, *to know* a person is to know and appreciate such a one not only in an intellectual way; it has to do with sharing deep psychic love with that person in an intimate personal affectionate way. And so the eternal life that Jesus gives in his hour seems to be the eschatological "*love-knowing*" spoken of by the prophets as the covenant of "*knowing*" which God would give to his people at the Final Age of history (cf., Jr 24:7; 31:33-34; Ho 4:6; 6:3, 6). Through Jesus' "hour" God will be able to put his caring, intimate, psychic love *into the hearts* of those who seek a new and ultimate covenant with him.

John is no pagan or Jewish "deviator" who believes in strange gods. The Father for him is the "one true God" (a Hebrew creedal expression proclaiming Yahweh as the one-only divinity and all other pagan deities as non-existent). But it is his deep belief that the *one true God* was humanly experienced in Jesus. In the human form of Jesus, God gave believers a visible *locus* where they could see and experience his love. The glory of God—his loving presence in power—was seen demonstrated in the works Jesus performed; it will be fully seen and demonstrated in Jesus' final work—his "hour." After his "hour" Jesus (as Wisdom did in the OT following her earthly sojourn) is to return to the "glory he had before the world began" (v. 5).

Jesus had glory from eternity. He had glory while on earth. He will have glory forever in heaven. But for that glory to be shared in, it must be *given*, and the "hour" is the mystery where it is given. It was encased in human flesh; that flesh must give it up "for love" of the brothers and sisters. It is in "*dying* that the seed becomes *fruitful*" (12:24). From human experience we know that love is communicated not by osmosis or ~~through some virus but by~~ "giving it up." Most humans give their love not fully but in percentages (even this is a beautiful thing to witness). Jesus, we know because of his human death, "gave it *all* up," and so "*all* of it" is there waiting to be shared in. Is Jesus in death "empty" of it? Lovers of such intensity are never empty; the more they give, the more there is to give. Jesus in giving his full love to the Father received of the Father's fullness, and that is there to be shared in too. Jesus is not returning to some left-behind glory; he is going through the mystery of death that makes his glory available to others (v. 5).

The Risen Jesus in verses 6-8, repeats the themes John has been establishing all through the gospel about Jesus' true identity. He is the revealer of the Father and his love, making his name (his presence, power and glory) knowable to the world (v. 6). Jesus is not here on his own; he comes from the Father and tells only what the Father lets him reveal (v. 7). Believers accepthis words as originating from God who sent him (v. 8). Jesus was while on earth, and is now in Resurrection, a person in "tandem union" with the Father. True believers "see" this.

And as Jesus reviews *his* tandem connection with the Father, he at the same time shows the *disciples* that *they* are now a part of this tandem mystery themselves. The Father *gives* disciples to Jesus (v. 6). They know that his words and gifts to them come from the Father (v. 7). They accept him as the Father's sole Agent on earth (v. 8). So to be a disciple is not to fasten faith on some chancy unknown; it is to opt for salvation through the one, sure, approved and sent revealer *of the Father*. If the Father is God and Savior he can be *humanly* encountered only in Jesus, not in some other person, form or place. By this time the disciples should be getting Jesus' drift. First, he identifies himself as the approved and only *locus* of God on earth. And now as Jesus departs, what he is and has is to go into the brotherhood. The brotherhood is to become the *locus* for God on earth after the "hour." Like Jesus before them, they are now indwelt by God, possessing his name, words, truth and knowledge (vv. 6-8). If the disciples wonder if they are or should be disciples, Jesus informs them that they are such by the very will and choice of the Father. As Jesus was part of the Father's plan, so are they! Because of the "hour" the Father, Jesus, and the disciples are all together in the Father's plan to save the world. People cannot separate themselves from Jesus, saying that they are settling for the Father alone. There is no Father alone! The Father is in tandem union with Jesus. Jesus is in tandem union with the brotherhood. To deny the reality of this interpersonal unity is to show abysmal ignorance of the Father and his plans for the world.

17:9-19

With verse 9, Jesus continues to reveal this mystery about the disciples; he is not selectively praying for them with no care for the world whatsoever (the world, as will be seen, is not excluded from Jesus' thoughts in the Last Discourse; cf., vv. 21, 23). The mystery is that the brotherhood is now a key part of the Father's saving work once Jesus departs "in the flesh." This part of the prayer, therefore, is "revelatory" and "commissionary." The disciples are receptive to God and thus "belong to him" (as creatures they certainly "belong to him"; but as receptive to his graces, as open to the revelations he gives them, they show they are more so a people who "belong to him"). He chooses to give them to Jesus. Why? Obviously so that they can become part of the Jesus-mystery in his post-Resurrection Mode. They are to be the *brotherhood of Jesus* joined to him transcendentally through faith; thus united to Jesus, they will carry on the Father's saving work through history. Jesus can take what is his from the Father and share it with the believing brotherhood at his death. The glory of God manifest in his earthly life is at his death now shared with the disciples and will be "seen" in their lives (v. 10).

To live out the mystery of being the visible *locus* of Jesus and the Father on earth, to do what the mystery demands of disciples, cannot be done on their own, so Jesus' prayer again becomes "intercessory" (vv. 11-12). They must know that they will be kept strong and safe in the mystery. The reader catches echoes of the Lord's Prayer as Jesus asks the *Father most holy to "keep them safe in his name"* ("may your name be kept holy," Mt 6:9). Once commissioned to be the visible *locus* of the invisible Jesus, they will know opposition and trials. They are surrounded by people who choose "darkness" over light, who seek always to oppose light, but the disciples must know that they are not alone against such opposition. They are united to the Father who gives them his name (his saving and strengthening presence) as he did to Jesus (three times Jesus prays for the "safety" of the disciples, vv. 11, 12, 15, so it must be that John's community is presently facing very stiff and dangerous opposition).

An allusion to Judas appears in the prayer (as noted, there seem to be Judas-types in John's community). He was obviously used as a "scandal" argument against the brotherhood (how could Jesus choose a disciple like Judas if he were the "high" Christ, etc.?). Early Christians could only answer the "scandal" by finding such defections as being "foreknown" by God and revealed in his Scriptures. This shows that defections do not reveal Jesus to be "unjust" or inadequate to save or to keep disciples. Defections are simply a mysterious part of the foreknown plan of God (John the dualist preacher and writer knows that people have the ability to follow either of two options in life, the good or the bad; otherwise there would be no sense to argue or debate over Jesus or even to write a gospel to safeguard and inform the faith of believers).

In verse 13, Jesus informs them that in the Resurrection Mode he reaches full joy. But he does not selfishly cling to it. His concern is that the brotherhood share in his joy. There is thus an ongoing relationship between Jesus and the disciples on earth. Jesus is still *their* Vine; the brothers and sisters are *his* Branches (c. 15). His Mode of realized joy is not apart, above or beyond them; they are joined to it radically if not completely. Their perseverance in trial will lead to a full sharing in his joy. However, since they remain on in a world of "darkness," they will know hatred as Jesus did (v. 14). But in this trial believers are not to combat hatred or "darkness" alone. Jesus is within them and he is invincible against such hatred, and so the brotherhood joined to him can defeat any hatred or opposition. Jesus here again seems to echo the Lord's Prayer as he prays that the disciples be "saved from the Evil One" ("deliver us from the Evil One," Mt 6:13) (v. 15). John's people would recall that the Jesus who says the prayer is the one who "defeated" the Prince of the World on the Cross (12:31; 16:11).

But disciples left in a world of "darkness" and feeling real persecution (ca. 90-95 AD) might feel alone and wonder about the realism of the Jesus-Father-disciples relationship (two in the relationship, after all, are transcendental and invisible). Do Jesus and the Father really keep them "safe" against evil? So Jesus must remind them that the relationship is indeed real, continuing and efficacious against evil. As disciples *they belong to* the *Jesus* of Mode #2, who is joined in joyful union with the Father. They do not "belong to the world" of "darkness" (vv. 15-16). If the Father got Jesus through the dark moments of his history, Jesus and the Father will get the disciples through their dark moments as well.

In verses 17-19, the prayer becomes "commissionary-revelatory" as well as "intercessory." The disciples must know that they are being made an essential part of the mystery of the glorified Jesus. Why was Jesus on earth so bold in his words, claims and promises? Because he was the *approved* and *sent* Agent of God (10:36). Jesus truly revealed in his visible works and audible words the Father's love and will for the world.

Now Jesus who is physically to depart must *appoint* and *send* the brotherhood to carry on his agency from the Father. The *locus* for God's words and works in the era of the Jesus of Mode #2 is the brothers and the sisters. Like Jesus, and because they are in Jesus and the Father transcendentally, they can carry on the Father's plan to challenge and hopefully save the world by announcing the plan and living it before the world. On the Cross, Jesus spoke the "truest" word about his and the Father's love for the world (this in sum was the revelation he was sent to give . . . "the Father so loved the world that he gave his only Son so that all who believe in him could have eternal life," 3:16). From Jesus' "consecratory act" of death flows the disciples' dedication to continue revealing this "truest word" to the world. As "sent" they carry within them the mystery of the "sender" and the "message" the sender spoke from the Cross, the message that says how much God loves the world and how much he wishes to give his love to the world (vv. 17-19).

17:20-26

The Jesus of the Last Supper now speaks to the believers of a later generation (certainly this would be John's community, but any believing community who met Jesus in the words and lives of other Christians would be the appropriate audience for these verses). What Jesus wants for those who come to believe in him through the preaching and love of the brotherhood is that they realize that faith brings them into the real spiritual unity that exists between Jesus-Father-and-the-present-brotherhood (vv. 20-21). There is a human community of brothers and sisters on earth that is in a real relationship of unity and love with the transcendental Jesus and the Father, a bridge community between heaven and earth. What greater unity, what better covenant could there be than this? The indwelling of God and Jesus in the brotherhood is surely what the prophets had in mind when they spoke of an inner covenant of "love-knowing" for the New Age (cf., again, Jr 24:7; 31:33-34, etc.).

If this community projects this mystery of love and unity outward to the world, then the non-believing world can "come to believe" in the mystery too (vv. 21, 23). The first believers saw this love in Jesus. Later generations (the post-Resurrection world) see this love in believers, who after all are Jesus in a new Mode, Jesus in the Mode of transcendentally dwelling with the brothers and sisters. Can this win over the world? It sounds unreal, so idealistic. History shows that it is the one sure thing that works, the one thing that draws the world to Jesus after his "departure." As an early example, one recalls Rome's first cynical reaction to Christians. Rome judged them an odd lot—"they love one another as though their precious Jesus were still with them." In time that cynicism gave way to belief, as the strong fraternal unity that characterized so many Christians brought Rome to believe that indeed a mystery was within them. It drew many non-believers to belief. The preaching probably didn't get any better, but the sincerity of the living and loving did, and so Rome took notice. (*John's community on the contrary, if one inspects the Epistles, indicates a lack of unity among some believers and shows that signs of fragmentation are present among some of them. Thus one can appreciate John's recalling of Jesus' strong plea for unity; not to profess it, not to live it is tantamount to denial of the fundamental Christian mystery*).

To be a disciple of Jesus seems risky in that it often brings persecution down on the believer; but radically it is the least risky thing one can ever undertake. The Father is behind the whole process of one becoming a disciple. He gives disciples to Jesus, so that Jesus in turn can bring them to his ultimate joy and glory (v. 24). And if Jesus, invisible and transcendent, seems in some sense "gone" from disciples, they are to know that his going is a "return to his glory," which glory in his return is being made sharable for them ("when the seed dies, it becomes fruitful"). Jesus is not off basking selfishly in glory. He is off making his glory "seeable," communicable to believers. And if "glory" is too lofty and abstract a term, let them know that it has mostly to do with "love." The plot of the Father and Jesus to draw believers to Jesus is all about love. Unless they can draw believers toward Jesus, they cannot give their own mutually shared love to them. Unless Jesus surrenders that love, it cannot be shared with believers through history. Unless there is a brotherhood to receive it there is no ongoing *locus* in which the world can find this love and experience a sharing in it. Jesus was the chosen *locus* while he was here. The brotherhood is the chosen *locus* until history becomes eternity. As believers love the brotherhood (keep the commandment; 13:34 f), they are loving Jesus and the Father. As they love one another, then the Father and Jesus are loving them through and in the brotherhood (vv.

25-26).

FURTHER PARTICULAR COMMENTS:

It has been noted that John's Last Supper account makes no reference to the Eucharist. Some few scholars see in chapter 17 a paraphrase of the words of institution in vv. 17-19. Others believe that Jesus' final prayer was composed against a eucharistic background. Community reception of the Sacrament symbolizes the indwelling unity of the brotherhood with Jesus and with each other. The imperative of the Eucharist is the same as the imperative of Jesus' final prayer . . . that believers remain united with him and each other in a unity of love, and that they project their unity and love outward toward the world.

Verse 3, *eternal life is in this* . . . Some scholars, knowing that John prefers the phrase "eternal life" to "Kingdom of God" see in this verse an echo of the Lord's Prayer, i.e., "thy Kingdom come."

Verse 11, *that they may be one, as we are* . . . These words are missing from early important MSS.

Verses 14, *any more than I belong to the world* . . . These words too are missing from early MSS.

Verse 15 . . . John is sometimes seen as a Christianized gnostic or as one who gnosticizes Christianity. This verse seems to dispute that notion. Jesus prays not to "deliver" his disciples *from the world*, but to keep them safe *in the world*.

Chapter 18

GENERAL COMMENTS (and reflections):

As Jesus concludes his Last Discourse, the gospel returns again to the Passion narrative and moves quickly towards his trial and death. A fast read-through of this and the next chapter shows that John follows the same general outline as the earlier gospels (the arrest, a hearing before the Jews, Peter's denial, a trial before Pilate, sentencing, crucifixion, death and burial). This is to be expected since most of the last moments of Jesus' life were witnessed publicly and recorded early. Once Jesus was believed to have risen from death, the religious significance of his final moments became all the more important, and Christians sought to solidify in memorable oral and written form the events that led to his death. Death was seen to be an integral part of the mystery of Resurrection. Christians felt redeemed from sin and gifted with new life in the Spirit because of Jesus' *death* as well as his Resurrection (cf., e.g. Ac 2:22-36; 3:12-26; 4:8-12, etc.). And of course the Passion as "scandal" had to be apologetically explained; thus Christians soon gathered accounts of those last days and hours.

It is on closer inspection that the reader notices that John tells the story of Jesus' final hours in a very distinctive way. To cite just a few examples (the commentary will call attention to his differences more in detail), one notices that John does not give an agony scene; his Jesus is more "talkative" than in the Synoptics (their silent "suffering servant" is only subliminally here); a formal trial before the "Jews" is missing; the trial before Pilate is given expansive and dramatic treatment and Jesus is scourged in the middle of the trial, not at the end; his mother and a faithful disciple are present not "at a distance" but near the Cross. In the gospel, Jesus is not mocked on the Cross and there is little feeling that he is undergoing prolonged *humiliation*. As befits one who is the "high"

Christ sent from heaven, he is in complete control of his "hour" and moves inexorably toward his death not as to a tragic and sorrowful event; his Cross is rather the instrument of victory, glorification and cosmic redemption. A few lines into the narrative, it becomes evident that it is not Jesus who is on trial and judged in these events. It is the "Jews," Pilate and the "world," and Jesus is *their* judge.

Since John's account is so "different" many regarded it as something of a "meditation" on the Passion more than an accurate record. Its historical value was judged less reliable than the earlier Synoptic accounts. Such is not the case today. Although there is no general agreement on where John gets his information, many now conclude that he is working with good sources and that these are different and independent of the Synoptics. Many feel his data is just as reliable as theirs, and in fact that it seems more plausible and balanced. Having said this, it is good to note that both traditions are not intent on giving exact documentary versions of events. They creatively adapt their material so that the theological truth and meaning of the events are conveyed for their own communities. John especially reworks his material for dramatic and theological effect. He is a master at drawing out the inherent drama, irony and symbolic content of his data. The result is a profoundly rich theological interpretation of Jesus' hour. The "high" Christology that John has established throughout the gospel continues through the Passion. John, up to now reticent to speak of the kingly aspects of Jesus' life and mission, is reticent no longer. It is during the Passion narrative that *Christ the King* emerges. His death will be a royal victory and conquest; his enemies so intent on his defeat will themselves be defeated and by their own weapon. His *rule* over "all people" is established in the "laying down of his life" and in his "being lifted up."

The Arrest: 18:1-12

Since John treats the sufferings of Jesus with great reserve, he records no "agony" scene. Scholars, however, point out that John spoke of Jesus earlier as being "troubled" (12:27; 13:21). This happened when "darkness" was close by. For John, Jesus' agony is the opposition of "darkness" and the "trouble-struggle" that ensues as he attempts to win people away from it. Evidence of the nearness of "darkness" to Jesus in this scene is discoverable in the time of arrest (it is night). Also, the mystery of "agony" can be found in the term "cup" mentioned by Jesus in v. 11. This is a Synoptic term for the Passion, the subject of Jesus' "agony" in these gospels (cf. Mt 26:39; Mk 14:36; Lk 22:42).

Judas does not feature prominently in John's version of the arrest. There is no "kiss," no dramatic confrontation between him and Jesus. He is simply the guide to where Jesus can be found. It seems John wants to show that the conspiracy of "darkness" against Jesus is wider than the "Jews" and a defecting disciple. And so, soldiers, priests and Pharisees (an alliance of the forces of "darkness") are involved in the arrest. The accompanying soldiers are Roman as well as Jewish (v. 3). It is John's thesis that Rome too is early concerned about Jesus. Just why is not clear. It is Passover time. Jesus has been gathering large crowds. Some will accuse him of being a "revolutionary" against Rome. This could be a worry to the authorities. The moral evil of the situation is underscored as Jesus' enemies, both secular and religious, come for him at night, with lanterns and torches. The irony of this is that for John, Jesus is the "light of the world." No one who has listened to him honestly would need such devices to find him (cf. 11:10; 12:35). And certainly he is no revolutionary. They have the weapons, not Jesus (v. 3).

With verse 4, the reader sees that Jesus is still the "high" Christ (he knows fully what is about to happen and is not hesitant to identify himself). He takes the initiative and asks whom they seek. It is obvious that all of his public preaching was lost on them as they say—"Jesus of Nazareth," as though they have found no "divine dimension" discernible in him at all. As if to remind them that there is another "origin" in his background besides Nazareth, he says the divine name, *ego eimi*, and the crowds fall back as though they have witnessed a divine epiphany. This of course is not John "exactly" recording an event (certainly the other gospels are silent on great displays of power during the arrest). It is John stating again what Jesus has displayed often enough in the gospel: that he is not alone, but is in union with his Father, whose name he bears and whose works and mission he carries out. Jesus is not being overcome by human power. As God's divine Agent he cannot be overpowered by human force (cf., 19:11). What superficially may look like humiliation or God's disapproval of Jesus, is not that at all. A divine mystery is about to unfold, not the arrest and destruction of a false prophet or blasphemer (vv. 4-7).

In verses 8-9, John seems to find in the fear (and implied flight) of the disciples a prophecy of the deeper meaning of the upcoming event. Even if Jesus will lose disciples momentarily, what is about to happen is destined ultimately to "save them" . . . "not one of them is to be lost" (cf. cross references: 17:12; 6:39) (v. 9). For the ultimate salvation of the disciples and the "world" . . . Jesus is the "one you want" (v. 8). The person being apprehended is actually the Shepherd who is to lay down his life for his sheep *so that* they will "*not be lost* in eternity" (10:28) (v. 9).

The next episode is in all the gospels: Peter is here identified as the impetuous defender of Jesus. Since he will soon deny him, it is evident that his understanding of Jesus and his mission from the Father is woefully inadequate. Jesus' function is to give life, not to injure or take it away. He is to take the world by love, not force (by his "cup" as he reminds Peter). The only weapon Jesus needs to overcome the world is his "death"—his "cup" is the container and communicator of his life-giving love. And since the "cup"is given him by the Father, the reader understands that the Father's love is to be contained in Jesus' death also. Besides the theology of his death, the incident obviously shows Rome that Jesus and his disciples are not revolutionary threats (vv. 10-11). It is only after Jesus has established his identity as "high" Christ, and implied the saving nature of the coming event, that he submits to be "bound" by the forces of Rome and Judaism (v. 12).

Jesus before Annas; Peter's Denial: 18:13-27

While John replaces the trial of Jesus before Caiaphas and the Sanhedrin (cf., Mt 26:57-68; Mk 14:53-65) with a short hearing before the former high priest Annas, he or his editors remind readers (v. 14), that the gospel has equivalently covered this trial(s) in other ways (since chapter 5, Jesus has been on trial "before the Jews"; charges have been made, witnesses demanded and given, verdicts and sentences handed out. Cf., e.g., 5:31-47; 7:26, 45-52; 8:20, 26; 10:24-25; 11:47-53). The "Jews" will make further political charges against Jesus during the trial before Pilate (for John, the critical trial); they will repeat their religious charges against him there also (18:33; 19:7) (vv. 13-14).

Peter's denial in all the sources seems tied in with the trial before the "Jews" and so John "wraps it around" the hearing before Annas. Peter's capitulation under stress will contrast dramatically with Jesus, who stands firm and unintimidated before his "captors." The nearness of Peter to Jesus also reminds readers that Jesus prophesied Peter's denial, 13:38; this reconfirms their belief that Jesus, even though arrested, is still the all-knowing "high" Christ. "Another disciple" is with Peter as he follows Jesus. Some see the disciple only as a device to get Peter inside the high priest's palace; others strongly suspect that the disciple is the "beloved disciple" who stands as an authoritative witness behind the gospel (this episode, like others, "pairs" him with Peter; the boldness of his action here seems consonant with the strong faith the "beloved disciple" displays by standing near the Cross). Peter by the end of the chapter and by day's break will have denied Jesus three times (all gospels record this incident, so it seems to be a troublesome and revealing historical incident, not *legend* as some suppose). John (i.e., his editors) further corroborates the "historicity" of the incident, as in c. 21, Peter will be forgiven this denial in the context of a *three*fold profession of love (in ancient times to say something three times publicly before witnesses was as "solemn and binding" a statement as one could make). This shows the depth of the denial, as well as the depth of the repentance and conversion (c. 21). Some see Peter's use of the "charcoal fire" as symbolic that he has forsaken the light from above for earthly light and safety. The threefold denial ends with the dramatic crowing of the cock—another reminder of Jesus' prophecy; it is the "high" Christ who has been denied (vv. 15-18, 25-27).

In verses 19-23, the reader seems to catch implications of what could be "honest" Jewish objections against Jesus. He is questioned about his "disciples" and his "teaching" (v. 19). Some "Jews" consider him to be a false prophet whose teaching is blasphemous. They worry about the political repercussions of his "movement" and its many adherents. Jesus in v. 20, reminds the "Jews" as well as the reader to recall his teachings (cc's. 2-12); they were neither secret nor blasphemous, if one accepts the premise that he is the "high" Christ. Nor are his disciples politically dangerous (cf., the recent cc's. 13-17, on Christian *discipleship* and the *commandment of love* . . . such disciples could hardly be called "seditious"). His words not only indicate that he is seeking the right to present his witnesses who will testify to the truth of his teaching(v. 21), but that he is reminding present disciples (ca. 90-95 AD) that they are now his "disciple-teachers" who should be proclaiming his message fearlessly as he does (even under stress).

Jesus in vv. 22-23, is struck by the police. During this hearing he does not remain silent and submissive as is the case in the Synoptic accounts (the *silent* "suffering servant" theme is strong in these gospels). There is nothing seditious about Jesus' message from the Father, and those who oppose it should be asked to show cause why they find a message of faith and love seditious. John's community is "being struck" undeservedly as was Jesus. Have they become silent and defensive about the gospel because of persecution? Jesus' reply should be a challenge to them. It is obvious that the more "talkative" Jesus is in control of his "hour." He is much less on trial than the high priest and the police. If Jesus goes "bound" to Caiaphas and Pilate, he goes not as a criminal but freely as one unjustly accused and unfairly treated (v. 24).

The Trial before Pilate Begins 18:28-40

John has made the reader aware of general Jewish objections to Jesus (cc's. 5-12). In his Passion narrative he will concentrate on the trial before Pilate. Here he will be able to show with high drama and irony how secular and religious forces, for different but still sinfully culpable reasons, joined forces to condemn an innocent person. John's sources, as noted, seem independent of the tradition behind the Synoptic gospels, but are no less accurate or reliable than theirs; his account in fact leaves far fewer blank spaces than the Synoptics about what really happened (e.g., why Jesus was brought to Pilate in the first place and why despite reservations he goes along with the execution of Jesus; his day for the sentencing and execution seems more plausible). Scholars of course realize that John works his material creatively; he is more concerned with theological interpretation of events than with presenting an exact replay of the trial.

If historians worry about how John would be aware of private conversations between Jesus and a Roman governor, the biblical scholar would see the conversations as being constructed from remembered public words between the two. The trial was witnessed by many, and words were exchanged (the Synoptics would tend to omit trial dialogue to develop the theological theme of Jesus as the *silent* "suffering servant"). Pilate is also being made a symbol of the "world," and his questions and replies to Jesus reflect the contemporary mentality of the "Roman world" (ca. 60-95 AD). Thus the trial not only gives John's understanding of what generally happened, ca. 30 AD, but also reflects the anti-Jesus, anti-disciple attitudes and accusations of a later period. As Pilate and the "Jews" are shown to be guilty of gross injustice, ca. 30 AD, their later counterparts, ca. 60-95 AD, are shown equally guilty, and contemporary Christians find in the trial their defense for Jesus and their own faith. John's account is based on the data available to him, but he uses it creatively to fashion a theatrical "morality play" on the events for his own time.

In this connection, scholars see, the whole trial is structured in seven dramatic scenes to highlight the conflicting forces of light and "darkness." The "play" is set on two stages: one outside the praetorium where the "Jews" bring Jesus to be tried before Pilate (the outer stage), and one inside where Jesus and Pilate meet together separated from the noise of the crowds (the inner stage). The Synoptics have only one arena for the trial before Pilate and it is outside. John finds his arrangement more dramatic. By naving Pilate come and go between the two "stages" he can through the inner stage show again the true identity and innocence of Jesus; Pilate away from "outside" pressure can see that Jesus is innocent of any political crime and is deserving of release. Then through the outer stage he can show the frenzied hatred of Jesus' opponents and how they exert political pressure on Pilate to change his mind about Jesus' innocence. Pilate in his coming and going is influenced both by the "stage" of light and truth and by the "stage" of hatred and "darkness." He hopes to satisfy the characters on both "stages," but in John's dualistic outlook this is impossible. Since he fails to take a committed stand for Jesus and truth in the inner stage, he ends up inevitably siding with the powers of "darkness" in the outer stage. As the trial comes to its inevitable conclusion, it becomes obvious that Pilate and the religious authorities and their disciples are on trial before Jesus and both end up guilty of an awesome crime—they reject and crucify the light and truth God sent to draw them to himself. In the years ca. 60-95 AD, the trial continues on; the "world" is still on trial with Jesus still innocent and the world guilty.

As noted, John has found much in the trial data that helps him draw out the mystery that Jesus is the long-awaited King that God has sent to begin his spiritual rule over the world. Jesus will be falsely charged as a pretender-king and unjustly executed as one. John sees a profound theological irony in this, for Jesus is no pretender; he is in truth the Messianic King of Yahweh. Six of the seven scenes draw attention to his kingly role and power.

First Scene (outer stage): 18:28-32

The "Jews" bring Jesus to the praetorium but refuse to enter the dwelling place of a Gentile on the grounds that by such entry they incur ritual impurity (v. 28). This, they say, could prevent them from eating the *Passover* supper. Scholars point out that it would be rather simple to remove the "impurity" by bathing before the supper. The surface irony of this situation is obvious. They are willing to use the profane office of a Gentile for the execution of an innocent Jew, but will not enter his house. The readers of the gospel recall a deeper irony. In c. 1, Jesus was identified as the Lamb of God who takes away all sin, all "impurity" (1:29) and yet the Jews worried about their "purity" seek to destroy the one God sent to "purify" them. The reader also knows that for John, Jesus is the Passover Lamb of fulfillment (cf., 19:14, 29, 36) and yet the "Jews" are more concerned about the "Passover" that is only a prophecy of Jesus. In c. 2, Jesus "took over the *purification* pots" at Cana, changing their cleansing waters into the purifying Wine of the New Testament. The "Jews" in Jesus have access to God's purifying Lamb and Wine and yet prefer lesser forms of *purification*.

Pilate, having sent police to arrest Jesus, must have some idea of the dangerous rumors that attach to his activity ("political liberators" were a special worry to him at Passover). But as judge over accused criminals he must have a formal charge and asks for one (v. 29). No charge is given in this scene. From the gospel the reader knows that the "Jews" have charged Jesus with blasphemy and according to their law (Lv 24:16), they can and should stone blasphemers. Why, then, not attend to this themselves? It seems (according to John) that Jews under Roman Law at this time are not allowed to execute anyone. If the offense is capital, Rome must carry it out. Rome could ridicule their "blasphemy charge."

So they do not offer it here. They (this seems to be John's reading of the evidence) attach a "political crime" to Jesus' religious offenses (this appears in v. 33; he is apparently brought to Pilate as a seditionary pretender-king).

Still, Rome could possibly grant them permission to execute their *blasphemer* their own way. They could try for this, but do not. Why? There seems to be an implication that some "Jews" at least prefer that Jesus not die the more traditional form of death by stoning. They want him to die the ignominious death of crucifixion, the Roman form of capital punishment which is considered by "Jews" an "accursed" death (cf. Dt 21:23; Gal 3:13). Some might think that such a death will destroy completely Jesus' credibility with the people. The irony of their wanting Jesus dead by crucifixion is evident in the fact that Jesus foreknows he will meet this manner of death, and rather than destroy his credibility, such a death will draw "all people" to him (12:32). John will continue to play on the words "hand over" throughout the trial. He finds it deeply ironical that all Jesus' enemies think *they* are in charge of his fate, when the reader knows that *Jesus* is in complete control of *his* life (cf., 19:11 and in 19:30, at death John says that it is Jesus who "*handed over*" his Spirit). The "lifting up" they ignominiously seek for his destruction actually brings him to the Father and will draw believers to him for all time (vv. 30-32).

Scene Two (inner stage): 18:33-38a

Pilate goes inside to confront Jesus personally. He is concerned about an inferred political offense that the "Jews" have added to Jesus' religious crimes; inferred because they have asked a Roman governor to put a Jewish "criminal" to death. Pilate asks the question found in all the gospels . . . "are you King of the Jews?" (Mt 27:11-14; Mk 15:2-5; Lk 23:2-5) Perhaps he knows that there is a religious connotation to the title (the expectation of a Davidic king to rule over Israel in God's name), but he seems worried only over the political possibilities. The title on the face of it implies sedition. Whereas Jesus in the other gospels admits that he is a King and refuses further comment, John's Jesus explains to Pilate the kind of King he is; he says that his kingdom is spiritual and *not* political. It is "not of this world" (v. 36). No rumblings of rebellion happened at his arrest. In fact Jesus is on record as being against political force (v. 11). One can almost see Pilate relax a bit at Jesus' statement. Jesus is a religious problem to the "Jews," but certainly not a political problem to Rome. But Jesus, who has fully admitted his spiritual kingship, does not leave it at that. As he has done with everyone he encounters in the gospel, Jesus challenges Pilate to open himself up to the truth of his "kingly" mission from God. The reader seems to hear in Jesus' *kingly* identification a challenge to Pilate that was also made to Nicodemus: to inquire about his *Kingdom* of new birth in the Spirit (3:3-8). Jesus has *truth* to reveal to Pilate, revelations about God; he has life, light and love from God to offer if he would "listen" (v. 37). Pilate is one of the "other sheep" Jesus the Shepherd-King invites to *listen* to his words and to join his flock (10:16).

But Pilate is not much interested in listening to revelations about "religious truth" or joining a flock, and in effect denies that Jesus has any kingly "jurisdiction" over truth that could affect him (v. 38). He becomes a symbol of the "world" that remains aloof and uninterested in the "ultimate truths" of religion, and as the story proceeds will illustrate how tragic his decision is to be neutral and unconcerned about such truth. Having rejected Jesus as the revealer of truth, he will proceed to make false and unjust decisions one after the other until finally he ends up crucifying the incarnation of "religious truth." The "Jews" already having rejected this Revealer-King, show that their expectations of messianic kings are much less "spiritual," much less concerned with "ultimate truth" than God intends. Just two scenes into the drama, and both Pilate and the "Jews" have rejected Jesus' offered "reign of truth" (cf. 3:18-21, 33-36). Who is really on trial here? Who is the false prophet?

Scene Three (outer stage): 18:38b-40

The Barabbas episode appears in all four gospels (the Synoptics speak of it as Pilate's custom; John calls it a Jewish practice). Though there is no extra-biblical evidence for this arrangement, it seems to make sense as a kind of "safety valve" for political passions at Passover. Pilate, convinced of Jesus' political innocence, seeks to free him and uses the "custom" as his means of doing so. Having shown so little interest in *truth*, he violates the *truth* of the situation right away. Jesus is no criminal and yet he presents him as a criminal candidate for amnesty. The Synoptics picture Barabbas as a murderer and revolutionary (Mk 15:7; Lk 23:19). The choice seems obvious to Pilate; the crowd will surely pick Jesus. But he has rejected an invitation to know the truth and equivalently has surrendered to "darkness." The plan thus backfires and "darkness" chooses Barabbas over Jesus. The irony is clear to John. Jesus has been falsely charged with sedition, and yet the "Jews" prefer a convicted seditionist. Pilate who hoped to release Jesus because he is guiltless of sedition, must release a proven seditionary enemy of Rome. The word "robber" is a cross reference to 10:1, 8, 10, where the Good Shepherd was contrasted with "robbers" who abuse God's sheep (given a choice between a Good Shepherd and a "robber" the forces of "darkness" naturally choose a "robber"). What Pilate says as a *sick joke*—" . . . should I release to you the 'King of the Jews'?"—truly identifies Jesus. He *is* the Kingly-Messiah whom God sent to Israel to fulfill the aspirations of Israel to be ruled by God and he is again rejected. In scene one he was the Lamb of God and was rejected. In scene two, Pilate rejects him as the Shepherd-King calling out to him, and here in scene three, the "Jews" reject him as King and with him their own aspirations to have a king sent from God. Curiously, Barabbas seems not to be a personal name (some think his name could have been Jesus and that Christians early expunged the name for obvious reasons, leaving only Barabbas which translates to "son of the Father"). Thus, on the face of the text, by choosing Barabbas they have also rejected Jesus as "Son of the Father."

FURTHER PARTICULAR COMMENTS:

Verse 5 . . . An editor seems to have inserted this repetitious reference to Judas as a cross-reference to 13:19.
Vv. 10, 26 . . . John knows that it was a servant of the high priest named Malchus whose ear was cut. In v. 26, he knows a relative of this servant who questioned Peter. Some commentators think such detailed data indicates that the "other disciple"with Peter in vv. 15-16, was the "beloved disciple" whom they see as the authoritative witness behind much of the data of the gospel.
Verse 27 . . . Peter's denial. Many commentators see this humiliating

account of Peter as nothing more than a contrasting example to Jesus: Peter is a weak, impetuous, failing disciple—Jesus is firm in purpose no matter what the dangers. Still, for early Christians Peter's conversion, much like Paul's, was something of a "probative sign" for the truth of the Resurrection. By the time the gospel was written, most Christians knew of the post-Resurrection life of Peter, how for thirty years he faithfully preached Jesus throughout the world and died a martyr. Peter's repentance to the Risen Jesus is chronicled in this gospel, c. 21. So it is not just a "bad example" that is being pointed up here. It is a "before-and-after-Resurrection Peter" that one sees in the gospel. Only the *Risen* Christ could account for such a remarkable conversion.

Chapter 19

GENERAL COMMENTS (and reflections):

The Passion of the "high" Christ continues. Jesus moves with serene and majestic calm toward the conclusion of his "hour." He is to lay down his life; it will not be taken from him (10:17-18). He is innocent of the religious and political crimes charged against him, and yet the forces of "darkness" still continue to push these charges to bring about his death. Jesus has often been accused of telling lies, of uttering blasphemies and corrupting the laws and values of the ancient Covenant. The chapter will dramatically and ironically illustrate that his enemies lie and blaspheme and deny the basic law of their Covenant, even setting aside their own expectations for a messianic King "greater than David"—all in an effort to destroy Jesus. But the reader knows that beneath the charges and the lies and blasphemy a cosmic mystery is taking place. "Darkness" fiercely seeks his death when ironically it will be his death that will defeat "darkness." It is when Jesus is "lifted up" that he will reach his "glory for others" and begin his spiritual rule over the world (12:32).

Scene Four (inner stage): 19:1-3

The data indicates that Jesus was scourged and mocked as a "pretender-king" by Pilate's soldiers (cf., Mt 27:27-31; Mk 15:16-20; Lk 23:11, 16, 22. Luke recounts that Jesus was also mocked as a king before Herod). Normally scourging would take place after conviction as a preface to crucifixion. John apparently chooses to rearrange or perhaps conflate the mockery-scourging data for dramatic and theological effect. He puts it in the middle of the trial. It illustrates that Pilate's neutrality about "truth" has brought him into an unwilling alliance with "darkness''; his sense of justice becomes warped and *untruthful* (18:37-38). If he hopes to solicit pity for Jesus and thus gain his release, it will not work. The *untruth* of the situation is obvious. Jesus is innocent by Pilate's own admission, and yet he has him whipped like a convicted criminal. John recalls the humiliating event because it serves to identify Jesus. He *is* in truth what this scene mockingly acknowledges him to be. And so he is crowned, robed and saluted as a King. The reader knows that in actuality Jesus is the King ''greater than David''; God as expected has sent him to Israel. Jesus will wear his kingly attire through the rest of the trial. His rule will begin when he mounts his throne (the Cross) which is symbolized here in the ''act of scourging'' and the ''slap of the soldiers.'' Jesus is not a *political* king (cf., 6:14-15; 12:32; 18:36); he is to rule over ''all people'' through the *drinking* of his ''cup'' (18:11) (vv. 1-3).

Scene Five (outer stage): 19:4-8

Pilate, an unprincipled man of devious stratagems, now leads Jesus still in his kingly costume to meet his ''subjects.'' Beaten and bloody, he hardly looks like a political threat or religious worry to anybody. Pilate again insists he finds no guilt in him (v. 4). Surely the crowds beholding his vulnerability will lose their taste for blood and take pity. Perhaps they will have second thoughts and take Jesus, not Barabbas. Pilate calls attention to his frailty—''behold the man'' (v. 5). Though scholars are not in agreement on the exact significance that John intends by this identification, the reader would remember Caiaphas' unconscious prophecy that one ''*man*'' must die *to save the people* (11:50). Jesus standing there in kingly robes is surely Caiaphas' ''*man*.'' Also, three references to the ''hour'' of the crucifixion (cf., 3:14; 8:28; 12:23, 32) foretold that the one to be ''lifted up'' was the ''Son of *Man*.'' What the crowds are ''beholding'' is actually the ''heavenly *man*'' (Dn 7:13-14) sent by God (the expected Messiah and more) who is shortly to be lifted up to the Father *for them*. The priests and police do not show pity; instead they shout for more blood (v. 6). Ironically what they shout for they actually need. His blood has his life ''within it.'' By seeking to destroy it, they will make it forever available to believers.

Pilate's stratagem backfires (having no interest in the deeper ''truth'' Jesus invited him to explore, 18:37-38, it was bound to).

Nevertheless, he restates his conviction that Jesus is innocent. His taunt to the crowds to do the "crucifying" themselves seems aimed at showing them that they are excessively violating innocence and should back off (v. 6). So now the "Jews" must inform Pilate that they will not back off because Jesus is a serious *religious* criminal. He pretends, they say (v. 7), to "be God's Son"—that is why he should die (10:33-36). He is a blasphemer!

This makes Pilate "fearful" (v. 8). His stratagems are not working and the situation is getting worse. There is too much hatred for Jesus and a just and successful solution is slipping away. He "fears" he may have to kill an innocent man to calm the situation (v. 6). Rome will not be pleased with the release of Barabbas, nor with the "ruckus" over Jesus. The possibility of a supposed "son of God" come to earth might strike "fear" in Pilate's pagan, superstitious heart (Pilate will be lectured about Jesus' *power* in vv. 9-11); but more likely he "fears" that the title attached to Jesus more officially belongs to Caesar (it seems close to one of the Emperor's titles—"son of the gods"). This further complicates his task. The irony of the scene seems obvious. Jesus *is* in truth the "Son of *Man*"—the "Messianic *King* of Israel"—"*God's Son*." The "pretense titles" are true and proper labels, correctly identifying Jesus.

Scene Six (inner stage): 19:9-11

Jesus is becoming much too difficult a problem for Pilate. Is it possible that another political jurisdiction could handle his case? Pilate asks where he is from (Luke says that Pilate temporarily referred Jesus to Herod on the grounds that he was from Galilee, the ruling province of Herod; cf. Lk 23:4-7) (v. 9). John uses Pilate's question to clarify the deeper mystery that is unfolding. Believers know where Jesus comes from (unlike non-believers who really are unaware of Jesus' true origins: cf., 6:42; 7:41-42; 9:29-30). Believers know that the ultimate power behind his fate is radically bound up with God and his will for the world, and is not subject to the various power jurisdictions of earthly rulers. Jesus told his disciples earlier that *he* has "power" to lay down his life and to take it up again (10:17-18). If Rome has any power it derives from God; Pilate is reminded of this (v. 11). The externals of crucifixion might be within his power, but there is a deeper meaning to Jesus' death and

Pilate has no jurisdiction over it whatsoever. Pilate thinks he is the judge of the situation and the controller of Jesus' fate. In the deeper sense of "power" and "fate," he is not. Jesus and the Father mainly control the "hour" (14:30-31) (vv. 10-11).

Scene Seven (outer stage): 19:12-16a

Pilate sees that Jesus is innocent of political crimes and is eager to release him. He is disinclined to execute him on religious grounds. What can change his mind and persuade him to put Jesus to death? Political pressure! Pilate is in Palestine by the grace of the Emperor; as the "Jews" remind, him he is a "friend of Caesar" (a technical term for a political appointee). He will lose favor with the Emperor if he lets a "pretender king" go free; a ruler who does this would automatically become "unfriendly to Caesar." Though Pilate knows the charge against Jesus is false, Rome does not know it and the "Jews," it seems, are willing to carry their *lie* all the way to Rome. Lies, as politicians know, are not easy to disprove or undo. Pilate's job and possibly his life could be on the line (Tiberius was known to be paranoid about personal loyalty). If Pilate were a man of political and moral principle, he would not yield to this "threat." The "Jews," however, know their man. They know that Pilate is expedient, a man more worried about position than principle, and so they have him where they want him. Pilate seems on the edge of capitulating to their desires. It is ironic in a way that Jesus may have to die "to save Pilate" (vv. 12-13).

But Pilate will make one last effort to free this "innocent" man and if the "Jews" insist that he must die, he will demand a high price for the surrender of Jesus to their will. He summons Jesus and seems to say to the "Jews": "I will give you this pretender-king if you tell me (and the Caesar you now are solicitous of) who your true king is." A great opportunity for them to own up to their spiritual King, Yahweh, and to admit that they also have expectations of an earthly vicar-king (the Davidic Messiah) that Yahweh is to send to them. But this is not forthcoming. What follows is the biggest blasphemy in the book. They shout back at Pilate . . . "we have *no king* but the Emperor." To get Jesus they turn their back on Yahweh, their own King (cf., e.g. Jg 8:23; I S 8:7; Is 26:13), and renounce their expectations of an earthly vicar-king "greater than David'' (cf., e.g., II S 7:11-16; Ps 2:7). *Jesus* they want dead because he lies and blasphemes. The scene eloquently shows that *they* have told the lies and uttered the blasphemy. The judgment of death for blasphemy should be on them, not Jesus. But they shout for *his* crucifixion. Ironically what they demand for Jesus will bring the Covenant they have just renounced to its fullest and highest form: Jesus' death will inaugurate the Messianic reign of God over the world and usher in the New Testament (vv. 14-15).

John notes in v. 14, that the day and time of Jesus' condemnation was at noon on the Day of Preparation. It was at this time that the lambs were being slaughtered for the Passover sacrifice. Jesus has already been identified as the ''Lamb of God'' (1:29, 36) and so John reminds the reader that Jesus is to die as the *sacrificial Lamb* who will take away the sins of the world. As the poured-out blood of the first lamb saved the Israelites from physical death and bondage, so the blood of the ''high'' Lamb will be poured out to free them from spiritual death and to give them new life in the Spirit. The irony of the situation is again clear. When they should be most solemnly celebrating and renewing their Covenant with Yahweh, the ''Jews'' have just renounced it and have opted for Caesar's ''slavery'' in favor of God's spiritual freedom available in Jesus. Doubtless the ''Jews'' were not subjectively conscious of the implications of their words and actions. John, the late-century dualist, however, is not about to let anybody subjectively off the hook (his naive psychology and either/or mindset cannot let him do this). Objectively, the words and actions were blasphemous and are depicted as such. And if Pilate was less guilty midway in the trial, his culpability intensifies as (after *three times publicly* declaring Jesus innocent) he now ''hands him over'' to be crucified (v. 16a).

Jesus' Execution, Death and Burial:19:16b-42

John's brief account of Jesus' crucifixion and death is narrated with great reserve. His Jesus again manifests a dignified serenity and calm. Although reworking data common to the Synoptic traditions, he seems to add material from his own sources. Still, he is quite selective, giving only seven short scenes. He downplays elements of excessive sorrow and cruelty: Jesus does not fall down, or cry out in desolation, nor is he mocked on the Cross. The "cosmic" repercussions of his death are discerned, not in quasi-apocalyptic phenomena (darkness, earthquakes, tombs opening, etc.), but in what happens to the dead Christ himself. His legs are not broken. His side is opened by a lance, with blood and water flowing from it (more on this below). The kingly theme continues. Jesus goes to the Cross, dies and is buried as a "King." Some also see a priestly-sacrificial theme emerging during these final moments.

The Way to the Cross

No mention is made of Jesus stumbling from weakness. No women lament his fate. He needs no help with his Cross (Simon of Cyrene appears in all the gospels but this one). This is the Shepherd "high" Christ who has "power" to lay down his life (10:18; 18:6; 19:9-11). John seems to stress the point that Jesus "carried the Cross *by himself*" (v. 17). Thus some scholars detect in the scene an "Isaac typology." Gn 22:6, has Isaac "carrying his own wood" to the altar on which he is to be sacrificed. John therefore could be making a theological statement that Jesus' "hour" is a sacrificial act, a victim-offering against sin, a victim-offering expressing the giving of his life and love to God for the people. Jesus has already been identified as the "Lamb of God" offered for sin (1:29). Reference was made to his decided-on *slaying* as simultaneous with the *slaying* of the Passover lambs (19:14). Some see his seamless robe, vv. 23-24, as an indication that Jesus goes to the Cross clothed as a *priest*, whose office is to offer "sacrifice" for the people (vv. 16b-17).

Jesus is crucified between two criminals, but they will not speak during the "hour." All attention is focused on Jesus (v. 18).

The Sign

All the gospels refer to the sign affixed to the Cross; it ambiguously states Jesus' *crime* (cf., Mt 27:37; Mk 15:26; Lk 23-38). He is the "King of the Jews.'" John and Luke (some Lucan texts) mention that it was written in the three languages that would be readable to all or most of the literate world of that time. The sign thus indicates the universal and "cosmic" nature of what is taking place on the Cross. The "Jews" object. The sign makes it sound like Rome is killing an actual Jewish king. Pilate refuses to change it; he has conceded as much as he intends to concede to these people. Rome will be pleased at his firmness with "Jewish kings." Ironically, readers know that Pilate's sign is profoundly true. Jesus *is* the Messianic King of the Jews sent to them by the Father. The sign is not a cynical joke; it is Jesus' authentic coat-of-arms recognizable to his world-wide subjects, Gentiles as well as Jews. He is mounted on the throne from which he will save and *rule* the world (cf., 3:14-16; 11:50; 12:32; 18:14) (vv. 19-22).

Jesus' Clothes Divided

This incident is in all the gospels (cf., Mt 27:35; Mk 15:24; Lk 23:34). John alone speaks of a seamless tunic that the soliders are reluctant to tear and so they toss for it. John must see this datum as fulfilling Ps 22:18. Knowing how selective he is in the use of material, some scholars detect in John's allusion a revealing symbolism. It is known that the high priest wore a seamless robe as distinctive of his office (he was principal offerer of sacrifices for the people), and so it seems that John again wishes the reader to know that Jesus' "hour" is not only an offering (cf., 19:14, 17; 1:29), but that Jesus is the offering priest. Jesus on the Cross is the supreme mediating-priest "for the world" before God. His death is *sacrificial* (an offering *against* sin, and *for* life). Some detect the untorn garment as a symbol of the unity Jesus wishes for those he leaves behind (cf., 10:15-16; 11:51-52; 17:11, 20-23). Others detect a continuation of the "kingly theme"; not that the item is luxurious *per se*, but *kings* would be more likely to have such garments (vv. 23-24).

Jesus' Mother and the Beloved Disciple

This scene is unique to John. The Synoptics have "women disciples" standing "at a distance" (cf., Mt 27:55-56; Mk 15:40; Lk 23:49), but John puts Jesus' mother and three believing women with the beloved disciple near the Cross. Though Jesus here on the historical level is providing for the care of his mother, he speaks with the solemnity of a biblical "revealer" indicating that a new relationship is to exist between his mother and the disciple, both of whom for John seem to be symbols of the Church which is created in the mystery of Jesus' "hour" (n.b., the biblical salute, "look here is," often states a person's new role identity; cf., 1:36, 47-51; I S 9:17).

Mary was Jesus' physical mother. She was the faithful Israelite who responded to God's call. She gave Jesus to Israel and to the world. Now Jesus reveals that Mary symbolizes the *mother* who will continue to bring him to Israel and to the world. Because of his "hour" now being consummated, a New Eve is being fashioned from the side of the second Adam (19:34) as the first Eve was formed from the side of the first Man (Gn 2:22-23). Mary is the symbol of the New Eve. She, like Eve, is called "woman" (Gn 3:15; Jn 2:15; 19:26). She, like Eve, is called a "mother" who is to give birth to the living (Gn 3:20; Jn 19:26-27). Mary then is the New Eve, the New Israel, Lady Zion (cf. Is 54:1; 66:7-11, etc.), in other words the Christian Church which brings the life of the glorified and transcendental Jesus of Mode #2 to the world. The beloved disciple through his steadfast faith in Jesus, now is *son* of Mary, *brother* of Jesus, because he is born of the Church. "Disciples" are "mothered" by the New Eve. And if the disciple is the main witness standing behind the gospel, then through his book he provides for the welfare of his mother, the believing community. As the disciple derives sonship-life from the Church, the Church is "cared for" by the disciple and his gospel (vv. 25-27).

Having created the New Eve through his "hour," Jesus then sees that "all is now finished" (v. 28).

Jesus Thirsts. He Hands Over His Spirit

During an act often extended to crucified victims, John knows that Jesus made a deeply symbolic remark as he neared death (cf., also Mt 27:48; Mk 15:23; Lk 23:36). There is nothing that he has failed to do to fulfill his Father's will for the world. "Aware that all was finished" and that the "Scriptures were fulfilled"—here Jesus seems to be challenging readers to review all the previous nineteen chapters. There they will see how fully he accomplished his Father's work and fulfilled the Scriptures. All that is left now is that he drink fully of the "cup" his Father has given him (18:11). It seems that Jesus is *thirsty* for this *cup* and not for the sedative of sour wine (cf., Ps 69:11; 22:15). In drinking it he knows he will be able to provide the "living waters" he promised to give the world if it would accept him (4:14; 7:37-39) (vv. 28-29). In fact, in a few short verses after his death, waters will flow from his side toward a "loving disciple" (19:34).

The *hyssop* reed is seen by some commentators to be an allusion to Ex 12:13, 22 (v. 29). As the blood of the lamb affixed to doorposts with *hyssop* saved the Israelites from physical death at the Exodus, so Jesus' blood can give eternal life to believers. Again Jesus dies as God's own Passover Lamb. His blood containing eternal life is a *sacrifice* to the Father for the people.

John's Jesus dies not with a loud cry of seeming anguish (cf., Mt 27:50; Mk 15:37). He dies with a sense of determined surrender that all that must be done has been done. The time has come now to lay down his life, to give it up for the good of the flock. In a sense the "Shepherd is dead" and in his death the sheep can now find life in the Spirit he has handed over. Jesus' last act from the Cross sounds much like Luke's description (Lk 23:46), except that the Father is not addressed. Some see here a distinct Johannine omission. It is taken for granted that Jesus must first return to his Father, but his Spirit is soon to be "handed over" to all (20:22) (v. 30).

Events Following Jesus' Death

Like his dying, the aftermath of Jesus' death is told with reserve and quiet majesty. As noted, there are no apocalyptic-like manifestations (darkness, Temple veils torn, earthquakes, tombs opening, etc.; cf., Mt 27:51-54; Mk 15:38-39; Lk 23:44-48). John discerns "cosmic" effects hidden in rather ordinary events.

The early Church had to assure its enemies that Jesus had truly died. Normally victims of crucifixion were left on the cross for long periods of time, even a day or so until they were dead. Sometimes for religious reasons (cf., e.g., Dt 21:23; Jews forbade the hanging of bodies on trees overnight) Rome permitted such victims to be dispatched mercifully on the day of crucifixion by letting their legs be broken. This hastened death by what was considered quick and merciful suffocation. Jesus was obviously dead, so this was not done. His side was jabbed and pierced to see if any life was left. There was none. Jesus, then, is certainly dead. John's recollection that the *crurifragium* was dispensed with serves a further theological purpose. It identifies Jesus once more as the Lamb of God; like the Passover Lamb of Exodus, his bones are to be *unbroken*. John sees the action as fulfilling Scripture (cf., Ps 34:20; Nb 9:12; Ex 12:46). Jesus' death was like the lamb's, *sacrificial* (an offering *against* sin, an offering *for* life; cf., also 19:14, 29).

Jesus' side was jabbed and pierced (again to certify death), but John notes that "blood and water flowed from his side" (cf., Zc 12:10) (v. 34). He is not calling attention to a post-mortem oddity. He obviously sees in the happening symbolism of great significance. He seems to see the meaning of Jesus' death and the spiritual effects that flow from it symbolically displayed in this event. The blood shows that Jesus gave up his life in death (life is in the blood, and it is flowing forth as the victim's blood in Jewish sacrifice must "flow" out of the victim). The "hour" in other words has happened; Jesus has *died* for the flock. But John notes "water" flows forth after it happened. His people reading and hearing this would be prompted to recall all the words of the gospel that spoke of water, especially "living, flowing water." Jesus had promised it to the Samaritan woman (4:10, 14) and to all believers (7:37-38). Jesus' water was not earthly water only, but water "of the Spirit" (1:31-32; 3:5), which Spirit was to be granted when Jesus consummated his "hour" (4:22-24; 7:39; 16:7).

The scene, then, is John telling his people that through his death Jesus has now passed into the Mode of his glory and is about to return to the world in the Spirit. The Jesus of Mode #1 is dead (no longer to be encountered in this Mode); but as Jesus is glorified in his death he can be encountered in the Spirit in his risen Mode through faith, a faith like that his mother and the disciple showed as they stood by the Cross. In full actuality Jesus is to return to give believers the Spirit in 20:22. In this scene we see the "mystery" of his death and return symbolically displayed. Because of his surrendered death (the blood flowing forth), believers are soon to receive his transcendental Spirit (the promised living waters that flow from his death). Scholars see verse 35 as being inserted by editors to show the reader that the symbolic event is not pious imagining; it happened and was witnessed by the respected authority who stands behind the gospel (21:24) (v. 35).

A later Church saw sacramental symbolism here also. The blood—a symbol of the Eucharist; the water—a symbol of Baptism. Did John intend this sacramental symbolism? Many would say yes, at least on a secondary level. It seems that by the years 90-95 AD, the word "blood" for this particular community would have eucharistic connotations (cf., 6:53-56); certainly the word "water" would connote more than the Spirit to them (cf., 3:5). As human spirits encased in human, fleshly symbols themselves (i.e., they have bodies and know spiritual reality through sensual symbolic experience), it would be natural for them to see and know transcendental truths and mysteries through their being *encased* in symbols. The Eucharist was Jesus' death and Resurrection encased in bread and wine; Birth in the Spirit was encased in the waters of Baptism. Doubtless the sacramental symbolism emerged after the primary symbolism was assimilated (in the first instance "blood" means the "hour"; "water" means the Spirit which is to come after and because of the "hour").

The Burial

All the gospels refer to Joseph of Arimathea as the one who claims Jesus' body after his death (John's Jesus is buried with an anointing; the Synoptics lack time for this and delay anointing until the Sabbath has passed; cf. Mt 27:57-60; Mk 15:42-46; Lk 23:50-53). In either case, one does not bury or anoint (or intend to anoint) the "living"; the *item* apologetically shows that Jesus is *dead* (not in a coma to be later revived by cunning disciples, etc.). The tomb is "new," "identifiable" (this too is apologetical evidence against Jesus being lost in some common grave). John seems to use Joseph and Nicodemus, up to now secret Christians, as examples for others. They are now publicly acknowledging their devotion to Jesus. Christians, having witnessed through the beloved disciple the blood of the "hour" and the "water of the Spirit" flowing from Jesus' side, can no longer justify *secret* belief. The episode illustrates that Jesus is drawing some secret believers out of the closet and the rest should come out too (12:32). The extravagant amount of spices and the new and unused tomb seem to continue the theme that Jesus is King, and that it is through his *death*, his "hour," that he *rules* over the hearts of believers (vv. 38-42).

FURTHER PARTICULAR COMMENTS:

Verse 13 . . . Scholars debate and disagree whether the verb "sat down" (on the bench of judgment) refers to Jesus or Pilate. If Jesus was told to sit down so that he could be mocked as a "kingly judge" then the scene illustrates John's irony, i.e., Jesus *is* what he is being mocked as. He *is* God's judge over his accusers. Others would see Rome as much too jealous of its judicial role in the world to use a judgment seat as an instrument for mockery.

Verse 14, 31, *Day of Preparation* . . . John differs from the Synoptics on the day of the crucifixion; for him it is the eve of Passover; for them it is Passover. In either case, Jesus seems to have died on a Friday (19:31).

Verse 16b . . . Some scholars think that John omits Simon of Cyrene to combat docetist belief. The scene shows that Jesus is *humanly* capable of this task and that it was *his flesh* that was fastened to the Cross. Some docetists had Simon being crucified.

Verse 23, Jesus' robe was seamless from "*top to bottom.*" This is quite similar to the way Matthew and Mark (Mt 27:51; Mk 15:38) describe how the Temple's veil was torn after Jesus' death. Could John have access to this traditional datum and see Jesus' tunic as a symbol of the eternal and untearable NT in contrast to the veil of the OT which by this act has been torn?

Verses 25-27 . . . Bultmann has an interesting interpretation of these verses. He sees Mary as a symbol of Jewish Christians, who because of exile and excommunication have "no home." They are now being entrusted to the care of the beloved disciple, who is a symbol of the largely Gentile Christian communities.

Verse 33, 36 . . . These verses would recall to Johannine readers verses 29 and 36 of chapter 1. They would see that JB's title "Lamb of God" is meant not only to identify Jesus as the "suffering lamb" of Isaiah (53:7) but to show that he is the "Paschal Lamb" as well. Verse 33: Jews who believed in resurrection after death would guard against breaking the bones of the righteous dead. The event thus would show these Jews that Jesus was "righteous" in death.

Chapter 20

GENERAL COMMENTS (and reflections):

This chapter is not written to prove that the Resurrection happened. It has been preceded by nineteen chapters of discourses and signs that revealed Jesus to be the "high" Christ. He existed eternally with God and has come from above with a message of life and love for the world. In death he has returned to his Father in glory. He has *promised* soon to return to the disciples to share his glory. His return is certain because he *is* the "high" Christ who existed before Abraham, who has power to lay down his life and take it up again, who has *promised* to return in "a little while" with gifts of Peace, Joy and the Spirit. How can he be dead and not Risen?

And yet, as the chapter opens there is no expectation of return or Resurrection, no sense of Joy, Peace or the Spirit about to be received. If Jesus could restore the dead Lazarus (11:43-44), how could death destroy him? Have the disciples forgotten that the seed must be surrendered (12:24) to give fruitful life to others? Were they even listening at the Last Discourse? (over four chapters of preparation for his death and Resurrection) Why such lack of belief that Jesus was soon to return?

Well, for one thing, Jesus foretold that no one can arrive at Resurrection-faith without his and the Spirit's help. For another, there is something about human death that is seemingly so absolute that it caused most believers to lose the faith given to a *live* Jesus. To believe in a living, breathing, talking, sign-working Jesus in historical Mode #1 is a lot easier than to believe in one seen dead on a Cross and stiff in a tomb. What seems to have happened is that human death in a way "disconnected" the faith-connection between believers and Jesus. All the events of the previous nineteen chapters, all the preparatory words of Jesus, seem to have been put *on hold* or to have fallen into a kind of limbo

because the familiar Mode of Jesus was no longer *there* to be encountered. The only Jesus they had ever known was now dead; they have
not yet "seen" a *beyond the grave* Jesus, a Jesus who exists in a New
Mode. This "New" Jesus must come to them and restore the faith-
connection by *revealing* his Risen Mode.

This chapter, then, is not a proof of Resurrection. It is a continuation
of the previous chapters. It is a further *revelation* of Jesus, but now in the
Mode of Resurrection. And since the "faith-connection" has been
loosened because of his death, he attempts to reconnect it in this chapter.
This *is* the chapter of the Jesus of Mode #2 who will that show he can be
spiritually encountered in his New Mode as he was in the old—*through
faith*. But what is wrong with the old Mode? Why not bring back the same
Jesus? Well, the Jesus who returns *is* the same Jesus but *New*. There is
still a world to win over, and as the world goes on Jesus must be present to
it in a Mode reachable to the ages. The chapter will establish that the Jesus
of the New Mode is present to believers *anywhere* and *everywhere*. All
the gifts promised by the Jesus of Mode #1 are given to disciples by the
Jesus of Mode #2 when faith is present. Though not "seeable" in the old
way, he is still "seeable" through faith and is able to provide believers
the life and love he promised them in his historically visible Mode. The
point of it all will be . . . "*Blessed* are those who do *not see* me [in that
Mode anymore] and *yet* who still believe" (v. 29).

Knowing what John is up to, it is sufficient to say that in his
Resurrection accounts he uses source material very much like that found
in the Synoptics (e.g., he will have two episodes at the "empty tomb"
and two episodes where Jesus appears to a group of gathered disciples).
Here Jesus' New Mode of existence and presence will be theologically
"described." The episodes will also help John show that Jesus seeks to
restore and re-establish the relationship of faith between himself and the
disciples which was momentarily interrupted by his death. For John, it is
of little importance that anyone know with great precision where he
derives the material for his episodes or how he justifies his arrangement
(more like an dited rearrangement). He would say, forget my creative and
dramatic expertise in these matters (you know I'm good at what I do);
don't worry about the precise geography, sequence, or ordering of
appearances in this chapter. Pay attention to the New Mode of Jesus'
presence. Pay attention to Jesus' concern about restoring adequate faith

that will make his New Mode of presence efficacious for the lives of believers. If you insist on knowing my sources, take a quick look at the Synoptics. You will find most of my material borrowed from their sources and slightly rearranged (cf., especially Mt 28:1-10, 16:20; Mk 16:1-8; Lk 24:1-12, 24, 36-49; and the Marcan Appendix, Mk 16:9-12). Obviously John reworks much of this material and puts a distinct Johannine cast to it. He arranges his accounts of Jesus' Resurrection in two acts, each with two scenes. The first scene in each act will feature two or more disciples and will speak generally about their faith-response to Jesus in his New Mode; the second scene in each act will focus on an individual disciple with specific problems of faith-response that Jesus overcomes in his New Mode.

At the Tomb (scene one): 20:1-10

The scene begins with Mary Magdalene coming alone to the tomb on the early morning after the Sabbath. She finds it open and presumes it empty. John's sources indicate that several women came to the tomb (cf., e.g. the "we" of v. 2; all the gospels narrate that women were the *first* to discover the tomb empty, so John works from a traditional source), but he narrows his account to *one* important early witness of the Resurrection for dramatic and theological effect. He will speak of a single apparition of Jesus to Mary at the tomb in vv. 11-18. Here she is used to bring the news of the "empty tomb" to the disciples.

The "darkness" of the scene points up the confusion and inadequacy of the faith of Mary and the disciples. Finding the tomb open, she does not think "Resurrection," but assumes that Jesus' body has been "taken away" and runs to inform Peter and the "other disciple" (they are not initially thinking "Resurrection" either; cf., Mt 28:13-15) (vv. 1-2). Apologetically this suggests that Christians were not mesmerized into believing in the Resurrection. It was an immense surprise to them and belief came *after* a period of disillusionment and disbelief. John (or his sources) seems to conflate two accounts of disciples coming to the tomb—one, Peter's inspection (cf., Lk 24:12); the other, the inspection of several disciples (cf., Lk 24:24) which John reduces to a single person, the beloved disciple. The combining of Peter's inspection with the disciple's provides John the theological contrast he needs to dramatize the early exemplary return of a "disciple" to faith against the slower, less exemplary return of Peter. Peter sees two signs of the Resurrection before he meets Jesus personally—the "empty tomb" and the "burial clothes"—and apparently does *not believe*. The beloved disciple, on the other hand, sees the same signs with no personal apparition of Jesus and yet *believes*.

It could be that John intends the two men "running side by side" (v. 4) to represent two groups of disciples that ultimately came to believe. Peter represents the Great Church whose leaders were the "twelve" and their disciples (reflected in the Synoptic gospels, the epistles of Paul, and the Book of Acts), and the beloved disciple represents the smaller and independent Church that John writes from and for, whose faith is greatly dependent on the witness of a specific "other disciple" (reflected in the Fourth Gospel). This disciple reaches the tomb *first* (v. 4), indicating, his deeper love and faith in the historical Jesus drew him to believe in the Resurrection *first of all*, even before the "twelve" and their disciples.

He looks into the tomb and sees the neatly folded burial clothes of Jesus. Putting the two signs together—the "empty tomb" and the "left behind clothes"—he reaches the faith-conclusion that Jesus is Risen. The body could not be "stolen" without the "clothes" (grave robbers would want these too). The tomb and clothes recall the historical Jesus (Mode #1). He was put in there dead wrapped for burial, but the "empty tomb" and "left behind clothes" show the disciple that Jesus has moved beyond the realm of "tombs" and "clothes" (he has passed on to Mode #2). The "signs" must trigger in his mind and heart the memory of Jesus' words about his origins, his purpose in coming to the world, his return to the Father, his re-coming to the disciples. All of those nineteen chapters forgotten in the traumatic happening of Jesus' death seem to return to him. No "angels" are necessary, no personal appearance of Jesus is needed to inform his heart or memory (both will be needed in the case of Mary, vv. 11-18). He "saw and believed." The loosened faith-connection has been reconnected, and of course the disciple's great love for Jesus makes the reconnection all the easier (vv. 4-8).

Peter is not so quick to recall or to believe. His "disconnected faith" is still not connected; his powers of recall are not responding. He will come to belief "*behind the disciple*" (v. 6). The disciple is, then, for the readers of the gospel the *model believer*. He believes without a "personal appearance'' of Jesus. All he needed was a ''revealing sign''; all the community of John, ca. 90-95 AD, needs are the ''revealing signs'' and the gospel that comes to them from the model believer. They have the Spirit and he will open to them the meaning of Jesus, the signs and the gospel.

This disciple not only contrasts with disbelieving Peter in this scene; he will contrast with disbelieving Thomas in the coming scene (vv. 24-29). The beloved disciple, unlike Thomas, does not demand the tangible evidence of Jesus' live body before he believes. He has the *words* of Jesus that come back to him as he views the *signs* of Resurrection—the ''empty tomb'' and the no longer needed ''burial clothes.'' With so much stress in the scene on the ''clothes'' the disciple must have recalled the scene at Lazarus' raising (11:44). Lazarus had come from the tomb still wearing his ''burial clothes'' (he was to die again); but Jesus' ''clothes'' are left behind. Clear enough revelation that Jesus will need them no more. It was at the ''tomb'' of Lazarus that Jesus spoke of himself as the ''*Resurrection* and the life'' (11:25).

Verse 9, seems to explain why Peter and the others (and the early Church generally) were slow to believe. The Spirit as the illuminator of the Scriptures was necessary to help them see the full meaning of Jesus' death and the inevitability of his Resurrection as a part of God's saving plan for the world (cf., e.g., Ps 16:10; Ho 6:2, etc.). The Church of John has access to the illuminating Spirit that brought the privileged but at first *unseeing* disciples to faith, and so they *do not need* tangible proofs or appearances or wonders in order to believe (in any event such evidence and appearances are *inefficacious* without faith or the Spirit to illumine them). Jesus will inform John's readers that *they* are as *happy* and fulfilled in the mystery of the Resurrection as the early Christians even though *they* have ''not seen'' (cf., an episode in Lk 24:13-33. It illustrates that Jesus had to ''open up'' the meaning of the Scriptures for the disciples; just being an early disciple was not enough) (v. 29). Moreover, John and his community know that any trouble they may have with regard to belief in Jesus' Resurrection can be overcome by ''asking'' his and the Father's help (14:13; 15:16; 16:23-24). Verse 10, clears the stage for an individual appearance of Jesus to Mary, vv. 11-18 (cf. Mt 28:1, 8-9; Marcan App., Mk: 16:9-11).

At the Tomb (scene two): 20:11-18

These verses constitute a Christian version of the "recognition story" (the recognition of a divinity in stages was a literary device used frequently in pagan literature as well as in the NT; cf., e.g. Luke's Emmaus episode mentioned above; Lk 24:13-33). It will serve to show that Jesus, true to his words, has returned to believers—but it will be a revelation of his New Mode of presence and will show believers that they must profess faith in him in his Risen Mode and not seek tangible access to his former Mode of presence.

Mary "weeps" (v. 11). This shows that the "death phase" of Jesus' "hour" has blinded her faith. She has all but forgotten his words and deeds that foretold, death was his and her path to glory. Her faith is "disconnected." So God, realizing she is a bit traumatized over Jesus' death, blesses her with a message ("angels" are the messengers of God's revelations and *two* witnessing "angels" would be a strong indication of his desire to draw her back to faith). She is asked why she weeps. The words and deeds of the previous nineteen chapters, the words especially of Jesus' Last Discourse do not call for weeping (will she remember and stop crying?). No, Mary is still overwhelmed by "death" and thinks only of a stolen, possibly desecrated corpse. There is no "recognition" yet. Thus Jesus himself appears to her. But note the New Mode of appearance. He is not wearing a disguise. He is different in appearance. He can be seen "in focus" only when people begin to believe, and by those who look for a Jesus of glory who comes from the Father as he promised (he is certainly not "seen" clearly by people who are *crying* over his missing corpse). Jesus tries to reconnect her faith. "Why do you weep?" And he asks another familiar Johannine question. "Who are you looking for?" (v. 15)—as much as to say, why did you stop believing and remembering all that I said and did, especially what I said at the final Supper? But death is still a "faith-stopper." Jesus to her is not *alive* and so the one who speaks to her must be the "gardener" (only believers *see* the Risen Jesus; non-believers *see* corpses, gardeners and the like). No "recognition" yet. How can Jesus restore Mary's faith, so strong before his death (in the time of Mode #1), and fasten it now on him as Risen (Mode #2)? He speaks to her as the Jesus of Mode #1 did and calls her by name (with the old inflexion?) (v. 16). The Shepherd is still alive; he knows the *names* of all his sheep and he calls and they come (10:3-5). Her "called name" is what jogs Mary to recall all of cc's. 1-19, and the "faith-connection" is restored. No longer does she think of corpses or gardeners . . . Jesus is *there*, she comes to her *still-living* teacher, "Rabbuni" and "clings" to him (vv. 16-17). "Recognition" at last! Faith is restored! Two "names," two living persons are related to each other in acceptance and love.

But Mary has one lesson yet to learn, and Jesus reveals it to her in the words: "Do not cling to me, because I must *ascend* to the Father" (v. 17). What Mary is clinging to is the Jesus of his former familiar earthly Mode (or at the least, she clings to the "apparition" Jesus). This is not the Jesus of the Last Discourse who "was to return" permanently to disciples (14:3, 18-20, 28; 15:4; 17:20-23, 26). No longer must faith be directed at the Jesus who had not yet gone through death and reached the glory of the Father. The Jesus believers must *cling to* is the Ascended (and returned from glory) Jesus. In that Mode he can catch believers up in the life of his Father. It is the Jesus of Mode #2 who makes *his* Father *Mary's* Father in truth and in fact (v. 17). It is that Jesus who (the reader will soon see, 20:19-23) breathes on believers his Spirit who will beget them into the inner eternal life, light and love of the Father (3:5; 6:62-64). It is this Jesus who fulfills the words of the prologue—"the one who *believes* is to receive power to become a *child of God*" (1:12). Note that Jesus urges Mary to return to his "brothers." This is the first time he calls the disciples his "brothers," for he and they now have a *common Father* by reason of the Spirit's "begetting." Brotherhood in Jesus within God's Fatherhood—this is the New and Eternal Covenant which Jesus offers Mary and the disciples and the world (cf., Jr 31:33; Ezk 36:28; Lv 26:12).

It should be noted that Jesus, having gone through his "hour," is already Ascended, but Mary is not "clinging" yet to Jesus *as* Ascended, so John's Jesus "points out to her" that her faith in him is not yet *full*. It will become full when she accepts him as the eternally Ascended One. The full cycle of Jesus' new glorified and glorifying Mode, to a degree, had to be sequentially "displayed" for early believers; thus— Resurrection appearances—Ascension—Pentecostal Return—are depicted as time and space sequential phases (Luke does this in more extravagant spatial and temporal terms than John, doubtless for catechetical reasons). John will "display" the Ascension-Pentecostal aspects of

Jesus' glorification in the next scene, vv. 19-23. There is a clear lesson for John's community. For them, it is the Ascended Jesus who encounters them in the Spirit. In the Spirit, Jesus calls them by name and grants them his eternal gifts—this is all they need to *cling* to. They need no appearances or additional signs or wonders.

Mary returns to inform the disciples. No one can consider a faith-encounter with the Risen Jesus a "private gift." It must be shared. As will be seen, the brothers and sisters are to be the continuing containment and visibilization of the Risen Jesus in the world (vv. 19-23). Mary, who first acknowledged Jesus with the quite minimal salute "Rabbi" (a very early title given to Jesus, cf., 1:38), finally speaks of the Jesus she encountered as "Lord," a Septuagint name for Yahweh (v. 18). Her faith is now *full*; in Jesus she has "seen" the *Father* (1:18; 14:9).

Jesus Appears to the Disciples (scene one): 20:19-23

In all the gospels Jesus appears to the disciples as a group (cf., Mt 28:16-20; Lk 24:36-49; Marcan App., Mk 16:14-18). In these accounts there is manifest *incredulity* on the part of some. John seems to work with very similar material (vv. 19-23, are in content quite close to Luke's account, Lk 24:36-49). He chooses to rework the material and cast it into two scenes. He can thus show Jesus in his Risen Mode where the reaction to him is good, where disconnected faith is re-established in short order. The gifts of Peace, Joy and the Spirit which he promised in his Last Discourse can be bestowed in an atmosphere of restored and joyful faith. He can further inform these receptive disciples that they are now his missionary agents who will continue his and the Father's work through history. Then, John will isolate in a separate scene the response of adamant "disbelief" on the part of a disciple who refuses to believe the *word* about Jesus given him by the disciples. Jesus will be able to undo this and lead the disciple to belief. This will provide a dramatic lesson of how John's own people are to believe. They are to find Jesus' Peace, Joy and the Spirit by belief in the word of the disciples, which Thomas refused to do and was corrected for not doing. Thomas wishes to *see* before he believes (a problem for some of John's community?). Jesus will insist: "happy those who *do not see* and yet who believe" (v. 29).

Where it takes Luke a framework of fifty days to *display* the

Resurrection-Ascension-Pentecost aspects of Jesus' "hour" of glory (cf., Lk c 24: Accc's. 1-2), John more compactly does it in one day, Easter, and, it seems, in a meal-room setting that will recall for the reader the ambience of the Last Discourse, for all of Jesus' important promises of that discourse are fulfilled during this appearance. John has the Risen, Ascended, and Spirit-bestowing Jesus appear to "disciples" and not specifically to the "eleven" (adaptation of his material seems to be in evidence here as the sources definitely speak of a special appearance to the "eleven"; cf., again the Synoptics; also Paul, I Cor, c. 15). John's Jesus gives the gifts of his glory to *all believers*; they are *all* his missinary agents. John, in a way, has avoided the specialized term "twelve-eleven" and thus seems less concerned than the Synoptics with any kind of "hierarchic structure" in the community.

Jesus comes, even though the doors are locked because the disciples feel somehow threatened by persecution. The Risen Christ can penetrate and overcome fears and persecution whether it happens in the year 30 or 90 AD. This is a Jesus who is "beyond doors and locks." He cannot be kept "spatially" separate from believers. He is universally accessible to all anywhere and everywhere (v. 19). And yet this is the Jesus of flesh and blood who was killed and buried; he will *display* his wounds and thus is no ghost or phantom. The disciples see the one and same Jesus, but they see him in a New Mode (v. 20).

Jesus' promises of Peace, Joy and the Spirit made at the Last Supper are now fulfilled (all true believers in the ancient Covenant would see these as the gifts God would grant his people at the *end-time*, and so for John the *end-time* begins with Easter). Jesus grants the disciples Peace and Joy (Peace promised, 14:27-28; 16:33; Joy promised, 15:11; 16:20-22). These gifts, as seen in chapters 14-16, were revealed to be not just earthly *shalom*-well being or ephemeral joy, but the "indwelling" of God's love and life. In such a living relationship with God, believers know the deepest Peace and Joy and now have it with Jesus' coming (vv. 19-21).

What Jesus substantively said at the Supper about the missionary office of Christians he says again (cf. 17:17-19). The disciples are to be his "sent" agents to the world, as he was the "sent one" of the Father (n.b., there is also a missionary motif in the Synoptic accounts of the Resurrection: Mt 28:18-20; Lk 24:47; Ac 1:8). Readers of the gospel would recall that as "sent," Jesus was always in tandem union with the Father who sent him. Now, they realize that as "sent agents" of Jesus, they are in the tandem mystery of Jesus-and-the-Father too. As they looked at Jesus and saw the Father, so now the world can look at disciples and see Jesus and the Father (Mode #2 now includes believers). Impossible to believe, had not Jesus next did what he does in v. 22 . . . he *breathed* on them and said "receive the Holy Spirit." The Spirit promised at the Supper (14:16-17, 26; 15:26-27; also implied, 7:39) is now given to the disciples. Jesus' *breathing* of the Spirit on the disciples obviously recalls Gn 2:7, when God *breathed* into the dust-formed Adam and gave him *life* (cf. also Ezk 36:25-27; 37:1-14; Ws 15:11). What is happening at Easter is the *New Creation* of God's people. Formerly they knew the gift of human life. Now through Jesus' triumphant "hour" they receive the Spirit, and through him are begotten into the life of God. The life of the Father flowing through Jesus is now flowing within them; 3:5 is fulfilled (and John would want readers to recall 6:39-40; 14:7—these verses would be fulfilled as well). The desired day of the coming of God's Spirit to the world has happened . . . the *end-time* is now!

Verse 23, picks up further echoes of the Last Discourse. There, Jesus spoke of himself as one whose coming and preaching revealed the Father and his love for the world, but many rejected him and his Father and thus knew *sin* and stood condemned as *sinners* for their refusal (for John the fundamental sin is refusing to see in Jesus the revelation of the Father) (cf. 15:22-24; 16:8-9). He promised to send his Advocate to his disciples. The Spirit in and through them would continue to *judge the world wrong* about Jesus. He would continue to convict the world of sin for its rejection of Jesus. The disciples now, with v. 22, possess the Spirit and so are "judges against the sins of the world" which refuses to believe in Jesus. Like Jesus who possessed the Spirit (1:32-33), they can in his name forgive sins and bestow Peace. Like Jesus, they stand as a judgment against those who sin by disbelief. The verse would seem to mean this.

But Christians, as is well known, differ in their interpretations of how the Church is a "judgment against sin." Most agree that the Church can in Jesus' name forgive sins through Baptism, and can provoke the world to repentance through its living and preaching and thus lead people to Jesus' forgiveness. In addition, some would see the verse as a variant of Mt 16:19 and Mt 18:18 (but expressed more understandably to a

Greek- reading audience) where Peter and the Apostles (say some) were given the power of "loosing" the excommunicated of their sins after a period of penitential "binding." It is obvious that sin as a Christian problem continues *beyond Baptism*. Jesus seeks the destruction of repented evil wherever he finds it (1:29). And the Church is not simply the provoker of penitence only, but is the *sent agent* (as he was) of Peace *and forgiveness*. Jesus, the Spirit and the Father live within the believing community and from *there* minister their forgiveness to sinful but penitent believers (cf., e.g., what seems to be a "disciple-agency" act of forgiveness of sin in Paul, I Cor 5:1-5; II Cor 2:5-8). There are two sides to the mystery of salvation—forgiveness and the gift of eternal life or Peace. For believers to have and be safeguarded in the latter, Jesus must always provide for them the former. Jesus does this and (now with chapter 20) it would seem that he does it in and through the brotherhood (so say many Christians).

Jesus Appears to the Disciples (scene two): 20:24-29

As noted, all the gospels recount an appearance of Jesus to the disciples as a group, with incredulity manifested on the part of some (cf. Mt 28:17-20; Lk 24:38-43; Marcan App., Mk 16:14). For dramatic effect John chooses to isolate the "doubt" of one disciple, Thomas. He has already been seen to be a bit skeptical in two former scenes: 11:14-16, 14:5. He can thus illustrate the "skeptical attitude" that Jesus condemns: "*you people will not believe*, unless you see wonders and signs" (4:48). Thomas refuses to accept the word of the disciples about Jesus' Resurrection. He will not accept Jesus' Peace and Joy or the Spirit from them. He seeks a direct encounter with Jesus and will believe only then. This attitude reflects the self-induced doubt and second thoughts of many second and third generation disciples (in John's time and through history). The scene will illustrate what Jesus thinks about such "doubt."

The opening verse of the episode seems aimed directly at some of John's own community. Like Thomas, they were "absent when Jesus came" (v. 24). And yet they refuse to believe the "community" (v. 25) that keeps telling them that they have "seen the Lord!" The Thomas-sin is in a way a refusal to believe that Jesus exists with the community in a New Mode. The disciples are the recipients of Jesus' Spirit and possess his Peace and Joy. They are his post-Easter "visibilization" to the world. But this does not impress Thomas. He exemplifies the skepticism Jesus abhors (4:48). He, like the beloved disciple, knows about the revelations of chapters 1-19, especially the promises of the Last Discourse (Peace, Joy, the Spirit, the Missionary Office). Both found the trauma and the seeming absoluteness of Jesus' human death a momentary "faith-stopper." But unlike the beloved disciple, he finds the "empty tomb"— the "clothes"—and *now* the visit of Jesus to the disciples—insufficient grounds for belief. He refuses to "reconnect" his faith. Ironically, the side of Jesus he seeks to put his hand into is the side that was opened by a lance (19:34), which provided another *revealing sign* that Jesus' death was not defeat but the means of bringing the Spirit to believers (v. 25).

A week later, Jesus visibly appears to the group and takes up Thomas' challenge (not to concede to his skeptical demands, but to teach future generations of Christians that they must not indulge in Thomas' attitude). They are to find him in the witness of his believing community (vv. 26-27). Jesus points out the key problem of Thomas—*disbelief*, even after hearing all the words of Jesus and witnessing his revealing signs and after hearing the witnessing words of his Spirit-filled brotherhood. The words—"do not remain in disbelief"—seem to trigger in Thomas' mind and heart all the words and deeds of Jesus in the previous nineteen chapters, because Thomas does not "touch" the body of the Risen Jesus as he insisted he must. In fact, he utters the most profound expression of disciple-belief in the gospel. What was revealed gradually over nineteen chapters is now *seen* by Thomas to be an *undoubtable* fact. He addresses Jesus: "My Lord and my God!" (heretofore a manner of speaking used only for Yahweh; e.g. Ps 35:23; 91:2).

The book has identified Jesus by many titles—"Rabbi," 1:49—"Prophet," 4:19—"Messiah," 4:26—"Savior," 4:42—"Holy One," 6:69—"Son of Man," 9:37—"Son of God," 11:27—"King of the Jews," 18:39; 19:19-20—and others, but none more profound than this—Jesus was and is the Incarnation of God. The gospel began with the identification of Jesus as God (1:1). It now ends with a disciple recognizing that Jesus is God in truth and in fact (20:28). And Thomas should speak for all the readers of the gospel. His profession of faith should be theirs. And they should see his words as fulfilling Jesus' prophecy that now all . . . "honor the Son *just as they honor the Father*" (5:32). And readers would hear other words of Jesus echoing off Thomas' profession, e.g., "when the Son of Man is lifted up then you will know that *I AM*" (8:23) . . . "when you see me you see the Father" (14:9). The words of Thomas are now the words of Christ's community responding to the New Covenant of Indwelling given to them by God in Jesus. "Doubters"— "people-not-my-people"—are *now* with God and have become his people, Jesus' brothers and sisters linked to God in the Spirit (Ho2:24) (v. 28).

With verse 29, one sees John's rationale behind all four scenes of chapter 20. They were aimed at the readers of the gospel. Those who were privileged with an eye-to-eye vision of the Risen Jesus are not more "with it" than later believers who "see" Jesus in his word and community, in its preaching and gospel, in its fraternal service and sacramental celebration. Yes, there is a Jesus of a New Mode and he is the Real Jesus and he exists to make his brothers and sisters "happy" (in the biblical sense of happiness) in the community indwelt by his Spirit (v. 29).

John, as he did his first book (12:37), formally closes the Book of Glory, and repeats again his rationale for recounting the few *signs* Jesus left of his Resurrection and New Mode. The gospel *in toto* reveals Jesus to be the Messiah of authentic Jewish expectation as well as the "not expected" *high* Messiah, literal Son of God (as per Thomas' profession of faith). The death of Jesus momentarily loosened the connection of faith,but Jesus and his *revealing signs* in chapter 20 have helped to restore the connection. Now Jesus in the belief of the disciples is truly the "low" as well as the "high" Christ, the sent source of the Father's life for them and for the world (vv. 30—31).

FURTHER PARTICULAR COMMENTS:

Verses 1-18 . . . Scholars discover several "inconsistencies" of narrative data in John's first two scenes (e.g., Mary assumes that Jesus' body is stolen without looking in the tomb; the "burial clothes" are described twice; angels appear in the second scene but not the first, etc.; vv. 19-29 will have "inconsistencies" too). This probably indicates that John is reworking two or more sources into a new theologically unified composition. He worries little about the historical "inconsistencies," since he is making theological points and not documenting the undocumentable.

Verses 1-2, 11f . . . All the gospels recount that women first saw the "empty tomb" and first experienced apparitions. In a way, this attests to the solidness of the "empty tomb" and apparition traditions, against the objections of those who say that this sort of thing was "contrived." If believers wanted to "contrive" witnesses, the first of them would surely have been *men* (the chauvinism of ancient times being what it was).

Verses 11-18 . . . There is a tradition in the Synoptics for such an "appearance" (cf. Marcan App., Mk 16:9; Mt 28:1, 8-10: Mary is in a group that experiences an apparition). Also the *weeping* of Mary would have some apologetical value, showing, believers were not gullibly expecting Resurrection. Some scholars call the scene a dramatization of John's often used device of "misunderstanding."

Verse 15 . . . Mary's "non-recognition" also reflects general Jewish belief about resurrection. In the view of some Jews the resurrected were to have a different appearance (cf., e.g., Paul's description of the "resurrection" of believers, I Cor 15:42f).

Verse 20, 25, 27 . . . Great stress is given to Jesus' hands, side, the nails, etc. This would have apologetical value, showing that the Risen Jesus is real and not ghostly (some objected that Christians "saw" what was not there).

Verses 22-23, *breathed* . . . Some commentators see this as equivalent to Baptism (3:5). "Breathing" on the baptismal candidate became a part of the early baptismal liturgy. Some see this verse, as well as v. 23 on "forgiving sins," as a distinct Johannine addition to his source material (although others note that Lk 24:47, includes a reference to "forgiveness of sins" and Mt. and the Marcan App. refer to "Baptism" which is a "forgiveness" Sacrament).

Verses 24-29 . . . This scene is also seen by some as a dramatized form of "Johannine misunderstanding." Some see it as "completely contrived." Others, as was noted, see it as a "separation" of the incredulity aspect found in the Synoptic accounts of the appearance to the disciples.

Verse 29 . . . Often called the second Johannine "beatitude." C. 13:17 is the "first" ("happy those who put it [i.e., fraternal service] into practice").

Chapter 21

GENERAL COMMENTS (and reflections):

Chapter 21 has always been included as part of the gospel text. However, most scholars see it as a later addition to an already finished book (20:30-31). The chronology, geography and disciple-reaction of the chapter do not fit in smoothly where they are; if anything, the appearance narrated in c. 21 should precede c. 20 (or at least 20:7f). Certainly disciples who have already seen the Risen Jesus and received his Spirit and who have been "sent" to bring his Peace and Forgiveness to the world should be "on the missionary trail," not back fishing. But if the chapter is something of a separate "afterthought," who wrote it and why was it added? It has a Johannine "sound" to it with familiar gospel vocabulary and themes (e.g., the Peter/beloved disciple pairing; the meal of bread and fish; the shepherd/sheep images; the emphasis on a reliable witness behind the book). But it lacks a smooth and creative integration of its narrative with the previous chapter and is probably the work of a post-John redactor. The redactor apparently sees some theological-pastoral value to the material and includes it for that reason.

If the chapter has pastoral value, what would it be? Scholars, who speak with little hesitancy about the pastoral context of the gospel proper, are more tentative in determining the context of c. 21. Some speculation about pastoral purpose proceeds along these lines. Verses 1-14, address the problem of the Risen Jesus' Mode of presence with the Church in the late first century. The Church is growing rapidly and includes great numbers of Jews and Gentiles of all types. This evangelical success should be attributable to Jesus' *presence* in the preaching and evangelization. The episode shows that the Risen Jesus is spiritually with the Church and is responsible for its remarkable evangelical growth. Also, the great number and variety of disciples should militate against the unity that

Jesus desires for his flock. The episode, however, reveals that Jesus can gain great numbers of disciples with all sorts of different backgrounds and still keep them together in spiritual unity. The episode also shows that Jesus' presence is manifest and experienced in the eucharistic gatherings of the community. Some of John's people may unreasonably desire a more *personal* form of Jesus' presence. So the episode reveals that Jesus is recognizably *present* in the community's mission-growth and preaching—in its unity in diversity—and in its eucharistic celebrations.

Verses 15-23, will talk more specifically about the "fate" and "role" of two disciples bound up with the destiny of this particular community (both introduced in vv. 1-14). These two persons are real disciples, but also apparently are understood by John's Church to be symbols of two "Churches" interacting with each other in a pastoral way in the late first century (the beloved disciple, a symbol of John's community; Peter, a symbol of the "Great Church" and its thriving communities). Jesus, in the second half of the chapter, will explain the role of each disciple (or Church) as he (they) relates to the other. Some see, for example, the Church of John as a bit "rudderless" with the death of the beloved disciple. His Church is seen as possibly investigating closer ties with the "Petrine Churches." Also, Jesus will comment on the *death* of the two disciples in such a way that pastoral lessons can be learned from their manner of death.

Sources

Scholars agree that the apparition at Tiberias, vv. 1-14, is a composite of two or three apparitions of Jesus to his disciples in Galilee. The Johannine tradition or the redactor-writer of c. 21 knew about the Synoptic sources that spoke of such apparitions (cf., Mt 28:10; Mk 16:7; also, it should be noted that although c. 20 of John is in the Jerusalem area, Jesus foretold in 16:32, that the disciples at his death would scatter and flee back "*to their own homes*"). These verses clearly recall a "pre-Resurrection" scene from Luke where Jesus is responsible for a miraculous catch of fish in Galilee involving Peter and others who are to become disciples (Lk 5:1-11). Luke's scene ends with Jesus calling and commissioning Peter and the others to be "fishers of men." Scholars believe c. 21 of John rightly identifies this Lucan scene as a Resurrection appearance in Galilee and believe that Luke placed it earlier for theological reasons.

Since Peter is important in the composite scene of vv. 1-14, and also features in the dialogue of the second part of the chapter, vv. 15-23, the scene at Tiberias would seem also to recall and adapt an apparition of Jesus to Peter. Such an apparition is spoken of in Mk 16:7; Lk 24:35; and Paul, I Cor 15:5, but never described in the Resurrection scenes of the Synoptics. This apparition is thought to contain elements of Peter's "rehabilitation" and his special "commissioning" by Jesus to be the spiritual leader of the community. Scholars think that traces of this apparition to Peter can be found in earlier "pre-Resurrection" scenes in the Synoptics (e.g., Mt 14:22-33; Mt 16:16-19; Lk 5:1-11); these commentators see these scenes (or parts of them) as originally a Resurrection appearance(s). So, if vv. 1-14, are a composite of two or three appearances, one of them would be this appearance to Peter. The "rehabilitation" and "commissioning" part of the appearance will be isolated in a separate section of the chapter, vv. 15-18. And vv. 9, 12-13, are an attempt to integrate into the Tiberias scene another apparition of Jesus to the disciples as a group (cf., Mt 28:10; Mk 16:14 f; Lk 24:28-35; I Cor 15:5). The setting was originally at a meal of bread and fish; this meal is translated by the redactor to the shore of Tiberias and put after the miraculous catch.

In vv. 15-23, the redactor, besides dramatizing the rehabilitation and commissioning sayings of Jesus associated with Peter, will further dramatize remembered words of Jesus about the beloved disciple. As noted, there seems to be some kind of "pastoral interaction" between the Churches these two people represent. Peter's role and value must be reviewed and explained to John's community. The beloved disciple's *book* and his theology of Jesus must be seen by Peter's community to be approved by Jesus. Perhaps the two Churches are in some sense coming together after the death of the beloved disciple, and John's people are bringing with them their *novel* gospel. Other pastoral lessons are contained in these sayings of Jesus and they will be discussed below.

Appearance of Jesus at the Sea of Tiberias: 21:1-14

As noted, the scene integrates possibly three appearances of Jesus to his disciples: one to them by the Sea, with a miraculous catch of fish (the redactor is properly locating the episode found in Lk 5:1-11); another to the disciples at a meal of bread and fish; another to Peter individually. *All* will "now" happen at Tiberias in c. 21.

It seems that the saying of Peter, "I am going fishing" (v. 3), has for John's community two meanings. One—the obvious one: the disciples, disillusioned after Jesus' death, did return to their homes and old occupations. They did go fishing, and saw the Risen Jesus for the first time after a fruitless night of fishing. In time the expression came to mean "to go evangelizing in Jesus' name" (Luke's telling of the miraculous catch of fish sets up Jesus' call to the disciples to come and be "fishers of men"; Lk 5:1-11). In the latter meaning, to go evangelizing without a sense of the "presence of Jesus" in the expedition is to doom the "mission" to failure. To go fishing "with Jesus," obedient to his commands, is to assure a "good catch." In the constructed scene the disciples join Peter. This shows that the vocation of all disciples is to "go fishing," i.e., to bring Jesus and his word to the neighbors and to the nations. The fishing is "at night" and this probably means that the disciples' "faith in the Risen Jesus" before his first appearance was almost non-existent; thus there is "no catch" (v. 3).

Jesus appears at daybreak (naturally!) but due to "lack of Resurrectional faith" he is not recognized. The Christian version of the "recognition story" demands *faith* before anyone *sees* Jesus. He will give them a *sign* of his Risen presence. He instructs them to cast their net on the right side of the boat (vv. 5-6). When they respond to his word a "great catch" is realized. The catch is so abundant (v. 7) that one of the fishermen, the beloved disciple, sees only one explanation—"It is the Lord!" In a sense, the one who made fish abundant in c. 6:5-12, has "done it again"—who else? John's Church, reading of this apparition, should see the "catch" in terms of the "abundant conversions to Christ" in their own time. As the first "catch" calls for the faith-response—"It is the Lord!", so the latter "catch" shows believers that Jesus is *present with* them in the New Mode of "evangelization." Note too, the beloved disciple sees Jesus *present in the sign*; he does not need a personal "fleshly" apparition of Jesus.

The disciple (and the Church he represents) is the one who informs Peter (and the "Great Churches" of the "twelve") that Jesus is *LORD*, i.e., that Jesus is not only the exalted "low" Christ . . . he is the eternally existing "high" Christ. Peter responds to the word of the beloved disciple and goes off to greet Jesus *as Lord*. This shows that the "Petrine communities," the Churches of the "twelve," in some way find the full meaning of Jesus in the belief of the Johannine community and its *book*. Note, Peter puts on his clothes; no one appears in naked informality or is irreverently "unclad" before the "high" Christ (v. 7). In a few verses Jesus asks the disciples to bring their fish to him (v. 10). This seems like a Johannine version of the Synoptic saying . . . "go forth to the nations and baptize them all in *my* name" (bring them all to me). To be as successful as they have been in doing this, shows John's people that they are not alone but are in tandem unity with the Jesus who *sends* them to the "fishing task." And if not alone, then Jesus is *present* with them in the Mode of "successful evangelization" and they should not seek more "fleshly" appearances, but be content with an experience of his *presence* in his *signs*.

In v. 11, the redactor finds a lesson for the community in the number of fish, 153, and in the fact that the net which holds them is "not torn." The symbolism of the 153 remains an exegetical mystery, but could indicate the abundance and variety of disciples that are to be brought to Jesus (some wonder if the ancients believed there were 153 different kinds of fish, or 153 different nations on the earth). Yes, Jesus' death and Resurrection "draws all manner of people" to him (11:52; 12:32), and despite the national, religious, and cultural differences of his many disciples, he can meld them into a community of faith (cf. c. 17). The *untorn* net, like the untorn tunic of Jesus (19:23-24), is seen as a *sign* that Jesus is Lord of unity, creator of community. Who else could bring it off?

In vv. 9, 12-13, the redactor attempts to integrate another Galilee apparition of Jesus—this time at a meal of bread and fish. John's readers would instinctively recall the *meal* of c. 6:5-11 (both that meal and this one take place at Tiberias); there the miraculous meal of bread and fish was a *sign*-revelation and lead-in to Jesus' discourse about the special *bread* he would provide for believers—the bread of his wisdom (6:35-51a) and the bread of the Eucharist (6:51b-58). This apparition, then, is also a *sign*—revelation of Jesus. As a New Mode *presence* was discernible in the "evangelical mission and growth of the community," so Jesus is also *present* in the preaching and the "eucharistic meal" eaten by the community in faith (a lesson, it seems, also taught by Luke: Lk 24:13-31). "Come and eat" (v. 12) seems a Johannine equivalent of the Synoptic "take and eat . . . do this in memory of me"; and of course in c. 6, John's Jesus invited disciples to eat and feed on the *bread* he brought "from heaven" (6:51a). The gestures here as in c. 6:11 ("took" and "gave") are very eucharistic (v. 13). And indeed the disciples seem to "recognize" Jesus in the *sign* of the offered bread. They hesitate to ask him questions (v. 12) because they know . . . "it is the Lord!" Jesus is not only at but *in* the meal.

The Tiberias apparition, then, shows John's community that the Risen Jesus is *present* to them in their "successful evangelization and preaching" (the "going fishing," "big catch" mystery)—in their unity in diversity—and in their Eucharists. Such *presences* (along with other forms of presence, e.g., Baptism, the "keeping of the commandment," etc.) should be the important "Jesus-apparitions" in their lives. They need no further dramatic and glamorous "personal" appearances (do some seek these?). This appearance of Jesus shows that he *calls* all disciples to the missionary task, to unity, and to his Eucharist.

Jesus and Peter: 21:15-19

As noted, scholars think that Jesus' appearance to Peter, spoken of but not described in the Synoptics and Paul (Mk 16:7; Lk 24:35; I Cor 15:5), involved Peter's rehabilitation and special leadership assignment (snatches of which seem contained in Mt 14:22-33; Lk 5:1-11; Mt 16:16-19—all seen to be relocations of a post-Resurrection appearance to Peter). The writer of c. 21 has access to this material or his own preserved version of this appearance, and chooses to dramatize the re-conversion and role-assignment of Peter in a separate scene. In a few verses he will "dramatize" a remembered saying of Jesus about the beloved disciple.

Why is it important for the writer to give the readers of a *gospel about Jesus* "information" about Peter and the beloved disciple? One cannot know for certain, but it seems that the sayings of Jesus to and about these two disciples answer pastoral problems the Church is experiencing. It could be something like this.

John's Church had as its shepherd and leader the beloved disciple who was a direct tie-in with Jesus. He was the first (or near first) to believe in Jesus' Resurrection. Through the Spirit's inspiration he came to know the full and eternal "high" character of Jesus. Many other Christian Churches were nearby and were recognized as authentic disciple-Churches also (the "Great Churches" of the "twelve"). John's group, however, was in a way singular in its early belief in Jesus as the "high" Christ; other Churches had not reached a conscious understanding of the eternal nature of Jesus' divine *persona*.

This disciple lived so long that the community never thought about what would happen to them when he died. Rumors, in fact, seem to have circulated that he would live until Jesus' fleshly "coming" *at the end* (and in such a case, Jesus would be everybody's Shepherd). But now the shepherd is dead and no one in this community, so dependent on his witness and charismatic presence, seems able to fill his shoes (cf., the factions that emerge in the Johannine Epistles; the troubles of the elder, etc.). The Church not only misses him; it needs a strong shepherd to lead them and to interpret his teaching and his book correctly. It is obvious to some of John's community that strong shepherding exists "out there." Does Jesus, then, want John's Church to seek closer ties with the "Great Church"? The isolated vignettes would seem to show that he does. Jesus has rehabilitated Simon and made him Peter—Rock and Shepherd of the flock. The beloved disciple never claimed to be a shepherd, so much as a reliable witness. But without anyone quite realizing it, while he was alive he did perform the shepherd's role. Now with his death, the Church needs a Jesus-approved, commissioned, graced shepherd. The "shepherd mystery" is important to the "Great Church" and works well there. This seems to be the case because Jesus wishes his flock to have good shepherds, and has provided the sheep with the *grace* of charismatic leadership. Dialogue about this with the "Great Church" is certainly in order.

Moreover, Peter's Church also *needs* the beloved disciple, and the second vignette, vv. 20-23, shows the "Petrine Churches" how Jesus loved the disciple and his community. Peter's Church needs the witness of the disciple and now that his witness exists in writing, Peter (and the Churches he represents) needs his book with its deeper and fuller understanding of Jesus as "high" Christ.

Simon is not here addressed as Peter, the Rock (perhaps this name, and Mt 16:16-19, where it is given, are "post-Resurrectional" after all—"Rock" being the Matthean equivalent to John's "shepherd of the flock"). Simon, to become the Rock and the Shepherd, must fulfill Jesus' norm for leadership. That norm is total love for him and the flock. Jesus asks *three times* if Simon loves him this deeply. *Three* inquiries indicate how important love is to Jesus. *Three* professions of love show that Simon is deeply committed to Jesus. The *three* inquiries and the *three* assignments to *feed and tend* his sheep show how serious Jesus is about this office (public "*threes*" are very solemn ways of saying things, to the ancients). Jesus' sheep must be fed and cared for, guided and protected, taught with dedication, served faithfully, even to the point of "dying for the flock" if need be (10:9-10, 16). Simon pledges this kind of love, and the *three* protestations of love seem dramatically to erase his *three* denials (vv. 15-16). Rehabilitated in his faith, Peter is given the office of Jesus' caring and serving leadership over the flock. Yahweh was Israel's Shepherd in the OT (Gn 49:24; Ho 4:16; Jr 31:10; Is 40:11; Ps 23). Jesus was the vbisibilization of the Father as Shepherd while on earth (10:11-18). The flock exists after Jesus' glorification and must still be cared for and led. Peter, then, is Jesus' "graced shepherd agent," the one who visibilizes Jesus as Shepherd of the flock after his Resurrection (a look at the Book of Acts, cc's. 1-12, shows the important shepherd role that Peter exercised in the early Church).

Jesus "sees" into Simon's heart. As the "high" Christ, he knows the inner thoughts of his disciples (v. 17). Peter earlier had boasted of his unfailing love (13:37; cf., also Mk 14:29; Mt 26:33). Could his spoken love be just another hollow boast? The community sees that Jesus knows that this time the "boast" is not empty (this is most evident in the upcoming v. 19, when Peter is to die for love of Jesus and the flock). From this episode John's community not only knows that Peter was rehabilitated, but they now see that Peter (and the "Great Church") accepts their "high" Christology (Peter sees that Jesus, like God, *knows all things*). They also see more clearly that Jesus bestowed the office of leadership on Peter. There can no longer be casual independence among the Churches, for Jesus spoke clearly of one shepherd and one flock (10: 16).

Verse 18, seems to be a proverb which Jesus applied to Peter that turned out to be prophetic of his life as shepherd of Jesus' flock. Youth has great freedom and few responsibilities. Old age (i.e., Christian maturity and leadership with its duties and community obligations) will *fasten* Peter to a life of *binding* "service." History proved (and most Christians would know this by 90-95 AD) that the proverb was also a prophecy of Peter's death (v. 19). He was not only "tied down" to dutiful "feeding and tending" of the flock, he stretched out his hands and was led off to a martyr's death. No wonder Jesus made him shepherd! Granted that he is weak and impetuous, he has the one necessary quality Jesus seeks from his shepherds. Like Jesus, he is willing to "lay down his life" for the flock (10:11; 15:13). As "high" Christ, Jesus foresaw that Peter would give him and the flock thirty years of service and finally his life; it was that ultimate "fate" of martyrdom that he had predicted in 13:36, even before Peter's denial (tradition has Peter dying a martyr in Nero's persecution, ca. 64-67 AD). The "follow me" of v. 19, and the fact that the reader knows Peter almost "literally" did follow Jesus in his manner of death seems conclusively to wash away any misgivings one could have about Simon Peter's faith. If John's Church saw God's *glory* manifest in Jesus' selfless death, they would see it present also in Peter's heroic giving of his life and thus Peter must have died as Jesus did, in tandem unity with God (cf., 7:39; 13:31-32; 17:4-5) (v. 19). Another reason for John's somewhat "shepherdless" Church to seek closer ties with the "Great Church" of Jesus' vicar-shepherd.

Jesus' Words about the Beloved Disciple: 21:20-23

These are the verses that indicate the beloved disciple has died. It is important that Peter (and the Churches he represents) learn about this disciple and the great love Jesus had for him (vv. 20-21). If Jesus loved him and he loved Jesus, then he is a Christian and should be dutifully cared for by Jesus' approved shepherd. It is also important that John's Church after his death realize that his long life did not mean that he was to live until Jesus' final coming, as rumors had it (v. 23). No, Jesus never spoke of his "remaining until I come back" (v. 22). (*Grounds for such rumors, however, could be found in Jesus' own "eschatological" words; cf., Mk 9:1; Mt 10:23; 16:28*). Jesus answers the rumor obliquely. Death is to overtake all disciples. They should be more concerned with how they "follow" Jesus than with how they are to die (v. 22). If superficial comparisons are made between the seemingly more heroic death of Peter (martyrs were by far the biggest heroes in the early Church) and the "old age" death of the disciple, Jesus tells all disciples that the two deaths are just different ways of "following" him. If one dies "loving and serving" him and the brothers and sisters, this is all that matters.

Conclusion

The writer of the added chapter informs the readers that the beloved disciple "wrote" the gospel and that his witness to its contents is true. There was mutual love between Jesus and the disciple. No rehabilitation was necessary in his case, for he never denied Jesus, but stood by him loyally even in death (19:35). "Wrote" does not preclude another and principal writer-evangelist (with other assisting editors). It could mean that the disciple is the principal authority behind the oral and written tradition that underlies the "picture of Jesus" set down in the gospel. "John" (as we have called him) could well be two individuals (the disciple and the writer-evangelist, with the disciple obviously the more important of the two, since he is the witness-authority that ties the book in with Jesus in a personal way). But we can only conclude that the disciple was a real person, highly revered and profoundly missed in death, not a created "ideal person." In v. 24, *his book* is defended by his community as a true and reliable account of Jesus ("*we* know *his* witness is true"). There seems to be a feeling that John's Church will enter into closer ties with the "Great Church" *only if* that Church accepts its book and its "high" Christology (which in time it did).

Verse 25, imitates John's own conclusion of 20:30-31, but with less reserve and some hyperbole. The implication is that Jesus is revealed in his own words and deeds, and can be met in the Church's continued preaching of them and in his sacramental symbols. The book has recorded enough of Jesus' words and actions to identify him as the Father's source of life and love for the world. The last chapter tells a Church sixty or more years removed from the Resurrection that this same Jesus is present with them and is sensibly experienced in the preaching, missionary life and sacramental celebrations of their community.

FURTHER PARTICULAR COMMENTS:

Verse 2, *Nathanael* . . . This might be a cross-reference to 1:50, and thus the chapter could be something of a Johannine postscript "inclusion."

There Jesus prophesied that Nathanael would see "far greater things" than Jesus' knowledge of his identity. Nathanael is about to witness the Resurrection, the "greatest thing of all."

Verse 7 . . . Peter's plunging into the Sea seems to echo Mt 14:22-33. There Jesus *saves* Peter from the waters when his faith falters. As noted, Matthew's episode is seen by some scholars as being in part a post-Resurrection event involving Jesus and Peter, transferred by the evangelist to a pre-Resurrection scene for theological reasons.

Verse 9, *charcoal fire* . . . Recalls 18:18, and the place of Peter's first denial. This reinforces the position of scholars who see the coming vv. 15-18, as not only a "commissioning" but a "rehabilitation" episode as well.

Verse 13, *took . . . gave . . . the fish* . . . These eucharistic ritual gestures recall 6:11; the multiplied fish of the miracle in time took on eucharistic connotations. Primitive iconography depicted "bread *and fish*" as symbols of the Eucharist.

Verses 15-17 . . . Does the Shepherd office endure after Peter? Peter will be dead nearly thirty years when the gospel is circulated. Why discuss him and the bestowal of his office unless his office is *still* relevant? The document known as First Peter (seen by some to be a late first-century document) indicates the importance of the shepherd's office in the "Great Church" of that time (cf. I P 5:1-4; and of course, the Book of Acts, cc's. 1-12).

Review Questions:
Material for Comment and Discussion

Introduction: What in general is a gospel? Does John's book qualify as one? How is it different from the Synoptics? Why does his Jesus *sound* different? Is he working from different sources? What seems to be his background? Hellenist-pagan? Gnostic? Stoic? Radically Jewish (orthodox, heterodox)? Discuss. The purpose of the book? Its makeup and divisions?

Chapter 1: Relationship of the prologue's Hymn to the full gospel? Does it depict Jesus as Stoic *Logos*? Gnostic redeemer? OT motifs behind the Hymn? Discuss. Why so much space given to JB? What does he call Jesus? The meaning of his titles? How does his baptism differ from Jesus'? Nathanael's attitude—a model for John's Church? "Son of Man"—a good title for John's Jesus? Discuss.

Chapter 2: Comment on John's use and theology of *signs*. The Cana episode—what is John saying about Jesus here? If the scene is one of *replacement* or *fulfillment*—what would this mean for John's community? Why does Jesus cleanse the Temple so early? What does the action say about Jesus and Christian worship?

Chapter 3: Comment on the *discourses* of Jesus. Is this the Real Jesus speaking? He *sounds* different. Comment. Nicodemus seems to be a symbol. Would his *type* be known to John's Church? Explain. How does John use the literary devices of "misunderstanding" and "irony"? The "Johannine presumption"—what is this? John's *dualism*—heavy but is it too heavy for a Christian gospel? Comment. How is Jesus a judgment on the world?

Chapter 4: What lessons are taught John's Church in the narrative about the Samaritan woman? Contrast the background and faith of Nicodemus and the woman. Lessons for John's Church? Worship and missionary themes here? A baptismal motif? Lesson for John's Church from the cure of the official's son?

Chapter 5: What does the cure of the cripple say about Jesus' identity? Comment on John's understanding of *eschatology*. What is going on in 5:19f—is Jesus on trial this early? His *crime*? How does he defend himself? Comment on John's use of the term "Jews." Is he anti-semitic?

Chapter 6: What particularly do the signs of the multiplication of the bread and the walking on the waters say about Jesus? How do scholars interpret the *Bread of Life* discourse? The meaning of vv. 51b-58? Where would these words more properly belong? Has Jesus left believers *two breads*? Comment. In sum, how does c. 6 illustrate the *replacement* theme of John? Again, comment on the predominant eschatology of cc's. 5-6. Is the Eucharist an example of eschatology? The chapter says that the "flesh" is useless. Is Jesus, then, not *in* the Eucharist as Zwingli and others say?

Chapters 7 and 8: What is the predominant theme of these chapters? The feast of Tabernacles—its meaning and relationship to this theme? What specific complaints do the Pharisees bring against Jesus? Do they reflect current problems, ca. 90-95 AD? Why is Abraham brought into the discussion? A baptismal motif to the chapters? Do they lend themselves to "flash-backs" and "flash-forwards"? Illustrate. Again, how is Jesus a judgment on the world? Comment on John's rationale for the frequent use of the phrase "*ego eimi.*"

Chapter 9: What does John seem to teach in the episode of the blind man? How would this story help his Church pastorally and apologetically? A sacramental motif? Crypto-Christians—what is the problem?

Chapter 10: Relate the feast of Dedication and its meaning to Jesus' identity as Good Shepherd. Traits of good and bad shepherds (Ezekiel 34)? What does the chapter say to John's people in their present situation?

Can non-Jews take comfort in c. 10? Jesus talks often in the Temple precincts and on feast days. Could there be a worship motif here? Discuss.

Chapter 11: The Lazarus episode—fiction or real? What is wrong with Martha and Mary's faith? Why is Jesus "troubled"? What does the sign say about Jesus beyond what the other signs say? Why is a "trial" put after this sign? Again, what theme(s) is illustrated here?

Chapter 12: Mary and her perfume—what does the scene say? A kingly theme seems to be emerging. Why now? The *why* of Jesus' Palm Sunday reception? What "corrective" elements does John bring to the episode? Why do the "Greeks" show up as Jesus nears his Passion? Why is his "hour" so important for them? Relate your answer to the Jesus of Mode #1, Mode #2. Again, how is the world to be judged?

Chapter 13: How is John's telling and celebration of the Last Supper different from the Synoptics? Can both be right? A Passover supper? Discuss the theological implications of Jesus' death near Passover. What seem to be the two levels of meaning for the "footwashing"? Why does Jesus see it as so important? A baptismal motif? Jesus gives a Last Discourse. Precedents and rationale for this sort of discourse? One discourse, or a collection? "Who" gives the discourse? Values of the discourse for John's Church? A Synoptic counterpart? How is Jesus' *commandment of love* different from the OT's? How do believers love the Risen Christ when he is absent?

Chapter 14: Jesus is called the *WAY*. What seems to be the meaning of the term? How can human persons know and love a God as transcendent as the Father? How can Christians do "greater things" than Jesus? Who is the Paraclete and what is his relationship to Jesus and to believers? What specifically is his role? What is the Peace he brings?

Chapter 15: Why would John want to insert a Vine/Branches passage in a Last Discourse? Possible source for the imagery? What does the passage say about Jesus—Mode #1 and Mode #2? About Christian morality? Why is the *new commandment* so important to Jesus? Why does John's dualism become even more pronounced in the Book of Glory? Why are Jesus' disciples bound to experience hatred? A theology of suffering and spiritual growth in c. 15? A eucharistic motif?

Chapter 16: The Spirit proves the world wrong about sin, justice, and judgment. How so? Why do you think the Paraclete is called the "Spirit of Truth"? Does he teach new truths about God? In 16:16-33, the disciples are "wondering." A pastoral problem for John's Church? Discuss. The probable meaning of Jesus' words: "in a little while you will see me"? What is the *Joy* Jesus promises?

Chapter 17: Jesus' prayer is "revelatory" and "commissionary"—what does this mean? Speculate on why Jesus must die to know his fullest glory. Does the prayer reveal why Jesus (and John) so often put the phrase "*ego eimi*" on Jesus' lips? How do Christians bring Christ to the world? A theology of the Church in cc's. 15-17?

Chapters 18 and 19: In general how does John's picture of Jesus during the Passion compare to the Synoptic picture? Lessons taught in the Arrest scene? Some apologetics in the Annas episode? Why and by whom was Jesus killed according to John? Comment on the rationale behind John's structuring of the Pilate Trial (inner and outer stages). What is Pilate's main sin as John sees it? The Jewish accusation against Jesus? Some irony here? Why does Pilate finally go along with the "Jews"? His revenge? Why is the kingly theme strong at this time? What theological statements does John seem to make in the following scenes: the way to the Cross? Pilate's *sign* over the Cross? the seamless robe? Jesus' "words" to his mother and the disciple? his final "words" from the Cross? Jesus' post-mortem piercing? his burial? Is Jesus' death sacrificial? Explain.

Chapter 20: What should the "empty tomb" and the "burial clothes" reveal to believers; what should be coming to mind as they see them? Compare Peter's reaction to the disciple's. Apologetical and pastoral lessons in their reactions? Lessons in the Magdalene episode—her problems?—their solution? Jesus' appearance to the disciples as a group and to them with Thomas present—what lessons here for John's Church? Jesus gives Peace and power over sin—a possible ecclesial motif here?

Chapter 21: Why is the chapter seen to be an addition? Sources for the "apparition"? Pastoral lessons in the episode? Speculate why there is so much Peter/beloved disciple material in a gospel about Jesus. In retrospect (cc's. 15-21) is the Johannine Jesus interested in "community"? If so, how is he *present* to it?

FOR FURTHER READING

COMMENTARIES

Brown, R., *The Epistles of John*, Anchor Bible (30) (New York: Doubleday & Co., 1982).
_____, *The Gospel According to John*, 2 Vols., Anchor Bible (29, 29a) (New York: Doubleday & Co., 1966/70).
Lindars, B., *The Gospel of John* (London: Oliphants, 1972).
Schnackenburg, R., *The Gospel According to St. John*, 3 Vols., Vols. I and II (New York: Crossroads Publ. Co., 1980), Vol. III (New York: State Mutual Book and Periodical Service, Ltd., 1982).

OTHER COMMENTARIES AND BOOKS

Barrett, C. K., *The Gospel According to St. John* (London: SPCK, 1967).
_____, *The Gospel of John and Judaism* (London: SPCK, 1975).
Brown, R., *The Community of the Beloved Disciple* (New York: Paulist Press, 1979).
Cullman, O., *The Johannine Circle* (Philadelphia: Westminster, 1976).
Dodd, C.H., *Historical Tradition in the Fourth Gospel* (New York: Cambridge University Press, 1963).
_____, *The Interpretation of the Fourth Gospel* (New York: Cambridge University Press, 1953).
Feuillet, A., *Johannine Studies* (New York: Alba House, 1964).
Kysar, R., *The Fourth Evangelist and his Gospel* (Minneapolis: Augsburg, 1975).
_____, *John the Maverick Gospel* (Atlanta: John Knox, 1976).
MacRae, G., *Faith in the World: The Fourth Gospel* (Chicago: Franciscan Herald Press, 1973).
Manson, T. W., *On Paul and John* (London: SCM Press, Ltd., 1963).
Marsh, J., *The Gospel of Saint John* (London: Harmondsworth, 1968).
Martyn, J.L., *The Gospel of John in Christian History* (New York: Paulist Press, 1979).
_____, *History and Theology in the Fourth Gospel* (New York: Harper & Row, 1968).
Schnackenburg, R., *Present and Future* (South Bend, Ind.: University of Notre Dame Press, 1966).
Taylor, M. J., *A Companion to John* (New York: Alba House, 1977).

RECENT POPULAR COMMENTARIES

Crane, T. E., *The Message of Saint John* (New York: Alba House, 1980).
MacRae, G., *Invitation to John* (New York: Doubleday & Co., Image, 1978).
McPolin, J., *John* (Wilmington: Michael Glazier, Inc., 1979).
Obach, R. E. and Kirk, A., *A Commentary on the Gospel of John* (New York: Paulist Press, 1981).
Perkins, P., *The Gospel According to John* (Chicago: Franciscan Herald Press, 1978).